High Definition Audio for the Digital Home

Proven Techniques for Getting It Right the First time

David Roach
Scott Janus
Wayne Jones

To Oren –
I hope this inspires some good drumming!

Intel PRESS

ISBN 0-9764832-2-X

This book is printed on acid-free paper. ♾

Publisher: Richard Bowles
Editor: David B. Spencer
Content Architect: Matthew Wangler
Text Design & Composition: Wayne Jones
Graphic Art: Wayne Jones (illustrations), Ted Cyrek (cover)

Library of Congress Cataloging in Publication Data:

Printed in the United States of America

10 9 8 7 6 5 4 3 2 1

First Printing May 2006

To Phil Pompa and Rich Bowles, who came up with the concept and put the wheels in motion to make it happen

Contents

Chapter 3 Basics of Surround Sound and Signal Processing 109

Foreword

We are fortunate to have two eminent industry representatives giving you their views on *High Definition Audio for the Digital Home*.

High-Fidelity Audio Everywhere

Digital technology is driving the development of new types of content, a variety of media distribution options and innovative digital devices, all of which point to the emergence of a new digital entertainment industry. As we focus on making digital entertainment easier to access and view on different devices throughout the home, a vast number of companies have an enormous opportunity to provide a wider variety of innovative devices, content and software than ever before. Intel® Viiv™ technology exemplifies this objective.

Intel Viiv technology marks the intersection point where innovation, a multitude of digital devices, first-class entertainment, and state of the art technology converge to put consumers in more control of experiencing digital entertainment on their own terms.

In the midst of these exciting opportunities for a wide new range of products and consumer experiences, it is important to remember quality. For nearly a quarter of a century, people have had digital audio in their lives in the form of compact discs. DVD-Video is widely popular today, and many people have high-performance surround sound systems in their living rooms. The bar for consumer sound quality has been set high, and media PCs must compete for a place in this environment.

It is no longer adequate for a PC to simply play sounds; it must play them well and at a quality level that meets or exceeds consumer's expectations for traditional living room devices. Historically, however, the engineers and architects who were good at building computers did not have a lot of experience in the field of audio.

This book remedies that discrepancy. It is an invaluable reference for making high-fidelity audio ubiquitous throughout the Digital Home. The authors have brought together decades of experience in both the worlds of audio and computer design to form a comprehensive handbook filled with both theory and practical advice. It contains a wide range of information, much of it never clearly documented. Whether you work on software or hardware, whether you are in engineering or in marketing, new to the field or experienced, this book is a handy companion.

The future of digital entertainment is filled with incredible possibilities. *High Definition Audio for the Digital Home* is a great tool for making those ideas come true.

Donald J. MacDonald
Vice President and General Manager,
Digital Home Group,
INTEL CORPORATION

High-Fidelity Audio for Everyone

Microsoft† welcomes technology advances that improve the PC user experience. Especially exciting to us are hardware developments that enable Microsoft to build new and exciting functionality into our Windows† operating system.

Intel's® next-generation High Definition Audio is a great example of such a technology and a wonderful result of collaboration between hardware designers at Intel and software engineers at Microsoft.

High Definition Audio delivers tremendous value to the PC ecosystem without adding significant cost. From the content creators and owners, the hardware manufacturers of the audio devices and the system vendors to the Windows end-user, the positive impact of the next generation audio design from Intel Corporation is undeniable. More channels, independent streams, higher quality formats, fully enumerated topology and room to grow are just a few of the great aspects of this new design. These exciting features create "sockets" for better quality and more immersive content. High Definition Audio also makes it easier and less expensive to incorporate easy-to-use audio content creation solutions in PC designs.

With this new extensible, discoverable and high-quality audio technology Microsoft can build ubiquitous device driver coverage for all Intel® HD Audio solutions into current and future versions of Windows and create new and exciting user scenarios that leverage the transparency and multi-steaming aspects of High Definition Audio solutions.

This book is an important part of the industry's move to this new technology. It offers a great way to familiarize yourself with all aspects of this great technology and is a "must read" for anyone interested in or working on PC audio. Microsoft would like to thank the authors for writing this book and for giving us the opportunity to contribute to it.

Amir Majidimehr
Vice President, Digital Media Division,
MICROSOFT CORPORATION

Preface

Audio in the personal computer has been evolving constantly since its introduction in the 1980s, and now it must compete with the high fidelity and ease-of-use that is expected from home entertainment systems and home theaters. The end of year 2006 will mark several milestones: close-to-100-percent adoption of High Definition Audio on PC motherboards, the proliferation of Intel's dual-core 64-bit processors, which will be a huge boost to audio processing on the PC, and the launch of Microsoft's† Windows† Vista† operating system, which has a totally new audio subsystem based in part on High Definition Audio.

Most computer engineers do not have a strong grounding in the fundamentals of audio. More often than not, the audio responsibilities for a system design are delegated to an individual with a good track record in PC design, but with no audio background. Even those who have audio experience often find it challenging to keep abreast of the rapidly evolving technologies of PC audio.

Up until now, there has been no single place to get the information needed to successfully design a PC audio subsystem; this book gathers together all the various disciplines needed to get good sound out of a PC, including software design and signal processing, hardware layout and interfacing, digital rights management, and surround sound.

The companion High Definition Audio System Diagram chart, available from this book's Web site and shown in miniature in Figure 9.7, is the first complete block diagram of the audio in a modern PC, showing analog, Intel® HD Audio bus, and software signal paths through the system, from jack to the application and back again.

Other concepts are also joined together for the first time. Verb tables and pin configuration defaults are documented together as a unit, rather than separately. Comprehensive recommendations for EMI and ESD treatment are joined to very-high-fidelity audio circuits.

This book is intended for practicing designers, engineers, developers, testers, project managers, and technicians who work in the field of PC audio.

Market Challenges and Motivations

Every portion of the PC is under cost scrutiny, and the audio subsystem is no exception. In the past few years, every possible cost has been extracted from the computer's audio subsystem, often to the detriment of the fidelity of the audio. Going forward, we can expect a portion of the market to demand the lowest possible cost.

However, we see a new emerging segment requiring audio fidelity on a par with the consumer electronics equipment that is currently available for the living room. To meet those requirements, the major ODMs[1] who design and build PCs for the major OEMs[2] must understand the value of higher quality audio and how to use it as a product differentiator. Even the lower cost systems can be improved considerably by paying attention to critical details.

Both Microsoft and Intel are focused on evolving PC architecture to support typical home usages that have previously not made technical or economic sense. One key concept is that of a single appliance in the living room, with a single remote control, providing music, movies, and even telephone service not only in the living room, but throughout the house. Setting aside the particulars of the implementation, audio becomes an important part of the effort to bring that concept to life.

The ubiquitous PC is being reassigned to be the core of the home audio and multimedia entertainment system. Historically, the PC has not been an optimal host for high performance audio. On the other hand, a user's expectations are high since traditional home-audio components have provided a high level of quality for many years at a relatively low cost. So while the consumer might appreciate the new advantages brought by the PC architecture, their tolerance of sub-standard audio quality is low.

---

[1] ODM stands for Original Design Manufacturer, the company which designs and builds the PC under contract to the OEM.

[2] OEM stands for Original Equipment Manufacturer, the company with the brand name which sells the PC to the public.

With their ever-shrinking size and power budgets, laptops are pressing the limits of what can be accomplished in PC audio. Mounting usable transducers, such as speakers and microphones, in the tiny spaces available inside the laptop is a considerable challenge, especially when it comes to minimizing noise pickup through the wiring to the transducers and jacks. Docking issues coupled with power supply and battery life issues make for some truly challenging scenarios.

With the record companies actually pursuing legal recourse against peer-to-peer music sharing and the emergence of online music buying services, digital rights management has become a significant component of PC audio. The upcoming launch of Windows† Vista will demand some new approaches.

Traditionally, considerable resources are expended on both software and hardware for any particular audio design. However, a third discipline is often not considered: the human factors that make products usable. The biggest cost center for most computer OEMs is now technical support, and in the arena of rising support costs, audio is one of the biggest culprits, and getting worse. Well-designed products emphasize good usability that prevents or eliminates expensive support calls.

Most computer designers and manufacturers no longer employ designated specialists in audio. Therefore, the task of implementing audio with high fidelity falls to the mainstream computer designers and implementers, for whom we have written this book. The biggest single piece of advice we can offer is this: *design with audio in mind*. It is close to impossible to retrofit an existing motherboard or system design with high quality audio if you have not followed basic guidelines during the initial system design stages.

Acknowledgements

Rarely is a book with this much information created by one person, or even three. Fortunately, we had help from numerous experts within both Intel® Corporation and SigmaTel, and from many more throughout the industry. For their direct contributions to the book, we would like to thank:

- Dr. Marcie Weinstein of Akustica, Inc. for the subsection on digital microphone implementation.
- Steven Tellman of SigmaTel for the section on Intel HD Audio for Linux

- Todd Hager of Dolby Labs for his expertise in the field of surround sound
- Chris Schrage of Intel for his review of Intel HD Audio details as well as his arcane knowledge of verb tables and front panel audio connectors and codecs.
- Hakon Strande of Microsoft for assistance on all things Microsoft in the book, and general support in this effort
- Richard Fricks of Microsoft for detailed explanations of previously-undocumented routings, both for volume controls and for DirectShow.
- Whit Hutson of SigmaTel for identifying and defining key subject areas, and for research assistance
- Thomas Mintner of NTI for detailed review of the book and specific suggestions for Chapter 11: Testing and Certification.
- Steven Harris for his review of the testing procedures in Chapter 11.

Special thanks to Dan Bogard, Rit Pitakpaivan, and Mike Doyle of SigmaTel and to Howard Millett of Intel UPSD for their exacting technical review of Chapters 5 and 6 on motherboard design and layout.

Numerous colleagues from SigmaTel, Intel, Microsoft and others in the PC Audio industry offered information, advice, and vision. We're listing them here.

SigmaTel: Antonio Torrini, Mark Harvey, Yumiko Ikeda Henson, Dave Collier, Jim Bowles, Paul Regier, Ty Kingsmore, Darrell Tinker, Roy Vargas, Mark Mills, Andy Lambrecht, Kevin Kilbane, Danny Mulligan, Vitaliy Kulikov, Stan Shkolnyy, Glenn Reinhardt, Enrique Wang, Imei Lin, Benny Hsieh, Jason Wang, Leon Lee, Richmond Hung, Gabriel Boals, and Janna Garofolo.

Intel: Daniel Borud, Devon Worrell, Jim Chu, Brent Chartrand, Phil Lehwalder, Bob Jacobs, Scott Bair, Ernesto Martinez, Ricardo James, Steve Pitzel, Darren Smith, Mark Gentry, Sona Mahavni, Dave Salvatore, Paul Parenteau, Chandramouli Narayanan, Bill Huffman, Mike Kruse, Steve Balogh, Thomas Loza, Greg Thomas, John Eley, and Andy Kopp.

Microsoft: Noel Cross, Frank Yerrace, Steve Ball, Ryan Bemrose, Josh Wexler, Mitch Rundle, Larry Osterman, Patrick Azarello, Dan Dinu, Martin Puryear, Frank Berreth, Trudy Culbreth Brassell, Dave Marsh, Soccer Liu, and Randy Granovetter

Project BarBQ Team:[3] Thanks to all the folks in Project BarBQ who helped cook up the original idea for the Intel HD Audio specification, especially those who were present at the beginning in October of 2001: Dan Bogard, Charlie Boswell, Brent Chartrand, David Crowell, Mike D'Amore, Todd Hager, Scott Kasin, Jim Rippie, David Roach, Steve Ball, and Aaron Higgins. You can view the original concept at:

`http://www.projectbarbq.com/bbq01/bbq01r6.htm`

Intel HD Audio Book Team: We put together a small team for this book, communicating electronically to accomplish the project. We did once have all three authors together in the same room for 20 minutes, but never did the whole team come together face-to-face, nor was it ever necessary.

Content architect and project leader Matt Wangler deftly negotiated the inner workings of Intel Press, while editor David Spencer did a terrific job of bringing the text to life and making it easier to understand. Wayne Jones deserves special mention for an outstanding job on the graphics throughout the book, as does Scott Janus for his trek in Chapter 10 through the sticky issues of digital rights management and copy protection. Thanks to Ted Cyrek for the cover design, and thanks also to Wasser Studios and all the folks—not quite so numerous as this sounds—at Intel Press for helping to make this book a reality

We could never even have started this project without Phil Pompa and Rich Bowles, who came up with the concept and put the wheels in motion to make it happen.

The Intel HD Audio book authoring team

David Roach

Scott Janus

Wayne Jones

Four or five different places somewhere in the Northern Hemisphere
November 2005.

[3] Project BarBQ is a 10-year old think tank consisting in any year of 50 movers and shakers in the computer audio area. Project BarBQ convenes once a year in the Texas hill country outside Austin.

High Definition Audio System Diagram – Companion to this book

Be sure to get your copy of the full color 17" x 22" poster illustrating the various layers of High Definition Audio and including other useful information. This poster is available at no charge to everyone who purchases a copy of this book. To obtain your copy, simply register your copy of the book on the Intel Press web site using the unique serial number at the back of this book. www.intel.com/intelpress/haud

Here is a small image of the poster:

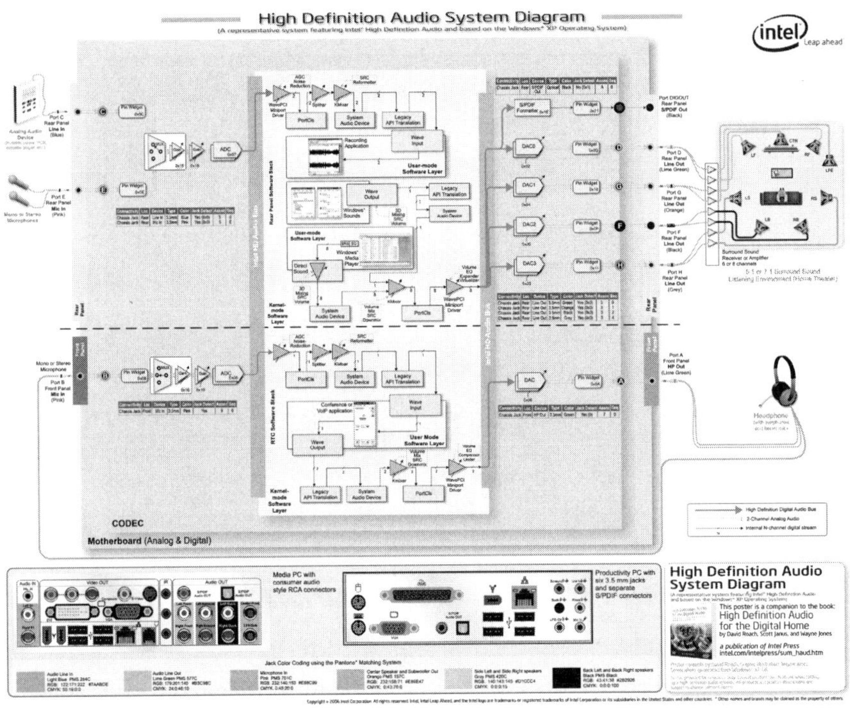

Chapter 1

Audio Basics

"An audio industry insider once told me there is nothing left to invent in PC audio. I couldn't disagree more. There are plenty of problems to solve and value to add to the platform. Intel HD Audio is only the beginning of audio innovation on the PC."

— Scott Bair; Intel Audio Enthusiast

Audio entertainment is an important part of our lives. Our voracious enjoyment of music has spawned a whole industry of artists, record labels, and equipment manufacturers. Audio is also a significant part of motion picture entertainment, with many new enhancements such as advanced surround sound adding to our enjoyment experience.

Intel® High Definition Audio (Intel® HD Audio), called Intel HD Audio for the rest of the book, is all about enhancing the perceived quality when audio entertainment is delivered by a PC, specifically making the listening experience richer, more realistic, and more enjoyable. This advancement in technology addresses two key issues for audio quality: how to achieve it and how to maintain it. Before diving into the details of storing, delivering, rendering audio content, and implementing Intel HD Audio subsystems, you should understand the underlying principles of audio quality and human perception of audio quality. This first chapter provides you with that foundation.

To establish a context, this chapter begins with a brief look backward at our roots in the history of electronically enhanced audio entertainment. Zooming forward to the present, it explores the many elements of Intel HD Audio. To understand the quality aspects and how to make the listening experience more enjoyable, you'll get a review of how we hear and what is important in human perception, followed by some of the metrics of analog and digital audio.

The Audio History of Entertainment

It is likely that the history of aural entertainment could be traced back to the cave dwellers, but let's start at the beginning of the 20th century when electronics was just starting to enhance the process of delivering artistic performance to listeners.

Prior to the 20th century, audio entertainment was live, experienced only when it happened and where it happened. If you wanted to hear musical instruments played professionally and had the means to afford it, you could attend a concert performance. If you felt an instantaneous desire to listen to a piano concerto, you either played it yourself, gathered in the parlor to hear a talented family member, or waited until a performer came to town. We now take for granted the ability to pull a CD from our collection or click on a file in our PC-based music library and within seconds listen to anything we want. And if we don't have it, a few more seconds and we can purchase it from the Internet and almost instantly enjoy it. The pictorial time line Figure 1.1 shows the evolution of home audio entertainment.

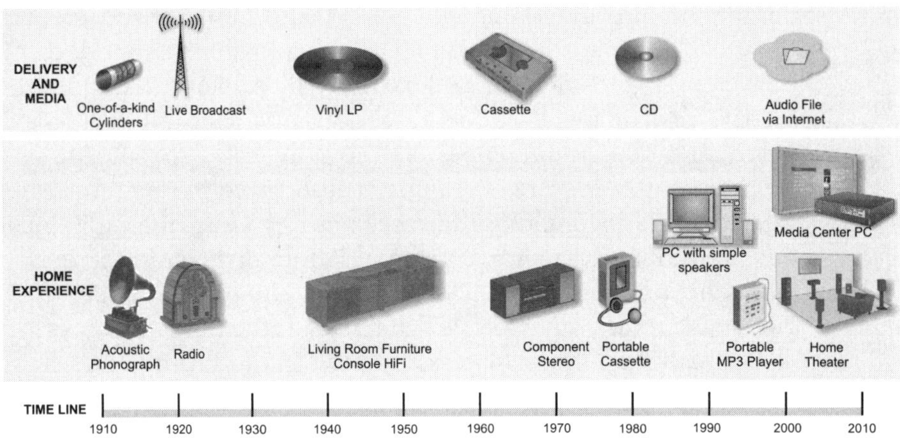

Figure 1.1 Timeline of Home Audio Entertainment Devices

Early Phonograph Players

Perhaps the first significant event was the invention of the phonograph as a means of delivering audio entertainment to an individual in their home. The first phonograph players appeared in the late 1800s, but of course they were mechanical with no electronics involved. No duplication facilities existed, so every cylinder or disc was an original. Sound was recorded acoustically and played back the same way—you had no volume control and fidelity was far from high. But with the advent of this technology, if you could afford it, you could listen to your favorite song at home when you wanted, not just when the performer was in town.

Radio

The second significant event was the use of radio broadcasting to deliver audio entertainment to a listener at home. Despite some debate over when the first broadcast of music entertainment took place, just before 1920 is a likely date. Broadcast music caught on quickly as home radio sets improved and became more available. Fidelity took a giant leap forward from the primitive acoustic phonograph; the radio could be loud enough for the whole family to hear. As the broadcasting industry grew, network connections between cities enabled a listener in Toledo, Ohio, to listen to a live symphony happening in New York. But initially, performances were live, because high-quality recording facilities had not yet been developed.

Record Players

In the late 1920s, electrified phonographs, later called record players, started to appear. The initial medium was the 78-rpm shellac record with a limited playing time. The late 1940s saw the introduction of the long-playing 33-rpm disc made of an improved material, polyvinylchloride. The record player was usually a large furniture item in the family living room. In the mid 50s, the stereo process was introduced to records. Audio quality improved with each new development. The availability of stereo prompted many people to upgrade their system. Audio entertainment was entering the *high fidelity* era and it was convenient and accessible.

Home Appliances and the Radio, Stereo System

In the mid 1900s, home audio entertainment was a single system in the living room. Perhaps one had a small "table radio" in the kitchen but only for listening to news The 1960s and 70s saw the introduction of *component* systems and later mini systems. As the costs of systems went down, families could have more than one system. Eventually every family member could have their own *personal stereo* although these appliances were not yet portable.

Electronic miniaturization coupled with improved headphones allowed high quality playback devices to be made small enough to fit into a pocket or purse so the personal entertainment device was now also portable.

Most of the initial growth of home audio was to enhance music listening. The other entertainment device in the home, the TV, likely still had only a single 4" speaker and audio quality was of little importance in the industry. But the development of the home video cassette recorder, and eventually, the spread of movie rental stores started a drive to improve the home video entertainment system to match the developments that had been happening in the movie theater. This drive started with improvements to the way audio was recorded on tape, improvements to the speakers and amplifiers, introduction of stereo to video programming, and better attention to audio production techniques during the creation of material.

Home Theater

Sound experience in cinemas went through many improvements in the 70s and 80s. Better speakers, replacement of the inferior optical sound track, environment equalization, and the introduction of multiple channels of surround sound made the listening experience in the theater far superior to the home TV or VCR. The development of the Digital Versatile Disk (DVD), with its superior digital audio quality and ability to handle multiple channels of surround sound, brought the theater experience into the home living room. Inexpensive and simple to set up, the home-theater-in-a-box systems made the new technology available to the mass market. Modified speaker spectral distribution inherent with surround sound technologies reduced the size and cost of surround speakers, allowing an easier integration into the home environment.

Home theater began as an evolution of traditional stereo receivers, adding surround sound, sub-woofer channels, and DVD playback capability. But while these systems deliver the quality and impact, they don't integrate well with the growing practice of digital audio music distribution. Consumers are migrating their existing CDs and building new music libraries in the form of files on their PCs or portable audio players. The convenience of instant access to thousands of songs, easily set up play lists, convenient family sharing, and easy distribution of music throughout the home made possible by inexpensive home networks—all these factors changed the way we store and listen to music.

Portable and "Personal" Stereo Devices (MP3 Players)

Consumers have wanted portable audio devices since the early days of home audio devices. If you can listen to audio at home, why not while you're at the beach or on a camping trip? The first answers to this question were portable tube radios that stretched the definition of the word "portable." Requiring three sets of expensive and heavy batteries with limited life, portable audio entertainment was an inconvenient luxury. The introduction of transistors in the 1960s made considerable improvements so that radios became small enough to fit into a pocket and needed only a single battery that would last for weeks. In 1979, Sony introduced the Walkman portable cassette player and now consumers could carry about an hour's worth of their own selection of music anywhere. If you wanted more than an hour of music, you had to carry more cassettes or wait another 20 years. In the early 1990s, the Fraunhofer Institute in Germany introduced the MPEG Audio Layer III audio compression format, better known as MP3. This digital compression technology—in conjunction with inexpensive digital storage—allowed more music in less space, faster downloads, and created the opportunity for the first portable MP3 players in 1999. Now, you could have hours of music in a device much smaller than the original Sony[†] Walkman.

PC Music "Jukeboxes" and Digital Home Media Centers

Before the 90s, PCs were seen as office appliances, word processors, accounting machines, maybe home game devices. The development of the MP3 compression format and introduction of Winamp music file organizer and player in 1998 changed that perception. It now became practical to play music on your PC while you worked on your word processor or spread sheet.

Sound cards also improved. Originally intended only to produce sound effects for games and the occasional PC warning beep, they were called upon to play high quality music now. Sound cards in the late 80s and early 90s were a mixed bag of quality, some very good, some with serious problems. In general, few were up to the quality level of traditional home audio systems.

PC music players and organizers, successors to the original Winamp, evolved in the mid-90s. The popularity of broadband Internet connections and home networks facilitated downloading and exchanging songs. The audio files could now be played on any home computer regardless of where they were stored. Suddenly a whole new wave of convenience was born as people transferred their CD and even vinyl music library to their PC. Music "jukebox" programs let listeners set up play lists and all members of the family had simultaneous but independent access to the complete library. On-line music purchase sites let you acquire music instantly without having to go to a retail store.

Parallel to this music listening evolution, home visual entertainment was expanding. Watching feature movies on rented VHS tapes on a small screen with questionable audio was not nearly as exciting as seeing the movie in a modern cinema venue with surround sound and big screen. Enter the home theater system! The introduction of the DVD, with its improved digital audio and ability to carry several formats of high quality surround sound, combined with the availability of less expensive larger screen plasma TV sets and DLP projectors meant that the consumer could now create a home entertainment environment in the league of commercial cinemas. This evolution began with traditional home entertainment devices—surround sound receivers, DVD players, and "home-theater-in-a-box" systems—but is now migrating to the PC as the media center. The PC adds accessibility, connectivity, a sophisticated user interface, and expandability that the traditional receiver cannot match.

Of course, now we're back to the subject of this book: Intel High Definition Audio. Now that the consumer has experienced high quality audio with traditional home entertainment systems, they are not likely to settle for anything less when the PC becomes the entertainment center. Audio quality, multichannel surround sound, consistent delivery, seamless resource sharing, and ease of use—the PC must meet customer expectations in all these areas of the home audio experience.

But first, how do we hear sounds? Have you ever considered what parameters are important for us to perceive audio quality and fidelity, and how we characterize them? Let's look at analog and digital audio basics, some of the technologies involved, and where problems can occur before we get to the important details of Intel HD Audio and how it is implemented.

Human Auditory Perception and Acoustics

When it comes to human auditory perception and how it relates to audio equipment design, specification, and quality management, our subjective perception is sometimes at odds with electronic measurement practices. So, here are the differences.

Frequency Range of Human Hearing

The generally accepted audio band is 20 hertz to 20 kilohertz, although few adults hear sounds above 12 kilohertz very well. To get a feel for how familiar sounds map to this spectrum, Figure 1.2 shows the audio band with the fundamental range of common musical instruments superimposed. At first look, you might say why bother with anything beyond 5 kilohertz or so since the chart shows no sound output from instruments above that point? But, the piano keyboard and musical instrument range bars refer only to *fundamental* frequencies. All instruments have rich harmonic structures that give them their unique timbre and character, and these structures extend their frequency range well beyond the fundamental range shown in this chart. And while human hearing at higher frequencies gradually degrades with age, it seldom disappears completely, so the upper range is important to reproduce instruments and other sounds faithfully and realistically.

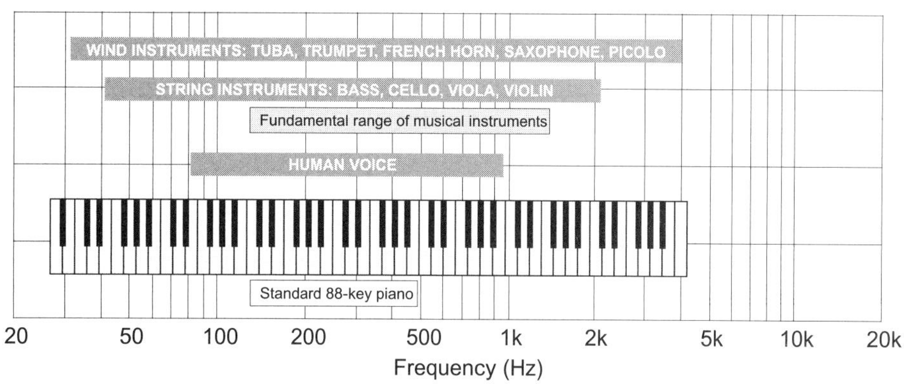

Frequently called the 20 hertz to 20 kilohertz audio band, the frequency range of common musical instruments and sounds are shown on the log frequency scale.

Figure 1.2 The Frequency Range of Human Hearing

Frequency or Pitch Scale

Human perception is inherently logarithmic while electronic circuits and measurements are usually linear. This difference becomes an issue when gathering and presenting measurement results. If you use the typical settings of a measurement instrument, the presentation of your results would appear skewed and it could mask important detail. For example, if we look at Figure 1.2, we see that the piano keyboard maps perfectly with the logarithmic frequency scale, as you can see from the fact that the keys are of uniform size on the diagram. Most instruments, such as spectrum analyzers, default to a linear frequency axis. If we were to redraw Figure 1.2 with the linear frequency scale shown in Figure 1.3, half of the graph depicts the top octave from 10 kilohertz to 20 kilohertz, which is far less important than the mid-range. On the other hand, most of the keys on the piano would be compressed into the lower 10 percent of the graph, obscuring this detail and presenting an image that is quite different from the way we hear it. Of course, the piano keys also are unevenly spaced; the lower frequency keys on the left are much smaller than the high frequency keys on the right.

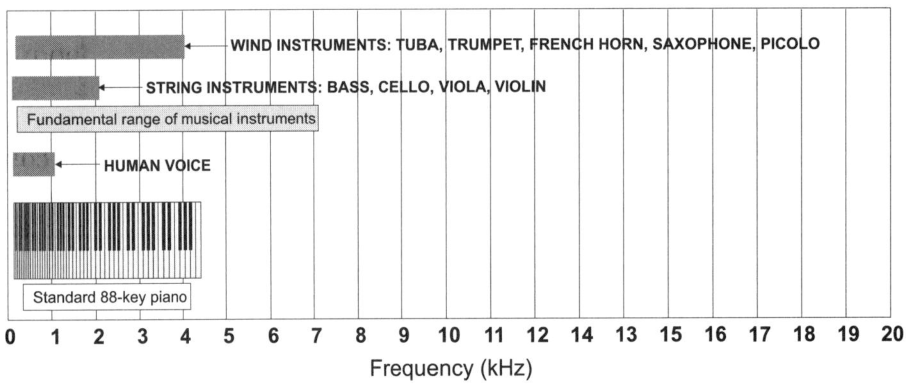

The same data is shown in Figure 1.2 is redrawn with a linear frequency scale. All the data is compressed into the left 20 percent of the graph, obscuring much of the important detail.

Figure 1.3 Frequency Range of Common Musical Instruments on a Linear Frequency Scale

Musical scales are expressed in octaves rather than hertz, where each increase of an octave is a doubling of frequency.

The Harmonic Series

Harmonics are secondary audible components, related mathematically to the fundamental range, that give a particular sound its character when the two are joined. It is rare to find a naturally occurring sound that has no harmonics. Indeed, the harmonic structure is what gives every musical instrument its unique timbre, distinguishing it from another even though they may have the same fundamental frequency range.

A *harmonic* is an integer multiple of the fundamental. For example, the second harmonic is twice the fundamental; third harmonic is three times the fundamental and so on. Most sounds contain a complex structure of several harmonics, each with its own unique relative amplitude and phase relative to the fundamental. We also have a varying appreciation for different harmonics. In general, even order harmonics such as second and fourth add warmth and body while odd harmonics may sound harsh or discordant. (See "Total Harmonic Distortion" later in this chapter.)

Amplitude Units (dB)

Before looking at amplitude and dynamic range, let's review the units used to describe those characteristics. Like human pitch perception, human sound intensity is also logarithmic, as you will see in the next few pages. To express audio amplitudes, we frequently use the logarithmic unit *dB*.

An abbreviation for deciBel, the dB is one tenth of a Bel. The Bel unit was named in honor of Alexander Graham Bell. Since the Bel is too coarse for most situations, the decibel (dB) was adopted as a more convenient unit.

Since it is a logarithmic unit, dB is more suitable for expressing perceived signal levels than linear engineering units such as Volts or Watts. We can convert voltage levels to dB using the formula $20\log_{10}(V_1/V_2)$ where V_1 and V_2 are the voltage levels of the two signal amplitudes that we are comparing. If we are comparing two power levels, the formula is: $10\log_{10}(P_1/P_2)$ where P_1 and P_2 are the power amplitudes of the two signal levels in Watts.

Several common ratios are handy to remember. For example, when dealing with the gain of an amplifier or loss of an attenuator, the ratio is often expressed as a ratio, for example: "a gain of 2 times" or "an attenuation of 1/10". Ratios of 2 or ½ are approximately 6 dB, ratios of 10x or

1/10 are 20 dB. Table 1.1 shows several common ratios and their equivalent dB values.

Table 1.1 Examples of Ratios and Their dB Equivalents

dB	Voltage Ratio or Gain or Loss	Power Ratio
60 dB	1000x	1,000,000x
40 dB	100x	10,000x
20 dB	10x	100x
10 dB	3.16x	10x
6.02 dB	2x	4x
3 dB	1.4x	2x
-10 dB	0.316x	0.1x
-20 dB	0.1x	0.01x
-30 dB	0.0316x	0.001x
-40 dB	0.01x	0.0001x
-60 dB	0.001x	0.000001x

Absolute dB units

Table 1.1 lists common ratios and their equivalent dB values. But what if we want to express absolute amplitude using dB units? The decibel is a ratio unit that is used to express the difference between two amplitudes. If one of those amplitudes has been defined as a *reference* amplitude, a special dB unit can be used to express the *absolute* amplitude of a signal. For example, if we assert our reference to be 1 milliwatt, we can express the amplitude of any signal relative to 1 mW and use the designation dBm, perhaps the most familiar unit. Other popular references are 1 Volt for dBV and 0.7746 V for dBu. So, 0.7746 V is the voltage amplitude of a signal that would produce 1 mW in a 600 ohm resistor, and it expresses the amplitude that a level meter calibrated in dBm would indicate.

Many AC level meters are calibrated in dBm, and it is common to see signal levels in audio equipment expressed in dBm. This usage actually is somewhat in error because this dBm unit refers to a power ratio and seldom is any power involved in audio circuits—excluding power amplifiers and speakers. The use of dBm is a holdover from early telephony engineering where audio or voice circuits actually did involve small amounts of power driving relatively low impedances of typically 600 ohms. Such power transfers have been replaced with so called "voltage transfer" interfaces, so dBm is no longer an appropriate unit. But old habits are hard to break. And because so many signal level meters display dBm, an alternative unit was developed. dBu is a voltage ratio unit where the reference is 0.7746 Volts, the same voltage that would be developed across a 600 ohm resistor if it were dissipating 1 mW. So the "dBm meter" is actually displaying dBu.

Another common unit is dBV, again a voltage ratio but with the reference set to 1 Volt. So 0 dBV is 1 V. +10 dBV is 3.26 V. -40 dBV is 10 mV, and
-60 dBV is 1 mV. This unit is perhaps the most appropriate measurement to use when specifying electronic audio signal levels.

So, all of these units can be used to measure absolute electrical signal levels or relative gains and losses such as one might find when measuring systems.

Acoustic Levels (dBSPL)

Acoustic levels, the physical sound levels of actual noise sources, are specified by measuring *sound pressure level*. Again, the log dB unit is the correct one to use, but one must develop an absolute unit of measure. For acoustic intensity, you would define a *reference* sound pressure level of 20 microPascals (µPa) and set this intensity to be 0 dBSPL.

Dynamic Range

The human ear has a remarkable dynamic range, significantly more than any man-made instrument. In fact, audio systems are challenged to preserve this dynamic range that naturally occurs in music and other sounds. The total dynamic rage of human sound level perception can exceed 120 dB although is more typically 100 dB, or 10 Bels. Such a wide range is greater than almost any electronic or electro-acoustic device can reproduce without using tricks. Figure 1.4 illustrates the range of sound intensities that we encounter day to day.

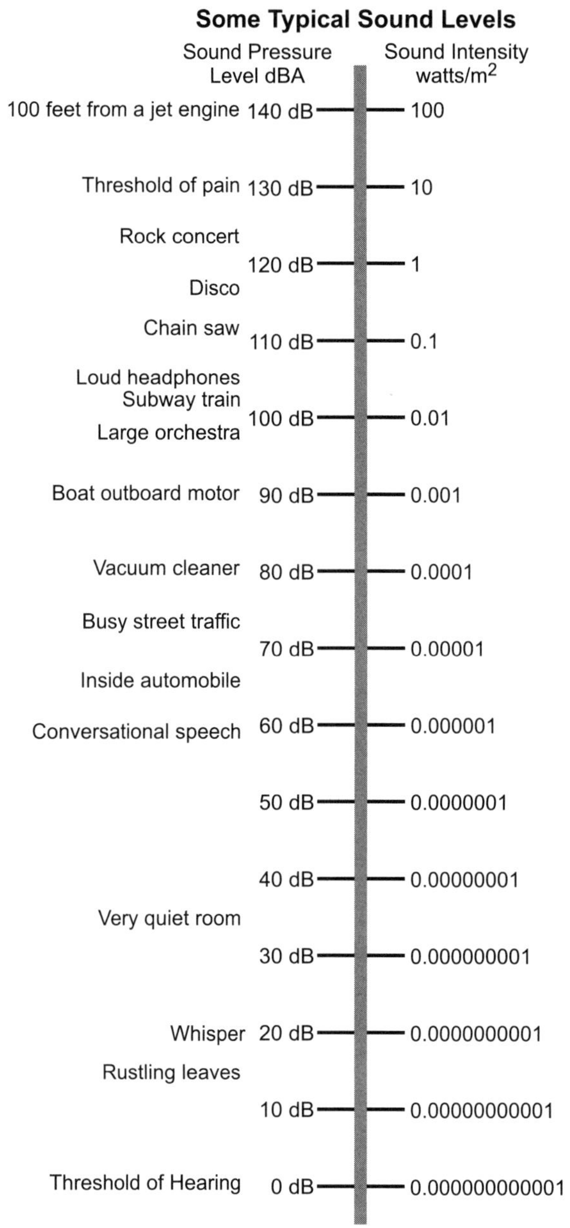

Figure 1.4 Typical Sounds and Their Levels in dB SPL and Intensity in W/m^2

Sound Levels

The same logarithmic perception of frequency scales is found with sound levels or intensities. How do we define and measure amplitude? If we are characterizing an electronic device, we might use volts, or if it is a power amplifier, watts. If we are referring to acoustic amplitude, we would use *sound pressure level* or *intensity*.

Humans can hear a remarkable range of intensities. For examples of the intensities of common sounds, see Figure 1.4. The bottom of the scale is defined as the *threshold of hearing*, meaning the lowest level sound that a human can just barely hear in an extremely quiet room. At the top of the scale is what, perhaps sadistically, is called the *threshold of pain*. An accurate expression: sounds this loud hurt, and sounds above this intensity are likely to damage the ear.

What is remarkable about this graph is its range. The scale on the right is expressed in watts per square meter, a linear unit. You can see how the numbers can get quite unwieldy with too many zeros to easily see the value. The scale on the left is in dB SPL, a logarithmic unit. Notice how much easier it is to understand level differences and express this wide a level range. One can see that the typical sound intensity examples are distributed somewhat evenly across the vertical scale. Now, imagine the scale redrawn with the right side values arranged in a linear distribution starting with 100 at the top, 50 at midpoint, and 0 at the bottom, as shown in Figure 1.5. With such a scale, almost every common sound would be clustered at the bottom and the bulk of the scale would describe very loud sounds. It would not be much value trying to understand sound level distribution.

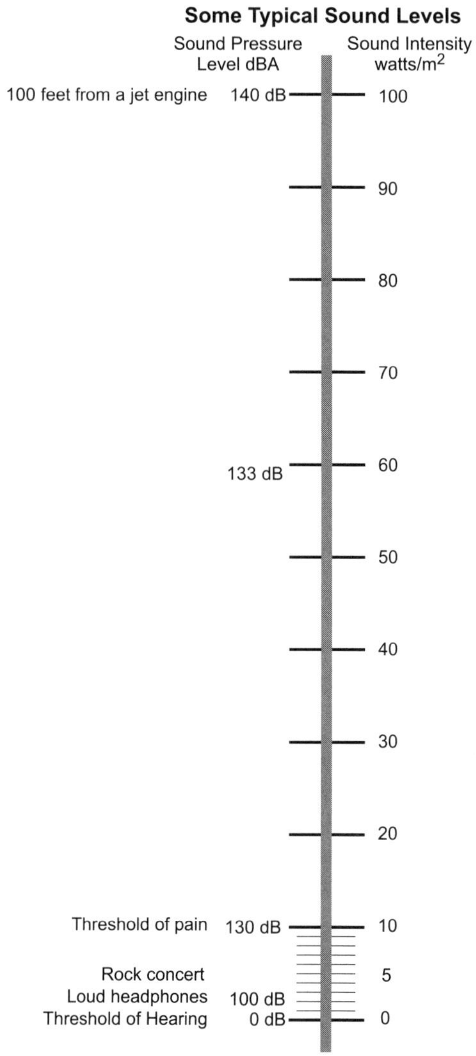

The scale from Figure 1.4 is redrawn as a linear scale showing its absurdity. All of the everyday mid-range intensities are compressed below the lower 10 percent of this scale.

Figure 1.5 The Typical Sound Intensity Levels Graph on a Linear Scale

The point here is to understand that just like frequency, sound levels perceived by human hearing are logarithmic and are best expressed in dB, not volts, watts, or percentage.

What does this point mean to the audio designer? For one, all level controls should have a dB scale with equal steps. Controls with this characteristic frequently are called *log taper* or *audio taper*, and they include volume controls, tone controls, mixer controls, and any others that control sound levels. Actually, most physical volume controls are not truly logarithmic because such a taper is hard to manufacture and not ideal from a user point of view. Typically, these controls are *modified log* or *audio taper*, which have an approximate logarithmic law over most of their travel except at the ends.

The second lesson is to always use a logarithmic (or linear dB) vertical scale and a horizontal log frequency scale when showing performance graphs such as frequency response. Such a graphical presentation better aligns the technical results with perceived performance. At times, this representation requires extra effort since most test instruments default to linear units such as volts and hertz. The better audio measurement instruments correctly favor log units for both measurement and results display.

Frequency Response vs. Audible Level

The *frequency response* of the human ear changes with amplitude. At low sound levels, the ear is not as sensitive to low and high frequencies. This phenomenon was investigated by two scientists at Bell Labs in the 1930s and their results are now well known as the *Fletcher-Munson equal loudness contours*, which are shown in Figure 1.6. This behavior drove the creation of *loudness-compensating* volume controls that were popular on early home audio systems. These controls would increase bass and treble as the volume was turned down in an attempt retain a perceived flatness to the material.

Notice that at the threshold of hearing, it takes about 70 dB more energy to hear a bass note than it takes to hear a mid-range note. However, at an average listening level of 90 to 100 dB SPL, the difference between bass and midrange is much smaller, making the highs and lows much easier to hear in relation to the midrange frequencies.

This behavior is important to know when characterizing audio devices, and it is often a source of considerable confusion in subjective listening. When measuring noise or dynamic range, frequency weighting should be used in order to more accurately model human perception. Frequency weighting reduces the sensitivity of the measuring instrument to low- and high-frequency signals to approximate the response of the ear to low-level signals. Since noise in a device generally is low-level, use of frequency weighting makes the noise test result a more accurate reflection of how noise is perceived.

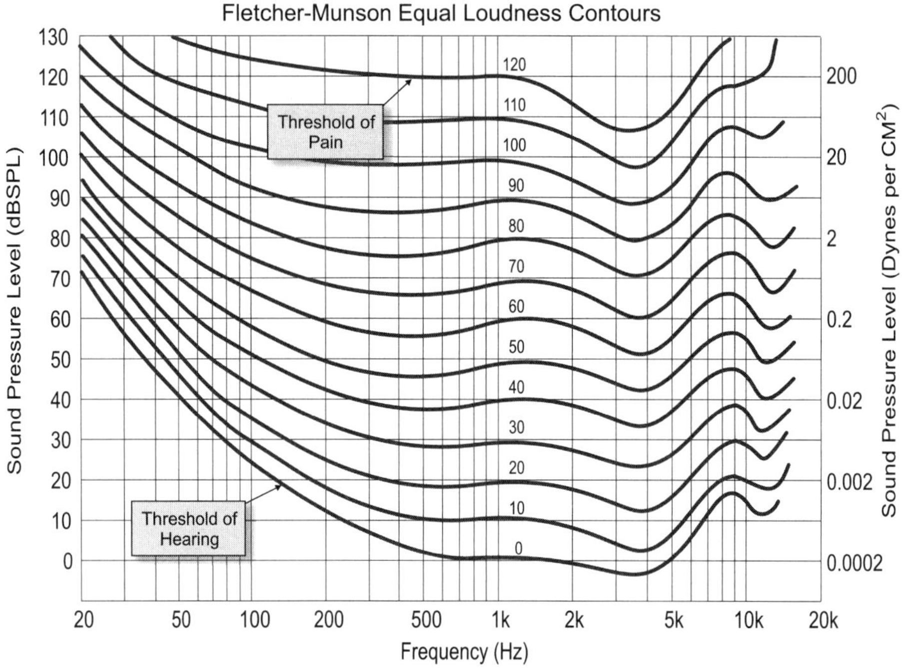

The graph describes the ear's sensitivity to various frequencies at different sound levels.

Figure 1.6 Fletcher-Munson Equal Loudness Contours

Masking

The concept of masking in the human ear is the primary basis for most lossy compression software codec technology such as the popular MP3, ATRAC, AAC, and WMA formats. Masking occurs when a dominant signal appears to cast a shadow over the nearby area, obscuring less dominant signals. Two kinds of masking are frequency and temporal. Frequency masking occurs when we are presented with two closely spaced frequencies of different amplitudes, and the ear only hears the louder signal. Experiments have been done to evaluate how close the two frequencies have to be for various amplitude differences. The results of these tests have defined *critical bands*, a cone-shaped response indicating the frequencies to be obscured by a close-by and louder tone. Early research identified 25 critical bands in the human ear that are distributed across the audio band. More recent studies suggest that these bands are not fixed, but they adapt to the current sound.

Temporal masking occurs when a loud sound is closely followed or preceded by a lower-level sound. The ear needs time to adapt to the low-level signal, and if it is too short a duration, we won't hear it.

When you take masking into account, you could analyze a music passage in which some of the information had been removed and you would not be able to detect its removal. That is exactly how perceptual coders work; they analyze a segment of the signal and throw away what falls within the critical band, processing only the remainder. As a result, a device needs to record or transmit less data than it would without such coding or compression.

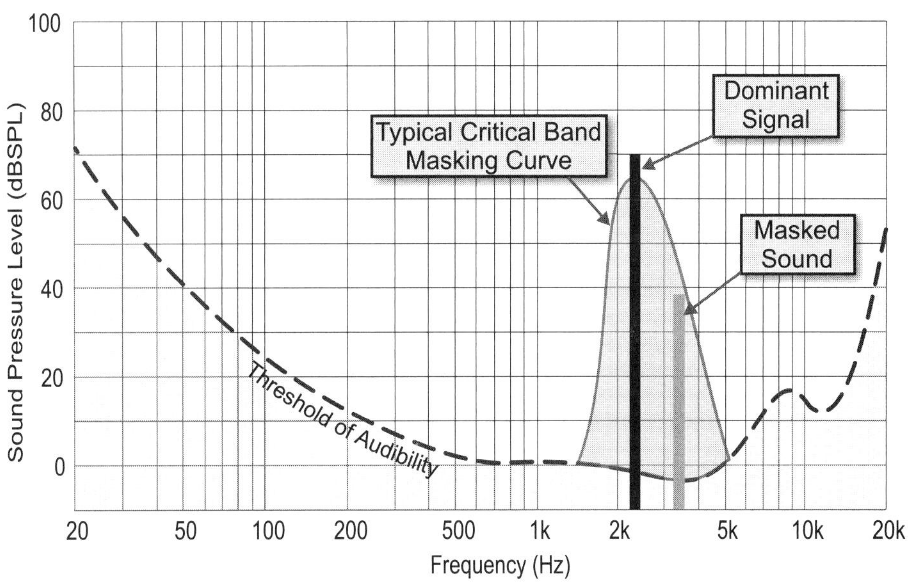

Sounds can be obscured if they fall within the curve of a dominant signal.

Figure 1.7 Typical Critical Band or Masking Curve

Analog Audio

This section shows you how to characterize an audio device, what factors may contribute to audio degradation, and what steps you might take to avoid such problems.

Critical Measurement Parameters

Part of any quality initiative is the establishment of metrics. We want to measure audio quality objectively so we can maintain or improve it, or know when it has been degraded. A well-established suite of tests provides a comprehensive characterization of an audio device. How the tests are performed is important, and interpretation of results may require explanation.

The three primary characteristics affecting audio quality are frequency response, noise, and distortion. Degradation in *frequency response*, a measurement of spectral uniformity or flatness, changes the character of a sound by emphasizing or suppressing parts of the spectrum. Poor frequency response invokes remarks about the sound being "muffled," "overly bright," or "thin." *Noise* is an unwanted addition to the sound that distracts from the listening experience. The noise could be broadband, such as hiss that is usually distributed across a wide audio band, or it could occur at particular frequencies, as does hum. Noise may be constant or only triggered by other events, perhaps by the primary signal itself. *Distortion* is the addition of new unwanted signals related to the primary signal. Different types of distortion invoke different degrees of annoyance, but virtually any distortion is unwelcome. Distortion causes listening fatigue, so it is no longer pleasurable for the listener to continue listening.

Establishing Reference Levels

If we are going to establish a set of metrics that can characterize an audio device, we need a standardized method of measurement and a consistent implementation. One area that is frequently overlooked but that has a significant impact on measurement results is the *reference level*. Virtually all objective measurements are intended to be done at a specific level, generally a standards-specified reference level. For results to be consistent and comparisons between devices to be accurate, you must determine this reference level properly. Usually, you establish the reference level by following guidelines that are defined in reference standards. A reference level is usually an amplitude that is close to full scale or to the clipping level in analog circuits. Sometimes, it is specified as the level at which the device first produces a specified level of distortion. With some complex systems where access to internal nodes is difficult or impossible, establishing a reference level can be difficult, and it must be done by inference.

Frequency Response

Frequency response characterizes the bandwidth and flatness of a device. It is perhaps the best known and understood measurement, and you often see frequency response graphs on consumer electronics packaging. The measurement is an easy one to make: simply stimulate the device under test with a series of test signals that span the band of interest or better yet, perform a continuous sweep, and measure the signal amplitude at the output of the device. Typically, the results are plotted on a log graph with the trace normalized to 0 dB at 1 kilohertz so deviations over the band of interest, usually 20 hertz to 20 kilohertz, are easily discernable. Expressed numerically, frequency response typically would be stated as ±n dB, 20 hertz to 20 kilohertz, where n expresses the maximum deviation such as ±0.5 dB. Figure 1.8 shows a graphical example of a two-channel frequency response. In this case, the peaks and dips are not symmetrical so this frequency response would be stated numerically as Frequency Response +0.1 dB, -0.7 dB, 20 hertz to 20 kilohertz. Frequency response usually is measured with a stimulus level of -20 dBR, that is, a level 20 dB below the established reference level.

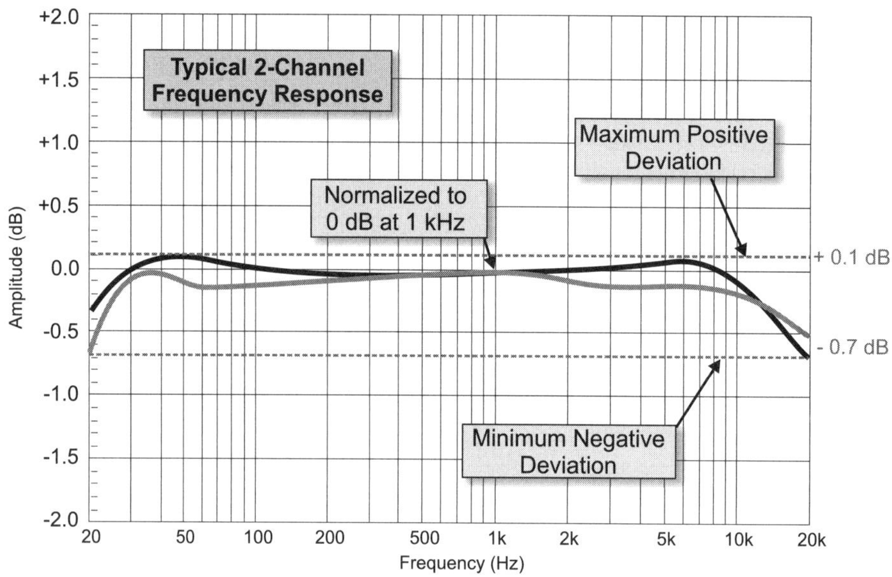

Figure 1.8. Frequency Response Graph with two Overlaid Channels

Any deviations from a flat frequency response indicates that the system is overly emphasizing or attenuating portions of the spectrum, which results in a *coloration* of the program material, as shown in Figure 1.9. For example, when bass response is inadequate, the audio sounds thin, a movie's sound effects seem to have less impact and music lacks a fullness and power that consumers might have enjoyed from a live performance or from their traditional home audio systems. Conversely, excessive boost of low frequencies can overemphasize movie sound effects or the beat energy in music, and in some cases, it can introduce unpleasant distortion by overdriving speakers.

The high frequency range of music provides the character and spatial imaging. The harmonic character of musical instruments is expressed at the higher frequencies. If these harmonics are suppressed or overly accentuated, the distinguishing features and characteristics of these instruments are lost. Our localization, or spatial perception, is almost completely derived from high frequency information. Our ability to separate distinct sounds is tied to high frequency content. Inadequate high frequency response removes clarity and sharpness, blurs stereo and surround sound imaging, and hampers the ability to distinguish subtle differences and nuances of musical performance.

Excessive high end response can make a system sound too bright. While a gradual boost of high frequencies adds unwanted brightness, a peaked boost adds unwanted color. If the peak boost becomes severe, significant degradation can occur. For example, if too much boost is applied, the "S" sounds in speech produces distorted sibilance. Accentuating high frequencies affects harmonic structure and can cause significant changes to the tonal character of instruments.

Mid-band dips, although a less common response problem, are just as troublesome. The sound lacks presence. The balance of voices is affected. Mid-band peaks, such as high frequency bumps discussed previously, change the character of the audio content, adding an unwanted and unnatural brightness. Similar effects can result from high frequency bumps, including generation of artifacts and sibilance.

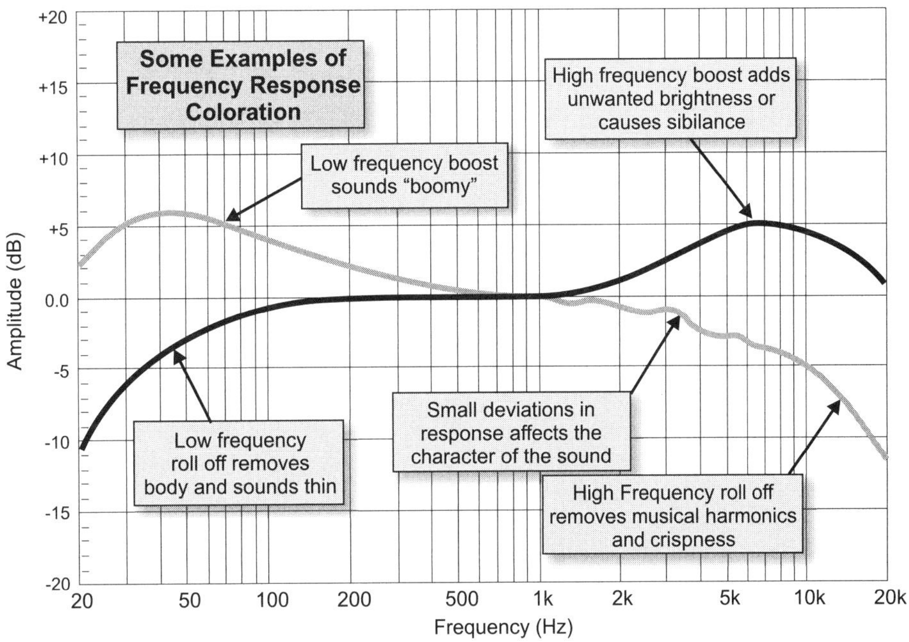

Figure 1.9. Example of Frequency Response Coloration

Pass-band Ripple

Many contemporary systems include a digital-to-analog converter (DAC). See "Digital Audio" later in this chapter for more detail. For now, just consider the frequency response implications these DACs have. Proper converter operation requires the use of anti-aliasing or reconstruction filters. Converters operating at a sample rate of 44.1 kilohertz or 48 kilohertz require high-order, low-pass filters at 20 kilohertz or slightly above. The optimal filter would have no attenuation at frequencies of 20 kilohertz or lower, and its infinite attenuation would be greater than 20 kilohertz. Of course, a practical filter design cannot achieve this optimal level, but the more poles that are used in the design of the filter, the closer a practical design can get to this ideal objective.

A side effect of a high order filter is *passband ripple*. In an effort to shape the filter to have minimal attenuation below 20 kilohertz and maximum attenuation above 20 kilohertz, small peaks and dips in the response below 20 kilohertz are created. You can minimize these peaks and dips by careful filter design, but component tolerances can exacerbate the problem. Figure 1.10 shows an example of passband ripple.

Newer designs are moving towards higher sample rates: 96 kilohertz and 192 kilohertz. The higher sample rates reduce the need for high-order filters, allowing a gentler roll-off characteristic with corner frequencies well above 20 kilohertz and diminishing passband ripple in the audio band. Measurement of passband ripple was an important criterion a few years ago since some filter designs were less than ideal and created significant ripple. Contemporary converter designs have reduced the ripple to almost immeasurable amounts.

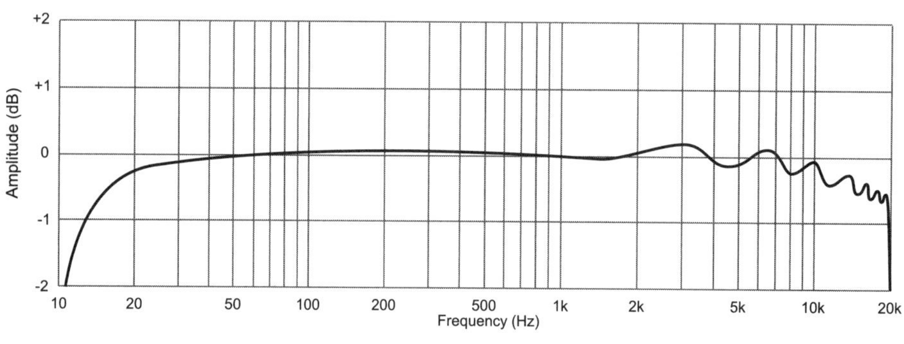

Figure 1.10 Passband Ripple Caused by the Anti-aliasing Low-pass Filter

Noise

Noise is unfortunately present to some extent in every device; when it is too loud, noise interferes with our enjoyment of the program content. Due to the various ways to specify noise in a device, comparing results can sometimes be confusing. One way to measure noise is to remove any signal source from the device, terminate the input, and measure the *absolute noise level* at the output of a device. You would specify this result in absolute units such as millivolts or dBV. While absolute noise is useful, it only gives us part of the picture. We really want to know how this noise compares to typical program level so we can judge how annoying it might be. This dilemma gave rise to the term *signal-to-noise ratio*, which gives us an understanding of how the absolute noise compares to typical signal level. Of course, the meaning of *signal level* must be defined and the level must be determined using a consistent method. The reference level helps to do both.

Signal-to-Noise Ratio (SNR)

For many years, the signal-to-noise ratio measurement technique has been used to characterize analog devices. Frequently, it is used to characterize digital devices, although this use is not correct.

To measure signal-to-noise ratio in a device, you must make two measurements, signal and noise, and then compute the ratio of the two. First, you establish the *signal level* part of this ratio, usually by following a published standard that defines a common industry-accepted method. For example, for analog tape recorders, reference signal level is the level that produces 1-percent third harmonic distortion. For audio power amplifiers, reference level is the point where the amplifier just produces an output of 1 watt at 1 kilohertz with the amplifier loaded to its rated load impedance. Thus, well-defined industry-wide procedures establish this reference level for various traditional audio devices. In general, the reference level is set as high as possible, as close to the maximum signal level as the device can handle. Of course, the higher this level, the better the signal-to-noise ratio result in published specifications that potential customers might use to compare competitive products.

Some loosely defined procedures may set the reference level as the *clipping level* of the device. The difficulty here is that results often are inconsistent because defining a crisp clipping level usually is impossible. Years ago when distortions levels were higher than they are on today's devices, engineers would use an oscilloscope to look at the signal waveform and with a 1-kilohertz tone, adjust the signal until they could just see a flattening or clipping of the waveform. Again, this procedure was not precise and was subject to inconsistencies as it is difficult to see 1-percent distortion on an oscilloscope.

You must establish the reference level with the device under test in a defined state and with prescribed external conditions. For example, if the gain of the device is user variable, one typically sets it to establish a particular system gain or output condition. If the device is a power amplifier, it must be loaded with its specified load impedance. If tone controls are present, they must be set to a flat condition. If signal processing is present, it generally is switched off. Each of these conditions is particular to the type of device and may be defined in a measurement standard or measurement procedure. Following these procedures should allow consistent and repeatable results to be achieved.

After establishing the reference level, you measure the second part of the ratio, the noise level. Here again, certain procedures must be rigorously followed. For analog devices, the signal source is removed from the input of the device and replaced with a *termination impedance*. Typically, this replacement is a resistor with a value the same as the typical source impedance of the usual source device. For example, if the device being measured is a microphone preamp that is designed to amplify a low-impedance microphone, the typical microphone would have a source impedance of 150 ohms. So, the input should be terminated with a 150 ohm resistor.

This termination impedance can influence the noise reading. High gain microphone preamps have a characteristic input noise current and noise voltage. Their design is optimized to balance these two contributors to noise for the intended source impedance. Simply *shorting* the input does not provide the correct operating conditions. See Figure 1.11 for a measurement procedure diagram.

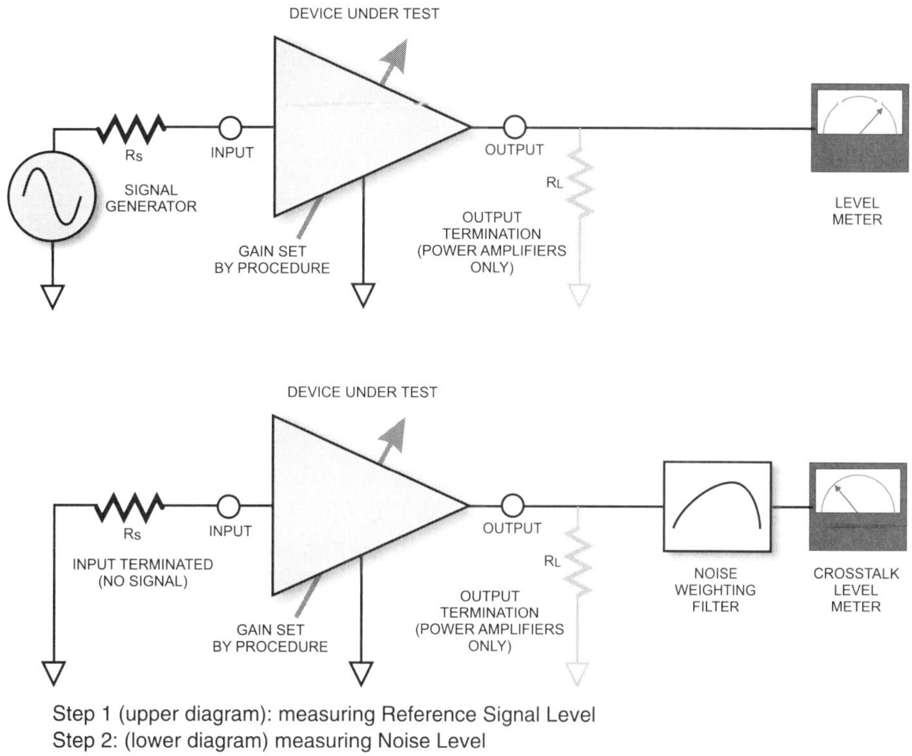

Figure 1.11 Signal-to-Noise Ratio Measurement

Dynamic Range (DR)

The signal-to-noise ratio measurement technique has been used successfully for many years to characterize analog audio devices. Digital devices, now making up the main stream of consumer audio devices, have certain operational characteristics that make the traditional technique of measuring signal-to-noise ratio inappropriate. Instead, the *dynamic range* measurement technique addresses the particular needs of digital devices.

The term dynamic range refers to the procedure used to characterize noise in a digital audio or mixed analog-digital device. The traditional signal-to-noise ratio method cannot provide correct results in a digital device. Most digital circuits or converters are smart and they shut down or reduce the gain of the channel in the absence of signal. So the analog technique of removing the signal from the input and measuring the remaining noise actually measures only the part of the circuit beyond the shut down portion. Since most of the noise in a typical circuit is at the input, the noise reading taken beyond shutdown is deceptively good and not representative of the device's actual operation.

Another difficulty when measuring a digital circuit is establishing the reference level. To understand digital reference level settings, you need to explore how digital circuits behave at and near their maximum level. Analog circuits exhibit a somewhat soft maximum limit. Yes, they do clip when the signal exceeds a particular voltage level, but near this point is a small region where distortion gradually increases with level. When the level is exceeded, the device begins to clip, which adds harmonic distortion to the signal.

Contrast this gradual onset of distortion with behavior of digital circuits near and at their maximum level. A digital circuit delivers its optimal performance near its maximum level. At that point, the full resolution is available, that is, all bits are contributing. But as soon as the level exceeds digital full scale, things turn very nasty. Unlike analog circuits, no gradual clipping or limiting occurs. The audible effect of exceeding digital full scale is far more objectionable than analog clipping. With this realization in mind, designers of digital circuits build in smart limiting that prevents the signal from ever reaching absolute full scale. In effect, the design mimics analog circuit behavior.

The problem is that early measurement recommendations suggested using digital full scale as the reference level. On the surface, choosing full scale seems wise—it is well defined as the maximum value of the digital word. In practice, digital full scale is unachievable in most cases because of the built-in limiting action. Current recommendations suggest that reference level should be established as the lower of two points: digital full scale or that level just producing a total harmonic distortion of -40 dB or 1 percent. Figure 1.12 illustrates a typical analog-to-digital converter's behavior near full scale. The upper graph shows the analog input to digital output transfer curve, indicating the gradual compression near full scale. The lower graph shows output digital Total Harmonic Distortion plus Noise (THD+N) as the analog input level is increased. Distortion is low over most of the range but rises sharply as the signal level approaches full scale. The digital output level that produces 1% THD+N is defined as the reference level. Interestingly, this behavior is very similar to that of an analog amplifier.

This process of determining a reference level by finding the -40 dB point can be challenging and is a complex process that is hard to automate. An alternative approach to establishing the reference level is to assert an absolute level as the reference, and then mandate that all equipment be able to operate within specification at that level. Some new certification programs are using this approach because it is more predictable, repeatable, and much easier to accomplish. The most popular choice for this absolute reference level is 0 dBV, that is 1 Volt. This establishes a level playing field for all manufacturers and removes much of the uncertainty and complexity from performing tests that require establishment of a reference level.

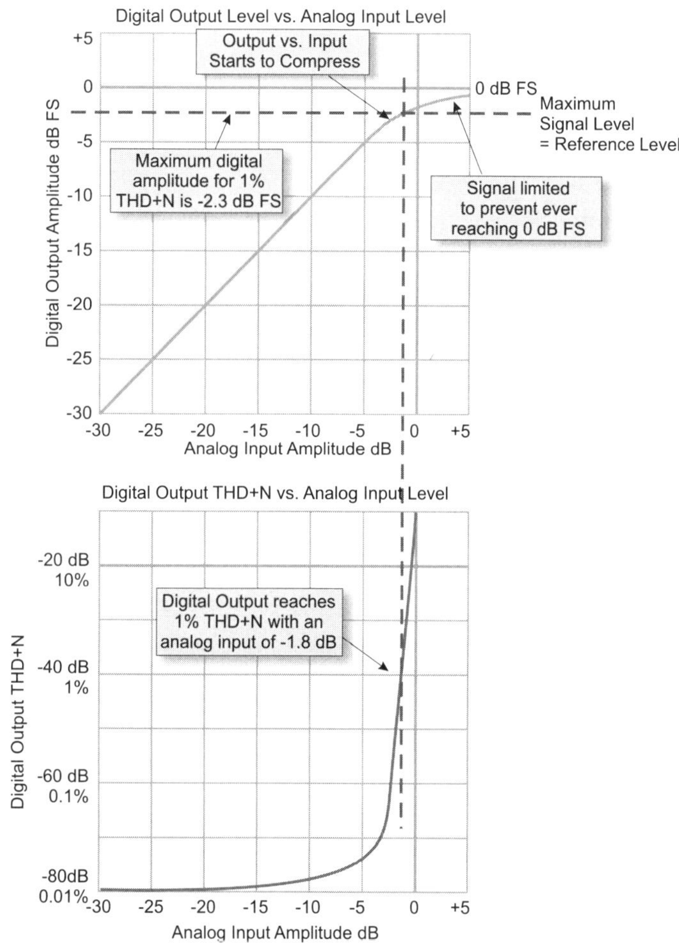

Figure 1.12 Example of "Digital Limiting" in an A to D Converter

Once the correct reference level is established, you can proceed with the dynamic range measurement. An honest noise measurement should express the amount of noise present when the system is operating in the conditions that are true while signal is present. The only way to make such a measurement in a digital circuit is stimulate the device with signal and measure the noise while this signal is present. This task seems difficult, but actually, it is a simple technique using any audio distortion analyzer. The device is stimulated with a low-level 1 kilohertz sine wave at 60 dB below the reference level.

The total harmonic distortion plus noise (THD+N) is measured using a THD+N audio analyzer and with an appropriate noise weighting filter selected. Because the stimulus signal is a very low level, the actual harmonic distortion components are very low. In fact, they typically occur well below the circuit noise of the device. Therefore, this measurement actually is a noise measurement, not a harmonic distortion measurement, and it accurately expresses the true system noise under real operating conditions. (See the "Non-linear Distortion" section for a detailed explanation of distortion measurement.) The dynamic range is the THD+N reading in dB increased by 60 dB, and it is the true dynamic range—the difference between the reference level and the noise floor in the presence of signal. Figure 1.13 illustrates the use of a typical analog THD+N analyzer to measure dynamic range.

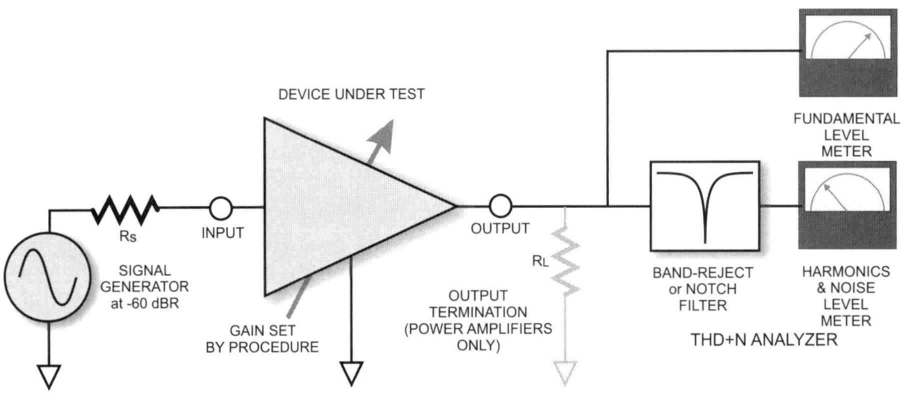

Figure 1.13 Dynamic Range Measurement Technique Using a THD+N Audio Analyzer

Noise Weighting

Figure 1.6 shows explicitly how the ear's sensitivity to high and low frequency signals at low levels is diminished. Noise in a device typically occurs at a low sound pressure level, which means that we do not hear low and high frequency noise components as well as mid-frequency components. When measuring noise, you should account for this fact. To do so, *weight* or filter the noise measurement. Again, measurement standards specify the type of *noise weighting filter* for particular measurements. In North America, *A-weighting* has been the most popular weighting curve used for many years. Although many in the measurement community feel that this weighting curve is out of date and not ideal for today's devices, it remains the most popular curve, and it does address the fundamental ear sensitivity issue while providing a consistency of measurement because of its popularity.

A second weighting filter that is more popular in Europe is the so-called *CCIR* filter. This filter had its origins in the CCIR-468 measurement standard. The CCIR group no longer exists but the large ITU standards organization has adopted this filter and it is now designated ITU-R468. Its general shape is similar to the A-weighting filter but it reaches a peak of approximately 12 dB at approximately 6 kilohertz. The original CCIR standard also specified a *quasi-peak* meter detection characteristic. Meters with such a detector were hard to come by and relatively expensive. In the 1970s, Dolby Laboratories proposed an alternative technique that used the same filter curve but set the unity gain point at 2 kilohertz rather than the more typical 1 kilohertz. Shifting the unity gain point made noise measurements approximately 6 dB lower than those made with the original CCIR-468 filter, but this shift avoided the meter overload problems that could occur because of the 12 dB gain of this filter. Dolby also suggested the use of what was then a more common *average responding* detector rather than the scarce quasi-peak detector. Most AC level meters in that era were "averaging responding, rms calibrated," so they could be used with this filter to make noise measurements according to the Dolby recommendation that they designated: CCIR-ARM.

Figure 1.14 illustrates the frequency response of the three common noise weighting filters. Most modern audio measurement systems include at least one, and often all three, of these filters and their corresponding detectors.

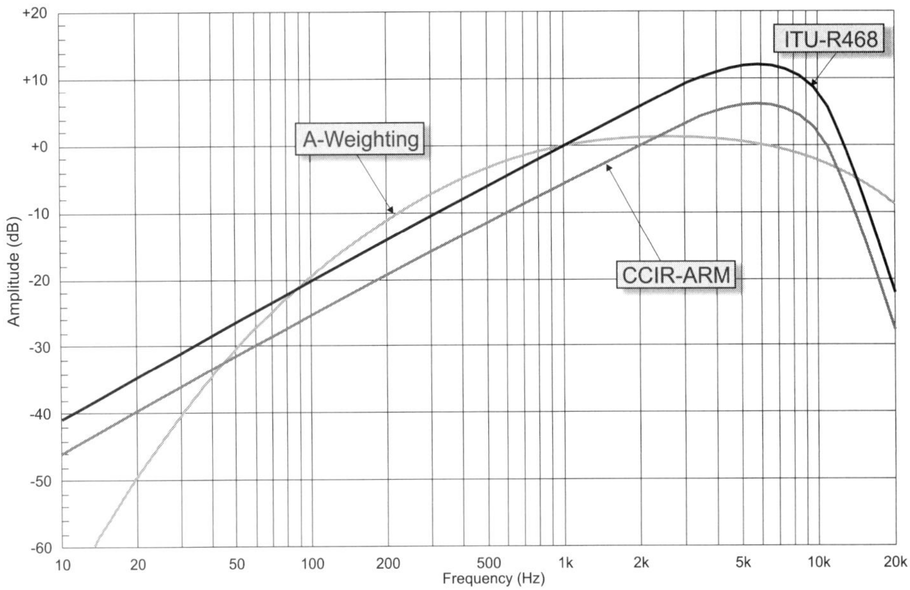

Figure 1.14 Frequency Response of Common Noise Weighting Curves

Headroom

Headroom is the difference between average program level and the highest level possible. Of course, this margin depends heavily on where we set average program level. Headroom is more commonly used in professional audio—recording and broadcast applications—where the average program level is constantly monitored and kept within a narrow range. With consumer equipment, the average program level depends on actual listening level, which in turn has a wide range of values. Figure 1.15 shows how headroom fits into the big picture that includes noise and maximum level.

In the professional world, it is common to strive for 20 decibels of headroom. During the music recording process, the recording engineer adjusts the level of each microphone to satisfy an artistic balance while maintaining the overall composite level within a narrow range. He or she monitors this level using a VU meter, a level meter optimized for monitoring continuously varying program content. The VU meter is calibrated in decibels with "0 dB" approximately 75 percent of full scale. The system design of the recording environment allows signals 10 to 20 decibels above this 0 VU level to be recorded undistorted. This margin is the headroom.

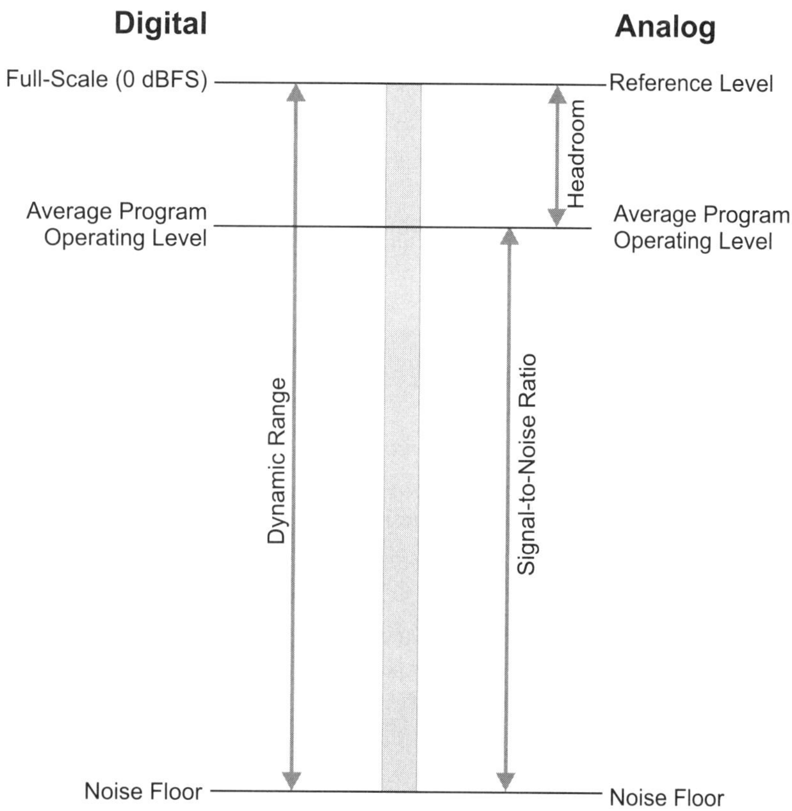

Figure 1.15 Various Reference and Signal Levels and Their Relationships

Nonlinear Distortion

Nonlinear distortion occurs when the device creates additional components that are not present in the original signal but are related to the original signal. This section addresses two types of distortion: harmonic and intermodulation.

Generally nonlinear components in the signal path cause distortion. These components may be active, such as amplification, or passive, such as capacitors.

We can safely say that distortion is virtually always an unwanted consequence of some part of the device not performing as desired. The only exception to this statement might be specialized effects devices, sometimes called *fuzz boxes*, used by musicians to achieve a particular sound.

Different types of distortion annoy the listener to differing degrees. Knowing this fact can help you make judgment calls on how much distortion is acceptable. Often a design or test engineer must make a tradeoff when deciding what constitutes a tolerable amount of distortion versus the cost of reducing all distortion or not shipping a product.

Digital components can present new challenges in distortion characterization. Before looking at measurements, let's define the two types of distortion.

- *Harmonic distortion* is the generation or modification of the harmonics of the original signal by the device. Reminder: harmonics are integer multiples of the fundamental.
- Harmonics can be classified further into odd and even. This distinction is relevant because we know that the annoyance from odd harmonics is greater than from even harmonics. It is also true that low-order harmonics are less objectionable than high order harmonics. So 7th, 9th, 11th and higher odd harmonics are less tolerated than 2nd and 4th even-order harmonics.
- *Intermodulation distortion* (IMD) is the generation of new components by the interaction of two or more signals. These additional components appear at the sum and difference frequencies of the original signals and at the sum and difference frequency of the harmonics of the original signals. In general, IMD is more objectionable than harmonic distortion.

Total Harmonic Distortion (THD)

THD is perhaps the most familiar type of distortion. THD is defined as the ratio of the square root of the sum of all of the squares of the magnitude of all harmonics to the magnitude of the fundamental harmonic. You can measure it with a spectrum analyzer or a wave analyzer by measuring the magnitude of all the significant harmonics, computing their root sum square, and expressing this as a ratio of the fundamental magnitude. This process can be a tedious although many spectrum analyzers perform this calculation automatically.

Use caution when characterizing the distortion performance of a contemporary high-performance audio device with a spectrum analyzer.

Unless the analyzer is optimized for audio performance, its residual distortion often exceeds the device under test. High quality audio devices can achieve THD numbers exceeding 100 dB, and some analog circuits go as high as 120 dB. On the other hand, it is rare to find a spectrum analyzer with inherent distortion better than 95 dB or so. Some specialized audio analyzers incorporate spectrum analyzers but precede them with low-distortion, analog band reject filters. This combination has the effect of lowering the inherent distortion by the amount of fundamental rejection contributed by the band reject filter.

For the most accurate results, particularly when measuring high performance devices, use a dedicated audio analyzer rather than a spectrum analyzer. The residual THD of the analyzer should be at least 6 dB less than the device under test.

Total Harmonic Distortion Plus Noise (THD+N)

THD+N is similar to THD but has an additional noise component. This designation was introduced because most audio analyzers, certainly all analog analyzers, actually measure THD+N, not THD. These analyzers use a band reject, or *notch,* filter that removes the fundamental and then measures everything remaining in the measurement bandwidth. Modern analyzers can achieve a notch depth exceeding 130 dB by using sophisticated servo tuning circuits. Figure 1.16 shows the process of characterizing THD+N using a notch filter.

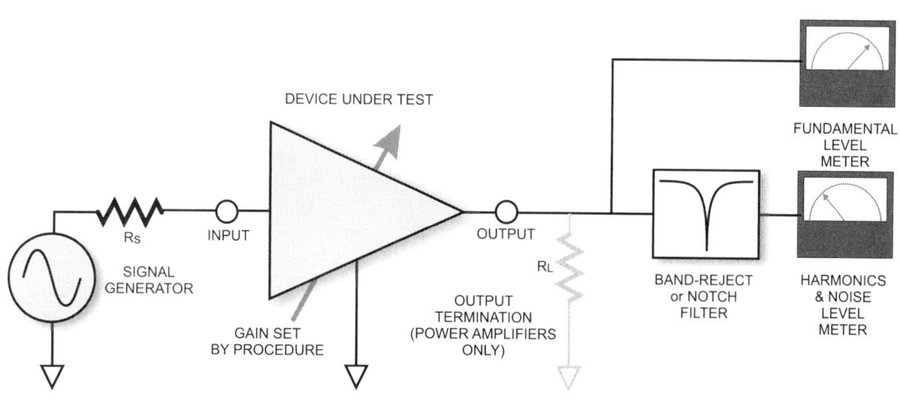

Figure 1.16 THD+N Measurement Configuration

When measuring THD+N with an audio analyzer, you should select the measurement bandwidth carefully. Most analyzers include a selection of low-pass filters to constrain the measurement bandwidth to something less than the typical 500 kilohertz unfiltered response. Since the THD+N measurement includes broadband noise, the bandwidth of the measuring meter has a strong affect on the result. Select a low-pass filter that is at least 5 times the fundamental frequency.

Limitations for THD in Band-limited Systems

The measurement of harmonic distortion requires the measurement of the fundamental amplitude and at least the second harmonic, but preferably also additional harmonics. Popular opinion suggests THD measurements should include up to the fifth harmonic for a true representation of perceived distortion. Capturing this many harmonics creates a problem in band-limited systems, that is devices whose frequency response rolls off sharply above the audio band. Many digital devices roll off abruptly between 20 kilohertz and 24 kilohertz or so, so they do not pass even the second harmonic of a 12 kilohertz fundamental. Therefore, measuring harmonic distortion at high frequencies of these devices gives meaningless results. The device still exhibits nonlinear behavior at these high frequencies, but we can't characterize this nonlinear behavior using harmonic distortion measurement techniques. Figure 1.17 shows THD measurements for two signals: a low frequency signal where all of the significant harmonics are measured and a high frequency signal where all the harmonics fall outside the measurement band.

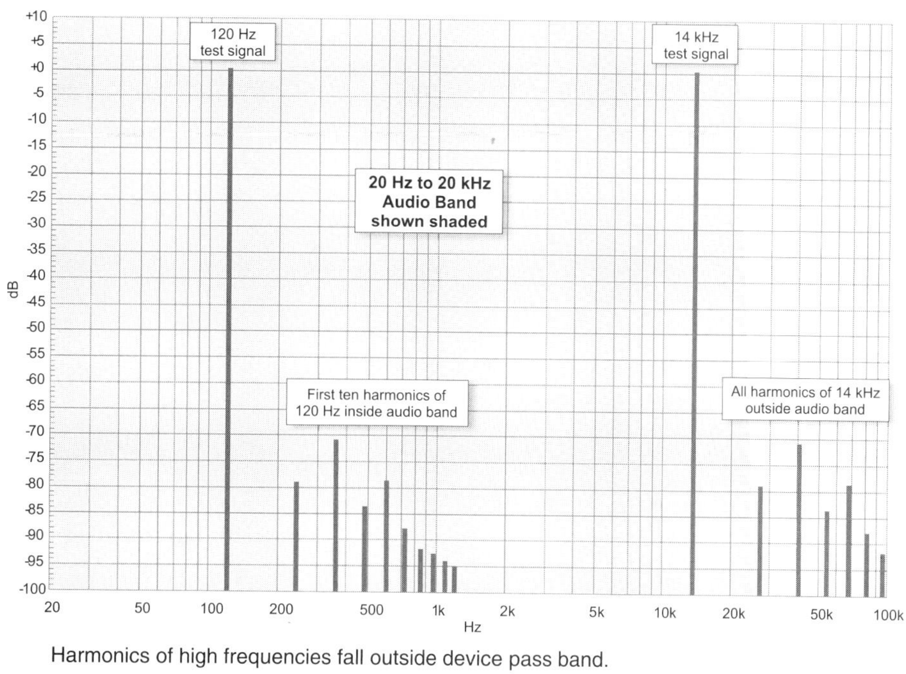

Figure 1.17 Harmonics in a Band-limited Device

Traditional analog audio devices were not band limited; their response extended well beyond the audio band, often beyond 100 kilohertz. They were not specifically designed to be wide band; there was simply no reason to intentionally reduce their naturally wide frequency response by adding an unnecessary low pass filter. So, it was common to measure the harmonic distortion of these devices over the complete audio spectrum, 20 hertz to 20 kilohertz, and achieve accurate and meaningful results. In fact, power amplifiers would often exhibit increasing THD at higher frequencies due to slew rate limitations. On the other hand, digital systems are band limited, since they include an analog-to-digital or digital-to-analog converter in the signal path, and they also must include a low-pass filter for proper operation. Typically, this filter limits the bandwidth of the device sharply at a frequency related to the digital sample rate.

So how should we characterize distortion at high frequencies in such devices? THD and THD+N measurements are completely adequate and useful for frequencies below approximately 10 kilohertz, but for higher frequencies, another technique must be used. Intermodulation distortion measurement is the answer. IMD is able to measure meaningful distortion behavior right up to the upper band edge of the device.

Intermodulation Distortion

Intermodulation distortion occurs when two or more signals interact to produce additional components. If a device exhibits nonlinear behavior, passing two signals at frequencies F_1 and F_2 produces distortion components at the sum and difference of these two primary signals; $F_1 \bullet F_2$ and F_1+F_2. Additionally, second order effects produce distortion components at sum and difference frequencies of the harmonics of the primary test signals. Table 1.2 following illustrates the components that can occur in a typical system stimulated by a hypothetical, but common, test pair of 18 kilohertz and 20 kilohertz. Figure 1.18 shows how significant IMD products could fall in-band even when the test signals are close to the upper band edge of the device.

While IMD measurement is useful for characterizing high-frequency distortion in band-limited devices, it has other merits as well. Some nonlinear behavior is less sensitive to THD+N measurements than IMD measurements and may escape detection. A test suite that includes both THD+N and IMD measurements provides additional confidence that the device has been adequately characterized.

Table 1.2 IMD Components for a Hypothetical Twin-tone Test Signal of 18 kilohertz and 20 kilohertz.

Signal	Order	Frequency
Test Signal F_1	Fundamental	20 kHz
Test Signal F_2	Fundamental	18 kHz
IMD component $F_1–F_2$	2nd order	2 kHz
IMD component $2F_2–F_1$	3rd order	16 kHz
IMD component $2F_1–2F_2$	4th order	4 kHz
IMD component $3F_2–2F_1$	5th order	14 kHz
IMD component $3F_2–3F_1$	6th order	6 kHz
IMD component $4F_1–4F_2$	8th order	8 kHz
IMD component $5F_1–5F_2$	10th order	10 kHz

This table only shows the components that fall below the test signals and within the device pass band. Additional IMD sum products also could be present.

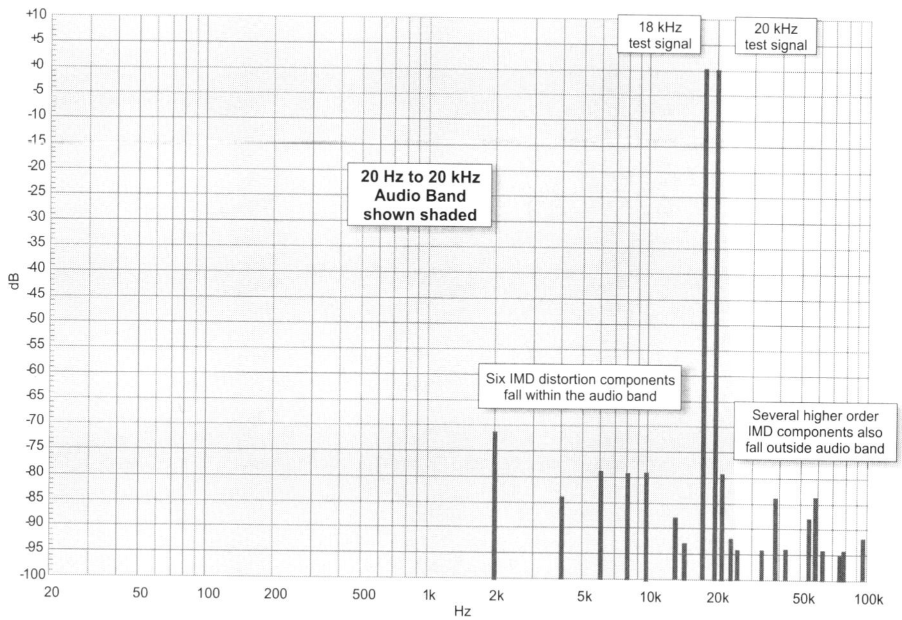

Although some IMD components fall outside device pass band, many fall within the pass band and provide important device distortion characterization near the upper band edge not possible with THD+N measurements.

Figure 1.18 IMD Components in a Band-limited Device

Crosstalk

Interchannel crosstalk characterizes the leakage of one channel into another. Such leakage can degrade the stereo or surround sound effect in a system. In the early days of stereo, this leakage was often called *separation* and the dominant contributor to poor crosstalk was the media: vinyl records and compact cassettes. Today's digital media have inherently low crosstalk. The most likely source for crosstalk problems today is the remaining analog circuits. Crosstalk can be caused by capacitive or inductive coupling between circuits, through common power supply rails, or even through common ground connections in system wiring or board layout.

Measuring crosstalk is similar to measuring frequency response with two notable differences: one or more channels receive the stimulus signal while the non-stimulated channel under test is measured with a narrow band filter tuned to the stimulus signal. This important filter rejects broadband noise and allows measurement of crosstalk signals below the noise floor. It is important to measure crosstalk across the complete audio band because it is usually changes with frequency. Figure 1.19 shows the measurement process for crosstalk measurements. Most analog circuits exhibit worse crosstalk at higher frequencies where capacitive coupling is more of a problem.

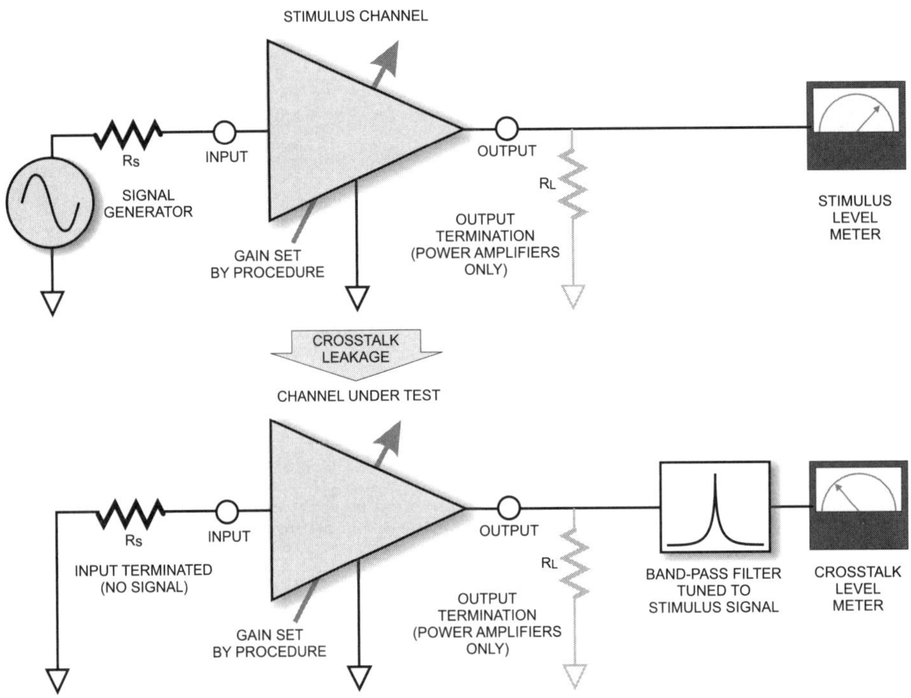

Figure 1.19 Measuring Crosstalk Between Two Channels

Interchannel Phase Difference

Interchannel phase difference characterizes the phase difference between the left and right channel of a stereo system or between pairs of channels in a surround sound system. Interchannel phase difference measurements are some of the most neglected measurements, yet they are particularly important in stereo and multichannel surround sound systems. Much of our spatial perception is derived by phase information. A significant phase difference between channels can destroy stereo and surround imaging and shift the apparent location of sounds.

Phase shift can be caused by poorly matched filters, by loose component tolerances, and even by incorrect digital design.

To understand the importance of phase in this context, you need to understand how human hearing perceives direction or location of sound sources. A sound at a particular location relative to the listener arrives differently at each ear, with slightly different levels and a small time offset based on the difference in distance between each ear and the source. The ear is remarkably adept at measuring this slight time and amplitude difference and inferring accurate location based on this difference. This process happens mostly at higher frequencies where the ear is most sensitive to time differences. Phase shift in electronic circuits represents a relative time shift. Thus, if one channel has a phase shift relative to another channel, this effect is equivalent to a frequency-related time delay between the two channels. It is easy to see how such a phase shift can substantially change the perceived location of a sound in a listening experience. The efforts and expense that were employed to try to duplicate the spatial image for the listener can be lost when channels are not phase matched.

As we mentioned, although this parameter is crucial to accurate spatial imaging, it is seldom characterized. The measurement is not difficult. In fact if the audio analyzer includes phase measurement capability, it can be measured as easily as frequency response, and often at the same time.

Interchannel phase difference is particularly important at higher frequencies where spatial location is more sensitive. The high frequency area is also the area most susceptible to circuit problems. The reconstruction low-pass filters present in virtually all digital audio entertainment devices are the biggest contributor to interchannel phase differences. Subtle component tolerance differences in these filters can cause sufficient phase differences to affect stereo imaging.

Although analog component tolerances are the biggest contributor to interchannel phase differences, digital system design can create problems occasionally. At least one popular sound card exhibits a substantial high frequency phase shift between left and right channels due to a design error. The stereo Digital to Analog converter (DAC) uses alternate clock transitions for the left and right channels giving a one-sample time offset between left and right channels. The one sample delay causes a progressive phase shift versus increasing frequency that is so significant beyond 10 kilohertz that all stereo imaging is lost.

When characterizing a stereo system, the measurement is a determination of the phase of the left channel relative to the right—or the opposite. However, for 5.1 and 7.1 surround sound systems, you have no common practice or standard specifying interchannel phase measurements. A sensible and sufficient measurement is to determine the phase shift of each channel relative to the front right channel. Figure 1.20 shows the measurement setup for measuring interchannel phase difference between two channels.

For thoroughness, phase measurements should be made across the audio frequency spectrum. However, if a phase sweep is not possible, measurements should be made at least at high frequencies where the errors are likely to be greater and accuracy is most important.

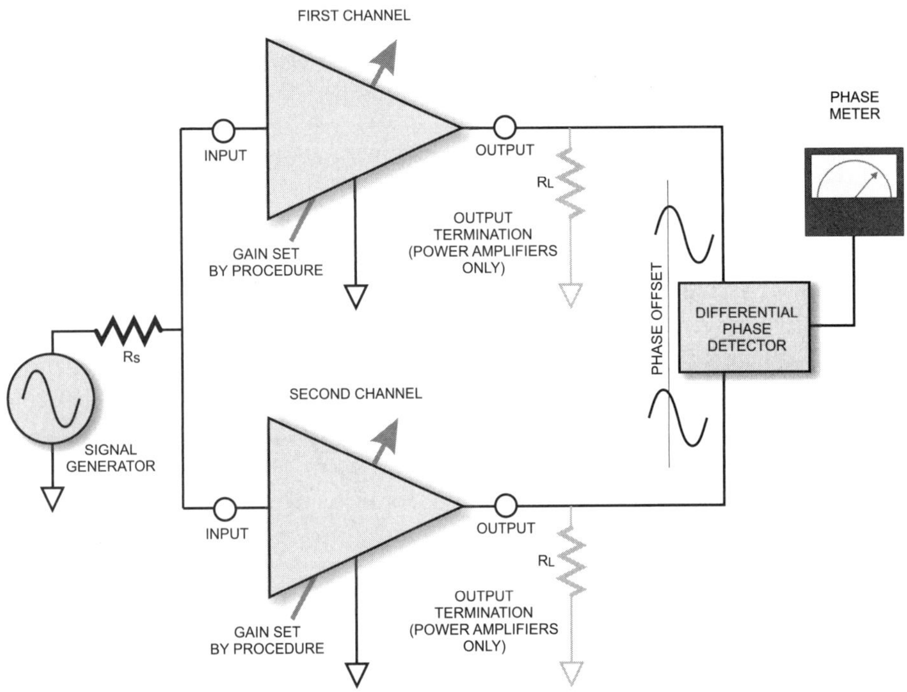

Figure 1.20 Measuring Phase Difference between Two Channels

Digital Audio

What is digital audio? Before we answer this question, let's step back to audio in its most primitive form: sound. Setting aside harmonic structure for the moment, natural sound has two primary attributes: pitch (frequency) and intensity (amplitude). Both of these parameters are continuous or have an infinite variety of values. Any musician will tell you that the reed or string in an instrument can be made to produce a sound at virtually any pitch and intensity within its range. An analog audio system will reproduce this sound with the same infinite values of pitch and intensity. A digital audio system on the other hand samples and quantizes sounds into discrete values represented by numbers or bits. The concept of continuous values is replaced by this finite range of discrete steps. However, if we have a sufficiently large quantity of steps—that is a sufficiently fine resolution—and if we sample frequently enough, we do not perceive steps, but we seem to hear a continuous signal and not discrete samples and quantized levels. The trick here is to know what sample rate and quantization resolution is sufficient to make the steps appear to be continuous.

Two parameters are fundamental to digital audio: samples and quantization. In other words, you would chop up continuous time into discrete time intervals and continuous intensities or into amplitudes into discrete levels.

Digital Audio Sampling Theory

Sampling digitizes a signal repetitively and regularly at a defined sample rate. By digitize, we mean the recording of instantaneous magnitude at the sample time. Intuitively, you can imagine that this sample rate must be frequent enough to capture the highest frequency that you want to digitize. What may not be intuitive is that the Nyquist theorem tells us that the sample rate needs to be just twice the highest frequency of interest to faithfully digitize the signal. So, to digitize the audio band to 20 kilohertz, you must sample at 40 kilohertz to capture all of the information. Hard to believe that only two time samples of a 20-kilohertz sound is sufficient, but it is. However, you need to know other factors about sampling, too.

Figure 1.21 shows a simplified representation of a continuous analog signal. The wavy line represents the values of an arbitrary analog signal as it changes over time. If you were to zoom in or enlarge the graph, you would see minute subtleties in this trace showing infinite detail. In other words, the range of magnitude values is an infinite or continuous, and time is also continuous.

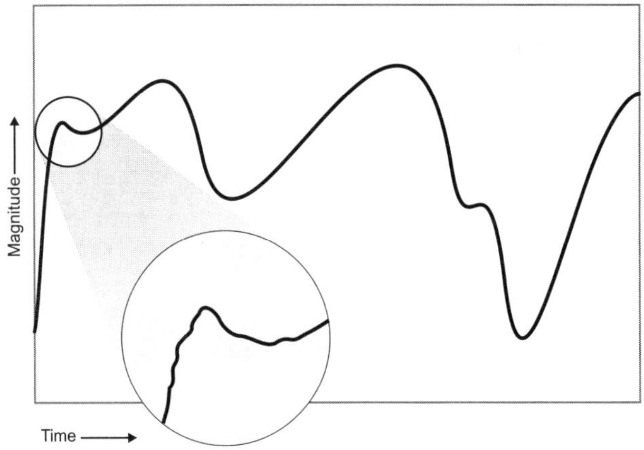

Progressive enlargements of the graph would reveal more and more detail.

Figure 1.21 Arbitrary Analog Waveform with an Infinite Set of Values

Figure 1.22 adds the concept of regular and repetitive sampling. Each vertical line represents a sample instant in time. The number of these per second is the *sample rate*. At every sample instant, you measure the magnitude of the waveform, that is, take a sample. The squares represent the samples. For an explanation of the way to assign an amplitude value, see "Quantizing" later in this chapter.

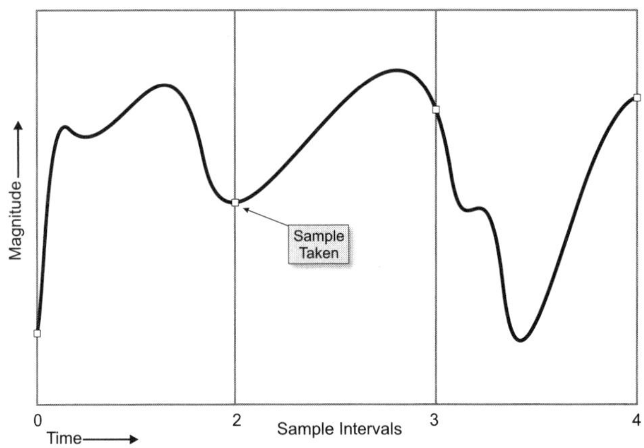

Each square represents a sample taken. Intuitively, you can see that the test has not taken a sufficient number of samples.

Figure 1.22 Sampling a Continuous Analog Waveform

Intuitively, it doesn't look like we have sufficient samples in Figure 1.22 to faithfully capture the analog signal and all its nuances. Let's triple the sample rate, as shown in Figure 1.23. This result looks better, but unless you accurately know the frequency components in the waveform and the sample rate, you can't be sure. But, it is clear that more samples, that is a higher sample rate, is better.

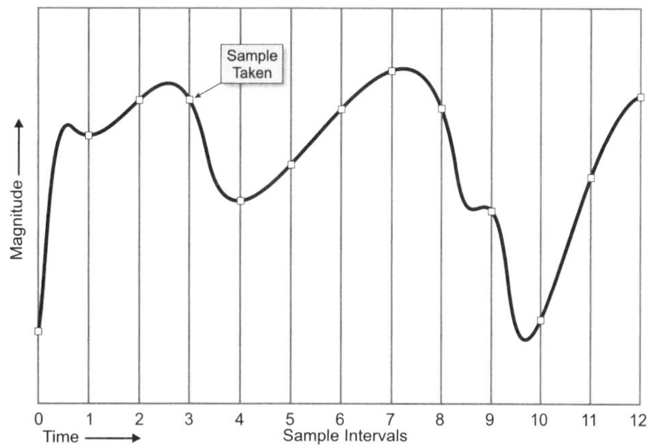

This analog waveform is the same as the one in Figure 1.22, but with three times the number of samples as before. This sample rate looks like it will record sufficient data for a faithful reproduction.

Figure 1.23 Continuous Analog Waveform Sample with More Samples

Nyquist Frequency and Aliasing

As stated previously, a sample rate twice the highest frequency of interest is sufficient to faithfully capture an analog signal. Also, any components higher than half the sample rate that are present in the signal are incorrectly digitized or *aliased*. When this incorrectly digitized information is converted back to analog, false frequencies become audible, making the result unacceptable. So once you establish your bandwidth of interest and your sample rate, you must remove all signals with frequencies above that band. You do so with a low pass *anti-aliasing filter*. This filter is inserted between the analog signal source and the digital conversion process to ensure that no content has frequencies greater than half of our sampling frequency.

Unfortunately, real-world filters are not perfect and they have a finite roll-off characteristic that is dependent on their design and on the number of poles. These characteristics start rolling off at the design frequency and then attenuate higher frequencies with progressively more attenuation dictated by the slope of the filter. It is possible to achieve some rather sharp slopes, but the steeper the slope, the more difficult the design and the more parts required. Analog filters require precision capacitors and resistors, and for sophisticated multi-pole filters, these additional components can get expensive. Even very sharp roll-off filters do not have infinite attenuation just above the cutoff frequency, so choose your digitizing band and sample rate to allow for this limit. Figure 1.24 shows two filter shapes for a simple 4-pole and an 8-pole filter design. Even the 8-pole filter, itself a non-trivial design and expensive to manufacture, has only about 50 dB of attenuation at 40 kilohertz, twice the 20 kilohertz cutoff point. We know that the signals above half the sample rate, even with some attenuation, will cause problems.

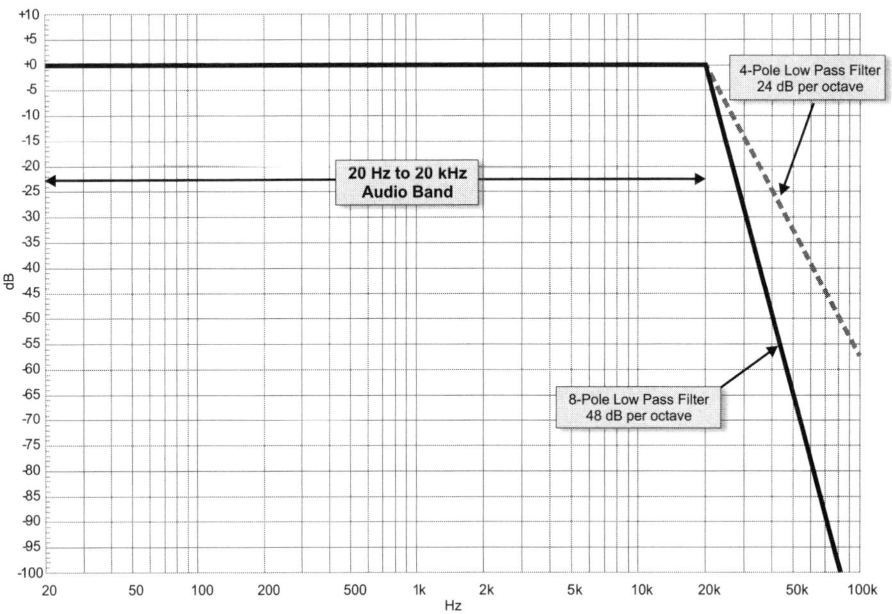

Low-pass filter shapes for two different quantities of poles.

Figure 1.24 Butterworth Filter Design

This simplified illustration uses a filter topology known as "Butterworth" that produces a smooth roll-off. Other designs, such as elliptic topologies, can achieve much steeper slopes close to the cutoff point, but they have lobes in their stop-band response and eventually achieve a similar ultimate roll-off at higher frequencies. However, typically they do provide a useful attenuation, in the range of 50 to 60 decibels or more, at just a fraction of an octave above their cutoff point. See Figure 1.25 for an example.

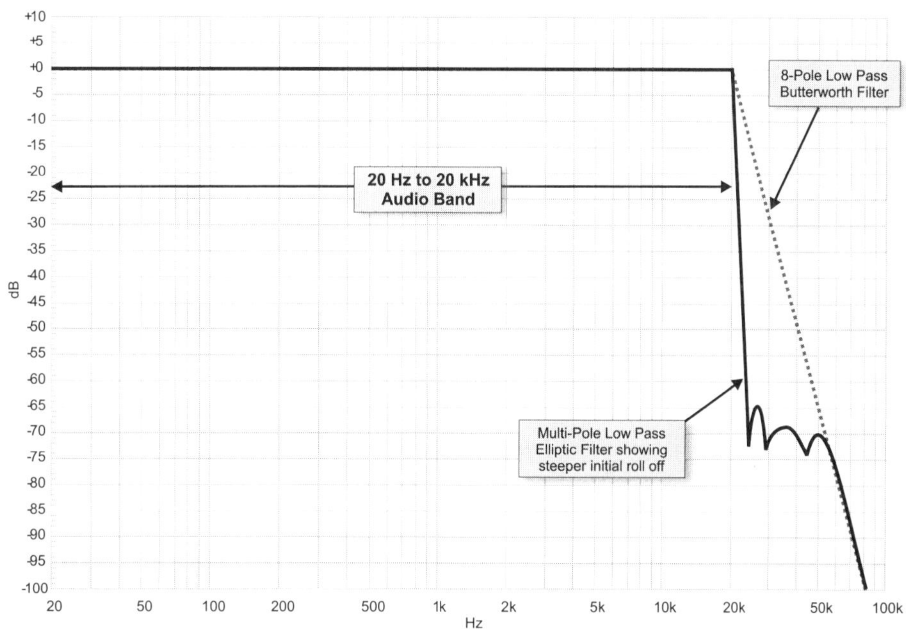

Comparison of the elliptical low-pass filter topology with the Butterworth shows steeper initial slope, yielding important attenuation close to the cutoff frequency.

Figure 1.25 Elliptical Low-pass Filter Topology Versus Butterworth

CD players, one of the first digital audio consumer devices, standardized a 44.1 kilohertz sample rate to capture a 20 kilohertz audio band. Professional devices choose a slightly higher sample rate, 48 kilohertz, to mitigate this filter design problem.

Another design and manufacturing difficulty with this anti-aliasing low-pass filter is passband ripple. Every filter has a specified cutoff point, that frequency where it starts to roll off. Defined by convention, the cutoff point is where the filter has an attenuation of 3 decibels. No filter has an abrupt change from flat response to its ultimate roll off slope. Each filter has a transition region when the roll off is gradual, and at some point, it rcachcs its asymptotic slope, continuing at this rate until the noise floor. With a multi-pole design, you could minimize this transition region and get closer to an ideal shape by staggering the poles and using *corner peaking*. An unfortunate byproduct of this optimization is *passband ripple*. By juggling the shape of each of the poles or sections of a composite filter to sharpen the corner transition, some passband flatness below the cutoff point is sacrificed. The composite effect of the adjustments of each of the poles shows up as ripple in the final octave or two just below cutoff. This error is exacerbated by increasing the quantity of poles and by component tolerances. Excessive ripple is a frequency response error and can add coloration to the high frequency content of music. Of course manufacturing cost is also an issue with sophisticated filters. Figure 1.9 shows an example of ripple from a low-pass filter that rolls off just above 20 kilohertz.

Oversampling

Oversampling techniques significantly reduce the low-pass filter design cost and the problems associated with this filter. Oversampling converters extend the sample rate well beyond the audio band, using sample frequencies of twice or four times previous rates such as 96 kilohertz or 192 kilohertz. Oversampling converters might be used for reasons in addition to low-pass filter issues, but this higher sampling frequency does significantly simplify the design of the anti-aliasing filter. If we sample at 96 kilohertz, the anti-aliasing low-pass filter needs to roll off only at 48 kilohertz. It no longer needs to have as steep a slope nor does it need to start very close to the top end of the audio band. This less demanding filter reduces the cost, passband ripple, and improves passband response flatness.

Of course sampling at four or eight times the Nyquist frequency means that the data rate becomes two or four times what it would have been with a traditional 2x sample rate. By implication, a storage capacity or transmission bandwidth also increases by two to four times the previous rate unless we *decimate* the digital signal. To reach the original bandwidth goal of an audio band with an upper limit of 20 kilohertz, you can afford to reduce the data rate that oversampling produces but still have sufficient samples to capture the audio band.

Adding a lower cost, digital low-pass filter can off-load some of the anti-aliasing burden from the analog filter. Sharp low-pass filters are easier to implement in the digital domain, and they don't suffer from the component tolerance problem of their analog counterpart. Figure 1.26 shows such an implementation. A simpler analog filter, a 4x converter, a digital LPF, and a 4x decimator bring the data stream back to what would it be with a conventional sampling technique.

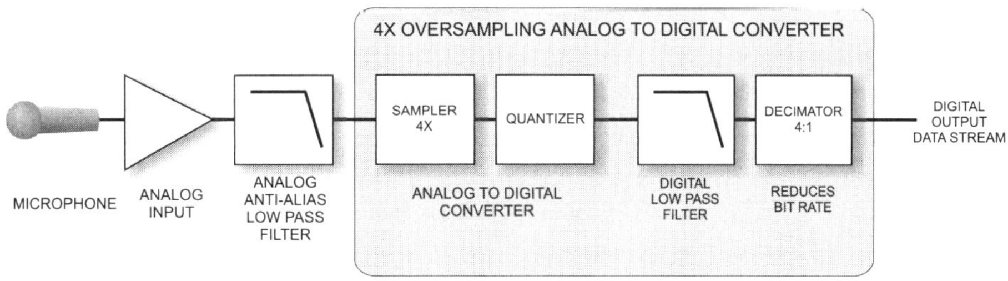

Figure 1.26 Oversampling Analog to Digital Converter

Quantizing

So far, we have discussed one of the two aspects of digitizing an analog signal: sampling, the conversion of a time-continuous signal into a finite number of discrete data. The second aspect is the instantaneous magnitude that is measured at the sample instant. Again, the method is sampling a continuous analog waveform that can have any instantaneous magnitude out of an infinite number of possibilities to assign a specific value from a discrete set of finite values. Figure 1.27 shows the same analog waveform but with an additional vertical scale representing amplitude values. This illustration has only five discrete values. Therefore, at every sample instant, you must assign and record the closest available amplitude value from this limited choice. The superimposed gray trace shows what a waveform reconstructed from these samples might look like—obviously not a very faithful reproduction.

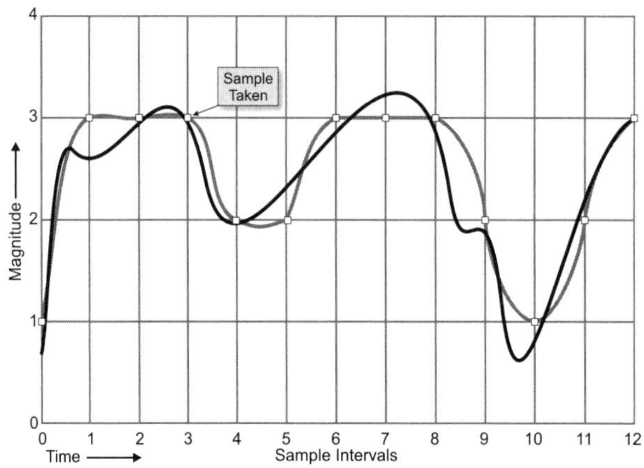

The gray trace is constructed using only the discrete samples. Obviously, it misses some details of the original black trace and adds new details not present in the original waveform. The result is far from "high fidelity."

Figure 1.27 Signal Level Quantization with Only Five Values

Now, suppose you increase the *resolution* or number of available amplitude values, as shown in figure 1.28. With almost three times the resolution, you can record and reproduce a much more accurate picture of the original analog waveform.

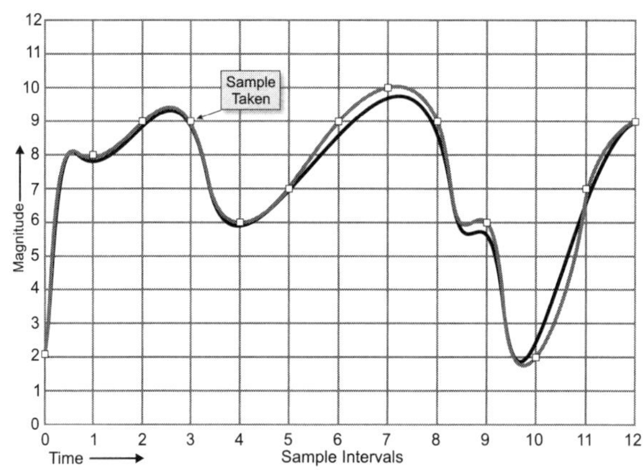

The increase improves the resolution. The reconstructed gray trace is now much closer to the original black trace with most of the details present and only some errors in magnitude.

Figure 1.28 Increasing the Quantization to 13 Steps

Quantization Error and Dithering

The difference between the magnitude of the original signal and the quantized representation at any given sample instant is the *quantization error*. For higher level signals, this quantization error is random and shows up as broadband white noise, not unlike other forms of noise present in all circuits. It is deterministic since you know the resolution of the converter. It gets to be a problem at low signal levels, where this noise begins to correlate to the actual signal and changes from random noise to a more objectionable signal-related distortion. Fortunately, you have a way to avoid this effect. Add a small amount of random noise to the signal, then even at low amplitudes, no correlation between signal and quantization error occurs. In effect, you trade more tolerable white noise for less tolerable distortion. The added noise is small, typically equivalent to the magnitude of one or two resolution steps. This process of adding small amounts of noise is called *dithering*.

Noise Shaping

An interesting byproduct of oversampling is that the quantization noise is distributed over a larger bandwidth now, thereby reducing the noise in the audio band. Using feedback techniques, the spectrum of this broadband noise can be modified to reduce the amount in the audio band in return for increased noise above the audio band. Of course, this inaudible out-of-band noise can be filtered out without affecting the audio band.

Resolution or Bit Depth

Resolution in the digital audio world is often referred to as *bit-depth*. The first examples of commercial digital audio entertainment devices had a resolution of 16 bits, which was the best available from converters at that time. Improvements in converter technology have increased this depth to 18, 20, 22, and even 24 bits. Every single-bit increase doubles the resolution. 16 bits provides 2^{16} or 65,536 discrete values while 24 bits produce 16,777,216 values.

Reconstructing Analog From Digital

Previously, quantization illustrations showed a reconstructed gray trace without any explanation of how it got there. Nyquist sampling theorem tells us that sampling at just over twice the highest frequency in our band of interest provides sufficient samples to reconstruct the original analog waveform. If you imagine plotting out a waveform using these samples, you might expect this reconstructed waveform to look quite crude and angular, not the gentle and smooth slope of the original waveform. But, if the reconstructed waveform has sharp features that were not present in the original, they represent added high frequency energy. But, no high frequency energy should be present beyond our constrained frequency band because a low pass filter intentionally limited it. If you use that same low pass filter on your crude reconstruction, it removes the extraneous high-frequency energy and smoothes out the curve to look like the original. We call this low-pass filter a *reconstruction filter*.

The reconstruction filter has all the same requirements and potential problems as the anti-aliasing low-pass filter, such as passband ripple and the need to optimize stop band attenuation, manufacturing cost, and passband fidelity.

Other Errors

Along with aliasing errors and quantizing errors, two other errors warrant some discussion here. Accuracy and jitter are both related to sample rate.

Sample rate accuracy refers to how close the DAC sample rate matches the ADC sample rate. A number of industry standard sample rates have been established, and devices must use one of these to be compatible with other devices. If the sample rate of the DAC or playback device is not exactly the same as the rate as that used in the ADC conversion, an unwanted pitch shift appears in the audio.

In addition to a fixed error in sample rate, small modulations of the sample rate or *jitter* can also degrade the audio quality. Several possible sources of clock jitter usually show up when connecting two separate devices. Clock jitter can introduce noise or distortion in the audio signal, and if excessive, it can even cause a system to loose frequency lock, shutting down the exchange of data.

Putting It All Together

This chapter covered each of the elements of the digital audio process. On the recording side, digital audio involves capturing the original sound with one or more microphones, amplifying the microphone signal and possibly mixing several signals together, restricting the analog bandwidth to less than half the sample rate, and finally converting this signal with an ADC converter operating at the sample rate and with a particular resolution. The output of this converter is a stream of digital words that flows into memory, is burned onto a transportable media such as a CD, or is sent to another location by digital broadcast or the Internet. On the receiving or playback side, the reverse process takes place. The digital stream is converted back to an analog signal by a D to A converter of the same resolution and at the same sample rate as the A to D process. The output of this converter is sent to a low-pass reconstruction filter, and finally, it is amplified to drive one or more speakers that convert the electrical energy back to sound. Figure 1.29 shows a block diagram of the complete process.

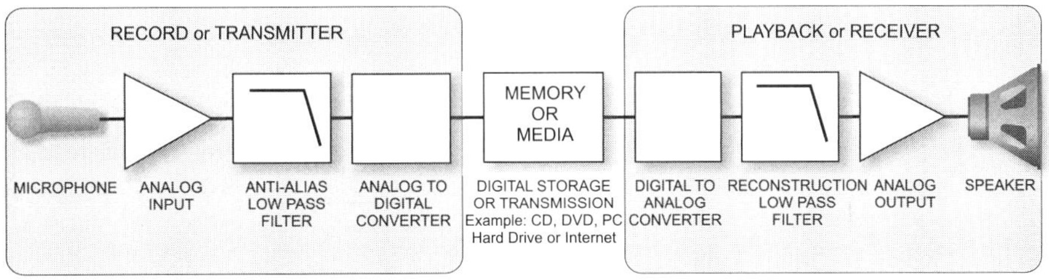

Figure 1.29 The Complete Digital Audio Process

Advantages of Digital Audio

Through careful choosing the sample rate and using a sufficient bit depth, you can accurately represent a continuous analog waveform by a series of digital values. One immediate advantage of this process is making additional identical copies by simply repeating these digital values. In fact, we can make multiple generations of copies from copies from copies, and the last copy is still identical to the first. This accuracy contrasts sharply with analog copying technology where each successive generation copy is a little inferior to the previous. Each copy adds some noise and distortion and reduces the fidelity.

The same is true for transmission of digital audio content. By transmitting a stream of digital values, the distant receiver can accurately reconstruct the original analog content with predictable and repeatable fidelity. As long as the transmission medium accurately transmits the digital values, the receiver reconstructs the original sound with the accuracy and fidelity that the sample rate and bit depth allow. Traditional signal quality parameters, such as frequency response, noise, and nonlinear distortion, are not degraded by the medium as is the case with analog storage and transmission techniques.

This preservation of quality has important implications for distribution of entertainment content. It lowers the cost of media duplication, makes it easier to preserve and manage audio quality, and opens additional distribution possibilities. Unfortunately for music distributors, it also allows easy and flawless copying by consumers. Since every copy is an exact replica of the original, pirating and illegal copies do not suffer from the quality degradation that was common with analog copies. This vulnerability has forced artists and entertainment distributors to add copy protection mechanisms to safeguard their property. This security is the subject of Chapter 10.

Chapter 2

Audio Interfaces

Engineers operate at the interface between science and society...

— Dean Gordon Brown; Massachusetts Institute of Technology

Audio interfaces in a PC environment can be daunting. Many may be new to PC designers and the wide variety of *analog* and *digital* connectors and supporting circuitry and protocols can be intimidating. The following pages describe the common interfaces that can be encountered in a PC that is intended to be used as an audio entertainment device, covering the connectors used, briefly looking at the interface circuitry, and discussing some common problems and their solutions.

Analog Interfaces

Until recently, the analog interface has been the only means of interconnection to PC audio. Sound cards and many motherboards have provided a line input, line output, and possibly a microphone input jack. Analog interfaces still include these primary connections but they have been expanded to include more outputs to support up to 6 additional channels of surround sound. While the majority of devices use the familiar 3.5-millimeter miniature phone jack, a number of popular connectors are used in PCs as well as in high-quality external audio equipment that can be connected to a PC using Intel HD Audio.

Analog Connectors

The audio entertainment industry has been around for many more years than the PC industry and has developed many varied connectors for particular audio needs. Not only could the physical connectors be new to the PC developer, the method of use and how they may be interconnected must be understood. The descriptions that follow should arm you with the knowledge of how to preserve audio quality while interconnecting a diverse range of traditional audio devices to a PC.

3.5 millimeter (1/8-inch) Miniature Phone Plugs and Jacks

This connector is probably the most recognized in the PC audio environment. It is almost always a 3-conductor type, often called *stereo* although in the case of microphones it may not always carry a stereo audio signal. While this type of connector often is referred to as 1/8-inch instead of 3.5 millimeters, the two are different: 1/8-inch is exactly 3.175 millimeters, so a plug that is exactly 1/8-inch in diameter will fit loosely in a true 3.5-millimeter jack, while a plug that is 3.5mm in size could damage a true 1/8-inch jack if someone forces it into the receptacle. For Intel HD Audio applications, you should always specify a 3.5-millimeter connector. When purchasing adapters and patch cords, always be sure to select a size that is exactly 3.5 millimeters.

The driving force behind the use of this connector comes from space constraints on plug-in cards and rear panel motherboard connector real estate. It is not the most robust connector around but is convenient and firmly entrenched in the PC audio environment because of its small space requirement. Since the 3.5-millimeter connector provides less overall surface contact than most other types of audio connectors, you can benefit from using gold-plated connectors for this type of jack, because gold is a better conductor than nickel and doesn't oxidize easily, thus ensuring a better connection. This connector is used for most PC analog interfaces, and it has no physical keying other than color to distinguish its different uses. Figure 2.1 shows some typical 3.5-millimeter plugs.

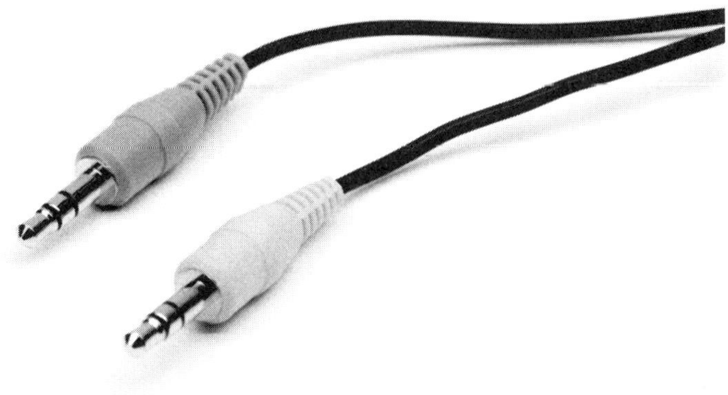

Figure 2.1 3.5 millimeter Miniature Phone Plugs

Wiring to an audio connector should always use shielded cable. If the circuit carries a stereo signal, each channel should be separately shielded to maintain low interchannel crosstalk. Sometimes, 3.5-millimeter stereo plugs are wired using a single two-conductor shielded cable. Although this cable provides shielding against external noise sources, the two signal conductors can cause crosstalk through capacitive coupling. The correct wiring for such a connector is shown in Figure 2.2.

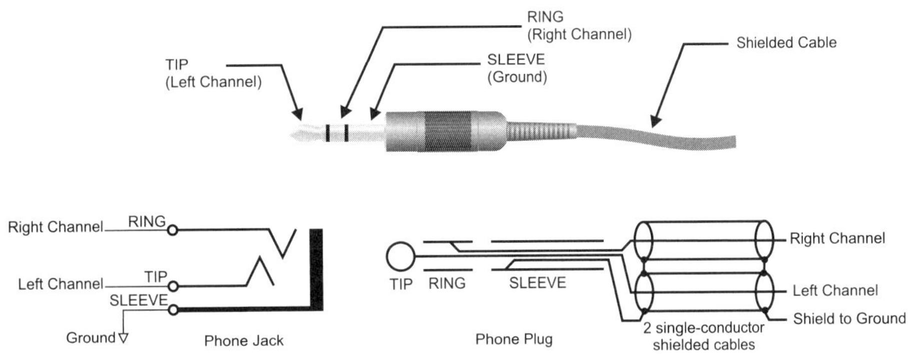

Figure 2.2 Wiring of a 3.5 millimeter plug and jack

2.5 millimeter (3/32-inch) Miniature Phone Jacks and Plugs

These plugs look almost identical to the 3.5-millimeter plugs, but are 1 millimeter smaller. Even though they are sometimes referred to as 3/32-inch jacks, they are usually exactly 2.5 millimeters. Unlike other jacks described here, these connectors support a mic signal with DC bias on one wire and a mono headphone signal on the other wire. Typically used for cellular phone headsets, these connectors are unsuited for Intel HD Audio because only one jack insertion signal can be activated, even though both mic and speaker are plugged in together. Therefore, the software layers cannot accurately identify what device has been plugged in, and could misbehave. These plugs and jacks are not recommended for PC applications. To interface a headset with a 2.5-millimeter jack to a PC, use an adapter such as Radio Shack's # 42-2428 adapter.

Phono or "RCA" Jacks and Plugs

This connector is perhaps the most common consumer audio connector. It was originally supplied by RCA as the connector to allow an external phonograph player to be connected to a receiver or amplifier, hence the name *RCA* or *phono*. The male plug is a coaxial connector that readily interfaces to a single conductor shielded cable preserving the shielding at the connector. This connector is also known as a "Cinch" connector in Europe, named for the connector company that was first associated with this part.

When used in an analog 2-channel stereo application, the plugs are usually color coded red and white or red and black. White normally denotes the left channel, while red denotes the right channel. The easiest way to remember this denotation: "red" and "right" both start with the "R" letter.

RCA plugs also are used on some PCs to connect the coaxial S/PDIF output signal. Usually, this jack is color coded orange. While standard RCA audio cables sometimes work acceptably in this application, it is always best to use a specially designed low-capacitance 75 ohm cable for this purpose. For S/PDIF, a single cable carries both the left and right signals.

You commonly find an RCA connector also used as an analog composite video connector, where it is usually color coded yellow. It sometimes is used for component video, too. In this case, three RCA jacks are used, and they are color coded red, green, and blue. Do not confuse a red jack used for component video with a red jack used for audio. Like the

S/PDIF cable, special low-capacitance cables are recommended for any of the video connections mentioned here.

Figure 2.3 shows some typical RCA plugs.

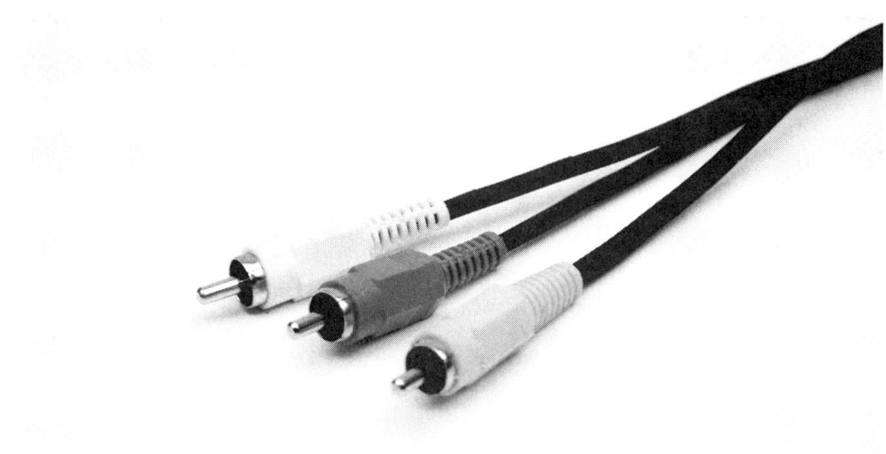

Note: the diameter of the cable attached to the yellow composite video plug on the right is larger to provide lower capacitance to properly support the higher-frequency video signal normally present on the yellow jack. While the yellow plug does work fine for audio, the white and red plugs this photo might cause some deterioration if used for video.

Figure 2.3 RCA-Phono Plugs

RCA jacks on audio equipment are used most often in clusters of red/white pairs for right/left inputs and outputs. Figure 2.4 shows a cluster of surround sound line outputs on an Intel HD Audio motherboard designed for use in a media PC. The traditional 3.5 millimeter jacks that usually are seen on PC motherboards have been replaced with RCA jacks that usually are associated with consumer audio equipment to produce an interconnect array more like conventional audio equipment.

On the left is an orange-colored S/PDIF coax output and above it, an optical S/PDIF output.

Figure 2.4 RCA Jacks on a Media Center PC Motherboard

RCA jacks are ideal inputs and outputs for PCs intended for the living room, as they match the connectors used on most living room equipment. To meet Windows Vista logo requirements, RCA jacks used on PCs must incorporate an isolated jack-detection switch, as shown in Figure 2.5.

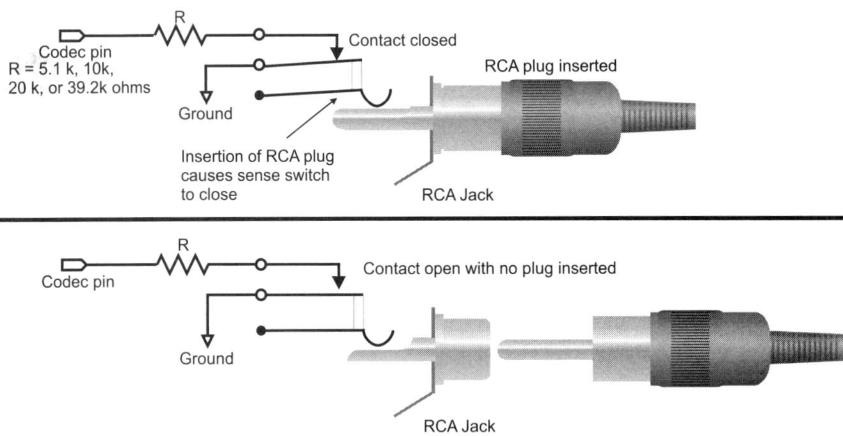

RCA jacks used for PC applications should contain an isolated jack-insertion switch which is closed whenever a plug is inserted into an RCA jack.

Figure 2.5 RCA Jacks with an Isolated Jack-Insertion Switch

XLR Connectors

The so-called "XLR" connector got its name from the part number prefix of its first manufacturer, Cannon, with the X identifying the series, L the latching property, and R the rubber insulation. Because of this origin, sometimes it's referred to as a Cannon plug. The connector is available in 3- through 8-pin versions, in both male and female forms, although the 3-pin version is certainly the most common for audio equipment. Often called a "balanced" connector because of its use in equipment employing balanced interfaces, it is one of the few popular connectors available with sufficient pins to accommodate a balanced circuit. This type of connector is very common in professional audio equipment for microphone and line-level interconnections. It is shielded, large enough to handle and terminate to a cable easily, robust, reliable, and latching to avoid accidental disconnect. It is not used in consumer audio equipment due to its higher cost and large space requirement.

The XLR connector is available in male and female genders and cable and chassis configurations. Circuit inputs are usually female and outputs such as microphones are usually male. Figure 2.6 shows typical cable mounted 3-pin XLR connectors.

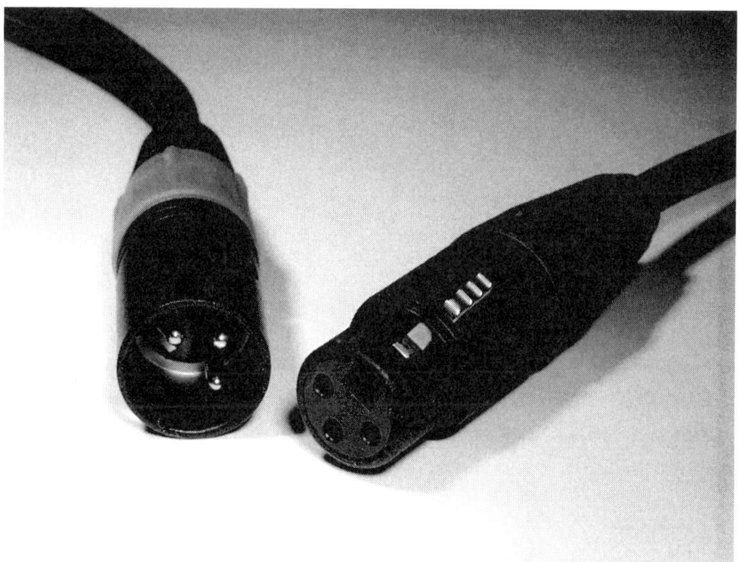

The common 3-pin type, male plug (output) is on the left; the female receptacle (input) is on the right.

Figure 2.6 "XLR" Cable Connectors

Figure 2.7 shows two female 3-pin chassis connectors mounted in a portable device.

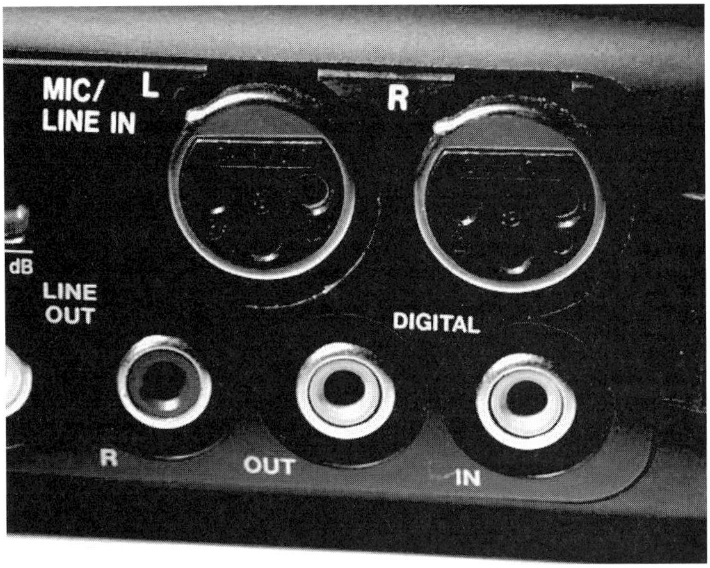

The 3-pin connectors mounted inside of the equipment are at the top of the photo. On the bottom are white and red RCA jacks for analog line out, as well as orange coaxial S/PDIF RCA connectors for digital input and output.

Figure 2.7 Chassis Type XLR Connectors in a Portable Device

¼-Inch Phone Jacks

The phone plug gets its name from its original use as a plug to interconnect telephone lines at the telephone company central office. It is now most commonly used as a connector for headphones. It is available in 2-conductor, often called "mono," and 3-conductor, often called "stereo" or "balanced." It is also very popular in musical instrument electronics, such as mixers and guitar amplifiers, where it is often used with 2-conductor wiring. In such mono applications, each connector carries a single signal and two plugs are used for stereo. This larger ¼-inch phone plug is not common in the PC audio environment that favors the smaller 3.5 millimeter miniature phone plug. It is, however, found in some professional audio sound cards that have balanced inputs and outputs.

Figure 2.8 shows a typical ¼-inch stereo phone plug.

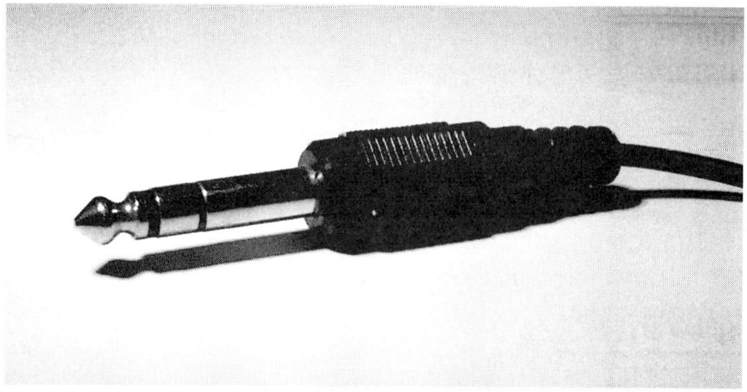

Figure 2.8 Typical ¼-inch Phone Plug

Like the 3.5 mm plug previously described, the wiring of a ¼-inch phone plug in a stereo application should always use two separately shielded cables. The tip is designated the left channel, the ring the right channel, and the sleeve as ground. See the diagram in Figure 2.9.

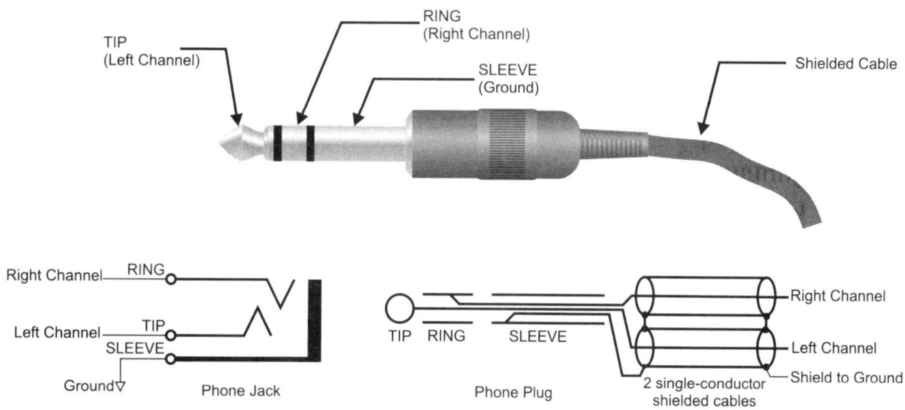

Figure 2.9 Standard Wiring for a ¼-inch Stereo Phone Plug

This stereo configuration is most commonly used for headphones, and is electrically identical to a 3.5-millimeter headphone jack. Other than for headphone jacks, this stereo configuration is rare on most audio equipment that might be connected to the PC. Usually a mono connector (with no ring) is used for each channel. Alternately, the tip and ring can be used to implement a balanced circuit that is almost identical electrically to the balanced connectors used in an XLR plug. The in-phase signal goes on the tip, and the signal that is 180 degrees out of phase goes onto the ring. When a mono plug is inserted, only the in-phase signal is connected, and the out-of-phase signal is shunted to ground. This optional shunting allows this configuration to be used for both balanced and unbalanced operation.

If a cable with a stereo 3.5-millimeter plug on one end and a stereo ¼-inch plug on the other end is connected from a ¼-inch balanced output to a stereo input on the PC, then the left channel of the PC receives the in-phase signal, and the right channel receives the out-of-phase signal. This arrangement is not recommended because it produces very confusing results.

Another common tip-ring-sleeve configuration for ¼-inch jacks is the *effects* insert point, where the output of one circuit is available on the tip, and the input of the following circuit is on the ring. The switch on the jack normally connects these two signals together but is disconnected when something is plugged in.

ATAPI Audio Connectors

ATAPI connectors provide internal PC connectivity to CD, AUX, TAD (telephone), and PC speaker. They may be found on a plug-in card or motherboard. They are a 4-pin header connector and two styles have been used. The style shown in Figure 2.10 is the most common and provides a latching capability. The style shown in Figure 2.12 is less common but can be found on some earlier plug-in cards.

As the signal connectivity from CD and DVD drives has migrated to a direct digital connection, these analog ATAPI connectors are gradually disappearing. Only the ATAPI header for analog CD input is found on many Intel HD Audio-based motherboards, and it is less likely to be used on future models, especially those intended for use with Windows Vista, which expects digital signals from the CD drive.

Figure 2.10 shows a typical ATAPI header on a plug-in audio device. This style connector provides latching retention of the cable.

These ATAPI headers are a 0.1" shrouded latching header style that is intended to accept 2-channel analog audio signals from a CDROM or DVD drive, AUX device, or telephone (TAD) device.

Figure 2.10 ATAPI Header for a Plug-In Audio Device

Figure 2.11 shows the wiring for the connector style shown in Figure 2.10. Note that the better designs provide a quasi-differential input configuration to minimize ground loops between the external device such as CD or DVD drive and the PC audio circuit. The shield pins do not connect to ground but go to the low side of a differential input amplifier, providing some common-mode rejection to accommodate ground differences between the analog circuit and the external device.

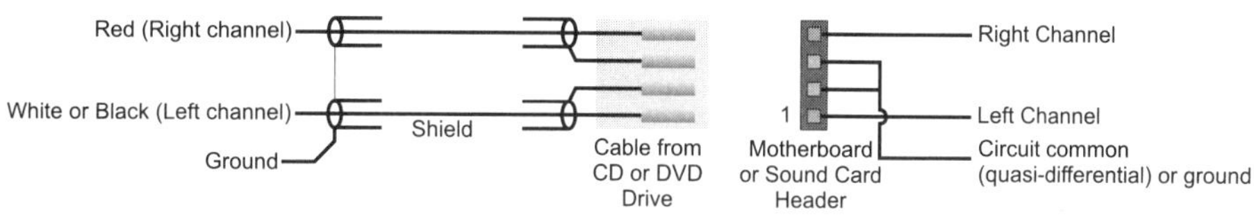

Figure 2.11 Wiring Schematic for the ATAPI Headers in Figure 2.10.

Another style of ATAPI header is shown in Figure 2.12. This miniature 4-pin header is common for CD drive to sound card connections. It provides a friction tight fit. This style header was rarely seen on motherboards.

Miniature shrouded header style is designed to accept a latching cable connector from a CDROM or DVD drive.

Figure 2.12 ATAPI Header for CD Drive to Sound Card Connections

The wiring for the header style in figure 2.12 is shown below in Figure 2.13 This wiring is not the same as the header style shown in Figures 2.10 and 2.11.

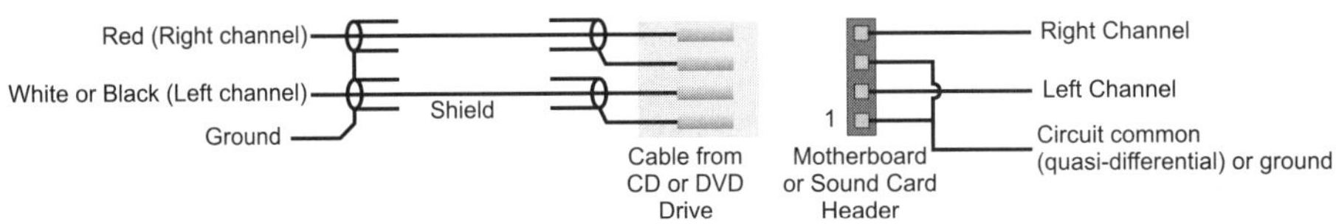

Figure 2.13 Wiring Schematic for the Miniature ATAPI Header in Figure 2.12

BNC Connectors

While BNC connectors are not intended for end users, they are the standard connector used in audio test sets. Analog cables that are used for audio test typically have a BNC connector on one end and a plug that matches the device under test at the other end. BNC connectors are similar electrically to RCA jacks or mono ¼-inch phone plugs in that they are unbalanced mono connectors. However, they also provide locking retention to ensure that they don't become unplugged unintentionally, and they provide superior shielding for the signal under test, especially at higher frequencies. They are a more robust connector than either the mini phone or RCA, providing tighter metal to metal contact and more metal contact surface area. For this reason, they are popular for use on test equipment. A BNC connector is shown in Figure 2.14.

Many test sets also use XLR connectors as well as BNC connectors. While it is certainly possible to use the balanced XLR connectors for test, the balanced circuit may in some cases provide better results than the BNC connectors. For Intel HD Audio devices that use unbalanced 3.5-millimeter or RCA jacks, the BNC connectors should always be used to ensure proper measurements.

Once it has been inserted and turned 90 degrees clockwise, the cable locks in place to prevent it from being pulled loose.

Figure 2.14 BNC Connectors on a Test Instrument and on the End of a Test Cable

PC Color Coding

Color coding is used on all external connectors on PCs to assist the consumer with connecting various external devices. Audio connectors have default color coding that is even more important since virtually all of the jacks are physically identical allowing any external device to be plugged into any jack. Table 2.1 indicates the standard color coding for various audio signals. Even if automatic retaskable jacks are provided, jacks should be color coded. Retaskable jacks are discussed in Appendix D.

Table 2.1 Intel HD Audio Jack Color Coding

Function	Channel	Wiring	Color	Pantone color	RGB values
Line In	Left	Tip	Light blue	284C	RGB: 122:171:222 Hex: #7AABDE
	Right	Ring			
Front Out	Left	Tip	Lime green	577C	RGB: 179:201:140 Hex: #B3C98C
	Right	Ring			
Microphone in (mono)	Mic In	Tip	Pink	701C	RGB: 232:140:153 Hex: #E88C99
	4V Bias	Ring			
Microphone in (stereo)	Left w/ 4V bias	Tip	Pink	701C	RGB: 232:140:153 Hex: #E88C99
	Right w/ 4V bias	Ring			
Side surround (not used for 5.1)	Left	Tip	Gray	420C	RGB: 209:204:196 Hex: #D1CCC4
	Right	Ring			
Rear surround	Left	Tip	Black	"Black"	RGB: 43:41:38 Hex: #2B2926
	Right	Ring			
Center speaker & LFE	Center	Tip	Orange	157C	RGB: 232:158:71 Hex: #E89E47
	LFE	Ring			

Desktop Color Coding

Desktop PCs incorporate 3.5-millimeter connectors either on a plug-in sound card or on a motherboard with integrated audio facilities. Connectors are generally located on the rear although mic and headset connectors may be available from the front. Figure 2.15 shows a typical set of connectors on a plug-in card.

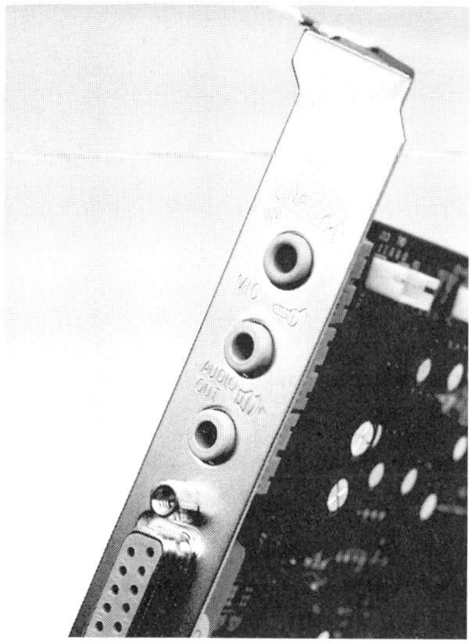

Figure 2.15 Color Coded Jacks on a Plug-In Sound Card

When integrated onto a motherboard, the connector array is grouped with other connectors on the rear panel as shown in Figure 2.16.

Figure 2.16 Color coded jacks on a typical Intel HD Audio motherboard.

Figure 2.17 illustrates two examples of the correct color coding for a motherboard surround sound implementation. The eight output channels (7.1) are distributed across four 3.5-millimeter jacks or an array of eight RCA jacks.

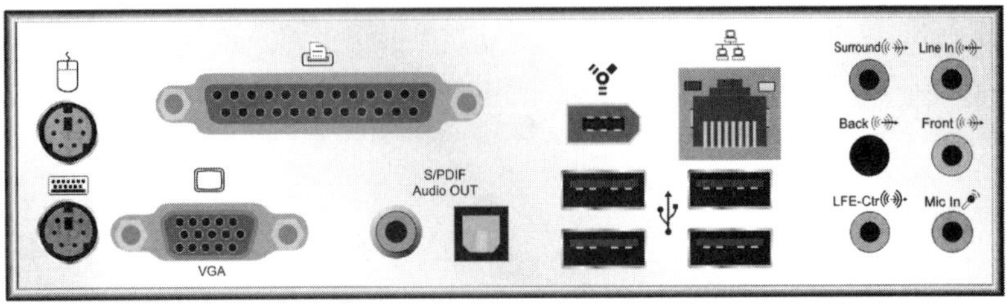

Productivity PC with six 3.5-millimeter jacks and separate S/PDIF connectors

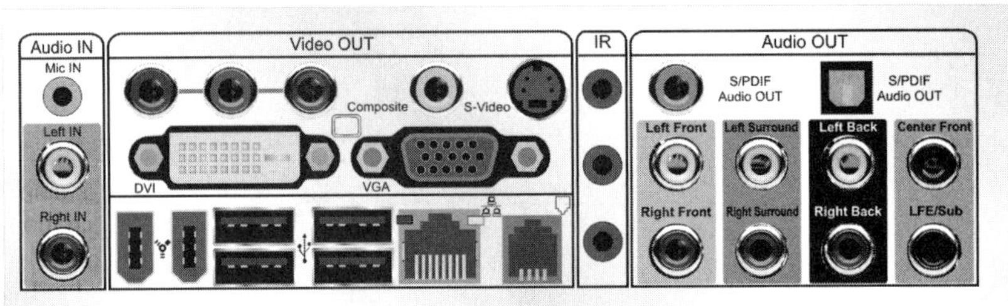

Media PC with consumer audio style RCA connectors

Figure 2.17 Typical Intel HD Audio Connectors Found at the Rear of a Productivity and Media PC

Notebook Computers

Figure 2.18 below shows a typical notebook computer sound jack configuration. Usually, only microphone input and headset output jacks are provided.

Typically, a microphone input and a headphone output are provided in a laptop. These red and green colors do not match the standard pink and lime color codes.

Figure 2.18 Miniature Phone Jacks in a Laptop Computer

Jack-Presence Detection

Jack presence detection—actually, it's *plug* presence detection—adds separate isolated contacts to jacks and simple circuitry that can alert the software that a plug has been inserted into a specific jack. This facility provides no information about what device is conncted to the plug, detecting only the physical presence of the plug in the jack. A set of auxiliary contacts in the jack close when a plug is inserted into the jack. A ladder network of four binary-weighted 1-percent resistors is used with each set of four jacks. As plugs are inserted into each jack, the composite resistance of the ladder network changes, allowing the codec to determine which jacks have plugs present. Figure 2.19 shows how the system works. The switches *must* be electrically isolated from the audio signals for this detection system to function correctly.

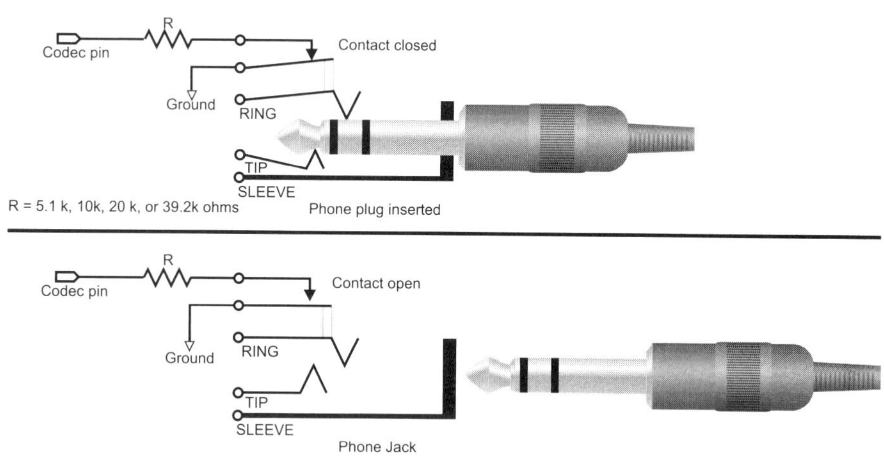

Figure 2.19 Plug Presence Detection Jack

Re-tasking Jacks

Re-taskable jacks are connectors which can provide multiple functions. For instance, a jack might allow the user to switch its function between line-in and surround-out. Or in the case of a traditional 3-jack stack, the re-tasking jack could be used to switch between 5.1 output and the standard line-out/line-in/mic-in combination found on many motherboards and sound cards.

The support in the Intel HD Audio specification for retasking jacks is incomplete, so retasking solutions usually rely on a codec vendor's driver to take advantage of custom functionality in the codec. The most basic form of retasking is to switch the jack's function based on a user command. An advanced form of retasking uses impedance sensing techniques to make a best guess of the actual device type that is plugged in and then automatically configure the jack.

Implementing retaskable jacks can be challenging, since many factors interact, especially for systems using impedance sensing. For detailed explanation of these issues, see Appendix D.

Circuit Topologies

While the physical connectors that can be used as audio interfaces vary widely, you have an equally large variation in circuitry behind the connectors to support them. The circuit topology is designed to be used with a specific external interface, cable, and interconnected equipment to preserve audio quality.

Voltage Transfer Versus Power Transfer

When a source device is connected to a receiving device, the signal energy is transferred from the source to the receiver. Early professional and broadcast installations using vacuum tubes employed a power transfer technique that often used 600-ohm impedances. The source had a 600-ohm source impedance, and the receiver had a 600-ohm input impedance. The line connecting the two had a characteristic impedance of 600 ohms. The later development of solid state circuits in the 1960s and of integrated circuit operational amplifiers in the 1970s changed much of this thinking. Sources could now have a low source impedance, usually well below 100 ohms, and receivers could have a high input impedance, generally above 10,000 ohms, and the signal transfer was now called a *voltage transfer* because almost no power was transferred. This technique inherently allows multiple receivers to be connected to a single source without significant loading or change in level. An additional benefit is that the contributions of the transmission line or cables were far less significant.

At audio frequencies, unlike RF or video frequencies, the characteristic impedance of the cable is insignificant. However, every cable has a certain capacitance per foot caused by the close proximity of the signal wires to each other. This capacitor interacts with the source impedance to form a low pass filter that rolls off high frequencies. However, if the source impedance is low, below a 100 ohms or so, typical cable capacitances would set this roll off well beyond the audio band.

Although voltage transfer techniques have been in common use for many decades, it is not uncommon to still see some holdovers of the old 600-ohm power transmission technology such as circuits including unneeded 600-ohm loads.

Designers should attempt to use the lowest practical output source impedance and highest practical input impedance in circuit designs. Operational amplifiers have an inherently low output impedance, less than 1 ohm in most cases. However, such a low impedance should not be used directly because it doesn't provide any short-circuit protection. Typically, a series build-out resistor is added to limit the output current to a safe value if the output is inadvertently shorted. This resistor might have a value between 50 and 200 ohms. The inherent input impedance of operational amplifiers is very high, typically over a mega ohm. Again, stray currents at these high impedances could cause a problem so a shunt termination resistor should be added with a value in the range of 10,000 to 100,000 ohms.

Unbalanced Interfaces

The unbalanced interface, also called the *single-ended interface*, is the most common in PC audio and consumer audio equipment. This interface uses two connections: signal and ground. It is the easiest to implement since all analog circuits naturally provide this configuration. Figure 2.20 illustrates a simplified analog audio device showing an unbalanced input and unbalanced output.

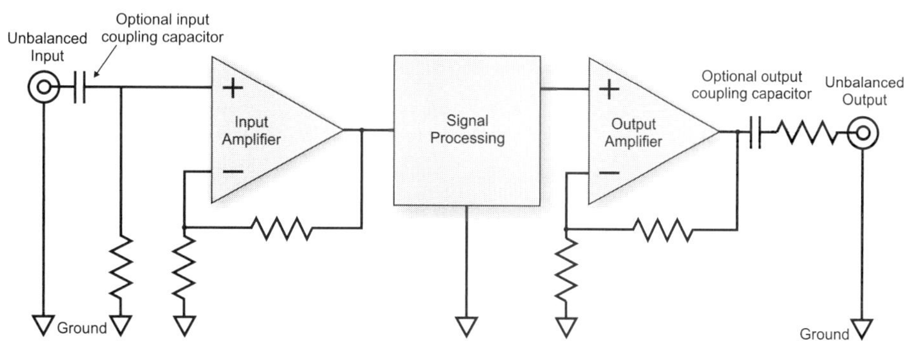

Figure 2.20 Example of an Unbalanced Device

Balanced interfaces

Unbalanced interface configurations have a distance limitation. Short runs of a couple of feet between devices that are common for consumer equipment don't pose a problem, but if longer runs, perhaps a few hundred feet are necessary, you must use a different technique. In addition to the actual distance, substantial differences are likely in the ground potential between the two devices. Professional and studio applications face these situations and use a balanced interface to overcome these challenges.

Balanced interfaces use three terminals, two for signal and a third for ground. Each of the signal terminals is "balanced" with respect to ground because they are identical in level but 180 degrees out of phase with the other. Balanced configurations are also called ***differential*** or occasionally ***push-pull***.

Noise Cancellation in Balanced Circuits

Long signal lines may pick up noise from interfering sources along the way. Such noise can appear equally in both of the signal wires creating what is called a ***common mode*** signal. As shown in Figure 2.21, the desired audio signal is present on both wires, but they have an opposite phase with respect to each other. This is called a ***normal mode*** signal. Balanced topologies get their noise immunity from the common mode signal rejection inherent with a differential input. This differential input rejects common mode signals—the unwanted interference—while accepting the normal mode signals—the desired program signal.

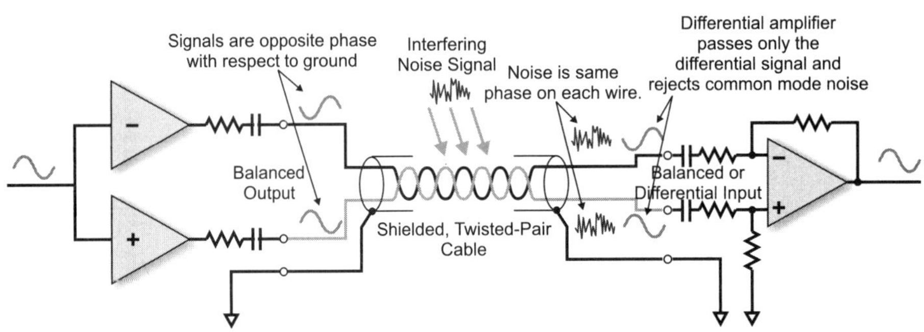

Figure 2.21 Balanced Circuit Eliminates Common-Mode Noise

Active Balancing

When balanced transmission line technology was first developed in the telephone industry many years ago, transformers were used to achieve the balance. Although transformers are still used occasionally in some professional audio applications, most contemporary equipment uses a less-expensive ***active balancing*** technique. Figure 2.22 is an illustration of a typical actively balanced input and output circuit topology. While many other circuit variations are in use, particularly for the output stage, their results are similar to this example.

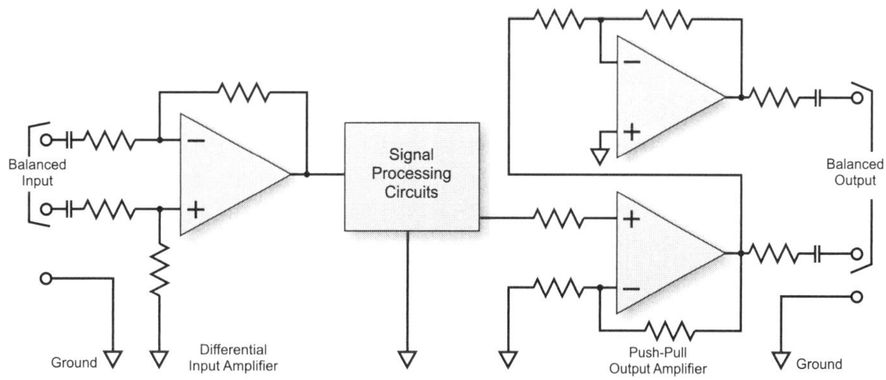

Figure 2.22 Example of a Balanced Input, Balanced Output Device

Occasionally, you need to connect "professional" balanced audio equipment, usually using an XLR connector, to consumer unbalanced audio equipment, usually with 3.5-millimeter miniature phone plugs or phono plugs. The confusion often arises: what pins to connect to what? Fortunately, differential or balanced inputs can be used without change for either balanced or unbalanced sources. In either case, the differential input correctly amplifies the signal. For unbalanced applications, simply connect either of the input signal terminals to ground and use the other terminal for signal.

Balanced outputs, however, present a different problem. You obviously can't simply connect one of the output terminals to ground—this would short out the signal. Some more sophisticated balanced output circuits set up a bridge configuration and do allow you to ground either side. To connect an unbalanced input to a push-pull balanced output, use ground and one of the two signal terminals ignoring the third terminal, as shown in Figure 2.23.

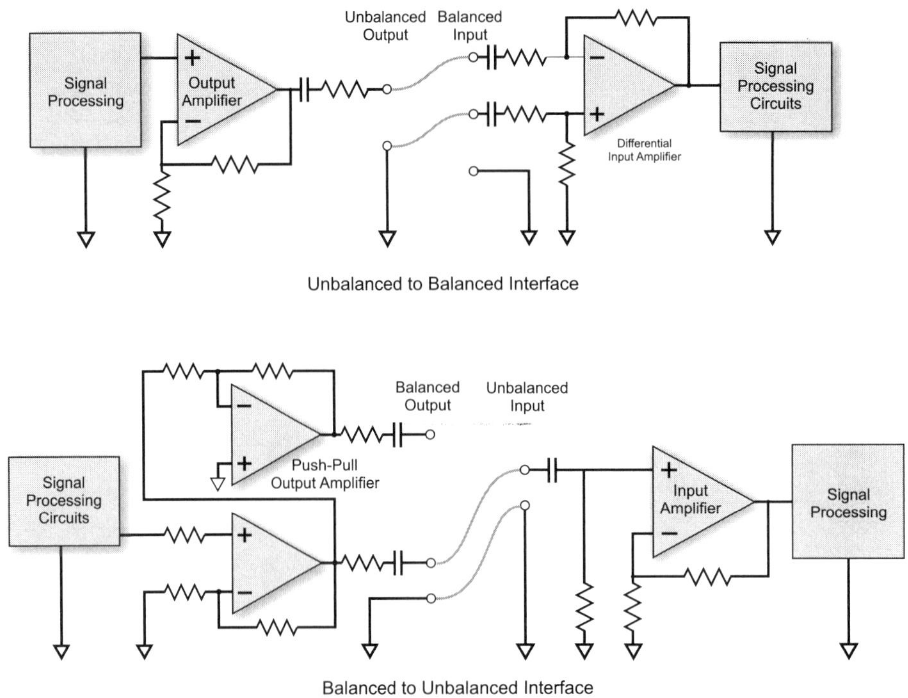

Figure 2.23 Connecting balanced and unbalanced equipment

Quasi-differential Inputs

The differential input amplifier is a powerful technique for reducing noise and eliminating ground loops. Many PC audio devices use a quasi-differential input for the ATAPI CD/DVD input that uses a total of 3 pins on the codec for a stereo signal. What appears to be the ground terminal actually is one side of the differential input, the other terminal being the other side of the differential input. When the three-wire cable from the CD/DVD device is connected, noise from the CD/DVD ground is rejected by virtue of the differential input. Figure 2.24 shows a simplified schematic of a quasi-differential input.

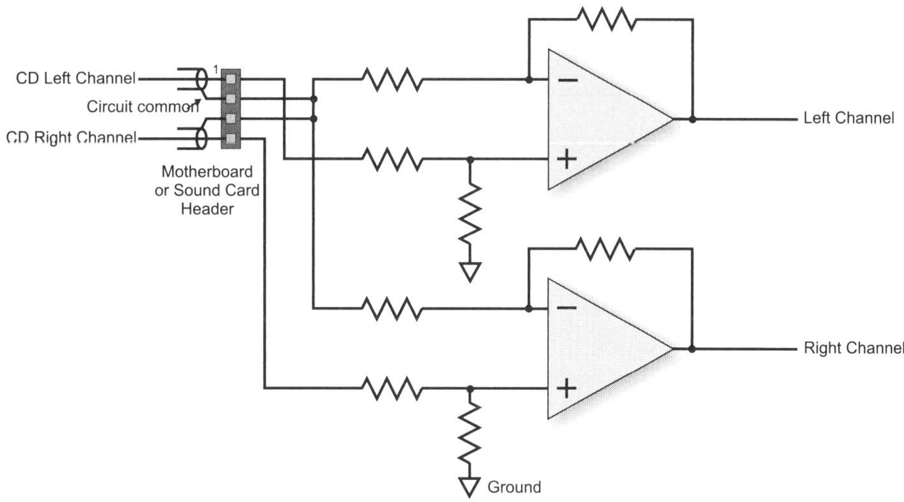

Figure 2.24 Quasi-differential Input for Analog Input from CDROM Drive

Headset Drive Amplifier

Line level outputs are expected to see only a high impedance load and therefore have little drive capability. A headset output on the other hand must drive a headset that typically has a low impedance of 32 ohms. This requires the output amplifier actually to be a small power amplifier and have a low source impedance. Some codec vendors recommend inserting a 5-ohm resistor in line with the headphone output, but this resistor limits the power delivered to the headphones. Higher-quality codecs often do not require this resistor.

Some codecs have the capability to run an output in either ***headphone*** mode or in ***line output*** mode. The advantage is that a line output does not need to source much current. Instead, it typically expects a 10-kiloohm load or higher, which makes it unsuitable for driving low-impedance headphones. Therefore, it can provide a very high quality signal, with good dynamic range and low THD+N. Amplifiers that are capable of driving headphones typically have higher THD+N, so if the codec can switch between these two modes, it should only be switched to headphone mode when headphones are intended. Headphone outputs also need large coupling capacitors, typically about 220μF. Details are provided in Chapters 5 and 6.

You could face a number of concerns when using the headphone amplifiers built into the codec. First of all, power dissipation can cause damage. While a codec may have headphone capability on more than one channel at a time, the standard 48-pin LQFP package generally is not capable of handling the thermal load caused by multiple headphone amplifier running simultaneously. While driving more than one headphone at a time may appear to work well, the additional current drain increases the heat dissipation and thermal stress. This increase is likely to cause metal migration within the codec's integrated circuits which in turn causes the codec to fail prematurely.

Another issue is how much current to output to a specific set of headphones. International law is not consistent on the subject of hearing damage caused by excessive sound pressure levels at the user's ear. France and Japan are thought to be more restrictive than other countries. The variability from one pair of headphones or earbuds to the next leads to even more confusion. Ideally, the codec should be capable of delivering enough power to the headphones to reach their loudest volume level.

If headphones are included with the PC, it may be prudent to measure the maximum output level at the ear to make sure that it doesn't exceed any legal limits for countries where the PC will be sold. As far as mixing and matching off-the-shelf PCs and headphones, just about anything goes. Headphone impedances can vary between 16 and 600 ohms, while the actual sensitivities of the headphones vary widely. You have no practical way to meet specific legal requirements if headphones are mixed and matched, except to limit the current output to somehow guarantee that no headphone exceeds the limit, which is likely to result in most headphones not being loud enough.

Speaker Power Amplifier

Most external speakers used with PCs are powered, that is, they contain their own power amplifier and are designed to be driven from the line output or headphone output of a PC audio device. If the PC includes a self-contained speaker or two, they should be driven from a 1- or 2-watt power amp contained in the PC. Make sure that the power supply to the amplifier is able to provide adequate current or the audio system could become unstable.

A movement in the industry wants to include high-power Class-D amplifiers inside a media PC chassis, so that the computer can fully replace the audio equipment in the living room. Instead of 3.5-millimeter or

RCA jacks on the back for the surround sound output, these systems would have spring-loaded clips for attaching speaker wires. For Class-D amps to be used successfully, significant redesign of the Media PC's power supply and cooling systems must take place.

Microphone Interface

Microphones can be constructed in a variety of ways. Until recently, the most common type of microphone for a PC was a dynamic microphone. Constructed like a loudspeaker, it has a diaphragm with an attached coil set between magnets. Sound vibrations move the coil and produce a small voltage output.

A less expensive type of microphone, the electret condenser mic, is now the most popular microphone for PC audio applications. This design uses the microphone diaphragm as one of the plates of a capacitor. Because its output level is so low, it requires a buffer preamplifier near the capacitor to increase the level to something that can be sent over a cable. This amplifier must be powered so the microphone input jack of a PC audio device must also provide a DC power or bias. The traditional method to provide this power on a mono microphone jack is to supply a nominal 4Vdc on the ring contact of the mic input connector. The tip contact is the signal from the mic and sleeve ground. Figure 2.25 shows a typical wiring.

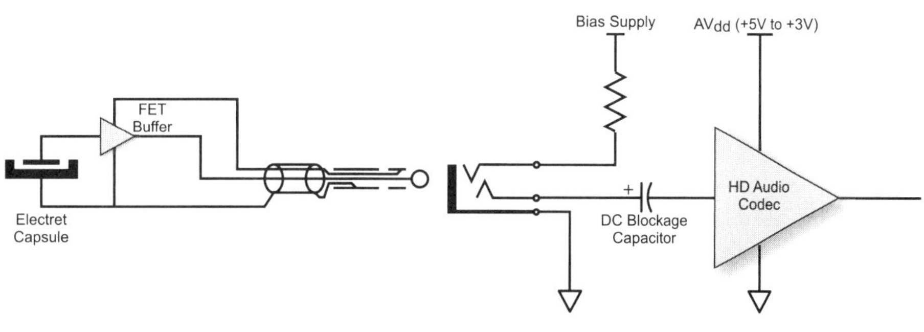

Figure 2.25 Mic Input with Electret Mic Powering

Current practice combines the signal and power on a single wire. This combination is possible since a capacitor isolates the DC voltage from the signal. This more efficient use of contacts also allows the microphone input to be stereo, like the line input. Figure 2.26 shows a schematic of a stereo powered mic input. Notice that a separate bias supply resistor must be used for each channel and the power supply should be well bypassed with a capacitor to prevent interchannel crosstalk. This capacitor also eliminates any power supply noise which would otherwise couple directly into the mic input.

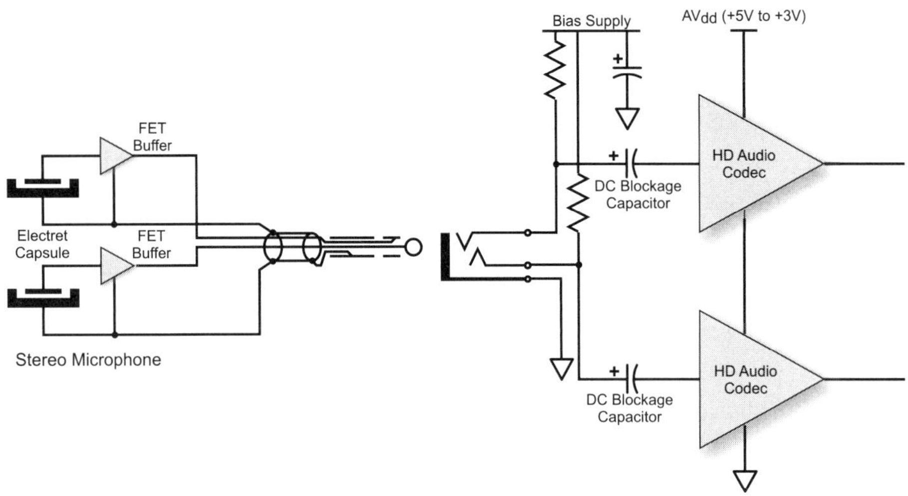

Figure 2.26 Stereo Microphone Input with Signal and Power Sharing the Same Conductors

Microphone Preamps

The microphone input must accept the low-level signal output from a microphone and amplify it to the same level as the line input. Microphone sensitivities can vary but they typically are between 20- to 60-decibels lower than a line input, so the preamp must have a similar gain range. Most designs provide a fixed gain and add a switchable *20 dB boost*. Some designs feature boost steps of 0, +10, +20, +30, and even +40 decibels. However, Windows[†] XP does not provide a suitable mechanism for engaging more than 1 or 2 of these gain stages. Most codec designs also include a variable gain stage; typically 16 steps of 1.5 decibels, for a total of 22.5 decibels. Overall available gain is therefore 62.5 decibels.

In general, adding gain should be avoided wherever possible. However, it is often necessary to accommodate unknown microphones plugged into the mic input jack. If the PC ships with a microphone, then the system should be preset to match the gain of that microphone. Microphones with higher output levels are preferred, especially if the circuit board traces are long. Chapter 5 explains additional details of circuit board layout to preserve audio quality.

The user interface to set microphone gain is a challenge. Most users do not understand how to set this gain and in fact often do not have the information to set it properly, even if they understand the principles. The safest approach is to establish a default for the gain at the ideal setting for whatever microphone is supplied with the system.

Signal Levels and Impedances

For optimal system compatibility, analog signal levels and impedances should be consistent and compatible. This compatibility should go beyond just PC audio devices since they are also connected to consumer audio devices. Line levels in consumer equipment have been well established, and in general, they are very compatible among themselves. Analog tape players, CD players, and VCRs usually can be connected to a receiver without problem—that is, levels appear balanced and compatible. The nominal line level in consumer equipment has been 2 Vrms for many years. Unfortunately, most PC audio devices provide 1-Vrms level outputs. Chapter 6 contains recommendations for implementing RCA jacks capable of handling 2Vrms in a PC environment.

While desktop PCs typically provide a nominal 1-Vrms line level, notebook PCs using low-voltage circuits and constrained by battery life struggle to deliver a 1 Vrms signal. No inherent quality reason forces the PC to operate at a 1 Vrms or 2 Vrms level, simply the signal-level convention established with most consumer audio devices and the consumer inconvenience when some sources produce a lower nominal program level.

Impedances are a parameter over which we have more control. We mentioned the voltage transfer principle earlier suggesting low-output impedances and high-input impedances for line inputs and outputs. Table 2.2 defines design goals for signal levels and impedances for analog interfaces for PC audio devices.

Table 2.2 Suggested Analog Interface Levels and Impedances

Parameter	Nominal Value	Range
Line Input Impedance	• 20 kΩ	10k to 100k
Line Input Maximum Level - CE devices	2 V rms	2 to 2.5 V rms

Line Input Maximum Level - PC devices	1 V rms	1 to 1.3 V rms
Line Output Source Impedance at codec	< 100 Ω	50 to 200 Ω
Line Output Load impedance	• 10 kΩ	6k to 100k Ω
Line Output Maximum Level – CE devices	2 V rms	2 to 2.5 V rms
Line Output Maximum Level – PC devices	1 V rms	1 to 1.3 V rms
Microphone Input Impedance at codec	• 4 kΩ	4k to 20k
Microphone impedance	600 Ω	300 to 1500
Microphone Input Maximum Level (w/ 20 dB boost enabled) at codec	100 mV	1 mV to 1V
Headset Output Source Impedance at codec	< 2 Ω	1 to 5 Ω
Headset Impedance	32 Ω	16 to 600 Ω
Headset Output Maximum Level at codec	50 mW	10 to 60mW
Speaker impedance (passive drivers)	8 Ω	4 to 32 Ω
Amplified speakers input impedance	>5k	3k to 20k
Speaker output source impedance at amplifier	< 1Ω	1 to 2 Ω
Speaker load impedance (passive)	8 Ω	2 to 16 Ω
Speaker output level	2W	1W to 10W

Digital Interfaces

While analog interfaces were the starting point and might still be the majority of audio interfaces in a PC environment, many new digital interfaces are being introduced. These new additions can offer many advantages over traditional analog interfaces such as better noise immunity, easier set up by the consumer, and fewer cables and connectors when multi-channel surround sound is involved.

S/PDIF Inputs and Outputs

The oldest and perhaps most common digital interface found on consumer electronics and PC audio devices is the commonly called *Sony/Philips Digital Interface* or S/PDIF. The professional version of this interface, used in recording studios and broadcast facilities, is designated AES 3, after the Audio Engineering Society standard that describes its characteristics. It was formerly referred to as "AES/EBU" after the two standards organizations originally defining the format. Both the professional and consumer version have nearly identical data formats but different interface levels, impedances, and connectors. Status bit protocol differs between the two implementations as you will see later. This format is also defined in IEC 60958, listed in "References."

The AES 3 format uses bi-phase coding which embeds the bit clock in the data and provides an average DC level of zero. Also the data is polarity insensitive, useful in professional applications as this allows two-conductor shielded cable to be used without regard to polarity.

Data Protocol

The AES3 format consists of a 192-frame *channel status block*. Each frame in turn consists of two sub-frames or channels. Each *sub-frame* is 32 bits long and consists of a 4-bit *preamble*, 24-bits of audio data, followed by four *status bits*. When audio data is less than 24 bits, zero padding is added. The preamble patterns identify the frames. Three distinctive preamble patterns are used:

- X, to identify the start of channel-A sub-frame
- Y, to identify the start of channel-B sub-frame
- Z, to identify the start of a 192-frame channel status block

Figure 2.27 shows the patterns of each of the three preambles and their position in the sub-frame.

Each data bit occupies a single time slot and is equivalent to one period of the sample clock. Every data bit starts with a transition and ends with a transition. If a data transition occurs during the time slot, the data is a 1; if no transition occurs during the time slot, the data is a 0.

The term *Unit Interval* signifies the shortest time interval between transitions. Each time slot has a duration of two unit intervals or 2 UI. Many timing parameters regarding the data are specified in terms of unit intervals since the UI is independent of sample rate. A frame has a length of 128 UIs. The preamble patterns violate the 2 UI pulse width rule and can have pulses up to 3 UI in duration allowing easy detection of the start of a frame.

As mentioned, 24 bits are reserved for audio data. Coded as two's complement, these bits typically are partitioned as 4 bits called auxiliary data, followed by 20 audio data bits. The 4 auxiliary data bits can be used for user-defined purposes such as low resolution voice annotation. If less than 20 bits are used for audio, the unused left-most bits are set to zero. The status bits define the use of these 4 plus 20 bits. Alternatively, all 24 bits can be used for a single high-resolution audio word.

The final 4 bits in a sub-frame contain metadata to instruct the receiver how to interpret the data stream. The *validity* bit is often a source of confusion, since it has been used for different purposes in different implementations. Typically, validity means that actual audio data is not present. For instance, it could be used to signal a recorder to only record when speech is present, so that silence is ignored. The user bits can contain special information defined by the implementer. IEC 60958-3 has defined a packet-based data format for consumer applications.

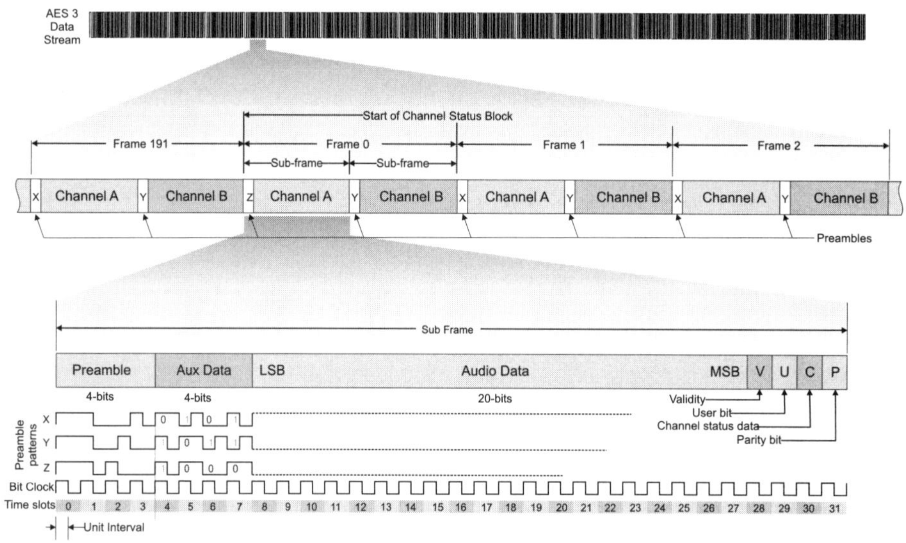

192 frames form a Channel Status Block. Each frame contains two sub-frames: channel A and channel B, which usually are the left and right, respectively. Each sub-frame contains 32 bits, including 24 bits that are reserved for audio data.

Figure 2.27 AES3 Data Format

The *channel status* bits are individually assembled over a 192-frame interval, starting with the start of the *channel status block* defined by the *z-preamble*. The first bit in the sequence identifies the stream as *Consumer* or *Professional*. The remaining bits are defined differently for consumer or professional formats. A *Copy Protection* bit enables or prevents copies. A *non-audio* bit identifies the 24 audio data bits as other than linear PCM audio data, such as might be the case with encoded data. For example, Dolby Digital (AC3), WMA Pro, and DTS use special encoding to fit six or eight channels of compressed data into the space normally used by the two-channel linear PCM data. A conventional two-channel receiver with simple linear PCM decoding is obviously unable to deal with this special data and this bit prevents an attempt to decode it. Table 2.3 shows the decoding of the channel status bits.

Table 2.3 AES 3 - S/PDIF Channel Status Bits

Byte	Bit 0	Bit 1	Bit 2	Bit 3	Bit 4	Bit 5	Bit 6	Bit 7
0	Prof/Con	Audio	Copy Protect	Pre emphasis			Status	
	0 = Cons 1 = Prof	0 = digital audio 1 = non-audio	0 = protect 1 = allow copy	000 = None 100 = 50/15 μs 2-channel 010 = reserved 2-channel 110 = reserved 2-channel xx1 = reserved			00 = mode 0 xx = reserved	
1	Category Code							
2	Source Number				Channel Number			
	0000 = unspecified 1000 = 1 0100 = 2 1100 = 3 …binary 1101 to 0110 = 4 to 13… 0111 = 14 1111 = 15				0000 = unspecified 1000 = A (left in 2-channel mode) 0100 = B (right in 2-channel mode) 1100 = C …binary 1101 to 0110 = D to M… 0111 = N 1111 = O			
3	Sample frequency				Clock Accuracy		Reserved	
	0000 = 44.1 kHz 0100 = 48 kHz 1100 = 32 kHz xxxx = reserved				00 = Level II ±1000 ppm 01 = Level III varable 10 = Level I ±50 ppm high accy			
4	Status	Word length			Reserved			
	0 = 20 bits	000 = not indicated 001 = 19 bits 010 = 18 bits 011 = 17 bits 100 = 16 bits 101 = 20 bits xxx = reserved						
	1 = 24 bits	000 = not indicated 001 = 23 bits 010 = 22 bits 011 = 21 bits 100 = 20 bits 101 = 24 bits xxx = reserved						

AES 3 Electrical Properties

The AES 3 serial digital interface can take two electrical formats and an optical format. As an unbalanced format, commonly called S/PDIF, the circuit has a 75-ohm characteristic impedance. For optimal data integrity, the transmitter source impedance, receiver termination impedance, and the cable used to connect the two must all have a 75-ohm impedance. This unbalanced format commonly uses RCA connectors although BNC connectors may also be used. The signal level for this format is 0.5 V pp.

In the professional, balanced format, the AES 3 interface has a 110-ohm characteristic impedance. Again, the transmitter source impedance, receiver termination impedance, and the cable used to connect the two must all have a 110-ohm impedance to preserve data integrity. Although when the format was developed, it was thought that common 2-conductor shielded microphone cables could be used, these do not have the correct impedance, a factor that is important at the frequencies used to transport this data. Cable manufacturers have developed 110-ohm cable optimized for use in this application. This balanced format always uses 3-pin XLR connectors. The signal level in the balanced format may be between 2 and 7 Vpp to comply with the AES 3 standard.

Figure 2.28 shows interface wiring for both the unbalanced S/PDIF and balanced AES 3 interface. Although the unbalanced format could get by without the use of a 1:1 transformer, eliminating this transformer invites trouble with noisy digital data leaking into the audio circuits because they now share a ground connection. The small and inexpensive transformer isolates these grounds and can save a lot of grief later trying to meet audio noise requirements.

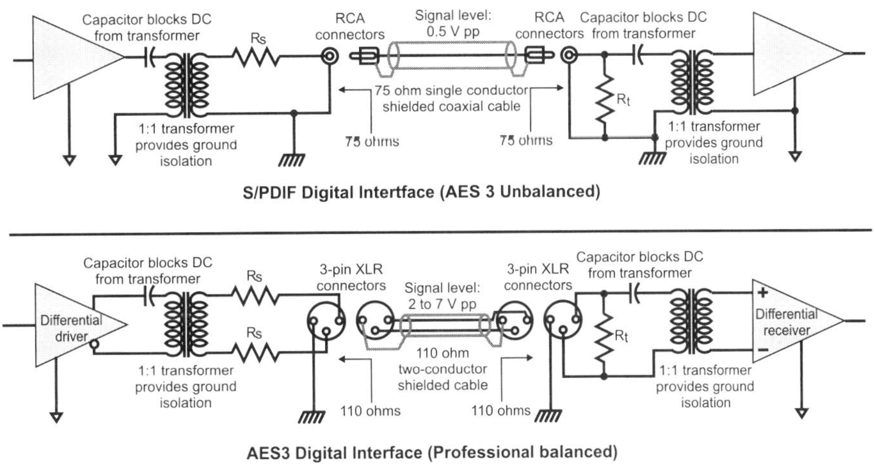

Note: transformers are recommended for both implementations.

Figure 2.28 S/PDIF (Unbalanced AES 3) and AES 3 Balanced Digital Interfaces

Optical

Serial digital data with AES 3 protocol can also be transported using an optical interface. Often called *TOSLINK*[†] after the initial implementer, Toshiba, this format eliminates all chances for a ground loop.

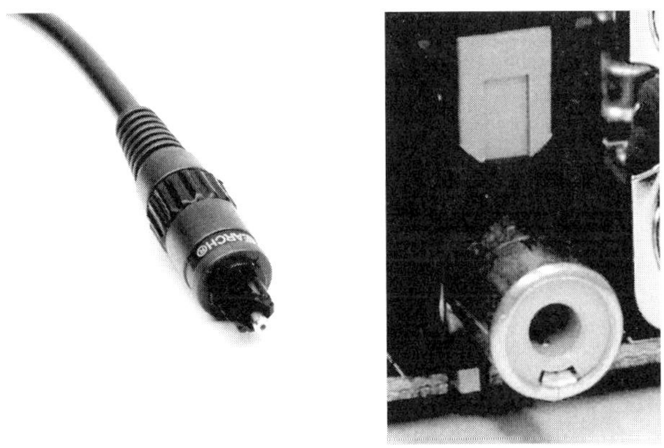

The image on the right shows an electrical coaxial connector with an optical jack above it.

Figure 2.29 Optical Connectors

Serial Copy Management System (SCMS)

As part of the overall definition of S/PDIF, different classes of devices are defined, along with different uses for the various control bits for each class of device. In the Japanese market, an important class of devices is the Minidisk player, which falls in the general category of optical storage devices. This class of device specifies the usage of particular bits to control copying from the PC to a Minidisk player over S/PDIF. The bits controlling SCMS are defined in EIC 60958-3 section 4.3. Copyright management is controlled by the combination of channel status copyright bit 2, category code bits 8-14, and the generation status bit 15 ("L" bit) as shown in Table 2.4.

Table 2.4 SCMS State Definitions

Bits	Copy Allowed	Copy Once	Copy None
Copy	1	0	0
L	1	1	1
CC6	0	0	0
CC5	0	0	0
CC4	1	1	1
CC3	1	1	1
CC2	0	0	0
CC1	1	1	0
CC0	0	0	1

Note: The default setting for the Japanese market should be "Copy Once". Bits designated by the gray shade do not change state when the SCMS modes are changed.

Because no API in Windows XP controls these bits, most codec vendors have collaborated with DVD Player vendors such as Intervideo (WinDVD) and Cyberlink (PowerDVD) to provide a proprietary API to manipulate these settings as different content is played.

For S/PDIF Output, simply setting these bits before transmitting is sufficient. For S/PDIF Input, you might have to limit copying based on the state of these bits. The OEM usually defines the behavior of SCMS if S/PDIF Input is supported.

S/PDIF Input

Although almost all Intel HD Audio codecs have designated Pin 47 as S/PDIF In, actually making use of this signal is problematic. The biggest problem is that S/PDIF is a self-clocking interface, and the clock signal is retrieved from the data stream. Therefore, the S/PDIF input receives everything asynchronously. As long as bandwidth is available on the Intel HD Audio bus, the incoming data can be passed through for storage. Typically, this data is not processed in real-time and is not routed to the PC's analog or digital audio outputs.

In addition, non-PCM formats are not supported by Windows for S/PDIF inputs, so while it may be possible to store the incoming data blocks for later processing, it is not possible to receive a Dolby[†] Digital or DTS stream and play it through multi-channel speakers.

For these reasons, most OEMs do not choose to implement S/PDIF input even if the feature is available on the Intel HD Audio codec.

Encoding

The AES 3 and IEC 60958 standards define a linear PCM data format with a resolution of 16 to 24 bits and two interleaved channels. To transmit more than two channels, as is required for 5.1 and 7.1 surround sound implementations, specialized encoding schemes have been developed by Microsoft, Dolby, DTS, and others.

Encoded Data Formats

The IEC 60937 standard defines the method for implementing alternative encoding protocols, such as Dolby Digital, using a standard IEC 60958 / AES 3 physical interface. The bits normally reserved for linear PCM audio are replaced with coded data in Dolby Digital format. The status bits in the AES 3 bit stream are set to non-audio to prevent conventional PCM linear decoders from trying to interpret this encoded data. Figure 2.30 illustrates the protocol stacks for the Dolby Digital format.

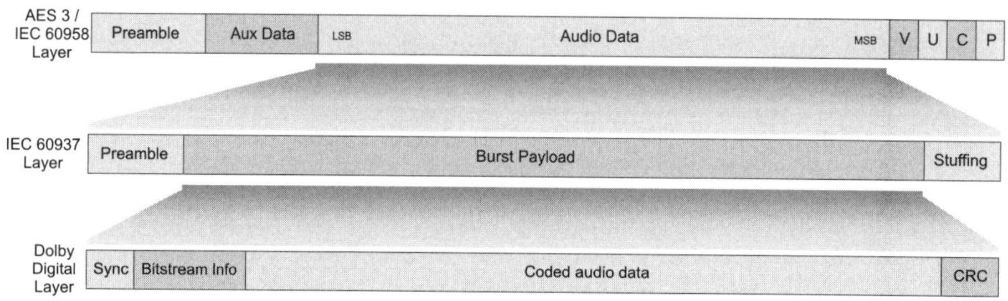

Figure 2.30 Protocol Stack Used by IEC 60937 to Transport Multichannel Data Using an IEC 60958 / AES 3 Format

The same basic approach is used for other non-PCM formats such as DTS and WMA Pro. The data in the stream is compressed in size using a lossy-compression algorithm much like MP3, and packets of data are passed down the line. The S/PDIF transmitter keeps the pipeline open by transmitting zeroes whenever no packet data is available. The non-PCM bit is set prior to sending the compressed data and cleared once the stream has stopped.

Windows maintains a list of tags that identify non-PCM formats. Dolby Digital (AC3) and WMA Pro are uniquely identified. DVD player software typically uses the AC3 tag to transmit DTS and other non-PCM formats. In this case, the receiving device at first only knows that the data is non-PCM, and must look inside the data packets to determine whether it can decode the data.

The act of passing non-PCM data to the S/PDIF output has the effect of making the S/PDIF output modal, which impacts usability. For instance, if the S/PDIF output is sending Linear PCM, then Windows own software-based kMixer would mix in system sounds, such as the beeps made when the user clicks on the remote control of a media PC. When a non-PCM stream is being played, then the system sounds are not heard at the digital output. This variation can be very confusing to the end user, who won't understand why the sound of pressing the button on the remote control comes and goes.

To make it even more confusing, the PC's master volume control has absolutely no effect on non-PCM data, as the contents of the data are unknown to the OS. Therefore, the volume buttons on the remote control have no effect.

Over the last few years, support of non-PCM formats has made sense for a number of reasons. The first reason is the ambiguity of "Who needs to pay the multi-channel decoder royalty?" If the decoder is in the A/V receiver, in firmware, then the receiver vendor pays it. If the PC decodes the stream in software, then the DVD player software vendor is responsible for the royalty, which they pass on to the OEM.

Another reason has been to minimize the CPU burden imposed by the decoder. Moore's law has made this a non-issue with modern CPUs.

For Media Center PCs that use the 10-foot user interface and don't expose the standard Windows GUI, the only DVD player that can be used is Windows Media Player. However, the AC3 and DTS decoders can be obtained independently from the same sources. In either configuration, the decoder usually is installed as a DirectShow filter that can intercept the non-PCM stream and decode it on the fly, providing multi-channel Linear PCM to kMixer and then to the driver. See Chapter 3 for more details on decoders and encoders.

The relatively recent development of software-based real-time encoders has provided some interesting ways to work around the usability issues caused by the Linear PCM/non-PCM modality. Dolby Digital Live, DTS Connect, and ADAT, which is described later in this chapter; all provide the ability to route six or eight channels of audio out of the TOSLINK or S/PDIF connector in real-time, with the OS and the driver receiving all the audio data in the Linear PCM format.

Therefore if Dolby, DTS, and WMA Pro decoders are all present, and the data is transmitted out the S/PDIF port using one of these three methods, then the remote control key clicks always can be heard, and the master volume control is able to control the volume of the clicks, regardless of the source format and number of channels.

Other Digital Audio Formats

While S/PDIF and AES3 serial digital interfaces have been the most prolific interfaces in PC audio to date, several newer digital interfaces are entering the mainstream. Multi-channel, preservation of audio quality and digital rights management issues are driving some of these developments. Additionally, other segments of the professional audio industry use unique digital interfaces developed to serve particular needs such as professional recording. You should find that understanding of these interface formats and how they compare proves helpful when interconnection is required.

ADAT Optical

The *Alesis Digital Audio Tape* (ADAT) digital audio format can carry 8 channels of low-latency 48-kilohertz, 24-bit audio by sharing a TOSLINK optical connector with an S/PDIF out jack on the PC. The ADAT Optical interface was developed in the mid-90s by the Alesis Corporation, for connecting multi-channel digital audio recorders to signal processing and mixing systems. It is the standard 8-channel digital interface shared between hundreds of multi-track audio devices made by manufacturers Alesis, Yamaha, Mackie, Steinberg, RME/Hammerfall, Echo Audio, Sek'D, Intel®, SigmaTel, Lynx, Behringer, PreSonus, Tascam, M-Audio, Kurzweil, Frontier Design, and many others.

Early versions of these recorders used standard S-VHS video cassettes but a proprietary recording technique to record eight channels of digital audio. The ADAT tape format has in recent years been supplanted by 24-track ADAT hard disk recorders, but the ADAT optical interconnect remains intact. Three separate ADAT connections are used to transfer all 24 channels.

The physical interface between ADAT devices is optical and uses the same connectors and optical cables as the TOSLINK S/PDIF format, although the data format itself is quite different than S/PDIF. The ADAT format, shown in Figure 2.31, can support 8 channels of uncompressed 24-bit audio at 48 kilohertz or 4 channels of 24-bit audio at 96 kilohertz. By comparison, the S/PDIF format can only support two channels of audio at these sampling rates. If ADAT is implemented, make sure to use a TOSLINK transmitter that supports the higher bit rates—most of them do.

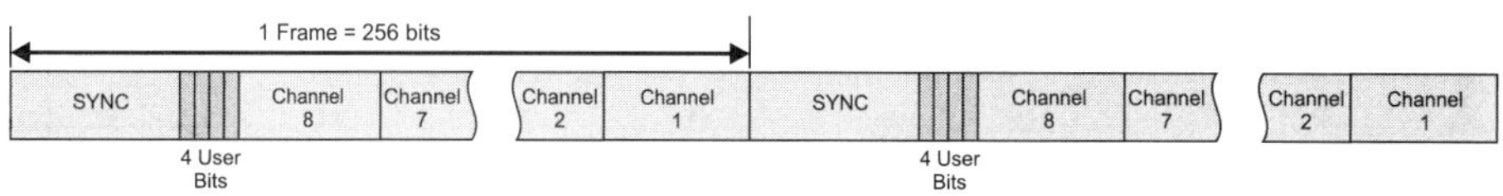

Figure 2.31 ADAT Data Format

The ADAT license is normally available on a royalty-free basis from Alesis Corporation if the ADAT logo is displayed on the end product.

I²S

The Inter-IC Sound (I²S) bus specification was developed in 1986 by Philips for connecting audio-related integrated circuits. For example, I²C is commonly used to internally connect components such as DACs, ADCs, DSPs, and filters within an audio device. The interface generally is not exposed for external device interconnection.

I²S consists of three signals:

- Continuous Serial Clock (SCK)
- Word Select (WS)
- Serial Data (SD)

Because the I²C separates the clock and data signals, the jitter is very low. The WS line is used to designate whether the current data is for channel 1 or channel 2. Because WS is only capable of specifying two channels, an I²S bus itself is limited to two channels. However, additional SD lines can be added in parallel to convey multi-channel surround sound.

The I²S specification allows for unlimited clock speeds. As long as certain clock waveform restrictions are met, the SCK can be run arbitrarily fast. As such, I²S is highly scalable, and sampling rates and depths of any size can be sent across it, provided that both the transmitter and receiver support the same clock speed.

The I²S interface includes support for transmitters and receivers supporting different bit depths. Each sample, or word, is bracketed by transitions of the WS signal. Each word is sent in two's complement format, with the most significant bit first. A receiver skips bits in a word that exceed its capability. If a receiver is sent fewer bits in a word than it can handle, the outstanding bits are set to zero automatically. Since the most significant bit is sent first, the least significant bits are discarded or extrapolated. Thus, a wide range of transmitters and receivers can be connected to one another, even though they may handle different word sizes. No sideband arbitration is needed; the word size is implicit in the number of SCK cycles between WS transitions.

Unlike Intel HD Audio, I²S does not inherently support control information such as volume control, sample rate selection, and the like. If such control is necessary, then an additional control bus such as I²C or Serial Peripheral Interface (SPI) should be used.

Also unlike Intel HD Audio, I²S pin counts increase with each additional channel pair. So while a stereo pair of I²S codecs can be implemented with only three signal wires, an eight-channel system requires four SD lines for a total of six signal lines. Eight channels of ADC would require another six lines, in addition to any analog I/O. By contrast, Intel HD Audio would require only five signal lines to accommodate both ADC and DAC functions, plus Intel HD Audio contains an advanced standardized control system as contrasted to proprietary controls bus implemented using I^2C or SPI.

For these reasons, Intel HD Audio is ideally suited for interconnecting controllers, DACs, and ADCs for consumer equipment as well as for PC audio applications.

DSD

When the Compact Disc (CD) was introduced in the early 1980s, its 16-bit linear PCM resolution and 44.1 kilohertz sample rate were state-of-the-art and seemed completely adequate for high audio quality. Since then, technology has advanced, resulting in the availability of inexpensive higher resolution converters and higher sample rates. Also, the original CD format only supports two audio channels and does not support 5.1 or 7.1 surround sound formats. Audio purists have looked for an improvement on the original CD format, higher bandwidth and more resolution, and two contenders were introduced in 1999 to fill that role: *DVD-Audio* and *Super Audio Compact Disc* (SACD). SACD uses a digital format called *Direct Stream Digital (DSD)*, which was created initially as a format for Sony to digitally archive its extensive library of analog tape and vinyl recordings.

Whereas the CD uses a bit depth of 16 and a sample rate of 44.1 kilohertz, the DSD format uses *Sigma-Delta* technology, which has a bit depth of only 1, but operates at a much higher frequency of 2.82 megahertz. Since this sampling rate is 64 times the original 44.1 kilohertz CD sample rate, this particular form of conversion is sometimes referred to as 1-bit 64X oversampling.

At first glance, it may seem that a 1-bit sampling depth is incapable of producing useful information. However, by examining Figure 2.32 you can see that the density of transitions from 0 to 1 is proportional to the slope of the input analog signal. This property is reflected in the sampling signal's name: *Pulse Density Modulation*. PDM should give you some sense that useful information can indeed be derived from a one-bit sample depth, provided of course that the sampling rate is sufficiently high.

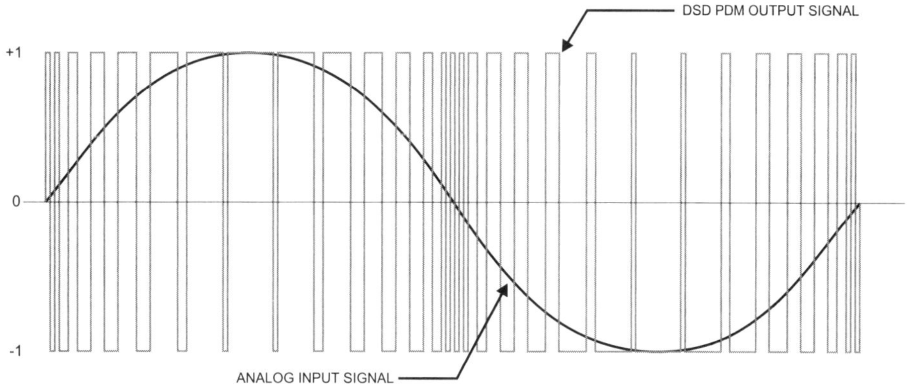

The one-bit Sigma-Delta sampling technique generates a Pulse Density Modulation (PDM) signal from an analog source.

Figure 2.32 SD Sampling

The raw serial output of the SD modulator is the DSD data stream. The 1-bit SD 64x conversion technology allows an analog audio frequency response up to 100 kilohertz and significantly reduces the demands for filtering as required in conventional converters. Figure 2.33 shows a comparison of DSD to conventional conversion. Notice how the DSD technique eliminates the need for the decimation and interpolation digital filters.

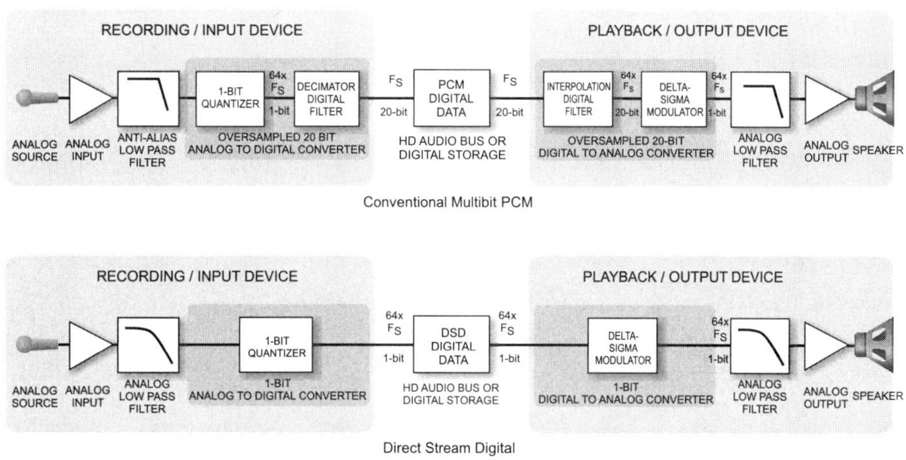

Figure 2.33 Conventional Digital Conversion Process versus DSD 1-bit 64x Fs Process

Direct Stream Transfer (DST) is the lossless data compression strategy that is designed to work with DSD data. DST compression and decompression are performed by dedicated hardware blocks.

While it is relatively straightforward to manipulate linear PCM data in software, DSD data is primarily intended for capture, storage, and playback. Processing DSD data in software on a processor which uses Intel® architecture is usually not practical because each bit in memory needs to be processed separately, which has the potential to tax even the most powerful CPUs. Therefore most DSD processing takes place in dedicated hardware units.

MIDI

The *Musical Instrument Digital Interface* (MIDI) is a control bus developed in the early 1980's to interconnect electronic musical instruments such as keyboards and synthesizers. MIDI also is used to connect instruments to computers. MIDI is not a digital audio interface because it does not transmit audio signals but instead provides control, timing and synchronization information that describe musical events to devices, which themselves may produce audio signals. In other words, MIDI is only suitable for conveying music; it is not a viable mechanism for transmitting arbitrary sounds.

The MIDI message protocol can include pitch and keyboard velocity information in addition to timing. MIDI files are a complete set of instructions of a song or sound effect for MIDI rendering devices such as synthesizers. Since the files contain no actual digital audio information, they are very small and efficient.

FireWire/IEEE-1394

The 1394 interface was originally developed by Apple Computer in 1986 under their trademark FireWire[†] as a multimedia bus to allow interconnection of audio and video devices, such as digital TVs, digital set top boxes, hard drives, and camcorders, to a PC. In 1995, the interface was adopted and standardized by the Institute of Electrical and Electronics Engineers (IEEE) as IEEE-1394. Since its introduction, it has undergone two revisions and is now IEEE-1394b. This format is also called iLink[†], a Sony trademark.

The 1394 interface provides peer-to-peer connectivity and a single 1394 bus can support up to 63 daisy-chained nodes of bi-directional traffic. It includes special provisions to handle multiple simultaneous tasks without disruption. The interface can handle diverse types of content including MPEG data, Digital Video (DV), and Internet Protocol (IP) and provides a guaranteed delivery and service quality. For example, a consumer may be watching a movie being streamed through a 1394 interface while another family member is transferring clips from a camcorder to a PC. As the second activity is stopped and started, the first person sees no disturbance to the movie audio and video stream.

IEEE-1394 is a "plug and play" interface allowing discovery and automatic configuration of devices plugged in or removed. It also includes support for Digital Transmission Content Protection (DTCP) to protect content from illegal copying. Chapter 10 provides more detail on DTCP implementations.

IEEE-1394a provides speeds of up to 400 Mbps over distances of up to 4.5 meters, and it can easily handle the 20 to 30 Mbps rate of compressed high definition video. IEEE-1394b has extended this bandwidth to 800 Mbps with architectural support to move the throughput speed all the way to 3.2 Gbps.

Physical connectors

IEEE-1394 can use a variety of connectors and cable types. The most familiar copper wire form is a 6-pin connector and cable that includes two twisted pair shielded cables, data and strobe, and two power wires providing power in the range of 8 to 33 V. An alternate form common with camcorders eliminates the two power pins and wires and uses a 4-pin connector. These connectors are shown in Figure 2.34.

The 6-pin is on the left, and the 4-pin variant for camcorders is on the right

Figure 2.34 IEEE-1394 Connectors

The 1394 interface can use an optical connector with fiber cable, too. The optical connections allow for high speed transfers over hundreds of meters. Different grades of plastic and glass and associated cladding are specified for different bandwidths.

Automotive Applications

A new interface with 1394 heritage is IDM-1394, with was developed for use in automobiles to distribute audio and video content among DVD players, video screens, camcorders, personal MP3 players, and other devices. It uses a Plastic Optical Fiber (POF) optical cable to keep noise from the electrically hostile automotive environment from leaking into the multimedia signals.

IEC61883-6 Audio and Music Data Streaming Protocol

The IEC61883-6 standard specifies packet formats for the following audio formats:

- Linear PCM (sample rates of 32 to 96k, 24 bits)
- IEC60958 (or AES3)
- 32-bit floating point
- MIDI

Synchronization is performed by creating time stamps[1] and inserting these time stamps into the isochronous packets with the audio sample payload. A receiver node uses these time stamps to reconstruct the audio clock by comparing the value of the time stamp to the receiving node's Cycle Time Register and issuing a pulse when they match. This pulse is fed to a PLL that multiplies the frequency to the audio master clock- e.g. 256xFs. This method of synchronization is commonly known in the 1394 world as SYT.

The IEC61883-6 standard was followed up by the *Audio and Music Data Transmission Protocol 2.1* (AMDTP2.1) specification published by the 1394 Trade Association. This specification is expected to work its way through the IEC and become a member of the IEC61883 suite. The AMDTP2.1 specification adds many new audio formats, including:

- DSD (SACD)
- Ancillary data for SACD and DVD-A
- SMPTE Time Code
- Multiplexed MIDI (up to 8 MIDI streams in one packet)
- High Definition Audio—8 Channels of 24-bit 192 kilohertz
- Compound packets that mix different formats (e.g. IEC60958 and PCM)

Digital Transmission Content Protection (DTCP a.k.a "5C")

The DTCP protocol adds a layer of encryption to the payload in IEC61883-x packets to prevent copying. The process begins when two nodes are told to talk to each other. They exchange keys to confirm that the other node is authorized to exchange the data—sort of a secret handshake. Once they qualify each other, data is exchanged using encryption.

During data transmission a random key challenge occurs on a regular basis to prevent someone else from snooping in on the transmission after the secret handshake was made.

---

[1] Basically, a timestamp is the instantaneous value of the transmitting node's Cycle Time Register when a transition occurs in the audio frame clock.

PC-Based Device Discovery and Connection Management

Many 1394 Audio devices are peripherals to personal computers. The Windows and Mac OS[†] operating systems discover devices through their plug and play mechanisms by reading descriptors in well-known address locations in each node and mapping these descriptors to OS drivers.

Consumer Adoption

In the consumer space, 1394 has been most widely adopted as compressed a multimedia interconnect. For instance, the DV video format uses 1394 to transfer video streams amongst digital camcorders, tape decks, and computers. 1394 is also used to convey protected video between digital satellite receivers and other components such as DVRs or some types of TVs. 1394 has not been widely adopted as a general purpose PC interconnect, although some peripherals, such as disk drives, do use it.

USB

The Universal Serial Bus (USB) was developed in the mid-1990s to replace existing serial (and parallel) interconnects on the PC. USB was intended to provide a single interface for connecting keyboards, mice, printers, game controllers, external modems, disk drives, and other peripherals. The first version was released in 1995 as USB 1.0. However, it was version 1.1 released in 1998 that gained wide popularity. Indeed, in 1998 the Apple iMac became the first computer to use USB ports in place of the legacy connections.

USB 1.1 adoption in the Windows environment was a bit slower, but today the USB interface is ubiquitous, appearing on virtually every new computer. USB 1.1 supports bit rates up to 12 Mbps. USB 2.0, introduced in 2002, added support for *Hi-speed USB*, with offered bit rates up to 480 Mbps.

USB uses a master-slave architecture, as shown in Figure 2.35. A *USB host* is in charge of the bus. Slave components known as *USB devices* attach to the host. A host may have multiple ports, but only one device may plug into a port. More ports can be added to a system by plugging a *USB hub* into the host. Unlike 1394, peer-to-peer connections are not supported; the system must contain a USB host.

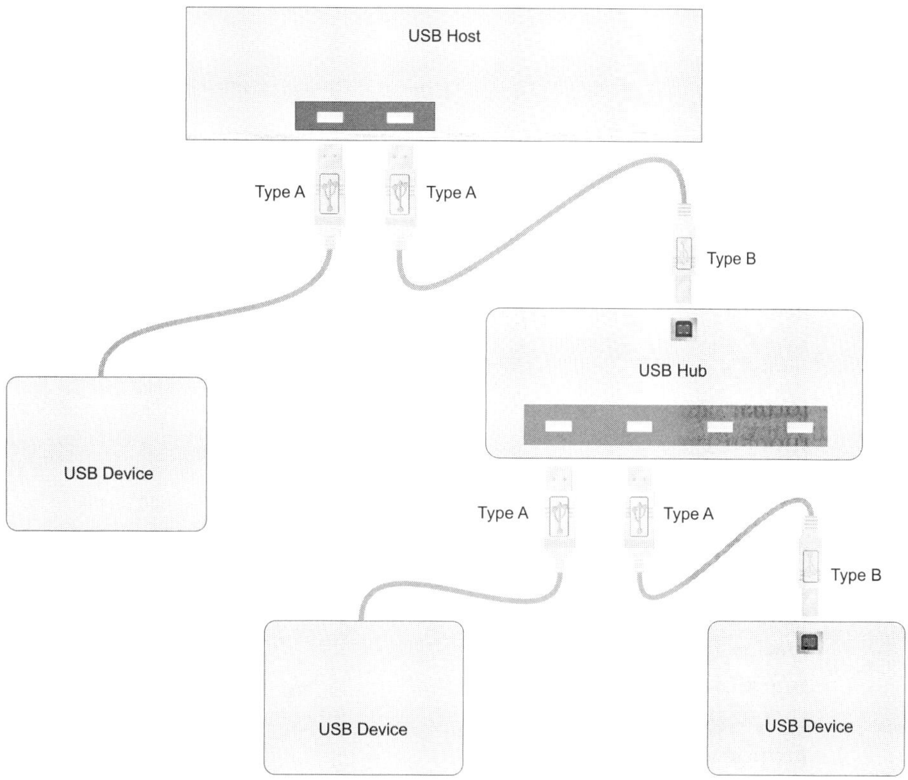

Figure 2.35 Sample USB Topology

Unlike many other external interconnects, the USB connectors are asymmetrical: the upstream connector located on the computer is known as a type A connector and it is distinct from the downstream type B connector, as shown in Figure 2.36. The unique connectors ensure that USB host and USB slave devices are always connected properly.

Smaller USB connectors are also available. Known as USB mini connectors, they also have type A and type B variants, as shown in Figure 2.36.

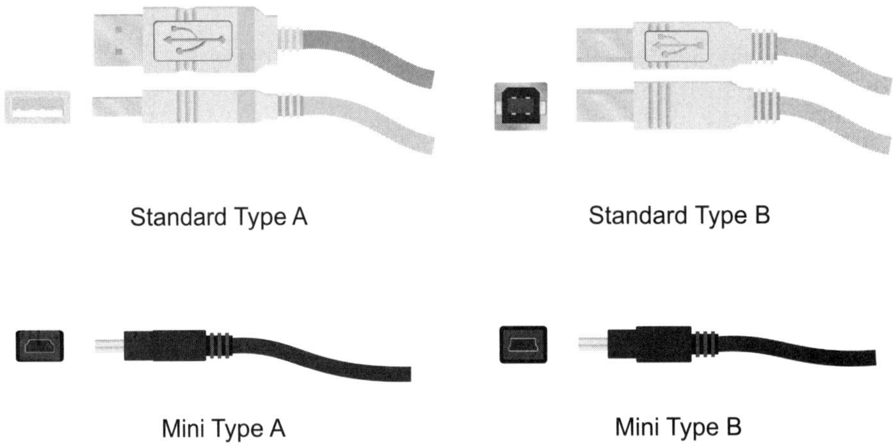

Figure 2.36 USB Type A and Type B Standard and Mini Connectors

Figure 2.37 shows examples of several USB connectors.

In order from left to right: Type A, Type B, and Mini USB.

Figure 2.37 Three USB Connectors.

The bit rates offered by USB make it suitable for audio use. One usage model is external sound cards that attach to a PC via USB. Such sound cards allow people to add high-performance audio capabilities to their computers without having to open the chassis and insert a card. These external cards are particularly suited to computers that do not have room for an internal card, such as a laptop or another small form factor PC. These USB sound cards typically are small boxes that use standard analog and digital connections to attach to speakers or amplifiers.

With the USB connection, audio data can be sent from the PC to the external card with no signal degradation over distances of several feet. Standard USB repeaters can extend this distance indefinitely, although such extensions are rare in the real world. Nevertheless, the lossless nature of the USB interconnects means that USB sound cards have the potential to produce high quality sound, and indeed some of them do.

A variation of the USB sound card is the USB speaker, which is essentially a USB sound card mounted inside a dedicated speaker, or, more commonly, a speaker pair. Since the final analog signal that drives the speakers only has to be carried a very short distance, a matter of inches, USB speakers also have the potential of excellent fidelity. Alas, most USB speakers are small, low-end devices with fair-to-average capabilities. Still, the USB speakers allow for convenient external sound reproduction in certain PC scenarios.

One advantage of USB speakers is that they may draw their power directly from the USB interface, and thus do not need an external power connection. USB power is limited to 2.5 watts per port, which means that speakers that rely exclusively on USB power generally use small diameter drivers and are not be capable of producing very loud sounds.

USB remains a viable and popular PC interconnect. Indeed, it is so popular that some Swiss Army knives even feature a USB connection to flash-based on-knife memory storage. USB is often used to transfer compressed audio from a PC to a portable media device such as an iPod. However, USB's use for streaming audio has been limited to a few niche applications.

HDMI

The High Definition Multimedia Interface (HDMI) interface is an all-digital audio/video interface that supports up to eight channels of uncompressed 192 kilohertz, 24-bit digital audio as well as standard, enhanced or high definition video. It evolved from the Digital Visual Interface (DVI) used to connect digital monitors to PCs. Compared to DVI, HDMI has the advantage of having smaller connectors and being able to carry audio over the same cable as the video. Thus, digital audio/video can be routed between components using a single small connector, rather than a larger DVI cable and separate audio cable.

The HDMI interface is primarily unidirectional: the video and audio flow from a source down to repeaters or sinks, as shown in Figure 2.38. The HDMI interface includes a sideband command and control channel, which is based on I^2C, to allow a source to discover the capabilities of attached sinks.

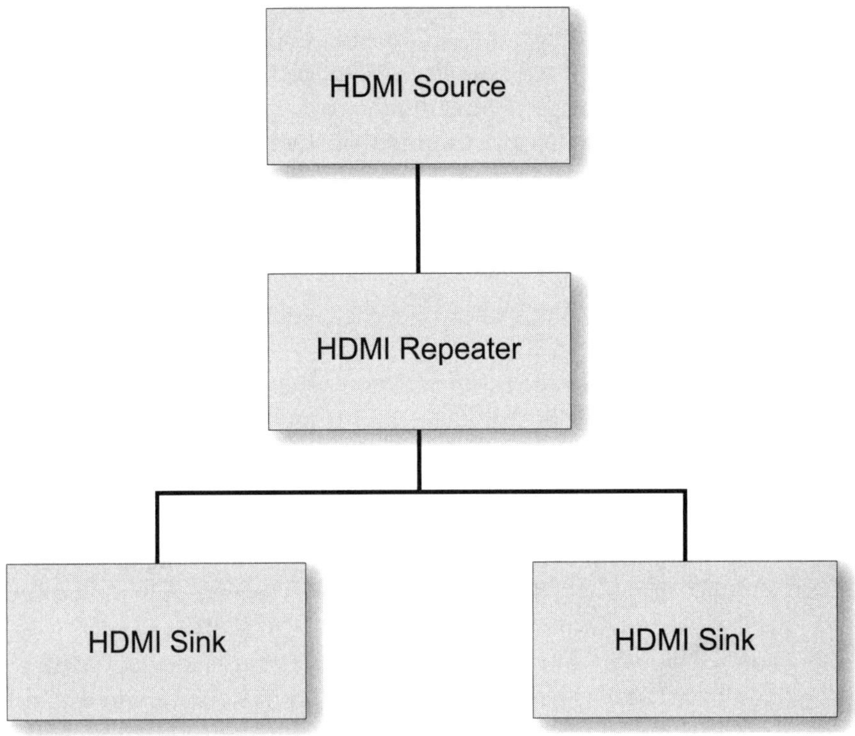

Figure 2.38 Sample HDMI Topology

Connectors

HDMI connectors come in two types: type A with 19 pins and type B with 29 pins, as shown in Figure 2.39. Type A connectors were originally intended only for CE devices, but have since been approved for PCs as well. Type A connectors are limited to a pixel clock of 165 megahertz, which is adequate to support all HDTV resolutions. Type B connectors are intended for use exclusively on PCs and are capable of supporting much higher resolutions. To date, type B connectors are very rare.

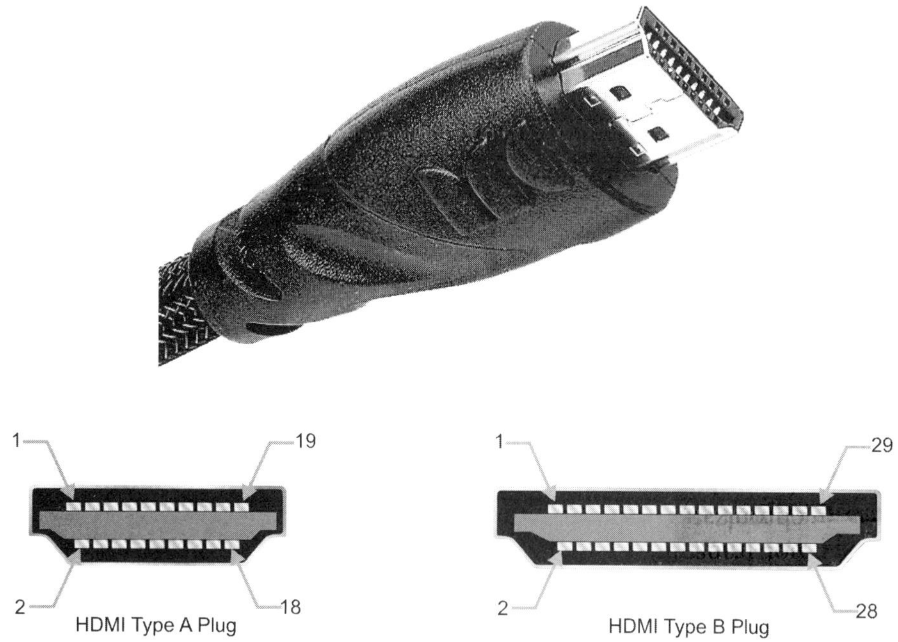

Figure 2.39 HDMI connectors

Protocol

HDMI is backwards compatible to DVI and basically uses the same scheme for transmitting information: Transition Minimized Differential Signaling (TMDS). HDMI has three channels for transmitting data and one for the clock, as shown in Figure 2.40. Each of these four channels uses a balanced differential pair in the cable to carry video, audio, and auxiliary data. The HDMI cable also includes a standard VESA Display Data Channel (DDC) to pass configuration and status information between source and sink.

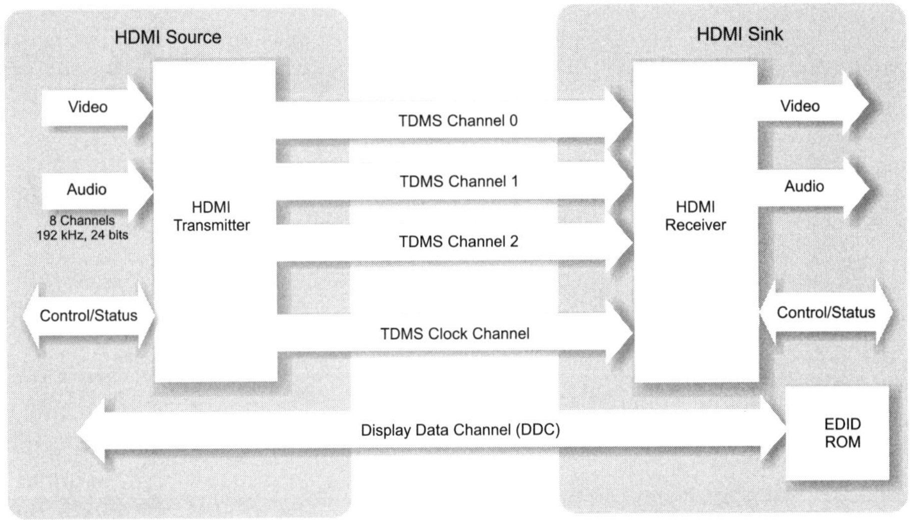

Figure 2.40 Block Diagram of an HDMI Source and Sink

No dedicated lines convey audio. Instead, HDMI takes advantage of the fact that video signals contain periods that are blank. These blank regions do not carry any video pixel information, but instead are used to give displays time to prepare for the next line or frame of video. For HDMI, the audio samples are carried in data packets embedded within the blanking intervals of the video timings, as shown in Figure 2.41.

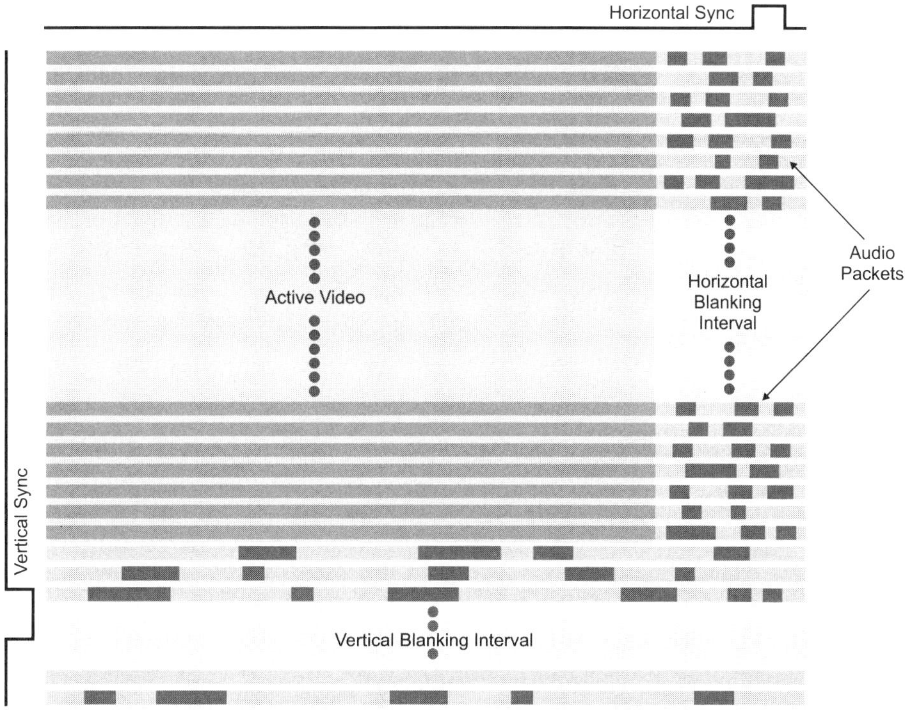

Figure 2.41 HDMI Audio Packets Transmitted During the Horizontal Blanking Interval

This embedded approach reduces the cost and size of cables and connectors by re-using the video signals for carrying audio as well. But the embedded approach brings with it two important implications. One is that certain audio formats do not fit within certain video timings. For instance, 8 channels of uncompressed audio at 192 kilohertz cannot fit within the lowest resolution video modes. You can compensate for this limitation by using pixel replication to double or quadruple the horizontal size of the active video and horizontal blanking interval; the increased blanking interval provides room for more audio data.

Another restriction of the HDMI audio approach is that the audio packets require a video carrier. Without a video signal, you have no place to insert the audio packets. As such, HDMI is not suited for audio-only applications.

That being said, emerging scenarios require HDMI devices that primarily deal with audio. Consider, for example, a digital player that sends video with surround sound to an AV receiver. The AV receiver plays the sound over speakers attached to it while simultaneously re-transmitting the HDMI stream to a TV for display of the picture.

Protection

High Bandwidth Digital Content Protection (HDCP) is available for use on HDMI. HDCP is covered in detail in Chapter 10, but in short it defines an encryption scheme which prevents data flowing across the HDMI cable from being copied. When activated, the HDCP encryption is applied to both the video and audio signals in the HDMI transmitter hardware; you have no way to encrypt just the video or just the audio signals. HDCP support is technically optional on HDMI, but as a practical matter, nearly every production HDMI sink supports it.

Economics

The manufacturer of the HDMI transmitter chip pays a fixed royalty to the HDMI organization for each chip sold. A substantial discount is available if the end product displays the HDMI logo. For a smaller discount, the device can only implement HDCP, which must be licensed from a separate entity. See the *hdmi.org* Web site, listed in "References," for up-to-date details on the licensing programs.

Audio Formats

Audio support itself is optional for HDMI devices. Again, most practical implementations of HDMI devices include at least some basic audio support. HDMI supports several different audio formats. Up to eight channels of uncompressed or compressed audio can be sent at sample rates of 32 kilohertz, 44.1 kilohertz, 48 kilohertz, 88.2 kilohertz, 96 kilohertz, 176.4 kilohertz, and 192 kilohertz. The uncompressed audio is very similar in format to IEC 60958. The compressed audio is very similar in format to IEC 61937, and it includes support for MPEG-1, MPEG-2, AAC, Dolby Digital, DTS, and ATRAC. Because of their common derivation, you can think of HDMI audio as four parallel encrypted S/PDIF channels capable of sample rates from 44.1 kilohertz to 192 kilohertz.

Audio Implementation

First generation PC HDMI implementations expected in the first half of 2006 are likely to connect the S/PDIF output of the Intel HD Audio codec directly to a digital input on the HDMI transmitter chip, which should take care of the HDCP and HDMI format conversions. This single S/PDIF path can provide Linear PCM, and can provide multi-channel if non-PCM data is passed to the S/PDIF output. This multi-channel data can be from a non-PCM pass-through or from a real-time encoder from Dolby or DTS, though using a real-time encoder.

Alternately, an ADAT signal from the codec could be routed to external circuitry that converts the eight channels of ADAT into four distinct S/PDIF signals, which can be connected to all four virtual S/PDIF inputs on the HDMI transmitter chip, allowing eight channels of Linear PCM at sample rates up to 48 kilohertz. Other proprietary approaches may offer up to 8 PCM channels at 192 kilohertz.

Usability Issues

Early adopters of HDMI are likely to use the HDMI connector much like a DVI connector, to transfer only video signals, as many of the earlier HDMI receiver designs support little or no audio. Even if audio is present in the receiving unit, it is unlikely to be multi-channel. Therefore, it could be important to allow the user to play multi-channel audio through the analog output jacks of the PC while delivering video over the HDMI link. Many different combinations will be put to the test as HDMI is adopted.

1394 versus USB versus HDMI

The three previously discussed protocols of 1394, USB, and HDMI have some similarities. They are all used on both PC and CE equipment as external interconnects. They can all transfer data at high bit-rates and support audio playback models. Despite these similarities, each interconnect has its own niche.

USB is typically used as a general purpose connection on PCs. Its typical uses for multimedia are PC-centric, including Web cams and external sound cards.

IEEE-1394's peer-to-peer capabilities allow 1394 devices to operate with a PC. As such, 1394 has been widely adopted for transferring compressed audio and video amongst consumer electronics devices, such as a between a DVD-Audio player and an AV receiver.

Over time HDMI is likely to become the preferred way to send uncompressed digital video from a consumer electronics device to a high-end display device. Certain types of media, such as DVD-Audio, might be practical to play only on HDMI-equipped PCs, since the format mandates that copy protection be present. The Intel HD Audio bus is not capable of providing an appropriate level of copy protection at this time.

Chapter 3

Basics of Surround Sound and Signal Processing

Digital signal processing (DSP), as applied to audio, is the modification of an audio input or output signal to achieve a desired goal or effect. While this processing could take place in a separate DSP chip or in dedicated hardware, most processing of PC audio takes place on the host CPU in the personal computer.

Surround Sound and Multiple Channels

Surround sound enhances the listener's experience beyond that provided by a conventional high quality stereo system by adding capability to recreate the localization experience that was present during the original performance. The surround sound technique goes beyond traditional 2-channel stereo implementation to define 6, 7, or 8 discrete channels with a specific speaker placement in the listening environment. These arrangements allow the listener to experience spatial position of musicians, the action events in movies, and the feeling of being immersed in the musical performance or action.

Surround sound techniques add additional side and sometimes rear speakers. The technique also adds a low-frequency speaker or sub-woofer and redistributes spectral energy to optimize the frequency response requirements of other speakers. When a movie portrays a fighter jet shooting past the center of the action from the behind the listener then veering off into the horizon at the right front, the sound of the jet actually follows this path. Even with eyes closed, the listener hears and senses this motion. Similarly, a large symphony orchestra seems to have surrounded the listener, as if one were standing next to the conductor where one could identify individual instruments by location as well as sound character.

Surround sound has been present in the cinema for many years so movie recording techniques are well established. But, how is surround sound implemented in the home environment as a part of high definition audio?

Historical Background

The home entertainment timeline presented in Chapter 1 showed the gradual evolution of home audio systems, including the effort to enhance spatial perception. The 1950s saw the major change from single-channel monophonic systems to two-channel stereophonic systems, moving listeners from a single-dimension point source to a two-dimensional presentation. Two decades later, the ill-fated quadraphonic experience attempted to expand the environment to three dimensions. This technique added two full-range rear speakers that complemented the existing two full-range stereo front speakers.

While the idea was well received, commercial success required several things that were not in place. For one, more than one proprietary technique was used to achieve four channels, and none of these techniques was compatible with the others. Source material was scarce, due in part to the requirement to make several retail versions to match particular formats. Since the range of each of the four channels was full frequency, each speaker and associated power amplifier had to be full size, doubling the cost of quad compared to stereo and making room placement difficult. The lack of standards and compatibility issues with legacy media and equipment exacerbated the problems, and now we look back at quadraphonic sound as nothing more than an interesting relic from the 1970s.

Multiple channels for a surround sound experience have been a successful attraction in movie theaters for many years, mostly due to techniques that allowed its gradual introduction into venues while preserving backward compatibility with existing films and existing non-surround installations. The cinema process added side and rear speakers to the existing front speakers, thereby enabling sound effects from action to emanate from the actual location at the sides or rear of the room. Virtually all feature films made in the last few decades have been recorded with 4-channel audio: front left, center, right and side/rear surround.

Consumers have been able to watch feature movies in their home since the 1970s, although without the realism and audio/visual quality that a well-equipped movie theater could provide. The quest to improve the quality of home systems started with "hi-fi audio" techniques for VHS and early Beta video recorders. This system replaced the low-quality linear audio tracks with an FM scheme that greatly improved bandwidth and dynamic range.

But while audio quality was better, the full cinema experience was still absent. Not wanting to repeat the industry quadraphonic experience, Dolby† Laboratories developed a matrix encoding technique, called "Pro Logic," that could add surround-sound information to the stereo channels while retaining compatibility with conventional stereo source material and listening systems. This format was designed to allow movies and music to be distributed using traditional two-channel media and traditional two-channel stereo systems without surround decoders reproduce compatible stereo material.

The early Pro Logic surround sound method was an analog technique for use with analog equipment. Newer and higher quality digital distribution systems opened the door to more advanced surround sound coding techniques.

Fitting 6, 7, or 8 Channels into 2

The early analog surround sound techniques used a matrix phase coding scheme to "hide" surround audio information in the 2-channel stereo information. It provided a credible surround experience, but it was not perfect—obviously, it is not possible to create 3 or 4 discrete channels from only 2 analog channels. Yet this new technique was very compatible; on a conventional stereo system, matrixed material would simply play in stereo since the surround information was hidden. But when a matrix decoder was present, the additional surround information could be extracted and fed to surround speakers.

Digital audio formats have more flexibility to encode additional channels. PCM digital audio, used in CDs and S/PDIF formats, is a serial data stream that interleaves the left and right channels as alternate frames in the stream. By encoding the data format or "payload", the system interjects additional channels where only two formerly existed. Using this capability, some digital surround sound coding schemes can compress the 5.1, 6.1, or 7.1 discrete channels into a format that can use existing S/PDIF hardware. In the case of movies, DVD standards were developed from the beginning to accommodate various encoding schemes. The initial format for DVDs provides for a 5.1 channel arrangement in addition to conventional 2-channel stereo. Later developments expanded this format to include 7.1 but maintain backward compatibility. So a DVD with Dolby[†] Digital EX 6.1 encoding plays just fine on an older DVD player that only supports Dolby Digital 5.1 although without the added benefits of the rear channel.

Channels and Bass Management

Current surround systems use 6, 7, or 8 channels designated 5.1, 6.1, or 7.1. The ".1" designations refer to the low frequency effects (LFE) channel that provides all of the bass information with the remaining 5, 6, or 7 channels providing the mid- and high-frequency information at the intended location in the room.

The human ear cannot discern localization information from low frequency sounds; all of our localization happens at the upper part of the spectrum. Thus, it is unnecessary to duplicate low frequency sounds at different locations in the room thereby reducing the frequency response requirements on the location-specific speakers. So, these "satellite" speakers can be made smaller, reducing their cost and making it easier for the consumer to find appropriate locations to install them in their listening room. A *bass management* program that is part of every surround sound system extracts the low frequency information in the source material and directs it to the LFE channel and the single sub-woofer speaker. Since location is not critical for this LFE speaker, it is easier to find a location for this larger device that is compatible with the furniture layout of the listening environment.

All surround sound formats retain the traditional front-left and front-right speakers found on any stereo system. They add a front-center dialog channel. If the system includes video, as any home theater system would, this front-center speaker usually is located directly above or below the video screen. This placement ensures that dialog always comes from the correct video source even when the listener is not sitting in the optimal center location, but is closer to the left- or right-front speaker. Finally, surround sound formats add a left- and right-side speaker for 5.1 and an additional rear-center for 6.1 or left-rear and right-rear for 7.1 formats. Figure 3.1 shows the speaker locations in a typical room.

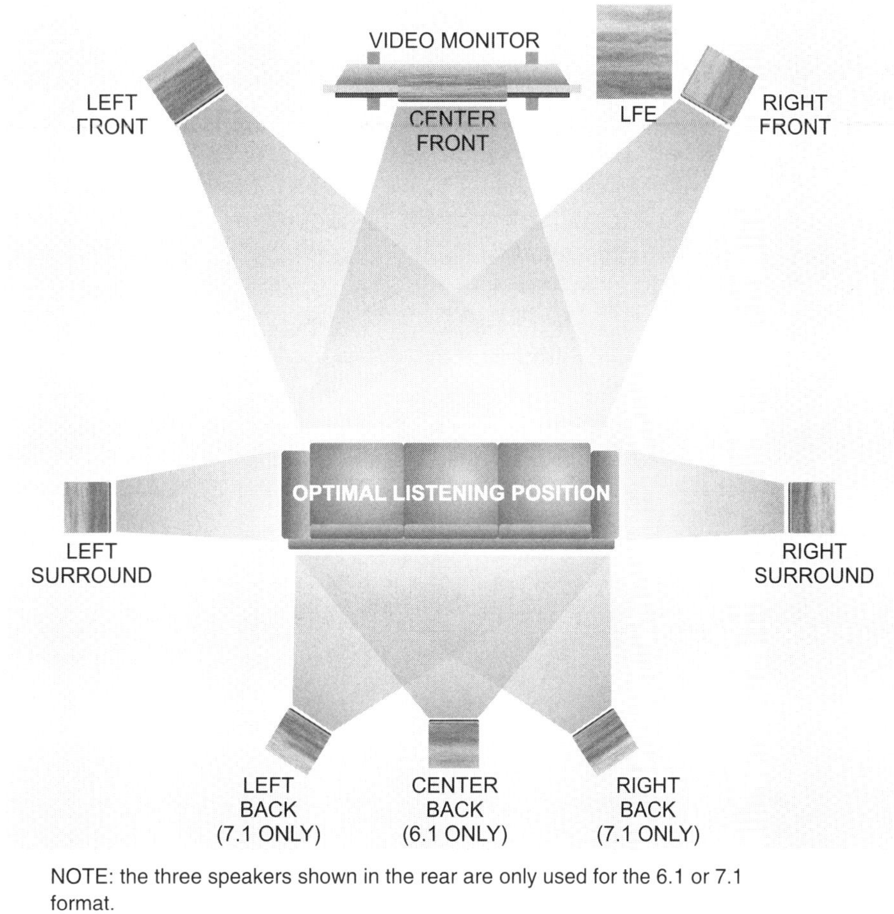

Figure 3.1 Speaker Placements for Various Surround Sound Formats

Spatial Perception

Surround sound systems are intended to create a spatial experience that reproduces as closely as possible the actual environment of the original performance. To understand how to make this recreation effective, you also need some understanding of human location, or direction perception, and of the elements necessary for accurate location fidelity.

We perceive direction cues by a number of means. Some cues are the result of situational expectations and visual stimuli, but the dominant cues are aural. The ear has a very refined temporal sense, enabling it to triangulate the location of a sound using the subtle timing differences between a sound's arrival at our two ears. This difference happens across the audio spectrum although we can only discern the difference at middle to high frequencies, where we can distinguish small phase differences between the two signals caused by these minute distance offsets. The fact that these differences occur only above low frequencies lets us use a single sub-woofer located at almost any arbitrary location in the room, thereby reducing the size and expense of the other speakers.

Because we perceive location by subtle phase differences between signals, electrical inter-channel phase shifts in the reproduction system are important. For more detail, see the explanation of testing in Chapter 11, but for now, you should be aware that phase consistency between channels is often overlooked during the design and verification phase. The relative phase differences between all of the channels of the system must be small across the audio spectrum to preserve position information.

Speaker Placement in the Listening Environment

With the wide variety of surround formats available, where in the listening room do you put the speakers to get the best surround sound experience? Since most of the speakers only need to reproduce middle to high frequencies, they can be physically small, making integration into the home environment and décor easier. And, you can place the larger LFE speaker assigned to reproduce low-frequency information almost anywhere. Figure 3.1 shows an optimal location for 6, 7, or 8 speakers. The three front speakers are always in the same location and provide most of the information. For best immersion experience, you should locate the side-surround and optional rear-surround speakers as close as you can get them to the positions shown in Figure 3.1.

Surround Sound Formats

Many different surround formats are in use, some analog, some digital, and with 4-to-8 channels. These have evolved over the years as media has evolved: analog TV broadcast, audio CDs, analog video tape, DVDs, PC audio, digital broadcast, and most recently, HDTV. The movement away from analog also opened new opportunities for enhanced systems and more channels. Through all of this evolution, various forms of audio media have retained a remarkable degree of compatibility, allowing the consumer to upgrade their system gradually to achieve new capability, without rendering legacy media obsolete. Table 3.1 summarizes the most popular of the current formats and related technologies.

Table 3.1 Table Summarizing the Various Surround Formats and Related Technologies.

Format	Technology	Quantity of Channels	Arrangement of Speakers	Application
Traditional Stereo (not surround; included here for comparison)	Analog Transport Format	2	Right front and left front. Optional subwoofer	Home and portable audio analog sources such as AM and FM broadcast, compact cassette, VHS video.
Traditional Stereo (not surround; included here for comparison)	Digital Transport Format (S/PDIF, AES3)	2	Right front and left front. Optional subwoofer	Home and portable audio digital sources such as CD, MP3, WMA.
Dolby Digital†	Digital Transport Format	5.1. (Also backward compatible with mono and stereo)	Right front, left front, center front, right surround, left surround, LFE.	Home audio/video receivers, PC, games, automotive, DVD Audio, DVD Video, North American Digital Audio HDTV, digital cable and DBS. DVB.
Dolby Digital Plus†	Digital Transport Format (6 Mbps)	7.1 or more. (Also backward compatible with 5.1, mono and stereo)	Right front, left front, center front, right surround, left surround, right back, left back, LFE.	HD-DVD Audio, DVD Video, Home audio/video receivers, North American Digital Audio HDTV, digital cable and DBS.
Dolby Surround†	Analog Transport Format	4 (with Dolby Pro Logic decoder) backward compatible with mono and stereo	Right front, left front, center front, mono surround	Home audio/video receivers, analog TV broadcast, VHS, home theater-in-a-box.
Dolby Digital Live†	Digital Real-Time Encoder (S/PDIF, AES3)	5.1	Right front, left front, center front, right surround, left surround, LFE.	PC, video games. (Optimized for low audio/video latency)

Dolby Digital EX†	Digital Transport and Storage Format	6.1 or 7.1	Right front, left front, center front, right surround, left surround, center back (or optional right back and left back), LFE.	Analog and digital cable TV, DBS video, DVD, Home audio/video receivers.
Dolby Digital Surround EX†	Digital Transport and Storage Format	6.1	Right front, left front, center front, right surround, left surround, rear surround, (optional dual mono rear surround), LFE.	Cinema theater Dolby digitally encoded film (not part of home entertainment systems).
Dolby Surround†, Dolby Pro Logic†	Analog Matrix Format	Decodes 4 surround channels from 2 stereo channels.	Front left, center, right and mono surround,	Home audio/video receivers, videotapes, analog broadcast, home theater-in-a-box
Dolby Pro Logic II†	Analog Matrix Format and Spreader	5.1 (also backward compatible with 2-channel stereo)	Front right, front left, front center, right surround, left surround, LFE.	Analog TV, digital cable, DBS video, Home audio/video receivers, multi-channel automotive, games, PCs
Dolby Pro Logic IIx	Analog Matrix Format and Spreader	6.1 or 7.1 (also backward compatible with 5.1 and 2-channel stereo)	Right front, left front, center front, right surround, left surround, center back for 6.1 or right back and left back for 7.1, LFE.	Analog TV, digital cable, DBS video, Home audio/video receivers, multi-channel automotive. Games, PCs
Dolby Digital Recording†	Digital (192 kbps or DVD 4.5 Mbps data rate). Non-Real-Time for creating DVDs	2-channel stereo. (Encodes stereo signals into Dolby Digital bitstream for DVD applications.)	Front left and right	Home entertainment: DVD recorders, DVD camcorders, Personal video recorders.
Dolby Digital Stereo Creator†	Digital (192 kbps or DVD 4.5 Mbps data rate).	2-channel stereo. (Encodes stereo signals into	Front left and right	PCs, DVD authoring software

	Non-Real-Time authoring tool.	Dolby Digital bitstream for DVD applications.)		
Dolby Digital 5.1 Creator†	Non-Real-Time authoring tool.	5.1	Front right, front left, front center, right surround, left surround, LFE.	PCs, DVD authoring software, DVD camcorders
DTS Digital Surround and DTS 96/24	Digital Transport and Storage Format	5.1	Front right, front left, front center, right surround, left surround, LFE.	Audio/video receivers, PCs, DVD audio players, DVD video players
DTS-ES† (Extended Surround)	Digital Transport and Storage Format	6.1	Front right, front left, front center, right surround, left surround, rear surround, LFE.	Audio/video receivers, DVD audio players, DVD video players.
DTS Connect†	Digital (S/PDIF, AES3)	5.1	Right front, left front, center front, right surround, left surround, LFE.	PC, video games. (Optimized for low audio/video latency)
DTS Neo:6†	Digital Matrix Format and Spreader	5.1 or 6.1 from stereo matrix source	Front right, front left, front center, right surround, left surround, LFE.	Analog TV broadcasts, VHS, stereo CDs, DVD players
SACD Stereo	Direct Stream Digital (DSD) Transport and Storage Format	2	Front left and right	SACD players, backwards compatible to any CD player
SACD Surround	Direct Stream Digital (DSD) Transport and Storage Format	5.1	Front right, front left, front center, right surround, left surround, LFE.	SACD players, backwards compatible to any CD player
DVD-Audio Stereo	Digital, 192 KHz, 24-bit lossless storage format	2	Front left and right	DVD-Audio players, usually backwards compatible with any DVD player

DVD-Audio Surround	Digital 96 kHz 24-bit Lossless Storage Format	5.1	Front right, front left, front center, right surround, left surround, LFE.	DVD-Audio players, usually backwards compatible with any DVD player
THX[†1]	Digital (can be Dolby Digital, DTS or PCM)	5.1	Front right, front left, front center, right surround, left surround, LFE.	Audio/video receivers, home theater, DVD, PCs, automotive, VHS, DBS, TV broadcast
THX EX[†1]	Digital (can be Dolby Digital EX, DTS-ES or PCM)	6.1 or 7.1	Front right, front left, front center, right surround, left surround, right rear surround, left rear surround, LFE.	Audio/video receivers, home theater.

[1] THX is a certification process, not a coding technology such as Dolby Digital or DTS.

Equalization

Equalization, or EQ, refers to modifying the frequency content of the audio program. The simplest type of EQ is the tone control on a stereo system. The bass control typically turns all the frequencies up or down, when they fall above or below a specified frequency known as the cutoff frequency. The treble control typically turns up or down all the frequencies above a separately specified cutoff frequency.

These types of controls are known as shelving controls because their graphical representation looks like a shelf that can be raised or lowered. Shelving controls are the most typical type of tone control to be used for treble or bass.

Figure 3.2 shows the shelving EQ high and low bands with boost and cut. You can see how the ends of the EQ looks like mechanisms for a shelf that is being raised or lowered.

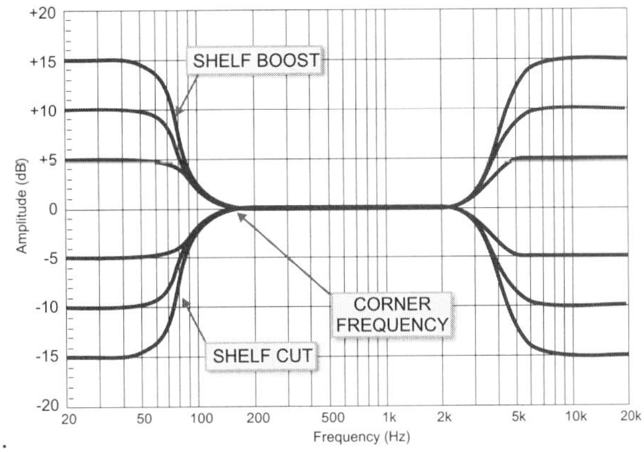

Figure 3.2 Shelving EQ for both High and Low Bands with Boost and Cut

Cut/Boost Bandpass EQ

For mid-range frequencies, a slightly different approach is needed. A bandpass filter can be inserted which can boost or cut at a specific frequency. It also has some effect on surrounding frequencies. The "Q" of this filter determines the width of equalization band. Q is usually represented in octaves. A passband of one octave is typical, but the range can be as large as 3 octaves or as small as 1/20th of an octave. You can see the effects of these different settings in Figure 3.3.

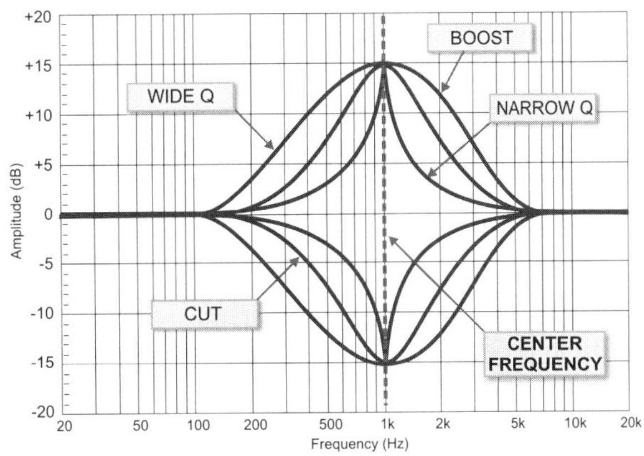

Settings of Q: 1 octave (boost), 3 octaves (boost), and 1/12th octave (cut)

Figure 3.3 A Single Band of Boost/Cut EQ with Various Settings

Graphic EQ

A graphic EQ is a collection containing more than 3 bands of EQ, typically 7 to 10 bands but possibly as many as 31 bands. Each band is a boost/cut bandpass filter operating on a different mid-range center frequency. A 10-band graphic EQ typically uses ISO-standard frequencies centered around multiples or divisors of 1 kHz, with spacing of one octave: 31.25 Hz, 62.5 Hz, 125 Hz, 250 Hz, 500 Hz, 1 kHz, 2 kHz, 4 kHz, 8 kHz, 16 kHz. Usually, the lowest band is a low-shelving filter rather than a bandpass filter, and the highest band is a high-shelving filter rather than a bandpass filter, although this is not always the case. Figure 3.4 shows a typical composite frequency response.

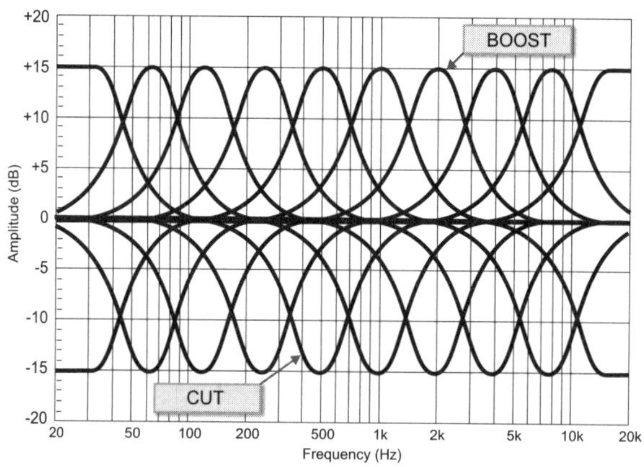

Figure 3.4 Variable Frequency Response of 10-band EQ with ISO Center Points

Parametric EQ

When each of the EQ parameters—frequency, boost/cut, Q, and filter type—is exposed to the user, you have a *parametric EQ*, which has one or more bands that can be completely and fully adjusted. While this type of EQ is an excellent choice for audio professionals, parametric equalizers are understood poorly by most end users, so you should avoid them in systems that are not targeted at audiophiles.

The user controls for a full-featured parametric equalizer are shown in Figure 3.5. These controls remain unchanged whether you implement the EQ in hardware or software.

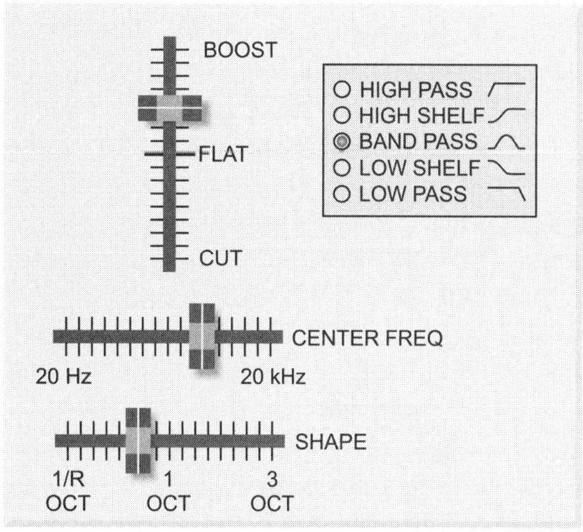

Figure 3.5 Controls for One Band of a Fully Parametric EQ

While equalizers can offer both boost (gain) and cut, oftentimes a "cut-only" option is the most sensible offering due to digital headroom constraints. If you add gain at a specific frequency to a digital signal that is already at full scale, distortion is the most likely result. For this reason, many equalizers offer only a "cut" capability, with no boost.

Another way to equalize the sound is to lower the overall gain by the same amount as the largest EQ gain setting. While doing so technically resolves the headroom issue, this solution is counter-intuitive, because increasing the gain of a particular band could result in lowering the overall volume, rather than raising it.

The best solution is to follow the EQ in the signal path with a compressor or limiter that can automatically compensate for the additional gain while avoiding any possible distortion issues due to overload. This method is covered in the "Dynamics Processing" section of this chapter.

Equalizer Implementations

In most cases, you can accomplish all of these various implementations using a bi-quad filter. You can design a bi-quad filter in such a way that it can be reconfigured to provide any of the functions listed previously, simply by changing the various bi-quad filter coefficients. The bi-quad filters are processed in a serial fashion, with each one further modifying the output of the previous filter. Therefore, mixing and matching the various usability models is possible so long as enough bi-quad filter stages are available.

PC OEMs implement EQ in a number of different ways. Many laptop manufacturers engage the EQ only when the internal speakers of the laptop are engaged, and the EQ is disengaged whenever headphones or line out are plugged in. The user has no EQ control panel in this case because operation is automatic. For this fixed EQ scenario, the engineer who is calibrating the EQ uses a special parametric control panel that is not available for the end user. The EQ settings are stored as part of the registry settings for the driver configuration, or in some cases, the BIOS provides a special area that the driver can read to determine the EQ settings. Often, this last technique is proprietary and involves a private communication between the audio driver and the BIOS.

Other OEMs implement a user-modifiable EQ as a graphic equalizer with a constant number of bands, usually 5 or 10. This type of implementation allows the user to adjust each of the bands individually, with low latency. Unlike the graphic EQ built into Windows[†] Media Player, this equalization affects all audio output through the digital-to-analog converters, regardless of which player application is used. EQ provided as part of the driver usually has much lower processing delays than the EQ provided with Windows Media Player, so the driver EQ usually has an audible effect while the slider is being moved, whereas the effect of the Media Player EQ could be delayed, which is confusing to the end user.

In a well-designed system, it is possible to implement both kinds of EQ: fixed and variable. The fixed EQ for the built-in laptop speakers would use some number of bi-quad filters, and the user-variable graphic EQ would use additional bi-quad filters. The bi-quad filters used for the speaker EQ would be switched in and out of circuit based on whether the speakers are on, while the graphic EQ bands would have the desired effect whether the speakers are on or off.

Bass Management

Bass management uses the same building blocks that EQ does, but the end result is somewhat different. The purpose of bass management is to allow the use of small satellite speakers in a 5.1 or 7.1 surround system by routing the bass signals to the subwoofer.

It's important to distinguish between the low frequency effects (LFE) track, which is normally routed to the subwoofer, and the low frequency portion of the music and dialog, which is intended for the surround speakers. Most movie producers use the LFE for explosions, shudders, rumbles, and the like. Typically, the LFE track, also called the ".1" track, contains only these sounds and does not contain low frequency portions of music or dialog because in a real movie theatre, the satellite speakers are full range and are capable of reproducing the bass signal without assistance from the subwoofer attached to the LFE channel. However, if the satellite speakers are small, as is the case with many home theatre systems, then they cannot reproduce the bass. So, bass management comes to the rescue by routing the low frequencies of the satellite channels to the subwoofer, in addition to the LFE signal.

Bass management is a useful and sometimes essential feature. However, it is important to note that many 5.1 and 7.1 surround speaker systems have bass management built into the speakers or amplifier. For best results apply bass management at a single point in the overall system. Figure 3.6 shows a block diagram for a simple bass management implementation.

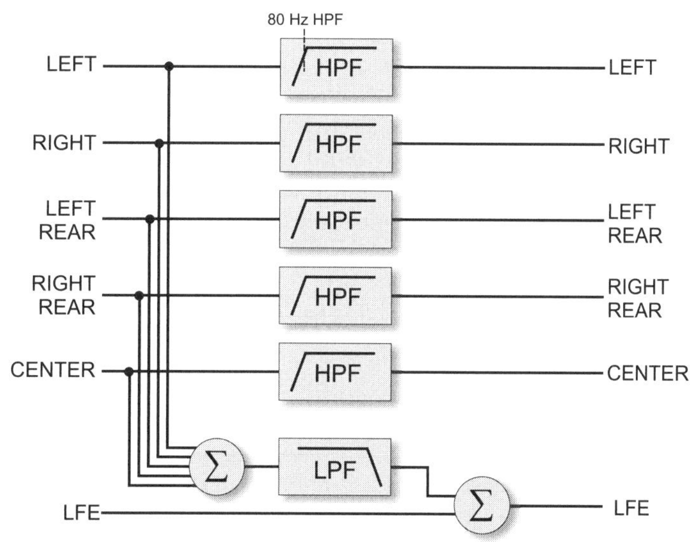

Figure 3.6 Bass Management Block Diagram

First, the signals going to the satellite speakers are summed together. Then, they are run through a low-pass filter and mixed with the LFE signal. This directs the low frequency signals from each surround channel to the subwoofer.

Each individual satellite signal is also run through a high-pass filter before being sent on to the satellite speaker. This filter removes low frequency signals that might cause distortion of the satellite speaker, protecting the speaker against damage from large speaker cone excursion.

Approaches to providing a graphical user interface for bass management are numerous, ranging from no interface at all to allowing the user to adjust each crossover point and summing node. The most common user interface is one where the user can specify the size of each pair of speakers being used.

Dynamics Processing

Dynamics Processing automatically varies a volume stage in real time based on the level of the input signal. The four basic types of dynamics processing are: compression, limiting, expansion, and noise gating. All four are derived from the same basic building blocks. Figure 3.7 shows how a level detector is used to determine the instantaneous level or volume of the audio signal, and a gain stage is controlled dynamically by the level detector to accomplish the processing. To avoid pops, clicks, and other artifacts, the gain stage always changes gradually and never uses a step function.

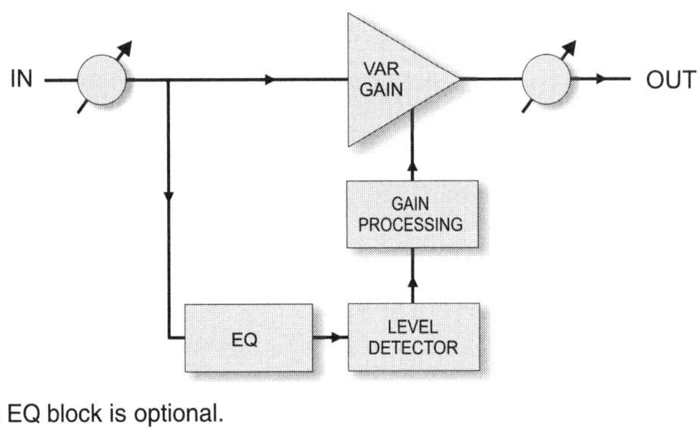

Figure 3.7 Dynamics Processor Block Diagram

Compression

Compression means constraining the dynamic range of a signal into a smaller dynamic range, which is especially useful for watching a movie on an airplane. By constraining the dynamic range, both soft and loud passages can be easily heard over the background noise of the airplane. If the signal is not compressed, the user usually turns up the volume when the dialogue is soft, in order to hear, but when the soundtrack gets louder for an action scene, the user often finds the sound to be too loud.

A compressor usually has four basic controls: Threshold, Ratio, Attack Time, and Decay Time. Signal levels below the threshold have no effect on the gain stage, but signal levels higher than the threshold cause the gain to be reduced by the Ratio control. Typical ratio controls are in the range of 1:1 (no compression) to 10:1 (severe compression). For example, if the ratio is 10:1 and the signal level is 10 dB above the threshold, the output signal level is only 1 dB greater than the threshold level. With a compression ratio of 2:1, the output signal level can be decreased to -5 dB when the input signal is at full scale (or 0 dB).

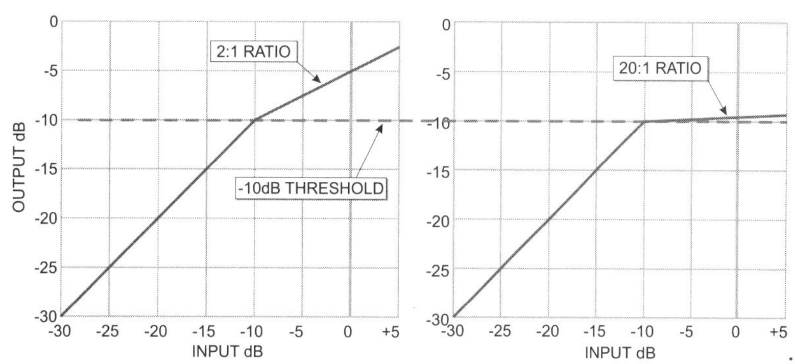

Figures 3.8 Compressor Transfer Curve and Limiter Transfer Curve

Usually measured in milliseconds, the *attack time* is the time it takes for the gain stage to change to the new level once the threshold has been exceeded. The *decay time* is the time it takes for the gain stage to return to unity gain (1:1) after the signal has dropped below the threshold.

Limiting

Similar to compression, limiting is used to ensure that a signal does not go above a specified level. For instance, it may be useful to apply a limiter which keeps an amplifier from going above the level that could cause clipping. The same four controls are used for limiting, but the typical ratios for limiters lie between 10:1 and 20:1. The threshold usually is set very close to the maximum signal level, so that the limiter has an effect only when the signal is very loud.

One well-established method for preventing the overloading of amplifier and speakers is to use a limiter that is calibrated to the clipping point of the amplifier. When properly set, this limiter can ensure that the output stage of the amplifier never clips. In addition to ensuring that the end user won't hear distortion, this limiter also helps control power peaks and could extend speaker life by avoiding distortion. This is especially true for high-frequency transducers, often called tweeters, which easily can be destroyed by excessive clipping.

Expansion

Expansion also uses the same four controls, but in just the opposite direction from compression. An expander makes loud sounds louder, and soft sounds softer. When the signal is below the threshold, the gain stage is reduced, and when the signal level is greater than the threshold, the gain stage does not change, so soft sounds stay the same. Ratios are typically 1:2 or 1:3. Generally, expansion is not used in a PC environment.

Noise Gate

Just as limiting is an extreme form of compression, noise gating is an extreme form of expansion. Signals below the threshold are attenuated completely, and signals above the threshold are unmodified.

A noise gate is useful for eliminating noise picked up by a microphone when the user is not speaking. The threshold is set at a level just below the average speaking level, so that when the talker stops talking, the gain stage is set to infinite attenuation, allowing no signal to pass. Figure 3.9 shows the gain transfer curves of both an expander and a noise gate.

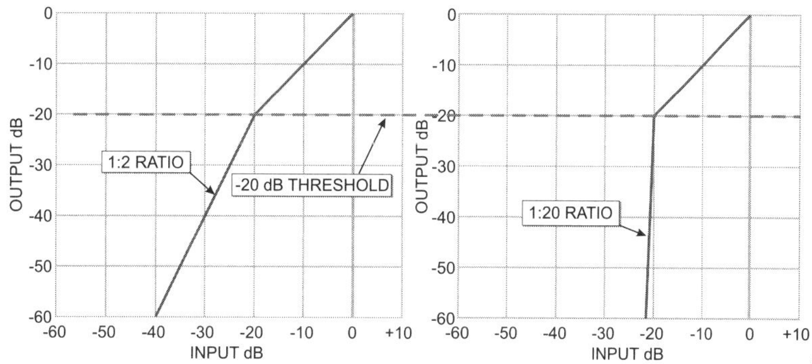

Figure 3.9 Expander Transfer Curve and Noise-Gate Transfer Curve

Multi-band Compression and Limiting

Have you ever wondered why some radio stations sound louder than others? It's probably because they are using a Multi-band Compressor/Limiter just before the signal goes to the transmitter.

To accomplish this bigger sound, divide the signal into 2 to 4 different bands, compress each band separately, then re-combine the different bands into a single output signal. This technique can help the sound system to avoid the "breathing" effect that can sometimes be heard as the gain stage of a single band compressor is changing. By breaking the signal into multiple bands, the listener perceives the overall signal content as louder without hearing the breathing effect of a single-band compressor.

Adjusting a multi-band compressor/limiter is a job best left to an audio professional experienced with this type of adjustment. The process is not intuitive, and often the novice inadvertently degrades the sound instead of enhancing it. Radio stations vie for the services of the pros that know how to set such a limiter properly; if you plan to implement a multi-band compressor/limiter in your design, be sure that you get a professional to set it up for you, unless you have lots of experience in this area.

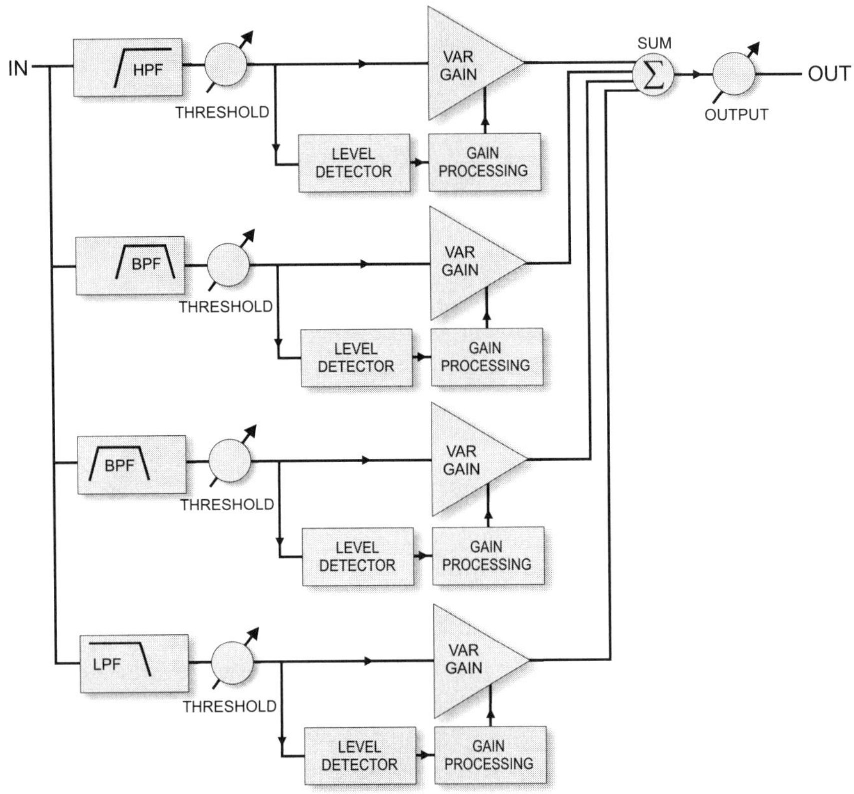

Multiple level detectors and multiple gain stages are shown. The only difference between each of the bands is the input filter configuration that divides the signal into four separate bands: Low, Low-Mid, High-Mid, and High.

Figure 3.10 Multi-band Dynamics Processor Block Diagram

3D Virtualization

Audio for games introduces the need to provide audio point sources relative to the player's point of view. One popular game series, Thief, uses audio cues to help determine where your assailants are as you creep through the dark.

These types of effects are created using 3D virtualization techniques. One popular method is Head-Related Transfer Functions (or HRTF). HRTFs take advantage of the time delays between when sound hits the left and right ears, and also takes the shape of the ear into account. Another approach is to model the reverbs of the virtual acoustic spaces. Each approach has both merits and shortcomings.

Using a stereo pair of speakers, the ear can be fooled into hearing sounds from far left and far right. The effect is much stronger when coupled with a video cue that matches the sound source.

3D virtualization was originally implemented on high-powered soundcards with hardware acceleration, but today this processing is almost always accomplished in software. Therefore, most games are integrating these effects into the game audio engine rather than counting on the audio subsystem to support this functionality.

2-to-N Spreaders

KMixer in Windows XP† is capable of down-mixing multi-channel content into stereo outputs, but it does not do anything to route stereo signals to any speaker pair other than the front left/right speakers; the other speakers remain silent. A spreader is used to route the stereo signal to these otherwise silent speakers.

A simple spreader might simply echo the front left and right channels to the side and rear surround speakers. This approach ensures that the speakers aren't silent, but doesn't really create a realistic ambiance. DTS Neo and the Dolby ProLogic family are examples of products which expand the stereo to multi-channel and provide a more realistic ambience to the resulting surround-sound mix. If the stereo signal contains matrixed information, then the spreader can do an even better job of making the sound appear more realistic.

Implementing a spreader reliably on Windows XP can be a significant challenge, because there is no easy way to know how many channels of input are arriving at KMixer, and therefore how many of KMixer's output channels contain silence at any given moment.

Encoders and Decoders for Compressed Audio

Like the word "codec", the word "compression" has a dual meaning in audio applications. The type of compressor described in the previous section is a *dynamics compressor*, which compresses the dynamic range of an audio PCM stream. The word can also be used to describe audio file or stream compression, which actually reduces the file size or stream bit rate. Compressed audio files are the basis of MP3's popularity, since the files can be easily exchanged over the internet. Later in this chapter you can find an example showing how easy it is to confuse these two very different types of compression.

Uncompressed Audio

At the hardware level, the Intel HD Audio subsystem in the computer uses uncompressed audio as the basis all of its operations, with the occasional exception of Dolby Digital†, DTS†, and WMA Pro† formats that are delivered in a compressed fashion to the S/PDIF output.

Intel HD Audio hardware typically performs no decoding on streams. All encoding and decoding is performed in software on a PC running Windows. Table 3.2 shows the comparative data rates for various uncompressed formats. Notice that CD-quality audio is the starting point for this table; other high-quality formats are even denser.

Table 3.2 Characteristics of Uncompressed Audio Streams

Sample Rate	Bit Depth	# of Channels	Mbytes/minute	Kbps	Classification
44.1 kHz	16	2	10.1	1,378	CD-Quality
48.0 kHz	16	2	11.0	1,500	Uncompressed WAV
48.0 kHz	16	6	33.0	4,500	5.1 Surround
96.0 kHz	16	2	22.0	3,000	Uncompressed WAV
96.0 kHz	24	2	43.9	4,500	Uncompressed WAV
96.0 kHz	24	8	175.8	18,000	7.1 Surround
192 kHz	24	2	87.9	9,000	Uncompressed WAV

Note: The storage calculations for Mbytes/minute are based on a 32-bit container for each 24-bit sample, which is the standard way of storing 24-bit audio data in RAM. The Intel HD Audio bus also carries a full 32 bits. Kbps calculations are based on 24-bit packed data arriving in a stream.

Lossless Compression

Because of the large data sizes that audio requires, it is often advantageous to reduce the file size using various file compression techniques. Generally, you want the audio signal after decompression to be 100-percent identical to the audio signal prior to compression.

A compression ratio of 2:1 is typical for lossless compression. That is, CD-Quality audio can be reduced in size from 10 MB/minute to 5 MB/minute by applying lossless compression. The Meridian Lossless Packing (MLP) algorithms which are part of the DVD-Audio specification are a good example of lossless compression. The Microsoft† WMA Pro format also incorporates lossless compression options for some encoding formats.

Lossy Compression

In the mid '90s, the only options for reducing the size of audio was to use lower resolution formats such as 8-bits, coupled with low sample rates. However, the ear is sensitive to the poor sound quality of these low-resolution formats, and these formats were not well received. PCs today rarely make use of 8-bit file formats. A 16-kilobit sample rate is still popular for some speech processing applications but rates lower than 44 kilobits are rarely used for music.

The big breakthrough for music over the internet came with the adoption of lossy compression schemes such as MP3, WMA, AAC, ATRAC, and even Dolby Digital Live (AC3). Rather than simply reducing the resolution, these compression formats are "smart" enough to throw away details that the ear cannot perceive, with a minimum amount of degradation to the sound.

All of these schemes function in basically the same manner, by using Fourier transformations to convert the audio from the time domain to the frequency domain. Once in the frequency domain, the conversion software monitors the audio spectrum for audio information that the ear can't hear and removes that information from the data set. Usually, a form of lossless encoding is performed on the remaining data to reduce the data set even further. See Figure 1.17 in Chapter 1 for more details.

The decoder decompresses the data set and performs an inverse Fourier transform on the data set to convert the signal back to the time domain. When the encoding takes place, the user has the option to specify the target bit rate, which in turn determines the overall audio quality. While the artifacts of lossy compression are often not noticeable in a casual listening environment, a trained listener can tell whether a lossy compression scheme has been used.

Lossy compression provides a big advantage over lossless compression. In Table 3.3, you can see that a compressed bit rate of 64 Kbps requires less than half a megabyte per minute, a ratio of 20:1 compared to the 10 megabytes per minute used for CD-quality audio. Therefore, the phrase "20:1 compression ratio" can be interpreted two different ways, depending on the context. If the context is dynamics processing, the 20:1 compression ratio would indicate that the processor is being used as a limiter. If the context is file size compression, the same phrase "20:1

compression ratio" most likely indicates that a data rate of 64 kBps had been specified when encoding MP3 or WMA data from an Audio CD.

Table 3.3 Characteristics of Compressed Audio Streams

Sample Rate	Bit Depth	# of Channels	Mbytes/ minute	kbps Compressed	kbps Uncomp ressed	Classification
44.1 kHz	16	2	0.47	64	1,378	Low-Quality WMA or MP3
48.0 kHz	16	2	.94	128	1,500	Moderate Quality WMA or MP3
48.0 kHz	16	2	1.41	192	1,500	Good quality WMA or MP3
48.0 kHz	18	5.1	2.82	384	5,184	Dolby Digital

Note: Storage calculations for Mbytes/minute based on actual data size with no padding. Dolby Digital LFE channel encodes only low frequencies, which allows 5 full-range and 1 bass-only channel to fit within the 384 Kbps limit.

Economics of Lossy Compression

The more popular lossy compression algorithms are covered by one or more patents, and each patent holder is eager to extract benefit from these patents. Because of this, all encoders and most decoders are bundled with specific software or hardware. WMA and WMA Pro decoders are bundled with versions of Microsoft's† Windows† Media Player. AAC encoders and decoders are included with the Apple† iPod and iTunes combination. Dolby† and DTS† decoders are available from DVD player software vendors, while Dolby and DTS encoders are available from Intel HD Audio codec vendors.

Under Windows XP, the Audio Compression Manager provides a translation layer for the recording and playing back of audio in different formats. Figure 3.11 shows the user's view of software codecs installed in the Audio Compression Manager.

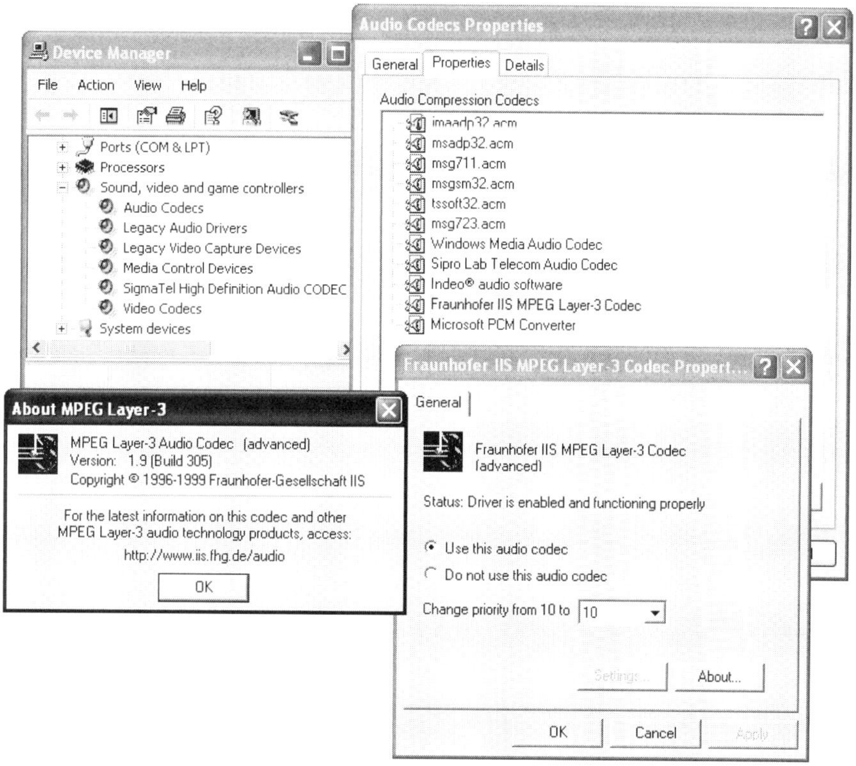

To see which audio software codecs are installed in Windows XP, double-click on the Audio Codecs category in the Device Manager, then select the Properties tab to see the list of installed codecs. This computer is able to decode MP3 files using the Fraunhofer IIS MPEG Layer Three Codec.

Figure 3.11 Software Codecs in the Audio Compression Manager

The use of the Dolby Digital and DTS formats should not incur license fees to the manufacturer of the PC if the compressed audio is delivered to an external A/V receiver through an S/PDIF connection. In this case, the actual decoder is inside the A/V receiver, so the royalty is paid by the A/V vendor.

If the Dolby Digital or DTS multi-channel decoding is performed on the PC, that capability always comes bundled with an enhanced version of DVD player software. Two prominent products are WinDVD by Inter-Video and PowerDVD by CyberLink. For Media Center PCs that rely on Windows Media Player for playback, the WinDVD or PowerDVD installation may also insert a decoder object into the DirectShow graph so that Windows Media Player can access the decoding on the platform. Unlike other Dolby or DTS processing on the PC, the multi-channel decoder never rarely implemented in the driver in Windows XP or in an Audio Processing Object in Windows Vista for licensing reasons.

Input and Capture

As the PC becomes a personal communication platform, the tight integration of speech-processing technologies is essential. Recording or capture of speech and music sources is a difficult process, one that often is not intuitive because you are not hearing the audio that is being captured and because the process of matching levels to an audio input is not understood.

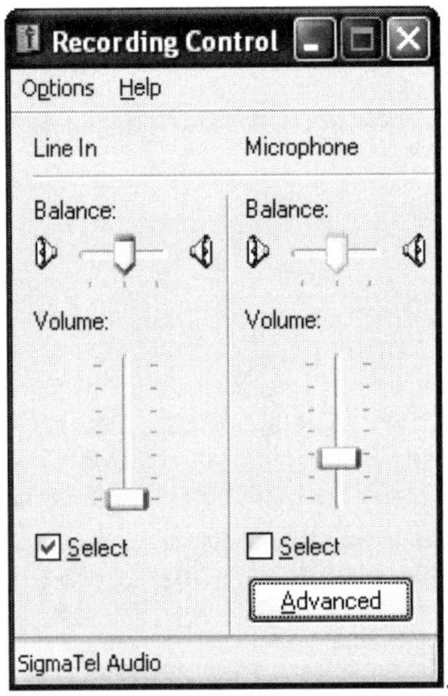

The Line In slider is set to the correct level, which is the *bottom* of the slider. Turning up the controls simply results in distortion unless the signal that is being recorded is abnormally low in volume.

Figure 3.12 Line Input and Microphone Input Recording Level Sliders

The gain control for the microphone is often useful, especially when interfacing to microphones with unknown characteristics. Microphone input stages often have an additional microphone preamp with adjustable gain stages of 10, 20, 30, and sometimes 40 dB of gain in addition to the 20 or so dB of gain that is available from the slider.

Clicking on the "Advanced" button shown in Fig 3.12 displays a checkbox controlling this additional gain stage. While this large range of gain allows interfacing to a wide variety of microphones, an untrained user often finds it more difficult to set the mic level properly. Windows XP has four different wizards for setting the input level properly, but they can conflict with each other sometimes. The audio subsystem in Windows Vista combines all into a single wizard that is easier for the end user to understand.

Speech Usage Scenarios

Four primary scenarios in which speech is used are:

- *Real-Time Communications (RTC)* or *Voice Communications* refers to basic telephony, with the computer acting as a telephone. Instant Messaging (IM) with voice and Voice over IP (VoIP) are good examples.
- *Voice Annotation* is the process of recording your voice. This capability might be useful for attaching a verbal statement to photos as a memo or for recording ideas that might pop into your head.
- *Voice Command and Control* uses speech recognition technologies to control your PC without needing to touch the computer. While included in most recent versions of Windows, this capability is usually left up to the user to enable, and should only be used when an appropriate microphone is present.
- *Voice Dictation* is also included with recent versions of Windows. However, using this feature might require a considerable amount of training before the error rate is acceptable. Voice dictation is a technology that is especially useful in the medical and legal fields.

All types of voice input are useful for mobile applications, such as a Tablet PC. Upcoming smaller form factors might require the use of voice as a primary input simply because other forms of input, such as keyboard and mouse, are simply too large to be useful with smaller devices. Figure 3.15 shows a complete implementation of a laptop PC using 4-mic beamforming microphone array with acoustic echo cancellation, noise suppression and speaker tracking.

Beamforming Array Microphones

One of the problems with using a single microphone is that it picks up audio from multiple directions. While this background sound could be useful in some circumstances, most often having the microphone focus only on the person speaking is more desirable. You can accomplish this focus by using an array of two, four, or even six microphones. The signals from the microphones can be combined using a signal processing technique that forms a "beam" that is sensitive to sound from a particular direction but rejects sounds coming from other directions. Two microphones are used in a configuration that rejects sounds from the either side. Four microphones can be set up in a row to do an even better job of rejecting sound from the sides, or you can set them up as the corners of a rectangle that can rejects sounds from left, right, top, and bottom. Six or more microphones are useful for scenarios where people are sitting around a table

Advanced beamforming implementations also might include the capability to determine who in a group is talking, and then not only focus the beamforming algorithm on the talker, but also provide coordinates for an intelligent camera to focus on the talker, which is useful for teleconferencing.

Beamforming technology provides a performance boost for all of the different types of voice capture listed in "Speech Capture Scenarios."

Acoustic Echo Cancellation (AEC)

Real-Time CommunicationsRTC (RTC) such as VoIP or IM often require acoustic echo cancellation (AEC) in the system. While not necessary for Voice Annotation, Command and Control, and Dictation, AEC is a requirement for any type of RTC device that does not use a close-talking microphone in a headset to provide acoustic isolation between speaker and microphone. If the microphone is more than a few inches from the talker's mouth, and the listening is taking place through speakers rather than through an acoustically isolated headset, AEC is critical for good sound quality. Of all these algorithms, a good AEC algorithm is likely to be one of the most difficult to implement successfully.

In the implementation shown in Figure 3.13, the basic idea is that software monitors the digital input(s) from the microphone(s) and the digital output that ultimately goes to the speakers. By synchronizing these two signals, the speaker signal can be subtracted from the mic signal, thereby removing any sounds from the speaker that are picked up by the microphone. To be useful in a VoIP scenario, the echo canceller needs to remove 35 to 40 dB of the speaker signal.

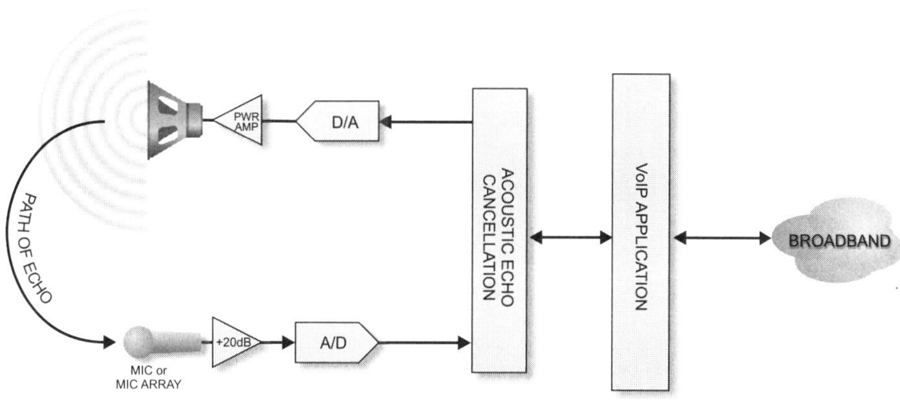

Figure 3.13 Block Diagram of Acoustic Echo Canceller

Noise Suppression

Sometimes, noise suppression is called Noise Reduction or Noise Cancellation. While this feature might be implemented a number of different ways, all methods reduce the noise in a speech signal to make the speech more clear. These techniques are often unsuitable for recording music.

The most typical implementation uses a Noise Gate dynamics processor as described earlier in this chapter. By inserting a bandpass filter tuned to match the range of human speech before the level detector, the processing lowers or eliminates any noises between spoken words. Careful setting of the threshold and ratio controls is necessary to accommodate both loud and soft talkers.

VoIP Application

A complete implementation for an RTC application is shown in Figure 3.14. The acoustic source—that is, the person who is speaking—is picked up by the four microphones, which are amplified and then converted to a four-channel digital stream. The beam-forming software combines these four channels into a single-channel stream that is sent on the acoustic echo canceller. At the same time, the speaker tracking module develops location meta data that can be sent to a videoconferencing application to focus the camera on the person that is speaking.

The acoustic echo canceller takes the single-channel input stream from the beam-forming algorithm, and then it "subtracts" a time-corrected version of the output stream going to the speakers. This signal is further processed by the noise suppression algorithm.

Theories conflict on the exact ordering of these algorithms, especially whether to place the AEC before or after the beam-forming algorithm. If placed before the beam forming, you need as many AEC instances as you have microphones. This duplication uses substantially more CPU bandwidth than a single AEC.

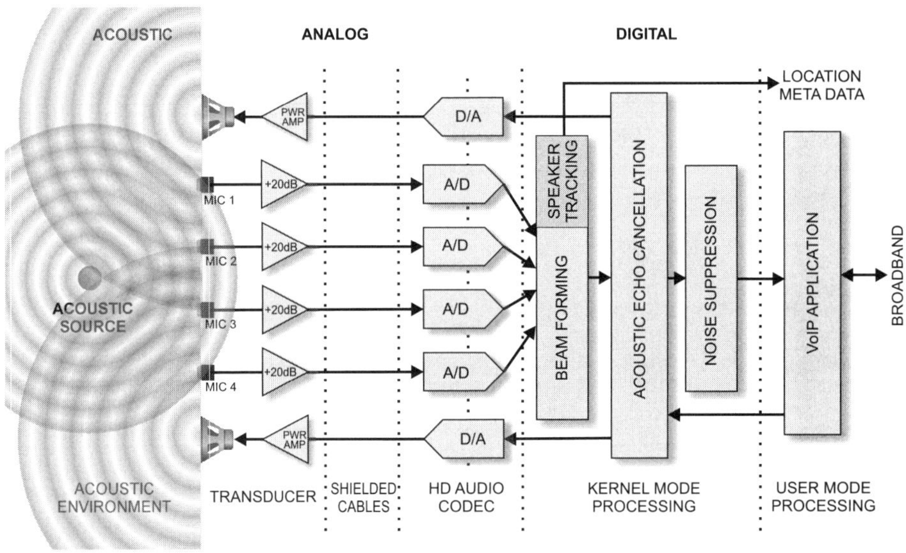

Notice that the Acoustic Echo Canceller is inserted in both the input path and the output path.

Figure 3.14 System Configured for a VoIP Application in Windows XP

Commercially Available Signal Processing for PCs

Moore's Law is one of the major contributors to the growth of audio processing in PCs. On modern systems, it is almost always more efficient to perform processing operations on the host CPU rather than on dedicated hardware, such as a DSP chip on a soundcard. In the long run, a general purpose CPU always wins out over a dedicated DSP, especially when used with modern operating systems.

Multi-core and hyper-threaded CPUs help audio processing considerably because a high audio-processing load does not drag the system performance down, while 64-bit extensions provide increased bandwidth for audio data processing. New multimedia timer services in Windows† Vista help provide resilience to glitches and dropouts.

A number of different signal processing algorithms are becoming commonplace on the PC, with a broad set of different offerings and a corresponding broad range of pricing for various solutions. Most of them are implemented in software.

Dolby† Processing Algorithms

In addition to the various transport formats listed earlier in the chapter, Dolby also provides processing algorithms for specific applications.

- *Dolby Headphone*† is a technology that provides a stereo output designed for headphone listening of 5.1 or 7.1 content, which is decoupled from the source content. This format could allow a traveler to listen to a 5.1 movie over headphones while on an airplane, and still be able to hear to surround sound effects intended by the movie producer.
- *Dolby Virtual Speaker*† is similar to Dolby Headphone, but is designed for use with a pair of speakers rather than headphones. The difference between these two algorithms is that Dolby Headphone can take advantage of the fact that each ear is isolated from the other while listening on headphones. When you are listening to a pair of speakers, each ear picks up the sounds from both speakers, although at varying levels. This format requires some adjustments to the algorithm.
- *Dolby ProLogic II*† and *Dolby ProLogic IIx*† are both capable of "spreading" two channels to multiple surround speakers. This spreading is possible regardless of whether the original stereo track includes material with matrixed surround content, though the surround effect usually is stronger when the stereo signal does have matrixed surround information. ProLogic II provides a 5.1 output, while ProLogic IIx provides a 7.1 output. Because 7.1 is common on many PCs but is not so common for a media storage format, ProLogic II is often used as the primary source of 7.1 output, synthesized from a wide variety of input formats.

- *Dolby Digital Live*† is a near-real-time encoder for Dolby Digital, also known as AC3, formatted streams. A typical application would be to render and encode a 5.1 or 7.1 output from a video game that is played on a PC to a digital S/PDIF output, which is in turn decoded by an A/V receiver that is receiving the S/PDIF signal. This sequence allows for a single cable—it can be either optical or coaxial—to be connected between the PC and an A/V receiver, instead of requiring 6 or 8 channels of analog output, which requires 3 to 8 cables to complete the connection. Overall encode and decode latency must be kept under 30 milliseconds, to ensure lip-sync with video.

Dolby† PC Entertainment Experience (PCEE)

In collaboration with Intel® Corporation, Dolby Laboratories has rolled out its PC Entertainment Experience program which makes a wide variety of Dolby products available on the PC. Complete PCs offer three basic levels of feature and performance, and boxed motherboards have an equivalent program. The following applications are offered:

- *Dolby Sound Room*† is intended for use on computers with only two channels of analog output. This program includes Dolby ProLogic II, Dolby Virtual Headphone, and Dolby Virtual Speaker. If discrete 5.1 output is available, the surround channels are down-mixed into Dolby Headphone when headphones are in use, or Dolby Virtual Speaker if headphones are not plugged in. ProLogic II converts 2-channel content into surround, which is fed into the Virtual Speaker or Headphone algorithms. S/PDIF Output of Dolby Digital streams is optional.
- *Dolby Home Theater*† normally requires 6 analog outputs to accommodate 5.1 surround, although some laptop designs with only two channels of analog output can qualify if the design has an S/PDIF connector to allow Dolby Digital to be routed out of the computer. The Home Theater program includes ProLogic IIx, Dolby Headphone, and Dolby Virtual Speaker. Dolby Digital Live is also included.
- *Dolby Master Studio*† builds on the Home Theater requirements to provide 7.1 output by substituting ProLogic IIx for ProLogic II. The audio fidelity output requirements for Master Studio require a high-quality audio codec coupled with a high-fidelity motherboard design. This level of fidelity requires significant attention to

motherboard design as well as choice of codec. The Dolby EX format is supported by the ProLogic IIx decoding. Figure 3.15 shows a complete system implementation for Dolby Master Studio.

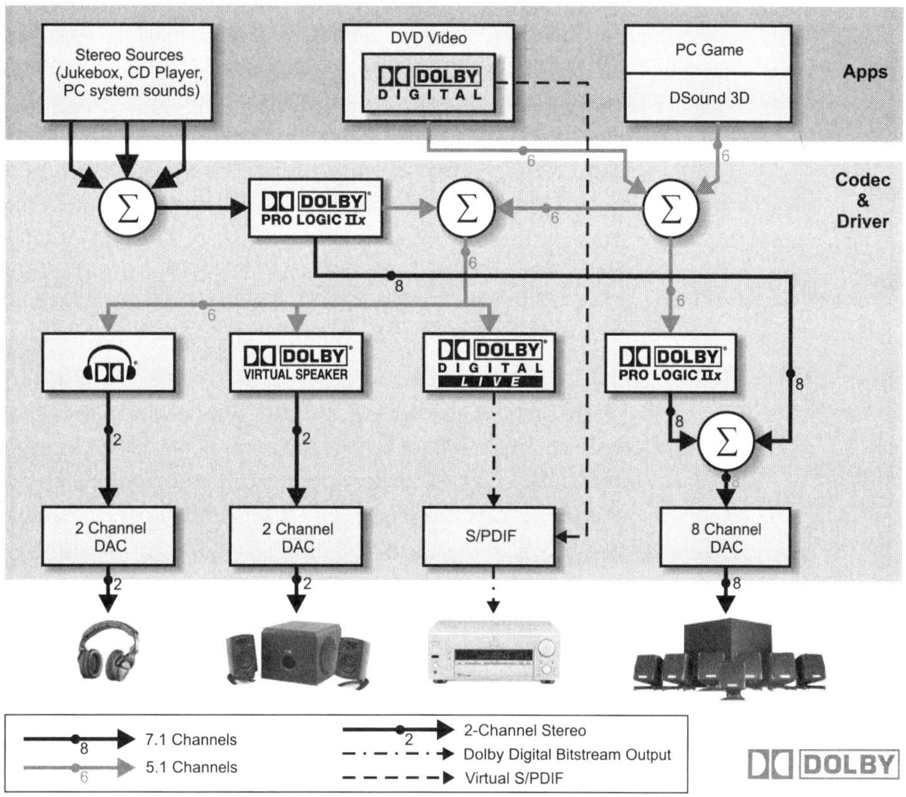

Figure 3.15 System Configured for Dolby† Master Studio† Operation

- *Designed for Dolby Home Theater*† is used for motherboards or bare-board computers that meet all the Dolby requirements for Home Theater and are ready to be built into a complete system.
- *Designed for Dolby Master Studio*† is used for motherboards or bare-board computers that meet all the Dolby requirements for Master Studio and are ready to be built into a complete system.

- *Dolby Digital Live*† is not by itself a part of the PC Entertainment Experience program but is available through a separate stand-alone license for computers with an S/PDIF output.

DTS

Digital Theater Systems, Inc., also known as DTS, also provides popular delivery surround-sound formats for movies and music. Unlike Dolby, DTS also provides high-quality surround-sound content in the form of music albums sold at retail.

DTS decoding technologies usually are included in the media player application, rather than as part of the audio subsystem. Like Dolby Digital, DTS surround-sound programs can be delivered to an A/V receiver using S/PDIF. Receivers that implement both Dolby and DTS usually are capable of determining the format that is being delivered and automatically switching to the appropriate format. Media player applications such as WinDVD and PowerDVD also could include both DTS and Dolby decoders and give the user a choice of which decoder to use if the DVD provides audio tracks in both formats.

DTS has recently rolled out a new program targeting PC applications. DTS Connect provides both a near-real-time encoder and a "spreader" for synthesizing multi-channel surround from a stereo audio stream.

SRS

SRS Labs provides a total of 12 different technologies intended for use on the PC platform, of which CircleSurround†, TruSurround†, and TruBass†, are the most popular. CircleSurround and TruSurround are similar in concept to Dolby ProLogic II, while TruBass provides a bass enhancement for smaller speakers.

The SRS technologies can be made available for installation either with the media play application or with the audio function driver. When they are installed in the media player application, the processing is available only when that media player application is being used. If they are installed with the audio driver or audio engine, the processing is available to all applications that play sound.

Sonic Focus

Sonic Focus takes a unique approach to audio processing on the PC, using techniques developed for the final mastering stages of professional recordings. The Sonic Focus ADRS—the acronym means adaptive dynamic refinement system—works to fill in the missing audio pieces created by lossy compression, while the surround sound expander is capable of accepting both 2-channel and multi-channel inputs and matching that to the current output configuration of the PC. This technique also ensures a listening experience that is pleasing throughout the entire sound field, and avoids *sweet spots*, where the user must be in a particular location to get the best benefit from the processing.

Sonic Focus processing is featured in the Intel® Audio Studio application, shown in Fig. 3.17, which is bundled with many of Intel's boxed motherboards that are sold through retail and reseller channels.

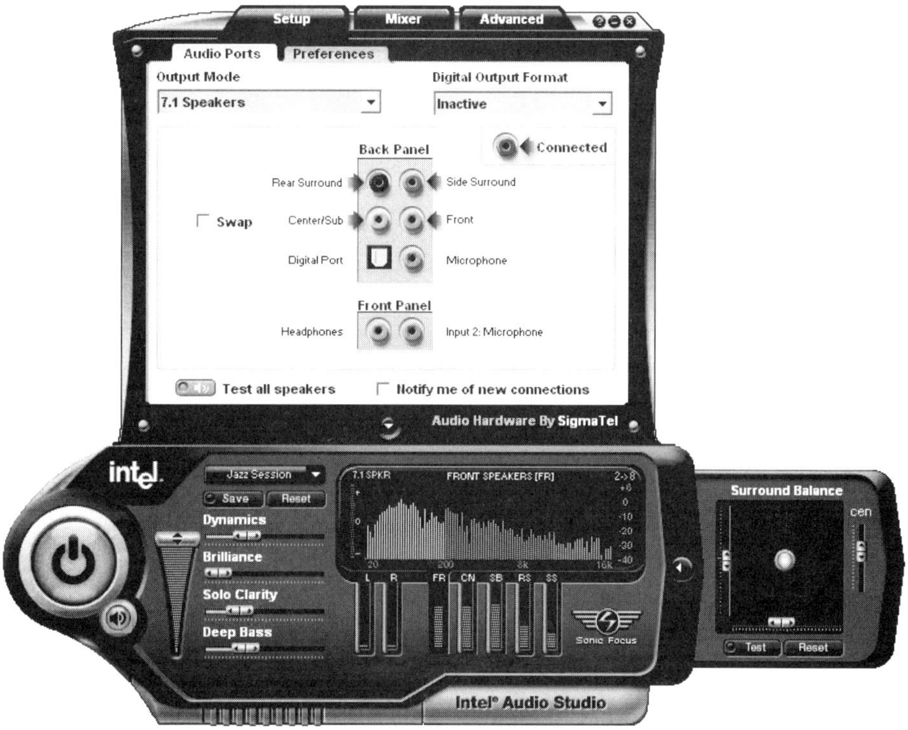

Figure 3.16 Intel® Audio Studio 2.0 Control Panel Featuring Sonic Focus

MaxxBass† by Waves

Waves has a long history of providing professional-quality audio processing plug-ins for computer digital audio workstations. The quality and convenience of these software solutions have allowed them to steadily replace dedicated hardware processing units in many professional recording studios.

For PC applications, Waves provides a patented MaxxBass† technology which uses the Phenomenon of the Missing Fundamental. Originally discovered by pipe organ builders in the 1700's, this psychoacoustic phenomenon stimulates the listener to hear bass frequencies below those that are physically generated. Figure 3.17 shows the processing stages taken during MaxxBass enhancement.

This software is not a bass boost technology, which increases peak amplifier power and speaker excursion requirements. Instead MaxxBass removes energy below the loudspeakers capability and reproduces this sound by generating a precise series of harmonics that the listener perceives as the original bass sound.

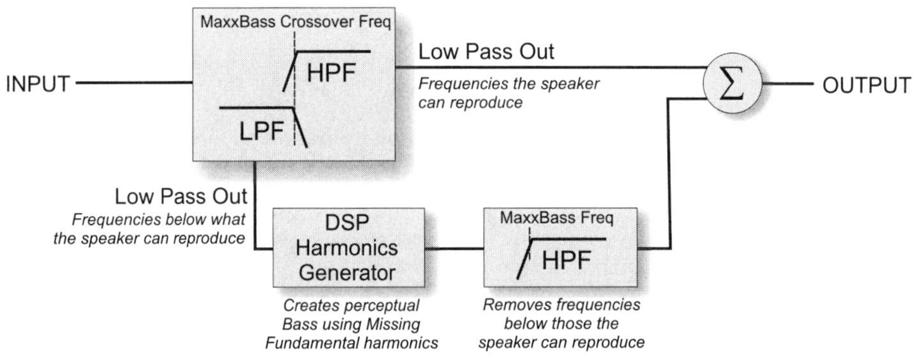

MaxxBass generates additional harmonics to be inserted back into the signal while extracting the original bass signal on which the harmonics are based.

Figure 3.17 MaxxBass Enhancement of Original Bass Signal

MaxxBass leverages our perception of hearing to improve the performance of audio systems. This method is similar to full color displays that leverage our sense of vision to require only red, green and blue pixels.

MaxxBass enables the audio system designer a new degree of flexibility. It can be used to increase the perceived bass frequency response by up to 1.5 octaves. Alternatively the speaker enclosure size and power consumption can be dramatically reduced by redesigning the acoustics with a smaller, more efficient loudspeaker with the same perceived bass response.

Intellisonics† by Knowles Acoustics

Parent company Knowles Electronics is known as a leader for precision microphones, especially for the hearing aid industry. Knowles Acoustics is the division charged with providing completed beamforming microphone array systems.

The Intellisonics software can be used with any good-quality microphone, but it shows its best results when coupled with Knowles SiSonics MEMS microphones. The Intellisonics software comes in four different configurations:

- DX-01 contains a noise-suppression software module and is intended for use with a single microphone.
- DX-01EC adds an acoustic echo canceller, which helps to enhance VoIP phone calls.
- DX-02 contains beam-forming software for two microphones as well as a noise suppression module.
- DX-02EC contains the beam-forming, acoustic echo cancellation, and noise suppression modules that are necessary for best quality on VoIP phone calls or audio-based instant messaging.

Professional Audio Applications

Professional audio applications such as Sonar† by Cakewalk or Nuendo† by Steinberg can take full advantage of a well-implemented Intel HD Audio system. Modern multi-channel Intel HD Audio codecs typically have eight stereo ports (a total of 16 analog I/O channels), eight or ten DACs, and four or six ADCs. This arrangement allows the simultaneous recording of six input channels, and the simultaneous output of 10 discrete channels which could be routed to a mixing console for further processing.

Applications in this category are expected to take over the entire system. In Windows XP, they use the DirectKS or ASIO interface to bypass KMixer. In Windows Vista, applications will call directly into the WASAPI layer, bypassing Media Foundation and the Streaming Audio Renderer.

System sounds and sounds from other applications will usually be disabled while these applications are running, which is as it should be. The last thing you need to hear in loud high-priced studio monitors is a loud "You've got mail!"

When running professional audio applications, be sure to turn off any microphone bias circuits and switch output amplifiers to line out mode if possible, to ensure the highest fidelity in the signal path. Retasking jacks should be avoided if possible.

Chapter 4

Introduction to Intel® High Definition Audio

Those parts of the system that you can hit with a hammer (not advised) are called hardware; those program instructions that you can only curse at are called software.

—Unknown

This chapter introduces the information needed to understand the hardware components that make up an audio subsystem in a modern PC, after the shift to chipset-based audio. It also addresses the attributes and constraints of several key hardware components such as converters and analog amplifiers. Finally, the Intel® High Definition Audio interface is introduced and explored in some detail.

In 2004, Intel® announced an Audio Codec 97 (AC97) replacement known as Intel® High Definition Audio (Intel® HD Audio). Introduced in 1997, the AC97 standard allowed sound-processing tasks such as sample rate conversion and mixing to be handled by the CPU. Logic known as the *AC97 digital controller* was added to the Southbridge or ICH chipset, as shown in Figure 4.1.

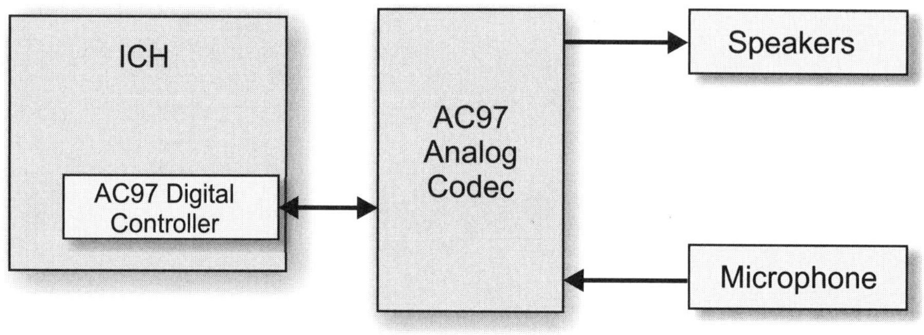

Figure 4.1 Addition of AC97

AC97 was originally known as *soft audio* or *host audio* because it offloaded many of the sound-processing tasks from dedicated hardware to software that is run on the general purpose CPU. Intel HD Audio is thematically similar to AC97 but includes support for many new features. For instance, Intel HD Audio can support 32-bit, 192-kilohertz surround sound out as well as multi-tasking, which is the ability to support multiple audio inputs and outputs simultaneously.

Quite a bit of the AC97 infrastructure is retained for Intel HD Audio. It uses the same five-wire serial link between controller and codec, as well as the same 48-pin package for the audio codec. Much of the analog circuitry in the codec remains the same, though better Intel HD Audio codecs have improved the audio fidelity of these circuits. While the Intel HD Audio specification allows for up to 16 input and output streams; today's chipsets typically support four input and four output streams. A separate DMA engine is required for each stream.

Hardware

The three key types of physical components in an Intel HD Audio solution are an Intel HD Audio Controller, an Intel HD Audio Link, and an Intel HD Audio Codec, as shown in Figure 4.2. The controller has responsibility for moving data to and from system memory via a memory controller. The link is the bi-directional interconnection across which audio data and commands flow. The codec interprets the commands and sends or receives data and to or from an attached acoustic device—that is, a speaker or microphone.

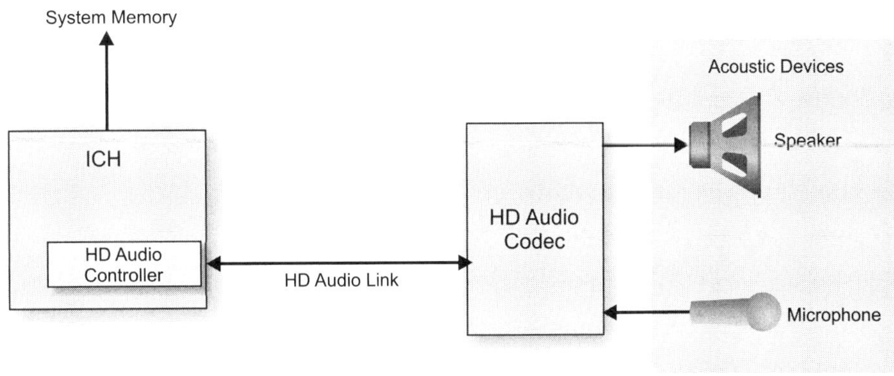

Figure 4.2 Intel® HD Audio Components

Multiple codecs can be attached to a single link. More rarely, a single system could have multiple controllers, each of which would have its own associated link and attached codecs. This situation might occur if a soundcard with an Intel HD Audio controller is inserted into a PCI or PCI Express slot.

Controller

An Intel HD Audio controller provides a capability for the system to discover and enumerate multiple Intel HD Audio devices connected to the Intel HD Audio link. It provides a capability to relay instructions to and from each codec, and it contains the Direct Memory Access (DMA) engines which stream audio data to and from the codec(s).

An Intel HD Audio Controller usually contains four or more DMA engines. DMA refers to copying data from one memory location to another without having to go through the CPU. In this case, the transfer goes from system memory to a codec or goes from a codec to system memory (see Figure 4.3). DMA transfers are faster than non-DMA transfers.

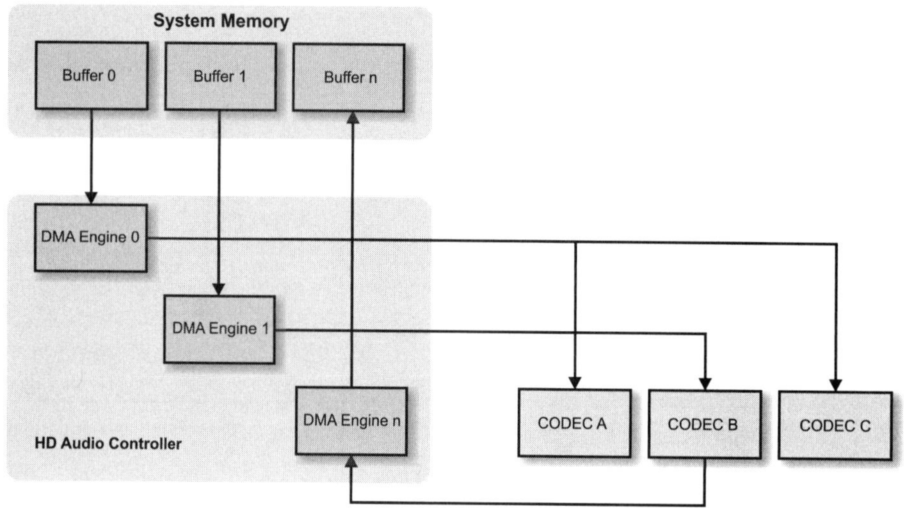

Figure 4.3 Controller DMA Engines

A DMA transfer from system memory to a codec is handled by a signal known as Serial Digital Out (SDO). DMA transfers in the opposite direction are handled by a Serial Digital In (SDI) signal. Controllers must provide support for at least one SDO line, up to a maximum of four, and at least one SDI line, up to a maximum of fifteen. The SDO and SDI lines are used to carry both commands and audio sample data, as explained in more detail in the "Command and Data Flow" section. In addition to the SDO and SDI lines, the controller must support bit clock (BCLK), frame synchronization (SYNC), and reset (RST#) signals.

The controller also contains a standardized set of memory-mapped registers that allow for command and control of the data streams and the codecs. The standardized nature of a controller's register makes it straightforward to write a universal Intel HD Audio Controller software driver that works for multiple instantiations of controllers, even if they are produced by different manufacturers, something Microsoft is utilizing for their windows class driver initiative, Universal Audio Architecture.

Link

The link itself, which connects a controller with one or more codecs, is a physical electrical interface consisting of the BCLK, SYNC, and RST# signals. It also consists of one to four SDO signals, denoted SDO_0-SDO_3 respectively, and one to fifteen SDI signals, and denoted SDI_0-SDI_N respectively.

Topology

The SDO lines can be multipoint; that is, a single SDO line can be attached to multiple codecs. In a configuration like the one in Figure 4.4, multiple codecs could receive the same audio data, thus allowing, for instance, a set of headphones and separate stereo speakers to receive the same program. However, the same physical topology could be used to send different programs to the headphones and speakers. The data sent from the controller can be targeted at a specific codec.

Unlike SDO, the SDI lines are point-to-point. Each attached codec's SDI must be wired to a unique SDI_n on the controller. Given that each codec must have at least one SDI, a practical upshot of these constraints is that the maximum number of codecs that can be attached to a particular link is limited by the number of SDIs the controller supports.

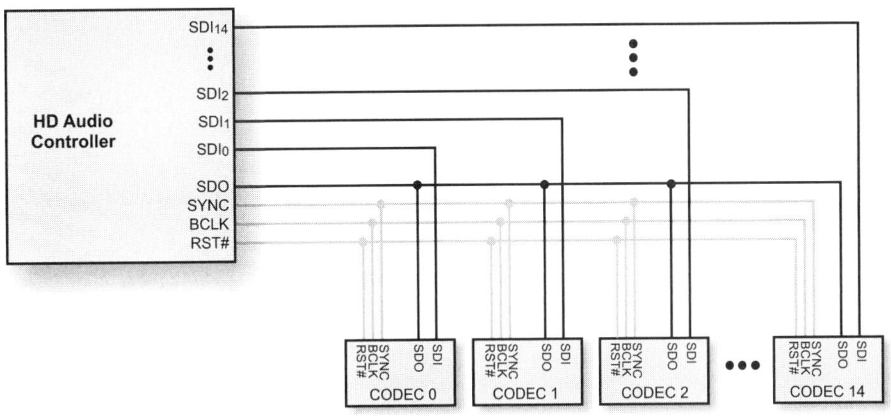

In this example, the controller's single SDO is wired to every codec's SDO. However, every SDI has a unique path—a fundamental requirement of the specification. More than one SDI line is optional for any particular system.

Figure 4.4 Sample Link Topology

Most, if not all, Southbridge chipsets that incorporate Intel HD Audio have at least four SDI pins, allowing up to four Intel HD Audio devices to be used in a system. The SDI pin that the codec is attached to determines the Codec ID used to address a specific codec. SDI0 is attached to Codec ID 0, SDI1 is attached to Codec ID 1, and so on. Intel recommends that SDI#2 be used for codecs mounted on the motherboard, and that SDI#0 be used for a modem codec, if present. SDI#1 and SDI#3 are reserved for future usage models.

To allow for future expansion, both the output and input data rates for Intel HD Audio are scalable. A single SDO or SDI provides the basic throughput, but *bandwidth scaling* is achieved by attaching multiple SDO or SDI lines to a codec (see Figure 4.5). The data bandwidth is essentially increased by the number of lines. For instance, four SDO lines offer roughly four times the bandwidth of a single SDO line. While technically feasible under the specification, no OS currently supports bandwidth scaling.

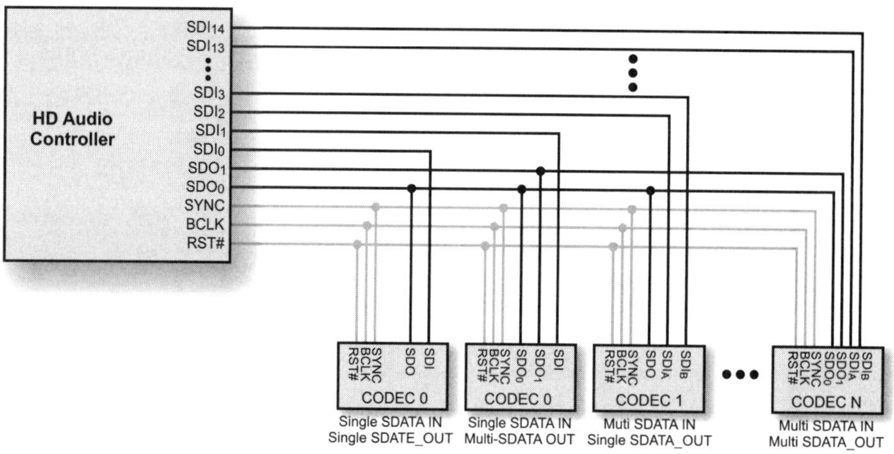

In this example, all four types of bandwidth-scaling codecs are attached to a link. Although the multiple in/out codecs only show two associated lines, it is possible to build systems with larger numbers of connections.

Figure 4.5 Bandwidth Scaling

With bandwidth scaling in mind, codecs can be classified into four categories:

- Single-SDO, single SDI
- Multi-SDO, single SDI
- Single-SDO, multi-SDI
- Multi-SDO, multi-SDI

Even in the case of a multi-SDI codec, the SDI lines remain point-to-point. Each SDI on the codec must be attached to a unique SDI on the controller.

In all systems, even those using bandwidth scaling, SDO_0 must be attached to all codecs on the link. This restriction ensures the basic operation of the system in the scenario of codecs that support scaling running with software that does not. The number of permitted SDO lines is 1, 2, or 4.

When building a system using codecs that are multi-SDO or multi-SDI, it is very important to attach all of the SDO and SDI lines from the codec to the controller. Failure to do so could result in reduced codec performance.

Data and Timings

The Intel HD Audio Link is isochronous, meaning that it can provide data at a predictable and fixed rate, rather than in bursts like most networks. The isochronicity is achieved in part from the use of a fixed bus clock (BCLK) that runs at 24.000 megahertz. Data transfers on the bus are broken into frames, each of which is exactly 20.833 microseconds. The frames are designated by the frame sync (SYNC) signal's falling edge, shown in Figure 4.6. Each frame ends with a SYNC signal going high for exactly four BCLK cycles, an event known as the frame sync.

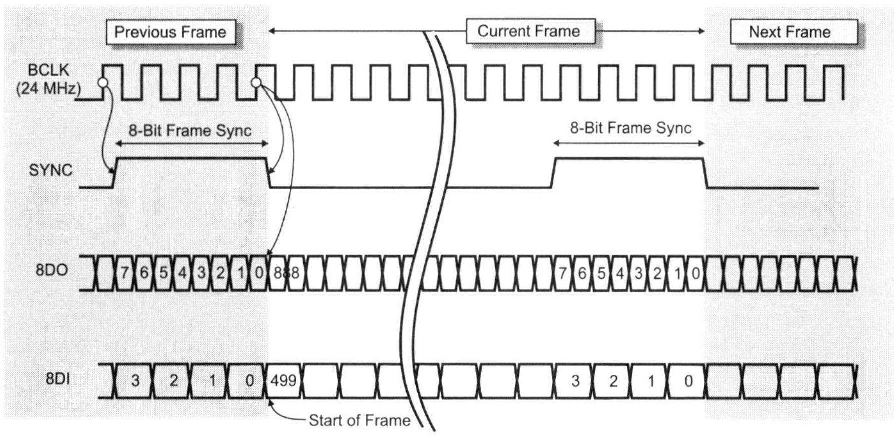

Figure 4.6 Link Signals

SDO is *double-pumped*, meaning that a unique bit of data can be sent on both the rising and falling edge of the reference clock (BLCK). Given that BLCK runs at 24 megahertz, a single SDO signal can convey 48 megabits per second. Each bit is contained within a timing window known as a *cell*. For SDO, each frame consists of 1,000 cells.

SDI is single-pumped. Only one bit is transferred per clock cycle. As such, SDI has half the bandwidth of SDO, or 24 megabits per second. Similarly, SDI has only 500 cells per frame.

The data within a frame can contain commands, status, and audio samples. The detailed structure of a frame will be examined more closely in the "Frame Format" section in this chapter.

Codec

Intel HD Audio Codecs are modular. They consist of a hierarchy of standardized modules. The number and types of modules, plus their connectivity, may vary from one codec to another. The codec architecture includes a discovery and addressing scheme that allows for a single driver to easily support a wide variety of codecs.

A *node* is either a single module within a codec or it is a collection of a module and all its children modules that are connected below it in the hierarchy, as shown in Figure 4.7. Each node has a unique address, known as a *node ID* (NID). An NID is usually 7 bits, but 15-bit NIDs can be used for very complex systems. Each node has a set of read-only capabilities, and each can be controlled and configured using commands targeted at that node.

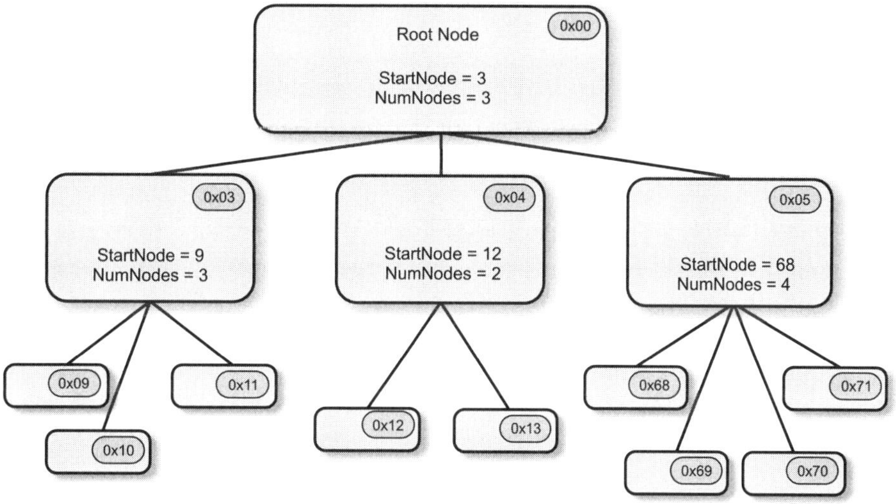

Figure 4.7 Codec Node Hierarchy

The *root node* is the node at the top of the hierarchy. It has an NID of zero. The root node has no other function than to serve as a pointer to the downstream nodes. The root node points to one or more *function group nodes*. A function group node is a collection of modules that perform a dedicated function and are designed to be controlled by a single driver.

The two basic function group types in use today are audio and modem; other function groups may be defined in the future. The remainder of this chapter focuses on the audio function group (AFG). The modem function group is outside the scope of this book. Some newer audio codecs support both audio and modem function groups in the same die, but each has it's own SDI pin on the codec, and they are treated as totally separate units.

Introducing...the Widget

Below each function group node is a collection of modules known as *widget nodes* or *widgets*. Widgets can be interconnected in many different ways, allowing a single AFG to support an arbitrary number of audio input and output channels.

A widget whose inputs are connected to the outputs of other widgets must contain a *connection list* that consists of the NIDs of the attached widgets. The connection list refers to the hard-wired topology of the interconnected widgets. If the connection list length is greater than one, the widget would have a *connection selector* that allows the run-time selection of input(s) to be used by the widget.

Thus, connection lists are always built from right to left in terms of conventional left-to-right audio flow. For output devices, you start with the output port and follow the connection list towards the Intel HD Audio bus. For input devices, you start with the ADC where it is attached to the Intel HD Audio bus and follow the connection lists widget by widget until you reach an input port.

Widgets are either 1-channel (mono) or 2-channel (stereo). An AFG as a whole can support greater than 2-channel sound by using multiple widgets.

The types of standardized audio widgets are:

- Audio Output Converter (AOC) Widget
- Audio Input Converter (AIC) Widget
- Pin Widget
- Mixer Widget
- Selector Widget
- Power Widget
- Volume Knob Widget
- Beep Generator Widget

An Audio Output Converter Widget converts audio data coming in over the link into an analog or digital audio format more suitable for transmission to an acoustic device. The key component of an AOC widget is a DAC for analog outputs or a digital formatter for digital outputs, such as S/PDIF. The widget may contain either an optional processing node or an optional amplifier with a mute capability or both, as shown in Figure 4.8. The data input to an AOC widget is always attached directly to the link.

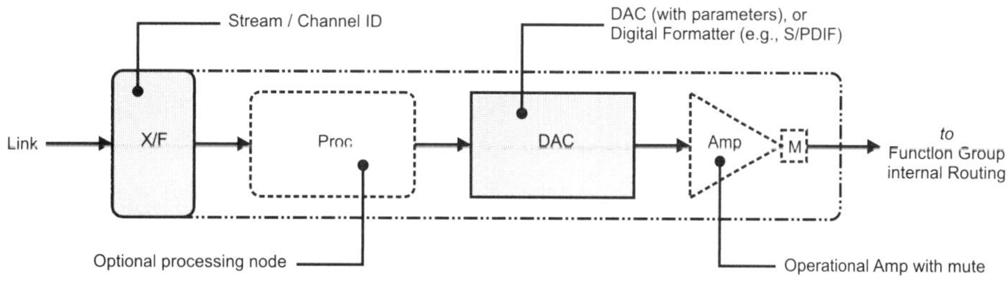

Figure 4.8 Audio Output Converter Widget

As you might guess, the Audio Input Converter Widget is the converse of the AOC. It converts analog or digital external formats into a digital format compatible with the link. As such, the main component of an AIC is an ADC or a digital sample formatter. An AIC may also contain an optional processing node and/or an optional amplifier with mute capability (Figure 4.9). The data output of the AIC attaches directly to the link.

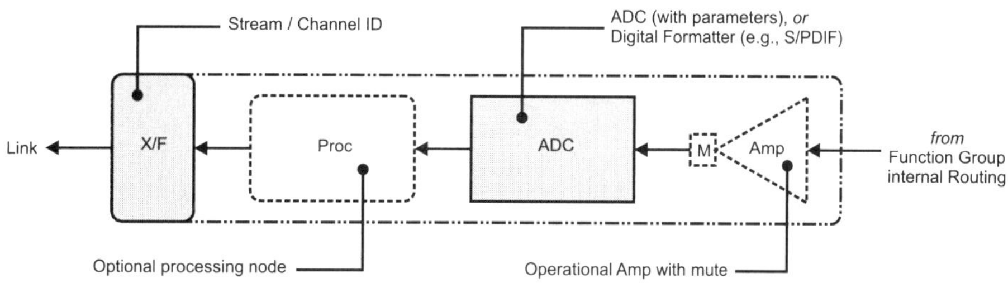

Figure 4.9 Audio Input Converter Widget

The Pin Widget shown in Figure 4.17 is a mechanism for sending to or receiving audio signals from a physical audio connector or sending them to a hard-wired connection to a dedicated acoustic device, such as a built-in speaker or a microphone integrated in a laptop bezel. The Pin Widget also supports other signals that are associated with the connector, such as *jack sense*—it detects the presence and type of the acoustic device that is plugged into the connector and VRefOut —used to switch microphone bias voltage on and off. The Pin Widget may contain optional outgoing and ingoing amplifiers. Alternatively, the Pin Widget is referred to as the Pin Complex Widget.

The Pin Widget is also very important because it can be used to convey detailed information about the associated connector. For instance, the type of connector, its location on the PC, and the color of the connector can all be communicated by the pin widget to the software stack. When such information is made available, very user-friendly interfaces can be designed which show computer users on-screen what connections are active or available on their computer. See "Pins, Pin Widgets and Ports" later in this chapter for more detail on pin configurations.

The Mixer Widget, also known as a Summing Amplifier Widget, is used to combine multiple signals into a single signal (see Figure 4.10). The number of inputs can vary. The relative intensity of the different inputs can also be altered.

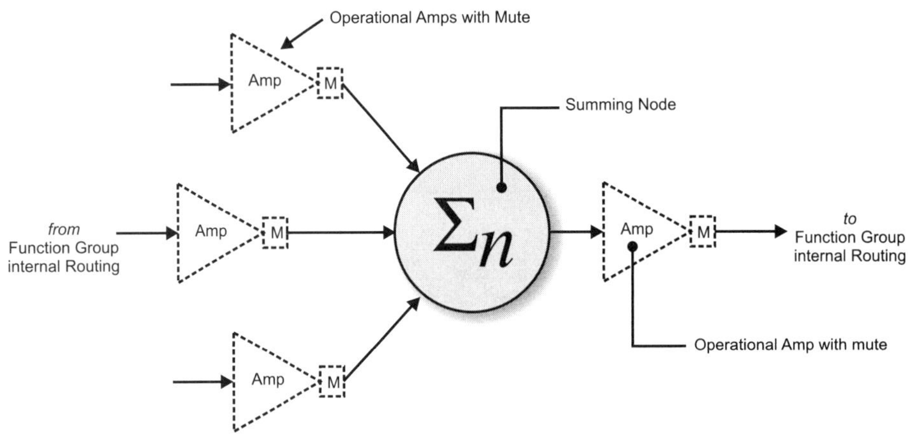

Figure 4.10 Mixer Widget

The Selector Widget is used to select a single signal from a multitude, as can be seen in Figure 4.11. Sometimes, the Selector Widget is referred to as a multiplexer widget (Mux for short). As it passes through the Selector Widget, the signal can be processed, amplified, or muted, if such optional capabilities are supported by the widget.

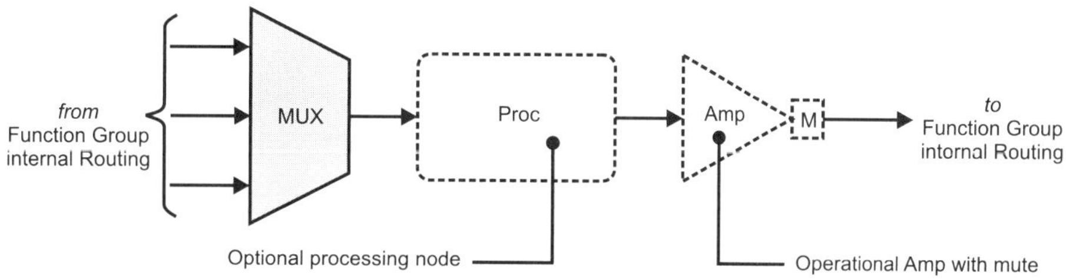

Figure 4.11 Selector Widget

Since most widgets already have implicit selection mechanisms via their connection lists and connection selector controls, the Selector Widget is not needed in most designs and has rarely appeared in actual codecs. However, a 1-input selector could be used to insert a processing/amplifier widget arbitrarily into a widget hierarchy.

The Power Widget provides a single point of control for power management of a subset of the widgets in an Audio Function Group, independent of the power management of the AFG as a whole. The Power Widget's connection list contains a static list of all the widgets under its control. The power state of those widgets can then be set independently of the AFG's power state, with the constraint that the Power Widget can never be at a higher power state than the AFG.

The Volume Knob Widget is used to report the state of a physical volume control. The control could either be absolute, as would be the case for a thumbwheel potentiometer, or it could be relative, as would be the case for + and - pushbuttons. The *Master Volume in Windows*† *XP* section of Chapter 8 includes details on how the Volume Knob Widget can be used with the Windows operating system.

The Beep Generator Widget is used to...generate a beep! The beep is derived from the 48-kilohertz reference clock on the link. A variety of frequencies can be created by specifying a divisor to be applied to the 48-kilohertz reference. The Beep Widget is not explicitly attached to other widgets via connection lists. Indeed, a Beep Widget is forbidden from appearing on the connection lists of other widgets. Instead, when the Beep Widget is activated, the tone that it generates must be applied to all active output pin widgets. The beep can either replace or be blended with other signals that might already be active on those pins.

Widgets in Practice

From the eight simple building blocks listed above, complex codecs can be readily constructed. Figure 4.12 shows an example of the widgets that are used in a real-world codec. This codec supports S/PDIF in and out, eight channels of analog out, multiple stereo inputs, I^{2}S out, ADAT out, and PC Beep.

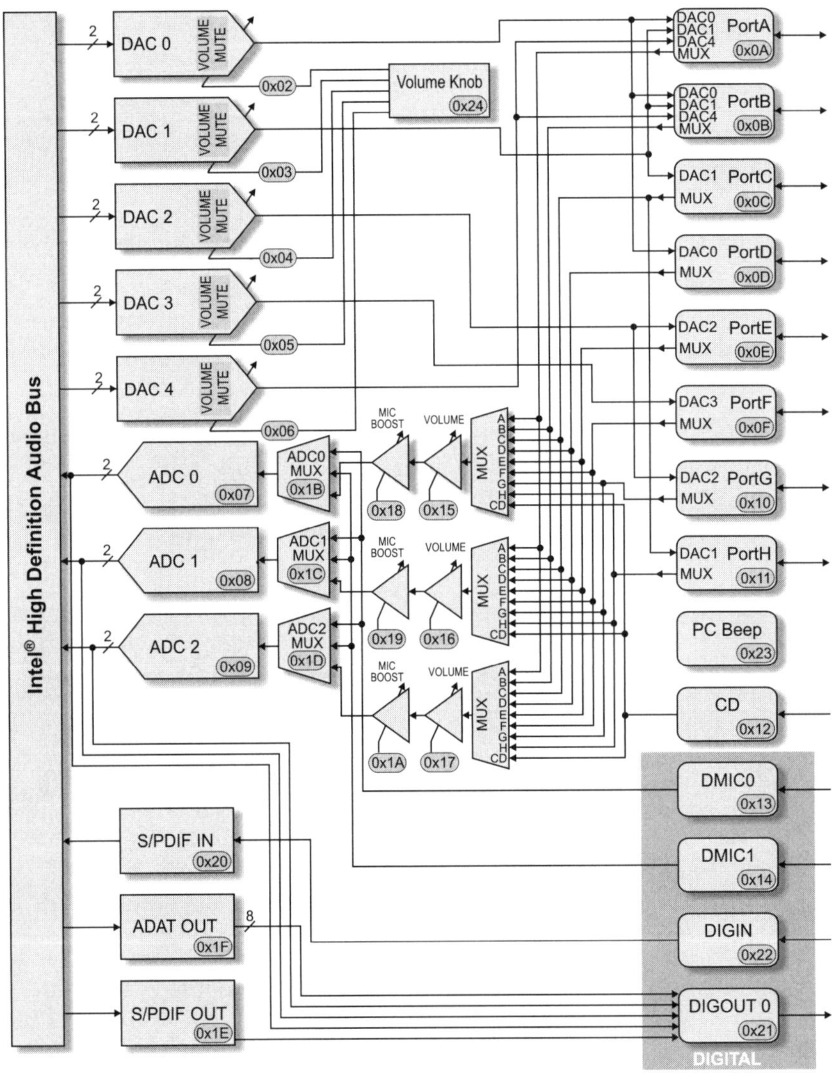

Figure 4.12 Sample Widget Diagram

Command and Data Flow

As mentioned, SDO and SDI carry both commands and audio data. The commands and their associated responses are low-bandwidth; the audio data is high-bandwidth. The two forms of data are interleaved, but the outbound protocol is slightly different than the inbound protocol.

To understand how these forms are multiplexed together, it is important to first understand the concept of a stream. A *stream* is a connection between a DMA buffer in the controller and a codec. A stream contains one or more audio channels from the same audio program. For instance, a stereo program would contain two channels.

Streams can either be output streams conveyed over SDO or input streams conveyed over SDI. Given the multipoint topology of SDO, it is not surprising to learn that output streams can be broadcast to multiple codecs. For instance, the same audio stream can be rendered concurrently on both headphones and speakers.

Verbs

These streams transport audio samples in both directions across the link. Although the audio samples take up the majority of the link bandwidth, they are useless without ancillary control data that is used to modify and direct the flow of the audio samples. The command information originates from the controller, which issues 32-bit commands known as verbs. Figure 4.13 shows the structure of verbs.

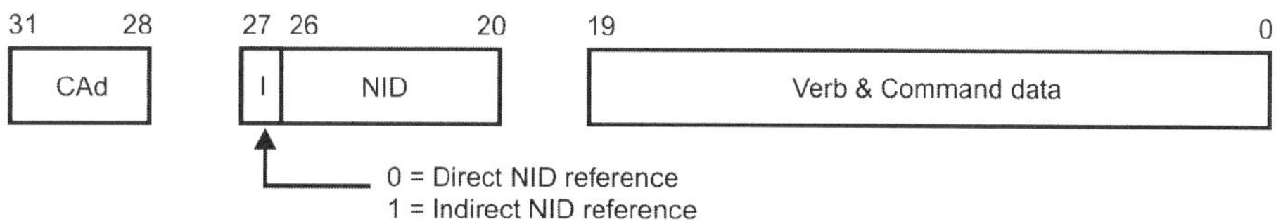

Figure 4.13 Verb Structure

The verb contains a 4-bit codec address that indicates the codec to which the command is targeted. A value of all ones in this field (`Fh`) is reserved to verbs that are intended to be broadcast to all codecs on the link. However, no such broadcast verbs have been defined in the current revision of the specification.

The verb also contains an 8-bit node address, which indicates the node at which the verb is targeted. Two different node-addressing schemes are supported: direct and indirect. If bit 27 of the verb is 0, the node ID (NID) is a direct address. Otherwise, it is an indirect address. However, an indirect addressing scheme has not yet been specified, so in practice, all verbs use direct addresses. The 7-bits allow a single codec to contain 127 nodes.

The final 20 bits of the verb command the actual command and its parameters. Verbs either have a 4-bit command identifier with a 16-bit payload or a 12-bit command identifier with an 8-bit payload. Not all types of widgets need to support all verbs. Table 4.1 is a summary of the verbs and whether or not they are required for the different widgets. Many verbs have get and set variations.

Table 4.1 Required Support for Verbs

Required Verb Support	Get Code	Set Code	Root Node	Audio Function Group	Modem Function Group	Vendor Defined Function Group	Audio Output Converter	Audio Input Converter	Pin Complex Widget	Mixer	Selector	Power Widget	Volume Knob	Beep Generator	Vendor Defined Wdiget
GetParameter	F00		R	R	R	R	R	R	R	R	R	R	R	R	R
ConnectionSelect	F01	701						C	C		C				
GetConnectionList Entry	F02							R	R	R	R	R	R		
Processing State	F03	##					C	C	C		C				
Coefficient Index	D	5					C	C	C		C				
Processing Coefficient	C	4					C	C	C		C				
Amplifier Gain/Mute	B	3					C	C	C	C	C				
Stream Format	A	2					R	R							
Digital Converter 1	F0D	70D					C	C							
Digital Converter 2	F0D	70E					C	C							
Power State	F05	705		R	R	C	C	C	C	C	C	R			
Channel/Stream ID	F06	706					R	R							
SDI Select	F04	704					X	X							
Pin Widget Control	F07	707							R						
Unsolicited Enable	F08	708					C	C	C	C	C	C	C		
Pin Sense	F09	709							C						

EAPD/BTL Enable	F0C	70C							C						
All GPI Controls	F10 – F1A	710 – 71A		C	C										
Beep Generation Control	F0A	70A												R	
VolumeKnobControl	F0F	70F											R		
SubsystemID,Byte0	F20	720		R	R	R									
SubsystemID,Byte1	F20	721		R	R	R									
SubsystemID,Byte2	F20	722		R	R	R									
SubsystemID,Byte3	F20	723		R	R	R									
ConfigDefault,Byte0	F1C	71C							R						
ConfigDefault,Byte1	F1C	71D							R						
ConfigDefault,Byte2	F1C	71E							R						
ConfigDefault,Byte3	F1C	71F							R						
Stripe Control	F24	724					C								
RESET		7FF		R	R	R									

R: Required.
C: conditional; required only if respective optional capability is declared to be available
X: required if codec supports multiple SDI signals.

Responses

Verbs are synchronous commands. For every verb that is issued from a controller to a codec, that codec must generate a 36-bit response on the following frame. The format of the response is shown in Figure 4.14. Bit 35 is the Valid bit. It must be set to 1 in order for the controller to process the response.

Bit 35	Bit 34	Bits 33:32	Bits 31:0
Valid	**UnSol**	***Reserved***	***Response***

Figure 4.14 Response Structure

The lower 32 bits of a response is a data payload. Responses to Set commands typically have a payload of all zeros, whereas responses to Get commands typically contain the information requested by the verb.

Bit 34 is used to flag a special type of response known as an *Unsolicited Response*. Unsolicited responses are asynchronous messages sent from the codec to the controller to signal an event, such as the attachment of an acoustic device. No verb is involved in the transmission of an unsolicited response.

Frame Format

Each frame contains a verb or response, one or more stream packets, and a null field. The exact formats of inbound and outbound frames differ slightly, but conceptually, both types of frames are organized as shown in Figure 4.15.

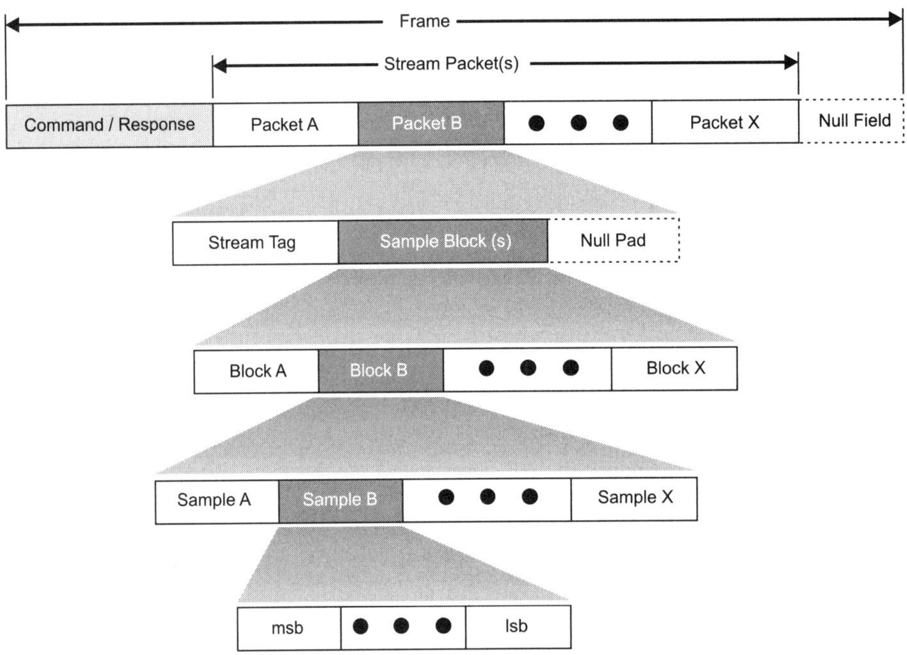

Figure 4.15 Frame Format

The stream packets are logical containers for the audio data streams. Each packet begins with 8-bit stream tag that uniquely identifies the streams. Codecs are programmed by software to send or receive a stream with the specified ID—for example, via the SetConverterStreamChannel verb. After the stream tag, the packet contains one or more sample blocks. Each block in turn contains audio sample data.

Hardware Volume Scaling

Volume controls on Intel HD Audio codecs can be present on almost any widget in the codec. Volume controls are optional and not required. A driver might or might not choose to expose any particular volume control, especially if the signal path contains multiple volume controls. Volume controls in Intel HD Audio codecs are required to default to unity gain, with neither gain nor attenuation. Therefore, volume controls that aren't manipulated by the driver pass through any audio in the signal path. You have no guarantee that the audio engine on the system will make use of the hardware volume controls. Many Intel HD Audio designs lock the hardware volume controls to unity gain, and they perform all volume and muting in software.

Almost every widget in the codec uses the Amplifier Capabilities response format shown in Table 4.2 to report its volume control characteristics. A widget that is retaskable may include both input and output volume controls, each with a separate set of capabilities. You must know the values in StepSize, NumSteps, and Offset for each widget in order to set the volume control correctly. You might need to read this information directly from the codec, as it is often not included in the codec datasheet.

Table 4.2 **32-bit** Amplifier Capabilities Response Format

31	30:23	22:16	15	14:8	7	6:0
Mute Capable	Rsvd	StepSize	Rsvd	NumSteps	Rsvd	Offset

The Amplifier Capabilities response formats are:

- Mute Capable (1 bit) reports whether the respective amplifier is capable of muting. Muting implies a minus infinity (-∞) gain, so that no sound passes, but the actual performance is determined by the Intel HD Audio codec.
- StepSize (7 bits) indicates the size of each step in the gain range. Each individual step may be 0-32 decibels specified in 0.25-dB steps. A value of `0` indicates 0.25-dB steps, while a value of `127d` indicates 32-dB steps.
- NumSteps (7 bits) indicates the number of steps in the gain range. The number could be from 1 to 128 steps in the amplifier gain range. (`0d` means 1 step, `127d` means 128 steps). A value of `0d` (1 step) means that the gain is fixed and may not be changed.

Because of this behavior, the name actually is incorrect; technically the name should really be "number of steps minus one."

- Offset (7 bits) indicates which step is 0 decibels or unity gain. With two or more steps, one of the step values must correspond to a value of 0 dB. The Offset value indicates the value which, if programmed in to the Amplifier Gain control, would result in a gain of 0 decibels.

For example, the AC97 specification defined master volume control as 32 steps of attenuation at 1.5 dB, where the maximum setting was unity gain. This definition is shown on the first row of Table 4.3. The next row shows a more capable volume control with a range of -96 to 0 dB in 0.75 steps. Following that is a volume control from –64 to 0 dB in 0.5 steps. This progression provides smoother steps due to the smaller step size, but the range is limited as a result, since both of these examples use the maximum of 128 steps. The following example shows a typical microphone input slider with a gain from 0 to +22.5 dB, and the final example shows a microphone preamp stage with variable settings of +0, +10, +20, +30, and +40 dB.

Table 4.3 Examples of Volume Controls Defined Using Amplifier Capabilities

Num Steps	Step Size	Offset	True Number of Steps	Lowest Gain	Highest Gain	Step Size	A gain value of 10 equals
31	5	31	32	-42.5 dB	+0.0 dB	1.5 dB	-27.5 dB
127	2	127	128	-96.0 dB	+0.0 dB	0.75 dB	-88.5 dB
127	1	127	128	-64.0 dB	+0.0 dB	0.5 dB	-59 dB
21	3	11	22	-10.0 dB	+10.0 dB	1.0 dB	-1.0 dB
15	5	0	16	+0.0 dB	+22.5 dB	1.5 dB	+15 dB
4	39	0	5	+0.0 dB	+40 dB	10 dB	+40 dB*

Note: The three columns on the left of the double line show the Intel HD Audio parameters, while the five columns on the right show the real world values of each example. The leftmost column shows the value of the NumSteps field, which is really the number of steps minus one. The rightmost column shows the effective gain in dB when a numeric value of 10 is written to the gain register in a widget.

The Set Amplifier Gain/Mute verb supports the 16-bit payload shown in Table 4.4, which is capable of specifying a number of simultaneous parameters for a stereo widget. You can set all of the volume controls in a widget to the same value in a single operation, or you can send multiple verbs to set each input and output control separately on each channel.

Table 4.4 **16-bit** Amplifier Gain/Mute Payload

15	14	13	12	11:8	7	6:0
Set Output Amp	Set Input Amp	Set Left Amp	Set Right Amp	Index	Mute	Gain

The bits in the Set Amplifier Gain/Mute verb are:

- Set Output Amp and Set Input Amp determine whether the value programmed refers to the input amplifier or the output amplifier in widgets which have both, such as pin widgets, sum widgets, and selector Widgets. A value of 1 indicates that the relevant amplifier should accept the value being set. If both bits are set, both amplifiers are set; if neither bit is set, the command is effectively a no-op. Any attempt to set a non-existent amplifier is ignored.
- Set Left Amp and Set Right Amp determine whether the left (channel 0) or right (channel 1) channel of the amplifier is being affected. A value of 1 indicates that the relevant amplifier should accept the value being set. If both bits are set, both amplifiers are set. Any attempt to set a non-existent amplifier is ignored. If the widget only supports a single channel, channel 1 bits have no effect and the value programmed applies to the left (channel 0) amplifier.
- Index is only used when programming the input amplifiers on Selector Widgets and Sum Widgets, where each input may have an individual amplifier. The index corresponds to the input's offset in the Connection List. If the widget being programmed is not a Selector Widget or a Sum Widget, or the Set Input Amp bit is not set, this field is ignored. If the specified index is out of range, no action is taken.
- Mute selects $-\infty$ gain (the lowest possible gain), but the hardware implementation determines the actual degree of mute provided. A value of 1 indicates that the mute is active. Generally, mute should default to 1 on codec reset, but in some circumstances, mute defaults to its off or inactive state. In particular, if an analog PC Beep Pin is used, the mutes of associated outputs must default to 0 to enable the beep signal prior to the codec coming out of

reset. This bit is ignored by any amplifier that does not have a mute option.

- Gain is a 7-bit "step" value specifying the amplifier gain, the actual decibel value that is determined by the StepSize, Offset, and NumSteps fields of the Output Amplifier Capabilities parameter for a given amplifier. After codec reset, this Gain field must default to the Offset value, meaning that all amplifiers, by default, are configured to 0 decibels or unity gain. If a value outside the amplifier's range is set, the results are undetermined.

To set a volume control to unity gain, follow these steps:

1. Simply copy the Offset from the Amplifier Capabilities response into the Gain field of the payload.
2. Set the Mute bit to 0.
3. Specify the input or output channel, the left or right channel, and the index (if needed).
4. Then send the payload to the widget.

Without knowing the offset, the only value you can reliably program in the gain field is the number zero (not 0 dB), which always represents the lowest gain available in the amplifier. A payload of `0xF080` mutes both input and output amplifiers on both left and right channels and sets the gain to the lowest possible value.

Pin Widget Control

In addition to the configuration default register, each Pin Widget also has a control register that the audio function driver uses to configure the port. Table 4.5 shows the contents of the Pin Widget Control register.

Table 4.5 Pin Widget Control Register

Bit 7	Bit 6	Bit 5	Bits 4:3	Bits 2:0
H-Phn Enable	Out Enable	In Enable	Reserved	VRefEn

The bits for the Pin Widget Control register are:

- H-Phn Enable stands for Headphone Enable, which disables or enables a low-impedance amplifier to be associated with the output. A value of one enables the amp. Enabling a non-existent headphone amp has no effect.

- Out Enable allows the output path of the port to be shut off. A value of one enables the output path. Enabling a non-existent output has no effect.
- In Enable allows the input path of the port to be shut off. A value of one enables the input path.
- VRefEn stands for Voltage Reference Enable, which controls the switchable microphone bias provided by the VRefOut pin that is associated with the port. A range of settings provide the ability to match specific microphones and to avoid crosstalk when the jack is re-tasked. Adjusting VRefEn sets the microphone bias voltage on the VRefOut pin to one of the following values:
  - Hi-Z (also known as floating, or tri-stated)
  - 100 percent of the analog power supply
  - 80 percent of the analog power supply
  - 50 percent of the analog power supply
  - Ground

Standard Packaging

As should be evident, the Intel HD Audio architecture is designed to allow a wide variety of controllers and codecs from potentially different vendors to operate using a universal software stack. Such a stack might only provide basic functionality. Codec vendors can provide value-add to their products by providing specialized drivers that take advantage of advanced features unique to their codecs.

Continuing this thread of interoperability, the Intel HD Audio specification includes the definition of a 48-pin package for codecs, as shown in Figure 4.16. While this package and pinout is not a requirement, most codec vendors follow it, which allows system integrators to have flexibility in selecting codecs. A motherboard designed to use a 48-pin codec can be populated with any compliant codec. For example, the same motherboard can be used to provide two different audio SKUs, one with basic stereo support and another with support for 7.1 surround sound. The different capabilities result from using a different codec for each SKU.

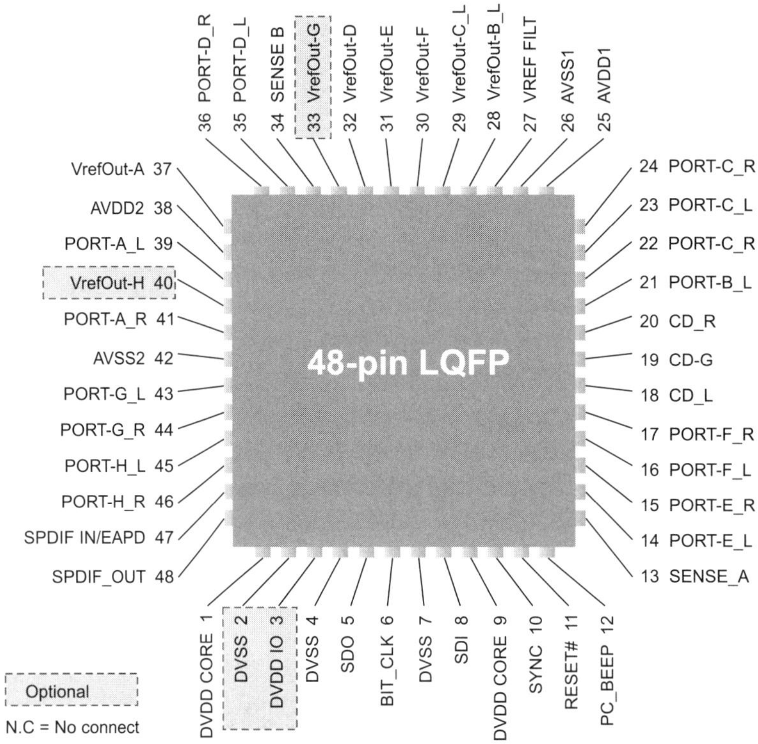

Figure 4.16 Recommended Pinout for 48-Pin Codec Package

Pins, Pin Widgets, and Ports

The word *pin* can be used in different ways when referring to Intel HD Audio systems. Audio software engineers use "pin" in many different contexts, some having nothing to do with audio. For purposes of this discussion, the term applies in the hardware context. But remember that if you hear a software guy using the word pin, it might mean something other than what is described here.

For integrated circuits, the word "pin" has traditionally been used to refer to a physical pin on a codec that is soldered down to a pad on the motherboard. The term *Pin Complex* was introduced in the Intel HD Audio specification to refer to a group of four or more hardware pins which are functionally linked together. You have an analog signal pin for the left stereo channel, an analog signal pin for the right stereo channel, a pin for a switchable microphone bias source, and a SENSE pin that is shared between groups of four analog ports. This functionality context is shown in Figure 4.17. These pins on the codec are often not located together physically, and they may be spread around all four sides of the codec package. See Figure 4.16 for more detail on individual pin locations.

"Pin widget" and "pin complex widget" both refer to the widget control node which controls a particular pin complex. The word *Port* is used to describe the group of physical pins that is associated with an input or output pin widget complex on the codec.

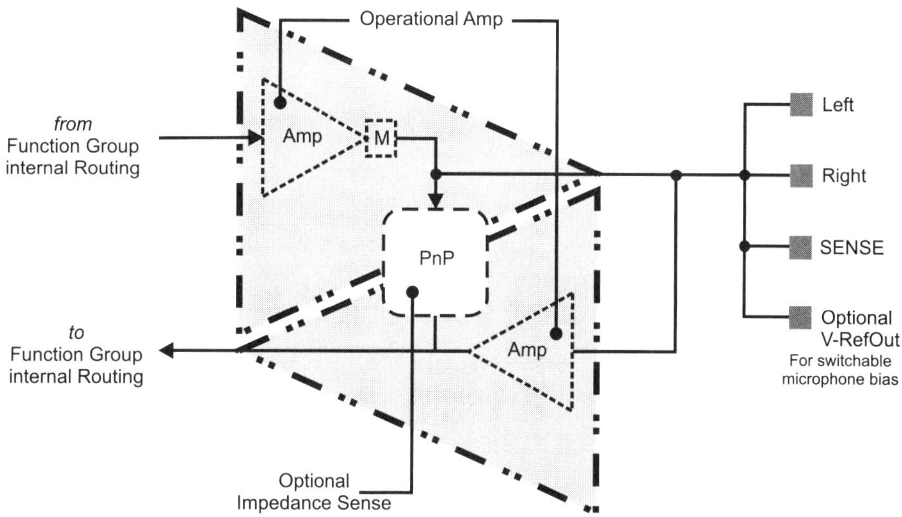

Figure 4.17 A Retaskable Pin Widget with its Related Port Shown on Right

For example, in Table 4.5 you can see that the physical pin numbers for Port A are 39, 41, 37, and 13. Pin 39 is the left audio channel, and pin 41 is the right audio channel. Pin 37 is the switchable microphone bias source (VRefOut_A), and pin 13 is the SENSE pin that is shared with Ports B, C, and D. Microphone bias is not available on ports G and H for this particular codec. Ports A through D share one SENSE pin, while ports E through H share a separate SENSE pin.

The designers of the codec in Figure 4.12 chose to use Widget IDs with hexadecimal values that match the alphabetical port names for the first 6 ports. While this choice is a nice touch that makes it a bit easier to work with ports A thru F, you should not expect to see this type of node-numbering on all codecs.

Table 4.6 combines information from the widget diagram shown in Figure 4.12, the codec pinout shown in Figure 4.16, and current Intel and Microsoft desktop platform recommendations for port assignments and functional color codes. The system should include an Intel HD Audio codec with at least eight analog ports, at least five stereo DAC pairs, and at least two stereo ADC pairs. This configuration is recommended for desktop PCs that are currently in design and production. This example is fully compliant with the Windows Vista Logo program, including multi-streaming support for Real Time Communication (RTC) applications such as VoIP or instant messaging.

You can make your life a lot easier by making a version of this table for each system you are working on, and filling in the appropriate Node ID numbers, hardware pin numbers, colors, and port usages. Check widget node IDs, schematic drawings, jack location and color, and pin configuration settings against this chart. Doing so provides a solid foundation for the pin configurations described next.

Table 4.6 Example of Ports, Pin Widget Node IDs, Pins, Colors, and Usages

Port	Pin Widget Node ID	Codec HW Pins	Color	Recommended Usage
A	0xA	39,41,37,13	Green	Front Panel Headphone Output
B	0xB	21,22,28,13	Pink	Front Panel Microphone Input
C	0xC	23,24,29,13	Blue	Rear Panel Line Input
D	0xD	35,36,32,13	Green	Rear Panel Front L/R pair (for 7.1)
E	0xE	14,15,31,34	Pink	Rear Panel Microphone Input
F	0xF	16,17,30,34	Black	Rear Panel Back L/R pair (for 7.1)
G	0x10	43,44,34	Orange	Rear Panel Center/LFE pair (for 7.1)
H	0x11	45,46,34	Grey	Rear Panel Side L/R pair (for 7.1)
S/PDIF Out	0x21	48	Black	Digital Out
S/PDIF In	0x22	47	Black	Digital In
CD In	0x12	18,19,20	Black	CD In (ATAPI connector on M/B)

The Pin Widget Node ID is usually different for each model of Intel HD Audio codec. This particular table matches the widget diagram in Figure 4.12, and the pinout shown in Figure 4.16. Items highlighted in grey are optional.

Verb Tables

A verb table is a list of 32-bit Intel HD Audio codec command sequences that are compiled into the BIOS as data. Each verb or command to be executed is hard-coded in assembly language as a list of 32-bit data values. This table allows the BIOS to transmit a variable-size list of codec commands in what appears to be a single operation. No mechanism for querying the codec or for error checking exists. The verbs are transmitted blindly. If a particular verb or a particular Node ID is not supported, the codec should skip over those verbs without complaint.

While not a part of the Intel HD Audio specification, verb tables are a very practical part of Intel HD Audio system implementation, and they are supported by most major BIOS vendors that support Intel HD Audio. Verb tables are defined in the *ICH7 Intel HD Audio Programmer's Reference Manual* (PRM); you can find a link to it on this book's companion Web site.[1] Verb tables are usually delivered as text files or code files, and are copied and pasted into the BIOS source code.

The verb table allows the audio team to provide the BIOS engineer with a table of codec commands to execute during system startup and during a return from S3 sleep state, while isolating the BIOS engineer from the details of Intel HD Audio codec implementations and motherboard schematic design. Completion of the verb table integration into the BIOS is a major milestone in the audio system development, since it should allow the Microsoft UAA class driver for Intel HD Audio to be used for bringing up the hardware. The "UAA Class Drivers" section in Chapter 7 contains additional details on the Microsoft UAA class driver for Intel HD Audio.

While verb tables are a handy way to deliver this information to the BIOS developer, verb tables are not particularly readable by humans. For this reason, it is important to provide as many comments as possible along with the code in the verb tables. In the absence of comments, deconstructing verb tables is a lengthy chore requiring your colleagues to consult the Intel HD Audio specification, the codec data sheet, the system schematics, and hexadecimal and binary calculators. This task is not trivial! Provide comments often and in as much detail as possible. The examples in this section contain an appropriate level of detail.

If the motherboard design has stuffing options for more than one codec, the BIOS for that motherboard should contain one verb table for each of the different codecs that might be installed, each of which con-

---

[1] The verb table and code examples in the currently available PRM describe an earlier version of the verb tables that actually are incorporated in many currently available BIOS distributions. Some of the details on how the header is formed are now out of date, but the way that the verbs are defined and placed in the tables remains current.

tains the codec ID as the first entry in the table. The BIOS reads the codec ID and matches it to a BIOS table in this fashion.

To be compliant with the Microsoft UAA class driver for Intel HD Audio under both Windows XP and Windows Vista, the BIOS must include a verb table which contains default pin configuration settings for *all* pin widgets in the codec, regardless of whether they are connected to anything or not. The BIOS must also program the subsystem ID register in the Audio Function Group (AFG). Since each of these registers is a 32-bit register, four verbs are used to program each register, byte by byte. In the case of a codec with eight pin widgets, a minimum of 36 verbs are necessary to program the codec at system startup.

Figure 4.18 shows the first set of four verbs in the verb table, which programs the subsystem ID register. This example sets the 32-bit Subsystem ID register to an arbitrary value of `0xAABBCCDD`. (See Chapter 7 for info on what values to use in a real system.) The four different verbs in this list are all directed to Node ID `0x01` on Codec ID#2, which is connected to the SDI#2 pin of the Intel HD Audio controller. This node is the audio function group for the entire codec, where the Subsystem ID register is located.

```
;Audio function group  (NID=01h), SDI#2
; set the 32-bit subsystem ID by writing four bytes to
; successive addresses. This examples writes 0xAABBCCDD
; to the subsystem ID register of the codec
;
: the four verbs to accomplish this are defined below
; with each of the 32-bit verbs stored as 32-bit data

      dd    201720DDh         ; Set bits  7:0  to 0xDD
      dd    201721CCh         ; Set bits 15:8  to 0xCC
      dd    201722BBh         ; Set bits 23:16 to 0xBB
      dd    201723AAh         ; Set bits 31:24 to 0xAA
```

Figure 4.18 Simple Verb Table Written in Assembly Language

To understand this list better, try breaking the first verb into its component parts:

```
2 01 720 DD
       0x2   = Codec ID number, that is the number of the
               SDI Pin to which the codec is wired
       0x01  = Node ID number
       0x720 = 12-bit command: write to bits 0:7 of
```

```
            the subsystem ID
    0xDD  = 8-bit payload
```

The second command in Figure 4.18 works in the same way, but uses a verb code of 0x721 to write the payload of 0xCC to bits 15:8 of the subsystem ID register in the codec, and so on down the list. Interestingly enough, it is possible to read all 32 bits of most codec registers in a single operation, but writing to them usually requires four separate operations.

Sending Verb Tables to the Codec

At startup, the BIOS reads the codec vendor ID and the codec ID, and possibly the codec revision ID, and then searches through a list of verb tables until it finds a verb table with a matching codec ID. If successful, the BIOS transmits the entire verb table to the codec. It also does this on returning from the S3 state.

A BIOS intended for desktop motherboards may also include logic or multiple verb tables to determine how to program pin widgets allocated to the front panel connectors that are optional on many new models. The BIOS can use a GPIO on the Southbridge to determine whether a front panel dongle is present. (See more details in Chapter 5, "Front Panel Considerations.") Additional logic in the BIOS is used to determine how to configure the pin widgets servicing the front panel. If the system has no front panel connectors, the BIOS sets the pin widgets to No Connectivity. If the front panel dongle is the older AC97 style dongle, with no presence to detect, the pin widgets are programmed to indicate no jack detect capability. Be aware that this implementation is not Vista-compliant.

While the driver normally is charged with maintaining the codec state during S3, you have no guarantee that a driver will be present and loaded during the transition into and out of S3, so for consistency the BIOS must always retransmit the verb table any time that power to the codec is removed and then restored. Otherwise, the Plug and Play ID becomes corrupted after resuming from S3, and the driver is unable to load.

If the system is using the codec hardware defaults or if the codec's digital power supply is kept powered up during S3, re-transmitting the verb tables when coming out of S3 is unnecessary; in all other cases the BIOS should retransmit the verb tables.

When coming out of S3, you have an additional consideration if a modem codec or other Intel HD Audio device generates a wake event. Because the OS needs to know which device caused the wake event, the BIOS must perform the following sequence when resuming from S3.

1. Store the contents of the controller's STATESTS State Change Status register, which contains info on which (if any) Intel HD Audio device caused the wake event.
2. Take the controller out of reset, program the configuration default and optionally, program the mute registers.
3. Restore the original STATESTS register contents.
4. Put the controller and Intel HD Audio link back into reset.

This sequence should restore everything in the codec to the state it was in when the wakeup event occurred, with the exception of the new values contained in the verb table.

Muting and Startup Work-arounds

One of the proposed requirements for Windows Vista Logo is for the BIOS to mute outputs during the power-up sequence. While not specifically defined in the PRM, the verb table mechanism can be used for this purpose. To mute a widget, you must send a verb which specifies the codec ID, the widget node ID, a Set Amplifier Gain/Mute command (`0x3`) and a 16-bit payload of `0xF080`. For instance, to mute the widget at Node ID `0x04` on codec ID #2, you would send `0x2043F080`. This value mutes both input and output volumes on both the right and left channels of the widget, as well as setting the volume controls on each pin widget to their lowest settings.

It's important to send these mute messages to the proper widgets. By studying Figure 4.12, you can see that the volume controls are implemented in the DAC widgets rather than in the pin widgets, which means that in this codec a mute command sent to a pin widget is simply ignored. Instead, you must send series of mute commands to all the DACs in the codec, as shown in Figure 4.19.

```
; MUTE ALL DACS on Codec ID #2
;
; the verbs are formed in groups of four in case the BIOS
; uses the count of pin widgets to determine how big the
; verb table is. The pin widget count should be increased
; by two to accommodate these additional commands
; The second group of 4 includes some repeated to make 4
```

```
;
dd     2023F080h            ; Mute DAC at Node 0x02
dd     2033F080h            ; Mute DAC at Node 0x03
dd     2043F080h            ; Mute DAC at Node 0x04
dd     2053F080h            ; Mute DAC at Node 0x05

dd     2063F080h            ; Mute DAC at Node 0x06
dd     2063F080h            ; Mute DAC at Node 0x06 (repeat)
dd     2063F080h            ; Mute DAC at Node 0x06 (repeat)
dd     2063F080h            ; Mute DAC at Node 0x06 (repeat)
```

Figure 4.19 List of Eight Verbs Which Will Mute All DACs in the Codec

Unlike the pin-configuration registers, the mute for each pin widget can be set with a single 32-bit verb, rather than a set of 4 verbs. If the BIOS requires you to specify the number of pin widgets in the verb table, you can fool it into supporting mute verbs by telling it that you have one or two additional pin widgets. You would add one to this count for every four mute verbs that you want to send. If you have an odd number of mute verbs to send, simply repeat the last one until they line up in sets of four. Some BIOS versions may use a terminator such as 0xFFFFFFFF to signify the end of the verb table, rather than specifying a count in the header. In this case, you can easily add as many verbs as you like without needing to restrict them to sets of four verbs.

Be sure to account for analog PC beep if it is implemented. For instance, if you want to be able to hear POST tones coming from the stereo outputs on the rear of the system, don't send a mute verb to that pin widget. Instead, you might send a verb that configures the output appropriately for the intended usage. If you are purposefully un-muting an output so that POST tones can be heard at startup, DO NOT set the volume control to unity gain. Instead, set it to 25 or 30 decibels of attenuation, so that if the system is attached to a high-powered speaker system, that the POST tones don't damage the speakers or the listener's ears. See "Hardware Volume Scaling" earlier in this chapter for more details on how to do so.

While the pin widgets may not contain volume controls, you can approximate a mute in many cases by disabling the pin widget's input and output circuits by writing to the Pin Widget Control register for each pin widget, as shown in Figure 4.20.

```
; Set all Pin Widgets on Codec ID #2
; to disable input, output, and VRefOut
```

```
;
; the verbs are formed in groups of four in case the BIOS
; uses the count of pin widgets to determine how big the
; verb table is. The pin widget count in the BIOS should
; increase by two to accommodate these additional verbs
;
dd     20A70700h          ; Disable Pin Widget 0x0A
dd     20B70700h          ; Disable Pin Widget 0x0B
dd     20C70700h          ; Disable Pin Widget 0x0C
dd     20D70700h          ; Disable Pin Widget 0x0D

dd     20E70700h          ; Disable Pin Widget 0x0E
dd     20F70700h          ; Disable Pin Widget 0x0F
dd     21070700h          ; Disable Pin Widget 0x10
dd     21170700h          ; Disable Pin Widget 0x11
```

Figure 4.20 Verb List to Disable Input, Output and VRefOut for All Pin Widgets

Notice that disabling a pin widget or muting the codec is not guaranteed to be a noise-free event, although it should be the case for a well-designed codec. In some cases, especially with a poorly designed codec, you might find that setting the mutes or disabling the pin widget ends up causing more noise than if you didn't write to the widget all. A number of factors come in to play in this situation, including the power supply sequencing and the rise time of the codec's DC levels for analog output and VRefOut.

Also remember that when the driver loads it may reset the Intel HD Audio link. If this happens, the codec registers return to their default state. This reset could also cause a pop or noise when abruptly changing from the settings written by the verb table at startup. You can isolate each noise source by disabling the audio driver, then removing power from the entire system.

After waiting at least one minute for all capacitors to drain off, start the system while listening through a good pair of speakers or headphones. Any noise that you hear is a function of the codec coming out of reset, the power supplies starting up, or the verb tables being written to the codec. Try changing the verb tables to see if this changes the noise behavior. Once you've characterized the startup noise sources, re-enable the driver. Any noises that you hear when the driver is started (and the codec is reset) could have an interaction with the verb table s programmed at startup. Try leaving out messages to the Amplifier/Mute register and the Pin Widget Control to further identify any interaction.

This ability to arbitrarily configure the codec at system startup can be very useful in cases where you are having problems with pops, clicks, or noises at startup before the driver loads. If you are using the Microsoft UAA class driver for Intel HD Audio, this period before the driver loads may be one of the few places where you can address these pops and clicks. You may want to experiment with other settings of the various pin widget controls. Each make and model of codec is likely to have some variation in how it responds to various settings while being powered up and initialized.

Sometimes, special cases require other verbs to be sent to the codec at initialization time, before the driver has been loaded, to address specific behaviors. Just about any command to the codec can be routed through verb tables, as long as it doesn't require any knowledge of the current codec state.

Pin Configuration Registers

The Pin Widget or Pin Widget Complex mentioned earlier has a special place in the relationship between Intel HD Audio and Microsoft's Universal Audio Architecture (UAA). The Microsoft UAA class driver for Intel HD Audio and some codec-vendor-specific drivers use the information that the BIOS programs into the Pin Configuration registers to determine the schematic design and layout of the audio subsystem and to automatically configure the driver topology based on the pin-configuration registers. Future versions of Linux drivers might also make use of these registers.

To meet both Windows XP and Windows Vista Logo requirements, the BIOS must program valid pin-configuration defaults into each pin widget contained in the codec. The codec hardware also has default configurations hard-coded into each of the codec's pin widgets, but these default configurations are only valid if the motherboard has been wired identically to the schematic used to generate the configuration defaults.

In almost all cases, the motherboard design does not match the codec's default pin configurations, so the BIOS has to program the pin-configuration registers during system boot-up. Often, the codec vendor provides the pin configuration defaults as part of the schematic review process. Like the Subsystem ID, each 32-bit configuration register requires four separate 8-bit writes to set the register, as shown in Table 4.7.

Table 4.7 Pin Configuration Default Register Fields

31:30	29:24	23:20	19:16	15:12	11:8	7:4	3:0
Connectivity	Location	Device	Connector	Color	Misc	Association	Sequence

The grey shading indicates each of the 8-bit segments used when writing to this register

The BIOS must therefore send four verbs for the subsystem ID, and an additional four verbs for each pin widget or port on the codec, regardless of whether the port is connected to anything or not. Figure 4.21 shows an example of a partial verb table which sets the pin configuration defaults that are shown in Table 4.8. A similar sequence must be repeated for each pin widget in the codec, whether it is connected to anything or not.

Be aware that the Subsystem ID Register and the Pin Configuration Default registers in each pin widget are not touched during a reset from any source, while other registers in the codec are reset to their default values upon a function group reset. The contents of these registers are only lost when digital power is removed from the codec; the BIOS must restore these registers when power is restored to the codec's digital power supply.

```
; Front Panel HP Out uses port A (NodeID = 0xA, SDI#2)
; Set Node ID 0x0A Pin Configs to 0x02214070
dd 20A71C70h ; Set 7:0   to 0x70 - Assoc 7, Seq 0
dd 20A71D40h ; Set 15:8  to 0x40 - Green, Jack Detect
dd 20A71E21h ; Set 23:16 to 0x21 - HP Out, 3.5 mm jack
dd 20A71F02h ; Set 31:24 to 0x02 - Front, chassis
```

Figure 4.21 Verb table and Pin Configuration for an Independent Stereo HP Out Jack on Front Panel

Table 4.8 Pin Configuration for an Independent Headphone Out Jack on Front Panel

Connectivity	Loc	Device	Type	Color	Jack Detect	Assoc	Seq
Chassis Jack	Front	HP Out	3.5 mm	Green	Yes (0)	7	0

For the most part, the individual fields of the Configuration Default register are independent of each other. These fields are sufficient to describe a static configuration, but they do not contain enough information to fully describe a retaskable jack.

The Port Connectivity field, shown in Table 4.9, allows you to specify whether the port is disconnected, connected to a jack, or connected directly to an integrated device such as a microphone or speaker amplifier. Though the Intel HD Audio specification allows for both a jack and an internal device to be attached to a single port, this configuration is not fully supported by the Microsoft UAA class driver for Intel HD Audio and should be avoided.

Table 4.9 Port Connectivity (Bits 31:30) of Pin Configuration Default Register

Bits 31:30	Value
00b	Port is connected to a jack (3.5 mm, ATAPI, RCA, etc)
01b	No physical connection for Port
10b	A fixed function device (integrated speaker, integrated mic, etc.) is attached.
11b	Both a jack and an internal device are attached. (Not recommended)

Note: Port connectivity settings that are highlighted in gray are not recommended.

The Location field consists of two subfields. Bits 29:28 are used to indicated whether the port is on the primary chassis, an external chassis, internal to the PC (not user accessible), or "Other," which includes microphones on the PC lid. Bits 27:24 are interpreted differently based on the contents of bits 29:24. This alternative results in a very large table of supported devices when decoded, but only a small subset of these possible devices is actually used in modern PCs. Most motherboard designs use only those locations not highlighted in gray in Table 4.10.

The Microsoft UAA class driver for Intel HD Audio uses the locations to build logical names for jacks, as well as to group related topologies. WHQL tests enforce Logo requirements by ensuring that two or more jacks of the same color are never in the same location or in the same association. It's OK to have a pink microphone input jack on the front, and another pink microphone input jack on the rear, but it's not OK to have two pink jacks on the front, next to each other.

When the Port connectivity bits are set to "jack" (`0x00`), the value in the high byte of the Pin Configuration Default register directly reads out the location. This result is true for any byte value for bits 31:24 that comes up to less than `0x40`.

Table 4.10 Location / Connectivity (Bits 29:24) of Configuration Default Register

b31:24	b31:30	b29:28	b27:24	Value
01h	00b	00b	1h	External jack on primary chassis: Rear
02h	00b	00b	2h	External jack on primary chassis: Front
03h	00b	00b	3h	External jack on primary chassis: Left
04h	00b	00b	4h	External jack on primary chassis: Right
05h	00b	00b	5h	External jack on primary chassis: Top
06h	00b	00b	6h	External jack n primary chassis: Bottom
08h	00b	00b	8h	External jack on primary chassis: Drive bay
18h	10b	01b	8h	HDMI Integrated (Direct S/PDIF trace to HDMI Encoder)
19h	00b	01b	9h	ATAPI Jack on motherboard
90h	10b	01b	0h	Internal: Speaker
B7h	10b	11b	7h	Other: Mic Inside Mobile Lid
B8h	10b	11b	8h	Other: Mic Outside Mobile Lid

Note: Uncommon combinations are highlighted in gray, and should be avoided. See Intel HD Audio Specification for complete description of the Location field.

The Default Device field shown in Table 4.11 describes the different functions that might be connected to a port. You rarely use any of the devices highlighted in gray in a modern motherboard. Items highlighted in gray are not supported by the Microsoft UAA class driver for Intel HD Audio.

Be sure to use speaker category only for devices that drive an amplifier that is outside the codec but inside the PC chassis. Either the speaker should be in the PC chassis as well, or it should be a passive 8-ohm speaker connected directly to speaker clips on the PC chassis, much like a stereo receiver. Devices such as self-powered 5.1 speaker systems that are connected through line-out jacks should be designated as line-out, not as speaker.

Table 4.11 Default Device (Bits 23:20) of Pin Configuration Default Register

Bits 23:20	Value
0h	Line Output Jack
1h	Internal Speaker (amplifier is built into PC chassis)
2h	Headphone Output Jack

Bits 23:20	Value
3h	*Analog CD Input (via ATAPI connector)*
4h	S/PDIF Out (optical or coaxial)
5h	Digital Other Out
6h	Modem Line Side
7h	Modem Handset Side
8h	Line Input Jack
9h	*Aux*
Ah	Microphone Input
Bh	Telephony
Ch	*S/PDIF In* (optical or coaxial)
Dh	Digital Other In
Eh	Reserved
Fh	Other

Note: Items highlighted in gray are not supported by the UAA class driver. Less common devices shown in italics should be avoided when possible.

The Connection Type field detailed in Table 4.12 describes the type of connector that is used. In practice, the highlighted subset of these connector types is rarely used on modern PCs.

The Microsoft UAA class driver for Intel HD Audio sets the outputs to a fixed maximum volume output level when an RCA jack is specified and the device type is set to Line Out. It labels the audio endpoint as *line connectors*, to indicate a multi-channel A/V receiver.

An RCA jack can also be used as digital connector for S/PDIF signals. The same connector code (`0x4`) is used in this case, but the device field is set to either S/PDIF In or S/PDIF Out, rather than Line In or Line Out. The Microsoft Intel HD Audio UAA Class Driver handles volume controls differently when an RCA jack is used, and it also displays a different name for the audio endpoint, which is typically a multi-channel A/V receiver.

The XLR connector is very useful for connecting professional microphones. It is typically mounted in a 5-inch wide content-creation audio bay on the front of the PC, in the spot where a CD or hard drive might otherwise be mounted. The XLR connector does not inherently have a jack detection mechanism, so this type of input should be treated as always connected.

Even though it's not indicated in the table, it's ok to specify a quarter-inch headphone jack on a content creation bay. As long as the quarter-inch jack is wired the same way that the 3.5-millimeter jack is wired for jack detection, this configuration will work well. Other standard quarter-inch jack configurations used in the audio industry do not match the way that 3.5-millimeter jacks are used on the PC. For instance, no pro-audio equipment uses a stereo quarter-inch phone jack for stereo line in. Instead, two quarter-inch jacks would be used for that purpose. In the audio industry, quarter-inch stereo jacks are more likely to be connected in a balanced configuration, which is rarely used in PC designs. Using quarter-inch jacks improperly can cause lots of confusion, and should be avoided.

Future versions of the Microsoft UAA class driver for Intel HD Audio could make use of these connector types, but these settings have little effect on the UAA class driver which ships with Windows Vista.

Table 4.12 Connection Type (Bits 19:16) of Pin Configuration Default Register

Bits 19:16	Value
0h	Unknown
1h	3.5 mm stereo/mono phone jack (incorrectly referred to as 1/8")
2h	¼" stereo/mono phone jack
3h	ATAPI Internal
4h	RCA jack (may be used for analog audio or for coaxial S/PDIF)
5h	EIAJ Optical or TOSLINK† connector for S/PDIF or ADAT
6h	Other Digital
7h	Other Analog
8h	Multi-channel Analog (DIN)
9h	XLR/Professional
Ah	RJ-11 (Modem)
Bh	Combination
Ch - Eh	Undefined
Fh	Other

Note: Uncommon connectors are highlighted in grey, and should be avoided.

Some classes of Microsoft Vista Logo compliance call for specific colors to be used for the various standard analog audio inputs and outputs on a PC. In addition to defining these colors, the Intel HD Audio specification also defines some additional colors which are not used for audio jacks on systems conforming to Vista Logo requirements. Avoid colors that are highlighted in Table 4.13 to help prevent WHQL failures.

Table 4.13 Color (Bits 15:12) of Pin Configuration Default Register

Bits 19:16	Value	Standard Usage	Associated Device
0h	Unknown	n/a	Don't Use
1h	Black	Rear Surround L/R	Line Out
2h	Grey	Side Surround L/R	Line Out
3h	Blue	Line In L/R	Line In
4h	Green	Line Out or HP Out L/R	Line Out or HP Out
5h	Red	Not used for audio 3.5mm jacks	Don't Use
6h	Orange	Center/LFE	Line Out
7h	Yellow	Not used for audio 3.5mm jacks	Don't Use
8h	Purple	Not used for audio 3.5mm jacks	Don't Use
9h	Pink	Microphone in mono or stereo	Microphone In
Ah - Dh	Reserved	n/a	Don't Use
Eh	White	Not used for audio 3.5mm jacks	Don't Use
Fh	Other	n/a	Don't Use

Note: Colors that are not Windows Vista Logo-compliant are highlighted in gray. Avoid using any of these colors in your pin configuration defaults.

Three of the four bits designated as Misc are currently undefined, and only one of the four is defined. This Jack Detect override bit is tricky, because it uses negative logic.

If the Jack Detect override bit is set, it indicates to the audio driver that it is not possible to detect jack insertion events on this jack. This result could be from using a connector that does not include an isolated switch, such as an RCA or XLR connector.

To meet Windows Vista Logo requirements, all 3.5-millimeter analog jacks must set the Jack Detection Override bit designated in Table 4.14 to zero, indicating that Jack Detection is present both in the codec and that the jacks on the motherboard have switches and are wired properly, even for front panel jacks. Analog outputs using RCA jacks and a device type of Line Out may set this bit to one, indicating that a switch on the jack is not present.

Table 4.14 Misc (Bits 11:8) of Pin Configuration Default Register

Bits 11:8	Value
00h	Jack detection through SENSE pins
01h	No jack detection implemented
2h – 7h	Reserved

Note: The 1.0 Intel HD Audio specification defines only bit 8 of the Misc fields. Bit 8 should be set whenever jack detection is not implemented for any reason. Setting Bit 8 on analog I/O ports may result in a WHQL failure under Windows Vista

Associations and Sequences

Each audio endpoint in complete system is defined by a separate association and sequence. Associations in the range of `0x1` through `0xE` can be used for multi-channel or stereo applications. Association `0xF` is reserved only for devices which expose a single pin widget. Each association must have a unique number. Although several pin widgets might use Association `0xF`, the Microsoft UAA class driver for Intel HD Audio treats each of the pin widgets in this association as a separate stereo device. The associations are evaluated in priority order, with association `0x1` having the highest priority and association `0xF` having the lowest priority.

The association is stored in Bits 7:4 of the Pin Configuration Default register. Associations that describe multi-channel audio streams can be represented by a 4-bit hexadecimal number from `0x01` to `0x0E`. Association `0x00` is reserved, and association `0x0F` is limited to a single pin widget. The sequence is stored in Bits 3:0 of the Pin Configuration Default register. A sequence must be unique in any particular association. Some special sequence values also are used to indicate specific behavior.

Associations built from a single pin widget should always use #0. Examples are Stereo Headphone Out, Stereo Line Input, Stereo (or mono) microphone input, Stereo Line Out, Stereo S/PDIF In, and Stereo S/PDIF Out. Multi-channel streams can be created by setting several pin widgets to the same association, and then using the Sequence numbers to define the individual channel pairs in the stream.

Associations can also be used to describe ADC multiplexer (Mux) inputs, ADC mixer (mix) inputs, mic arrays, and redirected headphone configurations. The audio driver uses the associations to determine how to make connections and allocate resources inside the codec. The audio driver evaluates each Association in numerical priority, starting with Association 0x01 and ending with Association `0x0F`.

Table 4.15 shows a possible set of association assignments for a complete system. If you prefer, you can mix and match any way that you would like, but you should try to set up a numbering scheme that is consistent across multiple systems, for ease of understanding, and that takes association priorities into account. Starting with one and skipping every other association number, as shown in the table, allows you to easily reorder priorities without renumbering the entire table.

Table 4.15 Example of a Set of Association Assignments in a Typical System

Association	Value
0h	Reserved, Do Not Use
1h	Integrated Stereo Speaker Pair
3h	Rear Panel Primary Line Out (may be stereo, 5.1, or 7.1)
5h	Rear Panel Primary Stereo Line In or ADC Mux In
7h	Front Panel Secondary Stereo HP Out
9h	Front Panel Secondary Stereo Mic In Jack
Ah	Rear Panel Stereo S/PDIF Out
Ch	Rear Panel Stereo S/PDIF In

Note: No standard requires this ordering, but you may wish to keep consistent between different models for ease of understanding.

One or more examples of each of these assignments follow. The association numbers shown in the examples match Table 4.15. You can use these examples to create your own verb table s directly.

Stereo Stream Associations

An association consisting of a single pin widget should always specify a sequence of zero. The association number should be unique, with the exception of `0x0F`, which supports multiple stereo associations. The example in Table 4.16 shows an association consisting of a single blue 3.5-millimeter stereo Line In jack on the rear panel of the computer.

Table 4.16 Pin Configuration for Rear Panel Line Input

Connectivity	Loc	Device	Type	Color	Jack Detect	Assoc	Seq
Chassis Jack	Rear	Line In	3.5 mm	Blue	Yes (0x0)	5	0

Note: See Appendix A for complete verb tables for this association.

While Table 4.16 shows the entire contents of the pin widget's default configuration register, this information is not enough by itself. The entries in the actual verb table also need to know the codec ID and the Node ID of the pin widget. For your convenience, completely assembled verb tables for each of the Pin Configurations shown in this chapter are available in Appendix A. These examples all assume that the Codec ID is #2 and that the Node IDs of the codec are the same as those shown in the widget diagram in Figure 4.12, where you can see that Node ID `0x0C` is used for Port C.

In this example, the pin widget attached to Port C is targeted. The Codec ID of `0x2` and the Node ID of `0x0C` can be seen at the beginning of each of the four commands in the verb list in Figure 4.22.

```
; Rear Panel Line In is port C (NodeID = 0x0C, SDI#2)
; Set Node ID 0x0C Pin Configs to 0x01813050
dd 20C71C50h ; Set 7:0   to 0x50 - Assoc 5, Seq 0
dd 20C71D30h ; Set 15:8  to 0x30 - Blue, Jack Detect
dd 20C71E81h ; Set 23:16 to 0x81 - Line In, 3.5 mm jack
dd 20C71F01h ; Set 31:24 to 0x01 - Rear, chassis
```

This verb list matches the line inputs in Table 4.16.

Figure 4.22 Verb List for Rear Panel Line Input Configuration

Table 4.17 shows the pin configuration for a green line-out jack on the rear of the computer. In this case port D is used, which is also assigned to Node ID 0x0D in the codec. In the corresponding verb table in Appendix A, you can see the "20D" at the beginning of each verb in the table. This pin configuration assumes that jack detection is wired correctly on the motherboard.

Table 4.17 Pin Configuration for Rear Panel Line Output

Connectivity	Loc	Device	Type	Color	Jack Detect	Assoc	Seq
Chassis Jack	Rear	Line Out	3.5 mm	Green	Yes (0x0)	3	0

Note: See Appendix A for an example of a completed verb table for this association.

Table 4.8 showed the pin configuration for a green headphone jack on the front of the computer. Node ID `0x0A` is used for this pin widget. Notice that a differently numbered association is used to denote the front panel headphone jack from the rear line out. This differentiation provides the option for a multi-streaming output configuration. This pin configuration assumes that the specified port is capable of driving headphones, that coupling capacitors large enough to drive headphones are present, and that jack detection has been wired correctly on the motherboard.

Table 4.18 shows the pin configuration for an independent micro phone input jack using Node ID `0x0B`, which in this case is also Port B. This configuration assumes that the microphone bias circuit and the jack detection circuit are configured properly on the motherboard.

Table 4.18 Pin Configuration for Front Panel Microphone Input

Connectivity	Loc	Device	Type	Color	Jack Detect	Assoc	Seq
Chassis Jack	Front	Mic In	3.5 mm	Pink	Yes	9	0

Note: See Appendix A for an example of a completed verb table for this association.

Table 4.19 describes a digital S/PDIF optical output jack using Node ID 0x15. No SENSE pin is associated with S/PDIF Out, so the Jack Detect bit is set to `0x1`, which indicates that jack detection is not available for this jack.

Table 4.19 Pin Configuration for Rear Panel S/PDIF Output

Connectivity	Loc	Device	Type	Color	Jack Detect	Assoc	Seq
Chassis Jack	Rear	S/PDIF Out	Optical	Black	No (0x1)	A	0

Note: See Appendix A for an example of a completed verb table for this association.

You should be able to put together a complete system featuring separate stereo input and output circuits on front and rear panels by using the preceding examples. Be sure to check the codec data sheet for the proper Node IDs for each pin widget, as they vary from codec to codec.

5.1 Surround Multi-channel Stream Association

Surround sound output with five satellite channels and a subwoofer can be accomplished by assigning three stereo line-out ports to the same association, but with unique sequence numbers for each pin widget in the association. Sequence numbers often have unique meanings; you cannot assign them arbitrarily as you can with association numbers. Additional information on multi-channel speaker configurations can be found in Chapter 7.

When used together in a single association, the set of sequence numbers (0, 1, 2) defines a 6-speaker configuration as shown on the left side of Figure 4.23, with speakers located at the Front Left (FL), Front Right (FR), Front Center (FC), Low Frequency Effects (LFE), Back Left (BL), and Back Right (BR) positions.

Similarly, sequence numbers (0, 1, 4) represent a 6-speaker configuration with speakers located at the FL, FR, FC, LFE, Side Left (SL), and Side Left (SR) positions, as shown on the right side of Figure 4.23.

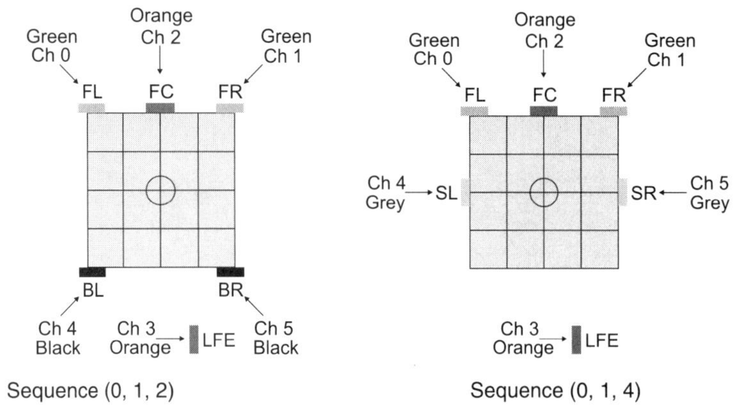

Figure 4.23 5.1 Surround Sequences for a Multi-channel Association

The Speaker Configuration control panel in Windows does not distinguish between the two 5.1 speaker configurations shown in Figure 4.23, which differ only in whether BL and BR speakers are used in place of SL and SR speakers. The control panel uses the label *5.1 surround sound speakers* to identify either configuration. The reason for not distinguishing between the back-speaker and side-speaker configurations in the control panel is that most listeners don't distinguish between these speaker positions, so having two different settings doesn't make a lot of sense.

Sequence (0, 1, 4) is the preferred configuration for Windows Vista. This configuration assumes that all ports in the association have jack detection circuitry implemented on the motherboard. Table 4.20 details the settings for this configuration.

Table 4.20 Pin Configuration for 5.1 Surround Line Outputs Using Sequence (0, 1, 2)

Connectivity	Loc	Device	Type	Color	Jack Detect	Assoc	Seq
Chassis Jack	Rear	Line Out	3.5 mm	Green	Yes (0x0)	3	0
Chassis Jack	Rear	Line Out	3.5 mm	Orange	Yes (0x0)	3	1
Chassis Jack	Rear	Line Out	3.5 mm	Black	Yes (0x0)	3	2

Note: The choice of sequence number determines the function of each port, which must be matched with the proper color for that function. See Appendix A for an example of a completed verb table for this association.

7.1 Surround Multi-channel Stream Association

Sequence numbers (0, 1, 2, 4) represent an 8-speaker configuration with speakers located at the FL, FR, FC, LFE, BL, BR, SL, and SR positions, as shown in Figure 4.24. Sequence 3 must not be used in this configuration. The *7.1 home theater speakers* configuration should be selected in the Advanced Audio Properties Speakers tab for use with this type of association.

Sequence numbers (0, 1, 2, 3) and (0, 1, 3, 4) represent now-obsolete multi-channel configurations known as *7.1 wide configuration speakers*. These sequences should not be used for new designs, nor should the speaker configuration control panel be used with this setting unless the speaker configuration is truly set up in this fashion.

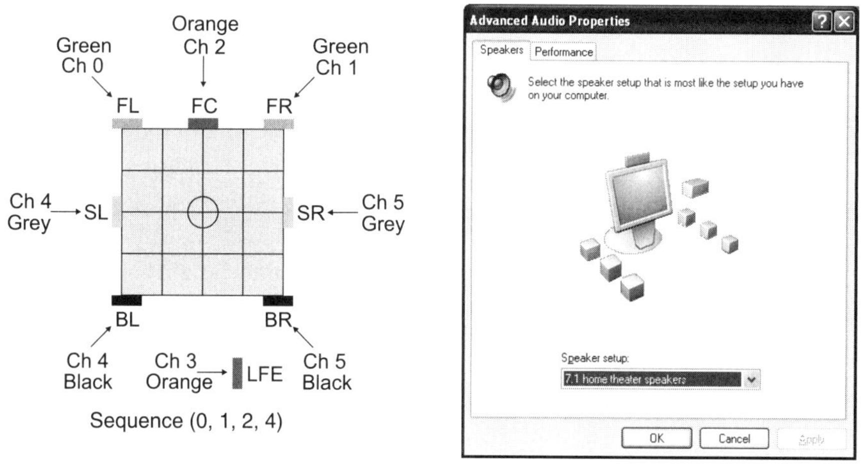

Figure 4.24 7.1 Home Theater Sequence for a Multi-Channel Association

Table 4.21 details the pin configuration defaults for the 7.1 home theater speaker configuration. Be aware that Microsoft uses the term *Home Theater* to denote a 7.1 configuration, while Dolby† uses *Home Theater* to denote a 5.1 configuration, and *Master Studio* to refer to 7.1.

Sequence (0, 1, 2, 4) is very similar to the recommended sequence of (0, 1, 2) for 5.1 surround. The addition of the grey side surround speaker jacks is the only difference. In sequence (0, 1, 2, 4), sequence 0 is always front (green), sequence 1 is always Center/LFE (orange), sequence 2 is always Rear Surround (black), and sequence 4 is always side surround (grey).

Table 4.21 Pin Configuration for 7.1 Surround Line Outputs using Sequence (0, 1, 2, 4)

Connectivity	Loc	Device	Type	Color	Jack Detect	Assoc	Seq
Chassis Jack	Rear	Line Out	3.5 mm	Green	Yes (0x0)	3	0
Chassis Jack	Rear	Line Out	3.5 mm	Orange	Yes (0x0)	3	1
Chassis Jack	Rear	Line Out	3.5 mm	Black	Yes (0x0)	3	2
Chassis Jack	Rear	Line Out	3.5 mm	Grey	Yes (0x0)	3	4

Note: The choice of sequence number determines the function of each port, which must be matched with the proper color for that function. See Appendix A for an example of a completed verb table for this association.

Resource Sharing

UAA guidelines generally discourage sharing of codec resources, such as ADCs and DACs, between multiple pin widgets because they might not always be available. This practice could be a cause of significant user confusion. A DAC or ADC should have an exclusive path to one and only one pin widget. The port controlled by that pin widget should be connected to one and only one jack or integrated device. This exclusivity allows the Microsoft UAA class driver for Intel HD Audio's topology parser to consistently and uniquely identify each audio endpoint.

The three exceptions to this rule support usability models that have long been established on the PC. In each case, a single DAC or ADC is associated with multiple pin widgets. Sequence numbers `0xE` and `0xF` are used to indicate this shared usage. While these special cases are not defined in the Intel HD Audio specification, they are part of the requirements for Microsoft's UAA Intel HD Audio class driver compatibility and are consistent with the Intel HD Audio specification.

Redirected Headphone Association

One common usage for headphones is that plugging headphones into the headphone jack disables the built-in speakers or the line-out jacks on the rear panel, as shown in Figure 4.25. In this case, the signal from the DAC at widget ID# 2 would switch from the line-out jack to the headphone-out jack whenever headphones are plugged in, and switch back when the headphones are unplugged, un-muting the line out again.

If a multi-channel configuration is used for line out, like that shown in Table 4.21, then plugging in the headphone would mute all of the multi-channel outputs on the same association. Depending on the driver configuration and what's playing, the headphones may contain only the Front Left and Front Right signals, or they may contain a mix of all the channels that are playing in the stream.

To use this configuration, you must use a DAC which is capable of being routed to either of the two pin widgets. The sequence number for the redirected headphone must always be `0xF`, which indicates to the Microsoft UAA class driver for Intel HD Audio topology parser that a redirected headphone configuration is being requested.

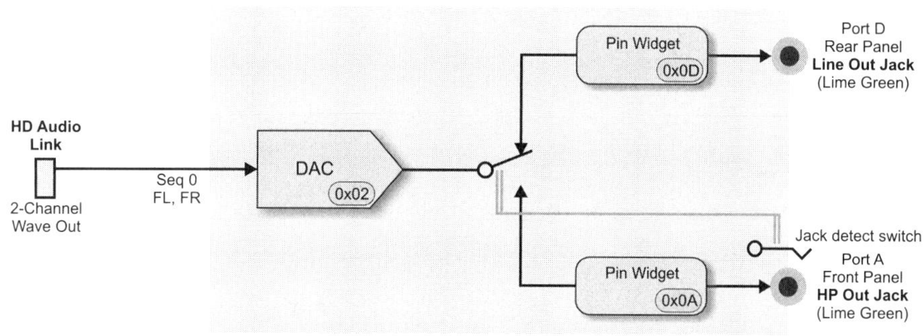

The DAC is routed to only one pin widget at a time. If the headphone jack is plugged in, then the signal from the DAC is routed to the Front Headphone Out and the Rear Line Out is disconnected. If the headphone jack is not plugged in, then the signal is routed to the Rear Line Out and the Front Headphone Out is disconnected.

Figure 4.25 Line Out jack and Headphone Out jack sharing a single DAC in a Redirected Headphone configuration

The redirected headphone configuration is shown in Table 4.22. Both jacks in this case are green, but this use of the same color complies with Logo requirements because one is on the front and one is on the rear.

Both jacks should support jack detection to meet Windows Vista Logo requirements, though the redirected function still works if only the headphone jack supports detection.

Table 4.22 Pin Configuration for Rear Panel Line Out with Redirected Front Panel HP Out

Connectivity	Loc	Device	Type	Color	Jack Detect	Assoc	Seq
Chassis Jack	Rear	Line Out	3.5 mm	Green	Yes (0x0)	3	0
Chassis Jack	Front	HP Out	3.5 mm	Green	Yes (0x0)	3	F

Note: See Appendix A for an example of a completed verb table for this association.

A similar configuration is desirable for PCs with a built-in speaker and a headphone jack. It matches the way that TVs and radios with a headphone work, muting the built-in speaker whenever headphones are plugged in. Figure 4.26 shows the block diagram of this configuration.

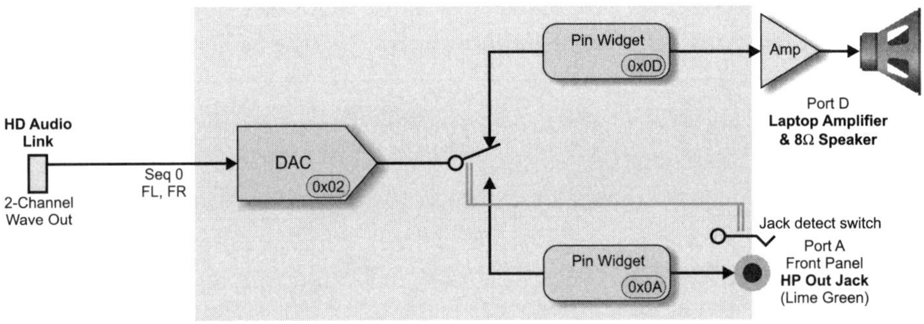

Figure 4.26 Internal Speaker with Redirected Headphone Output

From the codec perspective, the routing and the signal flow in Figure 4.29 are the same as shown in Figure 4.28. However, the pin configuration for the internal speaker is quite different from the line out configuration. No color is specified, and no jack detection is present. The location and connectivity registers are set to a unique value indicating a built-in speaker. Like the previous example, the sequence number for the headphone is set to `0xF` to indicate this behavior. Table 4.23 shows the configuration defaults.

Table 4.23 Pin Configuration for Internal Speaker with Redirected Front Panel HP Out

Connectivity	Loc	Device	Type	Color	Jack Detect	Assoc	Seq
Fixed Function	Internal	Speaker	Other Analog	n/a	No (0x1)	1	0
Chassis Jack	Front	HP Out	3.5mm	Green	Yes (0x0)	1	F

Note: See Appendix A for an example of a completed verb table for this association.

Redirected Line Out Association

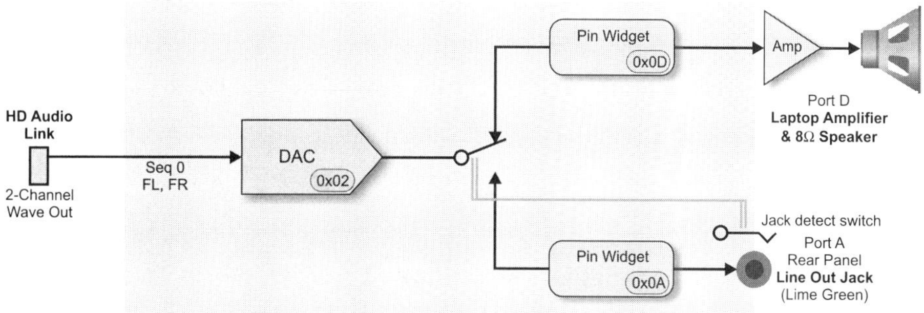

Figure 4.27 Internal Speaker and a Redirected Line Out jack Sharing a Single DAC

This configuration is very similar to the previous configuration. The primary difference is that the green jack is on the rear of the computer, and it is not capable of driving headphones. It is also possible for this configuration to be used with 5.1 or 7.1 associations. To allow for this, the internal speaker always uses Sequence `0xF` in the same way that the headphone output does in the previous examples.

Table 4.24 Pin Configuration for Internal Speaker with Redirected Rear Panel Line Out

Connectivity	Loc	Device	Type	Color	Jack Detect	Assoc	Seq
Fixed Function	Internal	Speaker	Other Analog	n/a	No (0x1)	1	F
Chassis Jack	Rear	LineOut	3.5mm	Green	Yes (0x0)	1	0

ADC Mux Association

Most Intel HD Audio codecs are designed to accept inputs on any of the analog audio ports A thru H, although typically only a few ports are dedicated to input functions. Each ADC usually has a selector that allows it to select one of these input ports to provide input. Figure 4.28 shows an association configured as ADC Mux. It is able to identify an ADC and the ports that ADC can choose to select its signal from.

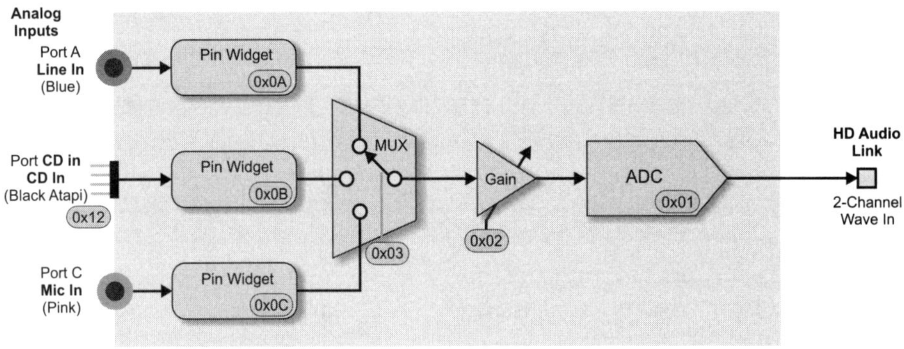

Figure 4.28 Three Pin Widgets Sharing a Single ADC in a Mux Pin Configuration

If there is only one gain control, as shown in the diagram, the OS stores a different gain value for each input to the mux. This feature gives the effect of having three separate gain controls without requiring all three to be implemented in hardware. If there are separate gain controls in each pin widget, then the OS keeps track of each individual volume setting. Table 4.24 shows the configuration defaults for this option.

Table 4.24 Pin Configuration for Shared Input Mux with Line In, CD, and Microphone In

Connectivity	Loc	Device	Type	Color	Jack Detect	Assoc	Seq
Chassis Jack	Rear	Line In	3.5 mm	Blue	Yes (0x0)	5	0
Fixed Function	ATAPI	CD In	ATAPI	Black	No (0x1)	5	1
Chassis Jack	Front	Mic In	3.5 mm	Pink	Yes (0x0)	5	E

Note: See Appendix A for an example of a completed verb table for this association.

Even though this example shows how to configure the analog CD analog CD is not recommended, and it might not be supported under Windows Vista. The ATAPI connector has no provision for jack detection. If no cable is plugged into the ATAPI connector, set the connectivity to No Connect.

ADC Mix Association

The ADC mix configuration block diagram shown in Figure 4.29 is very similar to the mux configuration. The big difference is that all three inputs are "live" at the same time, which requires independent gain controls for each input in order to adjust the relative level of each input. While allowable under both the Intel HD Audio specification and the UAA guidelines, most users find the mix configuration confusing since it doesn't match the way that A/V receivers are designed. A mix configuration is a poor choice for ease of use because it does not match the behavior of a typical A/V receiver, which uses a Mux to select between inputs. You should avoid using the mix configuration unless you have a specific reason to use it.

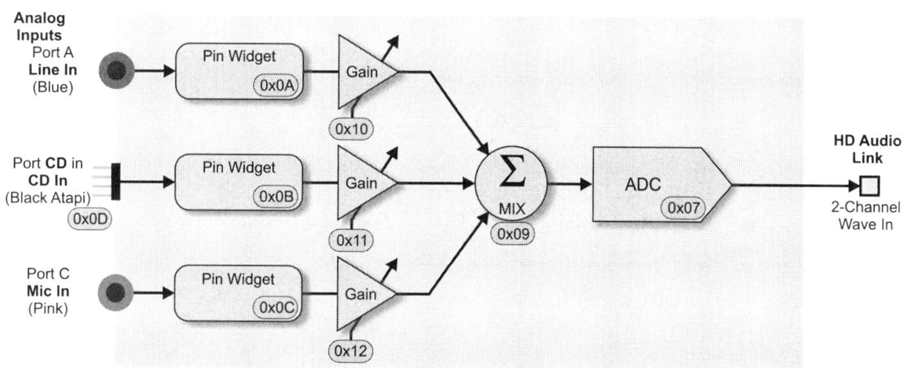

Figure 4.29 Three Pin Widgets Sharing a Single ADC in a Mix Configuration

Since each input port has an independent gain stage, they must have separately addressable widget node IDs, which increases the codec cost and complexity. In terms of the pin configuration shown in Table 4.25, the only difference between a mux and a mix configuration is that the highest sequence number is set to `0xF` rather than `0xE`, signifying mix rather than mux.

Table 4.25 Pin Configuration for Shared Input Mix with Line In, CD, and Microphone In

Connectivity	Loc	Device	Type	Color	Jack Detect	Assoc	Seq
Chassis Jack	Rear	Line In	3.5 mm	Blue	Yes (0x0)	5	0
Fixed Function	ATAPI	CD In	ATAPI	Black	No (0x1)	5	1
Chassis Jack	Front	Mic In	3.5 mm	Pink	Yes (0x0)	5	F

Note: See Appendix A for an example of a completed verb table for this association.

These configurations are but a few key ones that can be created from associations and sequences. Links to more detailed information are available at this book's companion Web site.

Resource Allocation

While hardware developers think of the I/O ports as the primary point of contact for the codec, software developers consider the DACs and ADCs in the codec to be the primary point of contact. Intel HD Audio codec designs have a somewhat flexible interconnection between analog I/O ports and resources such as DACs and ADCs that are directly addressed by the software.

The codec must have enough resources in the form of ADCs and DACs to build complete paths for each port, as specified in the default configurations. For instance, if four ports were to be configured as stereo line outputs, but the codec contained only three stereo DACs, the path with the highest association number (and therefore lowest priority) cannot be completed because the driver has run out of DACs to assign.

While most codecs have ADC muxes that can select any of the analog ports, it is not always true of the connections between DACs and ports configured for output. In many designs, a DAC can connect to only one or two ports.

If you are having trouble getting a particular pin configuration to work properly, study the block diagram or widget diagram of the codec to be sure that you have enough DACs and ADCs to fulfill your needs. If you're sure that resources are sufficient, try to isolate the problem by setting all other ports to No Connection. This setting releases any DACs, ADCs, or other elements claimed by these ports.

If your association now works properly with all ports set to No Connection, you have a resource conflict. Re-enable the other associations one at a time until the conflict re-appears, then study the codec block diagram to determine where the conflict is occurring. Or better yet, use colored highlighter markers on the codec block diagram to color code each association. Another approach is to reverse the priority of the associations that are in conflict. If a number of different paths are possible, you can often resolve the issue by causing the resources to be allocated in a different order.

Unsolicited Response

In place of a traditional interrupt request (IRQ), unsolicited responses are messages that are sent by the codec independently of any software request. Typically, they are triggered when the codec's SENSE pins change state because a jack was inserted or removed, but they can also be triggered by such events as when the listener changes a front panel volume control or when the codec latches onto a valid S/PDIF input stream.

The Intel HD Audio bus driver transforms the unsolicited responses into callback events that the function driver registers to receive. The Intel HD Audio bus driver calls the specified callback routine at IRQL DISPATCH_LEVEL, much like a traditional interrupt service routine. The driver can then dispatch events to user-mode applications that have registered to receive callbacks. At the higher levels in the OS, the unsolicited responses may be treated identically to a normal IRQ.

Jack Detection

The Intel HD Audio jack detection mechanism consists of two related but very different functions: jack-insertion detection and impedance sensing. Jack-insertion detection is required by the Windows Vista Logo program, but impedance sensing is optional and is supported only in some codec vendors' function drivers. In some limited cases, impedance sensing can be used to automatically reconfigure a jack to match the analog device that was plugged into the jack.

Jack-insertion detection is accomplished by using the resistor ladder shown in Figure 4.30 to share a single SENSE pin between four ports. The Presence Detect bit in the Pin Sense register inside each pin widget changes to a one whenever the corresponding switch is closed, indicating that a jack has been inserted.

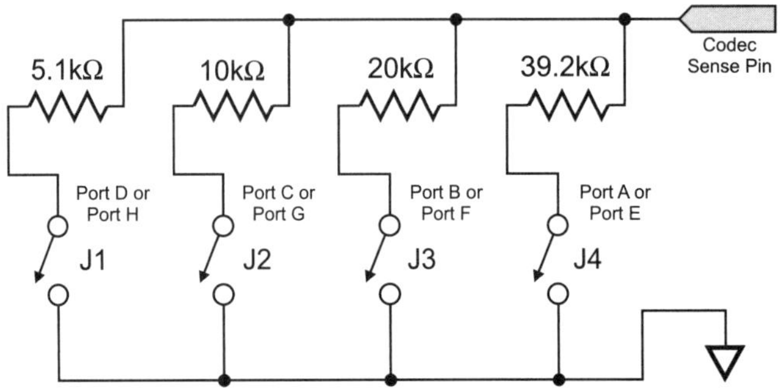

All resistors have a tolerance of 1 percent. Switches J1 thru J4 are closed when a jack is inserted in the associated port. The SENSE_A pin is used for ports A thru D, while SENSE_B is used for ports E thru H. The switches must be isolated from the signal paths of the port.

Figure 4.30 Resistor Stack Connecting Four Jacks to a Single Codec SENSE Pin

It is critical to use resistors with a tolerance of 1 percent or better, and to follow good layout and design practices for these circuits. Try to make sure that all four resistors are made using the same process, so that they track better together over temperature variations. If this circuit does not work properly, it could trigger WHQL failures under the Windows Vista Logo program.

Modifying the Pin Configuration in the BIOS

Often, when bringing up the system, you might find that the BIOS team cannot update the default configurations quickly enough to meet audio test deadlines. If the BIOS chip is mounted in a socket and not encrypted, it is relatively straightforward to modify configuration defaults in the BIOS, by using an external ROM programmer.

Remove the BIOS chip from the motherboard and use the ROM programmer coupled to a PC to read the BIOS contents into a hexadecimal file. Using a hexadecimal editor, search for a verb that you know to be present, such as `0x20A71C70`, which is the first verb in the partial verb table in Figure 4.21. You should be able to see the same verb table patterns that you see in the previous examples: sets of four similar 32-bit words all starting with 2 and followed by the widget ID.

Once you have located the verb table that you wish to edit, use the hex editor to edit the raw data, then blow the updated contents back into the BIOS chip, and put it back into the motherboard.

Most production BIOSes are encrypted, so this technique is unlikely to work with shipping products. However, it could prove to be very handy in meeting tight development schedules.

System Bring-up Trick Using the Microsoft UAA class driver for Intel HD Audio

In many cases, it may be sufficient to test with the Microsoft UAA class driver for Intel HD Audio. The class driver has an INF file mechanism to transmit a verb table just prior to normal driver initialization. This transmission allows the pin configuration registers to be programmed properly even if the BIOS is not programming them properly.

You can accomplish this transmission by editing a copy of the class driver INF file, HDAUDIO.INF. Be aware that this practice is only suitable for lab work; you cannot submit an edited HDAUDIO.INF as part of a Logo submission package. The mechanism is much like the verb table mechanism, but the surrounding syntax and structure is different. The formation of the verbs themselves is identical.

The InitVerbs registry entry is controlled by the HKR key in the HdAudInit.AddReg section of the HDAUDIO.INF file. Create one entry is for each verb that you want to send to the codec. You also must set a descriptor to indicate the total number of verbs, specified in hexadecimal. Each verb must be preceded by a unique ID number, starting with zero. These unique ID numbers are specified in decimal. An example is shown in Figure 4.31.

Just like verb tables written by the BIOS, you must know the codec ID and the Node ID for each set of commands. The verbs are sent blindly and with no error checking.

```
[HdAudInit.AddReg]
; Number of verbs to be sent to codec
HKR,InitVerbs,NumVerbs,0x00010001,0x00000004
;--Codec ID#2, Port C (NID = 0x0C)
; Set Node ID 0x0C Pin Configs to 0x01813050
HKR,InitVerbs,0000,0x00010001,0x20C71C50 ; Assoc 5, Seq 0
HKR,InitVerbs,0001,0x00010001,0x20C71D30 ; Blue, Jack Detect
HKR,InitVerbs,0002,0x00010001,0x20C71E81 ; Line In, 3.5 mm jack
HKR,InitVerbs,0003,0x00010001,0x20C71F01 ; Rear, chassis
```

This code matches the verb table in Figure 4.22 for a rear line input jack.

Figure 4.31 Verb Table Specified in the INF file of the UAA Class Driver

You can use this feature of the Microsoft UAA class driver for Intel HD Audio to pre-test verb tables before they are provided to the BIOS team or to test various potential configurations of the motherboard. Remember: any changes that you make to the HDAUDIO.INF file are for your own use and may not be submitted to WHQL as part of a Logo package. Instead, any verbs must be written by the BIOS in a production system capable of meeting Logo requirements. You must use an unedited version of the Microsoft UAA class driver for Intel HD Audio INF file to ensure system compliance with Windows Vista Logo requirements.

The examples provided in Appendix A include verb tables in both ASM and INF formats. You can use the examples to build a complete pin configuration for your system.

Chapter 5

Motherboard Layout Guidelines for Increased Audio Fidelity

"Microsoft intends to test the audio fidelity of Windows PC systems for the Designed for Windows Vista System Logo certification program".

— Hakon Strande, Audio Device Program Manager, Microsoft

In the past, integrated audio had a reputation for inferior quality. With the new and more capable integrated audio components that are now available, including parts designed in compliance with the Intel® *High Definition Audio Specification*, the systems that use these components can rival the audio fidelity of specialty PC audio cards and even of standalone consumer electronics equipment. The only obstacle to achieving a higher level of fidelity is poor system hardware design that fails to adequately address the potential causes of audio signal degradation in a PC environment that contains high-speed digital circuitry, stepper motors, and other sources of electrical noise.

The Art of Audio Design

As you read through this chapter and the next, it should become obvious that good audio design for a motherboard or PC system is as much an art as it is a science. You should follow the recommendations in this book and augment them with reference designs from the codec manufacturer.

Most codec manufacturers provide layout guidelines and well-tested circuit designs for their devices. They frequently recommend passive components to use with their devices. Even if two competing codecs have the same pinout, it doesn't always mean they will both work well with the same external components. Some words of advice:

- *Take special care* to achieve a motherboard layout with adequate shielding and isolation. Make sure that the power and ground return traces are of sufficient width. Try to achieve a "golden layout," even at the cost of an extra spin or two of a motherboard design, and when possible, use it in follow-on designs. In the long run, this effort pays off. This statement is especially true when you consider the increased emphasis on audio fidelity in the WHQL test cases for Windows† Vista.
- *Reuse "Golden" Designs.* Once you have perfected your audio design, continue to use it as the basis for new designs. Avoid trying to re-use existing designs that you know have audio problems—you will continue to have the same problems.
- *Start at the beginning.* Remember that audio must be designed into the system from the beginning, not added in at the end.
- *Consider your performance target.* Consumer equipment for the living room has a dynamic range of 115 dB or higher, but the dynamic range for existing PCs typically runs about 85 dB—it can be as low as 65 or 70 dB. For Windows Vista, PCs that are this noisy cannot meet the dynamic range requirements of the "Designed for Windows" audio fidelity tests.
- *Use good design and layout implementations.* Even when using codecs with high-quality analog circuitry, achieving high-fidelity audio depends on good design and proper layout of the motherboard and system.
- *Take care at every stage.* To realize theater-quality audio, apply careful design to every step of development, including schematic design and, in particular, layout.
- *Testing.* Ensure a proper testing environment, and with the equipment fully assembled in the final configuration, with every screw and every panel installed when possible. An audio test bench can be highly susceptible to ambient lab noise. You can improve the accuracy of the test results by moving the test bench to an isolated location, replacing any unshielded cabling with foil-shielded cables, and isolating the AC power supply from electri-

cal noise. Use incandescent lighting rather than fluorescent lighting.

- *Retain knowledge in the design team.* Try to assign the same engineer to the next design, or have him train the next engineer over the course of the next model. Document design decisions and tradeoffs so that the next person doesn't have to learn the same lessons all over again.

Multiple Complaints about Audio in today's PCs

A common complaint about audio subsystems in personal computers is that they are susceptible to electrical noise from other system components. Typically, some of the worst intermittent noise results from the electromagnetic interference (EMI) that is generated by moving the mouse or by the rotation of stepper motors on CD/DVD and hard disk drives. In addition, mechanical noise from cooling fans and hard drives can detract from the listener's audio experience. Look for more info in the section on EMI and ESD.

An inadequate power supply might be incapable of providing sufficient current to the audio circuitry, particularly if that circuitry is driving a large speaker load, such as built-in stereo speakers in a laptop computer, at high volume. As the power supply approaches its limits for supplying current, regulation fails and the DC-supply level sags, distorting supply levels and disrupting the audio signal.

Another problem for some audio subsystems is the loud thump, pop, or click that can be heard through the speakers when the system turns on or off. An audio system with a unipolar power supply typically uses DC blocking capacitors to isolate the speakers from the DC bias that the system adds to its internal audio signals. The thump results from the rapid charging or discharging of these capacitors as the DC bias level is applied or removed.

Poor system and motherboard layout commonly spawn other problems. Inadequate power supply traces can constrict currents from power supplies, thereby introducing transients into the local supply rails near circuits that undergo rapid changes in loading. Incorrect grounding of audio circuitry can dramatically reduce the signal-to-noise ratio and dynamic range while increasing harmonic distortion and noise. Circuits with inadequate ground return paths can shunt return currents to unrelated circuitry through ground loops. Ground loops are a frequent cause of audio degradation in boards that combine high-speed digital circuitry with analog audio devices.

In laptop systems, signals from internal microphones with long signal runs can degrade due to inadequate preamplification or noisy microphone bias supplies.

Everything Affects Audio

A PC hardware designer should treat audio as an integral part of the system. The integrated audio subsystem cannot be designed independently of the rest of the system. The entire system must be designed from the outset to accommodate high-fidelity integrated audio.

The layout of the audio subsystem is critical for isolating the audio circuitry from noise that is generated by the digital circuitry in the motherboard and other parts of the system. In addition, audio signals must be separated from each other to prevent crosstalk.

High-performance audio designs must avoid introducing digital noise into the audio subsystem through the power supply. Circuits that send or receive analog audio signals must have a power supply that is isolated from the power supply for the CPU and other digital circuitry. In addition, if the CD/DVD drive supplies analog audio signals to the audio subsystem, the power supply that powers these subsystems must also be isolated from the power supply for the digital circuitry and be free of noise.

Proper grounding and shielding are needed to reduce crosstalk and electrical noise. Of particular importance are case grounding, jack grounding, and techniques for suppressing electromagnetic interference (EMI) and electrostatic discharge (ESD).

For laptop systems, the external power supply and battery-charging circuit also can affect audio fidelity, especially if they cause a ground loop.

Choosing the proper Intel HD Audio codec is critical for achieving low noise. In general, an audio codec should have an internal layout which is optimized for high rejection of power supply noise at audio frequencies, along with digital-to-analog (DAC) and analog-to-digital (ADC) converters with greater than 16-bit resolution.

Motherboard Development Cycles

Motherboards often are developed in an iterative fashion. A design cycle includes each of these three steps: schematic design, Gerber plots, and hardware prototypes. The design cycle is repeated until the prototypes meet all of the product requirements. Typically, the design requires three or four iterations, though the ideal target is two iterations.

Each successive iteration is a refinement of the previous iteration, improving in those areas that didn't fulfill the requirements and validating that the iteration has not introduced new issues in the design. A motherboard is a very complex piece of electronics, supporting a wide range of advanced technologies, one of which is audio.

Usually, the audio design must be fundamentally correct, even in the first iteration, because the subsequent iterations usually don't allow significant changes to be introduced. For this reason, you should start the design process with audio performance in mind.

Schematic Design

The first stage of audio circuit design is the schematic design. Usually, the Intel HD Audio codec vendor supplies a reference schematic in Orcad file format. This schematic shows the proper component selections as well as a series of net lists to show how the components are interconnected. This file is often the best starting point for a new design.

Motherboards often are designed to accept several different models of codec. For instance, two different codecs from the same vendor could be used to support implementation of either a 2-channel or an 8 channel configuration. Alternatively, the motherboard could allow the use of similar codecs from multiple codec vendors. In either case, you should create a table of stuffing options, designating the components to be used with each codec.

Gerber Plots

Once the schematic design of the entire motherboard is complete, then the schematics are rendered into PC board layout files called Gerber plots. In this graphical representation of the circuitry of the PC board itself, each layer of the motherboard has a different Gerber plot associated with it. In addition to the information from the schematic, the Gerber plots also require knowledge of the size and pad locations for each component that will be used.

The automated tools that are used to convert a schematic and netlist into a Gerber plot file usually do not take into account any of the audio layout guidelines presented in this chapter. The board designer must make manual adjustments during this conversion process to ensure that the proper guidelines are followed. Otherwise, the probability of noise and distortion is very high.

The first iteration of the Gerber plot cycle is the most important step in designing a motherboard for good audio fidelity. The audio section of the motherboard must be isolated and good star grounding techniques have to be followed. While you can make small adjustments in later design iterations, doing so is often time consuming and costly. By taking the time to get it right during the first iteration, you will provide significant benefit to the audio fidelity.

Hardware Prototypes

Once the Gerber plots have been created, usually a few hundred motherboards are built and populated. At this point, the complete suite of audio tests should start immediately, so that you can identify and resolve any issue while you still have an opportunity to make significant changes. Since the cost of change increases dramatically with each spin of the motherboard, waiting until later in the cycle for full testing can become very expensive. Testing early and often during the design cycle is critical to ensuring good audio fidelity on a motherboard.

System Test

Full system testing in the final enclosure is often not possible until very late in the design stage, and often after the final spin of the motherboard. A re-spin of the motherboard at this late stage is often not an option, so make sure to leave some stuffing options available to solve potential problems. For instance, the EMI and ESD components may be left off the prototype builds, in the hope that the system as a whole will pass EMI and ESD testing. If an issue is identified during testing, then the components can be stuffed and/or adjusted until the system passes the test. If the pads for these components were not present, then an expensive and lengthy board re-spin might be necessary.

In terms of WHQL testing, the trend is moving towards system test. Under Windows XP, the test for the proper programming of the pin configuration registers by the BIOS occurs at system test. You can have a fully logoed audio driver and still fail this test, because HCT loads a special test driver to query the codec directly. Windows Vista is most likely to perform all audio testing, including audio fidelity measurements, as part of system test. Try to avoid situations where the audio implementation is not run through a complete system test (EMI, ESD, WHQL, QA) in the final enclosure before the final motherboard design is locked down. As simple as this seems, it rarely takes place.

Commonly Encountered Problems

Earlier chapters touched briefly on some of the barriers to increased audio fidelity. The following section dives considerably deeper in describing issues that exist on virtually every motherboard design. A good audio design distinguishes itself by directly addressing each potential source of degradation and guarding against it.

Electrical Noise Sources

When building a system or designing a motherboard, one of the biggest design challenges in achieving high-fidelity audio is removing or isolating sources of electrical noise from the audio subsystem.

Occasional or intermittent electrical noise usually comes from other major system components, such as the mouse, hard disk drives, CD/DVD stepper motors, RF circuits, memory (strobing), video display circuitry, and switching power supplies. Careful testing is needed to identify all potential problems emanating from these and other sources. During testing of the audio subsystem, be sure to check for noise while other system components are in use. Test for noise under the following conditions:

- While moving the mouse
- While running a disk defragmenter on each hard disk drive
- While copying large files to and from the CD/R drive
- While copying large files over the Wi-Fi link and LAN
- While exercising the memory
- While exercising the video display system

Passive Components

The amount of noise or distortion that a passive component such as a capacitor or resistor adds to a circuit is determined by the way that is the component is constructed or by the materials that go into it. Passive components that are perfectly suitable for use in digital circuits might not be suitable for audio.

Avoid using resistor, capacitor, ferrite, or inductor packs that have more than one device in a single package. These multi-device packages are possible sources of crosstalk. Use high quality film dielectric, ceramic, or electrolytic capacitors. The type of dielectric material affects the amount of noise that a capacitor generates. If a polarized capacitor is being used as a coupling capacitor, make sure that it is biased properly.

For microphones, be sure to use a low-leakage coupling capacitor because any leakage might cause a DC offset that can be amplified by the microphone preamplifier. Try to use non-polarized coupling capacitors wherever possible, especially in any circuits that are retasked between microphone and other usages.

Capacitors

Capacitors come in many different formulations, sizes and shapes. They are often sensitive to heat and cold as well as DC bias variations. While in theory a capacitor only provides capacitive reactance, many capacitors also exhibit some resistance, and in some cases they might exhibit inductance (the opposite of capacitance). Dielectric distortion is a significant source of distortion in audio circuits, so capacitors with low dielectric distortion are recommended.

For audio circuits, polystyrene or polypropylene film capacitors are preferred, though they are rarely found in PC audio circuits because they are more expensive than other types of capacitors. They exhibit the lowest resistance and inductance of the various types of capacitors used for audio, and they are usually less sensitive to variations due to temperature. They also exhibit the lowest dielectric distortion for audio applications in most cases.

Ceramic capacitors are common on PC's, but are often not the correct choice. The primary merit of these capacitors is their lower price and smaller size. Ceramic capacitors should be considered as a thermal noise source, and they should be properly evaluated before use. It is possible to make a good quality audio circuit using these capacitors if attention is paid to all the details and a good-quality capacitor is selected. Most ceramic capacitors are small and designed for pick-and-place assembly from a reel of parts. Ceramic capacitors are usually non-polarized. Ceramic capacitor values often vary widely with temperature, and tolerances may sometimes vary widely. Avoid using ceramic capacitors in the audio chain.

Aluminum electrolytic capacitors are often used when the circuit calls for 10 microfarads or more. Unfortunately, aluminum electrolytic capacitors do not always have consistent high-frequency audio response, so it is often good to add a 0.1 microfarad or a 0.01 microfarad capacitor in parallel to provide an unobstructed path for high frequencies. Aluminum electrolytic capacitors are usually polarized. If the polarity is incorrect, they could still appear to operate, but do so at a reduced level. The capacitor's lifetime may also be reduced significantly. Certain types of aluminum electrolytic capacitors can exhibit high DC leakage, which should be avoided to prevent pops and clicks. Aluminum electrolytic capacitors should be run close to their rated voltage, because the voltage across the capacitor helps "form" the dielectric.

Tantalum electrolytic capacitors often are used in applications where aluminum electrolytic capacitors would be too large, such as in laptop and tablet PC applications. Tantalum high-frequency response is usually good, and the design doesn't require any additional cap in parallel. Tantalums are usually polarized, and are extremely sensitive to reverse bias. Just a very short period of reverse bias can cause the capacitor to fail, so they are not recommended in re-tasking jack circuits, where DC currents might flow in different directions. Tantalums are usually much more expensive than aluminum electrolytic capacitors, so typically their use is limited to space-constrained designs. Some OEMs have a policy of not using tantalum capacitors in any product, because some countries consider the smoke emitted from a failed tantalum capacitor as a hazardous material.

Let's take a look at a simple coupling capacitor. In an audio circuit, the reactance of the capacitor affects the frequency response of the system. If a capacitor is used in series, it limits the low frequency response of the system, becoming a simple first-order high-pass filter, as shown in Figure 5.1. AC coupling capacitors are typically implemented using this configuration.

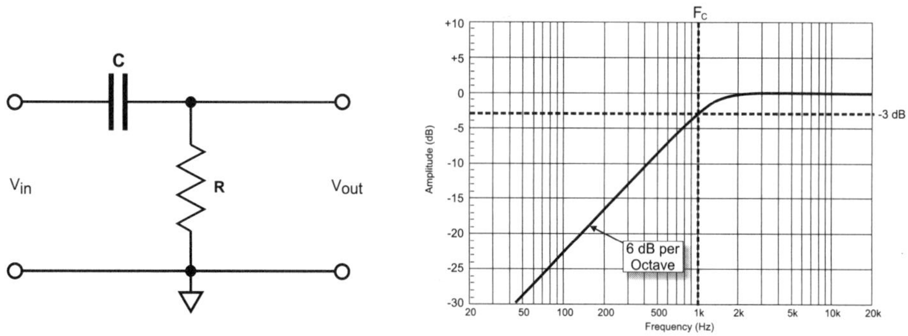

Figure 5.1 Schematic and Frequency Response of a Capacitor Used in Series

If the capacitor is used in shunt, the capacitor becomes a simple first-order low-pass filter, as shown in Figure 5.2. This configuration typically is used for power supply filtering, but you can also use it to adjust the frequency response of a circuit.

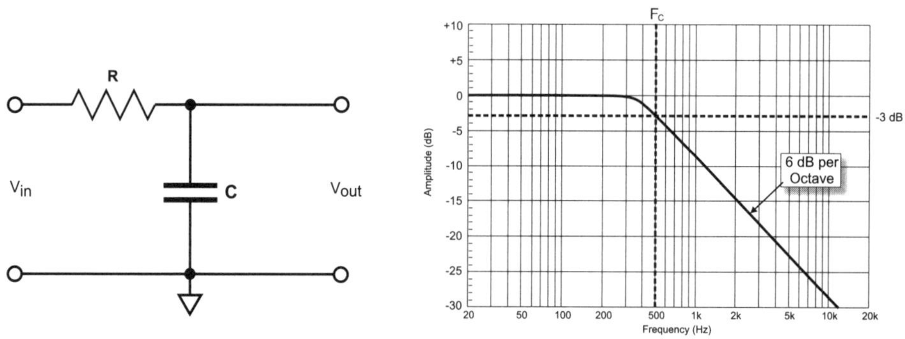

Figure 5.2 Schematic and Frequency Response of a Capacitor Used in Shunt

Figure 5.3 shows a simplified formula for determining the cutoff frequency for a given capacitance or the capacitance for a given cutoff frequency. The formulas are correct for both high-pass and low-pass configurations. These are first-order filters, so the roll-off is 6 dB per octave.

$$F_{co} = \frac{1}{2\pi \times R \times C} \qquad C = \frac{1}{2\pi \times R \times F_{co}}$$

These simple equivalent formulas determine the cutoff frequency or .capacitor value for a first order filter, where 2 Pi is roughly 6.283. Fco is the cutoff frequency in hertz. R is the resistance in Ohms, and C is the capacitance in Farads (not microfarads). These formulas are simplified. In practice, the load impedance and the input impedance must be taken into account.

Figure 5.3 Simplified formulas for Cutoff Frequency or Capacitor Value

For a headphone output circuit that is designed to drive a 32-ohm headphone, you would calculate the coupling capacitor value by taking the inverse of 6.283 (2 Pi) times the frequency of 20 hertz, times the resistance of 32 ohms, or 1/4021.24, which works out to 0.00024868. Converting from Farads to microfarads, we find that we need a capacitor size of at least 249 microfarads.

In practice, we find that most headphone output circuits use a commonly available capacitor size of 220 microfarads. Working backwards, we can calculate the cutoff frequency by taking the inverse of 6.283 (2 Pi) times 20 (hertz) times .000220 (Farads), or 1/0.02764. This calculation works out to roughly 36 hertz. Since most small headphones produce no sound below 50 hertz, this value is usually suitable. But for audiophile quality, you should use a capacitor larger than 220 microfarads. Since aluminum electrolytic capacitors don't pass high frequencies very well, an additional 0.1 microfarad ceramic capacitor should be added in parallel with the larger capacitor, to ensure that the high frequencies can pass through undisturbed.

Capacitor Tolerance and Variation

While the details of the numerous different types of capacitors lie beyond the scope of high definition PC audio, certain issues need careful attention. For one, the tolerance of a capacitor usually is plus or minus 10 percent. You need to consider the best and worst case values during the design phase. By simply factoring in a plus or minus 10-percent variation for the headphone coupling capacitor, you would have a range of 32 to 40 hertz, rather than an exact value of 36 hertz.

Some ceramic capacitors have a tolerance of minus 20 percent and plus 80 percent. If this tolerance were to be used for the headphone coupling capacitor, the cutoff frequency could vary between 20 and 45 hertz. Even worse, some newer ceramic capacitor formulations may vary their value based on the DC potential across the capacitor. For instance, a Taiyo X5R capacitor used in a first-order low pass configuration can see the cutoff frequency vary between 28 hertz and 100 hertz if the DC voltage across the capacitor is varied from 0 to 4 volts. This range of variation is in addition to the plus 20-percent or minus 80-percent tolerance variations that are characteristic of some ceramic capacitors. The good news is that most ceramic capacitors don't exhibit any DC sensitivity. However, if your design needs accurate and repeatable frequency response, capacitors with large tolerances and DC sensitivity should be avoided.

Power Supplies

Be sure to use an Intel HD Audio codec with a good power supply rejection ratio (PSRR) to minimize the coupling of noise from the power supply to audio signals. The PSRR should be at least 50 dB for supply noise at all frequencies used in the codec, including the digital clocks which run at 24 megahertz or higher. A high PSRR is especially important for audio designs that lack a dedicated voltage regulator. Avoid switching regulators; you should use linear voltage regulators for best dynamic range.

If careful attention is paid to design and layout, you can eliminate this linear voltage regulator and use a brute force RC filtered power supply to drive the external op-amp. For best effect, use a ferrite bead in series and a filter capacitor in shunt, as shown in Figure 5.4. You can string multiple LC or RC filters in a row to reduce power supply noise. In most cases a voltage regulator is less expensive and more effective than a series of brute force filters.

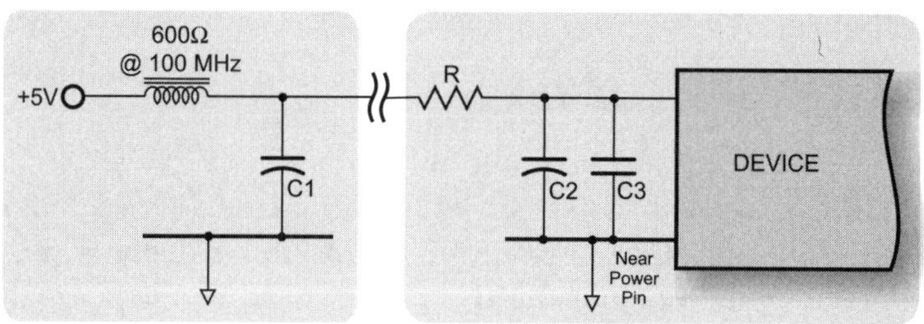

R = 2 to 10 ohms
C1 = 47 to 470 microfarads, C2 = 1 to 10 microfarads, C3 = 0.01 to 0.1 microfarads

Figure 5.4 Brute Force Power Supply, With No Regulator

If you use the brute force technique, be sure to choose a codec with a high power supply rejection ratio (PSRR) so that any remaining noise from the power supply is not coupled into the audio output.

Take particular care in selecting the power supply that provides the microphone bias voltage. Linear voltage regulators work best for this, switching regulators often are a poor choice. Any noises on this supply become amplified by the microphone preamplifier. For example, a small 10-microvolt noise on the supply rail, amplified by a typical preamplifier with a gain of 40 dB, results in a noise floor of -60 dB, which fails to pass "Designed for Windows" Logo requirements.

Whenever possible, leave a stuffing option for a voltage regulator to provide the analog audio supply, even if a voltage regulator is not planned as part of the final design. This precaution can prevent an expensive board re-spin late in the design cycle.

Analog audio power needs to be routed on an inner plane. All analog audio signals must be referenced to the analog power plane. Routing audio traces over non-audio planes induces noise and reduces the dynamic range.

Isolation

The Intel HD Audio Link is a 5-wire serial bus for connecting codecs to controllers. This connection forms the sole communication channel between a codec and the digital portion of the system. Apart from this link, the analog circuitry in the codec should be isolated from the digital circuitry in the system, and treated as a completely separate subsystem, even if it is located on the motherboard. Take advantage of this serial link by locating the codec as close as possible to the audio jacks, and as far away as possible from other circuits. Make a special effort to locate audio circuitry away from wireless LAN devices such as 802.11 and Bluetooth.

The digital circuitry often requires high-current switching voltage regulators, which can be noisy and should be positioned far away from the analog circuitry.

Connecting an analog supply rail to a noisy power source can degrade the dynamic range and increase the THD+N of analog signals. The best way to isolate the audio analog supply rail is with a simple linear voltage regulator. You should dedicate this regulator exclusively to the analog *audio* circuitry with an output of at least 5 volts. In general, higher analog supply voltages result in better dynamic range. Neglecting to provide capacitors to decouple low-frequency power rail transients can cause elevated low-frequency crosstalk and increase THD+N.

All analog audio circuitry should use the analog voltage supply, not the system voltage supply. Similarly, all analog audio signals' returns should connect to the analog audio ground, which is separate from the system ground.

Analog power should be routed to the audio circuitry on a plane located in an interior board layer. Make sure that the analog power plane encompasses the entire audio subsystem. Route analog audio traces on the signal layer that is closest to the analog power plane. Allowing the analog audio power plane to overlap non-audio planes degrades the dynamic range.

Try to eliminate any electrical coupling—albeit inductive, capacitive, or resistive—between the audio circuitry and the other circuits in the PC. Avoid routing audio traces near other circuitry, especially high-speed digital circuits. If possible, build a clearly defined boundary area around the audio circuitry, and don't allow any other circuits within this area.

Use twisted-pair shielded wires with the shield connected only at the input end. For analog connections to external devices such as port replicators and docking stations, avoid using ribbon cable or unshielded. Make sure that any connectors also provide shielding. Simple Molex connectors are not suitable for this purpose.

Do not use ribbon cable for analog connections to jacks or other connections not mounted on the motherboard. *Do not* share a cable harness with USB or other high speed digital signals.

Digital audio outputs should be electrically isolated. Use an optical S/PDIF output when the budget allows, otherwise use a transformer to interface an S/PDIF output with a coaxial RCA jack. When using a transformer for isolation, do not directly ground the output of this transformer; try to leave it floating. If the floating output causes excessive EMI, connect the output to ground through a bypass capacitor.

One Port, One Jack

Be sure that each port connects to one and only one audio source, destination, or jack. For compatibility with the Microsoft UAA class driver for Intel HD Audio, do not double-up on input or output ports in ways that cannot be exposed to the class driver through the information contained in the pin configuration registers.

Designs that use GPIOs under control of third-party function drivers must default to an appropriate hardware configuration when the Microsoft UAA class driver for Intel HD Audio is loaded in order to comply with the Windows Vista Logo program.

Ground Planes and Shielding

You can provide some degree of shielding for sensitive analog circuitry by locating a conductive surface—that is, an expanded metal trace—called a *ground plane*, in an interior board layer beneath the circuit. Ground planes should only be used for shielding, and they should be connected directly to the main ground *at a single point* beneath the codec. Ground planes should *never* carry any current! *Do not* use the ground plane to connect signal returns that carry any significant amount of current

Take special care with shielding around the audio jacks, as well as with EMI and ESD circuitry. A shield must be connected directly to the main ground and each shield must be grounded in only one place.

Analog audio circuitry should not share a ground plane with digital circuitry. Instead, the ground plane should be split into separate analog and digital planes. The analog ground plane encompasses the analog circuitry and the digital ground plane encompasses the digital circuitry. You can locate the digital and analog ground planes in the same board layer but they should be separated by a space of 1/8 inch to reduce capacitive coupling between the two planes. If the digital and analog ground planes are in separate layers, make sure that the planes do not overlap each other. The two planes should be connected through plated feed-through holes, called *vias*, to the main ground at a point directly beneath the codec.

Reminder: a can or other type of shield is an extension of the ground plane. Don't let the can touch the actual jacks; it should be connected to the ground plane with a single electrical connection in only one location.

Star Grounding

Star grounding is often counterintuitive for board designers who are unfamiliar with audio layout best practices. *Star grounding* is accomplished by running a separate trace for each analog ground (return) that appears on your motherboard schematic back to a central grounding point that is located underneath the codec. Connect the analog audio ground to the system ground through a set of vias located directly beneath the codec. Ensure that there are no "ground loops", where more than one return path can couple noise into audio signal paths.

The star-grounding topology keeps the ground for the entire audio circuit at the same potential. Ground return traces must be capable of handling as much current as each associated supply trace. A ground return trace of insufficient width can cause noise due to the voltage drop over the resistance of the trace.

Try to position the ground return trace for each circuit next to or directly beneath each associated signal trace. Figure 5.5 shows a return trace located under a signal trace.

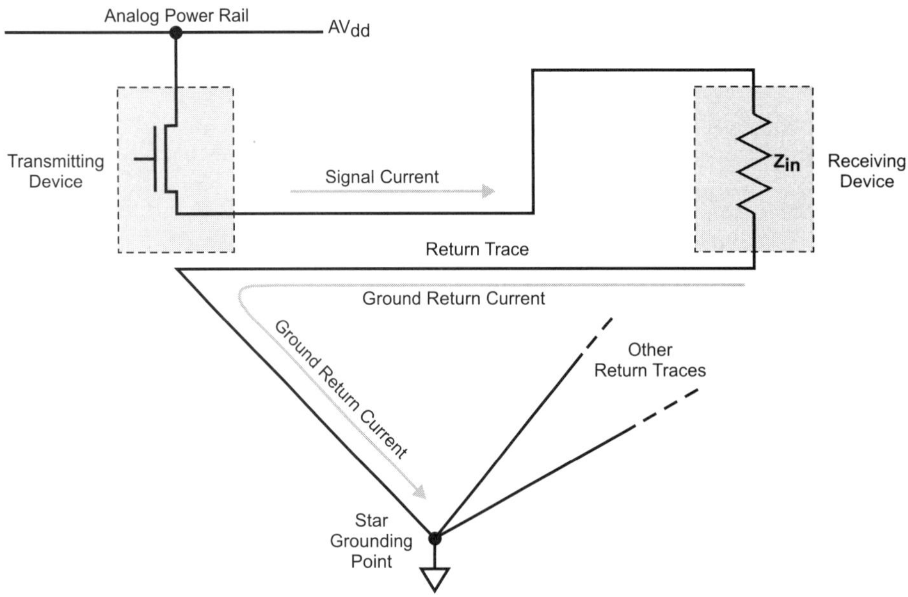

Figure 5.5 Star Grounding

As you can see, current flows from the analog power rail through the transmitting device, over the signal trace, through the input impedance, Z_{IN}, of the receiving device, over the ground return trace, and it finally arrives at the central grounding point for the star ground. The return trace follows the signal trace back to the transmitting device before connecting to the star grounding point. For best results, *do not* connect multiple ground returns to different locations in the ground plane.

Star grounding also applies for power supply paths. Treat the analog power supply (often designated as AVdd) as if it is a signal path, with separate dedicated returns. Do not connect the codec power supply return to ground except at the single point underneath the codec where the analog and digital ground planes are bridged. Both AVdd and analog ground should be wide low-impedance traces with no side-branches.

Laptops and All-in-One Systems

Designers of systems with built-in speaker amplifiers should make sure that the speaker amplifiers receive sufficient power. Users who view their screens from a distance tend to crank up the audio volume level accordingly; hence the larger the screen, the louder the expected listening volume.

Loud listening volumes require a well-filtered power supply that is capable of providing peak currents in excess of the maximum current consumption of the power amplifiers. If the power supply is not well-filtered and regulated, or if the power supply traces are not wide enough, then the output amplifier can become unstable at high volume levels.

Speech and Real Time Communications

Both Windows Vista and the Intel HD Audio spec provide enhancements for speech-based Real Time Communications (RTC) . Using a headset plugged into the front or side of the PC will provide the best acoustic interface between the user and the transducers, because the headset locates the microphone next to the mouth and the speakers cover the ears. However, the headset is not part of the computer and must be carried and stored separately. If the headset is not included with the computer at time of purchase, the analog interfaces levels and impedances are essentially unknown, and one or more software wizards must be used to assist the user in configuring the proper gain.

Also, the jacks on the headset are both 3.5-millimeter stereo phone jacks, and often aren't color coded. It's easy to make a mistake when plugging these two jacks into the computer. This potential stumbling block can be removed by using re-tasking jacks and automatic impedance, as discussed elsewhere in this book.

Front Panel Considerations

Many Windows Vista-ready designs will have jacks on the rear panel for multi-channel connections, and they also include a headphone and microphone jack on the front panel. For best results, use a separate Intel HD Audio codec for each location. This approach avoids long wiring runs and provides the best audio quality performance. While the extra codec may seem more expensive, you might find this cost is offset by the shielded cables and connectors and/or the additional preamp required for the mic signal that you would need in order to pass the audio fidelity tests that must be met to merit the WHQL Logo for the Vista OS. Also consider the cost of an expensive motherboard re-spin late in the product cycle if the quality is not capable of meeting Vista Logo requirements.

While a headphone jack on the front panel is not subject to many of the same limitations as microphones, it is important to use large send and return traces on the PC board or larger gauge wire that is capable of transferring the power to the headphone. Narrower traces act as a resistor and degrade the headphone performance. Narrower and/or longer traces may also increase the audio subsystem's susceptibility to electrostatic discharge (ESD) which is covered in detail later in this chapter.

If you decide against using a separate codec for the front panel application, then you have a choice of using one of two front panels designed by Intel. The Intel HD Audio version of the front panel includes jack switches for both jacks as well as a "presence" signal for the BIOS to detect whether a front panel is installed or not. The older AC97 version does not support any switches to indicate if the front panel is present or that jacks are plugged into it, and will not meet Vista Logo requirements.

The BIOS must be able to detect whether the front panel is installed or not in order to properly populate the Pin Configuration registers in the codec, so that the audio function driver can determine the configuration at load time. Specifications for recommended schematics and cables are available at the Form Factors Web site, listed in "References."

Analog Microphones

Keep the lengths of microphone connections to a minimum. Preferably, the codec should be located within an inch or two of the microphone or microphone jack.

A laptop system might contain an internal microphone element that is, for example, embedded in the bezel of the screen. The signal traces that connect the microphone to the codec might be long enough to require extra preamplifier or gain stages, which typically add between 20 dB and 62.5 dB of additional gain. If possible, use a microphone with a built-in preamplifier of 20 dB or more. Generally avoid preamplifiers that are not located inside or near the microphone. For external microphones, make sure that the microphone bias supply is well-regulated and noise-free.

When wiring a laptop system for internal stereo microphones, maintain as much isolation as possible between the bias supplies for the left and right channels to ensure low crosstalk. For beam-forming or phased-array microphones, isolating the individual bias supplies is especially critical because excessive crosstalk can cancel out the beamforming effect. However, avoid using diodes to isolate the left and right portions of the microphone bias supply, because as they could cause distortion if the jack is retasked for use as line in or line out. Appendix D contains more detail on microphone bias when used for retaskable jacks.

One commonly reported issue on laptop computers is that it is possible to record speech, albeit poorly, even if the microphone is not mounted in the circuit. While at first this sounds impossible, it turns out that this unintended recording can occur a number of different ways if the preamp on the codec is turned up to a high gain setting. One likely source of this problem is microphonic passive components, especially capacitors and inductors. For instance, if a capacitor changes its value slightly due to physical vibration, the capacitor becomes a microphone.

However, even if the capacitors and inductors are not microphonic, the traces on the motherboard could be microphonic, especially if the traces are long. You can avoid these types of problems by keeping any traces for microphones very short, or by using digital microphones.

Challenges in mic Array Implementation

Integrating a microphone array into a mobile PC presents a number of challenges, including electrical, mechanical, economic, and acoustical considerations. The result is often a mediocre compromise between selecting the acoustically optimal location for the microphone and the proximity of that location to interfering noise sources. Figure 5.6 highlights many of the noise challenges to successful microphone integration in a mobile PC.

Figure 5.6 Noise Sources Affecting Microphone Placement in a Mobile PC

The base of the laptop is a poor location for microphones because they are surrounded by a variety of noise sources such as fans and hard drives. Placing the microphone array near the speaker can also increase the likelihood of echo during real-time communications, such as VoIP. Additionally, a microphone array placed in the base of the laptop is not directly facing the user, which can reduce overall performance. A more ideal acoustic location for the microphone array is in the bezel of the laptop. This location mechanically isolates the microphone from all of the noise sources in the base and faces the microphones towards the mouth of the person speaking. In this position, the manufacturer can also expect the highest performance from the noise suppression algorithms.

Embedding the microphones into the bezel, while acoustically optimal, also has its challenges. This area offers little room for microphones in the ultra-thin bezels of today's laptops, and the microphones almost always share space with radio-frequency (RF) LAN antennas. RF noise can create a buzzing sound in a standard analog-output microphone. The traditional way to combat the RF interference would be to use shielded cabling to route the small analog microphone signals to a preamp close to the microphone, to boost the signal level. Then, the shielded wires are routed around the monitor and through the hinges to the base. However, shielded cabling can be thick, and for more than one microphone, it is difficult to squeeze several strands through the hinge pin. It also might have a limited lifetime due to constant flexing of the hinge. Braided shielding is more resilient to constant flexing but is less effective for shielding.

In a small number of microphone array implementations, considerable design time and cost has been spent to find a successful solution to the above challenges. However, recent advances in microphone technology have made it easier to overcome many of these challenges with significantly less time, effort, and in many cases, expense.

The Benefits of a Digital Microphone Array

Low-cost microphones with digital outputs have recently become available, which provide a much greater degree of flexibility in microphone placement. You can select a microphone location based on its acoustic merits rather than electrical or mechanical considerations. This flexibility comes from the robust digital output of these microphones, which are much less susceptible to interference from nearby RF or electro-magnetic sources. This choice eliminates the need for shielded cabling and allows the output wires from multiple microphones to easily fit through the thin hinge pins in many of today's mobile PCs. A number of different microphone manufacturers are producing or developing microphones with digital output capability, and codec vendors are starting to ship codecs with digital microphone input pins that can accept the input from any of these digital microphones.

Additional placement flexibility can be gained by using digital microphones based on recently introduced Micro-Electro-Mechanical Systems (MEMS) microphone technology. MEMS microphones are significantly thinner than a standard electret condenser microphone (ECM). The standard ECM is a metal canister with a height near 2mm which must be placed in a socket roughly 1-2mm high. All together, the standard ECM can require between 3-4mm of bezel thickness. Alternatively, MEMS digital-output microphones range in thickness from 1-2mm and do not require a socket since they are surface mountable components. Therefore, a MEMS digital-output microphone occupies 50 percent or less of the bezel thickness needed by the ECM, enabling embedded microphone arrays in the bezels of the smallest mobile PCs. MEMS microphones are surface mounted and can be installed by automated board assembly equipment, instead of the more expensive hand assembly required for ECMs.

Many MEMS digital microphones are multi-chip-modules with one transducer chip and a second IC containing the analog-to-digital converter. These two devices are then wire-bonded to each other within the MEMS microphone package. Figure 5.7 shows a newer MEMS digital microphone, which combines the transducer, a preamplifier, and an analog-to-digital converter on a single chip. EMI sensitivity is minimized by locating the transducer and the preamp only microns from each other.

A single chip contains the transducer, analog preamplifier, and an analog-to-digital converter. (Courtesy of Akustica®)

Figure 5.7 An Akustica† MEMS Digital-Output Microphone on a Single Chip

In addition to their smaller size, single-chip MEMS digital microphones normally have a lower degree of part-to-part variability compared with other types of microphones. This high degree of sensitivity matching and phase matching can make a big improvement in performance for most beamforming algorithms.

In general, digital microphones solve many of the acoustic and electrical noise issues that are commonly experienced when embedding a microphone array in a laptop. Consider using a digital MEMS microphone for applications with acoustical or space constraints; for use near the LAN and Bluetooth antennas in the top of the bezel; or to be able to use ribbon cable to connect through the hinge pin of a laptop.

Electromagnetic Interference and Electrostatic Discharge

Electromagnetic Interference (EMI) and Electrostatic Discharge (ESD) are subjects that are, for the most part, outside the scope of this book. However, you need to know about specific issues in order for your audio circuits to meet various regulatory requirements for ESD and EMI.

Since both EMI and ESD are normally tested at the system level; relatively few specifications apply directly to components such as the Intel HD Audio codec or controller. A poor layout can keep a well-designed codec from meeting these requirements, while a good design and layout can do a lot to strengthen a weaker codec design. The design and layout of the audio subsystem can have a significant effect on the EMI and ESD performance of a complete system, but there are many different factors to take into account.

The specialized facilities, equipment, and expertise needed to test completed systems for EMI and ESD regulatory requirements are well beyond the reach of a PC audio lab. Independent test labs are often the best option for comprehensive testing, though some larger OEMs and ODMs maintain their own dedicated test facilities.

The engineers associated with EMI and ESD testing labs will often make specific recommendations which can fix problems that they identify during testing. However, be aware that these recommendations do not usually take audio performance into account. For this reason, it is very important to perform a full round of audio testing both before and after any modifications are made to address EMI and ESD testing issues. By comparing before and after performance, you can easily determine whether any of the EMI or ESD fixes have created new audio performance issues.

For obvious reasons, complete system testing often occurs late in the design cycle, when fundamental design changes are difficult if not impossible. You can avoid this by observing the guidelines in this section.

All testing for ESD and EMI should be performed in the final chassis configuration, with all screws inserted and tightened properly, and all panels and covers in place. If you choose to test an open motherboard on the bench, for instance, be aware that you may get very different results than if the board is mounted in the target chassis.

EMI

For audio circuits, two basic categories of EMI issues are emission and susceptibility. Susceptibility occurs when the audio circuit's performance is reduced because of interference from frequencies much higher than audio frequencies. Radio frequency interference (RFI) usually refers to intended radio transmissions, such as Wi-Fi, Bluetooth, FM, AM, GSM, etc. EMI usually refers to signals from unintended radiators such as clocks and oscillators inside the PC or from adjacent equipment.

Emissions occur when an audio circuit becomes an unintended radiator. In the US, the FCC requires that all devices which contain clocks or oscillators which operate at a frequency above 9 kilohertz must be tested under FCC part 15 Subpart B, radio frequency rules and regulations. Similar requirements exist in most countries where Intel HD Audio-equipped systems are sold.

The purpose of the testing and certification is two-fold:

- To ensure that these electronic components do not interfere with devices that need to transmit or receive radio or wireless signals
- To ensure that the device being tested is not overly sensitive to external radio signals.

This testing is also valuable for audio circuitry, since high-energy RF fields can have unpredictable effects on audio circuits that are not designed to withstand strong RF fields. A PC environment contains numerous strong RF fields, and they are each a potential audio performance issue waiting to happen.

The FCC establishes two classes of devices, Class A and Class B. Class A devices are intended for use in a commercial, industrial or business environment, and are specifically not marketed for use by the general public or intended to be used in a home. Computer servers are usually designated as a Class A device.

Class B devices are intended for use by the general public, and have a more rigorous set of requirements that they must meet. Home and business computers must be tested with all standard components connected to the system. Individual add-on devices that are sold separately are tested separately from the PC. Figure 5.8 shows a typical testing site for outside open-air emission testing.

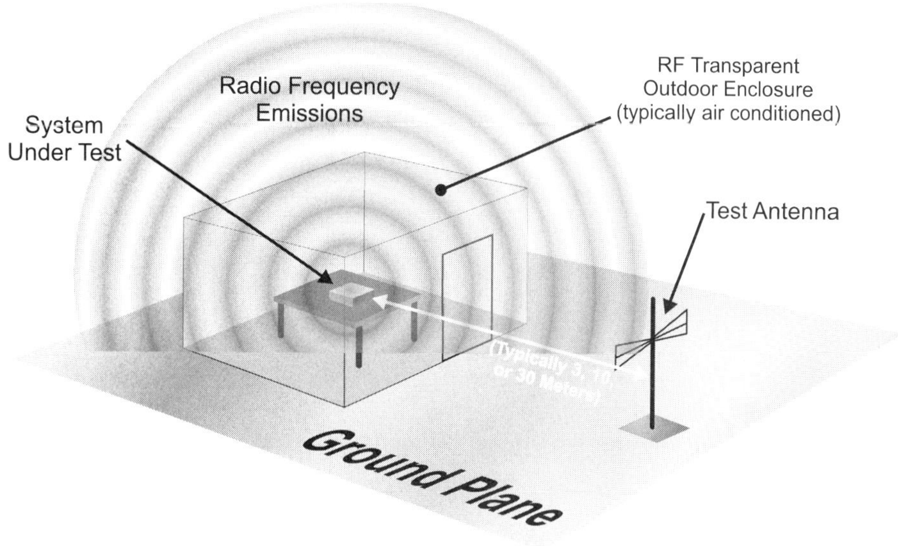

An open-air test sites (OATS) is the preferred method for FCC testing. Facilities such as this are usually located in rural areas far from sources of RF. It is also possible to perform this testing in an enclosed environment equipped with appropriate shielding.

Figure 5.8 Example of an Open Air Test Site

While a well-equipped audio test lab is unlikely to test for FCC compliance, a broadband spectrum analyzer is very useful for spot-testing of emissions. The analyzer should be equipped with three different categories of input devices: an antenna, a near-field probe, and a low-capacitance RF probe. An antenna is used as shown in Figure 5.8 to measure overall EMI emissions at a distance from the device under test.

While the antenna is useful as an overall measuring device, it does not always provide enough information for successful debugging. For this, a near-field probe such as the one shown in Figure 5.9 can be used to determine the exact location on the motherboard. The probe that is pictured is part of a set of near-field probes consisting of stub, ball, and loop configurations. If you don't have an analyzer which displays energy in the frequency domain, you can connect a near-field probe to the input of an oscilloscope and see signals on the scope as you move the scope closer to the device under test, though you are unlikely to see hard edges of a square wave, for instance.

The probe is taking an RF measurement without making contact with the circuit under test.

Figure 5.9 ETS Model 7405 Near-Field Loop Probe

You also need a specially rated low-capacitance, high frequency probe when you wish to measure the electrical signals on the board itself. Probes rated for RF are less likely to interact with RF signals on your board. On the other hand, RF probes are not always the best probe to use for measuring signals in the audio band, so be sure to choose the proper probe for the work at hand.

Before you take any measurements of the device under test, set up the antenna in its intended operating position and take a look at the signals that are present in your working area. Unless you are at an OATS facility or inside a specially designed room, you should be able to see lots of RF activity, including TV, FM, AM, 802.11, and Bluetooth signals, not to mention EMI emitted by other equipment in the lab. Take a set of baseline measurements so that you can compare with the measurements of the device under test; you will be looking for the deltas between these two measurements. Remember that radio stations and other sources come and go over the course of time and can vary significantly from day to night. Be sure to take a new baseline reading before each set of measurements, so that you are not chasing ghosts.

For the most part, regulatory testing focuses on the level of unintended emissions of the device under test. It is not uncommon for a product to exceed the limits for unintentional emissions. In some cases, a test failure can be resolved with very simple modifications, while other cases may require a significant redesign.

Few, if any, corresponding requirements relate to susceptibility, other than the standardized audio fidelity requirements for the target platform. You should normally spend more design and debug time on susceptibility than on emissions if you are working on a design with high fidelity targets.

Most of the layout guidelines in "Commonly Encountered Problems" focus on EMI susceptibility, as the inside of PC is a very harsh EMI environment. Many types of interference can be momentary or transient, so it is always best to test for susceptibility by turning on and of various EMI and RFI sources while repeatedly performing dynamic range and SNR testing for both inputs and outputs.

On a practical note, if you have a GSM mobile phone, you can easily test for RF susceptibility. Simply place the GSM mobile phone next to the audio jacks on the computer, and then call the phone from another number. Most computers made today emit a series of tones just before the GSM phone starts to ring, as it negotiates the call with the nearest tower. This tower negotiation is one of the most common sources of RF interference today, and it is an ugly sound. Your customers will appreciate it if your audio subsystem doesn't pick up this noise.

A more serious issue is when you have a built-in GPRS system. Like GSM, these radios can cause a lot of audio interference, especially when they are negotiating with the radio towers. If your design has an optional GPRS module, as many laptops do, then be sure to perform audio testing while the GPRS is connecting and disconnecting from the network.

ISOLATE

The first thing you can do to minimize both susceptibility and emissions is to isolate the audio section from all other circuitry in the computer. Treat the audio circuit as a separate subsystem, even though it may share space with other circuits on the same printed circuit board. If clock sources are located near the audio circuits, the audio circuit may become an inadvertent transmitter of these signals. In a laptop, one of the worst things you can do is to put your audio circuit next to the main 19-volt switching power supply. These supplies emit a strong EMI signal and often operate in the 100-kilohertz range, which is out of range for the EMI filter described later in this section.

In extreme cases, you can enclose the circuit or the jacks in a metal box, which can help combat both EMI and ESD if proper grounding rules are applied. Attach the box to ground at only one location to make sure that no currents are flowing through it. Don't let the box contact any other conductive surfaces. A poorly designed enclosure can cause more problems than it solves.

BITCLK

Once the audio circuitry has been isolated from other clocks, the Intel HD Audio bus becomes the dominant source of EMI. The BITCLK signal on the Intel HD Audio bus runs at a constant 24.000 megahertz. If 24 megahertz is identified as a problem frequency, make sure that the BITCLK circuit is tuned properly. Use a near-field probe to examine the entire length of the BITCLK trace to see if there are any hotspots.

You can also look at the BITCLK waveform using the low-capacitance probe to probe the BITCLK trace at several different points. It should look like a well-formed square wave without a lot of ringing at the edges. If the edges are not well formed, examine the BITCLK trace to see if has lots of turns or T-junctions. A short, straight trace is best to prevent the square wave from ringing.

A good layout can ensure that all of the energy in the signal is transferred from the Intel HD Audio controller to the codec. Any energy that is not transferred will be emanated as unwanted RF, which should be easy to detect using the near-field probe. It may be possible to terminate the BITCLK line with a series or parallel resistor near the codec to reduce the RF emanations from BITCLK and help "square up" this signal. Try several different values to determine which one minimizes the RF output.

While the other signals on the Intel HD Audio bus are less likely to present an EMI emissions problem, the same technique can be used for any of these signals. They work best with good sharp edges.

EMI and ESD Suppression Circuits

Each audio output jack should employ an EMI filter as shown in Figure 5.10. It is important to distinguish between the EMI filter installed very near the codec from the EMI and ESD circuits that are mounted very close to the jack. The 100 picofarad capacitor and the Transient Voltage Suppressor (TVS) mounted near the jack are connected in shunt to chassis ground, not analog ground. This capacitor functions to suppress both ESD and EMI. The chassis ground should be connected directly to the power supply at the point where power enters the box. The chassis should be treated as a shield.

The components in the EMI filter should be mounted very close to the codec, and connected in shunt to the analog ground. These components only affect EMI. This passive network should have little or no effect on audio frequencies, but should help to attenuate unwanted RF on the signal lines. During board bring-up you should perform tests with and without the EMI filter, and compare the results to make sure that the EMI filter is not affecting the audio adversely.

Because EMI and ESD testing can only be fully tested on a completed system, all of these components should be included in the original layout. To save costs, you may wish to depopulate these components (replace the ferrite bead with a 0-ohm jumper) before ESD and EMI testing. If the EMI and ESD tests pass with none of these components in place, you may decide to leave them off of the final product. However, you should wait to decide to remove these parts from the layout until you are sure that the system can pass EMI and ESD testing. If you do not leave these components in the layout and you have to solve an EMI or ESD issue, an unexpected and expensive board spin becomes necessary very late in the product cycle to fix these issues.

While the EMI filter in the diagram looks like a classic Pi filter, it doesn't really work that way. In modern equipment, inputs are usually very high impedance and outputs are very low impedance. The diagram in Figure 5.10 is good for a retaskable jack configuration, where the jack can be used as either input or output. If the jack is used only for output, the capacitors labeled C1 can be removed because they have no effect at low impedances. If the circuit is used only as an input circuit, the capacitors labeled C2 can be removed for the same reason.

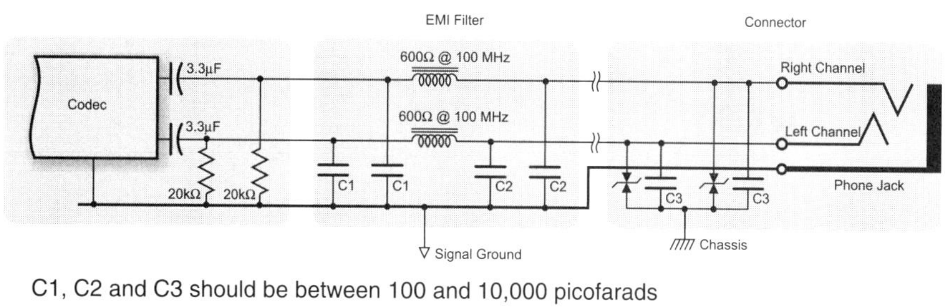

Figure 5.10 Output Circuit Treated for Both EMI and ESD

If you are experiencing excessive EMI from the audio jack, try using different types of ferrite beads to tune out troublesome frequencies, as well as adjusting the values of the capacitors. Always check the data sheet of the ferrite bead to ensure that the DC resistance is as low as possible. If the circuit is used for headphones, the ferrite bead should be capable of passing at least 70 milliamps. Line outputs don't need much current, so the current capability is not usually an issue.

ESD

Electrostatic discharge is more commonly known as static electricity. The shock you get after shuffling across a carpet and then touching a grounded conductive surface is an ESD event.

An ESD event can also cause a condition in the Intel HD Audio codec called "latch-up," where the part goes into an unknown state, possibly with high currents passing through paths not designed for it. A latch-up can sometimes cause the integrated circuit to fail. Other cases might require the power to be removed and restored to return the integrated circuit to normal functionality. In severe cases, the latch-up could permanently damage the circuit by burning through a trace. Such an event, regardless of the cause, is diagnosed as Electrical Overstress (EOS). Figure 5.11 shows damage caused by EOS.

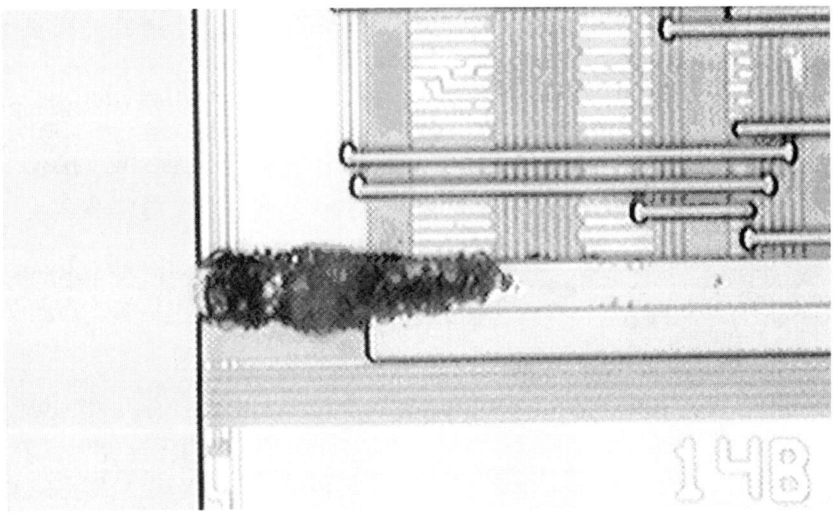

Figure 5.11 A Trace in Integrated Circuit Damaged by Electrical Overstress (EOS)

CAUTION

Testing for ESD sensitivity requires high voltage equipment capable of delivering 30,000 Volts at 30 amps for a short duration. If used improperly, this equipment is capable of causing injury or death. Do not use this equipment unless you have been trained by a qualified instructor, and follow proper safety procedures for working with high voltage.

- The PC industry has taken a number of different approaches to identifying and resolving sensitivity to electrostatic discharge events that result in temporary or permanent system failures.
- JEDEC standards for component-level ESD testing are intended primarily for manufacturing and assembly. The Human Body Model (HBM) was developed in the late 19th century to model the electrostatic discharge of the human body, and has been refined considerably since then. In this model, a small capacitor is charged from a high-voltage supply, and then the charge is routed to the device under test. HBM testing to JEDEC standards takes place with no power applied to the device, and is intended to ensure that an integrated circuit will not be damaged by contact with a human during the assembly process.
- A similar but more rigorous test methodology called the Machine Model was developed in Japan. It helps ensure that an integrated circuit is not damaged by static charges that might exist on automated assembly equipment which make direct contact with the leads of the IC. Like the Human Body Model, the Machine Model is normally used to test and qualify integrated circuits with no power applied, prior to be assembled into a system.
- More recently, the IEC 61000-4-2 specification has gained wide acceptance. The European Union requires compliance with IEC Level 2 performance. Unlike the JEDEC standards, this approach to ESD testing calls for stress testing a completed system both while powered and while not powered.
- Figure 5.12 shows the basic schematic used for HBM, MM, and IEC ESD testing. The schematic is basically the same for all three, but the component values are slightly different for each model. Some versions of the Machine Model use a 500 mH inductor rather than a resistor for R2.

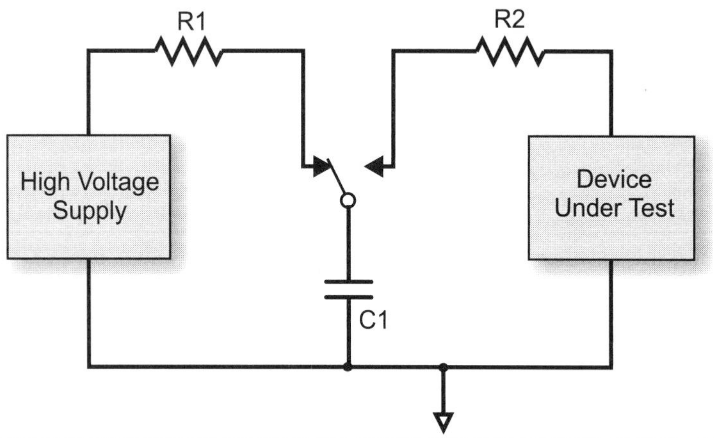

	R1 (ohms)	R2 (ohms)	C1 (picofarads)
Human Body Model	1M to 10M	1500 ± 1%	100 ± 10%
Machine Model	1M	0	200 ± 5%
IEC 61000-4-2	50M to 100M	330	150

The Human Body Model, the Machine Model, and the IEC 61000-4-2 model share the same basic schematic with differing values for key components.

Figure 5.12 Schematic for ESD Testing

The requirements for system testing are often much higher than the requirements for component testing. Why is that? A system can be designed to shield its internal components from ESD events. Therefore, the ESD ratings for systems are usually higher than the ratings for the individual components. Figure 5.13 shows an example of an Electrostatic Discharge Simulator test set.

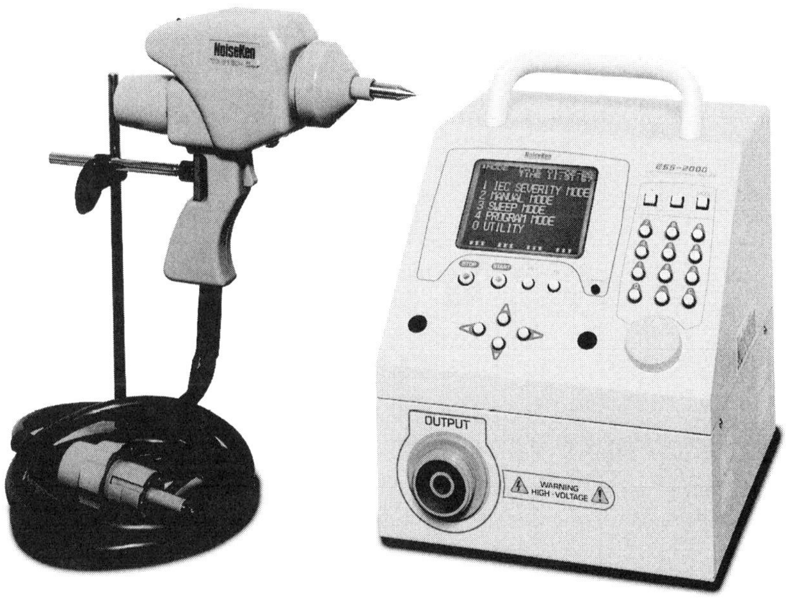

Courtesy of NoiseKen / Noise Laboratory Co., Ltd

Units shown are NoiseKen ESS-2002 Electrostatic Discharge Simulator and the companion TC-815R discharge gun.

Figure 5.13 Electrostatic Discharge Simulator Test Set

The contact discharge method is used for equipment with exposed conductive circuits, while the air burst method is normally used for systems with no exposed conductive surfaces. Figure 5.14 shows a typical setup for complete IEC testing of a PC.

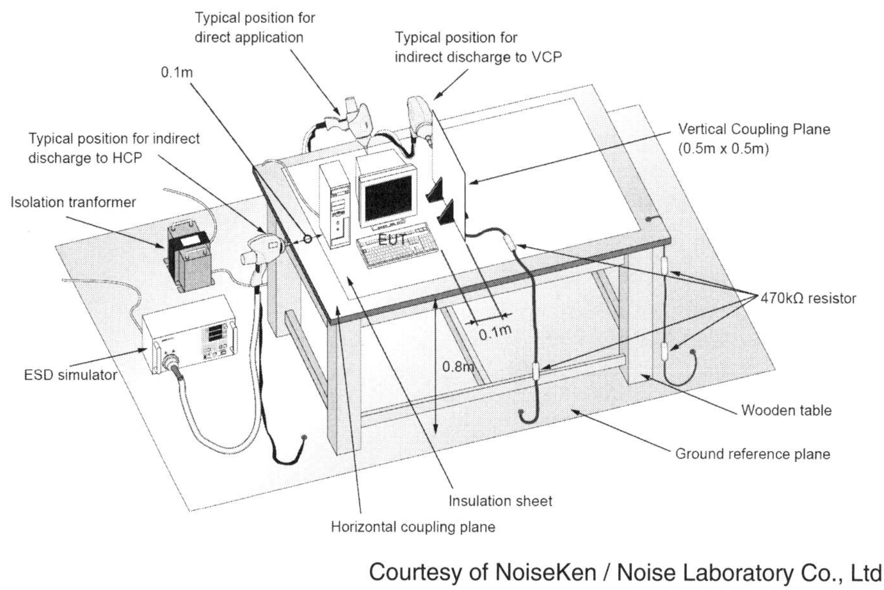

Figure 5.14 ESD Test Setup for IEC 61000-4-2 Testing

The IEC Level determines the characteristics of the ESD pulse that is applied. Table 5.1 shows that the ability for the system to withstand a 4 kV pulse is required to meet European Union requirements, while a system that meets IEC Level 4 can withstand 8 kV connected directly to the system, and 15 kV applied as an air burst in close proximity to the system.

Table 5.1 IEC 61000-4-2 ESD Stress Testing Compliance Levels

IEC Level	Contact Discharge (±kV)	Air Discharge (±kV)
1	2	2
2	4	4
3	6	8
4	8	16

Note: The European Union requires Level 2 compliance.

The results are classified into one of 4 classifications, as shown in Table 5.2. Result code 1 is the most desirable outcome, but result code 2 is usually considered acceptable. Result code 3 is usually not acceptable, and result code 4 is an indication of a poor system design or a poor component design, especially when testing at lower IEC levels.

Table 5.2 IEC 61000-4-2 ESD Test Result Classifications

Result Code	Description
1	Normal performance within specification limits
2	Temporary degradation or loss of function or performance that is self-recoverable
3	Temporary degradation or loss of function or performance, which requires operator intervention or system reset.
4	Degradation or loss of function that is not recoverable due to damage of equipment (components) or software, or loss of data.

Note: A result code of 1 or 2 is desirable. A result code of 3 or 4 is a test failure.

A few simple rules will go a long way in minimizing susceptibility to ESD. First, keep the traces between the codec and the jack short, straight, and wide. If possible, try to avoid any connectors or wiring between the codec and the jack, as this can increase ESD susceptibility.

Use Transient Voltage Suppressors (TVS) on each I/O port to keep harmful potentials from being applied directly to the Intel HD Audio codec. However, you must be very careful to use a TVS that does not introduce distortion into the system.

An ideal transient voltage for audio I/O will have zero leakage, a minimum of 5 Vrms minimum standoff, a fast reaction time of less than 20 nanoseconds, and a surge current capability of 15 or more amps at 8 kV. Be sure to perform distortion testing with and without the TVS installed. For best results, use a THD+N test at a 96 kilohertz or 192 kilohertz sample rate, or use an IMD test. Any differences between the readings are an indicator that the TVS is causing distortion.

Troubleshooting and Debugging

Even if you follow all the guidelines in the book, you almost always run into unique issues for each motherboard design that can be difficult to track down. The techniques outlined here provide you with some ways to dig even further, to insure that your audio design meets the original design goals for the PC.

Test Equipment

For troubleshooting a motherboard design, start with the test setup outlined in Chapter 11. If possible, use multiple pieces of test equipment connected to a single test probe. At a minimum, this setup includes an audio test set, an oscilloscope, a DC voltmeter, a set of good-quality powerful stereo monitor speakers, and a PC with a good pro-quality sound card.

This range of equipment is especially useful in situations where you are not sure exactly what you are looking for. As you probe the circuit, look at each piece of test equipment to check if the readings are as expected. For instance, if you probe a test point with an oscilloscope where signal should be present, also take a look at the DC voltage and make sure it's what you expect it to be.

Make sure to have a separate PC with a professional-quality soundcard with both analog and digital inputs and outputs that match the systems under test. Use this PC to record the output of the system under test. This soundcard-equipped PC is often more useful in first identifying issues than an oscilloscope or an audio analyzer.

Make sure that all of the test equipment and the system under test are properly grounded, and be sure to use some form of anti-static protection, such as an anti-static wrist strap grounded to the same point as the equipment under test.

Troubleshooting: Power Supply

If you are getting unexpected results, start with the power supply. Use both a voltmeter to measure the DC voltage and an oscilloscope set to high sensitivity to see if any AC voltages are present. Check at the output of the power supply and at the various input pins of the codec. Check both analog and digital supplies. AC signals on the analog supply could be an indicator of inadequate voltage regulation or insufficient capacitance in the power supply filter circuits.

Check the VAG voltages at the input and output pins of the codec. If they are not roughly 45 to 50 percent of the analog supply voltage, this variance is usually an indicator that the surrounding DC circuits are not functioning properly.

Play or record a full scale sine wave and again check the power supplies to make sure that you see no AC voltages. If the AC voltage is present only when playing audio, you should increase the size of the filter capacitor in the power supply. Bypass the filter capacitor with a small capacitor right at the pin if you are seeing very high frequencies on this trace. In some cases, you might need to widen the traces or insert some series resistance in the supply line to isolate the filter capacitor.

Do the same for various control voltages such as GPIOs, jack-insertion circuits, and microphone bias circuits. If you see AC voltages on any of these circuits, especially when audio is playing, then you need to analyze further.

If the design includes a dedicated power amp for speakers or headphones, probe the power supply to the amp while starting and stopping a full-scale sine wave. If the DC voltage varies at all, or if you see AC voltage, then either the power supply is insufficient, resistance in series between the power supply and the amp is too great, or the power supply filter has insufficient capacitance.

Troubleshooting: Signal Tracing

If an output signal is not present at the output jacks, or if an input signal is not showing up at the recording application, start by checking both AC and DC voltages at the codec pins. Be very careful when probing the codec pins, as they are very close together. Shorting two pins together with the probe could damage the codec and require it to be replaced before further troubleshooting can take place.

For output circuits, if the signal is available at the codec pin, probe at the output of the coupling capacitor next. You should see the same AC signal, but no DC voltage. If a pop-suppression circuit is installed, check before the circuit (at the output of the coupling capacitor) and after the circuit (usually at the output jack).

For input circuits, start at the input jack and verify the signal there. Then, check at the codec pin for correct AC and DC voltages. For any discrete circuitry such as a preamplifier or attenuator between the input jack and the codec, be sure to check on both input and output of that circuit.

Troubleshooting Pops and Clicks

Troubleshooting pops and clicks is often more difficult and time consuming than other types of troubleshooting. The test points should be at the output pins of the codec, rather than after the coupling capacitor or at the output jack. Pops and clicks are usually the result of a change in DC operating levels, and they cannot be easily quantified when the DC component is removed, as would be the case of testing at the other side of the coupling capacitor.

The easiest method is usually to solder two short wires directly to the output pins, and then clip the test probes to these wires. If possible, use an oscilloscope which is DC coupled and set to trigger on the pop. This way, the DC shift can be easily observed and quantified.

If driver source code is available, it is often a good idea to set a breakpoint in the debugger and single-step through the code, stopping when you hear the pop and analyzing the last instruction sent to the codec. However, doing so does not help with pops that occur prior to the driver being loaded, or after the driver is unloaded, since the BIOS is typically in control at these times.

If you are testing for pops in a built-in speaker, connect one pair of probes to the speaker terminals and connect another pair of probes to the codec output pins. Compare the results to determine where the pop is occurring. For instance, if the pop is not present on the codec output pins, then the pop is probably in the speaker amp circuitry.

Sometimes you can determine whether a pop or click is caused by hardware or software if the system has an S/PDIF output. Use a professional sound card running on a separate computer to record both analog and S/PDIF outputs of the system under test. Compare the results. Any pops and clicks that occur on both are taking place in software, any pops and clicks that are in only the analog output are taking place in analog.

Troubleshooting SNR and THD+N

A well-designed Intel HD Audio codec should have better SNR specs than the board on which it is mounted, primarily due to the harsh electrical environment inside a typical PC. Therefore, most SNR troubleshooting takes place at the board level.

One effective technique is to simply remove the codec from the motherboard and check the audio circuitry without the codec. Solder a pair of short wires to the pads associated with the codec port you wish to test, and clip your probes onto these wires. If you are testing an output port, connect the generator outputs of the audio test set to these wires and connect the signal from the associated output jack to the analyzer inputs of the audio test set. If you are testing an input port, connect the generator outputs of the test set to the associated input jack, and connect the two wires to the analyzer inputs of the audio test set.

Since no DACs or ADCs are involved when testing in this manner, you can test using an interactive line-to-line testing methodology, which is usually easier to set up and interpret the results.

If the circuitry by itself cannot meet the performance targets, then further investigation is necessary. The "divide-and-conquer" approach is probably most useful. Choose a point about halfway through the circuit and test at that point. It might be necessary to remove a component such as a coupling capacitor or series resistor in order to isolate a portion of the circuit. Test each half of the circuit to determine where the issues are occurring. If necessary, split this portion of the circuit into two sections and test again.

When testing without the codec installed, be sure to exercise all the different subsystems on the motherboard while testing: move the mouse, de-fragment the hard drive, transfer a very large file over the wireless network, run a video benchmark test, etc.

After testing without the codec has been completed, reinstall the codec and repeat the same tests. If the readings are not as good, there are a number of possible explanations. It could be an indicator that the codec performance is not as good as the board performance, and a codec with better specs should be considered, or it could be due to more complex interactions due to impedance changes in the circuit when the codec is reinstalled.

Troubleshooting Frequency Response

If a failure occurs in the frequency response or in the passband ripple tests, the culprit is almost always a coupling capacitor which is too small, which causes a failure at low frequencies.

If the failure occurs at high frequencies, carefully check for any capacitance in shunt at the output stage. Make sure to accommodate for capacitor tolerance as well as DC voltage and temperature variations that might affect the actual capacitance of the circuit.

Troubleshooting Active Outputs

Watch out for additional pops and clicks when interfacing to built-in speaker amps or headphone amps. Be sure to clip one oscilloscope probe to the codec output, and attach a separate probe to the output of the amp. Compare the two traces to see whether pops are present on both traces, or just on one. Set the scope inputs for DC coupling to see the pops and clicks more clearly.

"Golden" Passive Components

Because of extreme price pressures, often the least expensive passive components are used during the design cycle, since these are what will usually be used in production. However, you should keep a stock of higher-quality components for use while bringing up the board and during debugging phases. This group of golden parts includes film dielectric capacitors and low-noise precision resistors.

If you are having difficulty tracking down an audio performance issue, try replacing the passive components one by one with these golden parts. If the problem goes away, it should be easy to identify which component made a difference, allowing you to determine an appropriate course of action.

Chapter 6

Recommendations for Media PCs

To obtain a level of audio fidelity commensurate with top-end consumer audio equipment, your budget for the audio components must be about the same for each. Put simply, you cannot get the same performance as a $300 preamp using $2 worth of components. While existing low-cost approaches may yet be able to serve PC market segments such as the server market where audio is not of much interest, now Media PCs must compete directly with other equipment in the living room and the home theater. As a result, the overall system cost must be increased to meet the expectations of discerning customers and reviewers.

Audio Attributes of a Media PC

To truly compete against the audio equipment present in most living rooms and home theatres today, your design must have these attributes:

- *RCA jacks for line-level inputs and outputs.* They need to match existing equipment in the living room and provide a more reliable electrical contact that 3.5-millimeter miniature phone jack. Jack detection switches on the RCA jacks must be implemented in order to comply with the Windows Vista logo program. The Microsoft UAA class driver for Intel HD Audio sets the output to a fixed output level, with no master volume control, if the output jacks are specified as RCA jacks and the device type is set to line out.

- *2 volts RMS analog input and output levels.* This attribute avoids perceived loss of quality due to lower playback level. Refer to the Fletcher Munson curves in Chapter 1 for more details
- *No pops or clicks.* An absolute must for interfacing to high-powered high-fidelity audio systems: you need either shunt or series pop suppression circuits, with 3 to 5 second delays, to guarantee no pops and clicks in any PC audio circuit that uses a unipolar power supply.
- *No re-tasking.* RCA jacks should be fixed function, either input or output, just like those on existing equipment
- *Freedom from EMI and RFI interference.* No hums, buzzes, or static noises can be coupled in from other portions of the PC or radio signals.
- *Resilience to ESD events.* The system as a whole should conform to IEC 61000-4-2 Level 2 compliance. Level 4 is often required by leading OEMs.
- *Volume on Remote Control ALWAYS works.* A remote control, such as the Media Center PC remote control, must have the capability to adjust the listening volume in each and every user scenario, in order to achieve the goal of replacing multiple remote controls with a single remote control per living room. This single source of control should be the default behavior of a Media PC design. Some systems may offer the option to disable the remote volume control as a user preference, in much the same way as TV sets that allow the remote control volume to be disabled.
- *Digital master volume support.* If multi-channel compressed audio is being passed as non-PCM data over S/PDIF or HDMI digital interfaces, then a real-time encoder such as Dolby Digital Live or DTS Connect must be operating full time, and (under Windows XP) the DVD player application must have installed decoders for each non-PCM format that is intended to be supported. If non-PCM pass-through is attempted in this type of system, the remote control volume fails to work and the audio playback becomes stuck at full volume for the duration of the non-PCM data stream. The listener is forced to employ another remote control for the listening volume because the volume button on the Media PC's remote control has stopped working. Also, the clicks normally heard when the user presses buttons on the remote control cannot be heard whenever a non-PCM stream is playing.

Pops and Clicks

The terms "pop" and "click" refer to the unwanted audio-band transients that an input or output circuit produces during mode transitions. An ideal component would produce no audible artifacts during these mode transitions, but in practice, you always have a small but measurable artifact. The effect of this phenomenon varies, depending on the following things:

- The sensitivity of the output transducer (for speaker or headphone)
- The distance of the speaker from the listener's ear
- The listener's hearing
- The amount of gain applied after the signal leaves the computer

While it is very difficult, perhaps even impractical, to measure all of these system-related factors comprehensively; you can, however, with reasonable effort measure the electrical characteristics of the output circuit objectively. For a detailed explanation on how to perform these measurements, see Chapter 11, "Test and Measurements."

Unlike other types of noises, pops and clicks usually are caused by instantaneous DC voltage shifts rather than by anything that can be measured as AC voltage. Pops and clicks most often occur in analog circuits, but poorly designed signal processing software can also be a source.

To prevent pops and clicks, large concert sound systems and advanced hi-fi systems use power sequencing techniques to start up the system. Power strips with timers automate the process. For PA systems, first the outboard equipment is powered up, then the mixing board, then the racks of amplifiers, one by one. The power down sequence goes in reverse order. You can apply these same techniques to PC audio, just on a smaller scale.

The single biggest source of pops and clicks are the power transitions that take place during system startup, system shutdown, suspend, and resume. Most high-fidelity audio equipment contains bi-polar power supplies, with both positive and negative DC power supplies of equal potential. The AC signals swing back and forth around the zero point, as shown in 6.8. When the system is turned on and the positive and negative supplies are brought up equally and simultaneously, the net output voltage should remain at zero, and therefore pops or clicks are minimized.

On the other hand, PCs typically have unipolar power supplies consisting of 5VDC and 12VDC rails. Traditionally, the audio is run from a voltage regulator that is attached to the 5VDC rail, which is in turn referenced to analog ground. In this case, the AC signal swings back and forth between 0 VDC and the maximum analog supply, which varies from 3.3 VDC to 5VDC, centering around a point which is usually a little less than half of the analog power supply.

This voltage point is referred to as the Virtual Analog Ground, or VAG, and is the nominal DC offset present at the codec output. The AC output swings around this point symmetrically. Due to the differences between PNP and NPN transistor characteristics when both are used in a uni-polar power supply, the Virtual Analog Ground (VAG) is usually about 45 percent of AVdd. For instance, if the analog power supply is 5VDC, then the center point is 2.25VDC. This scenario explains the off-center sine wave swing seen on the right of Figure 6.1, showing positive and negative rails for both bipolar and unipolar power supplies.

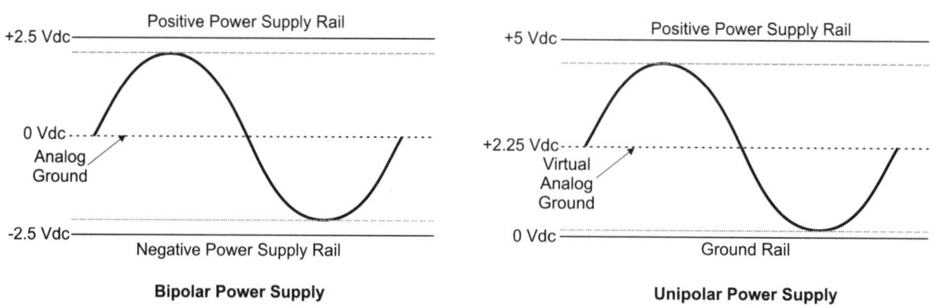

Figure 6.1 AC Voltage Swing for Both Bipolar and Unipolar Power Supplies

When the power is applied, the DC output voltage must change from 0 VDC to the normal DC voltage of VAG, when power is removed, the voltage must change from VAG to 0 VDC. If this voltage shift occurs instantaneously, a very loud pop is generated. If an amplified speaker system is connected to the PC and turned up to provide a full dynamic range of listening volumes, the pop could be astonishingly loud, especially if a powerful subwoofer is attached to the system.

This type of instantaneous voltage shift is known as an *impulse*, which has energy at all frequencies. One way to avoid an impulse is to ramp VAG from zero to its normal operating level over the course of many seconds. As the ramp is slowed down, the higher frequencies seem to disappear from the pop, and it sounds more like a thud.

The ramp timing is shown in Figure 6.2. If the ramp is slow enough, the impulse response is shifted below the range of human hearing, though you might still see the speaker cone of the subwoofer move as the power supply is ramped. It is important to monitor for pops and clicks using a powerful full-range loudspeaker because you might not notice a ramp of only a few seconds on small speakers, such as those found in a laptop. However, that same pop still could be audible when plugged into a powerful full-range surround system with subwoofer. For such a system, a line output from a unipolar device could need up to 30 seconds to settle for no pops or clicks to be heard on any speaker system.

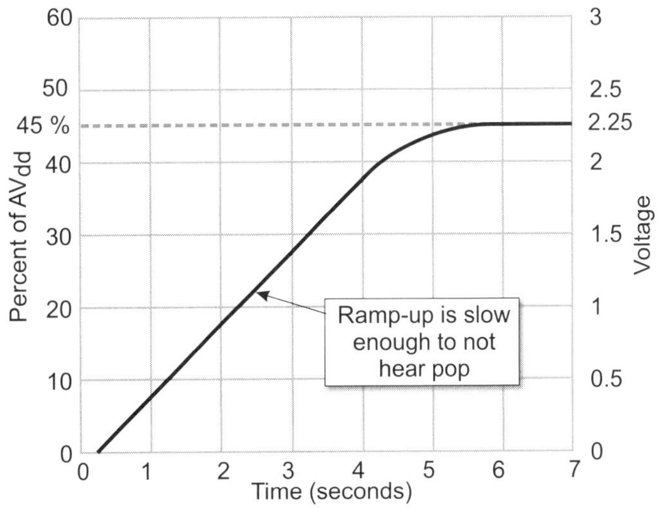

Figure 6.2 Virtual Analog Ground (VAG) Rise Time during Power-Up

Do not confuse this VAG rise time with power supply rise time. The AVdd power supply should be designed to reach full voltage within 15 to 100 milliseconds, which is much, much faster than VAG rise time.

Circuits with low impedance loads tend to ramp faster than circuits with high impedance loads. Circuits with large coupling capacitors take longer. For instance, the same headphone output circuit could be run to headphones or to a high impedance line input. The VAG rise time is much faster with the headphones plugged in than it is with the line input connected. Use a load resistor, as shown in Figure 6.3, to control these rise times. Be sure that you use a resistor greater than 4.7 kiloohms if the output is not headphone-capable or you could experience excessive distortion. Adjusting the size of the VRef Filter capacitor that is normally attached to pin 27 of the codec can also affect the timings.

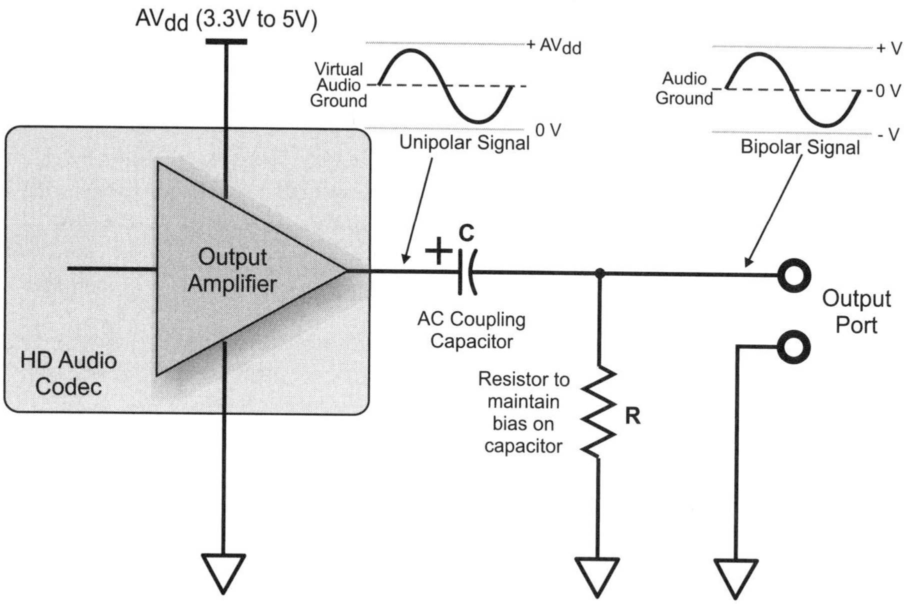

A load resistor in shunt with the output can help shorten the settling time. Use a 1-kiloohm resistor for a circuit with dedicated headphone drive capability and a large coupling capacitor. Use a 20-kiloohm resistor for line output with a smaller coupling capacitor.

Figure 6.3 Circuit to Shorten Settling Time

Because of the unipolar power supply architecture, you must perform a careful analysis at each of the four major power transitions: startup, shutdown, suspend, and resume. Each of these transitions can be the source of one or more pops, and each pop can manifest separately from the others. At loud enough amplitudes, these pops can damage loudspeakers, and, if they are loud enough, can even cause damage to the listener's ears. The better the amplified speaker system, the more noticeable are the pops and clicks, and the more costly it is to repair the speakers if damaged.

System Start-up (Cold Boot)

Starting up the system is the most problematic scenario due to the extensive system activity that occurs. During the early stages of boot-up, the hardware is under control of the BIOS, which sequences the power supplies, identifies the hardware that is present, starts up the audio codec, and populates the pin-configuration registers on the codec by sending verb tables to the Intel HD Audio codec.

Since the audio driver is not loaded until somewhat later in the process, the BIOS is responsible for ensuring that no pops occur during the early stages of system startup. For best results, the BIOS should first bring up the digital power supply (DVdd), then de-assert RESET#, and then mute all outputs and inputs by writing to the appropriate widgets for all of the jacks that are designated in the pin-configuration registers.

If an analog PC beep input is used for POST tones (not recommended), the BIOS should hold the codec in RESET# until the analog supply has ramped up. After that point the BIOS can open up the PC beep audio path, so that the listener can hear the POST tones. Then, the BIOS should transmit the verb tables containing the proper pin configuration defaults to each pin widget in the codec. Once this step is completed, the BIOS should then enable the analog power supply, so that the ramp-up of the supply voltage can begin as soon as possible.

The analog supply circuit for the codec and the VRef filter capacitor on the codec should be tuned for a ramp-up timing that happens as quickly as possible without hearing a click. The value of the capacitor that is connected to VRef must be large enough to ensure a slow ramp. Remember that if you monitor for the pops and clicks on small speakers, you can ramp the power supply much more quickly without hearing a pop. That same pop can easily be heard if the system is connected to powerful full-range speaker systems.

At some point later in the startup cycle, the Intel HD Audio bus driver is enumerated, which in turn enumerates one or more instances of the function driver. From this point on, the function driver can take control of the codec. The function driver should keep all inputs and outputs muted while reading the pin configuration registers and configuring the widgets in the codec. The outputs should be unmuted only after all other codec configuration is complete and the analog supply voltage has reached its full value.

System Shutdown (Power off)

The first thing that the audio driver should do, when notified that the system is going to shut down, is to mute all inputs and outputs. The BIOS should immediately disable the analog power supply, and VAG then starts ramping down at the same rate as it ramped up during start-up since the impulse response issues basically are identical regardless of the direction of the VAG ramping. The digital power supply to the codec should be removed only after the analog supply has fully ramped to zero. If the digital power supply is removed before this point, a pop could occur. It is also important to ensure that both analog and digital power supplies go completely to zero volts. Any lingering voltage could produce inconsistencies in minimizing these pops.

You have a special case to consider: powering the system up and down rapidly, which typically occurs only in testing labs and not in actual use. This situation has to do with powering the system up and down rapidly. If the system is fully powered down, and then restarted less than about one minute afterwards, a pop could occur because the power supplies have not fully settled. Specifically, if the analog supply is non-zero when the digital supply is brought up and the codec receives the RESET# signal, a pop could occur. No single comprehensive method guards against this type of pop. The good news is that most users don't perform this kind of power cycle very often, but it is likely to occur in testing laboratories where an impatient technician does not wait a full 60 seconds before starting the PC back up. This premature restart can result in false failures if the power to the system is cycled immediately back on after removing power from the system.

Some systems are designed so that the analog supply to the codec is powered up whenever power is applied to the motherboard. This connection is done in special cases to allow the analog audio output of the CD player or some other audio source to be routed through the analog circuitry of the codec, allowing the system to be used to play music even if the OS is not running. In such cases, the system designer must pay careful attention to the power sequencing and ramp times of the analog power supply. Fortunately, this type of implementation is becoming less common, ceasing to be an issue for most system designs.

While less common today than in the past, PC beep circuits on the motherboard can be another source of pops, because these circuits generate a series of square waves to provide POST tones and other audio feedback to the user when the BIOS is initializing. An analog PC beep circuit can also be used to generate key click sounds or to route an analog signal from a PCMCIA card on a laptop to the audio subsystem. The most common use for the audio output from the PCMCIA card cage are to provide audible notification of connect/disconnect status from a wireless network or to provide the call progress sounds heard when a modem is making a connection.

An especially troublesome aspect is that some PCMCIA cards generate a PWM stream, which, while heard as a somewhat distorted analog sound, also generates a noticeable pop when the sound starts and stops playing. For this reason, few modern systems connect the PCMCIA card cage output to the analog PC beep input.

While not always obvious to the board designer, it is absolutely necessary to use a coupling capacitor when connecting signals from the motherboard to an analog PC beep input. Otherwise, DC applied to this input can cause some spectacular pops before the driver is loaded while the audio subsystem is still under BIOS control. Analog PC Beep is a source of a number of audio problems, and you should avoid it in your design if at all possible. The Windows Vista Logo program may not allow analog PC beep.

Suspend

The sequence for supporting suspend events is quite similar to the shutdown sequence described earlier, but the code paths in both the driver and the BIOS are likely to differ. You should take care that the same sequence is applied in both cases.

Also, in the case of suspend, the driver is responsible for caching the current register settings so that it can restore them later. The driver should always mute all inputs and outputs before allowing the system to suspend.

Resume

The resume sequence is similar to the start-up sequence, but is expected to occur much more quickly. Unfortunately, the analog supply ramp time cannot be shortened without hearing a pop, so fitting in the resume sequence can be quite a challenge.

Unlike system start-up, the audio function driver is responsible for restoring all the codec settings that were cached during the suspend operation, including the pin configuration registers. However, the BIOS are also responsible for retransmitting the same verb tables that it transmitted during startup. See "Sending Verb Tables to the Codec" in Chapter 4 for details on how to preserve the modem's wake-on-ring state during the resume operation.

Software-induced Pops and Clicks

One of the easiest ways to get a pop is to play a .WAV file that starts at a non-zero point. Commercial audio content providers are very aware of this issue, and they go to great lengths to make sure that their content always starts at a digital zero level.

However, you have no guarantee that a sound downloaded from a Web site has been produced in this manner. You have no way to guard against such sound content, other than to be vigilant about what .WAV files are played on your computer. Certainly, you can create a .WAV file that can damage an unprotected high-powered speaker system because the impulse becomes quite load, as shown in Figure 6.4.

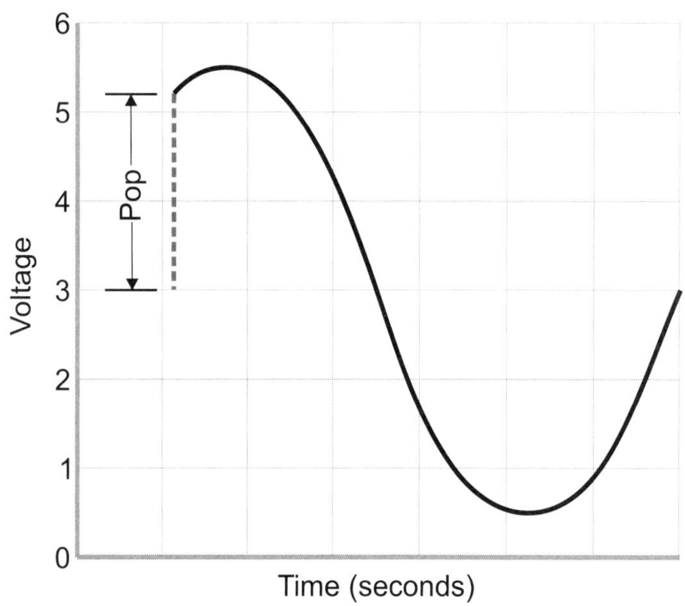

Figure 6.4 A Sine Wave Starting at a Non-Zero Point

Another problem can occur occasionally in Windows XP when the .WAV file is stopped or paused before it is done playing. While Windows XP's software-based KMixer is usually good about ramping these impulses down to zero, it doesn't happen in all cases, especially if only a single sound is played or paused in between long silences. In general, all signal processing stages must be sure to ramp to a zero value before ending the stream, otherwise this type of pop will occur in a seemingly random fashion, as it is content-dependent.

One important consideration for software-induced pops and clicks is that they are delivered accurately through digital interfaces, such as S/PDIF and ADAT, and that they are reproduced accurately by an external sound system, even if all the guidelines for analog pops and clicks have been followed religiously. Be aware that this type of noise is not heard when the sound stops playing, but it is heard when the next sound—one that was properly produced to start at a digital zero—is played, as shown in Figure 6.5.

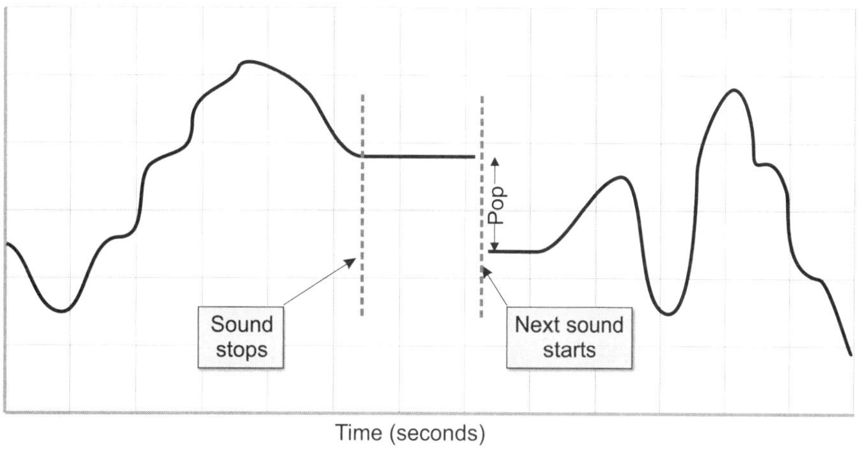

Figure 6.5 Pop from Sound Stopping and Re-starting After Pause

DC Offsets

Another source of clicks arises from minor DC shifts that occur as the audio codec switches between various modes of operation. For instance, even a slight change in DC levels, such as when the DAC starts and stops playing or when the mute control is turned on and off, is heard as a click. This phenomenon is identical to the pops previously described, but the magnitude of the DC offset is much smaller. These imperfections are due to the design of the codec, and typically, they are a function of the cost of the codec. The circuitry required to minimize such DC shifts is often removed in cheaper codecs to provide a cost savings. This DC shift circuitry is simply not a good place to cut corners.

Another source of DC offsets is the analog mixer, which some system designs still include for legacy reasons. In this case, the output signal from the codec is a combination of the DAC output and various analog inputs. If any of these analog inputs has a DC component, a click can be heard as the analog input is muted and unmuted, when its volume control is turned up or down, or even when the DAC is muted and unmuted. The use of analog mixing for Intel HD Audio systems is generally discouraged, and its presence may result in a test failure under the Windows Vista logo program.

Zipper Noise

Yet another source of noise is the gain step that occurs when the hardware volume control in the codec is manipulated, either while audio is playing or when a DC component s present on the output for whatever reason. The gain steps for hardware volume controls on an Intel HD Audio codec are between 0.5 and 1.5 dB per step. As a result, small impulses can be heard when the levels are being manipulated. This noise is called *zipper noise*.

One of the best ways to avoid zipper noise is to perform all volume scaling entirely in software and avoid the use of hardware volume controls. For this reason, some newer Intel HD Audio codec designs contain no hardware volume or mute controls. Typically, the software processing can use smaller increments for the gain changes. However, you should be aware that abrupt changes in level results in an impulse. Therefore, software-based volume controls should always ramp between volumes and never perform a step function.

External Pop Suppression Circuits

If you still have pops and clicks during power cycles remain problematic after tuning the ramp time, you might consider some possible solutions using external components. Two basic classes of external pop-suppression circuits exist: series and shunt. You can implement both classes with either electromechanical relays, which give the best performance, but incur the highest costs, or with silicon, a lower cost solution that comes with some performance tradeoffs). These silicon tradeoffs provide you with a wide range of solutions depending on the audio fidelity target and the cost target

Series Pop Suppression Circuits

One popular method is used in consumer electronics devices to eliminate startup and shutdown transients. You include a relay in series with each audio output, as shown in Figure 6.6. The control signal to the relay is timed to turn on the relay only after all turn-on transients have occurred. Control of this timing delay can be accomplished in one of two ways:

- A driver from the codec vendor can take advantage of general-purpose input/output (GPIO) pins on the codec to control the relays, but the Microsoft UAA class driver for Intel HD Audio does not make use of these pins.
- A better approach is to put a dedicated RC time delay circuit to delay the switch closure until between 5 and 35 seconds after AVdd has come up. The time delay is set to be just longer than the longest VAG rise time, which is typically usually measured under the condition of a termination resistance of 20,000 ohms or greater.

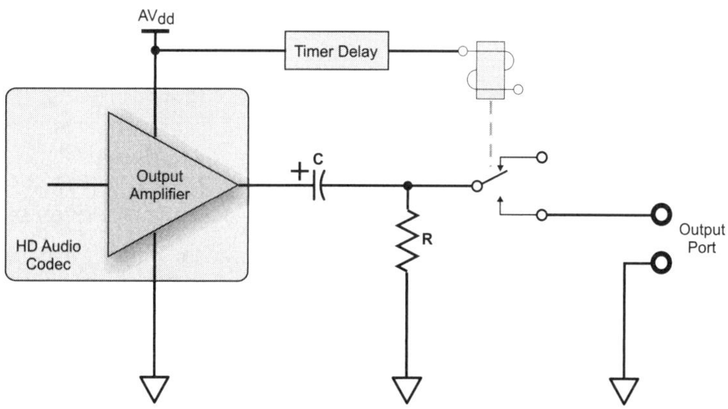

The terminating resistor is permanently connected to the coupling capacitor, so that the capacitor has a constant path to ground, regardless of the state of the relay. The relay is configured so that the contacts remain open until the timer delay has completed. The timer delay should be set between 5 and 35 seconds, or longer if the system is expected to drive line-level inputs to a high-gain, high-power speaker system that includes a subwoofer.

Figure 6.6 A Relay Circuit in Series with the Audio Output

No time delay is needed when AVdd is removed. It is better if the relay were to open slightly *before* AVdd is removed, which would require a more advanced circuit than the one shown here in order to support the Microsoft UAA class driver for Intel HD Audio. However, a codec-vendor-supplied driver controlling the relay using a GPIO can turn off the relay before AVdd is removed, at least in those cases when OS and audio drivers are in control when AVdd is removed.

Using an electromechanical relay in series with the output signal provides the highest degree of electrical isolation from the sources of the pops and clicks. Similar designs are used in many stereo receivers. End users are often reassured by hearing the time-delayed relay kick in, because they are used to this on their high-end audio equipment.

Because the audio signal must run through the relay switch contacts, the contacts themselves must be low impedance and rated for long life expectancy.

You could also implement this circuit using silicon components. For highest quality, use silicon switches that are designed for audio applications, such as the Analog Devices ADG841, to accomplish a similar result. Pay careful attention to the THD+N of the switch, since it could limit overall THD+N performance. Some switches list THD+N in percentages, such as 0.02 percent. As a quick rule of thumb, 0.01 percent is -80 dB THD+N, which is not particularly good performance for a media center PC.

A good analog circuit designer could also implement this type of switch in discrete circuitry using an FET or even a bipolar transistor, though the bipolar implementation would likely be much more difficult. If the output is intended for headphone use, the coupling capacitor and its associated currents could be large, and the open channel of the FET must be capable of passing all the current that the headphone draws. In many implementations, the silicon switch impedance is load dependent and may change with applied voltage.

However, unlike relays, an FET usually is not suitable for signals driving headphones, since the minimum resistance of an activated FET is 50 ohms or greater. This resistance interacts with the impedance of the headphones and causes a loss of 6 dB or greater, as well as requiring a large FET that is capable of dissipating the heat caused by the power that is consumed by this resistance.

Also, since the channel of an FET is normally on when no voltage is on the gate, careful power sequencing is required to turn the FET off as soon as power is applied, thereby keeping clicks from being transmitted to the output.

So an electromechanical series circuit can provide the best avoidance to pops and clicks—at the highest price and with high-quality relays. If a silicon-based switching solution is desired, a series implementation is probably not the best choice because of THD+N, current handling, and default switch polarity issues.

Shunt Pop Suppression Circuits

Instead of putting the switch in series, you also could put the switch in shunt. Using an electromechanical relay in a shunt configuration allows a reduction of pops and clicks second only to the electromechanical relay used in a series configuration. (See "Series Pop Suppression Circuits" in this chapter.) Some pops and clicks can still sneak through if the shunt path is greater than 0 ohms. This increased resistance could result from relay contacts deteriorating over time, or from use of a silicon switch with a non-zero impedance. However, even if the impedance is non-zero, the pops and clicks should be reduced significantly compared to putting no such switches in place.

Reminder: this configuration essentially puts a short on the output. As such, it should not be used for outputs driving low impedance loads, such as speakers or headphones. It is best suited for line level outputs.

In the shunt configuration shown in Figure 6.7, the signal path does not pass through the switch during normal operation. The relay contacts must be able to withstand the current surges during the VAG ramp-up and ramp-down cycles, when they are shunting all of the capacitor output currents to ground. The quality of the relay contacts is not as critical since they are not in the signal path, so you could use a less expensive relay compared to a series configuration, and the lifetime is not a significant consideration. In the shunt configuration, the relay should be normally closed, and it should be opened under timer or driver control once all the DC voltages have settled. A "snubber" circuit is used to minimize the difference in potential between the relay contacts when open. This snubber helps minimize transient currents when the contacts open and close, and it may help prevent arcing at the contacts if DC is present, which could extend the life of the relay contacts.

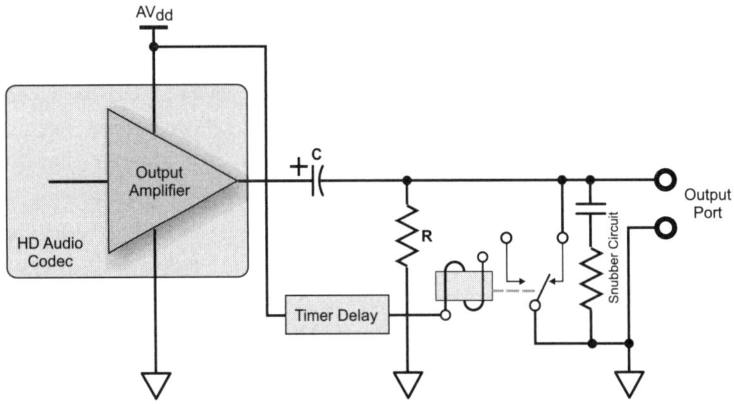

During power-up and power-down, the relay contacts should be closed to shunt any pops and clicks to ground. The relay contacts should open only after VAG has settled. The snubber circuit minimizes potential differences as the contacts come together.

Figure 6.7 A Relay Circuit in Shunt with the Audio Output

One benefit of this configuration is that the VAG ramp is faster than any other configuration because the output end of the capacitor is being held to ground during the ramp-up and ramp-down cycles.

When silicon solutions are used, the same basic considerations apply. Specially designed audio switches, such as Analog Devices ADG842, could provide easier design cycles and better performance, but FETs and bipolar circuits can also be implemented by a good analog circuit designer. If a discrete implementation is developed, be sure that the maximum amplitude AC output signal does not interact with the control node.

Compared to a series implementation, the THD+N of the switch is not so critical in overall circuit fidelity because the switch is in shunt with the signal when it contributes to the THD+N. The impedance of the silicon switch should be as close as possible to zero when the switch is closed, and the impedance should be at least 20,000 ohms when the switch is open. Higher impedance is better for this configuration.

The shunt configuration also favors the use of FET switches. Select an FET switch which is normally closed when no voltage is applied to the input, allowing the shunt to be in place while the equipment is powered up and down. The shunt is only removed once the system has powered up and a voltage is applied to the gate of the FET to open the switch.

Since the silicon switch must be on the other side of the coupling capacitor from the codec, it is not easily integrated into the codec. The timing issues when power is removed are the same for both series and shunt configurations; it is best to put the shunt on just before removing the power. Either a more expensive circuit must be used to trigger the switch before removing AVdd, or a codec vendor's driver must execute a custom GPIO action script to accomplish this sequence.

The shunt configuration works well with re-tasking jacks, since shunt to ground is the preferred standby state for inputs. However, care should be taken to limit the shunt impedance of the circuit to greater than 20,000 ohms when the shunt relay is not engaged, so that the input signals are not loaded down by any of the protection circuitry. Be sure that the shunt is open before perfuming any impedance sense functions.

In the shunt configuration, the coupling capacitor appears as a dead short when VAG first starts ramping. Make sure to use components that can pass the large transient currents that are generated as the coupling capacitor charges.

Be aware that the output amplifier must have internal short circuit protection or a resistor in series between the amplifier and the coupling capacitor. If the system has no output short circuit detection, the output amp could be damaged by running in this configuration.

The sets of 5.1 or 7.1 output jacks on a media PC are the most likely candidates for active pop and click suppression circuits. A dedicated headphone jack on the front panel, for instance, might not need this type of treatment. You must take a lot of factors into account when making this determination. Each channel requires a separate switch, so you need six or eight switches or relay contacts for 5.1 or 7.1, respectively. The prices for relays with multiple contacts appear to go up exponentially in relation to the number of contacts; using multiple pairs of 2-channel relays in shunt appears to be the best cost/performance tradeoff if electro-mechanical relays are used.

Pricing for these types of external circuits ranges from 5 cents to 50 cents per channel for silicon solutions, and 1 dollar and up per channel for electro-mechanical relays. Generally speaking, the overall fidelity and the resilience to pops and clicks both increase with cost.

Pop Suppression for Built-in Headphone and Speaker Amplifiers

In addition to analog outputs, many PCs also contain built-in speaker amplifiers. Currently speaker amps range between 1 and 5 watts stereo, although over the next few years multi-channel Class-D PWM digital amplifiers are expected to be integrated into media PCs, in much the same way that speaker amps have been integrated into audio receivers.

Even though most Intel HD Audio codecs contain an integrated headphone amp, some leading laptop designs have recently begun using separate capacitor-less headphone amps because these amps cost less than the small but expensive tantalum capacitors needed for headphone outputs for designs where space is at a premium. It is not uncommon to find both a separate headphone amp and a separate speaker amp in an Intel HD Audio-equipped laptop these days.

Interfacing to these amplifiers requires extra care. In many cases, the input impedance is much lower than a typical op-amp, and the coupling capacitor values become critical. Capacitors with performance variations caused by varying DC bias, heat, or loose tolerances almost always cause problems.

Power amps usually have one or more pins for power-down or standby control. In AC97 systems, the simplest implementation was referred to as External Amp Power Down (EAPD). Typically, Pin 47 of the codec would drive high to turn off the power amp and go low to turn it on. A pin with this name is available on some Intel HD Audio codecs, but the logic is inverted. Technically, it should now be called EAPU, for *External Amp Power Up*, since the pin is driven high to turn the power amp on. Most codecs use Pin 47 for S/PDIF in, though some codecs also allow this pin to be switched to use as EAPD.

Some power amps have two external control lines. One is for powering down the power amp, for maximum power savings. Depending on the amplifier design, a slight pop might occur when this signal is toggled. If a second control line is available, usually that line is used to mute the amp or puts it in standby. The use of the line allows a way to mute the output without clicking. With some designs, you could sequence these two signals with some delays to remove power to the amp without popping.

However, as with the relay circuits mentioned in "Shunt Pop Suppression Circuits," you might have to use a GPIO to control the external power amp, a solution that is not supported by the Microsoft UAA class driver for Intel HD Audio. If an EAPD pin is available on the codec and the codec is configured to use it instead of S/PDIF in, the class driver might support the use of the EAPD line. Otherwise, these control lines must be operated by timer delays, much like the relay circuits, or by a custom codec-vendor-supplied driver that includes GPIO support.

Interfacing to Consumer Electronics Equipment

Because of the 5V unipolar power supplies prevalent in PCs, the nominal output level of AC97 codecs as well as existing Intel HD Audio codecs is 1 Vrms, or 0 dBV. However, most consumer electronics (CE) devices run at a nominal 2 Vrms, or +6 dBV.

Until the relatively recent focus on PCs for the living room, this discrepancy hasn't been much of an issue. It is becoming a much bigger issue for media PCs because the end user is likely to switch often between multiple input sources on the primary receiver in the living room. In this situation, the analog output of the PC does sound weak compared to all of the other input sources available on a receiver, such as CD, DVD, TV, DVR, etc. With a 2 Vrms output, however, the PC would sound as loud as any of the other sources, so a perceptual disadvantage no longer exists.

Interfacing to 2V RMS Input Signals from Consumer Devices

It is a common misperception that an Intel HD Audio codec can attenuate a large signal received at its input without distortion. However, the same limits usually apply to both inputs and outputs, since both are based on the same unipolar power supply limitations that are shown on the right-hand side of Figure 6.8. If the input signal is greater than the normal working voltage range, then internal protection diodes turn on to contain the peaks of the signals within the power supply rails. This type of clipping results in a very nasty sounding distortion and should be avoided if possible.

Instead of depending on the Intel HD Audio codec to attenuate overly large signals the motherboard solution for a dedicated, or non-retasking, line input jack is simple. Create a 2-to-1 voltage divider as shown in Figure 6.8. This simple and inexpensive circuit attenuates the signal by 6 dB, converting a 2 Vrms signal at the jack into a 1 Vrms signal at the input to the coupling capacitor that is going to the codec line input.

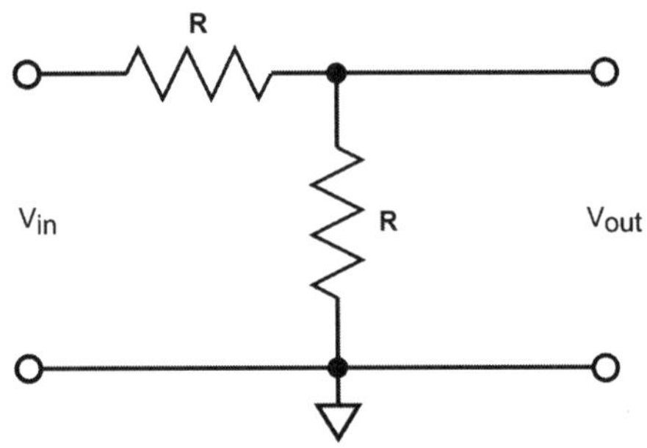

The dedicated circuit is used to convert a 2 Vrms (+6 dBV) signal at input jack to 1 Vrms (0 dBV) signal at codec input. Depending on the surrounding circuitry, R can vary between 10k and 100k.

Figure 6.8 Simple 2-to-1 (-6 dB) Attenuator Circuit

Unfortunately, this solution doesn't work very well for retasking jacks, especially if the re-tasking needs to support headphone out, because the series resistor in the attenuator network attenuates any output signals coming from the port, especially if the impedance is low. In a similar manner, the attenuator network does not interoperate with a mono or stereo microphone bias circuit.

Therefore line inputs which support 2 Vrms should be single-purpose dedicated line inputs with a 2-to-1 attenuator network between the input jack and the input coupling capacitor. RCA jacks are recommended for all inputs that can accept 2 Vrms signals. The supporting driver topology should not expose any boost or gain parameters for this type of line input, because the input level should remain fixed.

Interfacing 2V RMS Line Output to Consumer Devices

You cannot reasonably expect an Intel HD Audio codec powered by a 5V analog supply to drive a 2Vrms output. The power supply is simply not large enough, and if it were, the silicon processes typically used by most codec vendors are rated at 5V and are not designed for higher voltages.

However, you could use an external op-amp that is powered by a separate power supply can be used to increase the output voltage to 2 Vrms. You have a number of ways to do so. Designing the actual op-amp gain circuit is relatively straightforward; it should be possible to follow the application notes from the op-amp vendor to achieve a gain of 6 dB, which converts the output from 1 Vrms to 2 Vrms.

The tricky part is providing a power supply for the op-amp that is capable of providing the 7 volts needed to support 2Vrms output. In all of the following configurations, the codec must be capacitor coupled to the op-amp circuit because the DC potential at VAG does not match the DC operating levels of the op-amp.

The highest-quality approach is to add two 5V linear voltage regulators to the system, powered from the standard +12V and -12V supplies. Since the negative 12V supply is limited in the amount of current it can provide, take care to ensure that this supply is being run within spec. The op-amp power is then run in a bipolar power supply configuration as shown in Figure 6.9, while the codec continues to be run in the standard unipolar configuration. If a pop-suppression circuit is used, you should locate it after the coupling capacitor that is attached to the output of the op-amp.

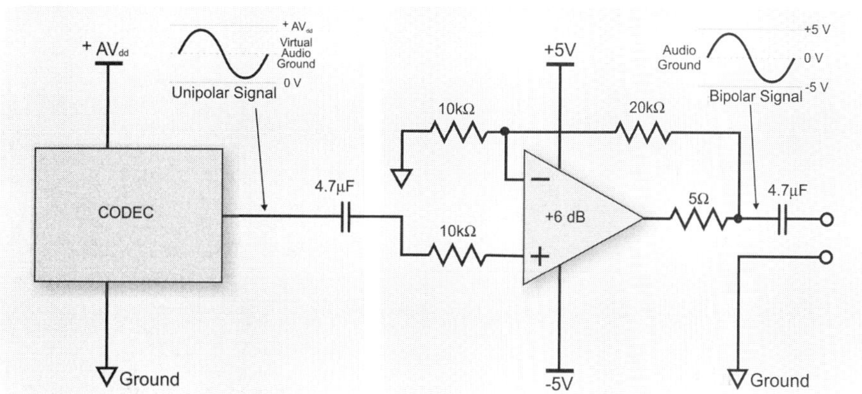

The unipolar output of the codec is capacitively coupled to the bipolar op-amp circuit which has a gain of 2 (+6 dB). Positive and negative voltage regulators (not shown) are needed to condition the power supply for the op amp.

Figure 6.9 External op-amp using bipolar power supply.

Another approach is to run the op-amp in unipolar mode, using a single 7V or higher linear voltage regulator fed from the +12V node of the power supply. As shown in Figure 6.10, this circuit is also viable, but you must pay special attention to the output coupling capacitor, since it must handle both DC and AC voltages that are higher than those in a design with a coupling capacitor connected directly to the codec.

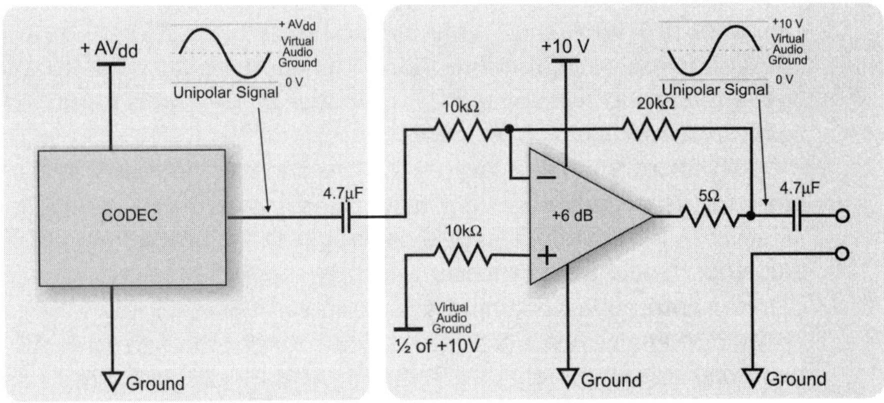

Figure 6.10 External Op-Amp Using 10 Volt Unipolar Power Supply

Like the 2Vrms input circuits, this solution doesn't work very well for re-tasking jacks. It also does not support headphone outputs, re-tasking or not, because the op-amp is configured for audio flow in only a single direction. In a similar manner, the op-amp does not interoperate well with a mono or stereo microphone bias circuit.

Therefore line outputs that support 2 Vrms should be single-purpose dedicated line outputs including an op-amp with 6 dB of external gain between the codec output coupling capacitor and the output jack. You should place a pop suppression circuit after the output coupling capacitor attached to the op-amp's output.

RCA jacks are recommended for all outputs that can drive 2 Vrms signals. The supporting driver topology should not expose any volume control parameters for fixed-volume RCA jacks which have been configured to not track the Media PC remote control's volume buttons.

Guidelines for RCA Jacks for Analog Line Level I/O

The RCA jack layout for a Media PC which supports 7.1 surround sound is shown in Figure 6.11.

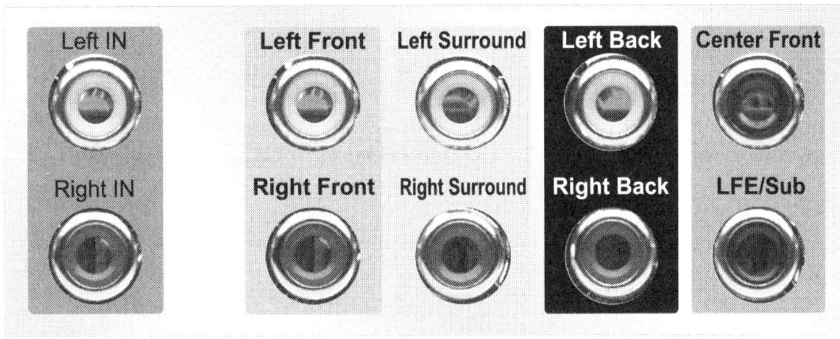

Each RCA stereo jack pair consists of a jack with a white center insert (left) and a jack with a red insert (right). The center and LFE inserts are black, to indicate that they are not a stereo pair. The panels surrounding the RCA jacks use the same Pantone colors that are specified for 3.5 mm phone jacks. From left to right, these color panels are blue, lime green, gray, black, and orange. You can download a color version of this graphic from this book's section of the Intel Press Web site.

Figure 6.11 RCA Jacks Rear Panel for a Media PC with 7.1 Outputs

Audio jack colors and functions are outlined in Table 1.3, which is derived from the Windows Vista logo program. Each jack pair should be mounted on a background color indicator which matches the standard jack colors in use for 3.5-millimeter jacks.

To allow proper interoperation with software, a jack insertion detection mechanism must be incorporated into the RCA jack, and it might be required by the Windows Vista logo program. This detection mechanism must consist of an SPST switch, which is normally open, and the mechanism is shorted to ground when a plug is inserted into the jack. The switch contacts must not be electrically connected to any of the signal wires, to avoid noises when a jack is inserted or removed. Figure 6.12 shows an example of such a switch.

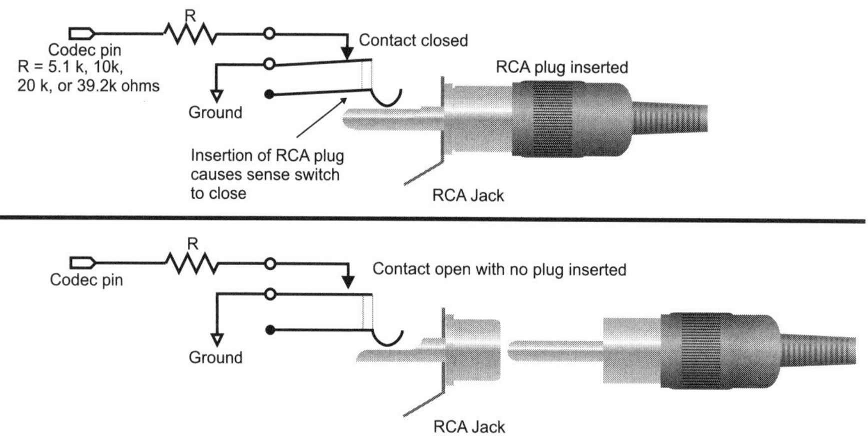

Figure 6.12 Jack Detection Switch for RCA Jacks

In typical Intel HD Audio implementations, the jack detection is accomplished by completing the circuit between a load resistor and ground. This detection is accomplished for both channels of a 3.5 mm jack. However, RCA jacks have separate jacks for each channel, which complicates the issue.

For best usability, the jack detection for stereo pairs should only take effect when both jacks in the stereo pair have been inserted. For this configuration, the two detection switches for the two jacks in the stereo pair should be wired in series.

Center and LFE require different treatment, as they simply share a cable, but are not considered to be a stereo pair. End users often have a subwoofer but no a center speaker, and less commonly, they might have a center speaker without a subwoofer. Ideally, the software would be able to identify each of these separately, but this identification is not possible in the case of a 3.5-millimeter jack. Therefore, the Intel HD Audio specification combines the jack detection for these two outputs.

To allow the use of center without LFE, or vice versa, and still provide the most jack-presence information, the jack detection switches on these two RCA jacks should be wired in parallel, so that plugging in either one of the two results in a positive jack detection. Table 6.1 provides a full description of the functions, colors, and switch wiring configurations for these jacks.

Table 6.1 **RCA** Jack Functions and Colors for 7.1 Outputs

Function	Channel	RCA Jack Color	Background Color	Pantone	Jack Detection
Stereo Line Input	Left	White	Light blue	284C	Wired in series requiring BOTH plugs.
	Right	Red			
Front Output	Left	White	Lime green	577C	Wired in series requiring BOTH plugs.
	Right	Red			
Side Output	Left	White	Gray	420C	Wired in series requiring BOTH plugs.
	Right	Red			
Rear Output	Left	White	Black	"Black"	Wired in series requiring BOTH plugs.
	Right	Red			
Center & LFE/Sub	Center	Black	Orange	157C	Wired in parallel requiring EITHER plug.
	LFE out	Black			

Figure 6.13 shows the recommended external circuitry for a single channel of an RCA line output jack used on a high-end Media PC, which embodies all of the attributes listed above.

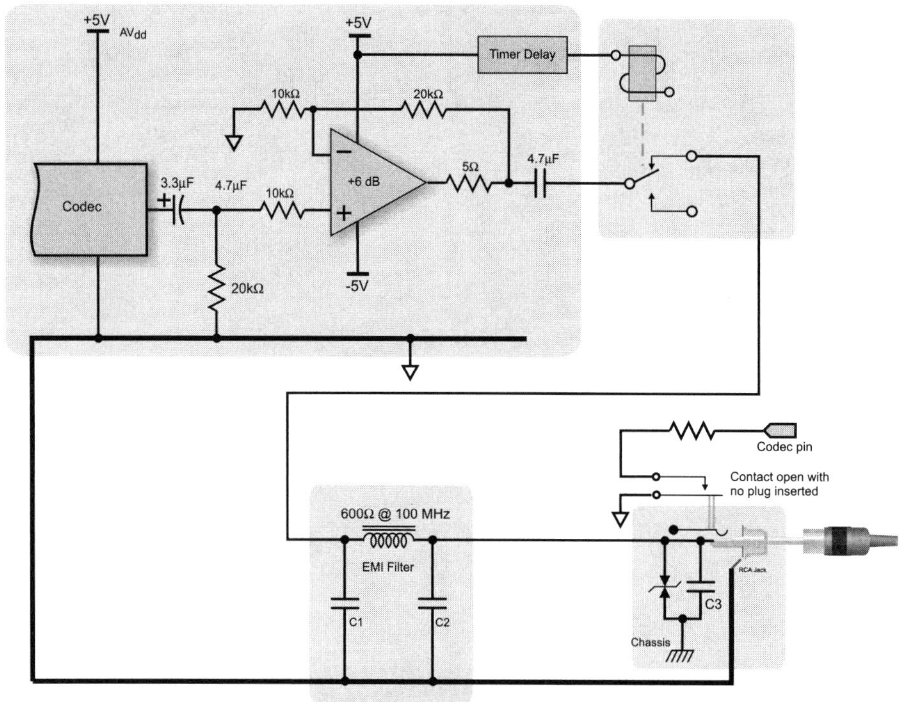

This circuit features RCA jacks, and external op-amp with 6 dB of gain and a bipolar power supply to provide 2Vrms output, circuit to control settling time, pop suppression circuitry using an electromechanical relay in shunt, jack detection switches wired in series, and EMI and ESD treatments.

Figure 6.13 One Channel of the Complete Output Circuit for Media PC

Figure 6.14 shows the equivalent line-level input circuit using RCA jacks. For the best capture quality, put a capacitor in parallel with the shunt resistor in the 6 dB attenuator to build a simple first-order anti-aliasing filter. This pre-conditioning helps prevent sum and difference tones that can be caused by aliasing.

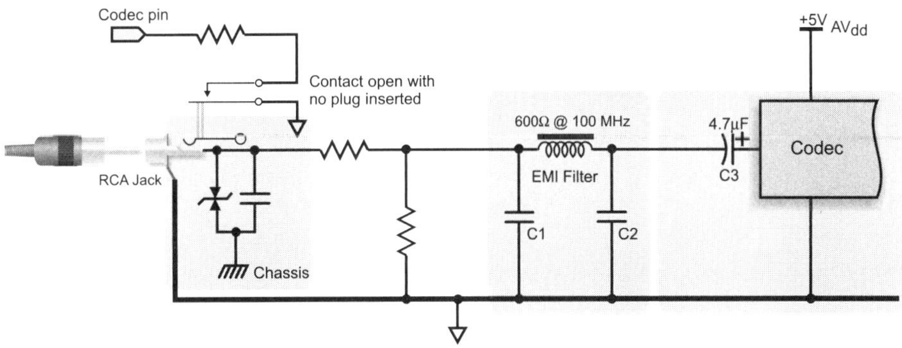

This input circuit features RCA jacks, a 6 dB attenuator to accept 2Vrms input, jack detection switches, and EMI, ESD, and anti-aliasing treatments.

Figure 6.14 One Channel of the Complete Input Circuit for Media PC

You can find other approaches to resolving these issues without following each of the recommendations outlined here, but each of the underlying issues must be addressed in order to meet the same levels of audio fidelity and freedom from pops and clicks that are the current norm for better audio equipment in home theaters and living rooms.

Chapter 7

Intel® HD Audio Software: Control Layer

The existing Windows[†] XP audio subsystem contains a rich legacy driven by backwards compatibility. Many of today's Windows XP audio "features" exist only because they were useful long ago and could not be removed. Windows Vista will completely restructure the audio subsystem and its release will be a much larger break from legacy applications than any that has ever taken place in Windows audio. However, to understand why the audio in Windows XP works that way it does, you need to first understand how it evolved. For a complete summary of audio driver evolution, see Appendix C, "Drivers from DOS to Windows XP."

As new audio functionality was added to each generation of Windows, the control of audio in Windows XP became distributed throughout a number of different control panels, often with no easy way to get from one to another, and with little or no end-user documentation. This chapter describes a few of the critical controls and what they do. Setting these controls improperly could cause failures during audio fidelity or usability testing. Most, if not all, of these control panels will change with the upcoming release of Windows Vista, which is described later in Chapter 8.

Sounds and Audio Devices Properties

Right-click on the speaker icon in the system tray and select "Adjust Audio Properties" to open the Sounds and Audio Devices control panel in Windows XP. You can also open it from the Control Panels on the start menu. Click on the Audio tab to see the dialog shown in Figure 7.1. From this dialog you can select the default audio playback device and the default recording device. Only the user can set the default devices; no API or programmatic method for an application exists to set the default devices. Click on the Voice tab to see a similar dialog for setting the default devices for voice applications.

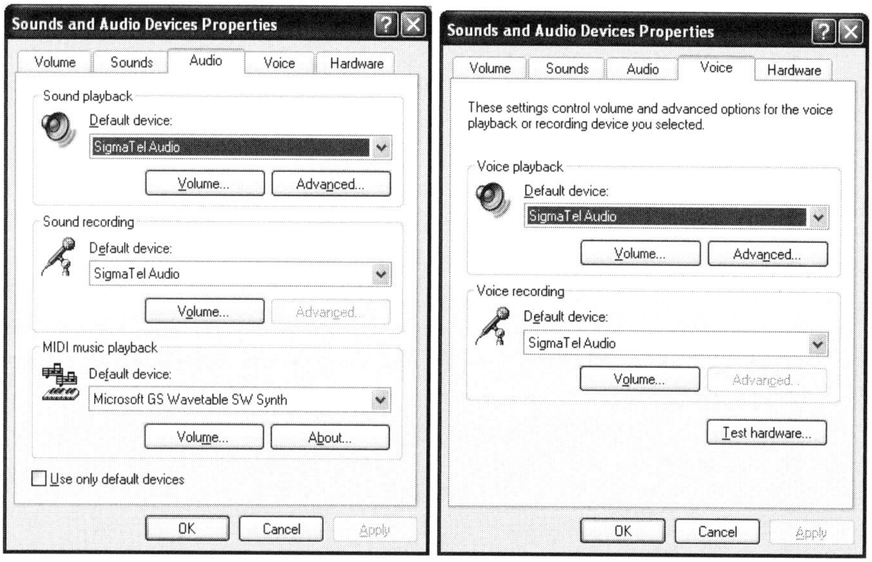

Figure 7.1 Audio and Voice Tabs in Sounds and Audio Devices Properties Dialog

Click on the Volume button under each device to bring up a SNDVOL32 window with a related view. Click on the *Advanced* button under the Sound playback device to set the speaker mode, the quality of the system sample rate converter (SRC), and the hardware acceleration mode.

Figure 7.2 shows the Speakers tab on the right and the Performance tab on the left. The top slider in the Performance tab controls the hardware acceleration settings. Four settings are possible, with the leftmost setting labeled None, and the rightmost setting labeled Full.

- *None/Emulation* forces DirectSound into emulation mode. In this mode, DirectSound applications run as though no DirectSound driver is present. All mixing is done by DirectSound in user mode, and the resulting audio data plays back through the WaveOut API. A large increase in latency typically results.
- *Basic* DirectSound interfaces are available, but hardware acceleration of DirectSound secondary buffers is disabled. While this setting avoids the increased latency associated with emulation mode, any 3D positional features that require hardware acceleration or a software equivalent are disabled.
- *Standard* uses DirectSound with KMixer, enabling hardware acceleration of DirectSound secondary buffers but disabling vendor-specific extensions that are exposed as property sets through the IKsPropertySet interface.
- *Full* enables full hardware acceleration, including 3D positional effects and vendor-specific extensions such as EAX. Even though this control is called "Hardware Acceleration", this name is simply not true for Intel HD Audio implementations. Any "acceleration" in the system is performed by a software layer included in the driver. These layers are not available for Windows Vista.

If a 3D positional effect is installed on your system, the Hardware Acceleration slider must be set to the Standard or Full positions in order to hear the effects. Except for compatibility with games designed for earlier versions of DirectX, this slider should always be kept in the Full position. This slider often appears to have no effect on modern systems.

The Sample Rate Conversion (SRC) quality slider in the bottom of the Performance tab is used to select from three different sample rate conversion algorithms for games and applications using the DirectSound interface. These settings can only be adjusted by the user; no API reads or sets them. Be aware that lower quality SRC settings can change the pitch of signals being played back slightly.

- *Good Linear Interpolation*. An efficient form of sample rate conversion, but has a grainy quality that is annoying to listen to. Only a single-sample history is used to determine the output.

- *High-end multipoint interpolation*. This simplified version of high-end multipoint interpolation is used to achieve a signal-to-noise ratio of approximately 70 decibels.
- *Best High-end multipoint interpolation*. This use of oversampling can achieve a signal-to-noise ratio of 90 decibels or more. Sample rate converters for Windows Vista are being designed for even higher quality than this setting.

Sounds that are played or recorded through the WaveOut API, Redbook CD, SoundBlaster emulator, or software synthesizer always use the high-end multipoint interpolation, and are not affected by this control

The better sounding algorithms use more CPU power. While this CPU demand was a big factor when these algorithms were introduced, systems using Intel HD Audio should not be affected by the small amount of CPU needed for the best SRC. In Windows XP, this slider is always defaulted to Best. You have no good reason to set this slider to a lower-quality setting on recently designed systems.

CD Audio: Analog or Digital?

In Windows XP, the redbook.sys driver is used to "rip" the digital audio data from the CD drive and route it to KMixer, which is the recommended way to play CD audio on modern systems. However, some systems could have a requirement to support an analog CD input on an ATAPI port. The CD cables and connectors increase system cost when implemented, and they are usually unused.

While the Windows XP driver topology supports switching between analog and digital CD, that operation is anything but simple. Unless you plan to pre-configure the system's OS for analog audio, you should not enable the analog CD input on the system and take the cost savings approach. The reason is that it is almost impossible for the end user by themselves to successfully switch between these two modes. In some cases, users might need to resort to calling the PC vendor for help in changing between these two modes. Any support call is expensive, but one where the support technician leads the user through 18 steps is more expensive than usual. The following list supplies the details of the 18 steps, and Figure 7.2 shows the 18 different screenshots that you see when switching between analog and digital CD playback settings. The last three steps are necessary only if you wish to record from the Analog CD input.

1. From the start menu, select the Control Panel.
2. From the control panel, double click on the System Icon.
3. In the System Properties dialog, click on the Hardware tab.
4. In the Hardware tab, click on Device Manager.
5. In the Device Manager dialog, click on DVD/CD-ROM Drives.
6. In the Device Manager tab, click on the name of the CD or DVD player.
7. In the CD/DVD Properties dialog, click on the Properties tab.
8. In the Properties tab, uncheck the "Enable digital CD audio for this CD-ROM device" checkbox.
9. Set the CD player volume to high (as shown), then click on the OK button to save the changes. Close all dialogs that remain open from executing this procedure.
10. In Windows MediaPlayer10, locate the invisible [ouch] drop down menu in the upper right corner of the window, select Tools, and then the Options menu item.
11. In the options dialog, select Devices.
12. In the list of Devices, select the DVD Drive or CD Drive that you wish to change to analog mode.
13. In the Drive Properties dialog, select Analog for Playback, and Analog for Rip.
14. When you select Analog for Rip, a dialog box will appear. Click OK.
15. Click OK again to apply all of the changes. Then, close all dialogs that were opened as part of this process.
16. To record from the Analog CD input, click on the speaker icon in the task bar to launch the Windows Volume Control panel. From the options menu, select Properties, then complete the following steps.
17. In the properties dialog, click on the radio button to adjust volume for recording. Make sure that the CD audio checkbox in the lower part of the window is checked. Then click OK. If no checkbox is labeled "CD Audio," recording from analog input is not supported on this system.
18. In the recording control mixer that appears, check the select checkbox underneath the CD Audio slider. Set the CD Audio slider at or near the bottom of its range. If you turn this volume up, the recorded CD audio becomes distorted. If the balance control is not already in the center, set it there.

Now you should be ready to play and record from the analog CD path. If you don't hear anything, check that an analog cable is connected from the CD or DVD drive's analog output to an ATAPI connector mounted on the motherboard and wired into the analog CD input pins of the Intel HD Audio codec.

If you have other music player applications besides Windows Media Player, you might need to set them for analog playback as well.

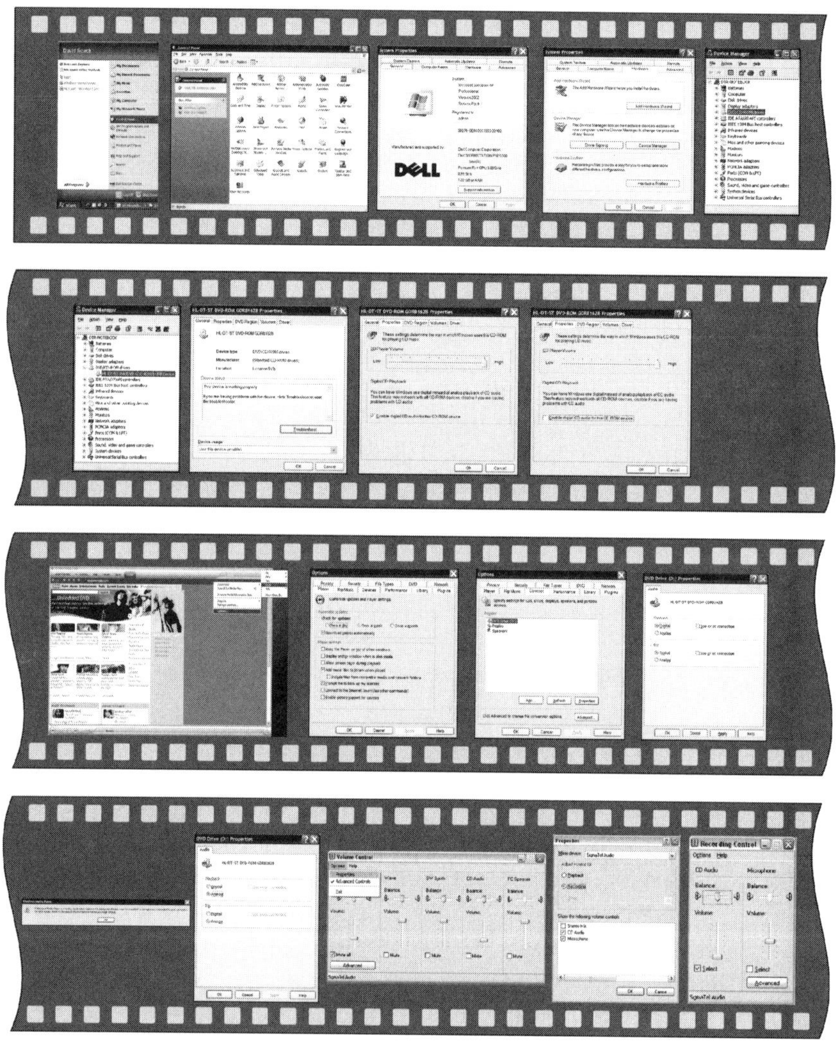

Figure 7.2 Screenshots Corresponding to the 18 Steps for Changing from Digital CD to Analog CD Playback

Sticky Keys, Toggle Keys, and the 8253 Timer

The accessibility options control panel in Windows XP shown in Figure 7.3 allows the user to specify system sounds that are associated with the state of special keys used for enhanced accessibility. Some government contracts require these sounds to be supported properly on the systems being purchased. However, these sounds may be generated using a very different method than any other sounds played by the computer.

On 32-bit versions of Windows XP and earlier operating systems, these sounds are formed by directly programming the 8253 timer chip and connecting the pulse wave output from this timer chip through a trace on the motherboard into the PC Beep input pin of the codec, if that pin is present.

When enabled, the ToggleKeys capability that is built into the OS causes a tone to sound when you press the CAPS LOCK, NUM LOCK, or SCROLL LOCK keys. Hold down NUM LOCK for 5 seconds to turn ToggleKeys on or off. To test the sounds, press CAPS LOCK repeatedly a few seconds apart and you should hear a short tone alternating between low and high frequencies.

The StickyKeys capability built into the OS assists those who are unable to hold down a modifier key such as ALT, CTRL, or SHIFT while pressing a second key. It allows the user to first press the modifier key and then to press the key being modified without needing to hold down both keys at once. StickyKeys has an option to play 3 different tones when a modifier key is pressed and the system is in "sticky" modes. The Sound tab is not used to control the playing of sounds; instead it provides a hearing-impaired user to specify a visual indicator that appears whenever a sound is played.

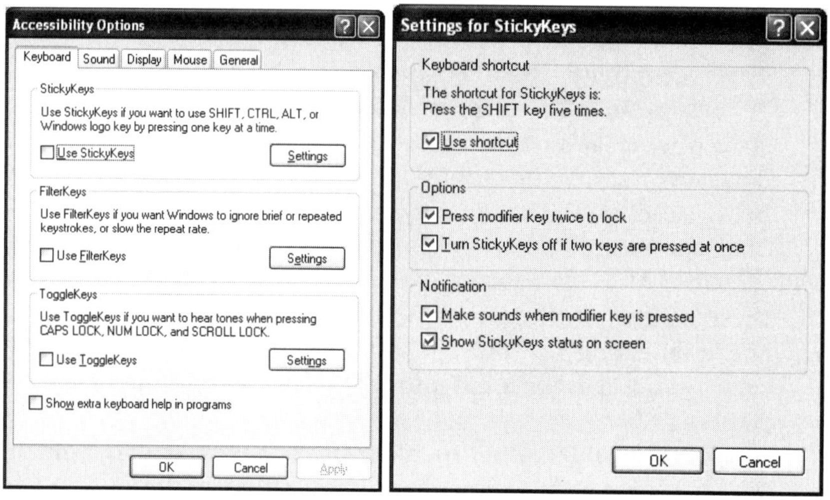

Figure 7.3 Sticky Keys and Toggle Keys Dialogs

The X64 versions of Windows XP and Windows Server 2003 do not directly program the 8253 timer. Instead, they play .WAV files just like the other system sounds. This is because many newer 64-bit platforms no longer include an 8253 timer, providing no way to generate the sounds.

SNDVOL32 also programs the 8253 timer to make sound in one particular case. Moving the master volume control with the mouse causes a system sound to be heard. The 8253 timer is used if the system sound configuration is set to "No Sounds."

The system BIOS may also program the 8253 timer to generate POST tones during boot and to generate key click sounds, which are also needed for some government contracts. The OS has no knowledge of these tones or how they are generated.

If the systems that you are designing are required to provide these accessibility tones in order to meet specific contracts, you will need to test these tones to make sure they are present and working properly. If you can't hear the tones, check in SNDVOL32 to make sure that PC Speaker or PC Beep is present and unmuted, and turned up. If you still can't hear it, it may not be connected on the motherboard. Some desktop motherboards connect the 8253 timer output directly to a buzzer mounted on the motherboard, rather than to the PC beep input pin. In this case, the accessibility tones appear to come from inside the PC rather than from the speaker. If the master volume for the system is handled in software, or when a separate buzzer is used on the motherboard, the master volume has no effect on these sounds.

Designs that do not have customer requirements for supporting these accessibility tones may choose to not connect the 8253 timer to the codec PC beep input pin, or they may choose to use a codec that does not support analog pc beep input, with the result that these sounds cannot be heard by the user.

While the analog PC beep input is not recommended for most systems, due to its low audio quality, it is the only way to meet requirements that the StickyKeys and ToggleKeys can be heard. Unless you have a specific reason that these sounds need to be available on a system's default configuration, you should default it to mute or to a very low volume setting. Otherwise, the high background noise from the motherboard circuits connected to the analog pc beep input creates an unpleasant sound, and the system could fail some WHQL tests. When possible, try to avoid using the PC beep input in your systems. The Microsoft UAA class driver for Intel HD Audio does not support analog PC beep.

WAVE_FORMAT_EXTENSIBLE

The ways to properly describe the various high-quality audio formats have steadily increased over time, with a number of older methods now becoming obsolete because they have been rolled into new types of descriptions. `WAVE_FORMAT_EXTENSIBLE` is a tag used to define the format of audio waveform data having more than two channels or higher sample resolutions than the older `WAVEFORMATEX` structure allows. The actual data structure used to store the information is `WAVEFORMATEXTENSIBLE`, without the underscores between the words. Figure 7.4 shows the growth of various waveform descriptors over the last twelve years.

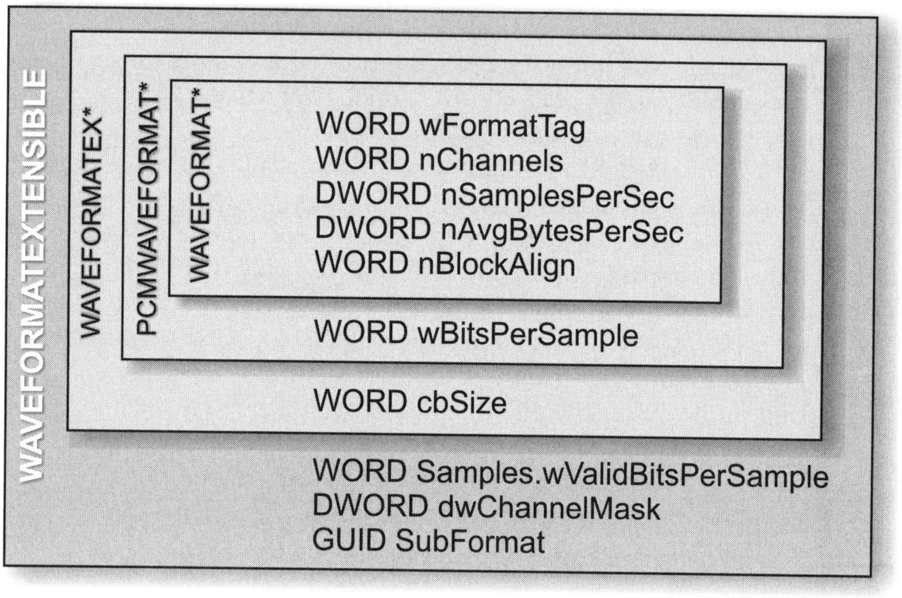

Figure 7.4 Extensible Wave Format Descriptors

You can easily see the progression of the fields that were added to existing structures as more complex waveform types were supported by Windows. Unlike previous versions, the WAVEFORMATEXTENSIBLE format allows arbitrary formats to be defined dynamically by providing a GUID field, which allows new unique IDs to be added. Doing so should give room for the `WAVEFORMATEXTENSIBLE` data structure to grow without needing to be replaced by another format any time soon.

Programs capable of generating multi-channel WAVEFORMAT-EXTENSIBLE files are rare, and test files are often difficult to generate. However, all multi-channel applications use WAVEFORMATEXTENSIBLE as the stream format sent to the audio output device. For instance, a DVD player application that includes a Dolby Digital or DTS multi-channel decoder opens a WAVEFORMAT-EXTENSIBLE stream, but it never needs to open a WAVEFORMATEXTENSIBLE file.

Table 7.1 shows the speaker ID codes and bit definitions that are used to build channel masks describing various combinations of speakers. Additional speaker positions are defined as part of this structure, but only the most commonly used ones are shown in Table 7.1. You can count the number of bits in the channel mask to determine the number of channels in the audio stream. Multi-channel streams containing WAVE_FORMAT_EXTENSIBLE data use interleaved audio with the channels presented in the order shown in this table. For instance, for stereo data the left channel is always presented first, before the right channel is presented. Color codes for jacks that match the Windows Vista Logo program are shown on the right. Speaker IDs FLC and FRC are part of the now-obsolete 7.1 Wide configuration, which has no matching color codes, so these speaker locations should generally be avoided.

Table 7.1 Common Speaker Locations Defined for WAVEFORMATEXTENSIBLE

Speaker ID	Speaker Name	Bit number	Hex Value	Jack Color
FL	SPEAKER_FRONT_LEFT	0	0x1	Green
FR	SPEAKER_FRONT_RIGHT	1	0x2	Green
FC	SPEAKER_FRONT_CENTER	2	0x4	Orange
LFE	SPEAKER_LOW_FREQUENCY	3	0x8	Orange
BL	SPEAKER_BACK_LEFT	4	0x10	Black
BR	SPEAKER_BACK_RIGHT	5	0x20	Black
FLC	SPEAKER_FRONT_LEFT_OF_CENTER	6	0x40	undefined
FRC	SPEAKER_FRONT_RIGHT_OF_CENTER	7	0x80	undefined
BC	SPEAKER_BACK_CENTER	8	0x100	undefined
SL	SPEAKER_SIDE_LEFT	9	0x200	Grey
SR	SPEAKER_SIDE_RIGHT	10	0x400	Grey

Channel masks consisting of one or more of these bits are used to indicate the channels that are present in multi-channel wave files, streams, and output configurations. Table 7.2 shows the most common channel masks. Channel masks highlighted in grey should be avoided.

Table 7.2 Standard Set of Channel Masks Defined in ksmedia.h.

Channel Mask Name	Channel Mask (Hex)	Speaker Positions
KSAUDIO_SPEAKER_DIRECTOUT	0x0000	None
KSAUDIO_SPEAKER_MONO	0x0004	FC
KSAUDIO_SPEAKER_STEREO	0x0006	FL, FR
KSAUDIO_SPEAKER_QUAD	0x0036	FL, FR, BL, BR

KSAUDIO_SPEAKER_SURROUND	0x010A	FL, FR, FC, LFE
KSAUDIO_SPEAKER_5POINT1	0x003F	FL, FR, FC, LFE, SL, SR
KSAUDIO_SPEAKER_7POINT1_SURROUND	0x063F	FL, FR, FC, LFE, BL, BR, SL, SR
KSAUDIO_SPEAKER_7POINT1_WIDE	0x00FF	FL, FR, FC, LFE, BL, BR, FLC, FRC

The KS_AUDIOSPEAKER_7POINT1_SURROUND channel mask is the most recent addition to the set of channel masks, and it is defined only in the most recent versions of ksmedia.h in the Windows DDK. This channel mask is used to represent the 7.1 home theater speaker configuration, which was added in Windows XP SP2. Previous versions of Windows supported only the older 7.1 wide configuration setting, which is now obsolete. While it was theoretically possible to create a wave file or stream with a channel mask of `0x63F`, the OS contained no formal definition for this channel mask and no standardized behaviors for using this format. Practically speaking, most computers are designed to support stereo, 5.1 surround, and 7.1 surround.

Multi-channel Speaker Configurations

The listener uses the Speakers tab to select the speaker configuration which most closely matches the speaker set attached to the PC, as shown on the right side of Figure 7.5. This global setting affects all applications that are playing audio. DirectSound also provides an API called `SetSpeakerConfig` that allows applications to set this same speaker configuration. The `SetSpeakerConfig` API should only be used by audio control applications included with an audio driver; other applications should not call this API. The speaker configuration is defaulted to Stereo Desktop Speakers after the OS is installed, although an OEM can configure a pre-install to be in any desired configuration.

Each speaker configuration has an associated channel mask, which is used to determine whether it is a match with the audio stream currently being played. If an exact match is found then KMixer passes the multichannel data through untouched, except for volume scaling. If the match is not exact, KMixer attempts to remap the source data to the available output channels. For instance, if the stream has a mask of `0x003F` (5.1 surround) and the speaker configuration is set to stereo desktop speakers, KMixer down-mixes the FLC, LFE, BR, and BL signals into the FL and

FR channels, so that all audio information can be present in the two speakers that are selected in the configuration. This down-mixing occurs even if the user has a complete 5.1 speaker system connected; audio only appears in the FL and FR speakers when the speaker configuration is set to any of the stereo settings. Wave files that are authored with Windows Media Encoder optionally may contain down-mix coefficients to be applied during this down-mix process.

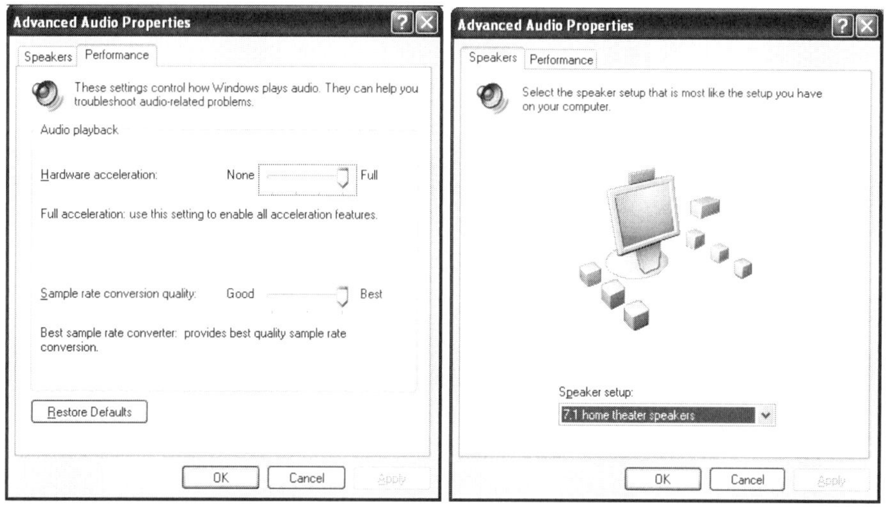

Figure 7.5 Advanced Audio Properties and Speaker Configuration dialog

The stereo speaker configurations have an additional geometry descriptor shown in Table 7.3 that is used only with stereo speakers, and is not used with headphone, mono, or multi-channel configurations. This parameter specifies the number of degrees in an arc from speaker to speaker relative to the user's listening position. A laptop's arc is relatively narrow and is defined to be 10 degrees of separation. A desktop usually has a little more distance between the speakers, so they are defined as having 20 degrees of separation. While Max and Min values of 5 degrees and 180 degrees, respectively, are defined, the settings in the speaker configuration dialog only make use of the 10 degree narrow and the 20 degree wide settings. These angles are passed to the driver, and a driver may decide to perform processing based on these angles. However, most drivers do not change their behavior based on this parameter.

Table 7.3 Speaker Geometries Defined in dsound.h

DSSPEAKER_GEOMETRY Settings	Hex Value	Decimal Value
DSSPEAKER_GEOMETRY_MIN	0x0005	5
DSSPEAKER_GEOMETRY_NARROW	0x000A	10
DSSPEAKER_GEOMETRY_WIDE	0x0014	20
DSSPEAKER_GEOMETRY_MAX	0x00B4	180

In addition to the channel mask and the geometries, the `SetSpeakerConfig` API uses the constants shown in Table 7.4 to determine the correct speaker settings. The name of each speaker setting in the speaker configuration dialog is shown in the leftmost column, while the names of the constants are shown in the second column. The stereo geometry settings comprise the upper 16 bits of the 32-bit data word that is used as the argument to `SetSpeakerConfig`, while the `DSSPEAKER` constants which define the number of channels are physically located in the lower 16 bits of the argument. The `DSSPEAKER_COMBINE` macro can be used to build up this 32-bit word. If the `DSSPEAKER_STEREO` flag is used along with a zero in the upper 16 bits, DirectSound assumes `DSSPEAKER_GEOMETRY_WIDE` by default.

Table 7.4 Standard Set of Channel Masks Defined in ksmedia.h.

Name In Control Panel	Speaker Configuration Name	Hexadecimal Speaker Configuration	Channel Mask	Matching Pin Config Sequence
No Speakers	DSSPEAKER_DIRECTOUT	0x00000000	0x0000	n/a
Stereo headphones	DSSPEAKER_HEADPHONE	0x00000001	0x0006	0
Desktop stereo speakers	DSSPEAKER_STEREO | DSSPEAKER_GEOMETRY_WIDE	0x00140004	0x0006	0
Laptop mono speakers	DSSPEAKER_MONO	0x00000002	0x0004	0
Laptop stereo speakers	DSSPEAKER_STEREO | DSSPEAKER_GEOMETRY_NARROW	0x000A0004	0x0006	0
Monitor stereo speakers	DSSPEAKER_STEREO | DSSPEAKER_GEOMETRY_NARROW	0x000A0004	0x0006	0

Monitor stand stereo speakers	DSSPEAKER_STEREO | DSSPEAKER_GEOMETRY_NARROW	0x000A0004	0x0006	0
Monitor mounted stereo speakers	DSSPEAKER_STEREO | DSSPEAKER_GEOMETRY_WIDE	0x00140004	0x0006	0
Keyboard stereo speakers	DSSPEAKER_STEREO | DSSPEAKER_GEOMETRY_NARROW	0x000A0004	0x0006	0
Quadraphonic speakers	DSSPEAKER_QUAD	0x00000003	0x0036	(0,2) or (0,4)
Surround sound speakers	DSSPEAKER_SURROUND	0x00000005	0x010A	n/a
5.1 surround sound speakers	DSSPEAKER_5POINT1	0x00000006	0x003F	(0,1,2) or (0,1,4)
7.1 home theater speakers	DSSPEAKER_7POINT1_SURROUND	0x00000008	0x063F	(0,1,2,4)
7.1 wide configuration speakers	DSSPEAKER_7POINT1_WIDE	0x00000007	0x00FF	(0,1,2,3) or (0,1,3,4)

Configurations highlighted in gray are uncommon and should be avoided for modern designs.

The sequence numbers that are used in the Pin Configuration defaults described in Chapter 4 are also related to the channel mask that is chosen, as shown in Table 7.5. Stereo channels should use a sequence of (0), 5.1 systems should use a sequence of (0, 1, 2), and 7.1 systems should use a sequence of (0, 1, 2, 4). A sequence number of 4 should only be used if the sequence number 2 is also used.

Table 7.5 Sequence Number encoding of Speaker Positions

Sequence Number	Left Channel	Right Channel
0	FL	FR
1	FC	LFE
2	BL	BR
3	FLC	FRC
4	SL	SR

The driver developer chooses how to resolve mismatches between the stream's channel mask and the channel mask of the current speaker configuration. KMixer negotiates with the driver to determine a common format, presenting the driver with different channel masks that the driver can accept or refuse. The negotiation continues until the driver has accepted a format from KMixer.

For a speaker configuration that is set to `DSSPEAKER_5POINT1`, the driver could refuse a 7.1 stream with a channel mask of either `0x063F` or `0x00FF`, but it could accept a 5.1 stream that was supplied by KMixer. In this case, KMixer determines which channels to either downmix or to exclude from the 5.1 stream sent to the driver. If the driver had chosen to accept the 7.1 stream, however, then it would be the driver's responsibility to decide whether to downmix or exclude two of the channels. The speaker configuration mask in the audio device, and much more, can be checked by using the KsStudio.exe application included with recent driver development kits.

The stereo down-mix behavior often differs depending on whether the application plays audio through the DirectSound interface like Media Player or through the WaveOut API like SoundRecorder. Make sure to test your system using separate wave files for stereo, 5.1, and 7.1, and play those files through both interfaces to verify correct down-mix behavior. Also, test each of these Wave files with each of the speaker settings from 7.5 that are not highlighted in grey. This procedure gives you a large matrix for testing, but it is the only way to conclusively verify multi-channel down-mix and mapping of multiple speaker configurations.

Also, remember that KMixer does not ever perform an "up-mix" or spreading function. If you play a stereo wave file through either DirectSound or Wave APIs and you are using a multi-channel speaker configuration, only speakers FL and FR produce the sound. The other speakers remain silent. A third-party spreading function must be supplied as part of the media player or part of the driver package if you want the user to hear sound out of any surround speakers whenever a stereo file is being played. If an upmix to from stereo to 7.1 is required, the speaker configuration must be set to 7.1 at all times. For this reason, some audio control applications constantly check the `GetSpeakerConfig` setting and change it back whenever a user changes it from 7.1. Some applications also monitor the "Wave" volume slider in SNDVOL32 and keep it set to Max at all times, because it affects only the front two channels of a multichannel stream, and the application can only reliably output multichannel audio when it knows that the Wave slider is set to maximum.

Whenever the user or an application sets the speaker configuration, a significant delay could occur before the new settings take effect. Depending on the conditions, this delay could be up to a week or longer. Here's why.

When the DirectSound speaker configuration is changed, or when an application creates a new DirectSound object, the DAC node of the driver is called with a request to change to the new configuration. If any stream is currently playing in a different format than the one in the configuration, the driver may choose to ignore the configuration call. The driver can return an error with no obvious consequences—that is the audio stream continues to play, and no dialog or alert is presented to the listener—but the driver configuration is not changed. An application calling the `SetSpeakerConfig` can see the error message, but can't do much about it.

The driver usually cannot take any action on the configuration request until all streams have stopped. An application has no programmatic way to know whether any streams other than its own are playing, and the driver has no way to force all streams to stop playing except by disabling or uninstalling the driver. If a poorly behaved application is keeping a stream open when it shouldn't or if the user has left Media Player tuned to an Internet radio station and forgotten about it, it could take days or weeks before all streams stop playing and the new speaker configuration is allowed to take effect.

A well-designed driver should remember this request and use it the next time the system transitions from no-stream-playing to stream-playing. If the driver doesn't remember this setting, the new setting takes place on the first DirectSound object opened. However, if an application starts playing sound through the Wave APIs first, then the new configuration does not take effect until all streams have again stopped. While it's possible to explain this type of behavior, it simply does not make sense to a typical end user.

To make this even more confusing, a bug in mm.cpl mixes up the 7.1 wide configuration and 7.1 home theatre settings, but only when the API is used. If an end user sets the speaker configuration from the dialog, everything works fine. If an application uses the `SetSpeakerConfig` API to set the system to 7.1 home theatre speakers, the channel mask is incorrectly set to 0x00FF, which is the channel mask for the obsolete 7.1 wide configuration.

As mentioned earlier, an audio control panel application which provides a spreading function from stereo to 7.1 must call the `SetSpeakerConfig` API to set the configuration to the obsolete 7.1 Wide configuration in order to properly set the channel mask of the speaker configuration to `0x063F`. The end user sees the obsolete 7.1 wide configuration when they open up the speaker configuration dialog, and if the user changes the configuration to a different setting, it automatically returns to the obsolete 7.1 wide configuration. Microsoft is aware of this issue and has provided a solution. A QFE has become available. You can find a link to it on this book's companion Web site, or by searching in the Microsoft Knowledge Base for KB909441.

A user account that does not have Admin privileges cannot set the Speaker Configuration. The Speaker Configuration is global, and affects all streams on a multi-streaming system. If your system is a multi-streaming configuration combined with multi-channel output on the rear panel, then you should set the speaker configuration to match the multi-channel configuration. This setting is the best compromise.

Bit Depths and Sample Rates for Windows XP

The audio function driver specifies a range of bit depths and sample rates that are supported. The bit depth of any particular node is determined when the driver is loaded, and it remains constant until shut down, disabled, or uninstalled. Intel HD Audio drivers should always set the bit depth to 24-bit integer representation, for best fidelity and compatibility.

Sample rates are determined at the time that a particular stream starts. KMixer provides format and sample rate converters to allow files to be played at their native rates, but the output of any stream from KMixer is coupled to DACs in the codec in a one-to-one relationship. The sample rate of this stream from KMixer's output to the codec hardware is controlled dynamically by the OS. Once a stream has started playing into KMixer, the sample rate will either stay the same or increase depending on what other streams are played, the sample rate never gets lowered. This process restarts every time that all streams have stopped playing.

For example, start with no streams playing. Start playing an audio CD digitally through redbook.sys. This feeds a stereo input into KMixer at 44.1 kHz, 16-bits. Because the driver specified 24 bits when starting up, and the speaker configuration mask is set to `0x063F`, for 7.1 home theater, and since the driver indicates that the hardware is capable of 44.1 kHz, KMixer opens an 8-channel 44.1 kHz output stream with a channel mask of `0x63F` and a bit depth of 24 bits. In the absence of any further processing, the CD content ends up in the upper 16 bits of the FL and FR channels in the stream, everything else is zeroes and is silent, although all 8 channels are present in the stream.

If the user then starts playing a well-recorded 96 kHz, 24-bit, 7.1 WMA Pro file using Media Player, KMixer negotiates with the driver to raise the DAC's sample rate to 96 kHz. KMixer then inserts a sample rate converter into the CD audio stream to convert to 96 kHz and mixes the CD audio with the FL and FR channels being played by Media Player. At this point, all eight channels of the stream going to the DACs contain a full 24 bits of data at 96 kHz.

When the user stops Media Player, the CD continues playing through the SRC at 96 kHz, and the six surround channels are again silent. The sample rate does not return to 44.1 kHz until all streams have been stopped. Then the process starts all over again.

Plug and Play

Unlike AC97, which only partially supported Plug and Play, Intel HD Audio fully supports Plug and Play. Each codec function group is enumerated as a separate device on the Intel HD Audio bus. For instance, if a single codec exposes both an audio function group and a modem function group, both appear as individual devices on the Intel HD Audio bus.

The Subsystem ID is a key part of the Plug and Play strategy, and the BIOS engineer must be sure to set this register properly. The following string is an example of an Intel HD Audio plug and play Device Instance ID string.

HDAUDIO\FUNC_*xx*&VEN_*yyyy*&DEV_*zzzz*&SUBSYS_*aaaabbcc*&REV_*deff*

The characters shown in italics in these examples represent hexadecimal digits. For example, "FUNC_01" is an example of a substring with the format "FUNC_xx". For Intel HD Audio, FUNC_01 represents audio function groups, and FUNC_02 represents modem function groups. Other function groups might be defined in the future.

The complete ID string is composed of a combination of values that are either hard-coded into the codec as part of its design, or from registers that are overwritten by the BIOS during system boot up. If multiple audio drivers are available, the system tries to choose the one that most closely matches the complete string. To do so, the Intel HD Audio bus driver builds up a list of hardware IDs and compatible IDs that it tries to match with the ID strings specified in the INF file of each available driver. For the string shown above, here is the order the PnP subsystem uses when trying to find the driver which matches best. :

```
HDAUDIO\FUNC_XX&VEN_YYYY&DEV_ZZZZ&SUBSYS_AAAAAAAA&REV_BBBB
HDAUDIO\FUNC_XX&VEN_YYYY&DEV_ZZZZ&SUBSYS_AAAAAAAA
HDAUDIO\FUNC_XX&VEN_YYYY&DEV_ZZZZ&REV_BBBB
HDAUDIO\FUNC_XX&VEN_YYYY&DEV_ZZZZ
HDAUDIO\FUNC_XX&VEN_YYYY
HDAUDIO\FUNC_XX
```

The OS starts with the ID string on top and tries to find a driver that can match the string. If no match is found, the OS keeps going down the list until it does find a match. If it gets all the way to FUNC_*XX* on the bottom, the Microsoft UAA class driver for Intel HD Audio is loaded by default, since that driver matches any UAA codec and/or motherboard, assuming that the pin configuration defaults are properly programmed. The first two ID strings in the list are considered to be hardware IDs because they include the SUBSYS information. The rest of the IDs are considered compatible IDs, which would probably work but might not provide a perfect match. The last two items in the list are a match only for the class driver; third-party drivers may not specify either of these as a matching criterion.

Table 7.6 shows the relationship between the PnP device instance ID string and the codec registers that provide this information. The ID string is built from various bit fields in different registers.

Table 7.6 Relationship Between PnP String and Codec Registers

Usage	PnP ID Name	Intel HD Audio Register	Bits
Vendor ID	VEN_*yyyy*	Vendor ID	31:16
Device ID	DEV_zzzz	Vendor ID	15:0
OEM/ODM ID	SUBSYS_*aaaa*	Subsystem ID	31:16
Board SKU	SUBSYS_*bb*	Subsystem ID	15:8
Assembly ID	SUBSYS_*cc*	Subsystem ID	7:0
Intel HD Audio Major Rev	REV_*d*	Revision ID	23:20
Intel HD Audio Minor Rev	REV_*e*	Revision ID	19:16
Codec Revision ID	REV_*ff*	Revision ID	15:9

The 32-bit Vendor ID register shown in Figure 7.6 is split into two 16-bit fields to form the VEN and DEV filed in the PnP ID string. The Vendor ID register in the codec is read-only, and it cannot be changed. Unlike AC97, the Intel HD Audio controller, which is usually located in the Southbridge, is not part of the PnP ID string, though it could be added in the future.

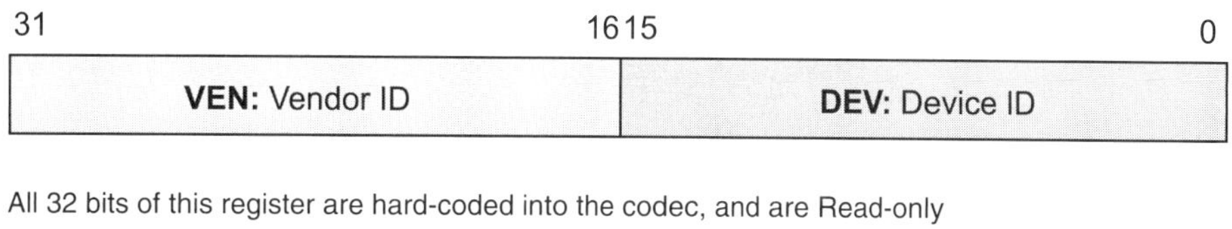

Figure 7.6 Vendor ID Register

Unlike the Vendor ID register, the Subsystem ID register shown in Figure 7.7 can be overwritten. For codecs mounted on the motherboard, the BIOS should always fill in the upper 24 bits of this register. The upper 16 bits should contain the PCI-SIG ID of the ODM or OEM. Bits 15:8 should contain a unique identifier for the audio subsystem and pin configuration defaults. Even if you use the same audio schematics and pin configurations on multiple SKUs, you should not use the same Board SKU number. This use of different numbers allows each OEM or ODM to develop up to 256 different Board SKUs for each Intel HD Audio codec device ID. The Assembly ID is currently unused in the PnP selection process, though it could be added in the future.

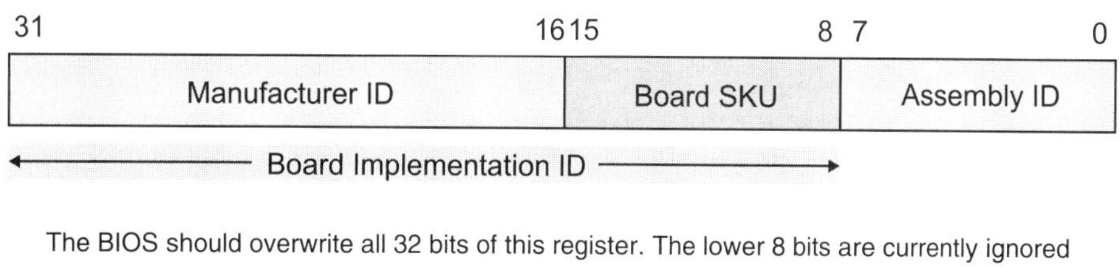

Figure 7.7 Subsystem ID Register

Figure 7.8 shows that the 16-bit REV field in the PnP ID string is derived from bits 23:8 of the codec's Revision ID register. Bits 23:16 contain the major and minor revisions of the version of the Intel HD Audio specification that the codec was designed to comply to. Bits 15:8 contain an 8-bit unique revision code for the codec. Bits 7:0 contain a stepping ID for the codec, which is not used by the PnP ID string. Thus, if a revision of a codec has an impact on software, positive or negative, the Revision ID field should be incremented. If a new codec revision is due to improved reliability, for instance, only the Stepping ID needs to be changed.

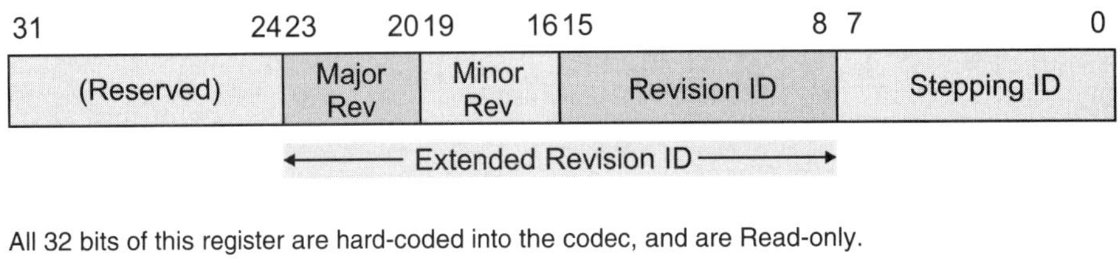

Figure 7.8 Revision ID Register

INF Files

Each audio driver consists of a minimum of two files, usually with the same name but different extensions. The .SYS files contain the executable driver code, while the .INF files contain the plug and play configuration information. A third .CAT file is included as part of the WHQL driver signing process, but it is not necessary for drivers that are not digitally signed by WHQL. Driver packages submitted to WHQL may continue additional files that are specified in the INF file. If any of the files specified in the INF are modified after the CAT file is signed, those changes invalidate the digital signature.

Each INF file contains a list of one or more Device Instance IDs, in a format that is identical to those generated by the Intel HD Audio bus driver. For all production models, make sure that the INF file provided by the codec vendor contains a line with a SUBSYS value that exactly matches one of the hardware IDs generated by the bus driver.

When an audio driver is installed, the INF file is copied into the INF directory in the Windows folder, and the file is renamed to OEM*x*.INF, where *x* is always an integer number which is the lowest unique number available in the INF folder. For instance, if OEM1.INF and OEM2.INF already exist, then the OS renames the new driver's INF file to OEM3.INF and copies it into the INF directory. At the same time, it copies the .sys file to the WINDOWS\system32\drivers directory and copies any associated files into the directory specified for each in the INF file. Removing these INF files from the INF folder effectively makes a driver invisible to the OS. You might wish to do this if you are trying to clean out older stale drivers on a test system under development. The Microsoft UAA class driver for Intel HD Audio's INF files are preinstalled in the INF folder by name

UAA Class Drivers

Microsoft's Universal Audio Architecture (UAA) supports three categories of audio device implementations: Intel HD Audio, USB, and IEEE-1394 (Firewire). A basic class driver is provided for each of these interfaces. Like the standard VGA driver that makes sure that you always get reasonable-quality video even if the graphics vendor's driver is not present, the Microsoft UAA Class driver for Intel HD Audio ensures that audio works properly in all cases, though advanced features might only be available with an audio function driver that the codec vendor supplied. AC97 and previously existing soundcards are not supported by UAA.

For Windows Vista, all WHQL tests must pass with both the Microsoft UAA class driver for Intel HD Audio and the optional codec-vendor-supplied audio function driver. Class driver testing and support is recommended for Windows XP, but not required.

The Microsoft UAA class driver for Intel HD Audio name is HDAUDIO.SYS, and its associated INF file is HDAUDIO.INF. The Microsoft UAA class driver for Intel HD Audio includes a topology parser module which uses the pin configuration default methods described in Chapter 4 to determine the topology from information that the BIOS writes into the configuration default registers of each pin widget. This topology parser is also available as a module that optionally can be compiled into any Intel HD Audio function driver.

The topology parser uses a set of predefined rules to determine an appropriate weighting for each path. All possible paths are evaluated and weighted for priority using the following rules:

- The lower the association number, the higher its priority.
- Known device types have higher priority than unknown device types such as "Digital Other In" or "Aux."
- A path with a wider volume control range has higher priority.

The highest sum of all weighted paths and associations is chosen as the best association resource mapping. For each logical device described the class driver builds a Windows Kernel Streaming filter to expose its audio functionality to the rest of the system.

Notice that the UAATest application used for WHQL loads a special audio function driver and bus driver for WHQL testing. The audio function driver for testing is named T_HDAUD.SYS, and the test version of the bus driver is named HDAUDBUSTEST.SYS. These drivers directly query the audio hardware to verify compliance with the Intel HD Audio specification.

UAA Intel HD Audio Bus Driver

The Microsoft UAA Intel HD Audio bus driver is required on all HD Audio systems running Windows, regardless of whether the UAA Class driver or a codec-vendor-supplied audio function driver is used. Whether it is WavePCI, WaveCyclic, or WaveRT, the audio function driver or the Microsoft UAA class driver for Intel HD Audio sits underneath the PortCls driver and on top of the HD Audio bus driver.

The HD Audio bus driver is named HDAUDBUS.SYS, and its associated INF file is named HDAUDBUS.INF. As a true Plug and Play bus driver, it enumerates each of the function groups in each device that is attached to the Intel HD Audio link. Microsoft has defined a device driver interface (DDI) that function drivers can use to communicate with the HD Audio bus driver.

The HD Audio bus driver becomes a native component in Windows Vista, but it is not included with Windows XP. Therefore, any HD Audio function driver or class driver must include the HD Audio bus driver as part of its installer. Microsoft makes the HD Audio bus driver available to OEMs and codec vendors as a Quick Fix for Engineering (QFE).

A license from Microsoft is required to redistribute this QFE. Each party in the delivery chain must possess a valid license to redistribute this or any other QFE. Rights granted to one party typically do not convey those rights to the next party. For instance, a codec vendor may have permission for Web redistribution of the QFE, but if the OEM does not also have permission for Web redistribution, the OEM is not allowed to post the codec vendor's driver on the OEM Web site legally. Be sure that you have appropriate redistribution permissions for all systems incorporating Intel HD Audio. These redistribution permissions normally cover both the HD Audio bus driver as well as the Microsoft UAA class driver for Intel HD Audio.

While it is technically possible to install the HD Audio Bus driver from a driver installer or audio applications installer, it should not be considered a part of the audio subsystem, but a part of the OS. Whenever possible, the QFE containing the HD Audio Bus Driver should be applied to the OS pre-install image.

Drivers for X64 Versions

Drivers for 64-bit versions of Windows are almost identical in design to 32-bit drivers. However, they must be recompiled in a 64-bit compiler, and any 32-bit assembly code must be removed. While 32-bit applications do run on X64 systems, 32-bit drivers do not run. A special section in the INF file is used to identify 64-bit drivers.

The Microsoft UAA class driver for Intel HD Audio and Intel HD Audio bus driver are available for both 32-bit and 64-bit versions of the OS. Most codec vendors also make both versions of their audio function driver available. The Secure Audio Path (SAP) may not be available on earlier X64 versions of the audio software stack.

Installing an Audio Driver

You have two basic ways to install an audio driver. One is to allow the system to enumerate all the hardware and automatically install the driver with the closest ID string match. But in a development environment, you often need to switch between two or more drivers, perhaps accommodating several different versions of each. Here's the easy way to switch between different drivers. This procedure could be repeated many times a day in a PC audio lab.

Start in Device Manager. Create a shortcut to the Computer Management Console (compmgmt.msc) which can be found in the WINDOWS\system32 folders. Then double-click on Device Manager in the window on the left to see the list of devices. Expand the *Sound, video, and game controllers* category, but don't click on the Audio Codecs item at the top of the list, that's the list of software codecs in the MS Audio Compression Manager, shown in Figure 3.12. Instead, look down the list and locate a driver which says Intel HD Audio or High Definition Audio in the name.

Right click on the driver and select *Update driver* from the menu. For the next four dialogs, always take the bottom and least obvious choice. Specifically, in the Hardware Upgrade Wizard, select *No, not this time*, then click *Next* to continue. In the second dialog, click on *Install from a list or specific location (Advanced)*, then again click *Next* to continue. In the third dialog, select *Don't search. I will choose the driver to install*, and again click *Next*. In the fourth dialog, ignore the list of drivers that might or might not appear and click on the *Have Disk* button. Navigate to the folder containing the desired .INF and .SYS files, select the appropriate INF file, and then click *Next* when finished selecting the file. If the driver is unsigned, a dialog appears asking if you're sure you wish to install. Click *Continue*.

It takes a few seconds for the driver to install, and then the wizard shows if the installation was successful. Sometimes you are told that you must restart before changes can take effect. This advice is rarely true; you can almost always safely ignore this message and continue on. Just try playing audio, if you hear sound then usually you have no reason to reboot. You can also enable and disable a driver, which causes it to return to the same state as after system startup.

You can limit the number of reboot requests when installing drivers by closing all audio streams and client applications before exiting the driver. If you install drivers often, you can make your life easier by creating a series of easily accessed folders containing the different audio drivers that you might need to install. When you click on the *Have Disk* button—that's the final driver update step listed previously—the browser comes up in the directory from which you last loaded a driver. If all of your driver folders are next to each other, it's easy to go back and forth between them.

The preceding method of switching drivers usually works well when switching between different versions of essentially the same driver. If you are switching between a third-party driver and the Microsoft UAA class driver for Intel HD Audio, you sometimes need to fully uninstall the old driver before installing a new one in order to get the driver friendly name and the driver topology to update on Windows XP.

Applications Installers

The type of installation described above is an INF-only driver installation. It does not usually install GUI applications, nor does it create an entry in the Add or Remove Programs control panel. In addition to an INF-only package, some OEMs and ODMs require the codec vendor to provide a double-clickable installer package that installs the previously-logoed driver and can also install one or more audio applications. Try to avoid including the Intel HD Audio bus driver QFE in the installer package if possible. The bus driver should be considered a part of the OS, and should be applied to the OS Pre-install image. Some system configurations only allow audio installers to operate when logged in as admin.

Linux and Intel HD Audio

The popularity and support of Linux has skyrocketed in the last few years. Linux has a strong presence not only in the server market, but as a platform for consumer electronics equipment. The Advanced Linux Sound Architecture (ALSA) Project is the software layer which provides the basis for audio in Linux. By building on ALSA, system vendors are able to provide impressive audio capabilities on a Linux-based system.

Linux and ALSA are open source development efforts, so the methods for obtaining and redistributing audio support are very different than those used by commercial operating systems. The most recent ALSA code is available directly from the ALSA site. At regular intervals, the ALSA code is also merged into the Linux kernel. This merge normally includes support for the most recent Intel HD Audio codecs.

While the Linux developer community continues to build a solid foundation for audio applications, some applications are already at the forefront of usability and capabilities. A program called X Multimedia System (XMMS) shown in Figure 7.9 is one of the most popular programs for general audio playback for MP3, WAV, AU, and other audio file formats. XMMS by itself is quite powerful, but a plug-in architecture expands its capabilities to include different interface skins, visualizations, audio effects, and support for additional file formats. XMMS is included in many major distributions of Linux, including RedHat Enterprise Linux and Mandriva. A newly rewritten version 2 is in the works.

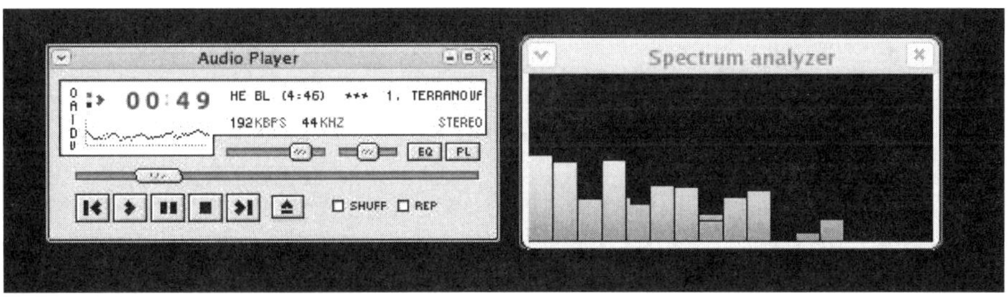

Figure 7.9 A screenshot of the X Multimedia System application

Another open source application is mythTV. By combining the stability of Linux with newly developed audio/video capabilities, you can make your own home theater PC. Through open source development and general enthusiasm for the product, mythTV has become fairly stable in the last couple years. It uses several components for A/V work, and ALSA is one of them. With skins and plug-ins, you can use mythTV to build a very capable and very stylish home theater PC.

Working with Audio Devices in Linux

Using the ALSA drivers from version 1.0.9 and on, most High Definition Audio devices configure themselves based on the pin configuration defaults contained in the BIOS verb tables. By employing this method, no custom work is needed to support a specific platform, and audio works properly out of the box. The BIOS method has a downside as well since it is heavily dependent on the correctness of the BIOS verb table. As long as the BIOS verb table is correct, the audio driver configures itself properly. See Chapter 4 for detailed information on programming verb tables and pin configuration defaults.

Linux has two main mixer devices: a GUI-based mixer and the ALSA mixer. The GUI-based mixer is available in most popular windowing systems, such as Gnome and KDE. A Windows-like mixer appears on the taskbar. In addition to this GUI-based mixer, ALSA supplies a full-featured text mode mixer that can be run on any Linux system, with or without a windowing system.

ALSA also provides a legacy layer for older applications that use the Open Sound System (OSS) audio architecture. You can download this additional support from the ALSA homepage. ALSA has two compatibility layers which support existing OSS applications – one in the kernel, and one in user-space. The kernel OSS layer works transparently, creating OSS device nodes corresponding to your ALSA devices, which can then be accessed directly by applications. It's not an ideal solution, but for games it works quite well. The only real problem with the kernel OSS emulation is that it sidesteps your `.asoundrc` user-customized startup options, so it disregards any configuration you've made, and it won't run applications through the dmix plug-in. The user-space OSS emulation addresses these issues by using a pre-loaded library that intercepts calls to OSS devices, routing them through the libasound module instead.

When configuring a system for Linux, you should install the standard distribution with the most recent kernel and then test. If everything works properly, then you are done. If things don't appear to be working right, then download the most recent stable ALSA build from the ALSA Web site and test with it. If that still doesn't solve your issue, you can try a development version of ALSA If audio is still not working as expected, try verifying the system operation under Windows using the Microsoft UAA class driver for Intel HD Audio. If the pin-configuration verb tables in the BIOS are not set correctly, then both the Microsoft UAA class driver for Intel HD Audio and ALSA would exhibit problems, so be sure that the verb tables are configured correctly. In addition, the ALSA project web site has a bug-tracking system where platform and driver specific issues are reported, to be resolved by ALSA contributors

Linux Applications for High Definition Audio

Linux is becoming popular in many embedded configurations, from small handheld devices to PCs masquerading as consumer electronics equipment. With the availability of high-fidelity Intel HD Audio solutions, Linux can be used for some very advanced audio functions. The Ardour project is an open-source digital audio workstation, while X-Lite, Kphone, and Skype all provide Voice Over IP functionality. Intervideo's LinDVD and CyberLink's PowerCinema products provide complete PVR and Media PC functionality. Some newer PCs are being built with instant-on capability, to work in Linux whenever Windows isn't running, so they come with both OSes enabled for audio.

Chapter 8

Intel® HD Audio Software: Signal Processing and Volume Control

BRIAN RUSSELL'S LAWS OF SOFTWARE RELATIVITY

- *As a software project approaches release, its mass increases.*
- *The energy required to release a software project is inversely proportional to the time before a scheduled release.*
- *It takes infinite energy to release a finished product on time; therefore, all software projects are both incomplete and late.*
- *Time is relative to the observer of a software project. The last month of development appears to an outside observer to take a year.*
- *If a software project becomes too large, it will collapse into a black hole. Time and money are absorbed but nothing ever comes out.*

—Usenet post

The interface between audio software and system hardware has three different areas of connectivity. The first is Direct Memory Access (DMA). The DMA controller is located in the Intel HD Audio controller, which is usually part of the input/output controller, also known as the Southbridge chip. The DMA circuitry in the controller gets the audio data from RAM and puts it on the Intel HD Audio bus. If the codec is properly configured, the controller can start and stop the DMA without any notification to the codec by other means than that the stream is starting and stopping. The audio codec receives no advance notice that the DMA stream is going to start or stop. The driver stack communicates only with the Intel HD Audio controller to manage DMA.

In fact, all communication from the driver to the audio hardware is routed to or through the controller. The Intel HD Audio codec is not addressable directly; it can be addressed only by way of the controller. Therefore, any commands to the codec actually are sent to the controller, which relays them through the Intel HD Audio bus.

The second class of connectivity is stream control. An Intel HD Audio codec can respond to various types of control. One control can set the sample rate for a particular ADC while another control can determine the specific channels in an eight-channel stream that a DAC is monitoring. These types of controls typically are changed when the DMA is not running.

The *topology controls* are another class of controls that can be manipulated while the DMA is running. The complete set of these controls is referred to as the system's audio topology. The topology is defined by the schematics of the audio circuit, by the settings of the pin configuration defaults registers, and by the codec design. Portions of the topology are exposed to the end user as part of the Windows mixer, as explained later in this chapter.

Modes of Operation

Audio drivers for Windows typically operate in kernel mode, a protected processor mode that is sometimes referred to as "Ring 0" or supervisor mode. Application software and DLLs run at a different protection level called user mode, or "Ring 3". Only software running in kernel mode can address the hardware directly. User mode software may communicate with kernel-mode components by calling a device Input and Output control (IOCTL, pronounced "eye-octal") which is a special interface that transitions between modes. Any data to be transferred must be copied from user mode to kernel mode. For Windows XP, all audio output data must be copied from user mode to kernel mode before it can be played. It is difficult, if not impossible, to share data buffers between user mode and kernel mode.

Kernel-mode elements in Windows XP are used to help isolate user mode applications both from each other and from the hardware. If an application crashes and is terminated, this isolation keeps its failure from causing the system or other applications to crash. For example, FPU exception handlers can resolve floating-point faults, such as a denormalized number, which is caused by a number that results from an FPU operation being too small to represent with the specified resolution. Kernel-mode code has no such FPU protection, so that the presence of a denormalized number in the FPU brings the system to a crawl. Software that performs floating-point processing in the kernel must be designed so that it never produces a denormalized number or that it has the capability to detect a denormalized number in some way other than relying on the FPU exception handler, which has no effect in kernel mode.

Poorly designed kernel-mode drivers and libraries are the primary cause of the dreaded Blue Screen of Death (BSOD). This Windows phenomenon happens because kernel mode, unlike user mode, has no underlying layers that can deal with detected programming errors. The Microsoft[†] Windows Hardware Quality Labs (WHQL) is the entity which administers Microsoft's hardware Logo programs. One of WHQL's primary missions is to ensure that the end user never sees a BSOD. Driver Verifier is the primary mechanism used by WHQL to banish the BSOD experience. Driver Verifier is a development framework that you can enable to monitor improper or unpaired memory allocations and deallocations and to keep track of other potentially poor driver behavior. The WHQL Hardware Compatibility Tests (HCT) turn on Driver Verifier and then, as a worst case scenario test, run all of the remaining audio tests at the same time. If the Driver Verifier monitor detects any improper behavior, then the test fails. A driver developer can also choose to enable driver verifier while he is writing and debugging his code.

Another operating mode that is invisible to the operating system is System Management Mode. When it executes instructions, the BIOS goes into this special CPU mode. For instance, consider the case when you hold down the power button for 4 seconds to power down a computer. The BIOS is polling the power button at a period of 10 to 100 milliseconds. Each time it notices that the button is down, it increments a counter. Each time it notices that the button is up, it resets the counter. Whenever the counter gets up to 4 seconds, the BIOS powers down the system. All of this logic occurs in System Management Mode. The OS is entirely unaware that the BIOS has taken periodic control of the system. The BIOS developer must ensure that the system is in System Management Mode for the smallest time possible whenever the OS is operating so that audio is uninterrupted.

The Differences Between ISR, DPC, and SMI

A hardware interrupt is a flag in the CPU that is set when a particular hardware event has occurred. For audio systems, the primary hardware interrupt is the signal from the DMA engine that indicates completion of the transfer of a block of audio data. For Windows XP, this signal occurs many times per second whenever the Intel HD Audio bus is carrying data.

The Interrupt Vector Table (IVT) in the CPU contains a list of interrupts and a corresponding list of Interrupt Service Routines (ISR), also known as interrupt handlers. When a hardware interrupt event occurs, the CPU stops what it was doing and jumps almost immediately to the ISR. The ISR is typically a very short piece of code that does two things. It resets the interrupt flag so that it is ready to be triggered again, and then the ISR calls the OS to schedule a Deferred Procedure Call (DPC). Thus, the time that the ISR spends servicing the interrupt is kept to a minimum. The only code that has higher priority than a hardware ISR is another hardware ISR with an even higher numerical priority.

The preemptive multitasking aspect of Windows is timer-based. At predetermined time intervals between 1 and 10 milliseconds, the Windows scheduler breaks in and takes a look around. If other tasks or threads with higher priority are pending, the current task is put on hold and the task with the highest priority is executed instead. A user mode thread cannot have higher priority than kernel mode. Of all the competing tasks in the kernel, a DPC has the highest priority. With one exception to be explained shortly, only a DPC with higher priority can preempt another DPC. For best performance, DPCs should be kept as short as possible.

For lowest latency, signal processing in the driver usually takes place in a DPC. If additional latency can be tolerated, the processing can be moved to a worker thread or some other lower priority. However, processing a signal inside a DPC has some drawbacks. Consider a single-threaded, single-core CPU. If the audio processing is using up ten percent of the CPU and the DPC is being queued up every ten milliseconds, the DPC would take one whole millisecond before it is completed and the whole system would be locked out of responding to other user interactions for one millisecond out of every ten. If ten or more different devices on the same PC took this approach, then the CPU would have no power left over for anything else. Multicore processors and hyper-threading do a lot to help distribute the load and prevent this type of issue, but those technologies can't stop it completely.

System tests being developed for the Windows Vista Logo program will measure both ISR times and DPC times. Any ISR time greater than 25 microseconds or any DPC time greater than 100 microseconds will trigger a test failure. Microsoft will include logs of ISR and DPC times in future versions of Internet-based Windows Error Reporting, so that it becomes possible to track down badly behaving ISRs and DPCs in the field even if they were able to pass WHQL testing.

System Management Interrupts, known as SMIs (rhymes with eyes), are the exception to the rule that only a DPC with higher priority can preempt another DPC. These SMIs are interrupts or other periodic processing that takes place in System Management Mode. The power-off example mentioned earlier uses a timer-based SMI to monitor the power button. As long as the SMI is as well-behaved, as an ISR should be, no issues arise. However, if an SMI takes an excessive amount of time to complete its processing, you could hear that delay manifested as a breakup in the audio stream.

Unfortunately, it is extremely difficult to determine externally whether an SMI is causing such problems, especially if the BIOS source code is not available or is poorly understood. Often, the BIOS engineer might not even be aware of a change in conditions that results in excessive SMI times. Frequently, the only way to confirm that an audio breakup issue is due to excessive SMI processing times is to fix the issue and then confirm that the new version fixes the noticeable problem. Try to eliminate SMIs in your design if possible.

Windows XP† Audio Stack

Microsoft Windows XP, in both Professional and Home versions, made the NT kernel available to the home user for the first time. This release also brought the audio improvements from Windows ME to the NT kernel, including full multi-channel support and a fully implemented Secure Audio Path (SAP). As a result, it became possible to qualify for a second digital signature as part of the Windows Logo process, with a DRM level of 1200. See Chapter 10 for details on SAP and DRM.

Windows XP also supports DirectKS, which is a special interface made available for recording studio applications that are capable of taking over all of the audio functions in the system. DirectKS is usually not appropriate for audio applications that must coexist with other audio applications, but can be useful for professional recording studio applications.

Unless otherwise stated, the details in the rest of this chapter refer to Windows XP with Service Pack 2 installed. Windows Vista will have significant enhancements that build on the information contained here, and which should fix a number of the problems identified here. Figure 8.1 details the WDM audio stack.

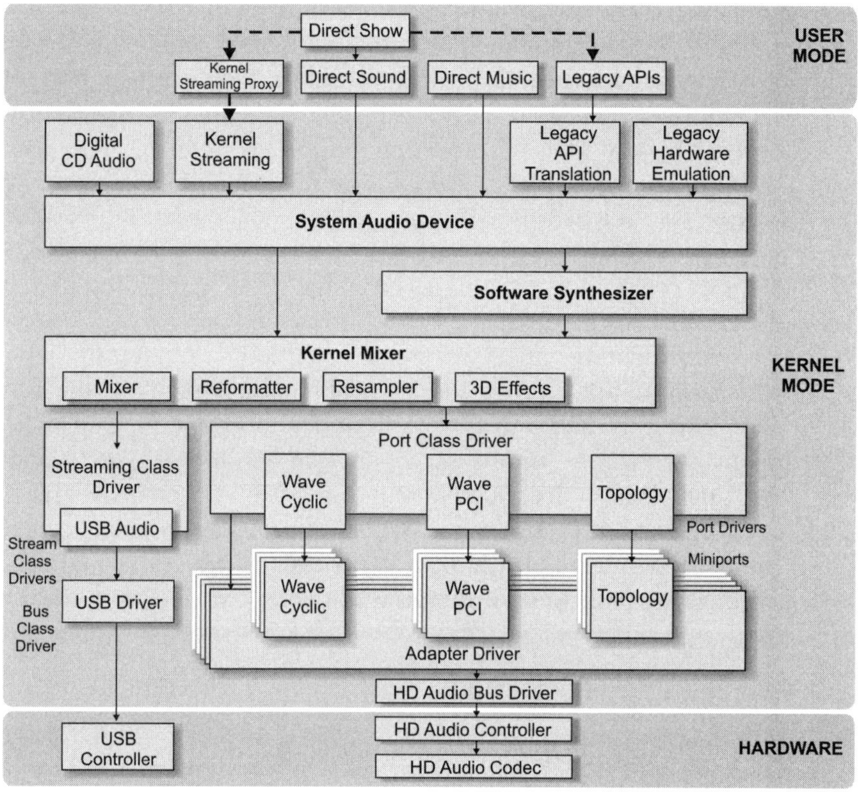

The top of the diagram shows both the Wave and DirectSound interfaces available to application programs. The legacy H/W Emulation includes the SoundBlaster Pro emulation in software. The port class driver can be seen on the lower right side. The port class driver provides a consistent interface to the vendor-supplied miniport drivers. The WaveCyclic or WavePCI miniport supports DMA and the Topology miniport driver exposes the audio topology of the system. The lower left section shows the differences in implementation of USB audio. Note that everything above the Kernel Mixer (KMixer) is the same regardless of whether USB or PortCls is used to communicate to hardware.

Figure 8.1 Windows XP WDM Driver Stack

SNDVOL32: The Misunderstood Windows Mixer

The topology miniport driver and the WaveCyclic or WavePCI miniport driver usually are combined into a single driver. The topology miniport driver is used to determine which audio volume and mute controls are made available to the user. It might not always be visible, but the application named SNDVOL32.EXE is the Windows mixer application, and it operates at all times. To see it, double click the speaker icon in the system tray, which usually is located in the lower right-hand area of your screen. In earlier versions of Windows XP, the speaker icon is hidden by default. In all other Windows versions, including Windows XP SP1 and SP2, the speaker icon is visible by default. When you double-click the speaker icon, the mixer appears in Playback view. Though it's not obvious, two or sometimes three alternate control views are really available from this application. SNDVOL32 supports multiple instances, each of which can be a separate view into a different or overlapping set of controls.

Select Properties from the Options menu to change the view. Playback and recording views normally are available, and sometimes a third "Other" view is also made available. Select the appropriate radio button to change to a new view. If you select the recording view, then click OK and the recording mixer is shown. Double-click on the speaker icon in the system tray again, and you can see the recording mixer and the playback mixer at the same time. While they often appear to have the same controls, they are in fact very different from each other, since one is used for adjusting the listening volume and the other is used for adjusting the recording volume. Figure 8.2 shows a typical Playback mixer panel for a notebook PC.

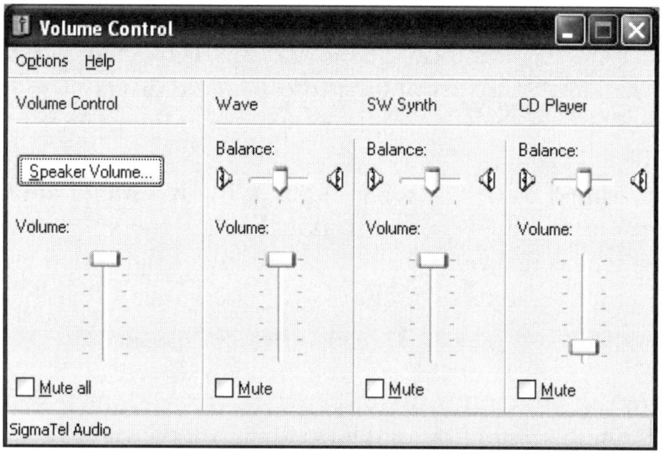

Figure 8.2 Playback Mixer Volume Control

It's important to understand both the playback mixer and the recording mixer, as well as what each control really does. The following controls usually appear in the playback mixer:

- *Master Volume and Mute.* This control must be present in every implementation. Originally, this control was mapped to the master volume and mute control of the codec, but more recent designs often perform this volume scaling in software. This implementation is only possible when no analog-through paths are in the topology. Instead of a balance control, Windows XP provides a way to individually control and balance each channel of a multi-channel audio stream. This capability is not available on Windows 2000 and earlier. While the master volume control still adjusts all channels of audio in most cases, Windows 2000 offers no mechanism for individually adjusting each channel of a multi-channel stream. Putting this slider to the maximum position should result in unity gain—that is, no boost, no gain—for the audio signals being output.

- *Wave Volume and Mute.* This control is still present in Windows XP for legacy reasons, but is largely useless for Intel HD Audio systems, especially those supporting multi-channel audio. This control is mapped to KMixer, and it performs a software volume scaling of the first two channels of any stream, stereo, or multi-channel. It has no effect on other channels in the multi-channel stream. For modern systems, this control should *always* be set to maximum, and the user should not be able to adjust it. When possible, it should not be displayed to the user. Adjusting this control to any setting other than full volume always puts multi-channel audio out of balance. It also reduces the dynamic range of a stereo stream. *Not Recommended. If present, always set to Max.*

- *SW Synth:* This control is used to adjust the software mixing volume of the MIDI software synthesizer included in Windows. It is normally turned up all the way, but can be adjusted if the user finds that the MIDI synthesis is too loud. This control is at unity gain when the slider is set to the Max position.
- *CD Audio:* This control has slightly different functionality depending on whether analog or digital CD input is used. For analog CD, it adjusts the hardware listening volume for the analog through path; for Digital CD, it controls the volume scaling of the CD audio stream in KMixer. Be aware that this slider controls both analog and digital gain if an analog input is implemented but the CD is in digital mode. Any noise on the analog CD input circuitry will be heard when the CD volume control is turned up, even if the CD is set to digital mode. A knowledgeable driver developer can set a topology option in the code to disable analog functionality, thereby eliminating this conflict. In digital CD mode, this control is at unity gain when the slider is at the Max position. In analog CD mode, this control usually adds 12 decibels of gain when at Max position, which often causes distortion. In analog mode, this control should be set to about one-third of the slider height to achieve unity gain.
- *PC Speaker or PC Beep:* This control, if present, determines the volume of sounds coming from the 8253 timer chip on the motherboard as well as sounds coming from the PCM/CIA card cage on some laptops. The signals available on this analog input line are usually very noisy, so it is best to keep this control muted except when it is needed.
- *Line In:* If implemented, this slider controls the analog-through volume of the line input jack. This audio path is no longer recommended, and implementing it results in a WHQL failure under the Windows Vista Logo program. Any audio signals routed through this path are not available to be modified or processed by

software, which can cause significant end-user confusion. Also, signals using this path are not available to be used for echo cancellation purposes. Signals using this path are also not available at the output of USB or 1394 audio subsystems. This control usually adds 12 decibels of gain when at Max position, which often causes distortion. If used, this control should be set to about one-third of the slider height to achieve unity gain. *Not Recommended.*

- *Microphone In*: If implemented, this slider has all the same issues listed above for Line In. If internal speakers are installed in the PC, turning up this control causes howling feedback as the speaker signal couples back into the microphone. To avoid feedback, this control should always be left muted to avoid feedback from the microphone. *Not Recommended.*

Many users never have seen the Recording Mixer, are actually unaware of it, and don't know what to do if/when recording doesn't work properly. The controls that usually appear in the recording mixer are listed below. Unlike the playback mixer, which mixes all of the inputs together, the recording mixer allows the user to select from one of the inputs displayed. Therefore, you have a checkbox that acts like a radio button below each slider. Only one input can be selected at a time. Figure 8.3 shows a typical Recording Control for a notebook PC.

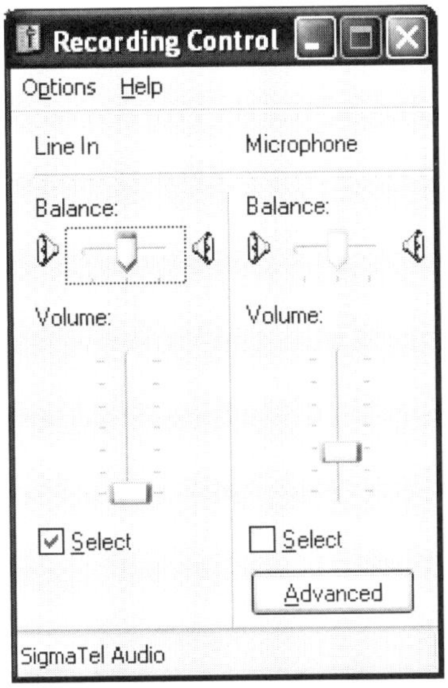

Figure 8.3 Recording Volume Controls

Unlike the playback levels, all of the controls in the recording mixer have gain, but no cut. In most cases, the best place to set the slider is at the very bottom of its range; setting the slider any higher than the bottom of its range causes unwanted distortion.

- *Line In:* This slider normally allows an analog boost of up to 22.5 decibels to be added to the line level input before the analog-to-digital conversion is performed. Since most analog line level signals are >= 1 volt RMS, adding this boost almost always causes unwanted distortion on a recording. Resist the urge to set this slider to any position other than the very bottom unless the line level input signal is abnormally weak. Newer designs may choose to eliminate a slider for line in, in order to behave more like an A/V receiver, which normally does not have separate volume controls for each input. .

- *Microphone In*: Most audio codecs have an additional microphone preamp stage that is used to interface to microphones with unknown output levels and impedances. Leading codecs may have selectable gain stages of 10, 20, 30, and even 40 decibels. Click on the options menu and make sure that the advanced controls selection is checked. This selection usually causes an

Advanced button to appear below the Select checkbox. Click on this advanced button to see a dialog for adjusting the microphone preamp. Just like the line-in slider, this slider also has 22.5 decibels of gain in addition to the 20 decibels of gain usually available from the microphone preamp. These controls should be set while running a recording application that shows the microphone level, or by running one of the four different microphone level-setting wizards included in Windows XP and accompanying software. The 10/20/30/40 dB microphone preamp is shared with the playback mixer, so adjusting the preamp also can cause feedback if the microphone input in the playback mixer is left unmuted. The 22.5 decibels of gain attached to the microphone recording slider does not interact with the playback mixer, nor does the microphone slider in the playback mixer have any interaction with the microphone recording slider.

- *CD Audio In:* If the driver developer has chosen to expose an analog CD input for the recording mixer, you can adjust it here. Many modern systems no longer allow this choice for the user, since applications such as Windows Media Player can read the audio CD directly, without using the analog input. Just like the line-in slider, this slider adds 22.5 decibels of gain to the signal when turned up, which almost certainly causes distortion. Keep this slider at the bottom of its range to avoid distortion. See "CD Audio: Analog or Digital?" for a detailed explanation of why to avoid exposing this slider in most systems.
- *Stereo Mix:* This functionality is a hold-over from AC97 implementations. Basically, this slider provides an analog mix of everything at the output of the codec, including the DAC output as well as any analog line or microphone inputs. If no analog microphone or line inputs are in the playback mixer, you have no reason to provide the stereo mix input. *Not Recommended.*

Some Intel HD Audio systems implement multi-streaming, where a separate audio device is instantiated for headphones plugged into the front panel, or if a microphone array is built in. These audio devices might appear and disappear depending on whether any jacks are plugged into the front panel, for instance. You can switch between multiple audio devices by going to the Options menu of SNDVOL32.EXE and selecting Properties. Click on the dropdown menu labeled Mixer Device at the top of the dialog to see a list of available devices. You might have to plug a jack into the front panel in order to see a front panel device onscreen.

MIXERLINE and SNDVOL32

The MIXERLINE API was introduced prior to Windows 95, and has changed little since then. This API preceded object-oriented programming, which makes it difficult to access from today's modern programming environments. If you are comfortable reading and compiling code, you could learn the most about MIXERLINE by building and tracing through Microsoft's MixApp sample code, which was originally released along with Visual C 6.0. You can download it from the Microsoft Web site, just search for MixApp.

The MIXERLINE interface is the layer directly underneath SNDVOL32. In addition to supporting the controls mentioned earlier, MIXERLINE provides a callback mechanism that allows multiple instances of multiple applications to access a particular control at the same time. You can see this mechanism easily by opening two instances of SNDVOL32 and moving the master slider in either instance. The master volume control of the other instance moves at the same time.

At the user-mode level, applications that need to be aware of the underlying volume level of an audio device need to register to receive the `MM_MIXM_CONTROL_CHANGE` message. When an application receives this message, it should query the specified control node to determine its new value and update its UI to reflect the change. Node in this context refers to a node in the Windows audio topology, which is separate and distinct from the widget or node ID in an Intel HD Audio codec. Don't confuse these two different types of nodes.

The volume levels in the MIXERLINE interface have a linear range of 65535 (maximum) to 0 (no sound). The value 32767 is 6 decibels lower than maximum, 16383 is 12 decibels down from max, 8191 is 18 decibels down from max, and so on. Each time the number is cut in half, the level is reduced by 6 decibels. Interestingly enough, the volume values that are passed down to the audio driver are in an exponential format, rather than the linear range used in MIXERLINE.

Master Volume in Windows XP†

It is a common misconception that the audio driver controls the master volume for the system, especially for volume buttons or keys on the keyboard, front panel, or Media Center Remote Control. In fact, the driver only receives messages from MIXERLINE to control the volume. With one exception, the driver does not generate any commands that affect the master volume based on user activity.

For instance, many laptops have dedicated volume up, volume down, and volume mute keys. Table 8.1 shows the scan codes associated with these functions. The scan codes are processed by the BIOS and the keyboard driver, causing a `WM_APPCOMMAND` windows message to be generated and broadcast to all applications every time one of these keys is pressed and released.

Table 8.1 Scan Codes and WM_APPCOMMANDs for Master Volume

HID Key Name	WM_APP COMMAND	Set 1 Make	Set 1 Break	Set 2 Make	Set 2 Break
Mute	APPCOMMAND_ VOLUME_MUTE	E0 20	E0 A0	E0 23	E0 F0 23
Volume Up	APPCOMMAND_ VOLUME_UP	E0 30	E0 B0	E0 32	E0 F0 32
Volume Down	APPCOMMAND_ VOLUME_DOWN	E0 2E	E0 AE	E0 21	E0 F0 21

Volume-up, volume-down, and mute buttons on the Media Center Remote Control also map into these same WM_APPCOMMANDs.

SNDVOL32, which is running all the time, even when no mixer window is displayed, receives and processes these three `WM_APPCOMMAND` messages and uses them to shift the master volume slider up, down, or to mute the master mute control. Any other applications that have registered a callback with MIXERLINE also trigger a notification whenever the master volume is changed, so you should see all of the master volume control sliders in these applications change as the Volume Up and Volume Down keys are pressed. The same `WM_APPCOMMAND` messages are also generated by clicking the volume up, down, and mute buttons on the Windows Media Center Remote Control if Windows XP Service Pack 1 or a recent version of Media Center edition is installed. Normally, you must press the button 26 times to go from minimum to maximum volume when using either the keyboard or the remote control.

One exception to the driver controlling volume can occur if the system makes use of the Volume Knob feature of Intel HD Audio, which allows the codec to support a volume knob or volume up/down buttons. In Direct mode, the Volume Knob is connected directly to one or more volume control stages in the codec, while in Indirect mode, the Volume Knob is sent up the driver stack, which eventually results in a new volume setting property that is passed to the topology miniport section of the Intel HD Audio function driver.

The system sends the `MM_MIXM_CONTROL_CHANGE` message in response to the volume control changing for one of two reasons:

- *Hardware event*. The driver signaled that a volume change occured by signaling the `KSEVENTSETID_AudioControlChange` event. This event results in the `MM_MIXM_CONTROL_CHANGE` message being sent to each registered application. This signaling method is used with the Direct mode of the Volume Knob control.
- *Software event*. A user-mode application or service called the `mixerSetControlDetails()` API. When this event happens, the `MM_MIXM_CONTROL_CHANGE` message also gets sent. This signaling method is used with the Indirect mode of the Volume Knob control.

Direct Mode and Hardware Volume Events

In the Direct method shown in Figure 8.4, pressing either the volume up or volume down buttons attached to the Volume Knob widget causes an immediate change in the DAC volume, and it also causes an unsolicited response to be sent by the Intel HD Audio codec. The unsolicited response is serviced by the topology miniport in the Intel HD Audio function driver, which converts this volume change into a `KSEVENTSETID_AudioControlChange` event, which is then redirected through PORTCLS.SYS to WDMAUD.SYS. This event bubbles up to WDMAUD.DRV, the user-mode counterpart of WDMAUD.SYS, which in turn causes `MM_MIXM_CONTROL_CHANGE` messages to be sent to all applications which have registered a callback.

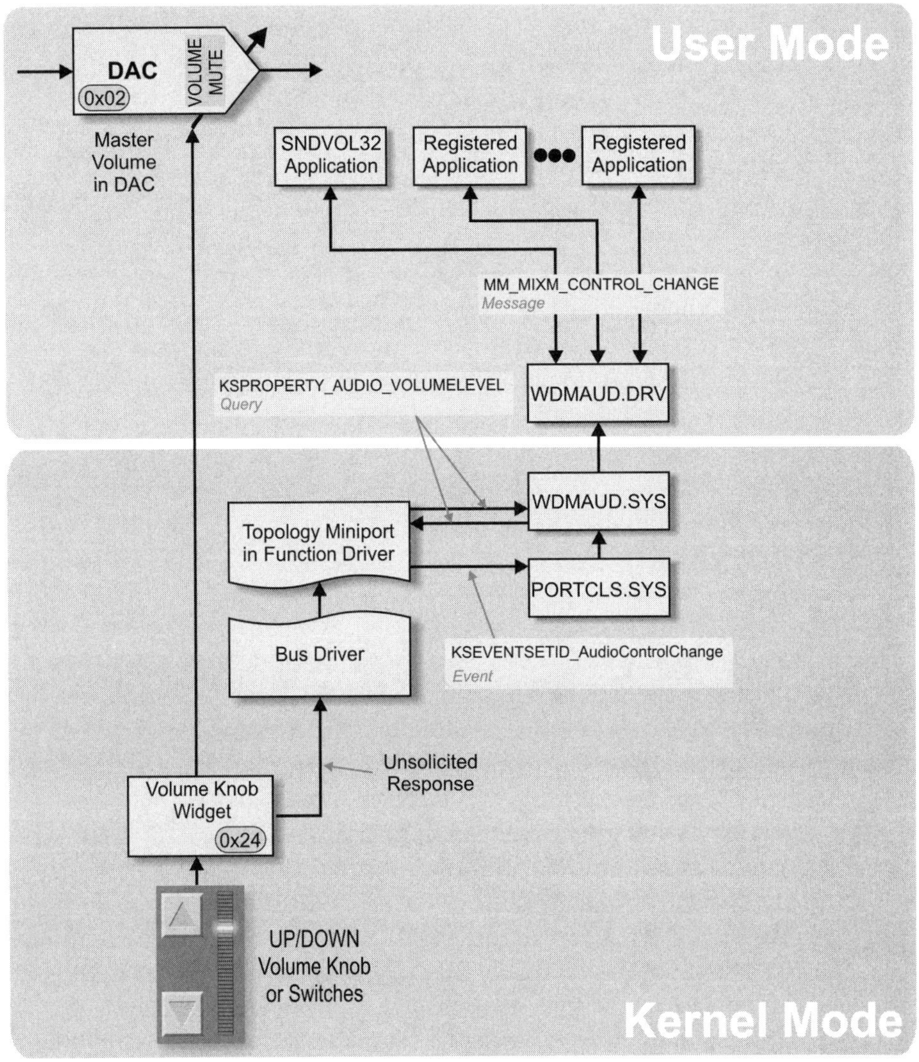

Figure 8.4 Direct Method Using Volume Knob with Hardware Events

Upon receiving the `MM_MIXM_CONTROL_CHANGE` message, each application calls back into the MIXERLINE interface to retrieve the newly updated volume value for the topology node that was specified in the `KSEVENTSETID_AudioControlChange` event, and subsequently in the `MM_MIXM_CONTROL_CHANGE` message. In the diagram, arrows representing this query go between the topology miniport driver and

WDMAUD.SYS. This query takes place for each registered application. In the SB16 sample, the property handler for this property reads the recently changed hardware register directly and converts it into decibels.

To support the hardware event method, your audio device must have an external volume knob that communicates directly to the audio driver, when its volume has been adjusted, by generating an unsolicited response. The audio driver then signals PORTCLS.SYS that the event occurred and PORTCLS.SYS then notifies any components that have registered with it to receive this notification. In the case of Windows XP, WDMAUD.SYS would have registered for this notification. When WDMAUD.SYS receives this event, it relays it to WDMAUD.DRV, which then sends the `MM_MIXM_CONTROL_CHANGE` message to those applications that registered to receive it.

To register the hardware event at system startup, WDMAUD.SYS in kernel mode queries each topology node to see whether it supports the event set `KSEVENTSETID_AudioControlChange` where the ID is equal to `KSEVENT_CONTROL_CHANGE`. The driver adds support for this event by including an Automation Table entry for every node that supports this type of notification. The SB16 sample in the *src\wdm\audio\sb16* directory in the Windows DDK provides an example showing how this support is accomplished. Search through all the files in this project using the string "`EVENT_SUPPORT`" to locate each of the elements that must be added to your driver to support the `KSEVENTSETID_AudioControlChange` event.

During setup, the callback routine that is provided by the driver in its automation table is called with the `PCEVENT_VERB_SUPPORT` and `PCEVENT_VERB_ADD` flags. After receiving the `PCEVENT_VERB_ADD flag`, the driver indicates to PORTCLS.SYS that it has started monitoring for changes to this topology node by calling `IPortEvents::AddEventToEventList()`. When a change in volume does occur, the driver must notify PORTCLS.SYS by calling `IPortEvents::GenerateEventList()`, passing in the specific event ID, which in this case is `KSEVENT_CONTROL_CHANGE`, along with the topology `NODE ID` that changed, which in this case would be the master volume control. Try looking these calls up in the SB16 sample driver to get a better picture of how they work.

Indirect Mode and Software Volume Events

To support Indirect mode and the software event method, the external volume controls need to expose themselves as HID devices. The Microsoft HID Service then generates `APPCOMMAND_VOLUME_DOWN` and `APPCOMMAND_VOLUME_UP` messages when the buttons are pressed. In response to those messages, the system calls the `mixerSetControlDetails() function` to change the volume level. When WDMAUD.DRV receives this call from `mixerSetControlDetails()`, it passes the call down to the driver. As a result, the driver changes the volume level and then WDMAUD.DRV sends the `MM_MIXM_CONTROL_CHANGE` message to notify applications that the volume level has changed.

In the Indirect method shown in Figure 8.5, pressing either the volume up or volume down buttons attached to the Volume Knob widget generates an unsolicited response. This response is reflected up to the HID device running in kernel mode, and then on to the HID service running in user mode. For Media devices, including Intel HD Audio, the HID service transmits `WM_APPCOMMAND` messages, just like those sent by a keyboard or Media Center Remote Control. These messages are received by WDMAUD.DRV, which sends `MM_MIXM_CONTROL_CHANGE` messages to all applications that have registered a callback. It also calls through WDMAUD.SYS to the property handler of the topology miniport driver with the new volume that was specified in a `KSPROPERTY_AUDIO_VOLUMELEVEL` structure. The topology miniport driver then converts this value to the Intel HD Audio codec volume format described in "Hardware Volume Scaling" in Chapter 4 before sending the volume command as a verb to the DAC widget.

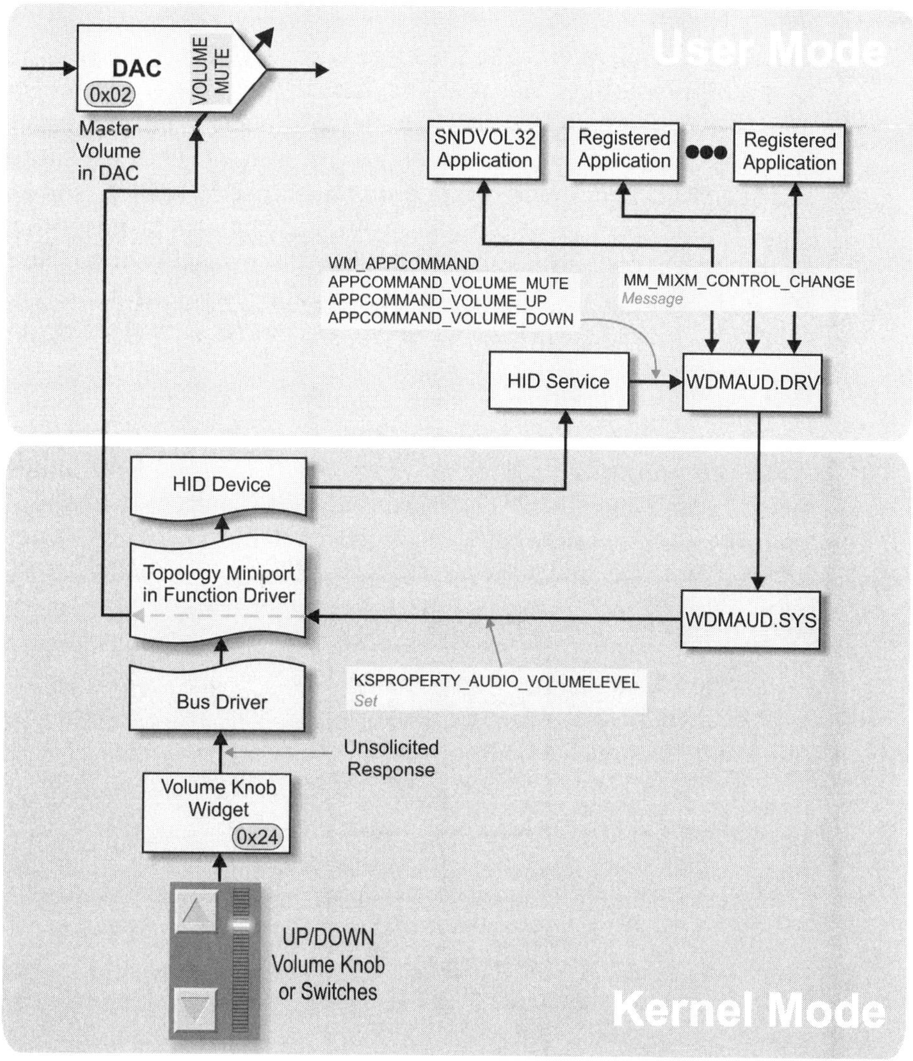

Figure 8.5 Indirect Method using Volume Knob with Software Events

No currently-available drivers have implemented this Indirect approach, it is shown to illustrate the big difference in approach from Direct mode using an event to signal the volume change.

Linear and Log Volume Scales

Figure 1.5 in Chapter 1 demonstrates how a linear scale does not accurately represent the way that the human ear works; while Figure 1.4 shows that a logarithmic scale results in a good match between the listener's perception and the measurement units of dB SPL. Unfortunately, the MIXERLINE interface is based on a linear scale, which is not an intuitive way for users to set listening volumes. Figure 8.6 shows the change in listening level as a result of adjusting the master volume slider. Since the scale is linear, the volume drops by 6 decibels each time the volume control is moved to half of its previous volume setting. The top half of the slider represents the top 6 dB of range, while the next 6 decibels takes up one fourth of the range, followed by the next 6 decibels being represented by only one eighth of the overall range. Thus, large changes to the control at the top of its range result in little or no difference in perceived volume, while very small changes at the lower range of the control make very noticeable changes in volume.

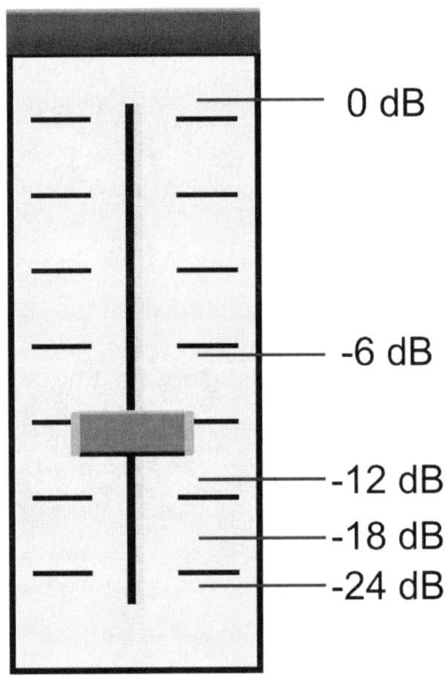

Figure 8.6 Linear Fader Attenuation Using SNDVOL32.EXE

The rightmost column of Table 8.2 shows the volume range for the MIXERLINE interface, which matches the slider behavior shown in Figure 8.6. The middle column of Table 8.2 shows the very different `KSPROPERTY_AUDIO_VOLUMELEVEL` and `KSAUDIO_MIXLEVEL` volume formats used by the OS to pass volume change messages to the driver.

Unlike the MIXERLINE interface, these formats are specified in decibels, and have considerably more dynamic range and significantly better resolution. Volume is represented as a 32-bit signed number, in which the 16 more significant bits are directly translated into decibels, either plus or minus. The lower 16 bits are treated as a fraction which is added to the whole number specified in the upper 16 bits. A value of `0x80000000` (-32768.000) is treated as a mute.

For example, •1.0 dBFS is represented as `0xFFFF0000`, and •1.5 dBFS is represented as `0xFFFE8000`. This format has a resolution of 1/65536 of a decibel, or 0.00001526 dB, and a dynamic range of +32767.9 dB to •32768.0 dB, far more than is needed for real-world audio applications.

Contrast this with the volume representation for MIXERLINE in the rightmost column. This format has a resolution of 0.453 dB when volume is near maximum, but the step size increases as the volume level is reduced. At about •80 dB the resolution becomes extremely coarse. The lowest level that MIXERLINE is capable of representing is •96 dB, all levels below that are treated as Mute or Off. In actual practice, an application which exposes a master volume control must specify the number of discrete steps in its volume range. The MIXAPP example uses 192 steps, while SNDVOL32 uses 500 steps. Dividing the maximum value of 65536 by 192 steps results in a linear value of 341 or 0x155. To convert from MIXERLINE units to decibels, use the formula 20 * log10 (volume / 65535). When 0x155 is converted into decibels, the result is •45.67 decibels. This volume is the lowest that can be passed via the MIXERLINE interface when the volume slider is implemented using the standard 192 steps. So even though the driver can receive volume messages with range and resolution that far exceeds what the ear can detect, the MIXERLINE interface significantly limits both the range and resolution, especially at the lower end of the volume range.

Table 8.2 Differences between driver and application volume ranges

Attenuation in dB	KSAUDIO_MIXLEVEL	MIXERLINE (Application)
0	0x00000000	0xFFFF
-0.00001526	0xFFFFFFFF	Out of range

Attenuation in dB	KSAUDIO_MIXLEVEL	MIXERLINE (Application)
-0.453	0xFFFFF463	0xFFFE
-1.5	0xFFFE8000	0xD7FF
-6	0xFFFA0000	0x7FFF
-12	0xFFF40000	0x3FFF
-18	0xFFEE0000	0x1FFF
-24	0xFFe80000	0x0FFF
-45.67	0xFFD25555	0x0155
-48	0xFFD00000	0x0104
-80	0xFFB00000	0x0006
-86	0xFFAA0000	0x0003
-90	0xFFA60000	0x0002
-96	0xFFA00000	0x0001
-100	0xFF8C0000	Out of range
-120	0xFF880000	Out of range

If the master volume control on the MIXERLINE side is implemented in the most standard way, with a minimum 0x0000, a maximum of 0xFFFF, and with 192 steps (0xC0), any values for MIXERLINE smaller than –45 dB are unavailable due to lack of resolution. To determine the number of steps needed for a specific resolution, divide the maximum value by the desired value from the MIXERLINE column. For instance, to support a user setting of –90 dB, the number of steps would need to 65535 (0xFFFF) divided by 2 = 32767 steps. To convert from MIXERLINE units to dB, use the formula 20 * log10 (volume / 65535)

Volume Tables for Audio Taper

SNDVOL32 uses a table of volume values to determine how to handle the `WM_APPCOMMAND` volume control messages. Whenever WDMAUD.DRV receives an `APPCOMMAND_VOLUME_UP` message, the volume is set to the next higher step in the table. The `APPCOMMAND_VOLUME_DOWN` message causes the next lower step to be selected. Usually, this table has a total of 26 steps, including full off and full on. For Windows XP and previous versions of Windows, the table was determined by dividing the MIXERLINE maximum of 65535 by 25, to derive a total of 26 steps including zero and max. However, the resulting values were not very usable because, at levels near maximum volume, pushing the volume up or volume down buttons did not result in a noticeable change in listening volume, while at lower settings the volume steps were too large.

Starting with Windows XP Service Pack 2, a new version of this table is inserted in the registry, as shown in Figure 8.7. However, the EnableVolumeTable key is defaulted to 0 (off), so that no change in volume behavior occurs when upgrading to SP2. System manufacturers have the option of enabling the volume table in new systems that they produce. Upcoming versions of Windows Media Center Edition and Windows Vista set the EnableVolumeTable value to true as the default.

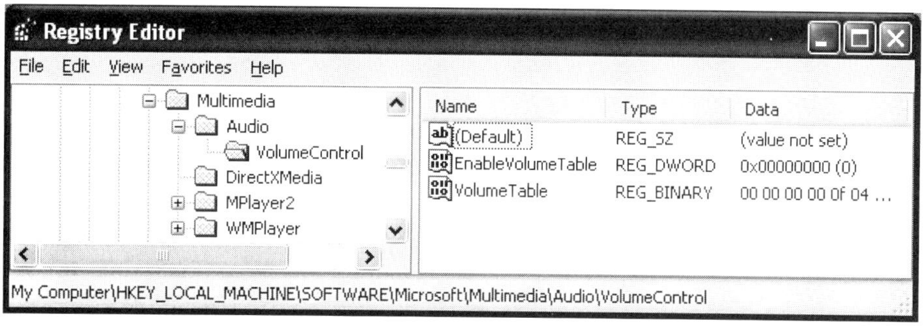

Figure 8.7 Volume Table Registry Entry installed by Windows XP Service Pack 2

Table 8.3 shows the standard Windows XP volume table that is enabled by default on the left side of the table and the new volume table installed by Windows XP Service Pack 2 on the right side of the table. Both tables have the same number of steps, but the newer table has a consistent step size of 1.5 decibels per step, which tracks the behavior of the ear more closely. Notice that SNDVOL32 does *not* reference this table to display its volume. This table is always linear, or not accessible, in all versions of Windows prior to Vista.

Table 8.3 Volume Taper Tables Before and After Windows XP SP2

Before				After			
Hex	**Dec**	**dB**	**Step**	**Hex**	**Dec**	**dB**	**Step**
0xFFFF	65,535	-0.00		0xFFFF	65,535	0.0	
0xF5C1	62,914	-0.35	0.35	0xD765	55,141	-1.5	1.5
0xEB84	60,292	-0.72	0.37	0xB53B	46,395	-3.0	1.5
0xE146	57,671	-1.11	0.39	0x987D	39,037	-4.5	1.5
0xD709	55,049	-1.51	0.40	0x804D	32,845	-6.0	1.5
0xCCCB	52,428	-1.94	0.42	0x6BF4	27,636	-7.5	1.5

Before				After			
Hex	**Dec**	**dB**	**Step**	**Hex**	**Dec**	**dB**	**Step**
0xC28E	49,807	-2.38	0.45	0x5AD5	23,253	-9.0	1.5
0xB851	47,185	-2.85	0.47	0x4C6D	19,565	-10.5	1.5
0xAE13	44,564	-3.35	0.50	0x404E	16,462	-12.0	1.5
0xA3D6	41,942	-3.88	0.53	0x361B	13,851	-13.5	1.5
0X9998	39,321	-4.44	0.56	0x2D86	11,654	-15.0	1.5
0x8F5B	36,700	-5.04	0.60	0x264E	9,806	-16.5	1.5
0x851E	34,078	-5.68	0.64	0x203A	8,250	-18.0	1.5
0x7AE0	31,457	-6.38	0.70	0x1B1E	6,942	-19.5	1.5
0x70A3	28,835	-7.13	0.76	0x16D1	5,841	-21.0	1.5
0x6665	26,214	-7.96	0.83	0x1332	4,914	-22.5	1.5
0x5C28	23,593	-8.87	0.92	0x1027	4,135	-24.0	1.5
0x51EB	20,971	-9.90	1.02	0x0D97	3,479	-25.5	1.5
0x47AD	18,350	-11.06	1.16	0x0B6F	2,927	-27.0	1.5
0x3D70	15,728	-12.40	1.34	0x099F	2,463	-28.5	1.5
0x3332	13,107	-13.98	1.58	0x0818	2,072	-30.0	1.5
0x28F5	10,486	-15.92	1.94	0x06D0	1,744	-31.5	1.5
0x1EB8	7,864	-18.42	2.50	0x05BB	1,467	-33.0	1.5
0x147A	5,243	-21.94	3.52	0x04D2	1,234	-34.5	1.5
0x0A3D	2,621	-27.96	6.02	0x040F	1,039	-36.0	1.5
0x0000	0	Mute		0x0000	0	Mute	

The newer table on the right has a consistent step size of 1.5 dB ranging from -36 dB to unity gain (0 dB). The lowest step on the left table is 6.02 dB, while the smallest step is 0.35 dB, much smaller than most listeners can discern.

These volume tables are used only by WDMAUD.DRV to respond to the `APPCOMMAND_VOLUME_UP` and `APPCOMMAND_VOLUME_DOWN` messages that result from pressing the volume up and volume down keys on a remote control or on a keyboard. An onscreen volume display, such as the one shown in Figure 8.8, can index into these volume tables if they are enabled, to determine how many bars to display on the screen. These volume tables are not used when the listener uses a mouse to move a volume slider in an application using the MIXERLINE interface. Applications should not modify the volume table registry settings.

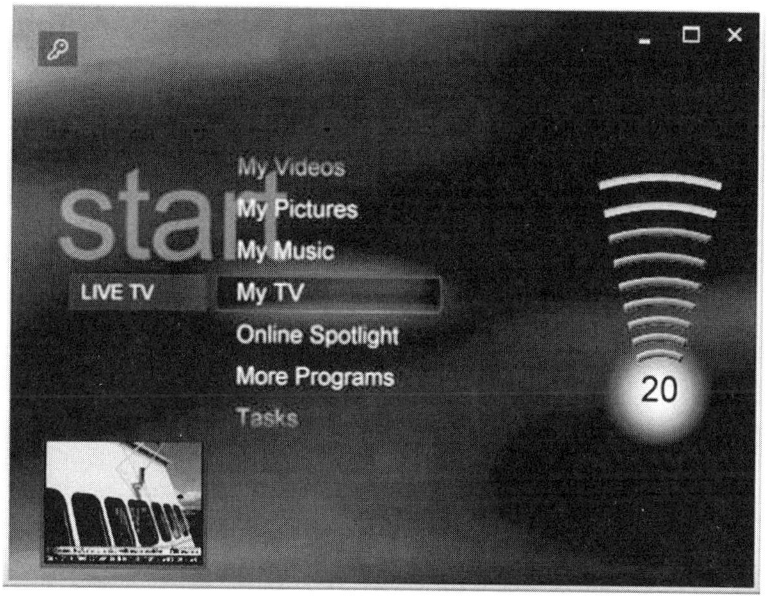

Courtesy of Microsoft Corporation

The display is for a remote control, as it would be shown on a ten-foot user interface used in Media Center.

Figure 8.8 Windows Media Center† On-screen Volume Display

Volume Remapping

Some system manufacturers require the driver developer to support a log curve within the driver, so that the slider behavior in SNDVOL32 follows an audio taper rather than the standard linear taper. Even though it is discouraged by Microsoft, some developers accomplish this tapering by remapping the 32-bit `KSPROPERTY_AUDIO_VOLUMELEVEL` value that is received in the topology miniport property handler, so that the linear movement of the volume slider results in a log taper. The application still treats the interface as linear, but the driver converts it into log. The driver provides no indication to the application that this remapping is occurring, which sometimes causes confusion.

Unfortunately, the alternate volume tables introduced with Media Center Edition and Windows XP SP2 don't coexist well with this custom strategy. Neither do they provide a solution for on-screen sliders which are adjusted by using a mouse. In some cases, it may be possible to disable the new log volume table and go back to the older linear table, letting the driver perform the volume remapping. This work-around is not recommended by Microsoft, however, and it may not always be a suitable solution.

Master Volume: Analog vs. Digital

Though most Intel HD Audio codecs include volume control registers, a surprising number of leading designs do not make use of these hardware volume controls and instead perform the volume control operations in driver software under Windows XP. Instead, the driver software processes the audio stream going to the DACs, scaling the output digitally while the audio signal is still in RAM, before the DMA engine passes it down the Intel HD Audio bus. When floating-point processing is used, this type of volume scaling can achieve higher fidelity than hardware-based controls, which typically have a resolution of 0.5 to 1.5 decibels.

Digital volume control is usually best for any system that does not include any analog pass-through paths. If an analog pass-through path is present—including one is not recommended—then the analog master volume control should be used, so that the master volume affects all audio signals. If the only signals going to the output are coming from the DACs, digital volume control works well. Digital volume control also can control the volume of digital outputs such as S/PDIF or ADAT as long as PCM data is being played. These digital outputs are not affected by analog volume controls.

Signal Processing in Windows XP†

In addition to digital volume control, signal processing in Windows XP can be applied at a number of different processing points throughout the signal path. Processing can take place in the application, in user-mode components, or in kernel-mode components. Chapter 9 contains overall signal flow diagrams showing the signal processing order for these various components.

Signal Processing in DirectShow

The DirectShow user-mode layer in Windows XP is largely beyond the scope of this book. While it contains extensive audio routing and processing capabilities, the DirectShow layer traditionally has been underutilized. Playback-oriented applications being developed for Windows Vista are expected to use the new Windows Media Foundation rather than using DirectShow. Modern PCs running Windows XP typically install any Dolby[†] Digital or DTS audio decoders in the DirectShow layers. DirectShow cannot affect any signals using the Secure Audio Path in Windows XP.

The GraphEdit (GRAPHEDT.EXE) utility included with the Windows DDK provides a graphical user interface into the DirectShow layer. Figure 8.9 shows an example of GraphEdit opening an input device, routing its digital output to a Waves Ultramaximizer signal processing module which is implemented as a DirectShow filter.

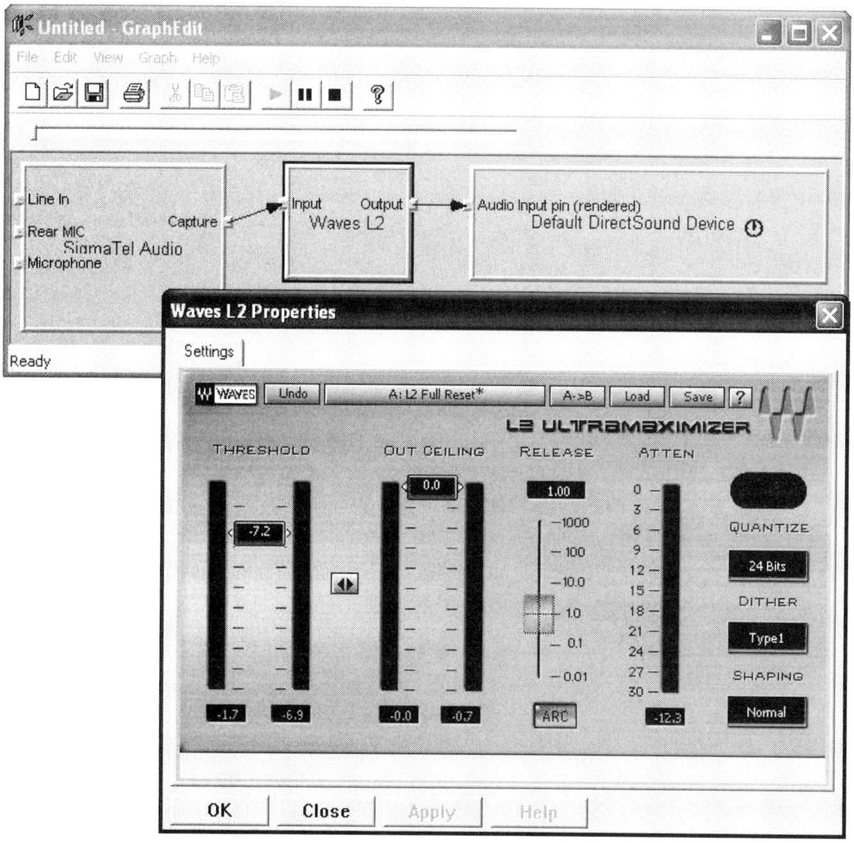

The Waves L2 Ultramaximizer compressor/limiter is inserted between the capture device and the playback device, processing the signal coming from the line input and routing it to the line output.

Figure 8.9 GraphEdit connecting devices in DirectShow

Signal Processing in an Upper Filter Driver

Sometimes signal processing in Windows XP is performed in an upper filter driver, which inserts itself in between PORTCLS.SYS and the audio miniport driver. The upper filter driver intercepts I/O request packets, called IRPs, while those packets are going to and from the audio driver, processes the signal in the audio data buffers being copied, and passes the processed audio data on to the next stage.

Unless included as part of a logoed driver package, an upper filter driver breaks the Secure Audio Path on a system, and the system becomes unable to play protected data intended to be delivered through the Secure Audio Path. An upper filter driver written to work on a WaveCyclic driver model is unlikely to work on a WavePCI driver model, unless specifically designed to work on either. Upper filter drivers do not work with the WaveRT driver model that is being introduced as part of Windows Vista because the audio data will be written directly and not copied into IRPs.

Signal Processing in the Miniport Driver

Since its inception, Windows XP and its Windows NT predecessors have been built on the concept of protected layers which are isolated from each other. As a result, any audio data must be copied as it crosses the boundary between user mode and kernel mode. Also, all informational traffic between OS and driver, such as the frequently called `GetPosition` function, incurs a transition between protection layers which incurs considerable overhead.

WaveCyclic

In the case of a WaveCyclic miniport driver, data from KMixer is copied from user mode to kernel mode as it is made available to the driver. Once inside the driver, a Deferred Procedure Call (DPC) which was scheduled from an ISR is executed, and the audio data is copied again from the input buffers to the proper location in the circular output buffer. If signal processing is applied, well-designed drivers include it during or just before this last copy operation, while poorly designed drivers perform yet another copy operation as part of the signal processing.

These separate copy operations each result in a measurable delay or latency that is added to the audio signal path. Some additional latency is also factored in for absorbing unforeseen delays and accommodating timing tolerances in the software-scheduling mechanism. This latency is in addition to KMixer's 30 to 80 milliseconds of latency.

WavePCI

A WavePCI miniport driver also copies the audio data from user mode to kernel mode, but usually it avoids a second copy operation and resultant latency because the OS prepares a list of memory mappings of various sizes for scatter-gather DMA. The pieces of audio data passed to the driver are scattered throughout physical memory, and a list of descriptors is used to locate each chunk of data as it is ready to be output. WavePCI was not intended as a processing node, but driver developers have created ways to perform processing inside the driver, usually requiring yet another buffer copy, and adding latency.

In general, the WavePCI driver can be configured for lower latency than the WaveCyclic driver, but both introduce latencies as a result of the data copies between user mode and kernel mode. Both WavePCI and WaveCyclic require a kernel-mode transition in order for the application to query the current output position pointer, which happens very often.

In most cases, the audio processing takes place inside a DPC, again to limit the latency. The problem with this approach is that audio processing can take a significant amount of time, and DPCs that execute for long periods of time can cause the OS to appear sluggish, since the DPCs are higher priority than normal threads.

Windows Vista[†]

Windows Audio has simply outgrown itself many times over since the original MME audio support was introduced in 1992. The Microsoft audio team working on Windows Vista was given the opportunity to start afresh, and build up an entirely new audio infrastructure predicated on reliability, fidelity, and resilience to external events. Inside Microsoft, this effort is known as Windows Audio Video Excellence, or WAVE. The new design broke with traditional Windows NT architecture, but in doing so was able to eliminate all buffer copies, kernel transitions, ISRs, and DPCs previously needed to play audio. The audio engine was relocated into user mode and new real-time scheduling services were developed to ensure that audio can be processed in a reliable way from within user mode.

A clever bit of audio software signal routing ensures a compatibility layer for older applications while newer applications can build on the new Windows Media Foundation services. One of the key considerations for the Vista audio team was to be sure that professional audio applications could be deployed on the platform and work reliably through standard system services.

What Won't Change In Vista Audio?

A number of Windows audios basics essentially remain unchanged from previous versions of Windows. For instance, multi-channel audio representations and channel masks using the WAVEFORMATEXTENSIBLE type do not change, the plug and play mechanism for loading an Intel HD Audio driver does not change significantly, nor does the Intel HD Audio bus driver.

WaveRT

To resolve the latency and reliability issues with existing WavePCI and WaveCyclic miniport drivers, Microsoft is introducing the WaveRT real-time driver model for Windows Vista and later operating systems. The WaveRT model shown in Figure 8.10 is a significant departure from previous models, and is specifically exempted from the requirements to copy data between user mode and kernel mode. It also adds a mechanism for the user-mode applications to query the hardware position register directly without incurring a kernel-mode transition.

Audio data flows directly between user mode and the audio hardware, without being "touched" by any kernel mode software components. With no opportunity to acquire and process audio data from within the kernel, all audio processing is relocated to user mode, and the driver performs no data copies and no processing. The new user-mode global audio engine, which replaces KMixer in Windows Vista, uses newly available real-time scheduling threads to mix and process all audio data in small chunks just before it is time for the audio to be played. It writes the data into a shared cyclic buffer just a few milliseconds before the audio DMA hardware is ready to play it.

The latency has two sources, designated in the diagram as A and B. Latency A is controlled by the Windows Vista Global Audio Engine, which tries to keep the write pointer and the read pointer as close to each other as possible while still avoiding data starvation and other audio glitches. This source of latency is between 3 and 10 milliseconds in time.

Systems with more processing power can sustain lower latencies without dropouts.

Latency B is the fixed latency of the controller and codec path. Typically, a codec contains a small FIFO and an FIR filter, which in combination are usually under 50 samples, usually less than a millisecond. The latency of an S/PDIF output jack is likely to be less, because normally no FIR filters are inline with the S/PDIF digital output.

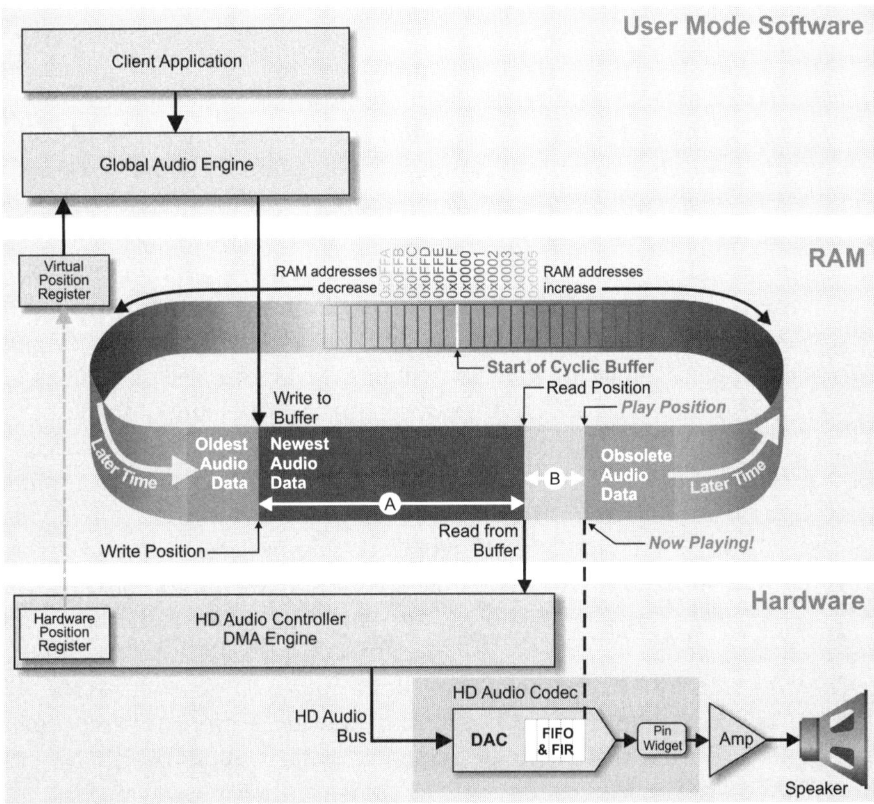

Elapsed time is shown from left to right on the bottom of the loop. The sound currently being heard is at the Play Position. Sound currently being read from the cyclic buffer by the Intel HD Audio DMA controller is shown at the Read Position. Sound currently being written to the cyclic buffer is indicated by the Write Position. Latency is shown in segments A and B, with the total latency being the sum of times A and B, which represents the total amount of time from when the Global Audio Engine writes a sample until the listener actually hears it.

Figure 8.10 WaveRT Latency Diagram

The wave position register is virtualized, allowing it to be exposed to user mode as a memory location which can be read directly. No kernel-mode transition is needed to query the current wave position. This approach makes it possible to eliminate all buffer copies and kernel-mode transitions during the normal playing of audio. The WaveRT audio function driver is responsible for starting and stopping the DMA engine, but it is incapable of touching the audio data for processing or metering. Any data manipulation takes place in the global User Mode Audio engine. The WaveRT driver architecture purposefully does not use DPCs and ISRs .

User Mode Audio (UMA)

The biggest change for audio in Windows Vista is the User Mode Audio stack. The old kernel-based audio stack has been removed from the OS. Kernel-mode audio components such as KMIXER.SYS, SYSAUDIO.SYS, WDMAUD.SYS, SWMIDI.SYS, DMUSIC.SYS, SPLITTER.SYS, AEC.SYS, and REDBOOK.SYS have all been replaced with a new user mode audio engine. Existing interfaces such as WaveOut(), WaveIn(), and DirectSound are connected to the UMA system through the use of "shims." That is, existing applications continue to work and existing audio drivers also continue to work, although they will not qualify for Vista Premium Logo.

A number of different reasons drove this change, not least being that Windows XP was simply not competitive with CE devices from a quality and performance standpoint, largely due to audio glitching when the system is under stress and the relatively high latency of the KMixer and the existing WaveCyclic and WavePCI driver models.

While UMA won't be finalized until Windows Vista is a shipping product, Figure 8.11 shows a preliminary view of the new layers. The global audio engine is designed to complement the WaveRT driver to produce low latency glitch-resilient audio. The new-to-Vista Multimedia Class Scheduler Services (MMCSS) provide a more reliable timer mechanism to prioritize audio and video streams. Check this book's companion Web site for links to new information as it becomes available.

Because the WaveRT driver does not generate any interrupts, the MMCSS timers are used to schedule the global audio engine so that it can stay in sync with the hardware output buffer. When a timer event occurs, the global audio engine reads the controller's position register, subtracts its previous position, and uses the difference to determine how many samples of audio to process. Because the MMCSS timer services are more reliable, the latency between the write position and the read position can be set to a small value without audio dropouts. The global mixer processing occurs more often, but with a correspondingly smaller set of samples being processed during each mixing pass.

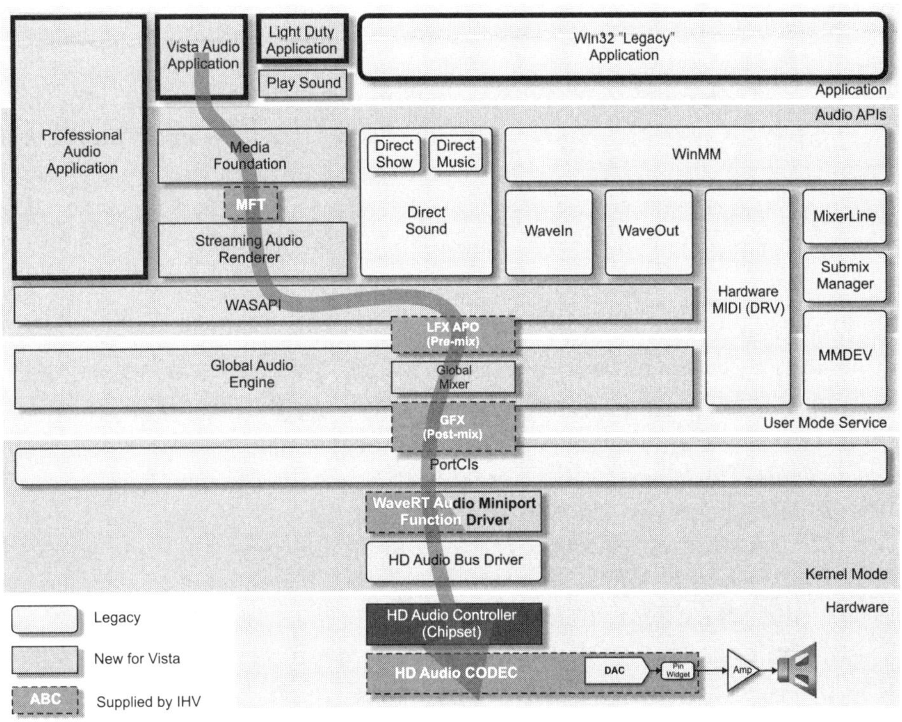

Each open audio application receives a separate instance of the LFX APO and all components above it, but there is only one instance of the GFX APO.

Figure 8.11 Preliminary Block Diagram of Windows Vista User Mode Audio

The Global Audio Engine runs as a user-mode service in its own process. The Windows Audio Session API (WASAPI) layer provides audio playback and capture services which are resilient to CPU and I/O stress. It has the lowest impact and is the lowest level of the public audio APIs to be included in Windows Vista. Pro-audio applications such as Sonar or Nuendo can benefit from the low-level WASAPI interfaces, but most audio-enabled applications should make use of the higher level Media Foundation APIs, which are able to make use of the new Streaming Audio Renderer (SAR). Applications that simply wish to play a system alert sound can use the simpler PlaySound API.

Per-application Volume Control

One of the major changes in Vista is per-application volume control. Each application can have its own volume control, so that it is possible, for instance, to turn down the system alert sounds while turning up the movie that is playing, something that can't be done in Windows XP.

Each on-screen volume control, whether associated with the application or with the audio endpoint, has a built-in volume meter that shows the level of the audio signal arriving at the input of the volume control. The level is always shown, even if the slider is turned down all the way or muted. This makes it very easy for the listener to see what is going on with audio in the system.

The Vista audio team has worked hard to create an "inductive" user interface, which can lead a user to solve a problem in simple digestible chunks. The combination of meter and volume control is a good example of leading the user to the correct conclusion and action. In this case, the listener can see that the application is playing sound, but the volume control is muted, with a clear path to access other volume controls in the system that might be affecting the sound.

The global volume controls at the system level are now associated with audio endpoints, such as headset, 5.1 speakers, or CD in. The plug and play idiom is extended all the way to the audio endpoints, again making it more clear to the user which volume controls affect what is actually being heard. Each audio endpoint is represented as a separate, independent device, with the exception of redirected headphones and redirected line out described in Chapter 4.

Audio Processing in the Global Audio Engine

Because of strict limits on DPC times in the Windows Vista requirements, processing inside the DPC of a WaveCyclic or WavePCI driver is no longer an option. Likewise, an upper filter driver is no longer an option for use with a WaveRT driver. However, Windows Vista has two new categories of audio processing blocks: MFTs and APOs.

In some ways you can think of an Audio Processing Object (APO) as a User-Mode Extension of the audio driver. An APO is installed along with the driver based on the same Plug and Play IDs that are used to load the driver. The APO is considered a part of the driver package, and it must be signed along with the driver. This requirement has the effect of locking any APO to a specific audio device.

An APO may be installed before or after the global mixer. An APO installed after the global mixer is called a global effect or GFX . Only one GFX can be installed per audio endpoint. Once the global mixer has completed the mixing process, it then executes the GFX synchronously to process the new data just before it is written to the circular buffer. A GFX normally has the same input and output data formats, as well as the same number of audio channels for both input and output.

An APO installed prior to the global mixer is called an LFX . Like the per-app volume, each application has a separate instance of the LFX for each open audio stream. Unlike a GFX, an LFX may have a different number of input and output channels, and it may also have different input and output data formats. An LFX is a good choice for a software spreader that expands two channels to 5.1 surround or for a downmix or virtualizer that converts a multi-channel stream to stereo.

The parameters of an APO typically are configured by the user through a global configuration panel. Applications do not have access to APO parameters. APOs are designed to be non-blocking, and they always locate both data and code in non-pageable RAM to prevent delays caused by memory paging.

A Media Foundation Transform (MFT) is a type of audio processing block that should take the place of the older DirectX Media Object (DMO) in the audio infrastructure, and is intended for general A/V extensibility. An MFT is intended for processing that the application is aware of and needs to control directly. An MFT is instantiated and controlled entirely by the application which loads it, and it is not available for system-wide use. While a driver package can install an MFT that can be loaded and used by an application, MFTs are more likely to be installed along with the application or as a set of general purpose processing blocks that can be accessed by any newer application which talks directly to the Media Foundation and Streaming Audio Renderer layers, rather than one of the older audio APIs.

Preparing Audio Subsystems for Windows Vista†

Disclaimer! This book was published before Windows Vista audio implementation and WHQL requirements were finalized. Some of the information contained is almost certainly going to have undergone changes between book publication and Windows Vista launch, but most of these recommendations should continue to apply.

Learn the Requirements

Along with the rewritten audio stack, a number of new audio requirements are contained in the Windows Vista Logo program (WLP) 3.0 document, which at this time of writing is at version 0.61. Be sure to monitor future versions of this document because it will be updated several more times prior to the release of Windows Vista. A link to the WLP documents is available on this book's companion Web site.

Determine Which Designs Will Need to Support Vista

Start right away. Look at all of your designs that currently shipping or at those your customers are currently shipping, as well as those designs that haven't shipped yet. Take a minute to make a list of those that must simply operate under Vista, and those that need to achieve a Logo under Vista.

Although Vista's Global Audio Engine is optimized for use with the WaveRT driver model, it is also designed to work properly with WaveCyclic or WavePCI drivers. Therefore, currently shipping systems that are intended to work properly under Windows Vista and that are not intended to pass the Vista Logo requirements should in theory be able to use the same audio driver packages that ship with Windows XP. You should start testing these systems with Vista Beta 1, and test both clean install and over-install behavior. If these systems do indeed work as they did under Windows XP, then you are done. Someone who purchases the machine can have audio work as well as it does in XP, at least if they are able to locate the audio driver package from Windows XP and install it on the Windows Vista machines.

Prepare and Test Pin Configuration Defaults

If the driver package from XP is not available, the UAA class drivers attempt to load on supported class IDs such as Intel HD Audio class and USB Audio class. If the verb tables in the BIOS that set the pin-configuration registers are not programmed correctly, the Microsoft UAA class driver for Intel HD Audio cannot function properly, and the system does not pass Logo testing. Start testing your systems with the UAA Intel HD Audio class driver version 1.1 for Windows XP when it becomes available. If the class driver configures the system topology successfully under Windows XP, odds are good that it would work properly under Windows Vista.

Determine the Logo level desired

The Standard or Silver level of Windows Vista Logo is roughly the equivalent of the current Windows XP set of requirements, although audio requirements in Vista have increased considerably because of the new audio focus in Windows Vista. The Premium or Gold Logo level is intended to assure customers they're purchasing a quality product that offers the richest, most compelling Windows experience. Microsoft's co-marketing efforts focus primarily on the Premium Logo level. Notice that the names gold, silver, standard, and premium are not final, and could change.

Another program allows a driver to be signed to show that the driver is reliable, stable, and compatible without receiving a Logo. The Driver Quality Signature (DQS) has a lower level of testing requirements. This level provides a driver signature, but does not earn a Logo.

Determine the Class of the System

The Windows Vista Logo program outlines four basic system configurations: Consumer Mobile, Business Mobile, Consumer Desktop, and Business Desktop[1]. In general, Consumer Desktop and Mobile are both expected to provide dedicated 5.1 outputs with very high fidelity, and both require a WaveRT driver model. The business categories could allow the use of a WavePCI or WaveCyclic driver and require only a stereo implementation. Strict limits on maximum DPC and ISR times restrict or eliminate the possibility of signal processing in a WavePCI or WaveCyclic driver.

Install the WDK and DTM

Install the Windows Driver Kit and the Driver Test Manager that are included with the Windows Vista Beta 1 release. These tools take the place of the HCT as well as the DDK and provide a powerful framework to manage testing and qualification of a large number of different machines. See Chapter 11 for more details on how to test with the WDK..

Install Windows Vista Beta2 As Soon As It Is Available

While Beta 1 of Vista contains the new global audio engine, as shown in Figure 8.11, it does not contain any of the new user audio interface bits,

---

[1] Indications are that the audio distinctions between different classes of systems may be minimized

nor does it include a WaveRT driver or documentation on how to use the new audio structures. Beta 2 is the first public release that will contain all of these pieces.

Migrate to WaveRT Driver

Prepare to migrate all classes of systems to the WaveRTdriver model. Even though the Standard Logo level and the business class systems in Premium level may not strictly require a WaveRT driver[2], the WaveRT driver simply makes for a better user experience.

Migrate all signal processing to GFX, LFX, or MFT

A WaveRT driver is not capable of performing any signal processing, and WaveCyclic and WavePCI drivers have strict ISR and DPC time limits that severely restrict the amount of processing that can be performed in the driver. Therefore, any signal processing needs to be migrated to a GFX, LFX, or MFT.

Migrate Driver Installation to the Driver Install Frameworks (DIFx)

Windows Vista does not support unsigned driver packages and only supports driver installation using the approved methods in the Driver Install Frameworks. Driver packages designed to the Vista device installation architecture help to ensure that drivers and associated applications are removed cleanly, without leaving files, state, or registry settings on the system that might cause instability or loss of functionality. Such driver packages also help preserve the stability and functionality of the system over time, as more devices are installed and uninstalled.

Adjust Usability Models and Documentation

Usability models are almost certain to change to adapt to new rules in Windows Vista. For instance, AC97 systems almost always route an identical signal to both S/PDIF and stereo analog output jacks, but this routing is not supported in Windows Vista. The change in usability models should be reflected in updated end-user documentation on the audio subsystem.

---

[2] The requirements for use of WaveRT driver on different classes of systems will be clarified in WLP3 v0.7 and later.

A transparent audio solution with independent audio endpoints would enable future operating system media policies to enhance the Windows audio user experience and make it more predictable.

Prepare for Audio Fidelity Testing as Part of the WHQL Requirements

Microsoft has announced its intention to perform audio fidelity testing as part of the Windows Vista Logo program. This testing is most likely to be integrated with the WDK and DTM. Make sure that your designs are capable of passing the audio fidelity tests. Gold or premium consumer PCs are held to a higher fidelity standard.

Prepare for Many Audio Tests to be Performed at a System Level, Rather Than a Separate Set of Audio Tests

Plan for much of the audio device testing to be performed as part of the overall system test, which changes the test flow as well as the driver delivery schedule. Any audio fidelity tests must be performed as part of system test.

Chapter 9

The Intel® HD Audio System as a Whole

Seeing is better than hearing a hundred times

百聞は一見にしかず

—Ancient Japanese Proverb

Seeing is better than hearing a hundred times

百聞不如一見

—Ancient Chinese Proverb

A picture is worth a thousand words

—Ancient English Proverb

While different cultures may say it in slightly different ways, a picture can convey certain types of information much better than the written word. In this case, the pictures are audio flow charts and block diagrams. While these visual aids are commonplace for most audio equipment, complete audio flow diagrams including motherboard, audio codec, and software routing all combined into a single picture have not been available. This chapter is intended to change that situation.

Any reputable piece of A/V equipment that is designed to go in the living room almost certainly includes these kinds of diagrams as a key part of the system design process. However, these documents rarely, if ever, exist on a PC system design. As part of your system design, you should create complete audio flowcharts of the audio paths for the primary usability models in your system.

Multiple Layers

Unlike most audio equipment, the PC has multiple different layers of signal routing to consider. It must interface to the outside world, establish connections from multiple jacks to one or more audio codecs, route the signals from the audio codecs through the Intel HD Audio controller and a complex software stack to the applications that are consuming or generating audio streams. Each stage along the way could insert gain, attenuation, or some sort of signal processing, and it is important to understand the headroom, noise floor, and resolution of each path, analog or digital, in order to provide reliable high fidelity audio from a PC.

To see the signal flow through all paths in a single glance, it is most convenient to think of them as layers much like the classic Russian dolls where each doll is enclosed inside a larger doll. The PC has multiple layers: the outside world, the motherboard, one or more audio codec layers, and one or more software layers, and finally the end user. Each layer fits totally within the next, with the user being in the center, as he or she should be.

The Real World Layer

The intersection between the real world and the motherboard occurs at the colored audio jacks in the system, or at any built-in microphones and speakers. The end user decides what device to connect to the PC, and how audio content comes to and goes from the PC. This layer is outermost in the system diagram. In Windows† Vista, these connections are referred to as audio endpoints, and the user experience is oriented towards the final source or destination in the real world, rather than being oriented to the jacks or the pins or DACs on the codec.

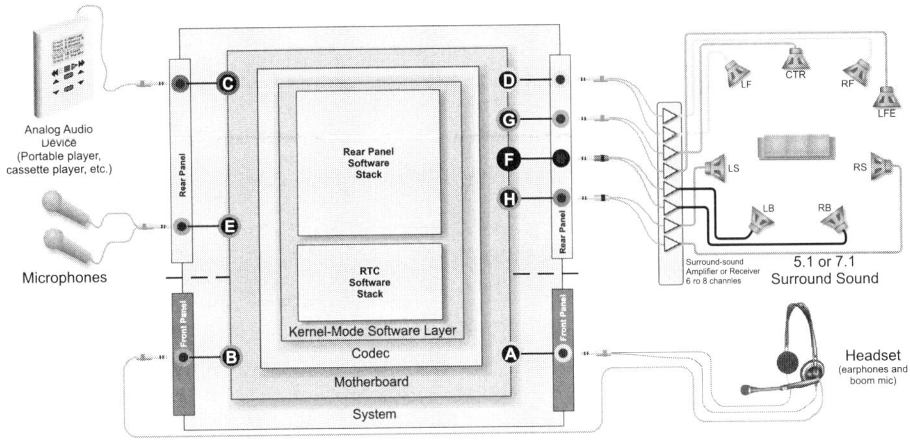

Figure 9.1 The Real World Layer

You should create a separate layer for each real-world usage scenario. For a system which supports 7.1 home theater, you should create a layer which pictures a target speaker system and all the jacks contained on it, with the connections going to the colored jacks on the PC. For a VoIP phone application using a headset, you should create a layer showing a headset plugged into the front panel jacks. If the user might have an expectation that the system must support both simultaneously, you should create a layer which shows both. Signals in this layer are predominantly analog, though digital signals such S/PDIF or ADAT could be present.

The Motherboard or System Layer

The intersection between the motherboard and the real world occurs at the colored audio jacks in the system, or at any built-in microphones and speakers. The intersection between the motherboard and the codec occurs at the codec's ports and pin widgets. You could argue that two layers exist here, since sometimes jacks are mounted on the chassis and not on the motherboard. The wiring between these jacks and the motherboard would constitute a fifth layer. Unless otherwise noted, these examples treat this intersection as a single layer and assume that all jacks are mounted directly on the motherboard.

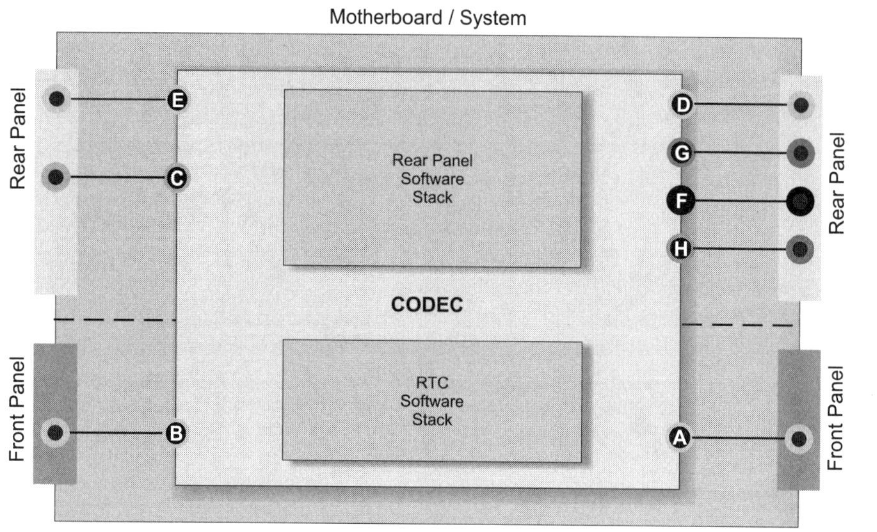

Figure 9.2 The Motherboard Layer

The motherboard design engineer generates the motherboard schematics, which define the routing and connections between the real world and the codec. While these schematics are a formal design document, the audio signal path is often only obvious to an electrical engineer who is trained in analog design and familiar with the chips in the circuit. By themselves, the schematics are not an adequate representation of the audio signal paths in the system, though they provide the underlying basis for this layer.

The motherboard design engineer also must generate a corresponding set of verb tables, which are compiled into the BIOS and used to program the default configuration registers in each pin widget in each codec during system startup. The pin configuration defaults describe the motherboard schematics to the software layer. The Microsoft UAA class driver for Intel HD Audio uses the contents of these configuration registers to determine how to expose audio devices in Windows.

The motherboard layer is fully contained within the real-world layer, and it fully contains one or more codec layers at its center. The audio signal routing on the motherboard is predominantly analog, though digital signals such as S/PDIF, ADAT and I^2S may be present. The layer shown in Figure 9.2 is relatively simple, since each signal from a jack is passed directly to a port on the codec. However, this simple, direct flow is not always the case; this layer can have considerable complexity associated with it.

This layer is likely to have the least audio fidelity of any of these layers, primarily because the inside of a computer contains many unintended EMI sources which can compromise the signal quality. Follow the layout techniques detailed in Chapters 5 and 6 to maximize the fidelity of this layer.

The Intel HD Audio Codec Layer

The intersection between codec and the motherboard occurs at the physical pins of the codec, which are soldered to the motherboard, and at the pin widgets in the codec. The intersection between the codec and the software layer occurs where the converter elements, such as DACs and ADCs, are connected to the Intel HD Audio bus.

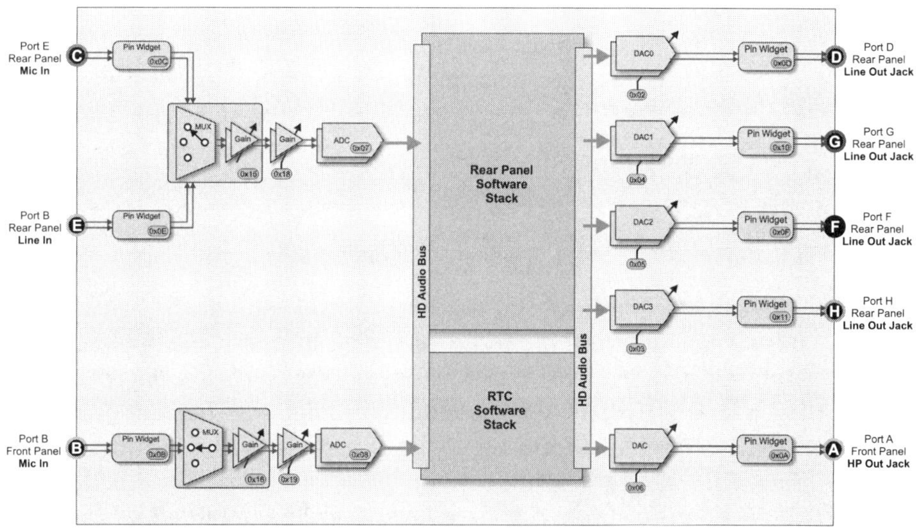

Figure 9.3 The Intel HD Audio Codec Layer

The signal flow between pin widgets and converters is determined by the audio function driver. The Microsoft UAA class driver for Intel HD Audio includes a codec topology parser module that uses the data contained in the pin widget configuration default registers to determine which internal signal paths should be used in the codec.

If a system is configured for independent multi-streaming and you wish to show both streams in the overall system signal flow, you would need to create separate layers, one on top of the other, with each one containing a software layer inside of it.

One or more codec layers are fully contained within the motherboard layer. Each codec layer contains a software layer at its center. The audio signal routing in a codec is primarily analog at Ports A through G, but digital signal such as S/PDIF, ADAT, I^2S, and PWM may also be supported.

The fidelity of the audio codec is largely a function of its design and implementation. Assuming clean, stable power supplies, the fidelity of the analog signals inside the codec normally is higher than the fidelity in the motherboard layer.

The Intel® HD Audio Bus, Controller, and Bus Driver

From a signal-flow perspective, the Intel HD Audio bus, as well its controller and bus driver, are transparent to the audio stream. No audio processing occurs while on the bus. In signal flow terms, you can think of the Intel HD Audio signal path as a straight wire with no loss. In terms of the flow chart layers, you can think of the Intel HD Audio bus as the boundary between the hardware and software layers. The signals on the Intel HD Audio bus are digital; no analog audio passes through this bus.

The Kernel-Mode Software Layer in Windows XP†

The intersection between the kernel-mode software layer and the codec occurs at the Intel HD Audio bus. The intersection between the kernel-mode software layer and the user-mode software layer occurs at the boundary between user-mode and kernel-mode. Buffers of audio data are copied across this boundary, with the possibility of processing the audio data while they are being copied.

The kernel-mode software layer is fully contained within each codec layer. Each kernel-mode software layer contains a user-mode software layer in its center. All of the audio signals in the software layer are digital. The fidelity of the signals in the software layers is a function of the bit depth and sample rate of the signal. Another potential source of fidelity degradation in the software layers is improperly implemented DSP blocks.

Figure 8.4 shows the signal flow for 7.1 surround sound playback using Windows Media Player (WMP) under Windows XP. You can see that the 8-channel signal passes through EQ and SRS processing which are extra processing modules built into WMP. The signal is then passed into the DirectSound interface which provides the transition to user mode. DirectSound is also capable of processing the signal, though it usually does no processing on streams coming from Windows Media Player. The signal passes through both the System Audio Device and the PortCls driver, but neither of these blocks performs any processing on the signal; they are the equivalent of a straight wire.

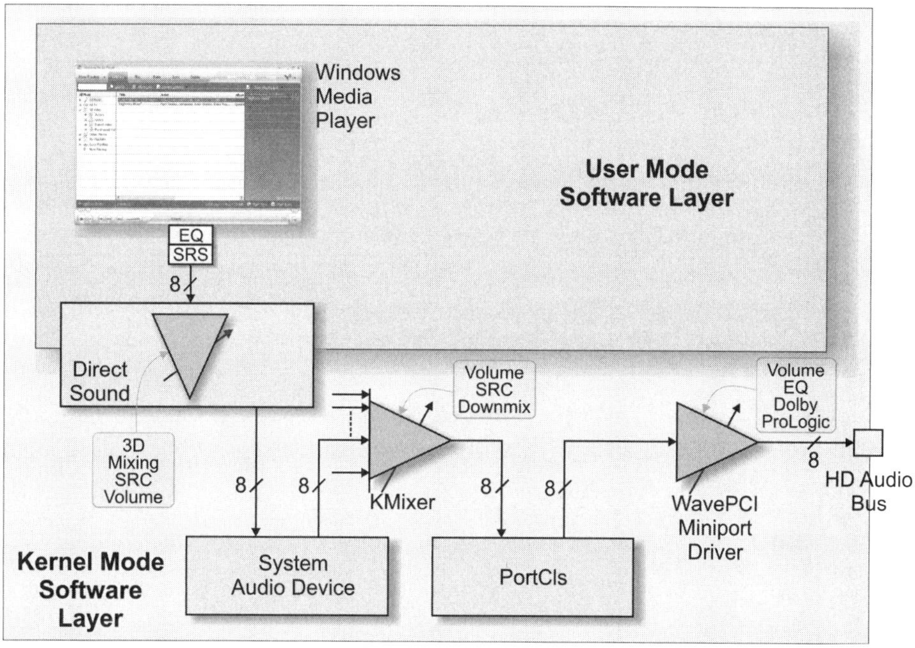

Figure 9.4 Windows XP playback of 7.1 Surround

KMixer performs processing on the signal. The volume scaling of the front two channels is controlled by the Wave slider. KMixer also performs processing to convert any given input stream into a format which can be mixed into the KMixer's output format. KMixer may also perform a downmix when the number of input channels exceeds the number of channels supported by the driver.

The final stage of processing in the kernel output may optionally take place in the driver. While the Microsoft UAA class driver for Intel HD Audio performs no processing, most drivers supplied by codec vendors for

Windows XP contain an option for various types of signal processing, such as those described in the last half of Chapter 3.

Figure 8.5 shows a similar diagram using Net Meeting for speech communications. A mono microphone signal is used as a speech input. The processing node in the miniport driver performs a noise reduction processing step, and then passes the signal through PortCls to the splitter module. This flow is the opposite of KMixer: where KMixer takes multiple input streams and combines them into a single output stream, the splitter takes a single input stream and provides it to multiple applications. If you were to open a wave recording application, this application could also receive the same signal from the splitter output. Functionally, the splitter is equivalent to a distribution amp used in a professional audio system. KMixer also provides different sample rates and formats to each calling application in much the same way that it does for output signals.

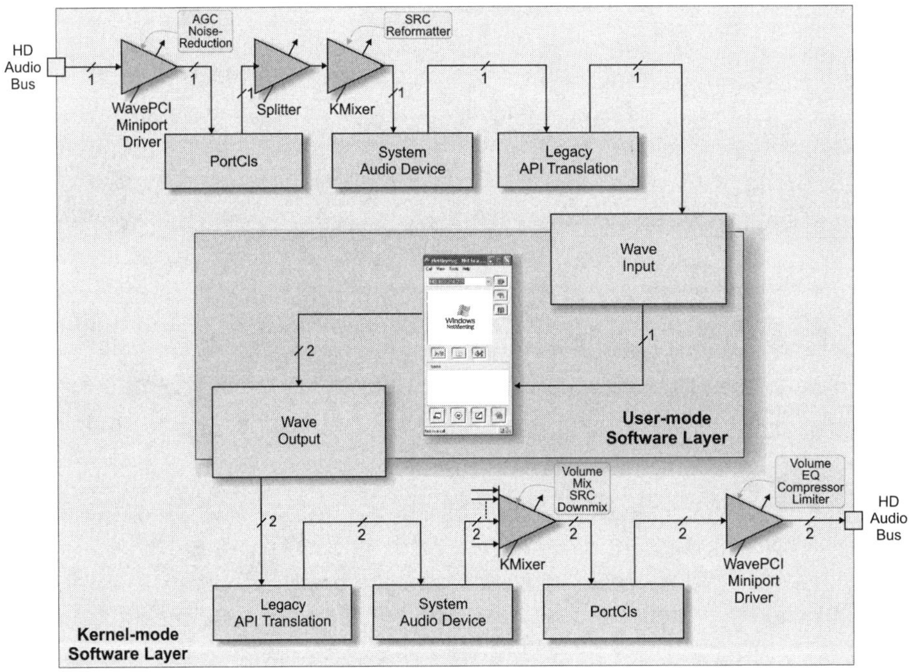

Figure 9.5 The Windows XP Kernel Software Layer for RTC

The System Audio Device, the Legacy API translation layer, and the WaveIn() port do not affect the audio signals passing through, they act like a straight wire in terms of signal flow.

The output circuit is much like the 7.1 output circuit, though in this case the application is using the WaveOut() API rather than DirectSound. Unlike DirectSound, WaveOut() does not perform any processing on the audio signals passing through it.

An additional level of detail is not shown in this chart. Each of the signal processing nodes can perform one or more types of processing, and the order of this processing could vary based on which order the processing is applied. Placing a compressor/limiter before an EQ provides a very different result from placing the EQ before the compressor/limiter. Each of the signal processing nodes shown in these diagrams could be expanded further to show the processing that occurs internally. Figures 8.4 through 8.7 show lists of typical DSP functions performed in each processing node, but they don't contain the additional internal details of the DSP routing.

For Windows XP, the sample rate and bit depth of the signal paths between the application and KMixer are determined by the application. The bit depth of the signal paths between KMixer and the audio codec is determined during driver initialization. The sample rate of the signal paths between KMixer and the audio codec is usually determined by the highest sample rate being played.

The User-Mode Software Layer in Windows XP[†]

The intersection between the kernel-mode software layer and the user-mode software layer occurs at the boundary between user-mode and kernel-mode. The intersection between the user-mode software layer and the user is through the graphical user interface (GUI) for each application that is running. This layer is normally the innermost layer on the audio flow chart.

The user mode software layer is shown in the center of Figures 8.4 and 8.5. Each application that is running should be shown in its own layer, with the outputs being mixed together at KMixer.

Any user-mode signal-processing objects such as DirectShow filters or Media Foundation Transforms normally execute within the process of the application that is calling into them, so they are considered to be part of the application.

The User Mode Audio Engine Layer in Windows Vista

The new WaveRT driver architecture allows direct communication between the audio hardware and the user-mode global audio engine, so the signal no longer flows through the kernel-mode layer. Conceptually, the global audio engine is treated as if it is a user-mode driver. For systems qualifying for the Windows Vista Logo program that use a WaveCyclic or WavePCI driver, the DPC and ISR time limits are so low as to prohibit any significant amount of signal processing in the kernel, so even if these types of drivers are used there is no opportunity to perform processing in the kernel.

Output signal processing occurs in the Media Foundation Transform (MFT), Local Effects (LFX), Global Mixer, and Global Effects (GFX) , in that order. Input signals use the reverse order, though the GFX is only available for output, not for input. A splitter functionality is included in place of the mixer.

Figure 8.6 shows the same usage scenario that is shown in Figure 8.4, but adjusted for the Windows Vista architecture. Windows Media Player performs its EQ and SRS processing in the MFT. The signal then passes through the Streaming Audio Renderer and WASAPI layers without any processing, before it is fed into the LFX, the Global Mixer, and the GFX, in that order.

The global mixer and the GFX each have a single instance for each audio endpoint which is exposed, while the MFT and the LFX have an instance for each application. The LFX is a good place for virtualizers, spreaders, and downmixers, since the number of input channels can be different from the number of output channels. The global mixer performs volume and mixing functions, but unlike KMixer does not perform any SRC. The GFX performs processing on the output stream in much the same manner that the miniport driver does in the Windows XP model.

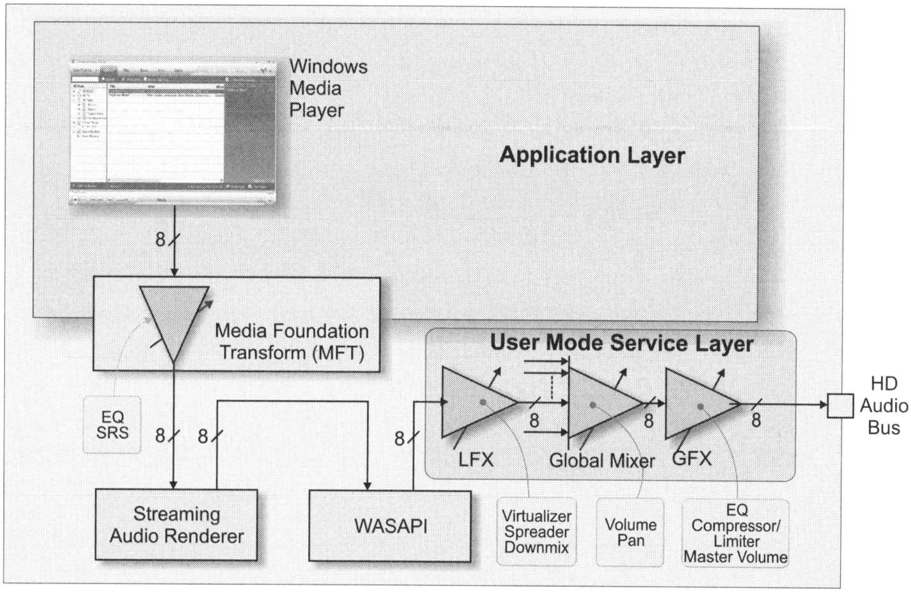

Figure 9.6 Windows Vista Software Layer during 7.1 Playback

The Application Layer in Windows Vista†

Normally the innermost layer in the flow chart, the application layer for Windows Vista consists of the application alone, since all elements from the MFT to the hardware are under control of the global audio engine. Each application that is running should be shown in its own layer, with the outputs being mixed together at KMixer.

Putting It All Together

Figure 8.7 shows all of the Windows XP layers put together in one. While the scale is very small, you can see the entire signal flow. Larger versions of this diagram are available on this book's companion Web site.

When conceptualizing the system audio flow, always try to think in terms of this complete diagram. Create a separate overall flowchart for each usage scenario, and check that the signal is not compromised at any point along the signal path.

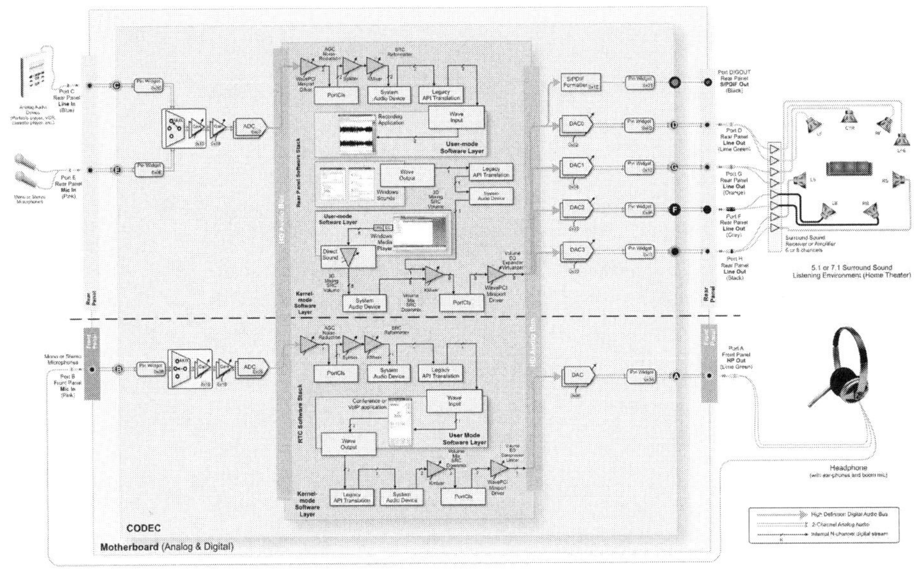

Figure 9.7 Complete System Diagram Showing All Layers Running Windows XP†

Figure 9.7 shows a shared ADC mux input on the rear panel being used to route a stereo line input through a stereo ADC to a recording application. At the same time, Windows Media Player is playing a 7.1 file (a total of 8 channels) at 96 kilohertz and 24 bits out of the green, orange, black, and grey jacks while the Sounds control panel is playing a 22-kilohertz, mono, 16-bit sound. This stream is mixed into KMixer and is played in the front two channels of the 7.1 speakers. Unfortunately, no separate volume control is available in Windows XP for the system sounds, so they may sound at a high volume unless they were recorded at lower-than-normal levels.

Ports A and B are connected to a headset which is running a separate Real-time communications stream using the Net Meeting application. Software processing of the speech signals takes place primarily in the miniport driver and in KMixer.

This usage is just one of the many that are possible for this physical configuration. You should create a similar diagram for each possible usage scenario for your system.

Chapter 10

Security and Content Protection

The Titanic will protect itself.

— Robert D. Ballard

Content protection (CP) refers to the general field of managing the distribution and use of intellectual works. These works include dramatic, artistic, and literary variations. In the PC world, content protection typically deals with managing audio and video content, such as pre-recorded movies and music. Content that needs protection usually has value and a clear owner.

Content protection is also known as *copy protection* or *digital rights management* (DRM).[1] Whether or not the three terms apply to slightly different aspects of technologies that are designed to manage the distribution of premium content is a fine-grained distinction. For our purposes, the term content protection serves as a catch-all descriptor.

Content protection is a very controversial field. Certainly, public awareness of the topic has increased since the Internet brought us the ability to rapidly and easily exchange digital copies of media. The last decade has seen a large increase in legal actions related to content protection. But, such content protection concerns predate the rise of the Internet. In 1983, for instance, Universal City Studios sued Sony[†] because

[1] Those forms of content protection that are associated primarily or exclusively with textual works, such as electronic books, are not included in this book.

the studio felt that Sony's Betamax VCR was a copyright infringement device.

The controversy stems from the fact that content providers typically desire a more restrictive usage of media than consumers want. For instance, many users feel they should be able to download all movies and music for free over the Internet. However, the owners of the content want to be compensated for their efforts, much in the same manner that if you put in a full week's worth of work at the office, you'd want to be paid for it. Content protection schemes are designed to enforce the content creators' desired usage models.

Originally, content protection was not a big deal, as the general public had no easy way to reproduce content. If you wanted to make a copy of a book, you'd need to wait for a group of monks to hand-copy it for you. And even then, chances are you were illiterate. Similarly, duplication of famous paintings required a great deal of time and skill. With the advent of technologies such as the printing press, the photocopier, digital imagery, and—more recently—the Internet, it has become much easier to duplicate and distribute content.

An ideal content protection scheme allows consumers to have a wide variety of usage models, yet producers still can prevent unauthorized uses of content. Consumers expect to be able to watch a movie on their DVD-Video player. However, most consumers don't expect to be able to make tens of thousands of copies and sell them for a profit on e-bay. Content providers are generally happy to support the first use case, but not the second. Much of the controversy is in the in-between cases. For instance, can consumers rip a DVD-Video that they own for viewing in a different venue, such as a Linux-based PC or a portable video player? That decision must be made in the arena of lawyers and courts and licenses. In short, an ideal CP system keeps honest people honest. It allows users to consume the content in acceptable ways, yet protects the intellectual property of the content provider.

What about those who feel that, because content protection schemes restrict usage, content would be much more widely available without content protection schemes? In fact, in the absence of CP, a great deal of premium content would not be available to consumers at all. For instance, Hollywood movie studios have been reluctant to release digital versions of their films unless they have some sort of mechanism in place to protect them.

Important Disclaimer

The field of content protection is much more subjective and nuanced than other technical disciplines, such as the straightforward playback of unprotected audio and video. Often, you have non-trivial monetary, legal, and political implications that are tied into the design and implementation of content protection. To that end, please bear in mind that this chapter is intended to serve as a rough primer to the field of content protection. Merely reading it does not make one an expert in content protection or its related fields. When working on projects involving content protection, it is a good idea to work with people experienced in the relevant technical and legal domains.

Content Protection Basics

Not all content needs to be protected. For instance, if you create a home video and want to share it with everyone in the world for free, you probably wouldn't want to use content protection. However, if you created a cool new music video and wanted to sell it to everyone in the world for $5, you might want to use some content protection scheme to make it harder for one person to buy the video and then send it for free to everyone else in the world.

So, what determines what the necessary protections for a particular type of content? In a word: licenses. For example, in order to make a DVD-Video player, the player manufacturer first needs to sign a license. The license grants to manufacturer the right to make the player, contingent upon them meeting certain requirements. If the DVD-Video player manufacturer fails to meet the requirements, they may be prohibited from shipping the product and/or have to pay financial penalties.

The requirements for content protection typically flow downward from a root license. For instance, the DVD-Video license describes how Macrovision must be used to protect certain types of DVD-Video content. Macrovision has its own set of licenses and requirements that describe how it must be implemented. The Macrovision[†] requirements do not describe how the manufacturer must meet DVD-Video requirements. In fact, Macrovision may be used for purposes other than DVD-Video. When working with content protection, it is important to understand such chains of licenses that are involved.

Compliance and Robustness

The licenses for content protection often include sets of rules for compliance and robustness. Compliance refers to a set of rules to which the system must adhere. For instance, a compliance rule may be "when playing premium content over an S/PDIF output, SCMS must be active." Robustness refers to how difficult it is make the system non-compliant. In this example, how difficult is it to play premium content over S/PDIF without SCMS being activated? If the only way to do it is to remove a blob of hardened epoxy encasing a particular chip, de-solder that chip, chemically etch away the outer layers, then use a multi-million dollar ion mill to generate a Focused Ion Beam (FIB) to cut some of the microscopic traces, carve new channels, and deposit new traces, then re-solder the whole thing back into the system—well, that system is fairly robust. However, if all you have to do to make the system non-compliant is hit buttons on the remote control, then that system is much less robust.

As a rule of thumb, compliance rules are testable. Robustness rules are not. Compliance rules say "in this specific situation, do this specific action." Robustness rules say "make sure the protection system cannot be com-promised easily." So, what exactly does "easily" mean? It depends. Even the most verbose of robustness rules are open to interpretation.

These robustness rules can make implementing content protection mechanism so frustrating from an engineering perspective. You have no effective way to measure unequivocally the robustness of a particular system. Furthermore, many of the content protection licensing bodies do not explicitly certify systems as being sufficiently robust! Typically, implementers are expected to decide whether or not the system they have built is sufficient. An insufficiently robust system typically is identified only after the product has been deployed and it becomes obvious that people are using that product to compromise content. At that point, the manufacturer could be immediately prohibited from shipping any more of the product until they have fixed the problem. Obviously, such injunctions can have a major impact to a company's profitability. In another scenario, the manufacturer might need to revoke systems already sitting in people's homes, even though the majority of the customers are not misusing the product. Such a situation would be a public relations nightmare for a company.

Open versus Closed Systems

Content protection licenses often distinguish between closed and open systems. *Closed systems* refer to products which are difficult to modify. For instance, a typical set-top DVD player is not designed to be opened by a consumer. It contains hard-wired electronic components, often interconnected with proprietary interfaces. Any software in the system is likely to be low-level firmware that works only on that particular product.

By comparison, an *open system* is one that can be readily altered by users. Most PCs are open systems. They run well-documented and well-understood operating systems. The behavior of the PC can easily altered by installing new software or hardware.

As a rule of thumb, closed systems are vulnerable to fewer attacks than open systems. Compromising a closed system typically requires a greater degree of skill than getting access to an open system. On the closed system, an attack could be mounted by soldering new components onto the system. Such a class of attack requires the attacker to have soldering skills and access to the necessary circumvention hardware. Conversely, an open system can sometimes be compromised by somebody downloading a piece of software off the Internet. This software-based attack can be mounted by anyone with basic computer skills.

You can see why content protection requirements are often different for closed and open systems. Please keep in mind that the concepts of security, threat modeling, and attack mitigation are very complex. But, knowing the basics can help you to understand the issue of content protection.

User Accessible Buses

One common theme in open systems is the concept of a *user accessible bus*—sometimes referred to as an *open bus*. This subject is very sensitive and must be approached with some delicacy. Like most CP terminology, the exact definition of a user accessible bus varies from one license to another. One definition of a user accessible bus is a data bus that is intended for end-user upgrades or accessibility.

Whether or not a particular bus becomes classified as user-accessible can often have major political and financial implications. Such classification must be left in the hands of experienced folks well-versed in the subtle nuances of content protection.

For certain buses, a particular content protection scheme determines whether or not they are explicitly defined to be user-accessible. For instance, the CSS procedural specification calls PCI a user-accessible bus but puts memory and CPU buses in the not user-accessible category.

Content protection schemes make the distinction between user and non-user accessible buses because of protection needs. A user-accessible bus typically requires increased protection, such as encryption, on data flowing across it. Using the CSS classifications as an example, it is much easier for someone to build a PCI-based mechanism designed to steal content than it is to build a mechanism designed to steal content as it flows across the memory bus. A large ecosystem is dedicated to the development of PCI devices: training books, de-bugging devices, and existing components. Memory buses are much more specialized. Furthermore, PCI is a multi-point bus explicitly designed to allow multiple devices to be added to it, whereas memory buses are point-to-point interconnects between memory and the memory controller. Most of the time, it is challenging enough just to get the memory bus working under normal conditions. Trying to tap that data flow is extremely difficult. Therefore, it makes sense to be more concerned about PCI-based attacks than memory bus-based attacks.

Types of Content

Content protection schemes often have different rules for the way that different forms of content needs to be protected. For instance, it is common for encrypted content to require few protections. The fact that it is encrypted is its protection. If the encryption scheme and associated key infrastructure were properly defined, you risk no harm in handing the encrypted content to anybody who wants it. As such, unencrypted content is generally deemed more valuable than encrypted content. After all, unencrypted content is typically what attackers are trying to get their hands on.

Content can also be compressed or uncompressed. Compressed content is sometimes deemed somewhat more valuable—and in need of more protection—than uncompressed, since compressed content is easier to capture and does not require recompression before distribution.

Some content protection schemes allow for degraded versions of the con-tent to be displayed with fewer protections than the full resolution version of the content. For instance, transfer of a 192-kilohertz audio stream might be permitted only over a protected output, but a down-sampled, or *constrained*, version of the audio stream might be permitted go over unprotected outputs.

Cryptography Basics

Cryptography plays an important role in most content protection schemes as it can be used to protect sensitive data using encryption. Cryptography can also be used to authenticate different components in a system and verify that they are authorized to receive premium content.

We provide a brief introduction to cryptography to give you a general feel for the concepts, not any detailed understanding of cryptography. Please keep in mind the words of noted cryptographers Niels Ferguson and Bruce Schneier, who wrote in their book *Practical Cryptography* that "Cryptography is fiendishly difficult. Even seasoned experts design systems that are broken a few year later.... Even though cryptography itself is difficult, it is still one of the easy parts of a security system."

Secret Key Encryption

In *secret key encryption*, both the sender and receiver use the same key to encrypt and decrypt data. For this reason, secret key cryptography is sometimes called *symmetric encryption*. The tricky bit is how to get the sender and receiver to agree on what the secret key they are going to use. They cannot simply send the secret key in the clear to each other because an attacker could intercept the key and then be able to decrypt all the messages without the sender or receiver knowing it.

One of the most commonly used private key encryption algorithms today is the Advanced Encryption Standard (AES). AES was standardized by the National Institute of Standards and Technology in 2002, replacing the older Data Encryption Standard (DES). AES supports key sizes of 128, 192, and 256-bits. By comparison, DES supported 56-bit keys. As a rule of thumb, the longer the key length, the harder it is to crack a cryptographic method.

Secret key encryption is typically used for three types of applications: block ciphers, stream ciphers, and message authentication codes.

Block ciphers are algorithms which take a block of data with a fixed size and create an encrypted block of data with the same size. AES is a block cipher. Block ciphers can be extended to create block cipher modes which are capable of encryption data of arbitrary sizes.

Block ciphers use the data to be an encrypted as an input to the cipher. By contrast, *stream ciphers* generate a pseudo-random sequence of numbers that are independent of the data to be encrypted. The pseudo-random numbers are then XORed with the message to create the cipher text. Stream ciphers are commonly used for high performance applications, like HDCP.

A *message authentication code* (MAC) is used by a recipient to verify that a particular message has not been altered in transmission. Altering messages is a security concern because a rogue agent could potentially change a message from something like "activate protection mechanism" to "deactivate protection mechanism." A MAC is calculated by using a secret key cipher. To provide message authentication, the MAC is sent along with the encrypted message. The recipient can use the shared secret key to compute the MAC on the decrypted message to verify that it is unaltered. Even if an attacker knows the MAC algorithm being used, he will not be able to create a valid MAC message to match a spoofed message without knowing the secret key.

Public Key Encryption

Public key encryption, also known as asymmetric encryption, is distinguished by the fact that different keys are used for encryption and decryption. This asymmetry can be leveraged to create some very useful solutions, as Whitfield Diffie and Martin Hellman noted in their 1976 paper that introduced the concept. Since the encryption key cannot be used to decrypt a message, you have no reason to keep the encryption key a secret. For that reason, the encryption key can be made widely known, and as such is known as a *public key*. However, the decryption key requires secrecy and is consequently known as a *private key*. Together, a public and a private key form a matched pair.

Public key encryption means that a person can publish their public key and anybody can encrypt a message using that key, but only the intended recipient can decrypt the message using his private key. Thus, the key distribution problem of symmetric ciphers is greatly alleviated. The sender and recipient need not agree on a secret key; only the person receiving the content needs to know the secret.

Considering only this first usage model, public key encryption may seem much better than secret key encryption. So, why not use public key encryption for everything? Alas, public key encryption requires significantly more computational power than secret key encryption. It also requires substantially larger keys in order to achieve the same level of protection as a secret key algorithm. In short, public key implementations are slower and more costly than secret key implementations.

As such, many security systems use public key cryptography as a mechanism to securely exchange a key, and then use secret key algorithms based on the exchanged key for bulk encryption.

In addition to encryption, public key cryptography can be used to provide a form of authentication. By using a message and a person's private key as an input to a special type of algorithm, a *digital signature* can be generated. Anybody can then send the message and the person's public key to a verification algorithm that confirms that the message was generated by the private key owner. In other words, a digital signature is the public key counterpart of a MAC.

One problem with public key cryptography is how to make sure the public-private key pair is truly associated with a particular person or entity. For example, a digital signature can mathematically confirm that a message was signed by private key X. However, the signature cannot confirm that private key X is owned by, say, John Smith.

A *certificate* is a signed message which asserts that a particular public key belongs to a specific person or entity. The certificate includes a copy of the public key in question; the signature of the certificate ensures that the public key will not be altered by an adversary. Certificates are issued by *certificate authorities*, who have their own public keys, which they use to digitally sign the certificates. VeriSign is an example of a certificate authority.

You may already have spotted the recursive nature of a certificate. To wit: a certificate uses a digital signature to assert that somebody owns a public key. So how do we know the public key used to generate the certificate's digital signature was valid? One answer is a have another certificate which verifies the public key of the first certificate's digital signature belongs to the correct certificate authority. This technique is actually valid, and it can be implemented with several levels of nest certification. Such a nested scheme is known as a *chain of trust*.

The topmost authority in a chain of trust is known as the *root of trust*. No cryptographic scheme can authenticate the credentials of the root of trust. Basically, you just have to trust them—or not. Most people, for instance, seem willing to make credit card transitions over the internet in sessions protected by the Secure Sockets Layer (SSL) protocol. SSL has VeriSign as a root of trust. Similarly, many computer equipment manufactures are willing to use Microsoft as a root of trust for WHQL certificates in their drivers. Presumably fewer people would be willing to trust Smilin' Bob's Shady Enterprises as a root of trust.

Contemporary Systems

Now that we have reviewed the basics of content protection and cryptography, let's discuss several of the current and upcoming content protection systems. It is important to understand these systems, as they dictate how contemporary premium content needs to be protected. More specifically, they impose engineering requirements that must be met in order to play premium audio.

SCMS

Serial Copy Management System (SCMS) is a mechanism for specifying the copy attributes of audio content. The protection attributes are specified by a single copy bit. When the copy bit is zero on every audio frame, the content is unprotected and may be copied freely. This state is sometimes referred to as "copy always."

When the copy bit is set to a `1` on every audio frame, the content is protected and the content is coming from the original source, such as an optical disk. Content in this state can be copied once, so this state is sometimes known as "copy once."

When the copy bit toggles between one and zero every five audio frames, it means that the content is protected and has already been copied. It can no longer be copied, and so this state is known as "copy never." There is an alternate implementation of SCMS "copy never" that is used for interfacing PCs to Minidisc players in Japan that is described in Chapter 3.

SCMS does not provide any cryptographic protection of the content. The copy protection status is merely carried as sideband information. A device that is not SCMS-compliant can simply ignore the bits and arbitrarily copy the content. SCMS is most commonly used on S/PDIF connections.

HDCP

High Bandwidth Digital Content Protection (HDCP) was developed by Intel® Corporation to protect data flowing across digital display interfaces. HDCP is managed by the Digital Content Protection LLC, and it has been approved for use on DVI and HDMI links. HDCP was originally defined to protect video data only, but was updated in the 1.1 revision to support audio protection in the context of HDMI.

HDCP-protected interfaces began appearing on DTVs in the United States in 2002. During that same time period, they began appearing on

CE DVD players. HDCP is expected to remain the primary protection protocol for digital uncompressed video links for the foreseeable future.

HDCP defines three types of devices: transmitters, repeaters, and receivers (Figure 10.1). As you'd expect, transmitters send HDCP-encrypted data, whereas receivers take in HDCP-encrypted data. Repeaters are receivers that include one or more transmitters. Up to 127 different devices can be attached to each other, with the restriction that the total depth from the root transmitter to the receivers does not exceed seven.

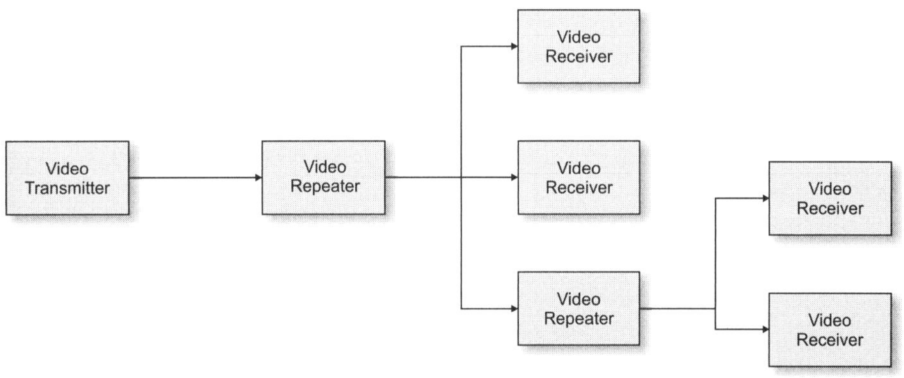

Figure 10.1 HDCP Transmitters, Repeaters, and Receivers

The HDCP framework has three key components: authentication, encryption, and renewability.

Authentication

Authentication is an exchange between the video transmitter and the video receiver that allows the transmitter to confirm that the receiver is authorized to receive the protected video. The mechanism relies on secret keys.

Each HDCP device, both transmitters and receivers, is assigned a unique set of forty 56-bit secret keys from the HDCP licensing body, the Digital Con-tent Protection LLC. The keys stored in transmitters are referred to as Akeys; receiver keys are known as Bkeys, as indicated in Figure 10.2. Each device is also assigned a unique 40-bit Key Selection Vector (KSV). The KSV is not a secret and it may be made publicly available.

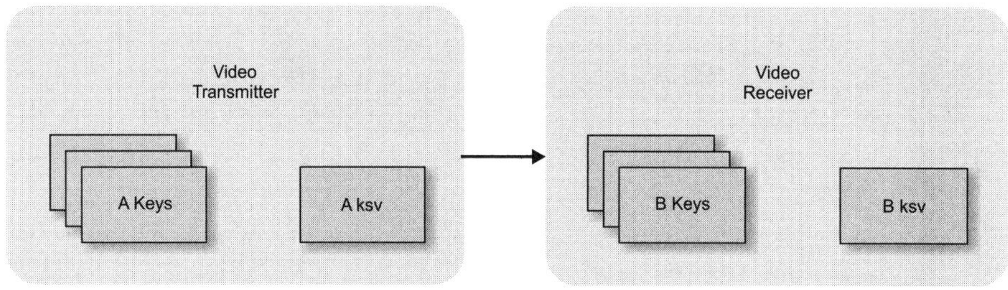

Figure 10.2 A keys and B keys

HDCP actually includes three types of authentication, known as the first part, second part, and, yes, the third part.

In the first part of authentication, two devices can use their KSVs and a 64-bit pseudo-random number to verify that they are both indeed licensed HDCP devices. They can create a shared secret, which allows them to communicate securely without another device being able to eavesdrop on them. The transmitter and receiver use this secure path to communicate the session keys used to encrypt the video data.

In the second part of the authentication, a protocol allows transmitters to gather a list of all the KSVs attached to it. This list has integrity; the transmitter can determine whether someone has tampered with it.

The third part of the authentication protocol transmitter is used to generate a new encryption key for every video frame. It also allows the transmitter to ensure that the receiver is still synchronized with the transmitter.

Encryption

Some content protection methods, such as CSS, keep the encryption algorithm a secret. The HDCP encryption algorithm, however, is public. Synchronized pseudo-random generators in the transmitter and receiver create 24-bit values for every pixel. These pseudo-random numbers are bit-wise XORed with the 24-bit pixel data to create 24 bits of encrypted information. The encrypted data is sent over the DVI/HDMI cable to the receiver, which XORs each encrypted set of 24 bits with the identical 24-bit pseudo-random number that was used by the transmitter, resulting in the original pixel data, as shown in Figure 10.3.

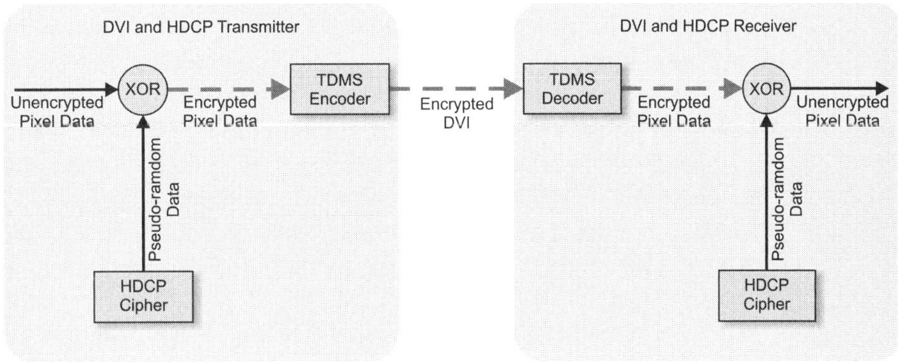

Figure 10.3 HDCP Encryption and Decryption

The 24-bit pseudorandom number is not transmitted across the DVI link. Instead, both the transmitter and receiver independently generate the number. To stay synchronized, the pseudorandom generators in the transmitter and the receiver must be initialized using the same keys. As the encryption algorithm is public, the security of the content relies on keeping the keys a secret.

Renewability

HDCP allows for the possibility that a set of secret keys may become compromised and subsequently used by unauthorized parts to decode protected content. In the event that a particular device's keys are compromised, the corresponding KSV is placed on a revocation list. As part of the authentication process, all HDCP video transmitters must check to see whether the receiver's KSV is on the revocation list. If it is, the authentication fails. Since each device has a unique KSV, other receivers not on the revocation list continue to function. DVD-Videos include support for HDCP revocation lists, which are called System Renewability Messages (SRMs).

Upstream Protocol

In 2001, the Digital-CP released the HDCP Upstream Protocol. As explained previously, it is harder to implement content protection schemes on open systems such as PCs than on closed systems. The Upstream Protocol was an attempt to create a standardized mechanism for supporting HDCP on PCs. Although proof-of-concept demonstrations of Upstream have been made to work, including prototypes running the on Intel® 845G chipset's integrated graphics, the feature has not been productized by any company.

Upstream Protocol support is not mandated by any license. An equivalent framework would be acceptable for HDCP on the PC. One such equivalent framework is Microsoft's Certified Output Protection Protocol (COPP), which became available on Windows†-based PCs starting in 2005. Another example is Protected Video Path-Output Protection Management (PVP-OPM), which is part of Windows Vista and is the successor to COPP.

Independent of the Upstream Protocol, the term *upstream* is used in the HDCP documents to refer to devices that are closer to the source. For instance, if an HDCP transmitter was attached to a repeater, which was in turn attached to a receiver, the transmitter would be upstream of both the repeater and the receiver. The repeater would be upstream of the receiver. So, be aware that use of the term upstream does not necessarily refer to the Upstream Protocol.

HDMI

HDMI is primarily a display interconnect, but it also has some unique content protection considerations that warrant discussion. Recall that HDMI is basically DVI with a smaller connector and optional support for HDCP and audio.

The implementation of HDCP over HDMI is extremely similar to HDCP over DVI. The keys and encryption scheme are the same, for instance. One key difference is that HDMI-HDCP includes support for encrypting the audio data. Since DVI does not include audio, it does not include such support.

In DVI-HDCP, only the active pixels are encrypted. The blanking intervals are unencrypted. Under HDMI, audio is sent in packets known as data islands in the blanking interval. These audio packets are also encrypted.

HDMI is thus the only widely available protocol for external digital audio connections that supports encryption of audio. SCMS allows copying rights to be sent along external digital audio links, but it does not obfuscate the data itself.

Windows† Media Digital Rights Management

Windows Media Digital Rights Management (WMDRM) is a comprehensive collection of technologies designed to support playback of premium content on computers, portable players, and networked players. Microsoft offers software development kits (SDKs) that allow content providers to create premium content distribution systems, which protect the content using encryption and license management infrastructure.

WMDRM is intended to support contemporary usage models, such as buying audio or video content over the Internet and downloading it to a PC for playback. Depending on the content provider's desires, the content can also be sent to non-PC devices for playback. It is also possible that the primary playback device is not a PC at all, which would be the case when dealing with ring tones for a mobile phone.

Licenses

Developers and manufacturers need to sign WMDRM licenses to build WMDRM products, but the term license is also used in the context of WMDRM to refer to a small chunk of data which describes the rules for playing back a piece of content.

Licenses are specific to an individual media file. They contain information such as the number of times the content can be played, the time window in which it can be played, the types of non-PC devices it can be transferred to, and the security level required for playback. The license also includes the key necessary to decrypt the media file.

The license can specify five different *protection levels* for digital audio outputs. A different protection level can be specified for both compressed and uncompressed digital audio. Some example protection levels in order of increasing security are:

- 100 Unprotected
- 200 Obfuscated
- 300 Encrypted low
- 400 Encrypted medium
- 500 Encrypted high

Level 200 can be achieved using Windows XP's Secure Audio Path (SAP), which is described later in this chapter, with digital outputs being allowed. Level 300 can be achieved using SAP with digital outputs disabled. In Windows Vista, the Protected User Mode Audio engine provides a similar protection level to Windows XP's SAP.

The output protection level should not be confused with the audio driver ***security level***. Licenses can also specify a required security level independent of any output protection levels. An SAP-compliant driver on Windows Millennium provides a security level of 1100. An SAP-compliant driver on Windows XP provides a security level of 1200.

The fact that the license can specify a time window in which the file can be played allows for a wide variety of usage models, such as:

- The license expiring a certain number hours after first playback
- The license only being valid on certain calendar days
- The license expiring a certain time interval after the file was downloaded onto the system

WMDRM also supports the concept of metering, meaning that licenses can expire after a piece of content has been played a certain number of times.

To ensure that the time-sensitive licenses are not circumvented by people resetting their system clock, WMDRM applications on the PC need to have an anti-rollback clock mechanism. Since the traditional PC on-board clock is very accessible, it alone is insufficient. Instead, a trustworthy time source such as Microsoft's time internet service must be checked periodically to ensure the player has an accurate time.

Portable Devices

In the context of WMDRM, ***portable devices*** are products that can play content without being connected to a computer or a network. Examples of portable devices are music players, often colloquially referred to as MP3 players, and mobile phones. The subset of WMDRM that applies to such devices is known as WMDRM Portable Devices (WMDRMPD). WMDRMPD was code-named Janus.[2]

One important feature of portable devices is that they must have a secure clock. Since these devices may be disconnected from any network for long period of time, an accurate clock is necessary to properly handle the case of licenses expiring while disconnected. Specifically, the secure clock needs to be accurate to within two minutes per month.

---

[2] No relation to the author. It did make for interesting status reports: "Janus reviewed Janus update."

Network Devices

In the context of WMDRM, the term *network devices* refers to products that can play content stored on a host computer. Content is streamed over a home network from the host to the network device. Network devices can only function over a local network; a network device in California cannot, for instance, play content streamed from New York. Network devices are also called digital media adapters, digital media receivers, and digital audio receivers. The subset of WMDRM that applies to such devices is known as WMDRM Network Devices (WMDRMND). WMDRMND was code-named Cardea.

Unlike portable devices, network devices cannot store content. They can only immediately render audio or video as it is streamed real-time over a local network.

On a related note, network devices do not need a secure clock. The host PC is already required to have a secure clock, and it does not send content to the network device if the license is not valid for the current time.

To enforce the restriction of the network device being attached over a local network, the host periodically confirms that the network device has an IP ping no greater than 7 milliseconds. If this proximity detection requirement is not met, the host does not send the network device any content.

The host also authenticates the device using a handshaking scheme based on 1024-bit RSA, SHA-1 MAC, and AES OMAC1. The content itself is encrypted using 128-bit AES.

Content Scramble System (CSS)

The Content Scramble System (CSS) is used to protect compressed video and audio data stored on DVD. The CSS infrastructure includes an encryption scheme for the data. The data is encrypted prior to being stored on DVD. Before the data can be decoded and viewed, it must first be descrambled. Descrambling is done by the decoder and requires retrieving keys from the DVD drive and the DVD-Video disc.

If you simply copy the contents of a scrambled DVD to your hard drive, you cannot watch them with a PC DVD player because some of the necessary security information cannot be copied from the DVD. Similarly, burning a copy of a scrambled DVD onto a DVD-R won't work, as that same security information still cannot be copied.

The CSS encryption scheme was famously cracked in 1999. Since CSS does not have a revocation scheme, the compromised keys can continue to be used to perform unauthorized decryption of CSS content. Even though methods to defeat CSS are available, manufacturers of DVD players and discs must still adhere to the CSS license.

Content Protection for Pre-recorded Media (CPPM)

DVD-Audio was originally slated to use an encryption mechanism known as CSS II. However, the very public cracking of the original CSS led content providers to ask four companies (IBM, Intel, Matsushita, and Toshiba) to develop a new scheme. These four companies—which came to be known as the *4C* in this context—developed the Content Protection for Pre-recorded Media (CPPM). Compared to CSS's 40-bit keys, CPPM uses 56-bit keys. CPPM uses the Cryptomeria Cipher (C2) to actually encrypt the disc content.

In addition to encryption, CPPM also includes a revocation mechanism. Each disc contains a large number of keys stored in a Media Key Block (MKB). Each DVD-Audio title has a unique MKB, and new MKBs are required to be used every three months. Every licensed DVD-Audio decoder has its own set of keys, known as device keys. A decoder uses its device key in conjunction with the disc's MKB to recover the actual key needed to successfully decrypt the disc.

If a particular decoder model becomes compromised, the MKB of future disks can be altered in such a way that the compromised device keys cannot recover the decryption key. In short, the decoder's ability to play back disks is revoked. It is still able to play older disks that were released prior to revocation, but it is not able to play any disks released after the revocation.

Closely related to CPPM is Content Protection for Recordable Media (CPRM). Whereas CPPM is designed for protecting mass-produced prerecorded content, CPRM is designed to protect content stored on recordable media such as optical discs and SD Flash. CPRM could be used, for instance, for taking premium content downloaded over the Internet and burning it to a disk. The CPRM-protected disc would be playable by compliant systems, but the content could not be copied off it.

When developing CPPM, the 4C strove to find a reasonable balance between consumer use and content provider restrictions. The 4C pushed for a consumer experience similar to regular audio CDs, which included making legitimate backup copies. For that reason, CPPM mandates that at least one full resolution copy of the content can be made.

Digital Transmission Content Protection (DTCP)

DTCP was developed by Hitachi, Intel, Matsushita, Sony, and Toshiba. The five companies in this context are known as the 5C. The 5C formed in February 1998 with then intent of developing a scheme to prevent "unauthorized, casual copying of commercial entertainment content." The goal of having such a scheme was so that movie studios would be comfortable releasing their content in a digital form for streaming and point-to-point applications.

In a nutshell, DTCP device encrypts the content before transmitting it. The content can only be decrypted by the receiver if it is a valid DTCP device. By design, DTCP is only one link in a complete solution. It has been mapped to the Internet Protocol (IP), 1394, USB, Bluetooth, and the Media Oriented Systems Transport (MOST). Intel has been advocating DTCP/IP as a means of securely transmitting media throughout a Digital Home.

By design, DTCP is only one link in a complete solution. It is not a source protection protocol, in that it does not protect content stored on a physical medium, but instead protects content as it flows between external devices. Examples of source protection protocols include DVD-Video, DVD-Audio, Windows Media DRM, and conditional-access TV cable.

DTCP-protected streams carry copy control information that conveys one of three protection levels: copy-one-generation, copy-never, or no-more-copies. They have no level equivalent to copy-freely. If the content can be copied freely, you need not use DTCP.

If the content is marked as copy-never, the sink device performs Full Authentication with the source. Full Authenticated Key Exchange (AKE) uses the Elliptic Curve Digital Signature Algorithm (EC-DSA) and Elliptic Curve Diffie-Hellman (EC-DH).

For copy-one-generation and no-more-copies content, the sink can use either Full or Restricted AKE. Restricted Authentication is intended for use on devices with limited computational bandwidth. Restricted Authentication is based on the sink and source sharing a secret, similar to how HDCP authentication is handled. The sink sends a random challenge and both the sink and source interpedently calculate an answer and check to see whether they both got the same answer.

DTCP also supports revocation. Revocation lists known as System Renewability Messages are distributed along with the content. Some types of DTCP devices are required to store a local copy of the most recent SRM and update it as more recent SRMs are sent down as part of the content stream.

Assuming authentication is successful and the devices in question have not been revoked, the premium content is encrypted and sent from source to sink. DTCP data is encrypted using a 56-bit M6 block cipher. Optionally, 128-bit AES encryption can be used.

Advanced Access Content System (AACS)

The Advanced Access Content System (AACS) is an infrastructure that is still under development. It is intended to protect pre-recorded content on both HD-DVD and BluRay disks. As such, AACS is a successor to CSS.

The founding members of the committee that are creating AACS are IBM, Intel, Microsoft, Panasonic, Sony, Toshiba, Disney, and Warner Brothers. AACS licensing is being handled by the aptly-named AACS Licensing Authority (LA). AACS was formerly known as the Advanced Copying Management System (ACMS).

At this writing, final definition and formal acceptance of AACS in the industry is still in progress. As such, many of the details are subject to change. But, at a high-level, AACS is based on industry-standard cryptographic protocols such as 128-bit AES, SHA-1 and hashing, and RSA digital signatures. It includes renewability, allowing compromised keys to be revoked.

New Usage Models

CSS was designed in a time when computers were just barely powerful enough to decode video DVDs and Internet connectivity was slower and rarer than it is today. As such, CSS supported a very basic playback mode. By contrast, AACS is designed to support new usage models and to accommodate the PC and Internet.

As an example, AACS supports the ability for consumers to unlock bonus content on disks they purchase by going on-line. AACS also supports *managed copies*, which allows consumers to make legitimate copies of premium content for distribution within a home media network. A third scenario under AACS is *burn-and-go,* where-in content is downloaded over the internet and the burned to a transportable medium, such as a recordable HD-DVD disc.

Content Protection on the PC

Many of the contemporary protection schemes discussed in the previous section have similar requirements for protecting premium audio. To facilitate support of a wide variety of premium audio, multiple frameworks for audio protection have been designed to work on the Windows operating systems. In this section we will examine content protection architectures that are or will be available on Windows XP and Windows Vista.

SAP

In the 1990s, an increasing amount of premium audio content was becoming available on the PC. With the simultaneous growth in popularity of the Internet, some audio content providers were concerned about how to make sure that their premium content was not widely distributed without permission. To address this issue, some audio player software was written that received encrypted audio, either streamed in real time over the Internet or downloaded in advance. The software could detect an authorized user, then decrypt and play the premium content.

This type of approach does offer some protection, in that even if the encrypted file is distributed, it cannot be played unless someone can crack the encryption.

However, if an authorized user is able to play the file, it becomes decrypted by the DRM client component and is then sent in the clear to the standard audio stack, which includes a sound card and associated driver. Someone wishing to copy the premium content can do so by capturing the unencrypted data, either by writing a simple plug-in that makes a copy of the data as it passes through the audio subsystem or by creating a modified audio driver that does the copy.

To provide a defense against these sorts of attacks, Microsoft created the Secure Audio Path (SAP) for the Windows Millennium and XP operating systems. SAP uses encryption and authentication to improve the robustness of the audio playback system.

As can be see in Figure 10.4, SAP allows for the creation of a DRM kernel component, so the content remains encrypted much further down into the audio chain. SAP provides additional protection because the content remains encrypted throughout the user-mode memory space, only becoming unencrypted in the kernel mode memory space. This protection derives from the fact that most applications can only access user-mode memory, and only low-level drivers can access kernel mode. Writing drivers is more challenging technically than writing applications.

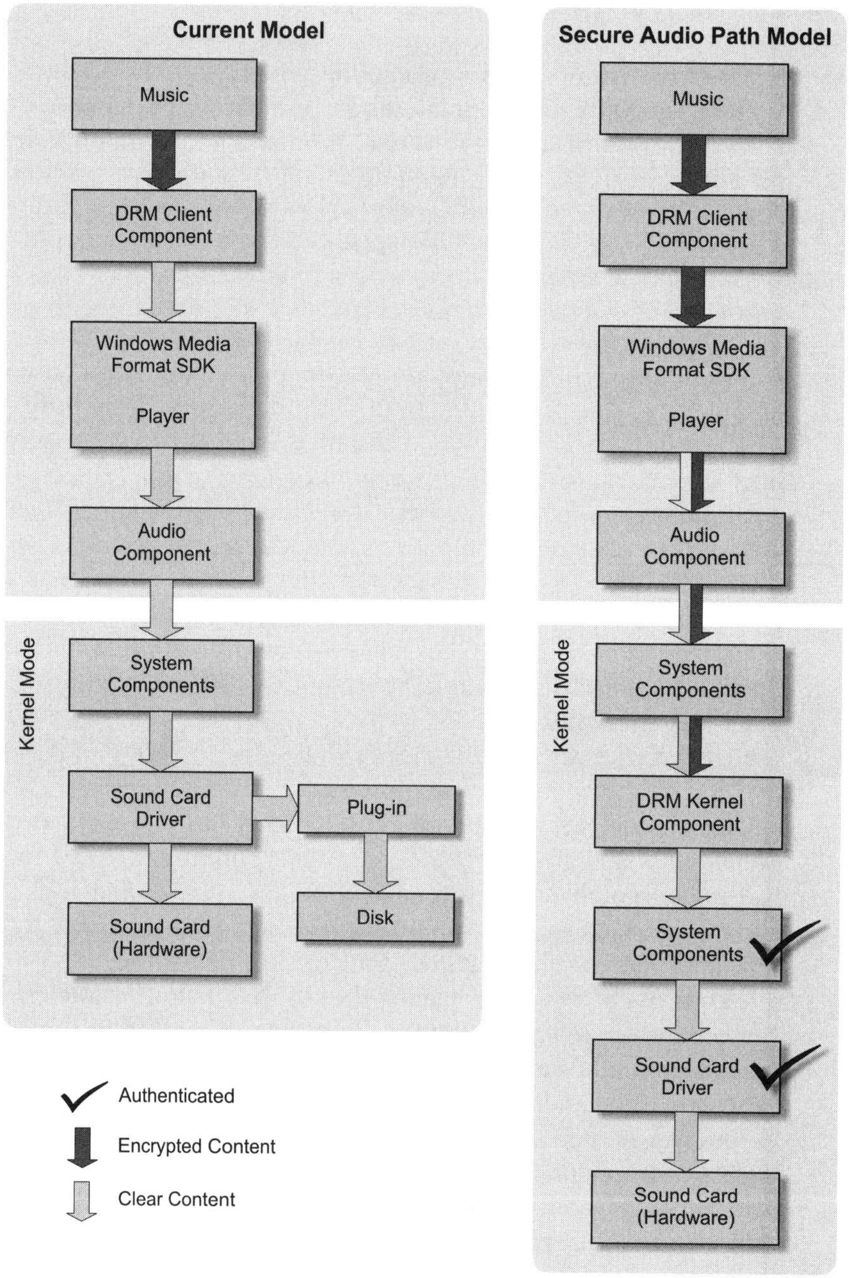

Figure 10.4 Secure Audio Path

Authentication is the second part of the increased protection that is offered by SAP. The DRM kernel component authenticates the system components and audio driver to ensure that both are SAP-compliant before releasing unencrypted premium content to them. SAP-compliant components contain a Microsoft-issued certificate indicating that they are secure and will not misuse the content sent to them.

Despite the protection offered by SAP, currently no content requires it. Furthermore, no applications have been written that make use of the SAP framework.

PMP

The Windows Vista operating system provides a fundamentally different and more secure infrastructure for the video and audio pipeline and drivers, compared to previous Windows operating systems such as Windows XP. The low-level details of the User Mode Audio (UMA) have already been covered in Chapter 8. This new architecture provides some fundamental improvements in the basic security of the operating system.

It so happened that the next generation optical disks (HD-DVD and Blu-ray) were scheduled to launch in about the same time frame as Windows Vista. In 2003, a Microsoft and Intel tiger team began meeting to explore ways to ensure that Vista, graphics hardware, and audio hardware would provide the level of security needed to meet the compliance and robustness rules for next generation premium content. The task of designing such a system was further complicated by the fact that these compliance and robustness rules were not yet finalized, and it still was not clear which of the two HD disk formats would prevail. Indeed, the outcome of the format war remains inconclusive, even as this book goes to print.

Despite these ambiguities, Microsoft publicly unveiled their Protected Media Path (PMP[3]) in 2005 at WinHEC. Supported in Windows Vista, PMP is designed to close many of the attack vectors that were possible under previous operating systems.

A high level schematic of PMP is shown in Figure 10.5. The four major components are the Protected Environment, Media Interoperability Gateway, the Protected Video Path, and Protected User Mode Audio.

---

[3] Pronounced "pump."

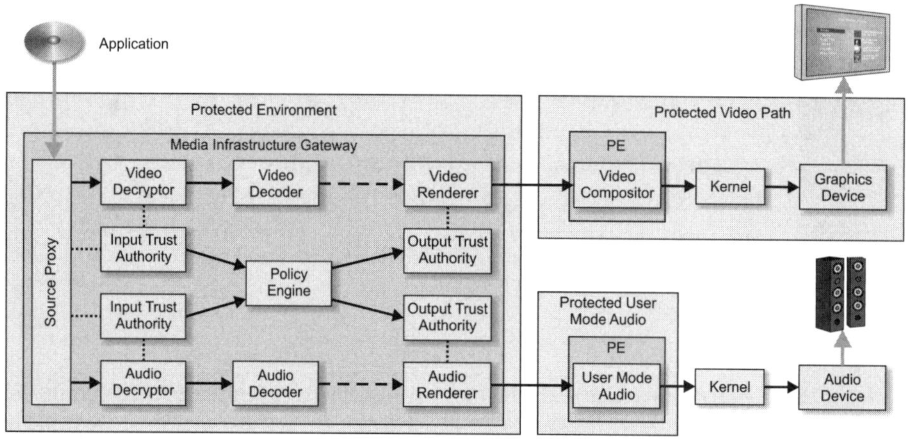

Figure 10.5 Protected Media Path

Protected Environment

The Protected Environment (PE) is a designed to carve out a safe haven of user and kernel mode space in which premium content can be handled. The PE achieves this security through a variety of techniques, including fundamental strengthening of many of the lower level processes and services of the operating system itself.

Signing

PE also checks each component, such as drivers, before they are loaded into the operating system. User mode *Participating Components*-that is, those components that will have access to premium content-must have a Protected Environment certificate that asserts that it meets the PE compliance and robustness requirements. Participating kernel mode drivers must have similar certificates. All non-participating drivers must be identity-signed, meaning that they can be identified using the certificate and verified that they have not been changed. However, an identity certificate does not itself make any guarantees about the behavior of the associated component. Loading drivers or other components that do not meet these requirements will mean the Protected Environment—and hence the PMP framework—will not be loaded.

The motivation for all these certificates is twofold. First, it ensures that only trusted participating entities will have access to the premium content[4]. Secondly, it allows for revocation of both participating and non-participating contents. If any component is found to be serving as an attack vector, it can be revoked, meaning that the PE no longer loads, and therefore content that requires it will not flow, if the revoked component is on the system.

Since participating components have direct access to the unencrypted forms of the premium content, they are required to have a PE-specific certificate associated with them, which asserts they will not misuse the content. Non-participating components, such as mouse and printer drivers, do not have direct access to the content, so they are presumed innocent and need only be identity-signed. However, if some attack is created that uses those components to somehow get access to the premium content, then non-participating components too can be revoked.

Revocation is an important point, in that every driver and every PE component on the system must be signed in some way. If the Protected Environment allowed an unsigned component to load, it would have no robust way of knowing if that component was an attack vector. Although a checksum of the file could be calculated, it would be trivial for attackers to create an arbitrary number of versions of the component, all of them having the same exploit functionality but different binary images.

It is further worth noting that the PE must check the components before loading them. If a compromised component was loaded, it could install a rogue Terminate and Stay Resident component that altered the behavior of the system, even if the component itself was subsequently unloaded. As such, if ever an unsigned component is loaded, then the PE cannot load until the operating system has been rebooted.

While the signing approach offers a high level of security, it comes at a price. Most notably, a certificate and signing infrastructure needs to be created, and participating component developers have the additional burden of participating in the signing programs. Another problem is that innocuous unsigned components cannot be loaded in the system if PE is to function. Thus, a user might have to choose at boot time between watching premium content or using a particular peripheral for which no signed driver is available.

---

[4] One security expert summed up this philosophy as "Don't let guys with guns into the bank."

Revocation and Renewal

As has been noted, the ability to unequivocally identify components in the operating system means that these individual components—and indeed even elements of the operating system—can be revoked. In the context of PMP, the list of revoked components is stored in the Global Revocation List (GRL[5]). The GRL is signed by Microsoft and includes a creation timestamp.

If a component is identified as compromising PMP security, its identifier gets added to the GRL, creating a new version of the GRL. Each GRL release is a superset of previous GRLs. The GRL is available via Microsoft's Windows Update and is made available on certain types of premium media as well.

In addition to revocation, PE also supports renewability. For instance, if a component is compromised, in most cases the component owner would have the ability to release a new version of the component that addresses the security hole. Thus, if a revoked component was identified, one usage model would have the player prompt the user to download an updated version of the component from an appropriate site to be able to play the premium content. Of course, if the revoked component was written expressly to defeat PMP, then renewing that component would make less sense.

Isolation

The PE's other key security measure is process isolation. Within PE, participating components with a valid PE certificate get instantiated in a protected process. Only protected processes have access to the unencrypted premium content. Unauthorized components in the system without PE certificates cannot create protected processes.

Media Interoperability Gateway

The Media Interoperability Gateway (MIG) is a collection of trusted components that together are responsible for decrypting the premium content and ensuring that the system state meets the requirements mandated by a particular piece of content. Such policies vary based on the content, as has been discussed earlier in this chapter.

The MIG is extensible, in that it contains components both native to the operating system and from third-party vendors. Furthermore, addi-

[5] Pronounced "grill."

tional components can be installed by the user to play new types of content, without requiring any changes to the PMP architecture itself. Again, each of these components will need a PE certificate in order to be loaded.

Key components of the MIG are decryptors, decoders, sinks, input trust authorities, output trust authorities, and the policy engine.

Decryptors and decoders are just what they sound like. Decryptors decrypt the premium content. For instance, when playing a DVD-Audio disk, the decryptor would unencrypt the C2-encrypted data stored on the disk. Decoders decode compressed media, such as MPEG.

An Input Trust Authority (ITA) basically describes a subset of the compliance rules for a particular type of content, such as CPPM content. The ITA details what conditions must be met for the associated content to be played. The ITA also may indicate a minimum GRL level that it requires.

An Output Trust Authority (OTA) is basically a mechanism for getting and setting output protection mechanisms such as HDCP for the audio and video sinks.

The Policy Engine takes the prerequisites laid down by an ITA for a particular piece of content and attempts to meet those conditions by negotiating with the OTAs. Assuming all conditions can be met, the policy engine reports success and the content can be played.

Protected Video Path

The Protected Video Path (PVP) secures content as it flows from the MIG to the video hardware. PVP requires the video drivers to authenticate that they are running on proper hardware, rather than rogue hardware designed to circumvent protection.

PVP includes Output Protection Management (PVP-OPM), which is basically a framework for setting video output protection mechanisms of HDCP, CGMS-A, and Macrovision. Its functionality is very similar to its Windows XP predecessor, Certified Output Protection Protocol (COPP). Compared to COPP, OPM offers a more robust implementation and includes additional functionality, such as support for HDCP repeaters, clone mode, and video resolution constriction.

For graphics hardware that is attached over a bus that a particular type of content might identify as being user accessible, PVP includes a User Accessible Bus (PVP-UAB) framework that allows premium content to be re-encrypted in the MIG before being sent out to the video hardware. Upon receiving the encrypted data, the video chip decrypts them using specialized hardware. Since the premium data is encrypted as it flows over the bus, it mitigates attempts to steal the content by snooping the bus. The two approved ciphers to date are the Advanced Encryption Standard (AES) and Intel's Cascaded Cipher (CC). PVP establishes session keys by running Diffie-Hellman independently at both the graphics chip end and the software end of the bus so that keys never need to be transmitted over the bus.

Protected User Mode Audio

Under Windows XP, audio processing is primarily handled in kernel mode, as has been discussed in Chapter 8. In Windows Vista, much of the audio functionality has been moved up into user mode to provide a more robust and extensible experience. Protected User Mode Audio (PUMA) is the PMP component that enhances user-mode audio (UMA) to a protection level that is equivalent to SAP. Indeed, any content tagged as requiring SAP can be played under PUMA. A schematic of PUMA is shown in Figure 10.6.

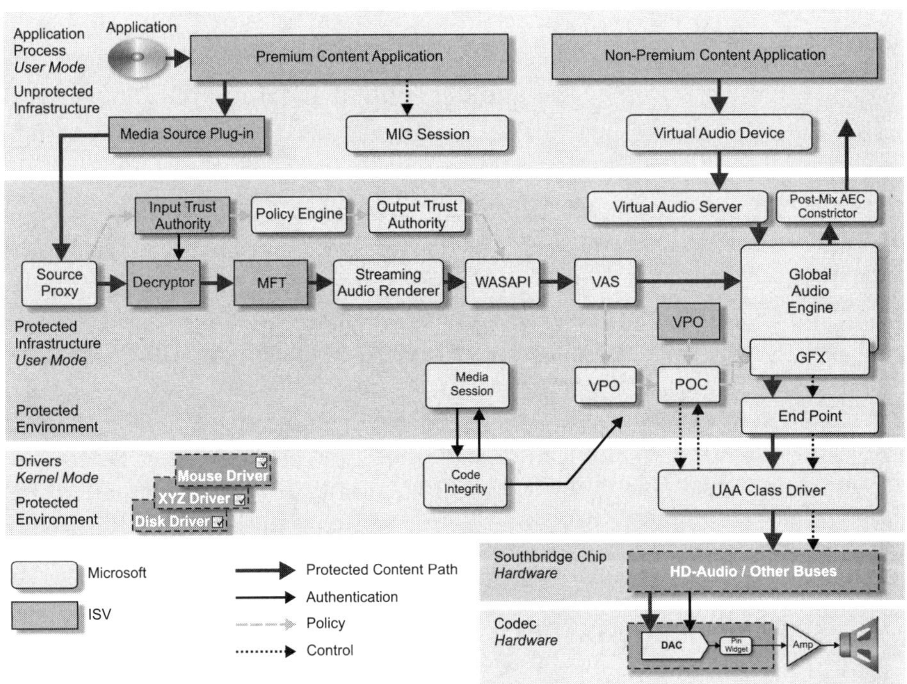

Figure 10.6 Protected User-Mode Audio

Microsoft UAA Intel HD Audio allows multiple clients to render audio streams concurrently. All the different sounds are mixed together into a single stream that is rendered to the speakers. PUMA maintains this type of flexibility and allows for the concurrent playback of both protected and unprotected audio. To allow for this mixing, the Audio Engine itself must exist in the Protected Environment.

A component known as the Virtual Audio Server (VAS) receives unprotected content from non-PMP applications. Another instantiation of VAS receives protected content from the MIG. The VAS feeds content to the Audio Engine for mixing. Any VAS that receives protected content from the MIG communicates with a Protected Output Controller (POC), which includes a Virtual Protected Object (VPO) module in the front end and an Output Encryption Audio Processing Object (APO) in the back end.

A VPO contains the policy for the associated content. It is functionally equivalent to an audio OTA, but it resides in the PUMA process rather than the MIG. Hypothetically, multiple VPOs could be active concurrently, each representing the rules required for different types of content.

The POC has responsibility for consolidating the policy requirements of all the active VPOs and setting up the appropriate audio hardware state. An example of a protection mechanism is configuring hardware to constrict the audio to a lower sample rate for transmission over an unprotected external output.

The Output Encryption APO will in the future encrypt content as it flows to the hardware. The APO is stubbed out in the first release of Vista, because such encryption is not necessary to meet the currently required security levels. Future versions of PUMA might include active APOs that aid in providing a very high level of security.

PAP

Protected Audio Path (PAP) is intended to be the audio equivalent of PVP-UAB. It is a logical extension of PUMA. Planned for release years after Vista, it is intended to bring additional security to the audio stack by providing encryption of the audio traffic as it flows from the MIG to the audio hardware. Figure 10.7 shows one possible architecture for PAP.

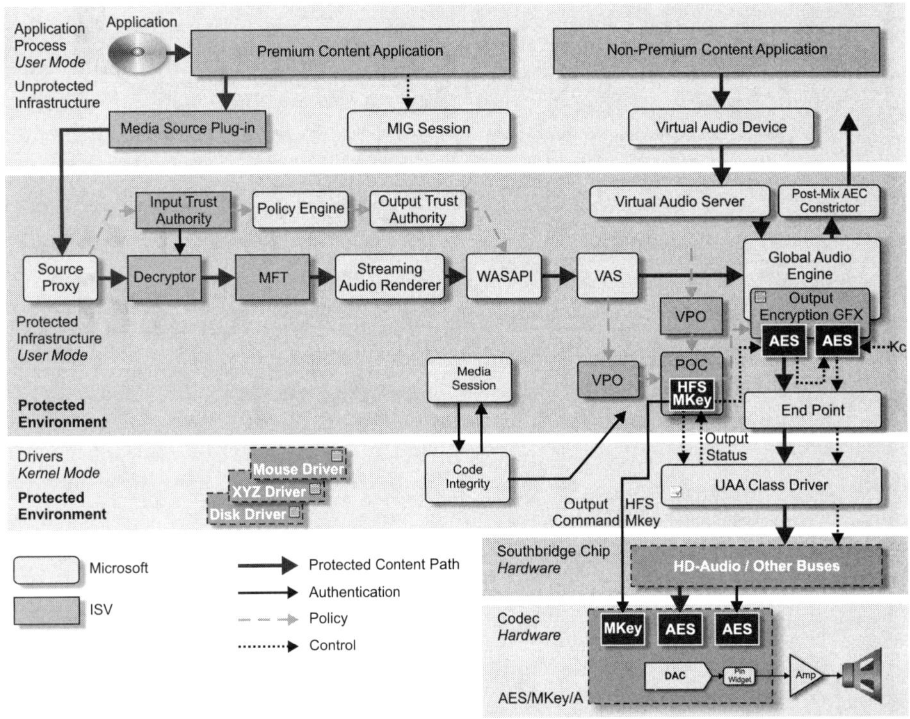

Figure 10.7 Protected Audio Path

It remains to be seen whether PAP ever becomes necessary. PVP-UAB is a reasonable technical solution for graphics chips, since those chips are already quite complex. Adding cryptographic functions to the graphics chips incurs additional expenses, but the cost is on par with other features available in the graphics chips. By comparison, Intel HD Audio codecs are much simpler devices, and adding cryptographic functions could result in a doubling the cost of the chip.

Chapter 11

Testing and Certification

An audio signal chain is only as good as its weakest link. Different parts of the audio subsystem are tested at different times in the development process. Testing might be to standards created by the OEM developing the system or to standards created by an external entity such as the Microsoft† WHQL program or Dolby† separate implementation and system-level testing. To make matters worse, you must test a wide degree of variability and functionality, with ever increasing combinations and permutations of options.

The Ever-growing Unwieldy Test Matrix

The options available on modern systems require a wide range of test coverage to ensure a quality product. This matrix has about ten dimensions, and that number appears to be increasing. Here are some of the dimensions:

- 64-bit OS versus 32-bit OS
- Choice of CPU Vendor
- Choice of Dual-core CPU versus Single-core CPU
- Choice of Intel HD Audio controller vendor
- Choice of Intel HD Audio codec vendor

- Windows Vista versus Windows XP versus earlier operating systems
- Mobility versus Portability versus Desktop
- The number of inputs and outputs
- Multi-streaming versus single-streaming
- Class Driver versus codec-vendor-supplied audio function driver
- Localization, usually required for 10 to 30 languages

The test manager must choose the proper set of target test systems to properly exercise the variables in this matrix. As a practical matter, it is close to impossible to provide complete coverage for all of these variables, but you can develop a strategy that covers the most likely failures. For instance, driver bugs are more likely to appear on a system with dual-core processors and hyperthreading, while usability bugs are more likely to appear on a system with a slow single-core CPU with no hyperthreading. You should make sure that your test platforms match your customer requirements. For instance, if the customer ships both 64-bit and 32-bit versions of Windows, you should include both types of systems in your test matrix.

Per-Unit Testing

Two basic categories of testing are:

- Per-unit testing is performed on each item that is manufactured.
- System-level design and validation testing is performed on a smaller number of units.

Various different audio testing stages exist in different parts of the design and manufacturing process. Testing often takes place globally, with each test stage conducted in a different country. Per-unit testing is a form of verification rather than validation, because each unit or system must be tested after it is manufactured to ensure that it meets the original design goals.

Audio Codec Manufacturing Verification Testing

The first point of testing comes as the audio codec is assembled and tested. Typically, an assembly facility takes the wafers from the fab, slices them up into individual die, assembles them into the packaging, adds the package marking, and then performs a functional test of the assembled chip. This type of testing is performed on a special tester built for the purpose of testing audio chips. The Teradyne Catalyst and J750 are popular platforms for this type of testing. A test program is used to establish test limits for the each codec being tested. The testing time per codec is typically two to 4 seconds, depending on the codec's complexity. Each second of test time has a cost associated with it. It is possible to reduce costs and increase yield by reducing the number of tests performed at this stage. However, such tradeoffs must be carefully considered in terms of the requirements of the end system. Specially designed test fixtures are needed to test dynamic range and THD+N above a level of 80 to 90 dB of dynamic range. Once codecs pass this test, they usually are mounted on tape and reel to support automated pick-and-place manufacturing techniques.

Motherboard Manufacturing Verification Testing

Once the codec has been soldered down to the motherboard, the entire motherboard assembly must be tested to ensure that all components in the audio path were assembled properly, and that all signal paths work properly. This test normally takes place at the end of the motherboard assembly line. Like the codec testing, the test time adds up to a significant measurable cost, so again you face a tradeoff between test coverage (quality) and test time (cost). Usually, you need not re-test the codec during this stage, nor do you need to test items that can be guaranteed by design.

Traditionally, this testing has been performed in real-mode DOS, as part of a batch script, to avoid the time it takes to boot into Windows. The testing application is normally provided by the codec vendor. However, some designs no longer support real-mode DOS, so Windows is becoming more common as a test framework at this stage.

System Level Verification Testing

A comprehensive manufacturing flow includes both a DOS-based test at the end of the motherboard manufacturing line, and a separate Windows-based test after the complete system is assembled. In both cases, most PC manufacturing flows use a special "medusa" cable which couples all inputs and outputs together so that any jack can work as either an input or an output for purposes of testing. No separate audio test equipment is part of the test flow. This approach is good enough to guarantee a minimum level of performance when testing any two ports consisting of a

DAC (output) and an ADC (input), but it cannot identify which component is at fault when a test failure occurs.

For systems that need to guarantee end-user performance greater than 100 dB, this self-test approach is not appropriate, and dedicated audio test equipment should be used at the end of the production line rather than the medusa cable.

If a system contains a built-in microphone or speaker, it must be tested during this stage. In general, automated tests inside an acoustically enclosed test chamber are much more reliable than tests where the test operator listens to a speaker and selects pass or fail.

System Design Validation Testing

Most other testing is part of the design validation process, where a small subset of systems or devices is rigorously tested for design errors. This type of testing may take hours or even days to complete, and usually, it is not practical to test each system that is being manufactured. Usability testing, functional testing, WHQL testing, acoustical emission testing, and audio fidelity testing—all fall into this category.

Usability Testing

Consumer electronics manufacturers usually place a heavy focus on usability testing. They do so because a happy customer is a repeat customer. It is no different for PC-based equipment that hopes to compete with or interface to consumer electronics equipment in the living room.

Usability design and testing is often counter-intuitive when compared to the standard top-down design common in the industry. Be on the lookout for the following indicators of usability problems.

- The system was designed by software and/or hardware developers, not specialists in human factors and usability.
- Written and measurable usability specifications were not part of the design.
- A strict top-down, functional decomposition approach was used.
- An iterative refinement process was not employed.
- The development cycle did not include any prototyping.
- The system design was not empirically evaluated by usability professionals observing typical end users..

Usability design and testing consists of identifying personas, such as entry-level, gamer, audiophile, or business user, and then identifying tasks that each of these personas might do to use the audio in the system. The next step is to get people that match each of the personas to perform the tasks and observe where they experience problems. Once the problem is fixed, you would test again with a new group of users to see if other problems occur. The five distinct phases of usability design and test are:

- Phase 1: Define
- Phase 2: Design
- Phase 3: Prototype
- Phase 4: Test
- Phase 5: Iterate

The prototype step is a critical step, but is often overlooked. It's best to prototype the system early and test the prototype against real users who are not developers or QA staff.

Acoustic Fidelity Testing

You can do a wonderful job of motherboard layout and design and still end up with terrible audio if you don't pay attention to the acoustic output of any built-in speakers, as well as the acoustic input of any built-in microphones. This attention to acoustics is especially difficult in laptop and tablet PCs, space to mount speakers is often very limited. While no specific requirements exist at this time, expect this type of testing to become prevalent in the future.

Acoustic Noise Emission Testing

You should measure the acoustic emissions of each system and attempt to quantify—and hopefully to minimize—the noise generated by the power supply and fans in each system under development. Systems intended for the living room should be especially quiet so that they do not interfere with quiet passages in movies and music.

While no specific requirements exist at this time, you can use a handheld sound pressure level meter in a quiet room to measure the relative loudness of each system configuration. You should measure from a distance of one meter. The room being used for measurements should have drapes on the wall and carpet on the floor to prevent audio reflections from influencing the measurements.

Functional Software Testing

Functional testing is the process of testing basic audio functionality and ensuring that the behavior conforms to the design. This behavioral test differs from usability testing in that functional testers are familiar with the normal operation of the system and are looking for places where the software does not work according to the design.

Functional testing usually includes exercising the audio applications that are included on a system, including Sound Recorder, Windows† Media Player, speech recognition, and Instant Messenger. All of the basic tasks defined in the usability test phase should be executed to verify proper operation.

Automated Software Testing

Since the year 2000, Microsoft Windows Hardware Quality Labs (WHQL) Hardware Compatibility Tests (HCT) have been the primary form of automated audio testing for PCs. The HCTs include tests for each major device category, including audio. A separate system test section also includes audio fidelity tests. Make sure to run both the system tests and the audio device tests for full coverage.

Automated testing is ideally tied to the software build process, with each new software build automatically triggering a new round of testing on a wide variety of target machines.

Windows† Driver Kit (WDK)

As part of the Windows Vista† launch, Microsoft† is combining the driver developer kit, the Windows Driver Foundation, the HCTs, and a test automation framework to create the new Windows Driver Kit (WDK). Not only does the WDK take the place of the HCTs for Windows Vista, it also replaces the HCTs for Windows XP once Windows Vista is released. If you haven't already started deploying the WDK in your organization, you need to start doing so.

The WDK includes the Driver Test Manager (DTM), which is the same testing framework that is used internally at Microsoft. DTM is scalable, from hundreds of test clients in a large test farm down to a single client system being debugged by a developer. The Automated System Installer (ASI) allows for hands-off installation of any version of Windows, while the System Imaging Tool allows automated installation of any hard disk image. A scheduling module provides automated job distribution, parallel test execution, and targets jobs to the available resources, while a packaging module collects test scenario information and provides an environment for collaboration and easy reproduction of test failures.

The WDK is included with the Beta 1 version of Windows Vista, which has already been released, and it will be updated with the Beta2, RC, and RTM releases of Windows Vista. The tests included with Vista RTM are the final version to use with all logo testing going forward, for both Windows Vista and Windows XP.

Given that the WDK and the DTM can have a large impact on your testing process, you should consider changes to your lab topology and development flow. If you haven't already done so, you should start using the WDK and DTM as soon as possible, as it becomes required for all system testing once Windows Vista has been released.

Audio Fidelity Testing

Several of the new functional tests that will be included with the WDK as part of logo testing are centered on audio fidelity testing. The most likely configuration for this testing will include the system under test (SUT), which is connected to the audio test set through analog cables, a second system that is used to control the audio test set, and a test server that controls the overall testing process. Software-based signal generators and analyzers running on the system under test are used in conjunction with hardware-based signal generators and analyzers on the audio test set to provide a comprehensive set of test vectors.

Audio fidelity characterization or quality testing can be challenging. The best way to assess that the desired level of quality is attained and maintained through to the manufacturing stage is to use a comprehensive suite of objective tests. However, the development and application of such a suite of tests is no simple matter. What tests should be done, how should they be done, what results can be expected or set as goals, and how do these test results correlate to perceived quality? How can we benchmark these metrics against quality levels, how can a comparison of different designs or different products be made given a large set of measurements? The next pages address these questions and describe in detail how to characterize audio systems.

Test Setup

The test environment, test set up, and cables can all contribute to the accuracy, repeatability, and quality of testing. Problems in these areas can significantly degrade test results, even when you are using high performance test instruments.

Cables

The type and quality of cables used to interconnect the test generation and measurement equipment to the system under test is important for consistent and accurate test results. Cables should be well shielded and use clean, high quality connectors. Follow the test equipment manufacturer's hookup instructions. In some cases, inputs and outputs are configurable to different formats, such as balanced or unbalanced, floating or grounded. The configuration that is chosen dictates the type of cable, its wiring, and the way that these cables connect to the system under test. If the test instrument has a dedicated ground terminal, use it to form a solid bond to the chassis of the system under test.

Cables should be as short as practical and should be kept away from noise sources, such as switching power supplies, computer monitors, and AC mains cables.

Grounding

Inadequate grounding is one of the biggest contributors to inaccurate and inconsistent test results. The ground connection between the system under test and the test instrument must be short and have low impedance. This connection can be a challenging task on a PC-based audio device, where the analog interface typically is done through 3.5 mm miniature phone jacks alone. Relying solely on these jacks for a ground connection usually causes noise and distortion, causing the test results to measure higher than they really are. The weak ground connection that is provided by these cables and jacks allows mains-induced noise to come through the mains safety ground and pollute the signal, which then shows up as high noise test results. The combination of a less-than-adequate ground path via the small audio cables and connectors and noisy power ground can often degrade noise and distortion measurements by up to 10 decibels! To solve this problem, add a supplemental ground connection between the PC audio device chassis close to the audio connectors and a solid ground connection on the audio test instrument. A stranded #12 AWG or heavier wire should be used to improve the integrity of this ground connection.

Shielding

The test environment can be rich with extraneous signals that can influence measurements and yield inconsistent test results. Packaged desktop and notebook computers typically include sufficient shielding, but if devices are being tested with covers removed or inside of test fixtures, shields might have been removed or compromised. All parts of an audio device must be enclosed in a grounded metallic case for proper shielding. If an open development board is being tested, completely enclose it in a metallic shield when making measurements.

While shielding is necessary and proper shielding can improve noise measurements, obvious sources of noise should also be minimized. Examples of these sources are PC monitors, switching power supplies, flat panel illumination, AC mains cables, fluorescent lighting, any cables carrying digital or clock signals and nearby radio or TV broadcast transmitters. Avoid letting these sources induce extraneous noise by keeping them as far from sensitive audio circuits as possible. You might need to dedicate a separate "clean" section of your lab for testing systems which are expected to exceed 90 dB of dynamic range, preferably with some sort of RF shielding. "Electromagnetic Interference and Electrostatic Discharge" in Chapter 5 provides more information on how to accomplish this.

AES17 Filter (Out-Of-Band Noise)

Almost every audio device that contains a digital-to-analog converter uses sigma-delta technology. This technique offers significant audio quality improvements, particularly lower noise, compared to older technologies. It does so by shifting the noise energy to a higher frequency, above the audio band where it can't be heard. However, while the human ear can't hear beyond 20 kilohertz, audio measurement instruments can have measurement bandwidths ten times that or more. The unusual noise floor spectrum at the output of such converters, more noise above 20 kilohertz than below, can confuse some measurement circuits causing them to produce inaccurate and erratic results. Figure 11.1 shows a typical noise spectrum from a sigma-delta converter with its characteristic steep noise floor rise above 20 kilohertz.

The Audio Engineering Society measurement standard AES-17 recommends the use of a high-order, low-pass filter with a steep roll off above 20 kilohertz when measuring digital audio circuits. This filter should be placed between the system under test and the measurement instrument to filter out this high frequency noise energy. The commonly called "AES-17 Filter" is a filter design challenge with specified performance of less than ±0.1 decibels response error from 10 hertz to 20 kilohertz and over 60 decibels of attenuation at 24 kilohertz. Some test equipment manufacturers can supply this filter as an internal option, which is a highly recommended practice that can save many hours of test troubleshooting in addition to ensuring that the best test results are obtained.

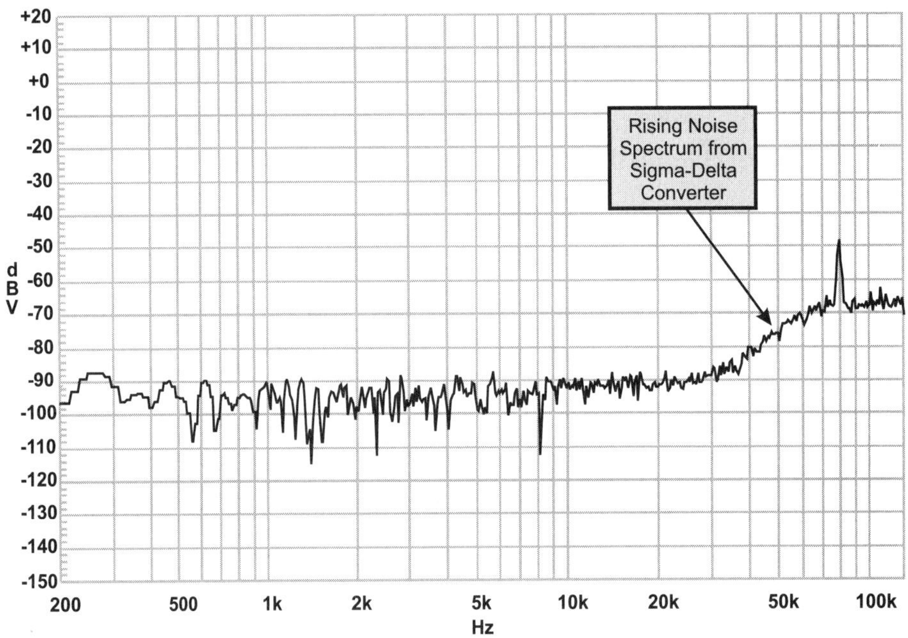

Figure 11.1 Typical Noise Spectrum from a Sigma-Delta Converter

Testing Switch-mode or Class-D Amplifiers

Switch-mode power amplifiers, such as Class-D amplifiers, offer substantial improvements in efficiency, power demands, and size. As a result, they are commonly used in multi-channel home theater systems and battery-powered personal stereo players. This switching design employs a high-frequency switching carrier operating in the 30 kilohertz to 200 kilohertz range, typically. This carrier produces a large *out-of-band* noise component, but more importantly, the fast-switching edges can cause problems at the analog input of a test system. The actual slew rate of these fast-switching edges can be in the hundreds or even thousands of volts per microsecond depending on the type of output filter included in the power amplifier. However, the maximum slew rate for a typical operational amplifier, such as might be used on the input section of an analog analyzer, is perhaps tens of volts per microsecond. The high slew rate of the incoming signal can cause the input stage of the analyzer to go into *slew rate limiting*, thereby putting it into non-linear state. In such a state, its behavior is unpredictable, and it is most likely to produce erroneous results. The test results produced by such an instrument in this mode would almost certainly be inaccurate.

The initial thought to remedy this situation might be to apply the low-pass filter described in the previous section. Unfortunately, doing so could be ineffective because the filter is located too late in the circuit to provide benefit, and the damage has already been done to the input stage prior to this low-pass filter. In fact, any active filter would suffer from the same problem as the input stage itself. What is needed is a high quality, passive low-pass filter placed between the output of the switch-mode amplifier and the analog input of the measuring instrument. It need not have many poles or provide a very sharp roll-off but it does need to be fabricated with high quality passive components and provide negligible inherent noise or distortion. Since it is used directly in the measurement path, quality degradation contributed by such a filter shows up in the measurement of the system under test. The inductors are the most common contributor to distortion in such a filter. Inexpensive, small inductors made with ferrite core material might be convenient to use, but they are inherently non-linear and can induce distortion into the measurement. Less efficient air-core inductors are more linear and should be used. When characterizing the distortion of such a filter, be sure to use the twin-tone IMD measurement technique with two test frequencies up near the cutoff frequency. THD+N measurements will be ineffective to characterize such filters as they roll off the harmonics giving a good but erroneous test result.

Measurement Standards

Several standards organizations have developed measurement standards and practices for characterizing audio entertainment devices. Here is a list of the most popular standards or reference documents:

- AES17-1998 (r2004): AES standard method for digital audio engineering—Measurement of digital audio equipment

- AES-6id-2000: AES information document for digital audio—Personal computer audio quality measurements
- IEC 61606-4: Audio and audiovisual equipment—Digital audio parts—Basic measurements methods of audio characteristics—Part 4: Personal computer (TC 100)

For PC Audio, the original document that formed the basis for several subsequent documents and recommendations was *Personal Computer Audio Quality Measurement* by Steven Harris and Clif Sanchez, at the time working for Crystal Audio Division of Cirrus Logic (Harris 2000). This document became a reference for later documents from Microsoft and Intel® and served as the starting point for AES 6id-2000[1], an Information Document published by the Audio Engineering Society (AES). The original document is now somewhat dated but provides an interesting historical note.

Microsoft has published a number of testing recommendations as part of their Windows Hardware Quality Lab logo certification program. The initial document was the *PC97 Design Guide*, created by Microsoft, Intel, and other industry leaders,, was later was revised to PC98, PC99, and finally PC2001, the last published version of this document. This series of recommendations covers all hardware and software parts of a PC while chapter 11 covers audio measurements.

Microsoft used the PC2001 document as the basis for the Windows Logo Program 2.0 (WLP 2.0) document which describes the logo requirements for Windows XP. The WLP 2.0 document refers to the PC2001 document, but stipulates that to resolve any discrepancies the WLP document prevails. The WLP 3.0 document contains the logo requirements for Windows Vista. It is currently in draft revision and becomes final when Windows Vista is released to manufacturing.

The International Electrotechnical Commission (IEC) standards organization has published IEC 61606-4 titled *Basic Measurements Methods of Audio Characteristics - Part 4: For Personal Computer*. This document is part of several standards in the 61606 series covering measurements of consumer audio devices.

The AES also publishes AES-17-2004, *Measurement of Digital Audio Equipment,* a reference document for measuring the audio performance

---

1 AES-6id has been updated and at the time of the printing of this book is in the final review stage by AES and soon to be released. The revised version is the most comprehensive and up to date document on the subject of PC Audio measurements. This chapter of the book contains much of the same information, but is focused specifically on measuring Intel HD Audio subsystems.

of all types of consumer and professional audio devices. This document provides valuable information on certain techniques that should be followed when characterizing digital audio devices. For example, this document specifies the use of a steep roll-off low-pass filter to remove out-of-band noise present in sigma-delta converters. The characteristics of this filter, which is known as an AES-17 brick-wall filter, must be less than 0.1 decibels attenuation at 20 kilohertz and greater than 60 decibels attenuation at 24 kilohertz and above, a challenging filter design exercise.

Testing Technologies

Testing methods spanning a wide range of technologies have been developed to optimize accuracy and test speed for specific applications. For example, you have special techniques for acoustic testing, newer sophisticated DSP-based techniques that deliver results fast enough to be used on high-speed production lines, and techniques that correlate better with subjective perceptions.

Single Tone, Stepped Sweep,

Perhaps the oldest and simplest test technique uses a single test signal, a pure sine wave. This test stimulus is set to the desired frequency and amplitude, and the analyzer measures the chosen parameter. Then, the generator is set to the next test frequency and the analysis is repeated. This process is repeated for each frequency to be tested. Most modern audio measurement systems can be set up to sweep automatically through a series of single test frequencies to produce a graph of the measured parameter versus frequency. The measurement system must dwell sufficiently long at each frequency for the test instrument and the system under test to settle to a quiescent state. At low frequencies, below a few hundred hertz, this settling can take as long as several hundred milliseconds. The best systems with optimized settling routines and other enhancements can produce a 30-point sweep in a couple of seconds. Some systems are able to measure two channels simultaneously and more than one parameter at a time yielding additional speed advantages.

Single frequency tests remain the workhorse of the industry. They are well understood, many instruments are available on the market, and results are usually consistent and repeatable. But while this technique is simple, it can't be used for acoustic testing, and many electronic testing situations demand faster throughput than this sequential method can support. This shortcoming has led to the development of several newer test technologies that improve speed, accuracy, or adapt to specialized needs.

The most common test frequency is 997 hertz, which is commonly used in place of 1 kilohertz, which should be avoided because it has an integer relationship with some of the codec sample rates. Signals which are a multiple or divisor of the sample rate will often interact with fast Fourier transforms (FFTs) that are used to measure audio fidelity. By using a sample rate which is not related to the sample rate, such as 997 hertz, you can avoid the measurement artifacts that will introduced if you use test tones which are integrally related to the sample rate.

Multitone

To gain a speed advantage, a special signal composed of several sine waves distributed over the band of interest can be all analyzed at once using special DSP measurement techniques. Rather than sequentially testing one frequency at a time, a parallel process can execute many tests and several frequencies at a time. The test signal is called a *multitone* since it is composed of several individual sine waves added together. The measurement process uses FFT spectrum analysis and DSP techniques to separate out the results of each frequency. Measuring the amplitude and relative phase of each of the individual tones yields the amplitude and phase frequency response. By carefully choosing the test frequencies, harmonics produced by each test signal do not fall on other fundamentals or harmonics. FFT spectrum analysis can target each of the resulting harmonics to derive total distortion versus frequency. Since more than one signal is used, distortion includes not only harmonic products but also intermodulation products. Finally, if the analysis is synchronous to the generation and the acquisition record length is twice the generator record length; every odd FFT bin contains only noise, not fundamental or distortion components. Thus, noise in the presence of signal across the spectrum can be measured by summing the energy in all of the odd bins.

The multi-tone measurement technique can yield significant speed advantages over the single tone method. A complete characterization from a battery of tests can be performed in about a second. This rapidity makes this method well suited to production line testing. The only downside of this method is that most test engineers are not familiar with it, and if an existing test procedure prescribes conventional single tone methods, they might be reluctant to use the multitone method. Also, distortion test results may differ from equivalent single tone test results since the device is stressed with a denser test signal. It can be argued that the multitone test signal is closer to actual program material than a single sine wave and thus produces a more realistic test result. But it may be difficult to correlate results produced by multitone distortion test results to traditional single-tone distortion test results.

Log Chirp

A new technique just beginning to gain acceptance is a very fast sine wave sweep sometimes called a *log chirp*. Special DSP techniques are used to generate the signal and analyze the results. With a sweep speed in the order of a second or less, this technique can be as efficient as the multitone technique, but it has the advantage of producing the same results as the conventional but slower single-tone methods. Commercial measurement systems have focused this technique on acoustic analysis applications, but the technique is just beginning to be used for electronic testing applications.

Perceptual (PEAQ)

Test engineers have faced an ongoing concern that objective tests might not always correlate well with subjective perceptions of audio quality. One might always question how much testing to do or how many frequencies to use to capture sufficient information to be able to judge the quality of a device.

Many types of tests can be used to characterize a device including several types of distortion measurements. The resulting battery of test results can present a challenge to interpretation. What test results are most important: frequency response, noise, or distortion? How much degradation of each of these parameters can be tolerated, and at what frequency, before most listeners would consider the quality unacceptable? Is it possible to distill all the common test results into a single figure of merit to assess quality?

Some hold to the opinion that only subjective testing can provide the definitive answer to what is acceptable audio quality. But such testing is very expensive and hard to conduct, and it is difficult to obtain consistent results. It requires hours of testing by trained listeners and a rating method to allow comparison of results. This approach is impractical for most routine engineering test applications.

The International Telecommunications Union (ITU) initially addressed this problem in the context of assessing telephone voice quality and devised a methodology to use objective measurement techniques to produce a single quality number that would agree with the subjective results obtained using the traditional panel of listeners. This technology has now been extended to include audio devices and is called *Perceptual Evaluation of Audio Quality* (PEAQ).

The technique uses short durations (4 to 8 seconds) of regular program material such as speech and music and a sophisticated analysis process that correlates well with perceived quality. The analysis evaluates a short sample of the original signal and the same signal after passing through the device under test. These two signals pass through a *perceptual model* that mimics human hearing to detect audibility. The two processed samples are then compared to extract the difference. This audible difference is then analyzed by a sophisticated *cognitive model* to derive a test score from 1 to 5 where 1 is unacceptable quality and 5 is best quality, indistinguishable from the original. The results from this quick objective test have been demonstrated to agree with the score that a panel of expert listeners would have assigned during a listening test that could take hours to conduct.

While this technique shows promise it does not yet enjoy wide acceptance. It is a new and unfamiliar test technique, and performing the test requires engineering skill. Measurement systems are relatively expensive. But, it is particularly useful for assessing the quality of perceptual codecs that cannot be characterized using conventional audio quality testing methods.

Acoustic Measurements

Electro-acoustical transducers such as speakers and microphones transfer energy between the electrical and physical domains. Various complex problems in assembly and materials may cause problems not only with normal audio parameters such as frequency response and distortion, but also in complex non-linear ways which are quite audible and annoying to humans. Although in PC audio applications, these transducers are typically a low-cost component unto themselves, they are frequently tested because their performance failure will cause the return of an entire laptop PC.

When testing acoustic devices, such as speakers and microphones, traditional sine waves cannot be used unless the testing environment is an anechoic test chamber. When performing such tests in a normal room, two problems can cause significant errors. First, reflections from the walls, floor, and ceiling could add and subtract from the direct signal causing substantial errors. Also standing waves, resulting from interactions of the room dimensions with the wavelength of sound at the specific test frequencies, cause increases and decreases to the measured response not related to the actual device response. Anechoic test chambers have specially treated non-reflective walls, floors, and ceiling to almost completely eliminate reflections and standing waves, at least above a low frequency limit. But such chambers are large and expensive and only available in the best-equipped laboratories.

To overcome this fundamental problem, a number of acoustic measurement techniques have been developed over the years. We won't review each of these—that is, a subject better suited to a book focused on speaker measurements—but we'll look at one of the current most popular and useful techniques.

Broadband Random Noise with Spectrum Analysis

A random noise test signal avoids the standing wave issues caused by a sine wave since the signal frequency is constantly changing and does not dwell at a specific frequency for any significant length of time. This measurement technique uses a ***pink noise*** test signal[2] and a ***real time analyzer*** or RTA to determine the energy in each band across the audio band. This technique was one of the earliest acoustic measurement methods and was first implemented using a parallel bank of band pass filters. Each filter is tuned to a different frequency and the frequencies are evenly distributed across the audio band. The filter bandwidths that determine the instrument's resolution are typically one octave, one-third octave, one-sixth octave, or one-twelfth octave. Later instruments used digitally implemented filters or FFT spectrum analysis techniques to reduce the hardware requirements.

While this technique is technically valid, it is slow and provides limited resolution. For accurate results, the signals measured at the outputs of the filters must be averaged over some period of time, usually seconds. The resolution is proportional to the number of filters used and their individual bandwidths with the highest practical resolution being one-twelfth octave and requiring many seconds of averaging. By replacing the random noise source with a special kind of random noise called pseudo-random noise, the measurement accuracy versus averaging time can be improved. Because pseudo random noise is a fixed sequence that is re-

---

[2] Pink noise has equal energy per octave whereas white noise has equal energy per hertz.

peated with every cycle, averaging need only take a single cycle with full confidence that all parts of the spectrum have been measured.

Maximum Length Sequence (MLS)

A more advanced variation of the random noise measurement technique uses a special digitally generated noise signal and digital analysis techniques. The signal is a mathematical sequence called a ***maximum length sequence*** (MLS) known to include and even distribution of all frequency components over the specified bandwidth. The analysis uses a cross correlation technique to compare the stimulus signal with the received signal and derive the impulse response. From this impulse response, the amplitude and phase frequency response can be derived.

This technique offers both speed and high resolution. Only a short MLS sequence of one or two seconds can provide a very detailed response, far exceeding the twelfth octave response of an RTA. The technique also offers high noise immunity, typically a 45 decibel improvement over a simple impulse noise measurement technique. The noise immunity also makes it well suited for use in a noisy factory production environment. Even with nearby worker conversations and fork lift truck noise, the MLS technique can produce respectable results. And the randomness of the test signal avoids the standing wave errors of sine wave testing. Since the measurement time is quick, it is possible to time window the analysis to reject reflections and the errors they would introduce. Like all acoustic measurement techniques, MLS has a minimum low-frequency point to retain accuracy. Below that point, reflections introduce errors.

Log Chirp

A newer technique, now the favorite of many acoustic engineers, uses a fast swept sine wave called a log chirp (see "Testing Technologies" in this chapter). As mentioned previously, a sine wave is swept over the audio band logarithmically in a second or less and sophisticated analysis techniques are used on the received signal to extract the amplitude and phase response and the distortion. Because the test time is short, the analysis is able to reject reflections from the measurement. This technique also inherently has high noise immunity and produces high-resolution results. Most of the latest generation acoustic audio analyzers use this technique.

Compatibility

With such a wide range of electronic and acoustic measurement techniques, how do results compare? Assuming the techniques are used as designed and within their constraints, amplitude and phase response results should align. Distortion test results can differ since the different stimulus test signals can provoke different behavior in the system under test. In this case, you have no simple way to know which test is more accurate. All of them might give a true representation of the behavior of the device. Then, the discussion might center around which test signal is the best choice. If the goal is to obtain an objective result that most represents the subjective perceived audio quality, one could argue that a test signal with the most similar characteristics to program material, such as music and voice, would be appropriate. Unfortunately, the most common test signals with many years of legacy are simple sine waves, the least similar to program material.

So the compatibility question has no simple answer. The test engineer should be aware of the differences and the difficulty of comparing valid, but different test results and choose a technique suited to the application.

Acoustic Noise Emission testing

The acoustical testing techniques just described relate to audio quality issues, the performance of speakers and microphones forming part of the system. Other acoustical measurements relate to determination of the acoustic noise level produced by parts of the PC system such as the fan and hard drive. A noticeable whine of a fan will certainly detract from listening pleasure. To characterize such noise, use a precision sound level meter or acoustic spectrum analyzer.

Unfortunately, using only a Sound Level meter does not give any information on the frequency and selective intensity of the emissions. Also this should note that sound pressure levels may be taken either "Flat" with no weighting or with a variety of noise weighting curves. Inexpensive handheld audio analyzers are now available which include either selective (1/3 octave) Real Time Analyzers or even FFT spectrum analysis, which each give a better picture of exactly what noise sources are contributing to the overall acoustical noise output. Figure 11.2 shows a handheld acoustic sound level meter and spectrum analyzer that can provide information on both the intensity and frequency spectrum of emitted acoustic noise. The graph on the screen is an FFT spectrum analysis showing the spectral distribution of the noise from the fan of the PC system under test.

Audible Mechanical Defects (Rub & Buzz)

Other complex and very audible defect/failure modes for speakers and microphones are collectively grouped under the category of "rub and buzz." They are part of what may be called aperiodic, non-linear distortions, not easily detectable with any normal distortion measurement methodology. Because they are physically related to the mechanics or technology of a specific transducer type, they could appear only at certain levels and/or with certain stimuli. In addition, their strong correlation to product reject rates is because they are so audible to end users. Their relative audibility is in turn related to the same psychoacoustic masking principles that are known in other areas of the audio arts. Because of this high visibility, certain specialized testing methodologies and systems are used to stimulate transducers with signals that are designed to elicit rub and buzz defects and to analyze them with psychoacoustic masking sensitivities in mind.

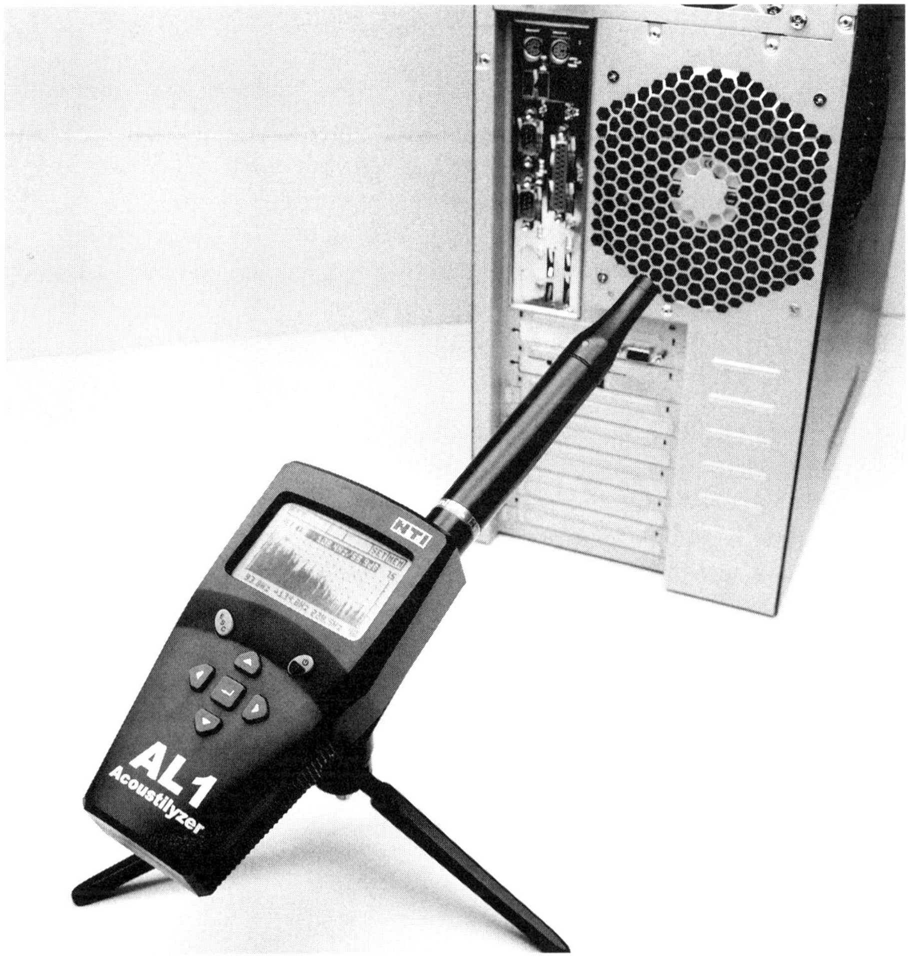

Figure 11.2 Acoustic Level and Spectrum Analyzer from NTI

Testing Intel® HD Audio Systems

You have a frequent need to characterize audio quality and performance of Intel HD Audio systems. During the design stage, it is important to not only assess the relative merits of different designs but also be sure other parameters are not compromised while improving the primary parameter. During the prototype and eventual manufacturing stage, all parameters contributing to audio quality need to be monitored. Marketing departments need to evaluate competitive products comparing performance in the light of target customers. Often, comparing test results can be challenging especially when incomplete information on the test environment is provided.

In addition to obvious factors of the quality of the test equipment, many other factors can influence the accuracy of the test results. The interconnections between the system under test and the test instrument, noise sources close to the test environment, and how the test equipment is set up can all have a significant impact on the test results.

Interfacing to the System Under Test

All audio signal performance measurements on Intel HD Audio systems are cross domain tests. That is, they either use an analog source and digital signal analysis (ADC record or transmit path) or a digital test signal and an analog analysis (DAC playback or receive path). Unlike earlier AC97 systems, Intel HD Audio systems often have no *analog loop through* to permit an analog test signal to be sent to the system under test, looped back to the playback path and tested at the analog output. While such a path may facilitate systems testing using an analog-only test system, it does not separate the paths, and thus makes it impossible to diagnose the source of failed tests. Also, if only the analog input and output is examined, you gain no knowledge of the signal level in the digital domain.

Proper testing requires that this level be accurately set to a prescribed value. This section describes the details of interfacing to both the analog and digital paths to enable optimal establishment of test levels and independent measurements of individual paths.

Analog Interface

Several analog interfaces are on an Intel HD Audio system: at least one stereo line input, one microphone input and at least two independent stereo outputs. Systems intended to be used for entertainment or home theater applications could have additional inputs and outputs. Proper interface to the analog ports ensures reliable and accurate test results.

The analog portion of the Intel HD Audio system includes specific interfaces such as microphone, line, or headset. Each of these may have specific impedances, levels and other conditions that are important for proper testing. Intel HD Audio devices include retasking than can reassign most jacks to different functions. For simplicity when discussing test setup wiring, one assumes a static condition with every jack in a known and fixed state; testing jacks with retasking functionality is more complex.

In Chapter 2, we indicated that analog interfaces used a *voltage transfer* methodology, not power transfer as had been used with early tube-based circuits or that is still used with RF interfaces. This approach suggests that all generator sources have low source impedance and all analyzer inputs have a high input impedance. Since impedances in general are not significant at audio frequencies, you need not *match impedances* as is necessary at higher frequencies such as RF. Although impedance matching is not necessary, constraints still exist on the impedances that are used in test fixtures and in the test instrument for reasons other than matching. The test setup, including all cables, switching, and test instruments, should appear to the system under test similar to the typical external devices connected to it, such as stereo components, headsets, and microphones. Also, loads must be applied to outputs, not for impedance matching, but to stress them as they would be under actual operating conditions.

Figure 11.2 shows a typical test setup connection from an Intel HD Audio system under test to a dual channel audio analyzer. The low-pass filter is shown on each input. This sharp 20-kilohertz low-pass filter is specified by AES-17 to substantially reduce the large out-of-band noise components present in most DAC fed analog outputs. Although this filter is shown in this diagram as an external device inserted between the system under test and the analyzer input, in practice, it is usually included inside the analyzer. It is usually an option, commonly called "AES-17 Low Pass Filter" available on many contemporary audio analyzers.

For line outputs, which include all surround sound outputs, the load impedance should be approximately 10,000 ohms. This is the typical load presented by a stereo component that may be connected to the line-level outputs. Almost all contemporary audio measurement systems have an input impedance of 100,000 ohms, and we assume that the low-pass filter would preserve this input impedance. Adding a parallel 11,000 ohm resistor brings this load impedance to 10,000 ohms. The actual resistor value would have to be 11,111 ohms to achieve 10,000 ohms, but the small error, less than one-percent, caused by using a standard value of 11,000 ohms is insignificant.

If headset outputs are being tested, they should be loaded with a 32 Ω resistor with sufficient power handling capacity to accommodate the power output of the device. Figure 11.3 shows the test setup.

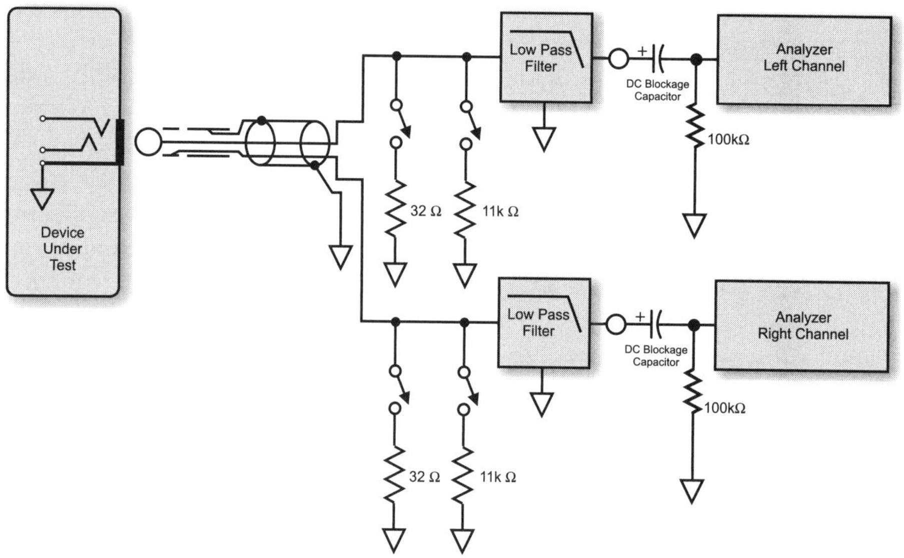

Figure 11.3 Interfacing System Outputs to Audio Analyzer Inputs

Figure 11.4 shows the connection from a two-channel audio generator to a stereo input of an Intel HD Audio system. This diagram represents the typical wiring for either line or microphone inputs, although microphone inputs would require the additional bias voltage testing circuitry shown in Figure 11.5.

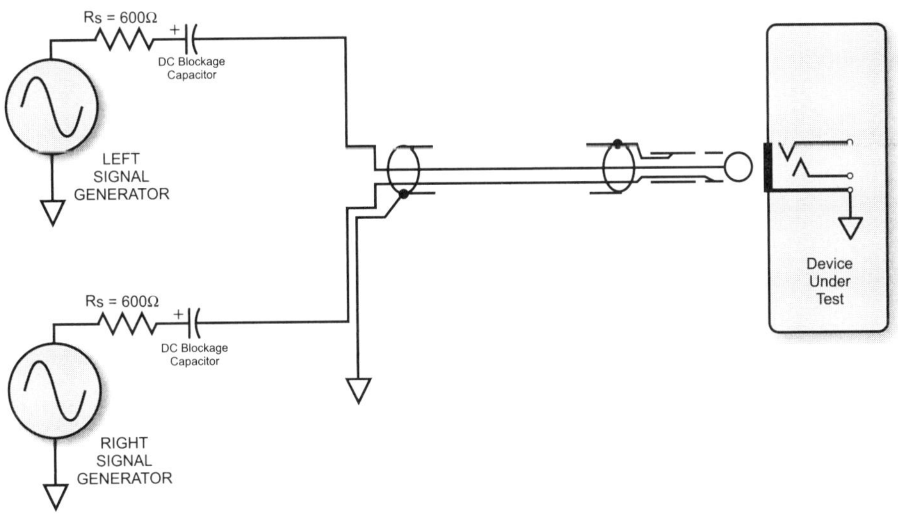

Figure 11.4 Interfacing Audio Generator Outputs to System Inputs

Microphone Input

To test microphone inputs, two parameters must be measured: the audio channel performance and the DC bias supply. To test audio performance, the audio signal generator should have a source impedance of 600 Ω to simulate the impedance of a typical microphone and be able to provide signal levels at a low level, typically -60 dBV to -40 dBV. Figure 11.5 shows the test connections for a mono microphone input. Since the microphone input often has a DC bias supply voltage on the same wire as the signal, the generator must have an AC-coupled output, which generally is accomplished by using an output capacitor as shown in the diagram. The bias supply voltage, usually present on the ring of the 3.5 mm phone jack, must provide an unloaded voltage not exceeding 5.5V. This voltage is typically 4V. The bias supply must also be able to source a current of 800 microamps with a voltage not less than 2 VDC. By applying a load resistor of 2500 ohms and measuring a voltage of 2 VDC or greater under this loaded condition, the required current sourcing ability can be confirmed.

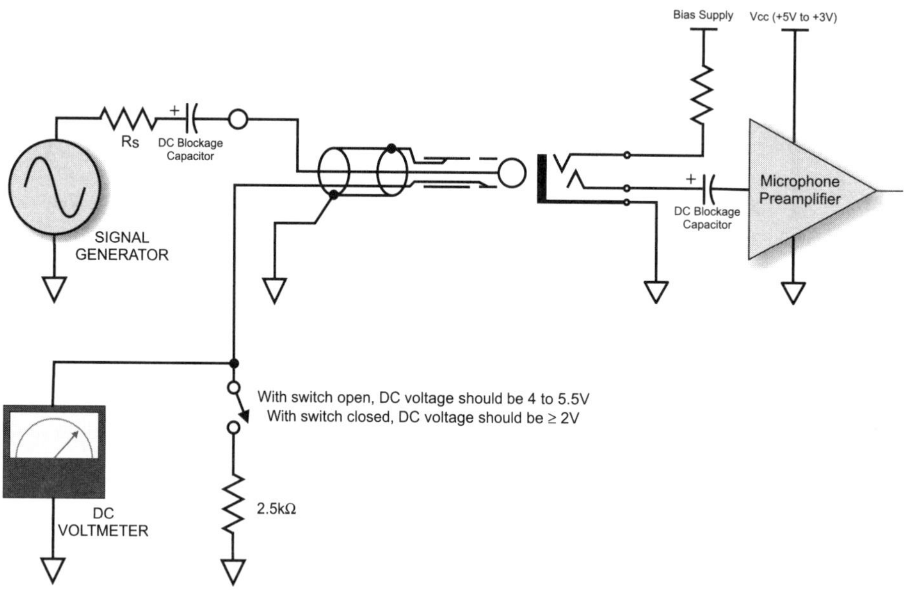

Figure 11.5 Test Setup for a Mono Microphone Input

For a stereo microphone input, the signal and bias supply share the same wire. Figure 11.6 shows the test setup for a stereo microphone. Although the diagram for simplicity shows a single test generator and a switch to select the channel to be tested, testing efficiencies can be achieved using a dual channel generator. Although the signal generator output coupling capacitor might not be required in all mono applications, it is required in all stereo applications because the bias DC voltage is always present on the signal path.

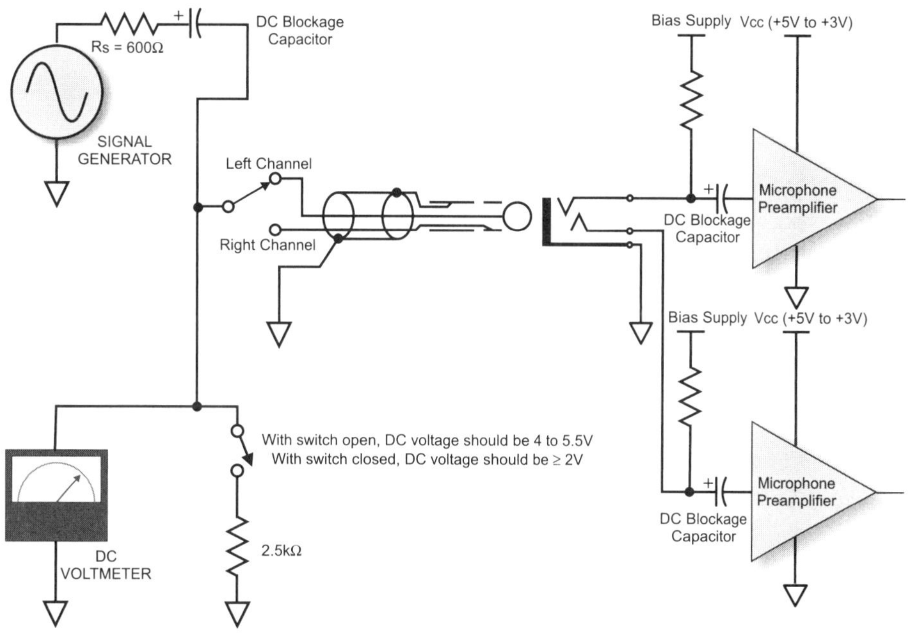

Figure 11.6 Test Setup for a Stereo Microphone Input

Digital Interface

Intel HD Audio systems may have some combination of S/PDIF output and/or S/PDIF input. These may be electrical, often called coaxial and appearing on orange color coded RCA jacks, or optical using TOSLINK† connectors. The most common configuration is to provide a single S/PDIF output, either electrical or optical.

Interfacing to the Digital Domain

All tests are cross domain. As such, connectivity must be established between the test instrument and the digital bus in the Intel HD Audio system. While connectivity to all of the analog signals easily is accomplished using the readily accessible appropriate analog jack, interface to the digital domain is not as obvious or consistent among systems. S/PDIF interfaces are not commonly present for both inputs and outputs. You have four methods to accomplish connectivity to the digital domain. Here is a description of each.

S/PDIF Interface

If both the system under test and the audio measurement system include S/PDIF digital inputs and outputs, establishing connectivity using these interfaces is the easiest. The only downside to this technique, apart from the fact that not all devices provide these interfaces, is that the path is not direct to the DAC or from the ADC but must pass through the AES3 transceiver. Also, the standard routing in a PC audio system does not allow for an ADC's digital output to be connected directly to the system's S/PDIF Outputs, or for the system's S/PDIF input to be connected directly to the digital input of a DAC. While some codecs do include this routing as a possible option, special software would be required to activate these routings, as they are not useful to end users, and would only be confusing if made available as options.

Some devices may include additional processing or sample rate conversion that may influence the embedded signal making it difficult to diagnose the source of errors. Using S/PDIF Inputs and Outputs instead of ADCs and DACs is especially useful for testing software audio fidelity, since it excludes all sources of analog signal degradation. See Figure 11.7 for a simplified test setup diagram.

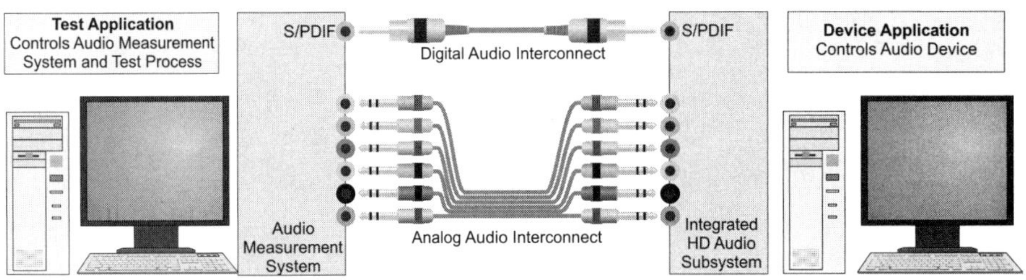

Figure 11.7 Digital Connectivity by S/PDIF Interface

File Transfer

If the audio measurement system includes the ability to generate test signals as .wav files and analyze the embedded audio in a .wav file, this method may be used. Test signals are developed by the audio measurement system and saved as test files. These files may be played back through the digital-to-analog converters to produce analog signals which are then fed to the analog analyzer. To test the record side, an analog test signal is developed by the audio generator, fed to the analog inputs of the system under test, and the signal is recorded on a hard drive. This file is then sent to the analyzer for analysis.

The downside of this method is that it is not real-time. Several successive steps and impromptu changes to the test signal require generating new files, a time consuming process. Figure 11.8 illustrates the concept.

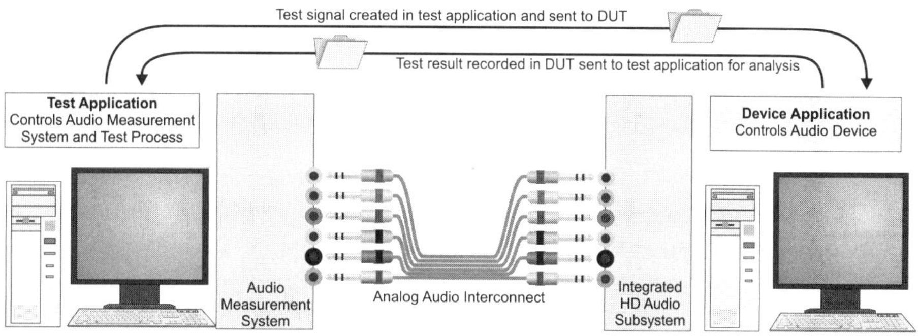

Figure 11.8 Digital Connectivity by File Transfer

Software Generator and Analyzer

This technique runs an application on the system under test that generates signals and feeds them to the DAC and analyzes signals from the ADC. No commercial products are available to do this testing with sufficient quality and provide the variety of test signals and analysis needed for comprehensive testing. The application must be compatible with the operating system that is running on the system under test. Microsoft uses this technique in various WHQL audio tests, and the quality is suitable for most basic measurements. Figure 11.9 show the software technique.

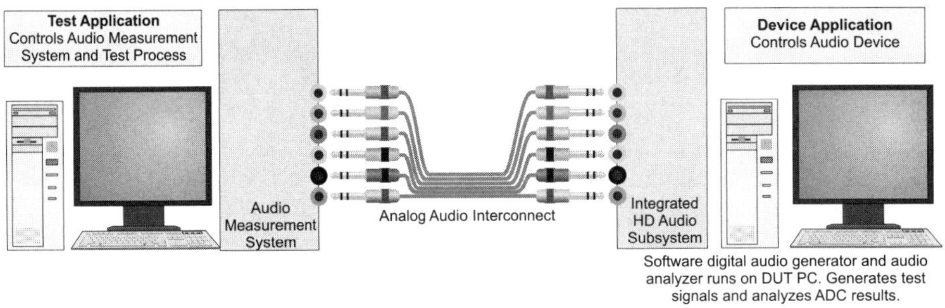

Figure 11.9 Digital Connectivity by Software Generator and Analyzer

DCOM Connectivity between the SUT and the Test Instrument.

This method establishes a Distributed Common Object Model (DCOM) or Remote Procedure Call (RPC) link between the PC system under test and the PC running the test application software. This method is the most flexible and efficient, but it is not commonly available.

Microsoft uses this approach in conjunction with software analyzer and generator on the SUT to accomplish audio fidelity testing. This method is used for the Lullaby/ACPI audio tests in Windows XP, as well as for upcoming Windows Vista logo tests. Figure 11.10 shows digital connectivity by DCOM.

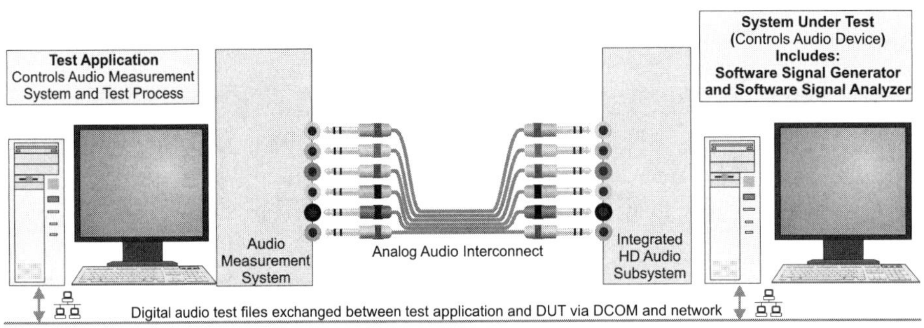

Figure 11.10 Digital Connectivity by DCOM or RPC Network Interface

Separating the Paths

To properly characterize a High Definition Audio system, the individual paths should be separately evaluated. These paths may be divided into record, or A to D paths, and playback, or D to A paths. Additionally, several of each of these paths must be independently evaluated.

Test Setup

Figure 11.11 illustrates a typical test setup. The system under test is shown in the center. The shaded area illustrates the minimal paths that must be present in an Intel HD Audio system. A home theater media PC is likely to have most or all of the paths shown in this block diagram.

Surrounding the system under test are signal switchers used to route the generator test signals to the system under test (SUT) inputs and to route the SUT outputs to the audio measurement system. Most contemporary audio measurement systems are two-channel while Intel HD Audio systems are six (5.1) or eight (7.1) channels, requiring that pairs of channels be selected in sequence. The quality of these switches must be such as to not degrade the audio signal and inter-channel crosstalk must be below the residual of the test instrument (typically better than -120 decibels). This test method requires careful switcher design, close attention to grounding details, extensive shielding, double path relay switches, and careful circuit board layout not found in simple signal switches. Audio test equipment manufacturers can supply such special purpose switchers.

In addition to signal switching, particular channels might have to be loaded with specific impedances to simulate actual use conditions. For example, line outputs should be loaded with 10 kΩ and headphone outputs with 32 ohms. Microphone inputs require that the bias supply be measured open circuit and loaded. When you add the fact that most of the analog jacks are retaskable, this switching facility can be formidable. The following diagram illustrates a typical test set up. It does not address the switching required for testing retaskable jacks.

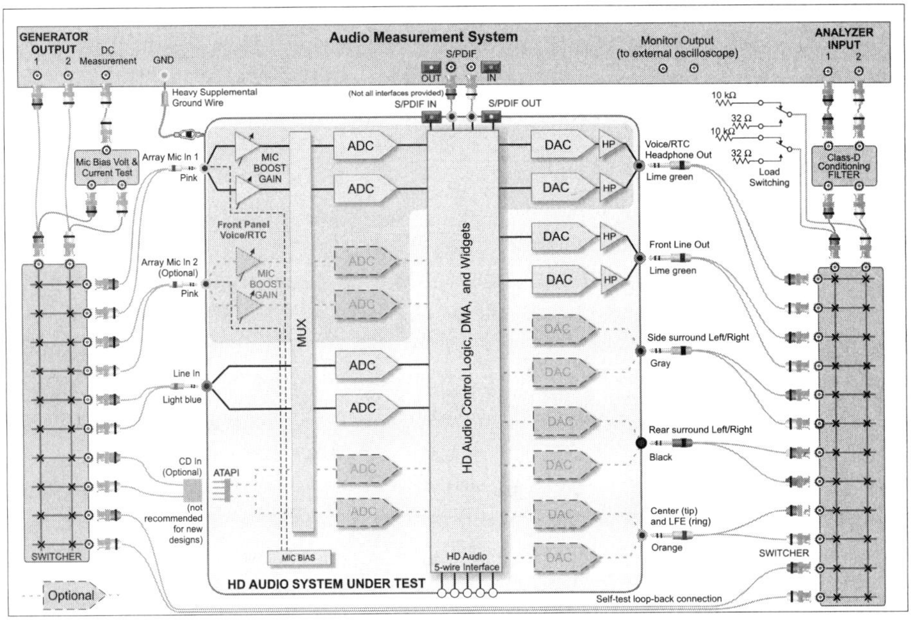

Figure 11.11 Typical Test Setup

Establishing Reference Levels

Almost all measurements require that a level reference first be established. In Chapter 1, we introduced the concept of Reference Levels and how they influence Dynamic Range and Signal-to-Noise measurements. We explained some of the difficulties establishing a reference level when the system included digital limiting (see Figure 1.12). Standards define the test level that should be used for a particular measurement and dynamic range, and distortion measurements are made with respect to a defined reference level.

For digital audio circuits, the reference level is generally established as *digital full scale*, which is the level that produces the maximum digital code value. For analog circuits, different recommendations have been used over the years but most refer to a level *below clipping*, the analog equivalent of *full scale*. Unfortunately, the signal level that causes clipping in an analog circuit can often be soft, subject to some interpretation. Add to this the fact that many digital systems include some compression algorithms that prevent the level from ever reaching digital full scale.

This precaution should be taken against the unpleasant audible effects that would occur if music program content reached and tried to exceed this level. As a result, an accurate and definitive establishment of reference level requires a definition more complete than simply *full scale*.

AES 17, the reference standard for digital audio measurements, recommends that *full-scale amplitude* be established as that level that just produces • 40 decibels, or 1 percent, THD+N or 0.3 decibels of compression, which would apply only if a compressor or limiter is implemented in the converter. This amplitude effectively defines a repeatable method for establishing a universally agreed maximum level, full scale level, or clipping level.

Determination of this level is the first step in any characterization exercise. Accurately establishing this level ensures that noise and distortion measurements are repeatable and consistent.

A number of assumptions can be made when testing integrated Intel HD Audio systems that simplify the process of establishing reference levels.

- Desktop PCs use a 5V analog power supply for the codec, while laptops typically use a power supply between 4.0 and 4.75 volts. This difference has a practical effect of limiting maximum RMS voltage of the codecs to just under 1.4V RMS, or +3 dBV.
- The Intel HD Audio specification requires all volume widgets to default to their unity gain settings and also provides a mechanism to reliably set the codec to unity gain.

Thus, most systems can be directly referenced to 1 volt, or 0 dBV, thereby simplifying the measurements by allowing the readings to be taken directly in units of dBV and dBFS. This approach eliminates the need for a complex and tedious reference-setting procedure, and ensures a uniform absolute noise floor when this approach is applied to many computers.

Use absolute dBV values for a true comparison of noise floors between two different computers. The unit with the higher noise floor measured in dBV sounds noisier when plugged into the same high-quality speaker system. If the dynamic range is calculated relative to 1-percent distortion level, you can't really compare the noise floor of the two units, especially if the resulting reference levels are very different.

Detailed Test Procedure Descriptions

Up to now, we have discussed testing practices in general, how to avoid common problems, what tests should be performed, and how they relate to perceived quality. The following pages describe in detail how to apply these tests to characterizing High Definition Audio systems.

ADC Frequency Response

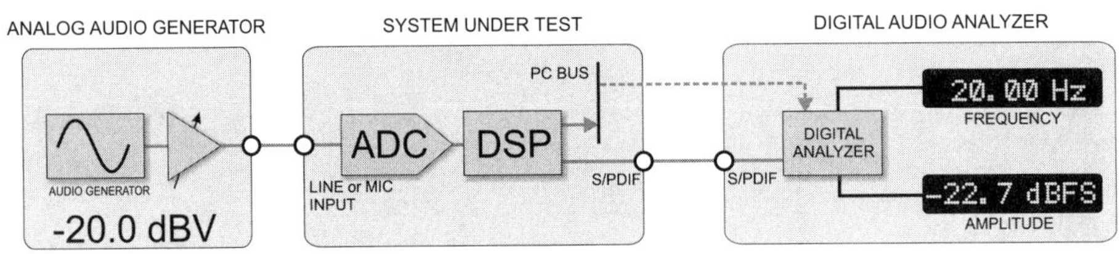

Figure 11.12 ADC Amplitude Frequency Response Setup

Description: This test characterizes the amplitude frequency response of the record or Analog to Digital path of a PC audio system. This test should be performed on each analog input or channel of the system.

Test Signal: The test signal is a single sine wave that is swept across the audio band.

Measurement Process: The measurement records the amplitude of the digital audio signal at the output of the ADC and plots this reading against the test frequency on a graph.

Setup Notes: The test signal is connected to the analog input of the system. Access to the digital signal at the output of the ADC can be either by using the S/PDIF serial digital output if available or by tapping into the PC digital bus.

Procedure: Normally, this test is conducted at a level 20 dB below digital full scale. First, establish what analog level at the input to be tested is necessary to produce a full-scale digital output from the ADC. Then set the audio generator to a level 20 dB lower than this full-scale level and sweep its frequency from 20 Hz to 20 kHz while measuring the amplitude of the digital audio signal at the digital output. If you are measuring using the S/PDIF serial data stream, the measurement is of the amplitude of the digitized embedded audio in the data stream, not the data carrier.

Reporting results: Test results may be reported as a graph or numerically. Graphical results should display a graph with a log frequency axis from 20 Hz to 20 kHz and a vertical axis linear in dB. The mid-point of the vertical axis should be 0 dB. The top and bottom limits of the vertical axis should be such that they show response variations over the frequency range. Typical axis values would be ±2 dB or ±5 dB. The response trace should be normalized such that the response at 1 kHz passes through 0 dB.

Numerical results should indicate the maximum normalized deviation relative to 1 kHz over the 20 Hz to 20 kHz frequency range. The graph in Figure 11.13 is a typical report.

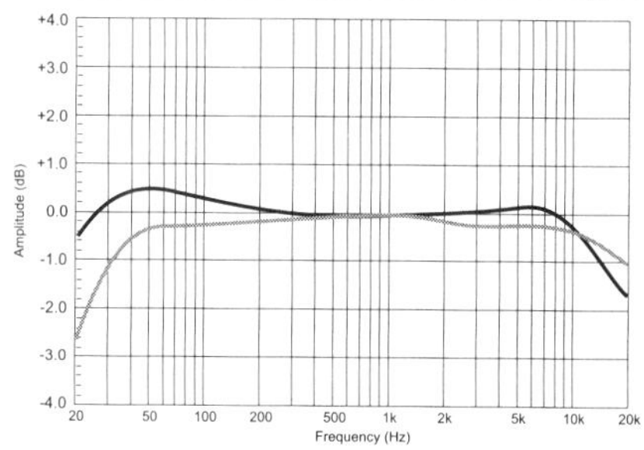

Frequency Response, 20 Hz to 20 kHz:	± 2.5 dB, relative to 1 kHz

Figure 11.13 Typical Report for ADC Amplitude Frequency Response Test

ADC Dynamic Range

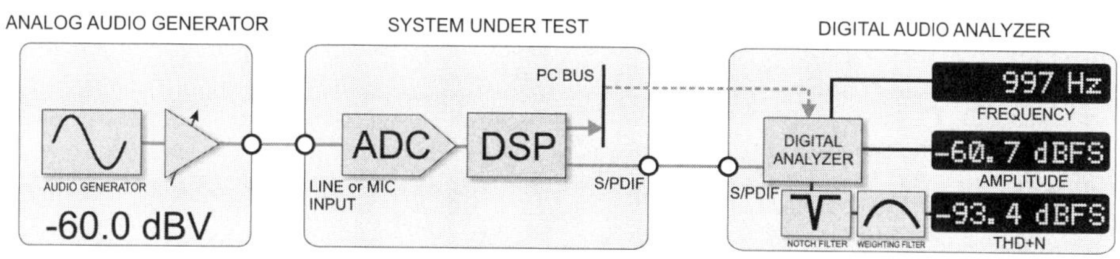

Figure 11.14 ADC Dynamic Range Test Setup

Description: This test characterizes the dynamic range of the record or Analog to Digital path of a PC audio system. This test should be performed on each analog input of the system.

Note

Dynamic range is similar to and is a replacement for the traditional "signal-to-noise ratio" test used to characterize analog systems.

Test Signal: The test signal is a single low-amplitude analog sine wave at 997 kHz. Except when testing microphone gain stages, the ADC input level should be set to 0 dB or unity gain, which is often the lowest setting of the input gain slider.

Measurement Process: The measurement acquires the digital audio signal at the output of the ADC and measures the THD+N of this signal. Since the amplitude of the test signal is very low, distortion components are below the noise floor and the measurement is actually noise.

Setup Notes: The test signal from the analog generator is connected to the analog input of the SUT. Access to the digital signal at the output of the ADC can be either by using the S/PDIF serial digital output if available or by using a software signal analyzer installed on the SUT.

Procedure: This test is conducted at a level 60 dB below reference level. First, establish what analog level at the input to be tested is necessary to produce a full scale digital output from the ADC. Then set the audio generator to a level 60 decibels lower than this full scale level and a frequency of 997 hertz. If taking readings relative to one volt RMS, simply use an analog signal level of -60 dBV. Measure the THD+N of the digital audio signal in dB or dBFS at the digital output of the ADC. Use a noise weighting filter for this measurement. If you are measuring using the S/PDIF serial data stream, the measurement is of the THD+N of the digitized embedded audio in the data stream, not the data carrier.

Reporting results: Test results are reported numerically as a negative number. Report the results in dBFS if the reading is taken referenced to one volt RMS (0 dBV) or report the results in relative dB (no suffix) if they are taken relative to a reference level other than 1 volt RMS. The following is a typical report.

Dynamic Range	-93 dBFS, A-weighted

ADC THD+N Distortion

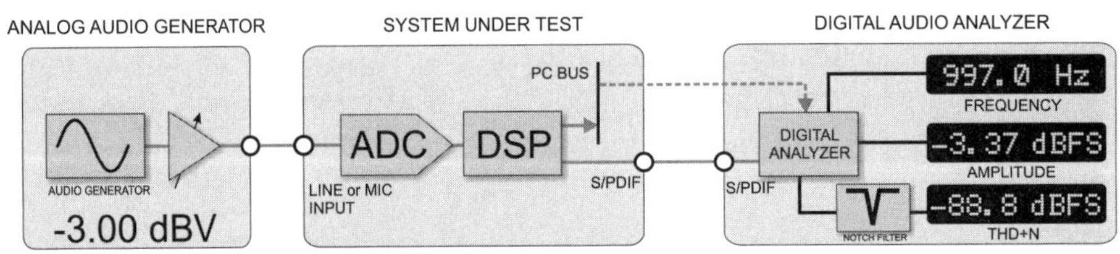

Figure 11.15 ADC THD+N Test Setup

Description: This test characterizes the total harmonic distortion plus noise (THD+N) of the record or Analog to Digital path of a PC audio system. This test should be performed on each analog input of the system.

Test Signal: The test signal is a single sine wave at several test frequencies from 20 Hz to 1/3 of the maximum bandwidth of the system. Except when testing microphone gain stages, the ADC input level should be set to 0 dB or unity gain, which is often the lowest setting of the input gain slider.

Measurement Process: The measurement acquires the digital audio signal at the output of the ADC and measures the THD+N of this signal. The measurement technique may use a DSP implemented notch filter or FFT spectrum analysis to derive the amplitude of harmonics of the test signal.

Setup Notes: The test signal from the analog generator is connected to the analog input of the SUT. Access to the digital signal at the output of the ADC can be either by using the S/PDIF serial digital output if available or by using a software signal analyzer installed on the SUT.

Procedure: This test normally is conducted at a level 3 dB below digital full scale. First, establish what analog level at the input to be tested is necessary to produce a full-scale digital output from the ADC. Then set the audio generator to a level 3 dB lower than this full-scale level and sweep the frequency from 20 Hz to the maximum fundamental test frequency, which should be one-third of the device bandwidth, typically 20 kHz. If measuring relative to one volt RMS, simply use an analog signal level of -3 dBV.

Measure the THD+N of the digital audio signal in dB or dBFS at the digital output. If you are measuring using the S/PDIF serial data stream, the measurement is of the THD+N of the digitized embedded audio in the data stream, not the data carrier.

Reporting results: Test results should be reported graphically and numerically. Graphical results should display a graph with a log frequency axis from 20 Hz to 10 kHz or less and a vertical axis linear in dB. The top and bottom limits of the vertical axis should be such that they show THD+N variations over the frequency range. Typical axis values would be -100 dB to -40 dB.

Report the results in dBFS if the reading is taken referenced to one volt RMS (0 dBV) or report the results in relative dB (no suffix) if they are taken relative to a reference level other than 1 volt RMS. The graph in Figure 11.16 is a typical report:

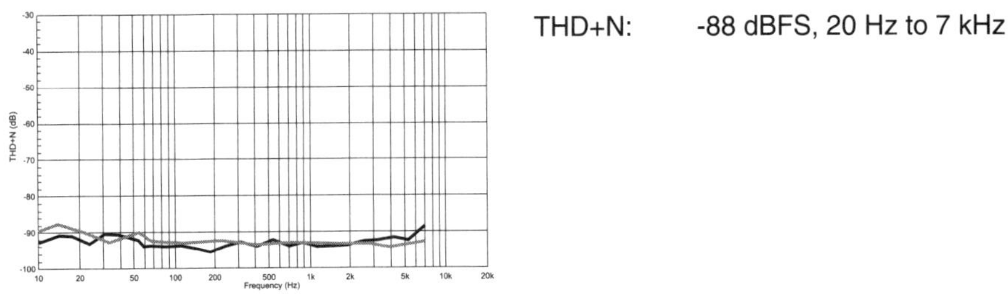

Figure 11.16 Typical Report for ADC THD+N Test

ADC Intermodulation Distortion

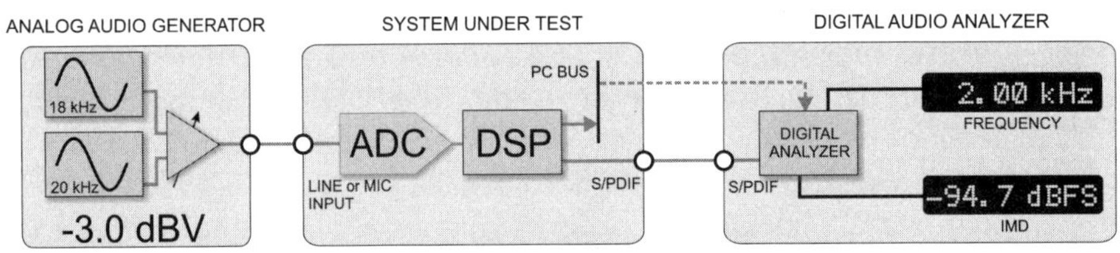

Figure 11.17 ADC IMD Test Setup

Description: This test characterizes the intermodulation distortion of the record or Analog to Digital path of a PC audio system. This test should be performed on each analog input or channel of the system. This test is useful to characterize the high-frequency distortion of the system since THD+N techniques are not able to determine distortion above approximately 7 kHz.

Test Signal: The test signal is a twin-tone signal composed of two equal amplitude sine waves of 18 kHz and 20 kHz. Except when testing microphone gain stages, the ADC input level should be set to 0 dB or unity gain, which is often the lowest setting of the input gain slider.

Measurement Process: The measurement acquires the digital audio signal at the output of the ADC and measures the IMD of this signal. The process measures second, third, and fourth order difference IMD components.

Setup Notes: The test signal from the analog generator is connected to the analog input of the SUT. Access to the digital signal at the output of the ADC can be either by using the S/PDIF serial digital output if available or by using a software signal analyzer installed on the SUT.

Procedure: This test is normally conducted at a level 3 dB below digital full scale. First, establish what analog level at the input to be tested is necessary to produce a full scale digital output from the ADC. Then set the audio generator to a level 3 dB lower than this full-scale level and a twin-tone frequency of 18 kHz and 20 kHz. If measuring relative to one volt RMS, simply use an analog signal level of -3 dBV.

Measure the IMD of the digital audio signal in dB or dBFS at the digital output. For stimulus frequencies of 18 and 20 kHz, IMD components occur at 2 kHz, 4 kHz, 14 kHz, and 16 kHz. If you are measuring using the S/PDIF serial data stream, the measurement is of the IMD of the digitized embedded audio in the data stream, not the data carrier.

Reporting results: Test results are reported numerically. Report the results in dBFS if the reading is taken referenced to one volt RMS (0 dBV) or report the results in relative dB (no suffix) if they are taken relative to a reference level other than 1 volt RMS. The following is a typical report.

Intermodulation Distortion -94 dBFS, (18 kHz and 20 kHz)

ADC Interchannel Phase Response

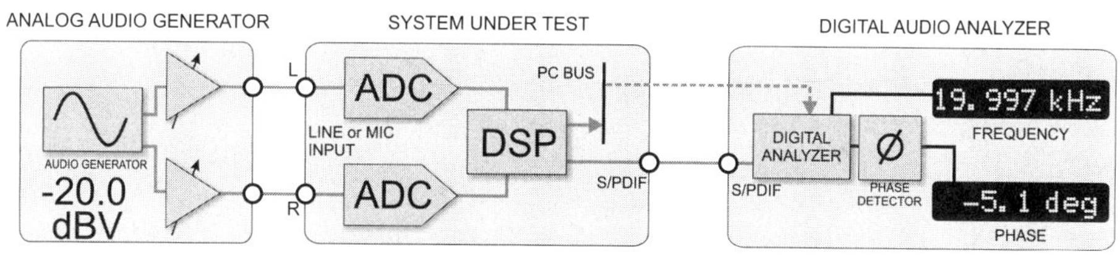

Figure 11.18 ADC Interchannel Phase Response

Description: This test characterizes the phase difference between two channels of the record or Analog to Digital path of a PC audio system. This test should be performed on each analog input or channel of the system with respect to a reference channel. The reference channel can be any of the available channels. The right-front channel is the most common reference.

Test Signal: The test signal is a single analog sine wave swept over the audio band, typically 20 Hz to 20 kHz, and fed simultaneously to the two channels being tested. Except when testing microphone gain stages, the ADC input level should be set to 0 dB or unity gain, which is often the lowest setting of the input gain slider.

Measurement Process: The measurement acquires the digital audio signal at the output of the ADC. An S/PDIF signal contains two channels of information sent in alternate frames.

Setup Notes: The test signal from the analog generator is connected to the analog input of the SUT. Access to the digital signal at the output of the ADC can be either by using the S/PDIF serial digital output if available or by using a software signal analyzer installed on the SUT.

Procedure: This test is normally conducted at a level 20 dB below digital full scale. First, establish what analog level at the input to be tested is necessary to produce a full scale digital output from the ADC. Then set the audio generator to a level 20 dB lower than this full-scale level and sweep the frequency from 20 Hz to 20 kHz. If measuring relative to one volt RMS, simply use an analog signal level of -20 dBV. Measure the phase difference between the two channels at the digital output. If you are measuring using the S/PDIF serial data stream, the measurement is of the phase of the digitized embedded audio in the data stream, not the data carrier.

Reporting results: Test results can be reported graphically and numerically. Graphical results should display a graph with a log frequency axis from 20 Hz to 20 kHz and a vertical axis linear in degrees. The top and bottom limits of the vertical axis should be such that they show phase variations over the frequency range. Typical axis values would be ±20 deg.

The graph in Figure 11.19 is a typical report.

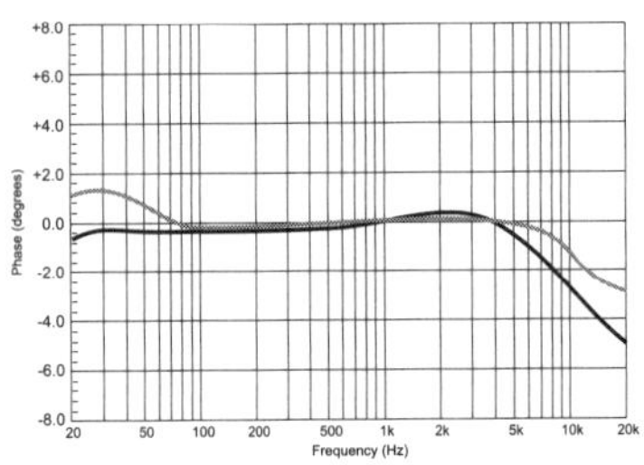

Interchannel phase difference (left to right)	±5 degrees, 20 Hz to 20 kHz

Figure 11.19 Typical Report for ADC Inter-channel Phase Response Test

ADC Interchannel Crosstalk

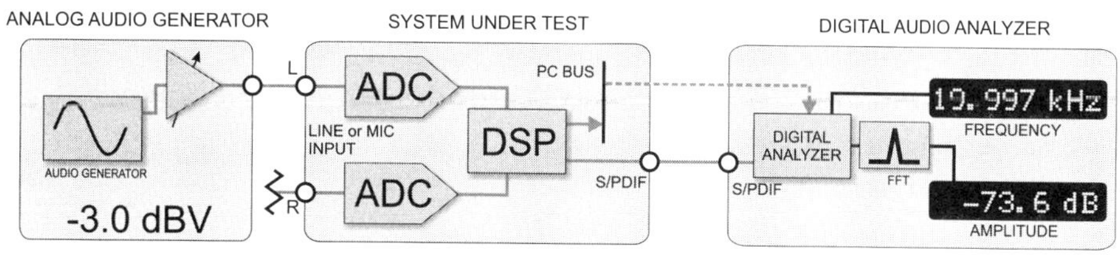

Figure 11.20 ADC Interchannel Crosstalk Test Setup

Description: This test characterizes the leakage of one channel into another channel of the record or Analog to Digital path of a PC audio system. This test should be performed on each analog input of the system.

Test Signal: The test signal is an analog sine wave swept from 20 Hz to 20 kHz. Except when testing microphone gain stages, the ADC input level should be set to 0 dB or unity gain, which is often the lowest setting of the input gain slider.

Measurement Process: The test signal is applied to one or more active inputs or channels while the channel under test receives no signal and has its input terminated. The measurement acquires the digital audio signal at the output of the ADC and measures the level of the signal in this terminated channel compared to stimulated channels. A band pass filter tuned to the stimulus signal is used to suppress broadband noise and enhance the accuracy.

Setup Notes: The test signal from the analog generator is connected to the active analog input(s) of the SUT, and the input under test is terminated. Access to the digital signal at the output of the ADC can be either by using the S/PDIF serial digital output if available or by using a software signal analyzer installed on the SUT.

Procedure: This test is conducted at a level 3 dB below digital full scale for best noise immunity, normally. First, establish what analog level at the input to be tested is necessary to produce a full-scale digital output from the ADC. Then set the audio generator to a level 3 dB lower than this full scale-level and sweep the signal from 20 Hz to 20 kHz. If measuring relative to one volt RMS, simply use an analog signal level of -3 dBV.

Measure the level of the digital audio signal in dB in the test channel at the digital output. If you are measuring using the S/PDIF serial data stream, the measurement is of the crosstalk of the digitized embedded audio in the data stream, not the data carrier.

Reporting results: Test results are reported graphically and numerically in relative dB (no suffix). Graphical results should display a graph with a log frequency axis from 20 Hz to 20 kHz and a vertical axis linear in dB. The top and bottom limits of the vertical axis should be such that they show crosstalk variations over the frequency range. Typical axis values would be -100 dB to -40 dB.

Figure 11.21 is a typical report.

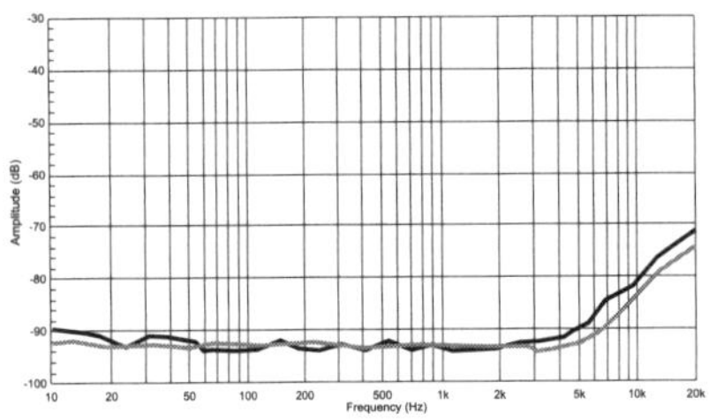

Crosstalk (left to right):	-74 dB, maximum over 20 Hz to 20 kHz

Figure 11.21 Typical Report for ADC Inter-channel Crosstalk Test

Digital to Analog (Playback) Paths

The following tests characterize the digital to analog converter or playback path of the system under test.

DAC Frequency Response

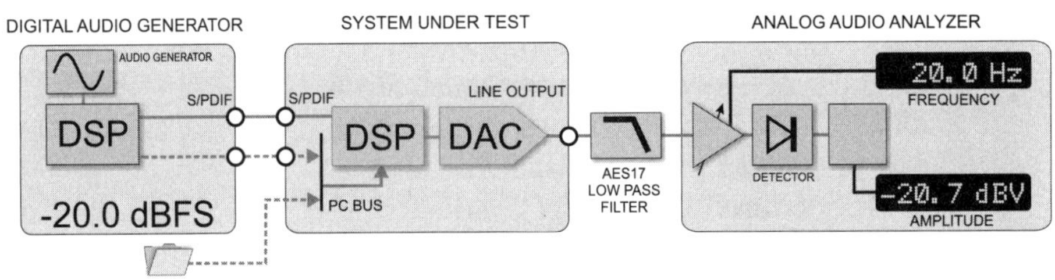

Figure 11.22 DAC Frequency Response Test Setup

Description: This test characterizes the amplitude frequency response of the play or Digital to Analog path of a PC audio system. This test should be performed on each analog output of the system under test.

Test Signal: The test signal is a digital sine wave that is swept across the audio band. It may be supplied to the SUT from a software signal generator directly driving the Intel HD Audio bus or from a file in memory of the PC that is played back.

Measurement Process: The measurement records the amplitude of the analog audio signal at the output of the DAC and plots this measurement against the test frequency on a graph.

Setup Notes: The test signal is sent to the digital input of the DAC using either of test signal methods outlined above. A 20 kHz low pass filter, such as specified by AES-17, should be included in the measurement path, either between the SUT and the measurement instrument, or as part of the measurement instrument itself.

Procedure: This test is normally conducted at a level 20 dB below digital full scale. Set the digital audio generator to a level of -20 dBFS and sweep its frequency from 20 Hz to 20 kHz while measuring the amplitude of the analog audio signal at the line output. Alternative, use a .WAV file that contains a swept sine wave at -20 dBFS and set the analyzer to *external sweep mode* so that it tracks the analog sweep.

Reporting results: Test results may be reported as a graph or numerically. Graphical results should display a graph with a log frequency axis from 20 Hz to 20 kHz and a vertical axis linear in dB. The mid-point of the vertical axis should be 0 dB. The top and bottom limits of the vertical axis should be such that they show response variations over the frequency range. Typical axis values would be ±2 dB or ±5 dB. The response trace should be normalized such that the response at 1 kHz passes through 0 dB. Numerical results should indicate the maximum normalized deviation relative to 1 kHz over the 20 Hz to 20 kHz frequency range. The report in Figure 11.23 is typical.

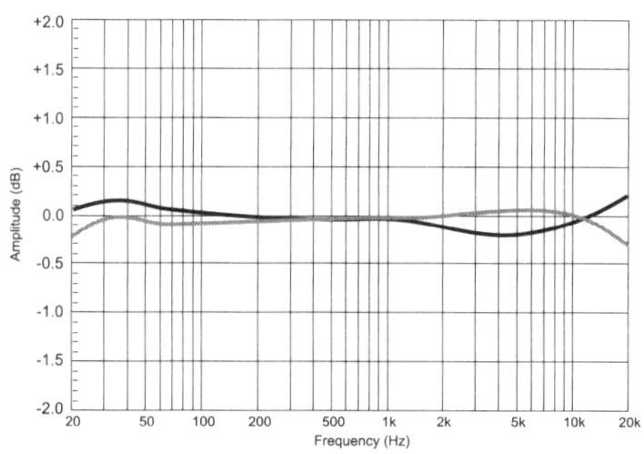

Frequency Response, 20 Hz to 20 kHz — ± 1 dB, relative to 1 kHz

Figure 11.23 Typical Report for DAC Frequency Response Test

DAC Dynamic Range

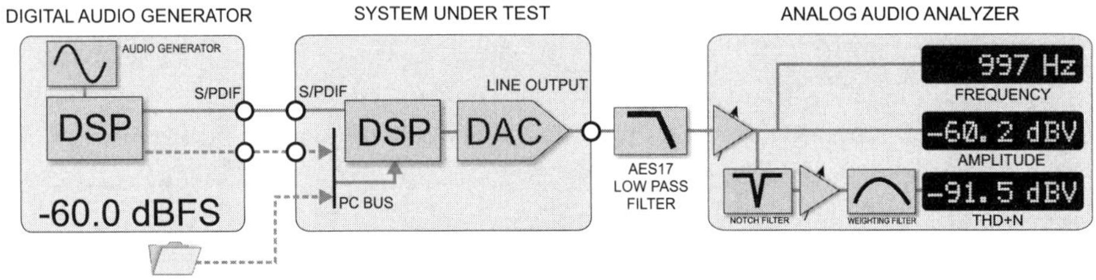

Figure 11.24 DAC Dynamic Range Test Setup

Description: This test characterizes the dynamic range of the play or Digital to Analog path of a PC audio system. This test should be performed on each analog output of the system. Be aware that dynamic range is similar to and a replacement for the traditional "signal-to-noise ratio" test used to characterize analog devices.

Test Signal: The test signal is a single low-amplitude digital sine wave at 997 kHz. It may be supplied to the SUT from a software signal generator directly driving the Intel HD Audio bus or from a file in memory of the PC that is played back. All volume controls–including Wave in Windows XP–should be set to unity gain, which is normally the maximum setting. For hardware testing, all signal processing should be disabled.

Measurement Process: This process measures the analog THD+N at the line out of the system. Since the amplitude of the test signal is very low, distortion components are below the noise floor and the measurement is actually noise.

Setup Notes: The test signal is sent to the digital input of the DAC using either of test signal methods outlined above. A 20 kHz low pass filter, such as specified by AES-17, should be included in the measurement path either between the SUT and the measurement instrument or as part of the measurement instrument itself.

Procedure: This test is conducted at a level 60 dB below digital full scale. Set the digital audio generator to a level of -60 dBFS and a frequency of 997 kHz. Measure the THD+N of the audio signal in dB or dBV at the analog output of the system under test. Use a noise weighting filter for this measurement.

Reporting results: Test results are reported numerically. Report the results in dBV if the reading is taken referenced to one volt RMS (0 dBV) or report the results in relative dB (no suffix) if they are taken relative to a reference level other than 1 volt RMS. The following is a typical report.

Dynamic Range -91 dBV, A-weighted

DAC THD+N

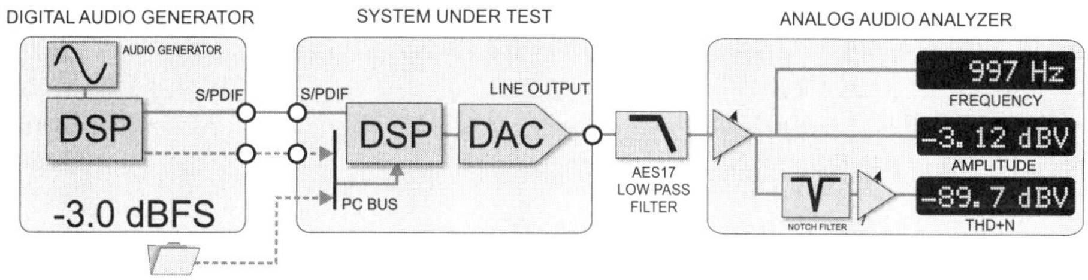

Figure 11.25 DAC THD+N Test Setup

Description: This test characterizes the THD+N versus frequency of the play or Digital to Analog path of a PC audio system. This test should be performed on each analog output of the system.

Test Signal: The test signal is a digital sine wave that is swept across the audio band. It may be supplied to the SUT from a software signal generator directly driving the Intel HD Audio bus or from a file in memory of the PC that is played back. All volume controls–including Wave in Windows XP–should be set to unity gain, which is normally the maximum setting. For hardware testing, all signal processing should be disabled.

Measurement Process: The process measures the THD+N of the analog line out signal at the output of the DAC. A notch filter is swept across the audio band tracking the stimulus test signal.

Setup Notes: The test signal is sent to the digital input of the DAC using either of test signal methods outlined above. A 20 kHz low pass filter, such as specified by AES-17, should be included in the measurement path, either between the SUT and the measurement instrument, or as part of the measurement instrument itself.

Procedure: This test is normally conducted at a level 3 dB below digital full scale. Set the audio generator to a level of -3 dBFS and sweep the signal from 20 Hz to approximately 1/3 of the bandwidth of the system. Typical sweep range for a 20 kHz band limited system will be 20 Hz to 7 kHz. Measure the THD+N of the audio signal in dB or dBV at the line out.

Reporting results: Test results are reported graphically and numerically. Graphical results should display a graph with a log frequency axis from 20 Hz to 10 kHz or less and a vertical axis linear in dB. The top and bottom limits of the vertical axis should be such that they show THD+N variations over the frequency range. Typical axis values would be -100 dB to -40 dB.

Report the results in dBV if the reading is taken referenced to one volt RMS (0 dBV) or report the results in relative dB (no suffix) if they are taken relative to a reference level other than 1 volt RMS. Figure 11.26 shows a typical report.

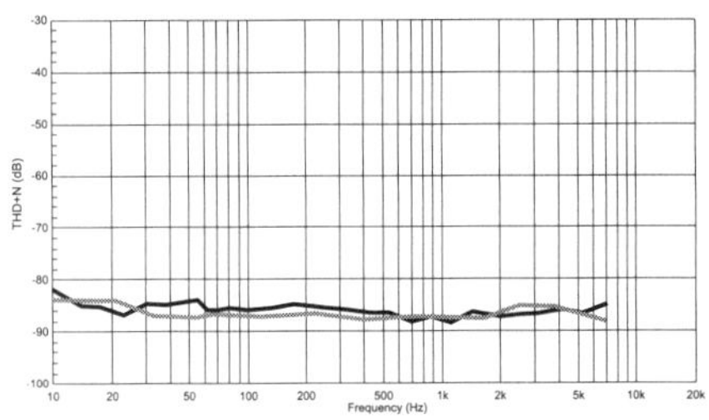

THD+N (20 Hz to 7 kHz)	-89 dBV

Figure 11.26 Typical Report for DAC THD+N Test

DAC Intermodulation Measurement

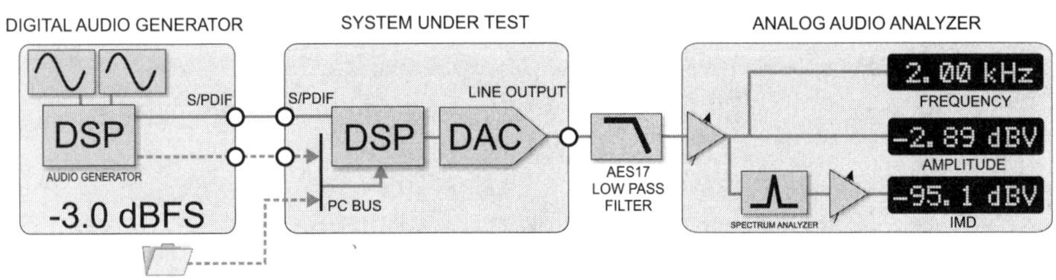

Figure 11.27 DAC IMD Test Setup

Description: This test characterizes the IMD of the play or Digital to Analog path of a PC audio system. This test should be performed on each analog output of the system. This test is useful to characterize the high-frequency distortion of the system since THD+N techniques are not able to determine distortion above approximately 7 kHz.

Test Signal: The test signal is a digital twin-tone signal composed of equal amplitude two sine waves of 18 kilohertz and 20 kilohertz. It may be supplied to the SUT from a software signal generator directly driving the Intel HD Audio bus or from a file in memory of the PC that is played back. All volume controls—including Wave in Windows XP—should be set to unity gain, which is normally the maximum setting. For hardware testing, all signal processing should be disabled.

Measurement Process: The process measures second, third, and fourth order difference IMD components of the analog signal at the line out.

Setup Notes: The test signal is sent to the digital input of the DAC using either of test signal methods outlined above. A 20 kHz low pass filter, such as specified by AES-17, should be included in the measurement path, either between the SUT and the measurement instrument, or as part of the measurement instrument itself.

Procedure: This test is normally conducted at a level 3 dB below digital full scale. Set the audio generator to a level of -3 dBFS and frequencies of 18 kilohertz and 20 kilohertz. Measure the IMD of the audio signal in dB or dBV at the line out. For stimulus frequencies of 18 and 20 kilohertz, IMD components occur at 2 kilohertz, 4 kilohertz, 14 kilohertz, and 16 kilohertz.

Reporting results: Test results are reported numerically. Report the results in dBV if the reading is taken referenced to one volt RMS (0 dBV) or report the results in pure dB (no suffix) if they are taken relative to a reference level other than 1 volt RMS. The following is a typical report.

Intermodulation Distortion (18 kHz and 20 kHz, -3 dB): -95 dBV

DAC Interchannel Phase

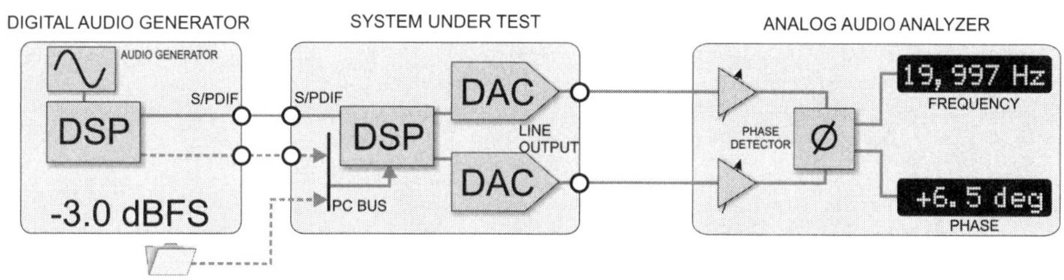

Figure 11.28 DAC Inter-channel Phase Test Setup

Description: This test characterizes the interchannel phase difference of the play or Digital to Analog path of a PC audio system. This test should be performed on each analog output of the system.

Test Signal: The test signal is a sine wave swept from 20 Hz to 20 kHz sent simultaneously to the two channels being tested. It may be supplied to the SUT from a software signal generator directly driving the Intel HD Audio bus or from a file in memory of the PC that is played back. All volume controls–including Wave in Windows XP–should be set to unity gain, which is normally the maximum setting. For hardware testing, all signal processing should be disabled.

Measurement Process: This process measures the phase difference between two sine waves at identical frequencies at the DAC output.

Setup Notes: The test signal is sent to the digital input of the DAC using either of test signal methods outlined above. For phase measurements, the usual AES-17 20 kHz low-pass filter should not be used as it introduces phase errors.

Procedure: This test is normally conducted at a level 3 dB below digital full scale. Set the audio generator to a level -3 dBFS and sweep form 20 Hz to 20 kHz. Set the analyzer to measure phase difference between the two channels under test.

Reporting results: Test results are reported graphically and numerically. Graphical results should display a graph with a log frequency axis from 20 Hz to 20 kHz and a vertical axis linear in degrees. The top and bottom limits of the vertical axis should be such that they show phase variations over the frequency range. Typical axis values would be ±20 degrees.

Figure 11.29 shows a typical report.

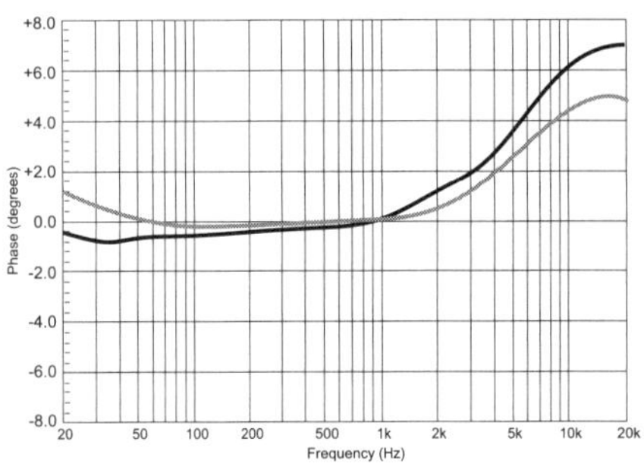

Inter-channel phase difference (left to right):	±7 degrees, 20 Hz to 20 kHz

Figure 11.29 Typical Report for DAC Inter-channel Phase Test

DAC Inter-channel Crosstalk

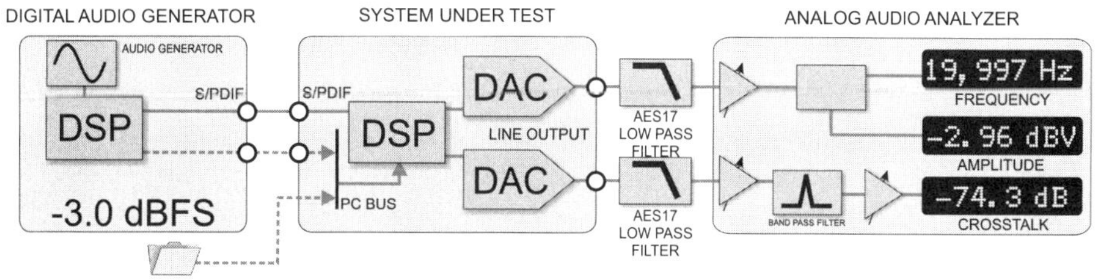

Figure 11.30 DAC Inter-channel Crosstalk Test Setup

Description: This test characterizes the interchannel crosstalk of the play or Digital-to-Analog path of a PC audio system. This test should be performed on each analog output of the system.

Test Signal: The test signal is a sine wave swept from 20 Hz to 20 kHz sent to one of the two channels being tested. It may be supplied to the SUT from a software signal generator directly driving the Intel HD Audio bus or from a file in memory of the PC that is played back. All volume controls—including Wave in Windows XP—should be set to unity gain, which is normally the maximum setting. All signal processing should be disabled.

Measurement Process: The test signal is applied to one or more active inputs or channels while the channel under test receives no signal and has its input terminated. This process measures the residual amplitude in the test channel compared to stimulated channels. A band pass filter tuned to the stimulus signal is used to suppress broadband noise and enhance the accuracy.

Setup Notes: The test signal is sent to the digital input of the DAC using either of test signal methods outlined above. A 20 kHz low-pass filter, such as specified by AES-17, should be included in the measurement path either between the SUT and the measurement instrument or as part of the measurement instrument itself.

Procedure: This test is normally conducted at a level 3 dB below digital full scale. Set the audio generator to a level -3 dBFS and sweep the signal from 20 Hz to 20 kHz. Measure the amplitude of the terminated audio signal in dB at the line out. Use a tracking band pass filter tuned to the stimulus feeding other channels.

Reporting results: Graphical results should display a graph with a log frequency axis from 20 Hz to 20 kHz and a vertical axis linear in dB. The top and bottom limits of the vertical axis should be such that they show crosstalk variations over the frequency range. Typical axis values would be -100 dB to -40 dB.

Figure 11.31 shows a typical report.

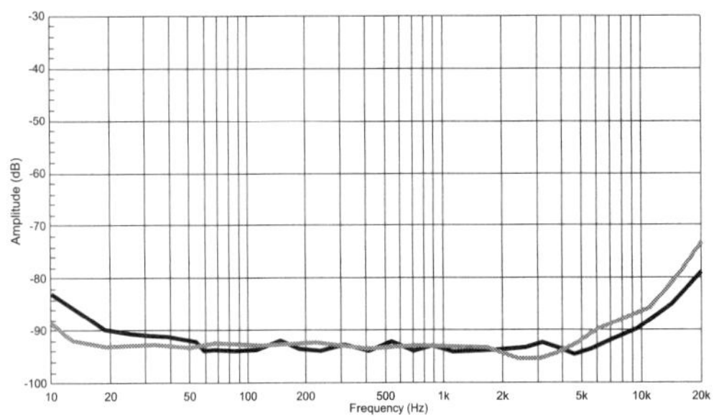

Crosstalk (left to right):	-74 dB, maximum over 20 Hz to 20 kHz

Figure 11.31 Typical Report for DAC Inter-channel Crosstalk Test

Additional Tests

The previously described tests are common ones that have wide industry acceptance. Characterization of certain other behaviors requires special techniques. Many of these behaviors are random and particular to PC audio, and they cannot be characterized by traditional testing methods. Yet they can be of sufficient annoyance that characterization is required.

Glitch Detection

Although the term "glitch" is not well defined, it usually refers to an interruption or disturbance in the delivery of an audio stream. With error correcting facilities, an interruption or silence can be replaced by a repetition of previous data, though this is hardly an ideal solution. The only true solution is to ensure that glitches do not occur under normal situations, and to do so requires the ability to detect and measure glitches. Resilience to glitching is one of the primary focuses of the new Windows Vista audio architecture.

This problem is completely unique to digital audio program distribution. Traditional consumer analog equipment has no equivalent. Although consumers may have become familiar with this type of error from cell phone and internet audio delivery experiences, they are not likely to be very tolerant to such disturbances when listening to high quality audio or watching a movie on a home theater.

A major cause of glitches is sharing of resources. This behavior is particularly evident in PCs with applications running while file transfers, hard drives, and other activities are competing for computational resources. Operating systems have been improving how they manage resources to reduce this problem, but it still occurs. Simpler devices like MP3 players may have less contention for resources but still have the potential for the glitch problem.

Characterizing glitches can present a test problem. It can be difficult to hear, let alone detect, a glitch using music program content. However, a powerful and sensitive technique can be implemented using almost any audio analyzer. The procedure uses a sustained single sinewave signal as the stimulus. The analysis is simply a THD+N measurement using the common notch-filter method monitored over time. Even the slightest disturbance of a single cycle of the test signal is easily detected and measured. The technique for measuring THD+N with a notch filter employs a servo tuned notch filter that will lock on to a test signal. To achieve the 120-decibel notch depth required for a low residual THD measurement, the servo is monitoring two parameters and constantly correcting to maintain accurate tuning. Should the stimulus signal change slightly in amplitude or frequency, the servo readjusts the filter tuning quickly but with its own internal time constant. Any disturbance or glitch during the delivery of this sustained signal shows up as a momentary large increase in distortion residual while the servo adapts to the change. By detecting the magnitude and duration of this increase in residual, an accurate metric of the glitch can be determined.

A good test frequency to use is 10 kHz although other frequencies may be used. Of course, the objective is not to measure actual THD+N, only to detect disturbances. So, the absolute sustained level of the residual or measured THD+N is not important. You are concerned only with how much it increases and how long it lasts when a glitch is detected. Figure 11.32 shows the test setup.

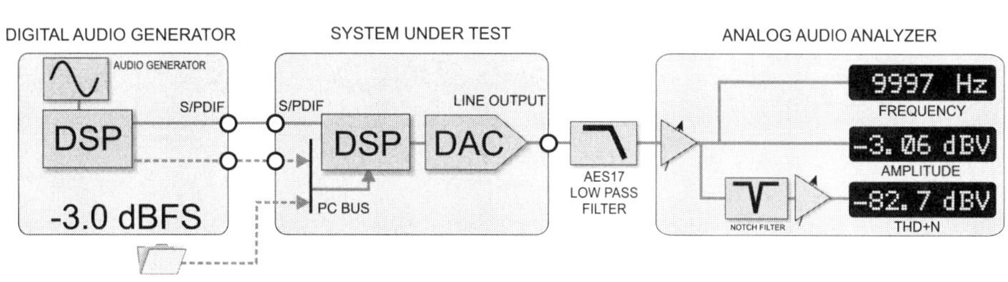

Figure 11.32 Glitch Detection Test Setup

Description: This test characterizes any disruption in the delivery of program material in the playback or Digital to Analog path of a PC audio system. Interruptions can be dropouts, repeats, or signals not part of the original program material.

Test Signal: The test signal is a sustained digital sine wave at 10 kHz. It may be supplied to the SUT from a software signal generator directly driving the Intel HD Audio bus or from a file in memory of the PC that is played back. All volume controls–including Wave in Windows XP–should be set to unity gain, which is normally the maximum setting. All signal processing should be disabled.

Measurement Process: The measurement monitors the analog audio signal at the output of the DAC and measures the THD+N of this signal. This process involves a continuous amplitude and frequency monitoring of the 10 kHz test signal. Any amplitude, phase, or frequency disturbance of this signal shows up as an error that can be measured and logged.

Setup Notes: The test signal is sent to the digital input of the DAC using either of test signal methods outlined above. A 20 kHz low pass filter, such as specified by AES-17, should be included in the measurement path either between the SUT and the measurement instrument or as part of the measurement instrument itself.

Procedure: This test normally is conducted at a level 3 dB below digital full scale. Set the audio generator to a level of -3 dBFS and a frequency of 10 kHz. Measure the THD+N of the digital audio signal in dB at the digital output. Record the amplitude of the residual signal after the notch filter against time. Exercise the system to stimulate disturbances that may cause a glitch and note any change in residual level.

Reporting results: Test results are reported graphically and numerically. Graphical results should display a graph with a linear time axis and a vertical axis linear in dB or dBV. The top and bottom limits of the vertical axis should be such that they show residual THD+N variations over time. Typical axis values would be -100 dB to -40 dB.

The report in Figure 11.33 is typical.

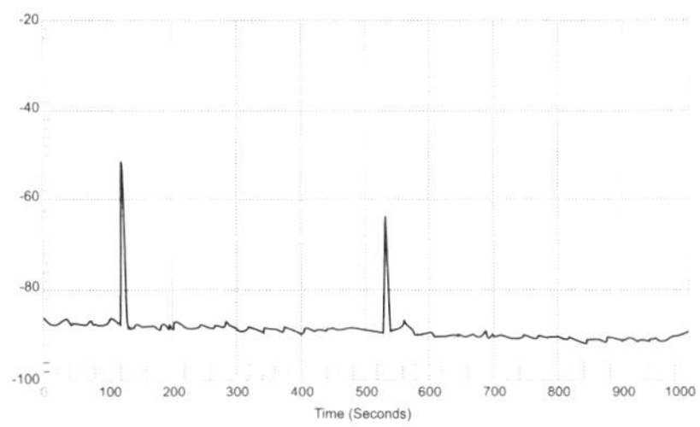

Glitches per 1000 seconds:	2
Maximum glitch amplitude:	-45 dBV

Figure 11.33 Typical Report for Glitch Detection Test

Clicks, Pops, and Thumps

Impulse noise can be disturbing when listening to music content or watching a movie. An excessive impulse when wearing earphones can even be damaging. Pops, clicks, or thumps can have many possible causes, but usually the cause is a sudden change in DC level at the output jack which sounds like a high-energy click or pop.

What can cause a change in DC level? Applying or removing power to the Intel HD Audio codec is the most common cause. When a device is off, the DC level at the output is zero. Depending on the design of the circuit, the output terminals could assume a new DC level when power is applied. The inclusion of an AC coupling capacitor on the output eliminates long-term DC offset at the output but does little to eliminate this instantaneous DC transition.

Retasking jacks can be a source of sudden DC shift when they switch between different functions. Microphone inputs typically have a DC bias voltage of 2 to 5 volts and include a DC blocking capacitor to keep this voltage out of the microphone input. But if a low impedance load such as a headphone is connected, the DC energy stored in this capacitor must be dissipated. Depending on circuit configuration, this stored energy might get dumped into the chip itself or back into the headphones. A capacitor discharging a 5V DC level into a typical headset can produce a very loud click that would be obnoxious at best and damaging at worse. The same energy dumped into a chip can cause catastrophic failure.

Another source of clicks or pops could be power supply disturbances. Unless a supply is extremely well regulated, sudden load changes can affect its output. For example, when a hard drive motor starts, the instantaneous current demand can be large which could cause a momentary change in output voltage of the power supply. If the audio chip is sensitive to this power rail change, it may pass on a pop or click to its output.

Since such impulse events can be difficult to characterize if only determined subjectively by listening with a headphone or speakers. Engineers at Maxim Semiconductor have suggested an objective technique to allow comparisons of systems for click and pop magnitude. A link to this article is available on this book's companion web site. This technique uses an A-weighting filter to integrate the impulse and better sensitize it to human hearing. This technique works for any situation where the cause of the click or pop can be controlled, such as power turn on or shut down.

To use this technique, the system under test is cycled through two defined states such as power on and power off, or suspend and resume. The audio output of the system is connected to the input of an audio analyzer, as shown in Figure 11.34. All auto-ranging in the analyzer is disabled and the input range is fixed at a level appropriate for the level of the click or pop. The A-weighting filter is enabled to sensitize the measurement. You select a relatively fast reading rate of 32 readings per second and peak detection, rather than the usual RMS detection. You set units to dBV. The impulse noise from the system under test should then produce a level reading in dBV that can be used as a relative *figure of merit* and allow objective comparisons between systems.

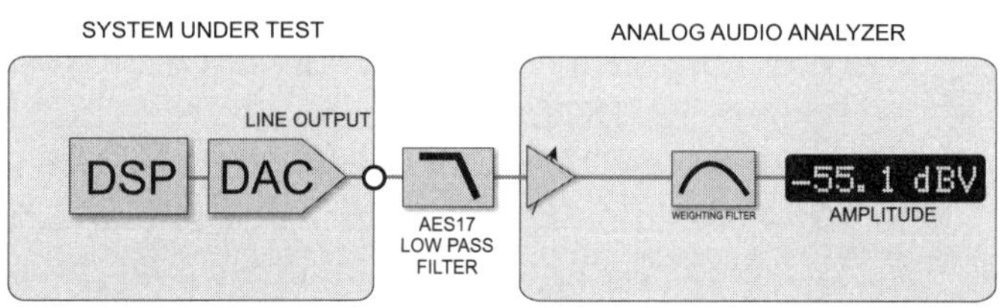

Figure 11.34 Clicks and Pops Test Setup

Description: This test characterizes the magnitude of clicks or pops of the playback or Digital to Analog path of a PC audio system during state changes. This test should be performed on each channel of the system.

Test Signal: No test signal is used for this measurement. All volume controls–including Wave in Windows XP–should be set to unity gain, which is normally the maximum setting. If testing only the hardware, all signal processing should be disabled.

Measurement Process: The measurement monitors the analog audio signal at the output of the DAC and measures the weighted amplitude of all signals present over time. Any audible clicks or pops that exceed the quiescent weighted noise of the system are quantified.

Setup Notes: A 20 kHz low pass filter, such as specified by AES 17, should be included in the measurement path, either between the SUT and the measurement instrument, or as part of the measurement instrument itself.

Procedure: The A-weighted audio level at the analog output of the system is measured and recorded over time. The state of the system is changed, such as powering on or off, while monitoring the audio amplitude. Clicks or pops are integrated by the A-weighting filter and indicate an amplitude that can be used to compare the subjective amount of clicks or pops from various systems.

Reporting results: Test results can be reported graphically or numerically. Graphical results should display a graph with a linear time axis and a vertical axis linear in dB or dBV. The top and bottom limits of the vertical axis should be such that they show weighted noise variations over time. Typical axis values would be -100 dB to -40 dB.

Report the results in dBV if the reading is taken referenced to one volt RMS (0 dBV) or report the results in pure dB (no suffix) if they are taken relative to a reference level other than 1 volt RMS. The report in Figure 11.35 is typical.

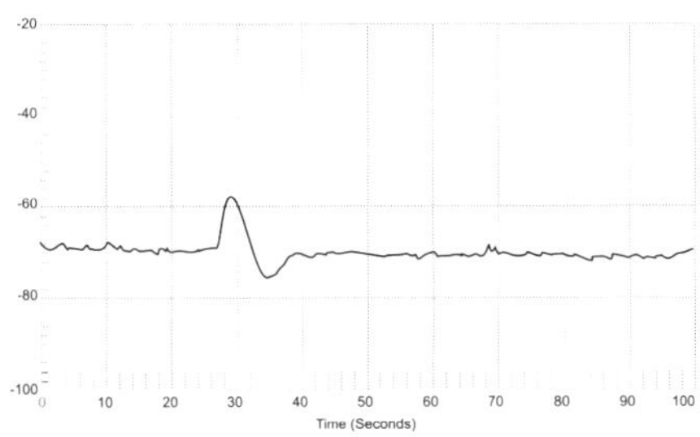

Click and Pop amplitude	-55 dBV, A-weighted

Figure 11.35 Typical Report for Clicks and Pops Test

Appendix A

Pin Configuration Verb Tables

Chapter 4 introduces the concept of verb tables and how the BIOS uses them to transmit default configurations to each pin widget in each Intel HD Audio codec in the system during startup and during resume from standby. The examples in this appendix provide partial verb tables for a number of different configurations which can be assembled to define a complete system like the one detailed in Chapter 9.

Each example in this appendix presents a block diagram, a summary of the pin configuration, a verb table in assembly language format, and a verb table that can be added to a copy of the Microsoft UAA class driver for Intel HD Audio INF file. This approach might be useful in early hardware bring-up stages if the proper verb tables have not yet been programmed into the system BIOS. For this technique to work, each verb programmed into the INF file must be sequentially numbered. If you combine verb tables from multiple INF examples in this appendix, be sure to include all verbs in a single section, and make sure that they are numbered in sequential order and that each number is unique.

Using the INF file to program the pin configuration default registers of the codec is only useful as a workaround, the Windows Vista Logo program requires the BIOS to program these registers during startup and resume from standby. Chapter 4 contains detailed information on how to understand and create verb tables containing pin configuration defaults for a system under development.

Subsystem ID

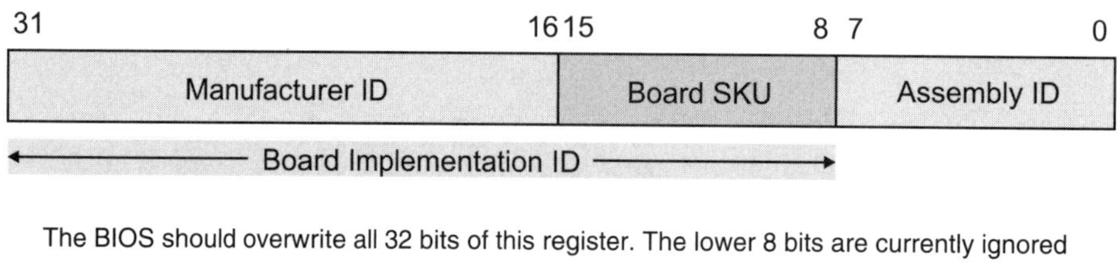

Figure A.1 Subsystem ID Register

```
Audio function group  (NodeID = 01h), SDI#2
; set the 32-bit subsystem ID by writing four bytes to
; successive addresses. This examples writes 0xAABBCCDD
; to the subsystem ID register of the codec
;
: the four verbs to accomplish this are defined below
; with each of the 32-bit verbs stored as 32-bit data

      dd     201720DDh          ; Set bits  7:0  to 0xDD
      dd     201721CCh          ; Set bits 15:8  to 0xCC
      dd     201722BBh          ; Set bits 23:16 to 0xBB
      dd     201723AAh          ; Set bits 31:24 to 0xAA
```

Figure A.2 Partial Verb Table Written to Set Subsystem ID to 0xAABBCCDD

```
[HdAudInit.AddReg]
; Number of verbs to be sent to codec
HKR,InitVerbs,NumVerbs,0x00010001,0x00000004

;--Set Node ID 0x01 Pin Subsystem ID to 0xAABBCCDD
HKR,InitVerbs,0000,0x00010001,0x201720DD ; Set b31:24 to 0xDD
HKR,InitVerbs,0001,0x00010001,0x201721CC ; Set b31:24 to 0xCC
HKR,InitVerbs,0002,0x00010001,0x201722BB ; Set b31:24 to 0xBB
HKR,InitVerbs,0003,0x00010001,0x201723AA ; Set b31:24 to 0xAA
```

Specify the verb table in a copy of the UAA class driver INF file as a temporary workaround if the BIOS is not programming the pin configuration default registers properly. You cannot use this to pass Windows Vista Logo.

Figure A.3 Partial Verb Table specified in the INF file of the Microsoft UAA class driver for Intel HD Audio

Front Panel Headphone Output

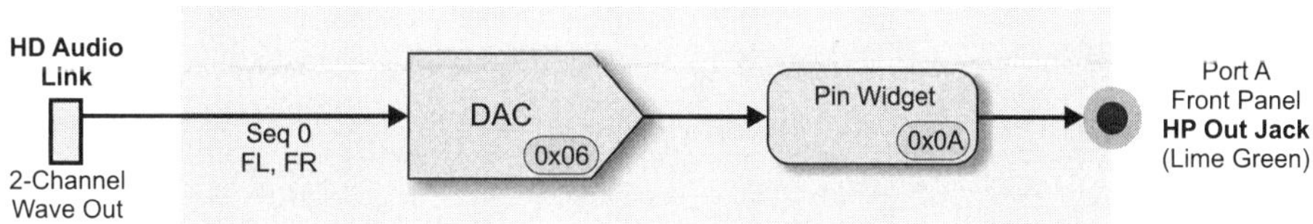

Figure A.4 Codec Topology for Front Panel Headphone Output

Connectivity	Loc	Device	Type	Color	Jack Detect	Assoc	Seq
Chassis Jack	Front	HP Out	3.5 mm	Green	Yes (0)	7	0

```
; Front Panel HP Out uses port A (NodeID = 0xA, SDI#2)
; Set Node ID 0x0A Pin Configs to 0x02214070
dd 20A71C70h ; Set 7:0   to 0x70 - Assoc 7, Seq 0
dd 20A71D40h ; Set 15:8  to 0x40 - Green, Jack Detect
dd 20A71E21h ; Set 23:16 to 0x21 - HP Out, 3.5 mm jack
dd 20A71F02h ; Set 31:24 to 0x02 - Front, chassis
```

Figure A.5 Partial Verb Table and Pin Configuration for an Independent Stereo HP Out Jack on Front Panel

```
[HdAudInit.AddReg]
; Number of verbs to be sent to codec
HKR,InitVerbs,NumVerbs,0x00010001,0x00000004

; Front Panel HP Out uses port A (NodeID = 0xA, SDI#2)
; Set Set Node ID 0x0A Pin Configs to 0x02214070
HKR,InitVerbs,0000,0x00010001,0x20A71C70 ; Assoc 7, Seq 0
HKR,InitVerbs,0001,0x00010001,0x20A71D40 ; Green, Jack Detect
HKR,InitVerbs,0002,0x00010001,0x20A71E21 ; HP Out, 3.5 mm jack
HKR,InitVerbs,0003,0x00010001,0x20A71F02 ; Front, chassis
```

Specify the verb table in a copy of the UAA class driver INF file as a temporary workaround if the BIOS is not programming the pin configuration default registers properly. You cannot use this to pass Windows Vista Logo.

Figure A.6 Partial Verb Table specified in the INF file of the Microsoft Intel HD Audio UAA class driver

Rear Panel Line Input

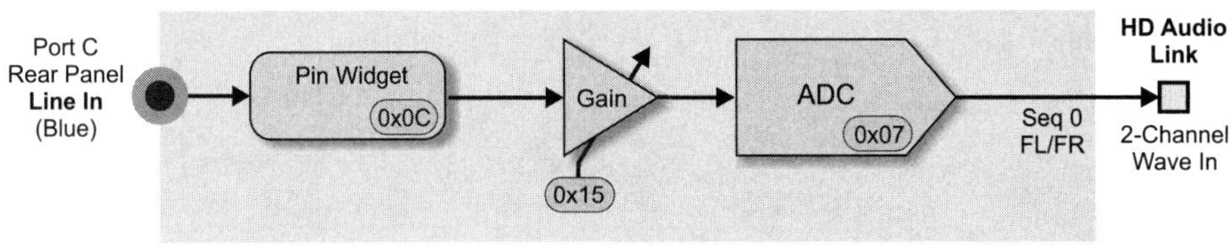

Figure A.7 Codec Topology for Rear Panel Line Input

Connectivity	Loc	Device	Type	Color	Jack Detect	Assoc	Seq
Chassis Jack	Rear	Line In	3.5 mm	Blue	Yes (0x0)	5	0

```
; Rear Panel Line In is port C (NodeID = 0xC, SDI#2)
; Set Node ID 0x0C Pin Configs to 0x0x01813050
dd 20C71C50h ; Set 7:0   to 0x50 - Assoc 5, Seq 0
dd 20C71D30h ; Set 15:8  to 0x30 - Blue, Jack Detect
dd 20C71E81h ; Set 23:16 to 0x81 - Line In, 3.5 mm jack
dd 20C71F01h ; Set 31:24 to 0x01 - Rear, chassis
```

Figure A.8 Verb table and Pin Configuration for a Stereo Line In Jack

```
[HdAudInit.AddReg]
; Number of verbs to be sent to codec
HKR,InitVerbs,NumVerbs,0x00010001,0x00000004

; Rear Panel Line In is port C (NodeID = 0xC, SDI#2)
; Set Node ID 0x0C Pin Configs to 0x0x01813050
HKR,InitVerbs,0000,0x00010001,0x20C71C50 ; Assoc 5, Seq 0
HKR,InitVerbs,0001,0x00010001,0x20C71D30 ; Blue, Jack Detect
HKR,InitVerbs,0002,0x00010001,0x20C71E81 ; Line In, 3.5 mm jack
HKR,InitVerbs,0003,0x00010001,0x20C71F01 ; Rear, chassis
```

Specify the verb table in a copy of the UAA class driver INF file as a temporary workaround if the BIOS is not programming the pin configuration default registers properly. You cannot use this to pass Windows Vista Logo.

Figure A.9 Partial Verb Table specified in the INF file of the Microsoft UAA class driver for Intel HD Audio

Rear Panel Line Output

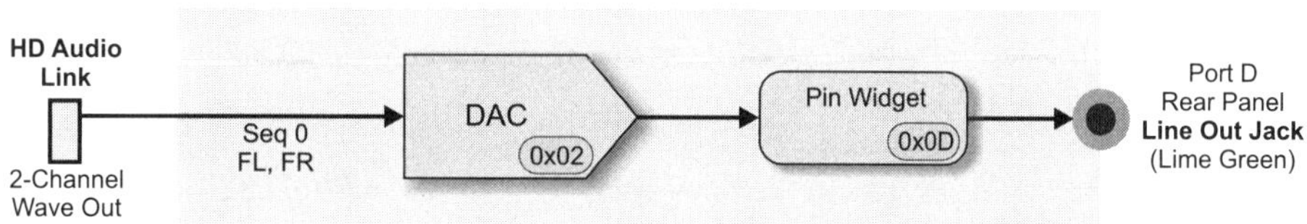

Figure A.10 Codec Topology for Rear Panel Line Output

Connectivity	Loc	Device	Type	Color	Jack Detect	Assoc	Seq
Chassis Jack	Rear	Line Out	3.5 mm	Green	Yes (0x0)	3	0

```
; Rear Panel Line Out is port D (NodeID = 0xD, SDI#2)
; Set Node ID 0x0D Pin Configs to 0x01014030
dd 20D71C30h ; Set 7:0   to 0x30 - Assoc 3, Seq 0
dd 20D71D40h ; Set 15:8  to 0x40 - Green, Jack Detect
dd 20D71E01h ; Set 23:16 to 0x01 - Line Out, 3.5 mm jack
dd 20D71F01h ; Set 31:24 to 0x01 - Rear, chassis
```

Figure A.11 Partial Verb Table and Pin Configuration for a Stereo Line Out Jack

```
[HdAudInit.AddReg]
; Number of verbs to be sent to codec
HKR,InitVerbs,NumVerbs,0x00010001,0x00000004

; Line Out is port D (NodeID = 0xD, SDI#2)
; Set Node ID 0x0D Pin Configs to 0x01014030
HKR,InitVerbs,0000,0x00010001,0x20D71C30 ; Assoc 3, Seq 0
HKR,InitVerbs,0001,0x00010001,0x20D71D40 ; Green, Jack Detect
HKR,InitVerbs,0002,0x00010001,0x20D71E01 ; Line Out, 3.5 mm
jack
HKR,InitVerbs,0003,0x00010001,0x20D71F01 ; Rear, chassis
```

Specify the verb table in a copy of the UAA class driver INF file as a temporary workaround if the BIOS is not programming the pin configuration default registers properly. You cannot use this to pass Windows Vista Logo.

Figure A.12 Partial Verb Table specified in the INF file of the Microsoft UAA class driver for Intel HD Audio

Front Panel Microphone Input

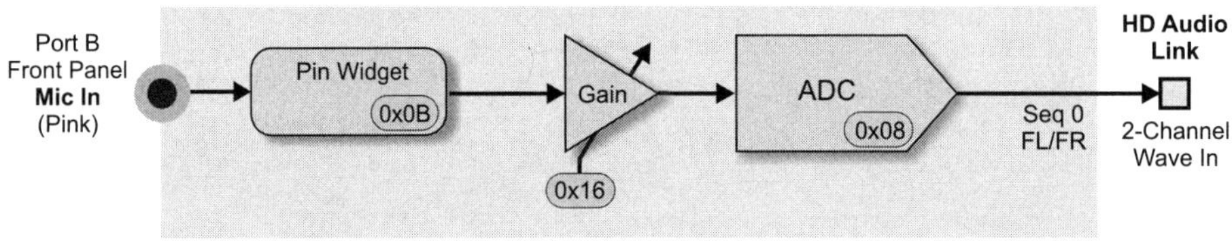

Figure A.13 Codec Topology for Front Panel Microphone Input

Connectivity	Loc	Device	Type	Color	Jack Detect	Assoc	Seq
Chassis Jack	Front	Mic In	3.5 mm	Pink	Yes	9	0

```
; Front Panel Mic In uses port B (NodeID = 0xB, SDI#2)
; Set Node ID 0x0B Pin Configs to 0x02A19090
dd 20B71C90h ; Set 7:0   to 0x90 - Assoc 9, Seq 0
dd 20B71D90h ; Set 15:8  to 0x90 - Pink, Jack Detect
dd 20B71EA1h ; Set 23:16 to 0xA1 - Mic In, 3.5 mm jack
dd 20B71F02h ; Set 31:24 to 0x02 - Front, chassis
```

Figure A.14 Partial Verb Table and Pin Configuration for a Mic In Jack on Front Panel

```
[HdAudInit.AddReg]
; Number of verbs to be sent to codec
HKR,InitVerbs,NumVerbs,0x00010001,0x00000004

; Mic In is Port B (NodeID = 0x0B, SDI#2)
; Set Node ID 0x0CB Pin Configs to 0x02A19090
HKR,InitVerbs,0000,0x00010001,0x20B71C90 ; Assoc 9, Seq 0
HKR,InitVerbs,0001,0x00010001,0x20B71D90 ; Pink, Jack Detect
HKR,InitVerbs,0002,0x00010001,0x20B71EA1 ; Mic In, 3.5 mm jack
HKR,InitVerbs,0003,0x00010001,0x20B71F02 ; Front, chassis
```

Specify the verb table in a copy of the UAA class driver INF file as a temporary workaround if the BIOS is not programming the pin configuration default registers properly. You cannot use this to pass Windows Vista Logo.

Figure A.15 Partial Verb Table specified in the INF file of the Microsoft UAA class driver for Intel HD Audio

Rear Panel S/PDIF Output

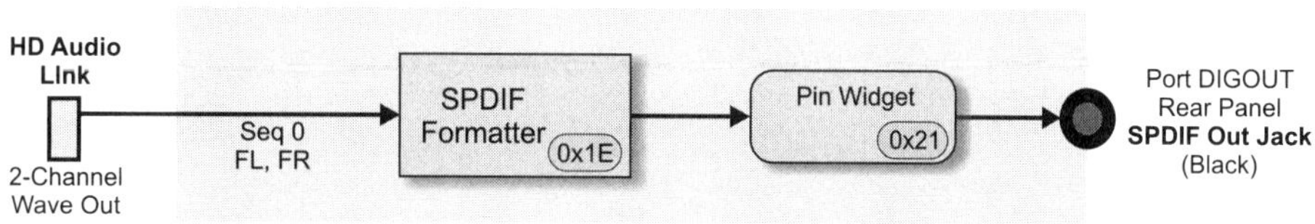

Figure A.16 Codec Topology for Rear Panel S/PDIF Digital Output

Connectivity	Loc	Device	Type	Color	Jack Detect	Assoc	Seq
Chassis Jack	Rear	S/PDIF Out	Optical	Black	No (0x1)	A	0

```
; S/PDIF Output port (NodeID = 0x21, SDI#2)
; Set Node ID 0x21 Pin Configs to 0x014511A0
dd 22171CA0h ; Set 7:0   to 0xA0 - Assoc A, Seq 0
dd 22171D11h ; Set 15:8  to 0x11 - Black, No Jack Detect
dd 22171E45h ; Set 23:16 to 0x45 - S/PDIF Out, Optical
dd 22171F01h ; Set 31:24 to 0x01 - Rear, chassis
```

Figure A.17 Partial Verb Table and Pin Configuration for an Optical S/PDIF Out Jack on Rear Panel

```
[HdAudInit.AddReg]
; Number of verbs to be sent to codec
HKR,InitVerbs,NumVerbs,0x00010001,0x00000004

; S/PDIF Output port (NodeID = 0x21, SDI#2)
; Set Node ID 0x21 Pin Configs to 0x014511A0
HKR,InitVerbs,0000,0x00010001,0x20D71CA0 ; Assoc A, Seq 0
HKR,InitVerbs,0001,0x00010001,0x20D71D11 ; Black, No JackDetect
HKR,InitVerbs,0002,0x00010001,0x20D71E45 ; S/PDIF Out, Optical
HKR,InitVerbs,0003,0x00010001,0x20D71F01 ; Rear, chassis
```

Specify the verb table in a copy of the UAA class driver INF file as a temporary workaround if the BIOS is not programming the pin configuration default registers properly. You cannot use this to pass Windows Vista Logo.

Figure A.18 Partial Verb Table specified in the INF file of the Microsoft UAA class driver for Intel HD Audio

Rear Panel 5.1 Surround Line Outputs

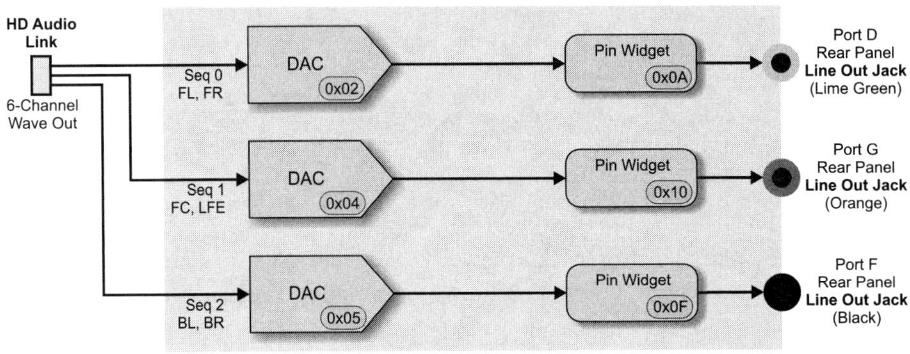

Figure A.19 Codec Topology for 5.1 Output

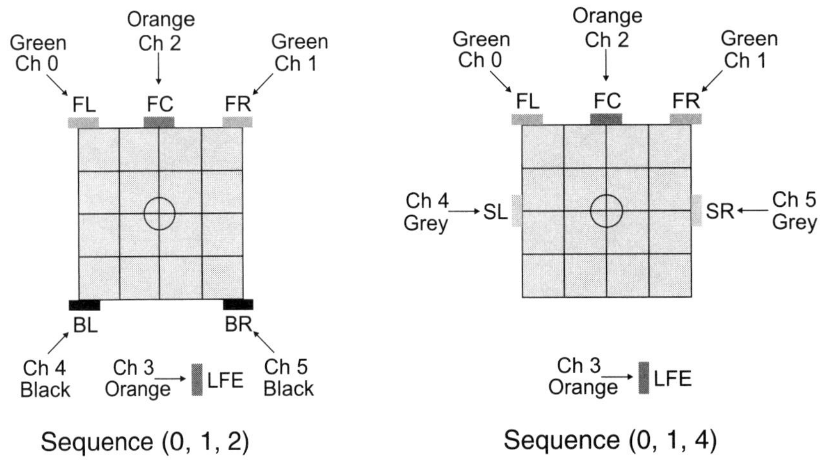

Figure A.20 5.1 Surround Sequences for a Multi-channel Association

Connectivity	Loc	Device	Type	Color	Jack Detect	Assoc	Seq
Chassis Jack	Rear	Line Out	3.5 mm	Green	Yes (0x0)	3	0
Chassis Jack	Rear	Line Out	3.5 mm	Orange	Yes (0x0)	3	1
Chassis Jack	Rear	Line Out	3.5 mm	Black	Yes (0x0)	3	2

The choice of sequence number determines the function of each port, which must be matched with the proper color for that function.

```
;configure 5.1 surround sound

; Port D (NID = 0x0D): Green, Front L/R
; Set Node ID 0x0D Pin Configs to 0x01014030
dd 20D71C30h ; Set 7:0   to 0x30 - Assoc 3, Seq 0 - FL,FR
dd 20D71D40h ; Set 15:8  to 0x40 - Green, Jack Detect
dd 20D71E01h ; Set 23:16 to 0x01 - Line Out, 3.5 mm jack
dd 20D71F01h ; Set 31:24 to 0x01 - Rear, chassis

; Port G (NID = 0x10): Orange, Center/LFE
; Set Node ID 0x10 Pin Configs to 0x01016031
dd 21071C31h ; Set 7:0   to 0x31 - Assoc 3, Seq 1- FC,LFE
dd 21071D60h ; Set 15:8  to 0x60 - Orange, Jack Detect
dd 21071E01h ; Set 23:16 to 0x01 - Line Out, 3.5 mm jack
dd 21071F01h ; Set 31:24 to 0x01 - Rear, chassis

; Port F (NID = 0x0F): Black, Back L/R
; Set Node ID 0x0F Pin Configs to 0x01011032
dd 20F71C32h ; Set 7:0   to 0x32 - Assoc 3, Seq 2- BL,BR
dd 20F71D10h ; Set 15:8  to 0x10 - Black, Jack Detect
dd 20F71E01h ; Set 23:16 to 0x01 - Line Out, 3.5 mm jack
dd 20F71F01h ; Set 31:24 to 0x01 - Rear, chassis
```

Figure A.21 Partial Verb Table and Pin Configuration for a 5.1 Surround Sound Configuration Using Sequence (0, 1, 2)

```
[HdAudInit.AddReg]
; Number of verbs to be sent to codec
HKR,InitVerbs,NumVerbs,0x00010001,0x0000000C

; Line Out is port D (NodeID = 0xD, SDI#2)
; Set Node ID 0x0D Pin Configs to 0x01014030
HKR,InitVerbs,0000,0x00010001,0x20D71C30 ; Assoc 3, Seq 0
HKR,InitVerbs,0001,0x00010001,0x20D71D40 ; Green, Jack Detect
HKR,InitVerbs,0002,0x00010001,0x20D71E01 ; Line Out, 3.5mm jack
HKR,InitVerbs,0003,0x00010001,0x20D71F01 ; Rear, chassis
```

```
; Codec ID#2, Port G (NID = 0x10
; Set Node ID 0x10 Pin Configs to 0x01016031
HKR,InitVerbs,0004,0x00010001,0x21071C31 ; Assoc 3, Seq 1
HKR,InitVerbs,0005,0x00010001,0x21071D60 ; Orange, Jack Detect
HKR,InitVerbs,0006,0x00010001,0x21071E01 ; Line Out, 3.5mm jack
HKR,InitVerbs,0007,0x00010001,0x21071F01 ; Rear, chassis

; Codec ID#2, Port F (NID = 0x0F)
; Set Node ID 0x0F Pin Configs to 0x01011032
HKR,InitVerbs,0008,0x00010001,0x20F71C32 ; Assoc 3, Seq 2
HKR,InitVerbs,0009,0x00010001,0x20F71D10 ; Black, Jack Detect
HKR,InitVerbs,0010,0x00010001,0x20F71E01 ; Line Out, 3.5mm jack
HKR,InitVerbs,0011,0x00010001,0x20F71F01 ; Rear, chassis
```

Specify the verb table in a copy of the UAA class driver INF file as a temporary workaround if the BIOS is not programming the pin configuration default registers properly. You cannot use this to pass Windows Vista Logo.

Figure A.22 Partial Verb Table specified in the INF file of the Microsoft UAA class driver for Intel HD Audio

Rear Panel 7.1 Surround Line Outputs

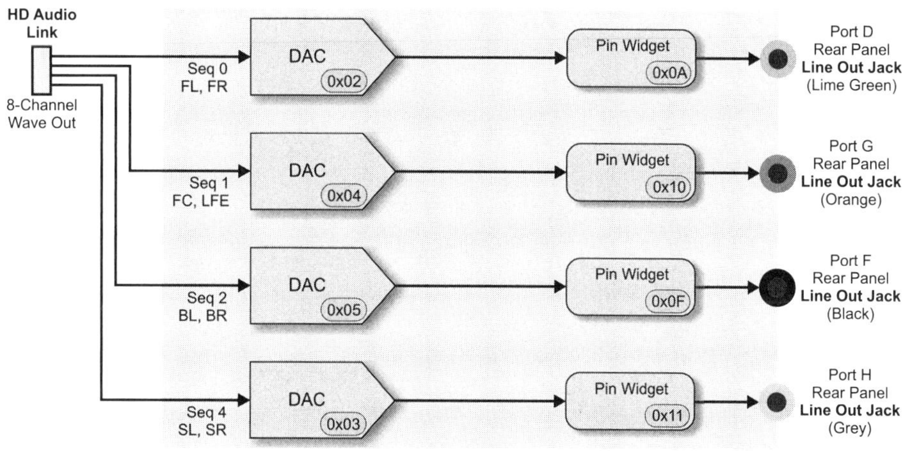

Figure A.23 Codec Topology for 7.1 Output

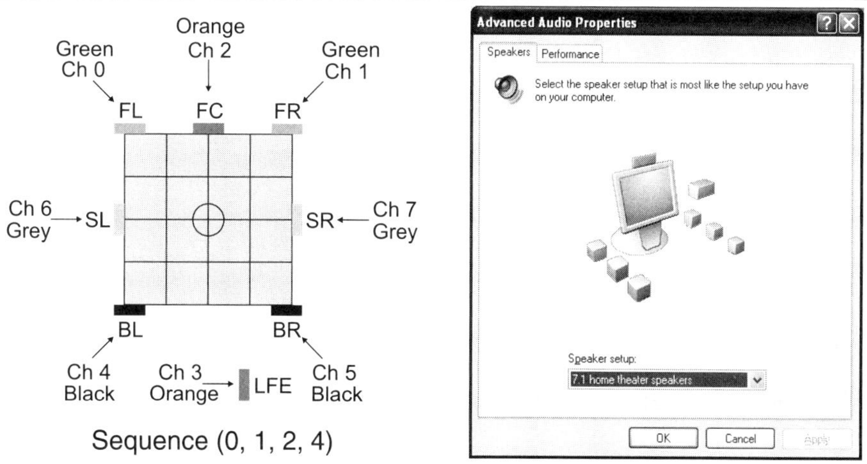

Figure A.24 7.1 Home Theater Sequence for a Multi-channel Association, Along With the Speaker Configuration Dialog That Is Used To Activate It

Connectivity	Loc	Device	Type	Color	Jack Detect	Assoc	Seq
Chassis Jack	Rear	Line Out	3.5 mm	Green	Yes (0x0)	3	0

Chassis Jack	Rear	Line Out	3.5 mm	Orange	Yes (0x0)	3	1
Chassis Jack	Rear	Line Out	3.5 mm	Black	Yes (0x0)	3	2
Chassis Jack	Rear	Line Out	3.5 mm	Grey	Yes (0x0)	3	4

The sequence number determines the function, which must be matched with the proper color for that function.

```
;configure 7.1 Home Theatre

; Codec ID#2, Port D (NID = 0x0D)
; Set Node ID 0x0D Pin Configs to 0x01014030
dd 20D71C30h ; Set 7:0   to 0x30 - Assoc 3, Seq 0 - FL,FR
dd 20D71D40h ; Set 15:8  to 0x40 - Green, Jack Detect
dd 20D71E01h ; Set 23:16 to 0x01 - Line Out, 3.5 mm jack
dd 20D71F01h ; Set 31:24 to 0x01 - Rear, chassis

; Codec ID#2, Port G (NID = 0x10
; Set Node ID 0x10 Pin Configs to 0x01016031
dd 21071C31h ; Set 7:0   to 0x31 - Assoc 3, Seq 1- FC,LFE
dd 21071D60h ; Set 15:8  to 0x60 - Orange, Jack Detect
dd 21071E01h ; Set 23:16 to 0x01 - Line Out, 3.5 mm jack
dd 21071F01h ; Set 31:24 to 0x01 - Rear, chassis

; Codec ID#2, Port F (NID = 0x0F)
; Set Node ID 0x0F Pin Configs to 0x01011032
dd 20F71C32h ; Set 7:0   to 0x32 - Assoc 3, Seq 2- BL,BR
dd 20F71D10h ; Set 15:8  to 0x10 - Black, Jack Detect
dd 20F71E01h ; Set 23:16 to 0x01 - Line Out, 3.5 mm jack
dd 20F71F01h ; Set 31:24 to 0x01 - Rear, chassis

; Codec ID#2, Port H (Nid = 0x11):
; Set Node ID 0x11 Pin Configs to 0x01012034
dd 21171C34h ; Set 7:0   to 0x34 - Assoc 3, Seq 4- SL,SR
dd 21171D20h ; Set 15:8  to 0x20 - Grey, Jack Detect
dd 21171E01h ; Set 23:16 to 0x01 - Line Out, 3.5 mm jack
dd 21171F01h ; Set 31:24 to 0x01 - Rear, chassis
```

Figure A.25 Partial Verb Table and Pin Configuration for a 7.1 Home Theatre Using a Sequence of (0, 1, 2, 4)

```
 [HdAudInit.AddReg]
; Number of verbs to be sent to codec
HKR,InitVerbs,NumVerbs,0x00010001,0x00000010

; Line Out is port D (NodeID = 0xD, SDI#2)
; Set Node ID 0x0D Pin Configs to 0x01014030
HKR,InitVerbs,0000,0x00010001,0x20D71C30 ; Assoc 3, Seq 0
```

```
HKR,InitVerbs,0001,0x00010001,0x20D71D40 ; Green, Jack Detect
HKR,InitVerbs,0002,0x00010001,0x20D71E01 ; Line Out, 3.5mm jack
HKR,InitVerbs,0003,0x00010001,0x20D71F01 ; Rear, chassis
; Codec ID#2, Port G (NID = 0x10
; Set Node ID 0x10 Pin Configs to 0x01016031
HKR,InitVerbs,0004,0x00010001,0x21071C31 ; Assoc 3, Seq 1
HKR,InitVerbs,0005,0x00010001,0x21071D60 ; Orange, Jack Detect
HKR,InitVerbs,0006,0x00010001,0x21071E01 ; Line Out, 3.5mm jack
HKR,InitVerbs,0007,0x00010001,0x21071F01 ; Rear, chassis
; Codec ID#2, Port F (NID = 0x0F)
; Set Node ID 0x0F Pin Configs to 0x01011032
HKR,InitVerbs,0008,0x00010001,0x20F71C32 ; Assoc 3, Seq 2
HKR,InitVerbs,0009,0x00010001,0x20F71D10 ; Black, Jack Detect
HKR,InitVerbs,0010,0x00010001,0x20F71E01 ; Line Out, 3.5mm jack
HKR,InitVerbs,0011,0x00010001,0x20F71F01 ; Rear, chassis
; Codec ID#2, Port H (Nid = 0x11)
; Set Node ID 0x11 Pin Configs to 0x01012034
HKR,InitVerbs,0012,0x00010001,0x21171C34 ; Assoc 3, Seq 4
HKR,InitVerbs,0013,0x00010001,0x21171D20 ; Grey, Jack Detect
HKR,InitVerbs,0014,0x00010001,0x21171E01 ; Line Out, 3.5mm jack
HKR,InitVerbs,0015,0x00010001,0x21171F01 ; Rear, chassis
```

Specify the verb table in a copy of the UAA class driver INF file as a temporary workaround if the BIOS is not programming the pin configuration default registers properly. You cannot use this to pass Windows Vista Logo.

Figure A.26 Partial Verb Table specified in the INF file of the Microsoft UAA class driver for Intel HD Audio

Rear Panel Line Out w/ Redirected Front Panel HP Out

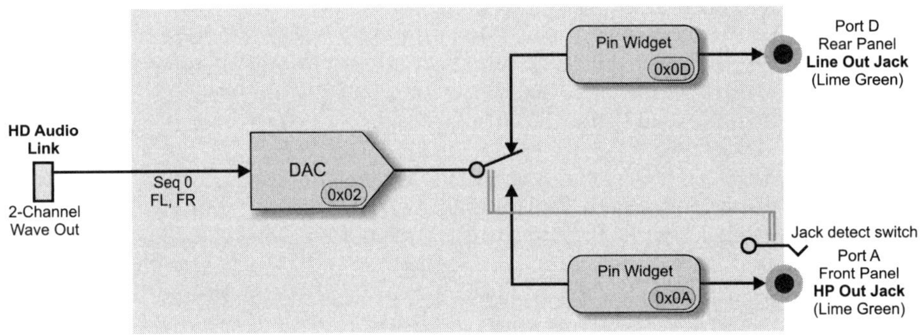

The DAC is routed to only one pin widget at a time. If the headphone jack is plugged in, then the signal from the DAC is routed to the Headphone Out and the Line Out is disconnected. If the headphone jack is not plugged in, then the signal is routed to the Line Out and the Headphone Out is disconnected.

Figure A.27 Line Out jack and Headphone Out jack sharing a single DAC in a Redirected Headphone configuration.

Connectivity	Loc	Device	Type	Color	Jack Detect	Assoc	Seq
Chassis Jack	Rear	Line Out	3.5 mm	Green	Yes (0x0)	3	0
Chassis Jack	Front	HP Out	3.5 mm	Green	Yes (0x0)	3	F

```
;configure Redirected Headphone / Line Out

; Line Out is port D (NodeID = 0xD, SDI#2)
; Set Node ID 0x0D Pin Configs to 0x01014030
dd 20D71C30h ; Set 7:0   to 0x30 - Assoc 3, Seq 0
dd 20D71D40h ; Set 15:8  to 0x40 - Green, Jack Detect
dd 20D71E01h ; Set 23:16 to 0x01 - Line Out, 3.5 mm jack
dd 20D71F01h ; Set 31:24 to 0x01 - Rear, chassis

; HP Out is Port A   (NodeID = 0xA, SDI#2)
; Set Node ID 0x0A Pin Configs to 0x0221403F
dd 20A71C3Fh ; Set 7:0   to 0x3F - Assoc 3, Seq F
dd 20A71D40h ; Set 15:8  to 0x40 - Green, Jack Detect
dd 20A71E21h ; Set 23:16 to 0x21 - HP Out, 3.5 mm jack
dd 20A71F02h ; Set 31:24 to 0x02 - Front, chassis
```

Figure A.28 Partial Verb Table for a Line Out jack and a Redirected Headphone Output jack

```
 [HdAudInit.AddReg]
; Number of verbs to be sent to codec
HKR,InitVerbs,NumVerbs,0x00010001,0x00000008

; Line Out is port D (NodeID = 0xD, SDI#2)
; Set Node ID 0x0D Pin Configs to 0x01014030
HKR,InitVerbs,0000,0x00010001,0x20D71C30 ; Assoc 3, Seq 0
HKR,InitVerbs,0001,0x00010001,0x20D71D40 ; Green, Jack Detect
HKR,InitVerbs,0002,0x00010001,0x20D71E01 ; Line Out, 3.5mm jack
HKR,InitVerbs,0003,0x00010001,0x20D71F01 ; Rear, chassis

; HP Out is Port A   (NodeID = 0xA, SDI#2)
; Set Node ID 0x0A Pin Configs to 0x0221403F
HKR,InitVerbs,0004,0x00010001,0x20A71C3F ; Assoc 3, Seq F
HKR,InitVerbs,0005,0x00010001,0x20A71D40 ; Green, Jack Detect
HKR,InitVerbs,0006,0x00010001,0x20A71E21 ; HP Out, 3.5mm jack
HKR,InitVerbs,0007,0x00010001,0x20A71F02 ; Front, chassis
```

Specify the verb table in a copy of the UAA class driver INF file as a temporary workaround if the BIOS is not programming the pin configuration default registers properly. You cannot use this to pass Windows Vista Logo.

Figure A.29 Partial Verb Table specified in the INF file of the Microsoft UAA class driver for Intel HD Audio

Internal Speaker w/ Redirected Front Panel HP Out

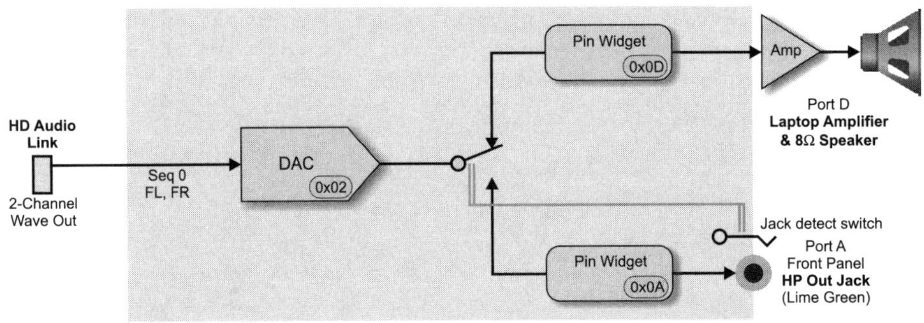

Figure A.30 Internal Speaker and Redirected Headphone Out Jack Sharing a Single DAC

Connectivity	Loc	Device	Type	Color	Jack Detect	Assoc	Seq
Fixed Function	Internal	Speaker	Other Analog	n/a	No (0x1)	1	0
Chassis Jack	Front	HP Out	3.5mm	Green	Yes (0x0)	1	F

```
;configure Redirected Headphone/speaker
; Internal speaker amp is Port D (NodeID = 0xD, SDI#2)
; HP Out is Port A   (NodeID = 0xA, SDI#2)

; Set Node ID 0x0D Pin Configs  to 0x90170110
dd 20D71C10h ; Set 7:0   to 0x10 - Assoc 1, Seq 0
dd 20D71D01h ; Set 15:8  to 0x01 - unknown,No Jack Detect
dd 20D71E17h ; Set 23:16 to 0x17 - Speaker, Other analog
dd 20D71F90h ; Set 31:24 to 0x90 - Internal Speaker

; Set Node ID 0x0A Pin Configs to 0x0221401F
dd 20A71C1Fh ; Set 7:0   to 0x1F - Assoc 1, Seq F
dd 20A71D40h ; Set 15:8  to 0x40 - Green, Jack Detect
dd 20A71E21h ; Set 23:16 to 0x21 - HP Out, 3.5 mm jack
dd 20A71F02h ; Set 31:24 to 0x02 - Front, chassis
```

Figure A.31 Partial Verb Table and Pin Configuration for an Internal Speaker and Redirected Headphone Output

```
 [HdAudInit.AddReg]
; Number of verbs to be sent to codec
HKR,InitVerbs,NumVerbs,0x00010001,0x00000008

;--Codec ID#2, Port D (NID = 0x0D)
; Set Node ID 0x0D Pin Configs  to 0x90170110
HKR,InitVerbs,0000,0x00010001,0x20D71C10 ; Assoc 1, Seq 0
HKR,InitVerbs,0001,0x00010001,0x20D71D01 ; unknown,NoJackDetect
HKR,InitVerbs,0002,0x00010001,0x20D71E17 ; Speaker,Other analog
HKR,InitVerbs,0003,0x00010001,0x20D71F90 ; Internal Spaker

;--Codec ID#2, Port A (NID = 0x0A)
; Set Node ID 0x0A Pin Configs to 0x0221401F
HKR,InitVerbs,0004,0x00010001,0x20A71C1F ; Assoc 1, Seq F
HKR,InitVerbs,0005,0x00010001,0x20A71D40 ; Green, Jack Detect
HKR,InitVerbs,0006,0x00010001,0x20A71E21 ; HP Out, 3.5mm jack
HKR,InitVerbs,0007,0x00010001,0x20A71F02 ; Front, chassis
```

Specify the verb table in a copy of the UAA class driver INF file as a temporary workaround if the BIOS is not programming the pin configuration default registers properly. You cannot use this to pass Windows Vista Logo.

Figure A.32 Partial Verb Table specified in the INF file of the Microsoft UAA class driver for Intel HD Audio

Internal Speaker w/ Redirected Rear Panel Line Out

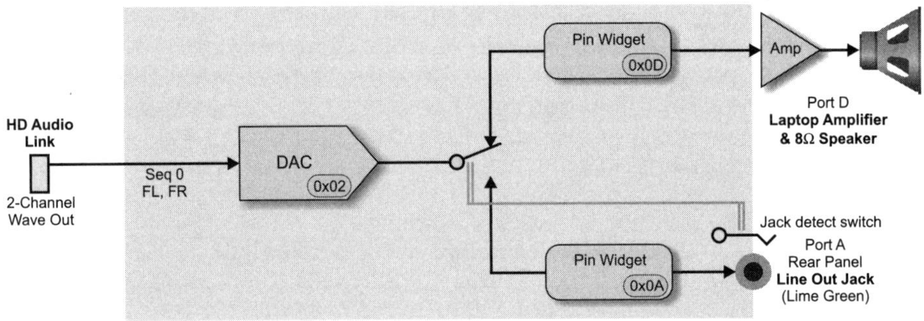

Figure A.33 Internal Speaker and Line Out jack Sharing a Single DAC

Connectivity	Loc	Device	Type	Color	Jack Detect	Assoc	Seq
Fixed Function	Internal	Speaker	Other Analog	n/a	No (0x1)	1	F
Chassis Jack	Rear	LineOut	3.5mm	Green	Yes (0x0)	1	0

```
;configure Redirected Line Out/Speaker
; Internal speaker amp is Port D (NodeID = 0xD, SDI#2)
; Line Out is Port A   (NodeID = 0xA, SDI#2)

; Set Node ID 0x0D Pin Configs  to 0x9017011F
dd 20D71C10h ; Set 7:0   to 0x1F - Assoc 1, Seq F
dd 20D71D01h ; Set 15:8  to 0x01 - unknown,No Jack Detect
dd 20D71E17h ; Set 23:16 to 0x17 - Speaker, Other analog
dd 20D71F90h ; Set 31:24 to 0x90 - Internal Speaker

; Set Node ID 0x0A Pin Configs to 0x01014010
dd 20A71C1Fh ; Set 7:0   to 0x10 - Assoc 1, Seq 0
dd 20A71D40h ; Set 15:8  to 0x40 - Green, Jack Detect
dd 20A71E21h ; Set 23:16 to 0x01 - Line Out, 3.5 mm jack
dd 20A71F02h ; Set 31:24 to 0x01 - Rear, chassis
```

Figure A.34 Partial Verb Table and Pin Configuration for Internal Speaker and Redirected Line Out

```
 [HdAudInit.AddReg]
; Number of verbs to be sent to codec
HKR,InitVerbs,NumVerbs,0x00010001,0x00000008

;--Codec ID#2, Port D (NID = 0x0D)
; Set Node ID 0x0D Pin Configs  to 0x9017011F
HKR,InitVerbs,0000,0x00010001,0x20D71C1F ; Assoc 1, Seq F
HKR,InitVerbs,0001,0x00010001,0x20D71D01 ; unknown,NoJackDetect
HKR,InitVerbs,0002,0x00010001,0x20D71E17 ; Speaker,Other analog
HKR,InitVerbs,0003,0x00010001,0x20D71F90 ; Internal Speaker

;--Codec ID#2, Port A (NID = 0x0A)
; Set Node ID 0x0A Pin Configs to 0x01014010
HKR,InitVerbs,0004,0x00010001,0x20A71C10 ; Assoc 1, Seq 0
HKR,InitVerbs,0005,0x00010001,0x20A71D40 ; Green, Jack Detect
HKR,InitVerbs,0006,0x00010001,0x20A71E01 ; Line Out, 3.5mm jack
HKR,InitVerbs,0007,0x00010001,0x20A71F01 ; Rear, chassis
```

Specify the verb table in a copy of the UAA class driver INF file as a temporary workaround if the BIOS is not programming the pin configuration default registers properly. You cannot use this to pass Windows Vista Logo.

Figure A.35 Partial Verb Table specified in the INF file of the Microsoft UAA class driver for Intel HD Audio

Shared Input Mux with Line In, CD In, and Microphone In

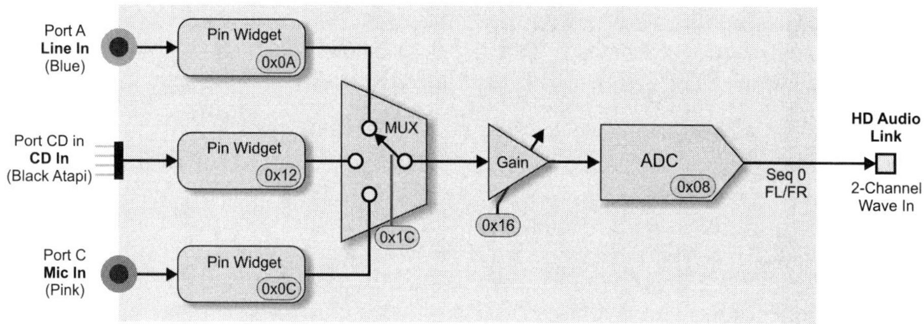

Figure A.36 Three Pin Widgets Sharing a Single ADC in a Mux Pin Configuration

Connectivity	Loc	Device	Type	Color	Jack Detect	Assoc	Seq
Chassis Jack	Rear	Line In	3.5 mm	Blue	Yes (0x0)	5	0
Fixed Function	ATAPI	CD In	ATAPI	Black	No (0x1)	5	1
Chassis Jack	Front	Mic In	3.5 mm	Pink	Yes (0x0)	5	E

```
;configure shared ADC with Muxed inputs

; Line In is Port A (NodeID = 0xA, SDI#2)
; Set Node ID 0x0A Pin Configs to 0x01813050
dd 20A71C50h ; Set 7:0   to 0x50 - Assoc 5, Seq 0
dd 20A71D30h ; Set 15:8  to 0x30 - Blue, Jack Detect
dd 20A71E81h ; Set 23:16 to 0x81 - Line In, 3.5 mm jack
dd 20A71F01h ; Set 31:24 to 0x01 - Rear, chassis

; CD In  is Port CD_IN (NodeID = 0x12, SDI#2)
; Set Node ID 0x12 Pin Configs to 0x19931151
dd 21271C51h ; Set 7:0   to 0x51 - Assoc 5, Seq 1
dd 21271D11h ; Set 15:8  to 0x11 - Black, No Jack Detect
dd 21271E93h ; Set 23:16 to 0x93 - CD, ATAPI
dd 21271F19h ; Set 31:24 to 0x19 - ATAPI Jack on M/B

; Mic In  is Port C (NodeID = 0xC, SDI#2)
; Set Node ID 0x0C Pin Configs to 0x02A1905E
```

```
dd 20C71C5Eh ; Set 7:0   to 0x5E - Assoc 5, Seq E
dd 20C71D90h ; Set 15:8  to 0x90 - Pink, Jack Detect
dd 20C71EA1h ; Set 23:16 to 0xA1 - Mic In, 3.5 mm jack
dd 20C71F02h ; Set 31:24 to 0x02 - Front, chassis
```

Figure A.37 Partial Verb Table for a Shared ADC Mux Pin Configuration

```
[HdAudInit.AddReg]
; Number of verbs to be sent to codec
HKR,InitVerbs,NumVerbs,0x00010001,0x0000000C

; Line In is Port A (NodeID = 0x0A, SDI#2)
; Set Node ID 0x0A Pin Configs to 0x01813050
HKR,InitVerbs,0000,0x00010001,0x20A71C50 ; Assoc 5, Seq 0
HKR,InitVerbs,0001,0x00010001,0x20A71D30 ; Blue, Jack Detect
HKR,InitVerbs,0002,0x00010001,0x20A71E81 ; Line In, 3.5 mm jack
HKR,InitVerbs,0003,0x00010001,0x20A71F01 ; Rear, chassis

; CD In  is Port CD_IN  (NodeID = 0x12, SDI#2)
; Set Node ID 0x12 Pin Configs to 0x19931151
HKR,InitVerbs,0004,0x00010001,0x21271C51 ; Assoc 5, Seq 1
HKR,InitVerbs,0005,0x00010001,0x21271D11 ; Blue, Jack Detect
HKR,InitVerbs,0006,0x00010001,0x21271E93 ; CD In, ATAPI
HKR,InitVerbs,0007,0x00010001,0x21271F19 ; ATAPI Jack on M/B

; Mic In is Port C (NodeID = 0x0C, SDI#2)
; Set Node ID 0x0C Pin Configs to 0x02A1905E
HKR,InitVerbs,0008,0x00010001,0x20C71C5E ; Assoc 5, Seq E
HKR,InitVerbs,0009,0x00010001,0x20C71D90 ; Pink, Jack Detect
HKR,InitVerbs,0010,0x00010001,0x20C71EA1 ; Mic In, 3.5 mm jack
HKR,InitVerbs,0011,0x00010001,0x20C71F02 ; Front, chassis
```

Specify the verb table in a copy of the UAA class driver INF file as a temporary workaround if the BIOS is not programming the pin configuration default registers properly. You cannot use this to pass Windows Vista Logo.

Figure A.38 Partial Verb Table specified in the INF file of the Microsoft UAA class driver for Intel HD Audio

Shared Input Mix with Line In, CD In, and Microphone In

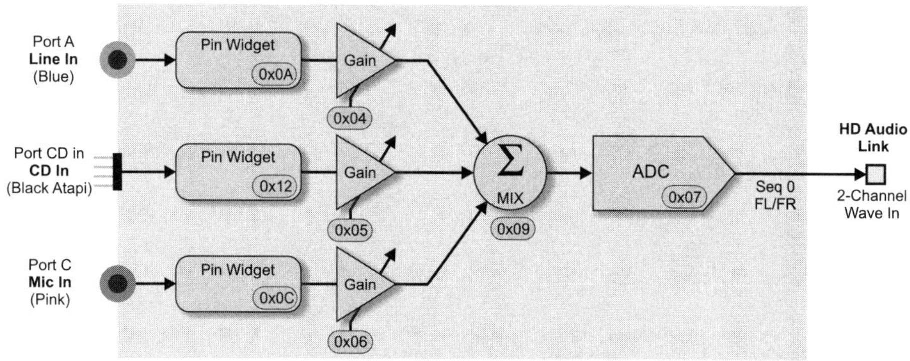

Figure A.39 Three Pin Widgets Sharing a Single ADC in a Mix Configuration

Connectivity	Loc	Device	Type	Color	Jack Detect	Assoc	Seq
Chassis Jack	Rear	Line In	3.5 mm	Blue	Yes (0x0)	5	0
Fixed Function	ATAPI	CD In	ATAPI	Black	No (0x1)	5	1
Chassis Jack	Front	Mic In	3.5 mm	Pink	Yes (0x0)	5	F

```
;configure shared ADC with Mixed inputs

; Line In is Port A (NodeID = 0x0A, SDI#2)
; Set Node ID 0x0A Pin Configs to 0x01813050
dd 20A71C50h ; Set 7:0   to 0x50 - Assoc 5, Seq 0
dd 20A71D30h ; Set 15:8  to 0x30 - Blue, Jack Detect
dd 20A71E81h ; Set 23:16 to 0x81 - Line In, 3.5 mm jack
dd 20A71F01h ; Set 31:24 to 0x01 - Rear, chassis

; CD In is Port CD_In  (NodeID = 0x12, SDI#2)
; Set Node ID 0x12 Pin Configs to 0x19931151
dd 21271C51h ; Set 7:0   to 0x51 - Assoc 5, Seq 1
dd 21271D11h ; Set 15:8  to 0x11 - Black, No Jack Detect
dd 21271E93h ; Set 23:16 to 0x93 - CD In, ATAPI
dd 21271F19h ; Set 31:24 to 0x19 - ATAPI Jack on M/B

; Mic In is Port C  (NodeID = 0x0C, SDI#2)
; Set Node ID 0x0C Pin Configs to 0x02A1905F
```

```
dd 20C71C5Fh ; Set 7:0   to 0x5F - Assoc 5, Seq F
dd 20C71D90h ; Set 15:8  to 0x90 - Pink, Jack Detect
dd 20C71EA1h ; Set 23:16 to 0xA1 - Mic In, 3.5 mm jack
dd 20C71F02h ; Set 31:24 to 0x02 - Front, chassis
```

Figure A.40 Partial Verb Table for a Shared ADC Mix Pin Configuration

```
[HdAudInit.AddReg]
; Number of verbs to be sent to codec
HKR,InitVerbs,NumVerbs,0x00010001,0x0000000C

; Line In is Port A (NodeID = 0x0A, SDI#2)
; Set Node ID 0x0A Pin Configs to 0x01813050
HKR,InitVerbs,0000,0x00010001,0x20A71C50 ; Assoc 5, Seq 0
HKR,InitVerbs,0001,0x00010001,0x20A71D30 ; Blue, Jack Detect
HKR,InitVerbs,0002,0x00010001,0x20A71E81 ; Line In, 3.5 mm jack
HKR,InitVerbs,0003,0x00010001,0x20A71F01 ; Rear, chassis

; CD In  is Port CD_IN  (NodeID = 0x12, SDI#2)
; Set Node ID 0x12 Pin Configs to 0x19931151
HKR,InitVerbs,0004,0x00010001,0x21271C51 ; Assoc 5, Seq 1
HKR,InitVerbs,0005,0x00010001,0x21271D11 ; Black, No JackDetect
HKR,InitVerbs,0006,0x00010001,0x21271E93 ; CD In, ATAPI
HKR,InitVerbs,0007,0x00010001,0x21271F01 ; Jack on M/B

; Mic In is Port C (NodeID = 0x0C, SDI#2)
; Set Node ID 0x0C Pin Configs to 0x02A1905F
HKR,InitVerbs,0008,0x00010001,0x20C71C5F ; Assoc 5, Seq F
HKR,InitVerbs,0009,0x00010001,0x20C71D90 ; Pink, Jack Detect
HKR,InitVerbs,0010,0x00010001,0x20C71EA1 ; Mic In, 3.5 mm jack
HKR,InitVerbs,0011,0x00010001,0x20C71F02 ; Front, chassis
```

Specify the verb table in a copy of the UAA class driver INF file as a temporary workaround if the BIOS is not programming the pin configuration default registers properly. You cannot use this to pass Windows Vista Logo.

Figure A.41 Partial Verb Table specified in the INF file of the Microsoft UAA class driver for Intel HD Audio

Rear Panel 5.1 Surround Line Outputs with Redirected Front Panel Headphone Output

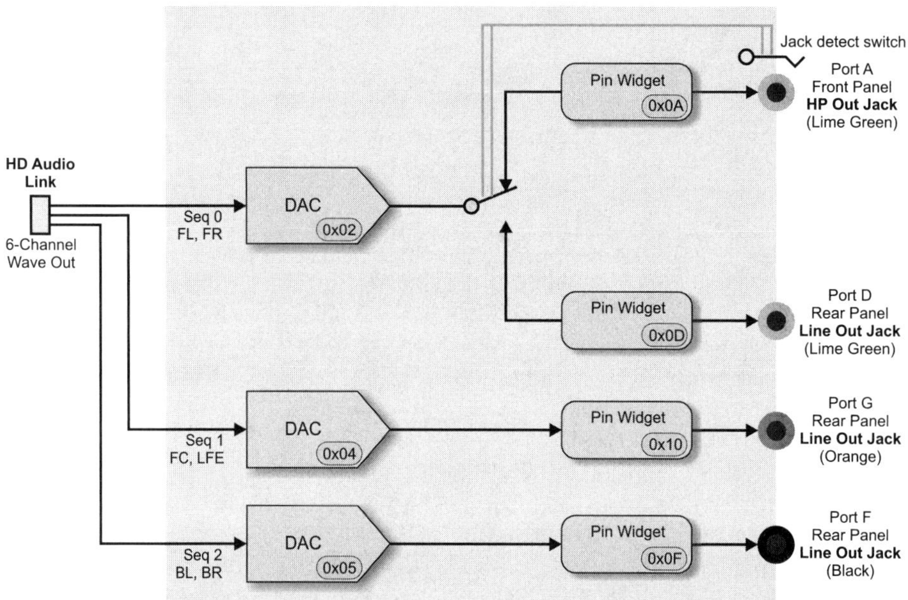

Figure A.42 Codec Topology for 5.1 Output with Redirected Front Panel Headphone Output

Connectivity	Loc	Device	Type	Color	Jack Detect	Assoc	Seq
Chassis Jack	Rear	Line Out	3.5 mm	Green	Yes (0x0)	3	0
Chassis Jack	Rear	Line Out	3.5 mm	Orange	Yes (0x0)	3	1
Chassis Jack	Rear	Line Out	3.5 mm	Black	Yes (0x0)	3	2
Chassis Jack	Front	HP Out	3.5 mm	Green	Yes (0x0)	3	F

The choice of sequence number determines the function of each port, which must be matched with the proper color for that function.

```
;configure 5.1 surround sound

; Port D (NID = 0x0D): Green, Front L/R
; Set Node ID 0x0D Pin Configs to 0x01014030
dd 20D71C30h ; Set 7:0   to 0x30 - Assoc 3, Seq 0 - FL,FR
```

```
dd 20D71D40h ; Set 15:8  to 0x40 - Green, Jack Detect
dd 20D71E01h ; Set 23:16 to 0x01 - Line Out, 3.5 mm jack
dd 20D71F01h ; Set 31:24 to 0x01 - Rear, chassis

; Port G (NID = 0x10): Orange, Center/LFE
; Set Node ID 0x10 Pin Configs to 0x01016031
dd 21071C31h ; Set 7:0   to 0x31 - Assoc 3, Seq 1- FC,LFE
dd 21071D60h ; Set 15:8  to 0x60 - Orange, Jack Detect
dd 21071E01h ; Set 23:16 to 0x01 - Line Out, 3.5 mm jack
dd 21071F01h ; Set 31:24 to 0x01 - Rear, chassis

; Port F (NID = 0x0F): Black, Back L/R
; Set Node ID 0x0F Pin Configs to 0x01011032
dd 20F71C32h ; Set 7:0   to 0x32 - Assoc 3, Seq 2 - BL,BR
dd 20F71D10h ; Set 15:8  to 0x10 - Black, Jack Detect
dd 20F71E01h ; Set 23:16 to 0x01 - Line Out, 3.5 mm jack
dd 20F71F01h ; Set 31:24 to 0x01 - Rear, chassis

; Port A (NID = 0x0A): Green, Front L/R
; Set Node ID 0x0A Pin Configs to 0x0321403F
dd 20A71C3Fh ; Set 7:0   to 0x3F - Assoc 3, Seq F - FL,FR
dd 20A71D40h ; Set 15:8  to 0x40 - Green, Jack Detect
dd 20A71E21h ; Set 23:16 to 0x21 - HP Out, 3.5 mm jack
dd 20A71F03h ; Set 31:24 to 0x03 - Left, chassis
```

Figure A.43 Partial Verb Table and Pin Configuration for a 5.1 Surround Sound Configuration Using Sequence (0, 1, 2) with Redirected Headphone

---

```
[HdAudInit.AddReg]
; Number of verbs to be sent to codec
HKR,InitVerbs,NumVerbs,0x00010001,0x00000010

; Port D (NID = 0x0D): Green, Front L/R
; Set Node ID 0x0D Pin Configs to 0x01014030
HKR,InitVerbs,0000,0x00010001,0x20D71C30 ; Assoc 3, Seq 0
HKR,InitVerbs,0001,0x00010001,0x20D71D40 ; Green, Jack Detect
HKR,InitVerbs,0002,0x00010001,0x20D71E01 ; Line Out, 3.5mm jack
HKR,InitVerbs,0003,0x00010001,0x20D71F01 ; Rear, chassis

; Port G (NID = 0x10): Orange, Center/LFE
; Set Node ID 0x10 Pin Configs to 0x01016031
HKR,InitVerbs,0004,0x00010001,0x21071C31 ; Assoc 3, Seq 1
HKR,InitVerbs,0005,0x00010001,0x21071D60 ; Orange, Jack Detect
HKR,InitVerbs,0006,0x00010001,0x21071E01 ; Line Out, 3.5mm jack
HKR,InitVerbs,0007,0x00010001,0x21071F01 ; Rear, chassis
```

```
; Port F (NID = 0x0F): Black, Back L/R
; Set Node ID 0x0F Pin Configs to 0x01011032
HKR,InitVerbs,0008,0x00010001,0x20F71C32 ; Assoc 3, Seq 2
HKR,InitVerbs,0009,0x00010001,0x20F71D10 ; Black, Jack Detect
HKR,InitVerbs,0010,0x00010001,0x20F71E01 ; Line Out, 3.5mm jack
HKR,InitVerbs,0011,0x00010001,0x20F71F01 ; Rear, chassis

; Port A (NID = 0x0A): Green, Front L/R
; Set Node ID 0x0A Pin Configs to 0x0321403F
HKR,InitVerbs,0012,0x00010001,0x20A71C3F ; Assoc 3, Seq F
HKR,InitVerbs,0013,0x00010001,0x20A71D40 ; Green, Jack Detect
HKR,InitVerbs,0014,0x00010001,0x20A71E21 ; HP Out, 3.5mm jack
HKR,InitVerbs,0015,0x00010001,0x20A71F03 ; Left, chassis
```

Specify the verb table in a copy of the UAA class driver INF file as a temporary workaround if the BIOS is not programming the pin configuration default registers properly. You cannot use this to pass Windows Vista Logo.

Figure A.44 Partial Verb Table specified in the INF file of the Microsoft UAA class driver for Intel HD Audio

Set All DACs to Mute

```
; MUTE ALL DACS on Codec ID #2
;
; the verbs are formed in groups of four in case the BIOS
; uses the count of pin widgets to determine how big the
; verb table is. The pin widget count should be increased
; by two to accommodate these additional commands
; The second group of 4 includes some repeated in order
; to end up with a table size which is a multiple of 4
;
dd    2023F080h        ; Mute DAC at Node 0x02
dd    2033F080h        ; Mute DAC at Node 0x03
dd    2043F080h        ; Mute DAC at Node 0x04
dd    2053F080h        ; Mute DAC at Node 0x05

dd    2063F080h        ; Mute DAC at Node 0x06
dd    2063F080h        ; Mute DAC at Node 0x06 (repeat)
dd    2063F080h        ; Mute DAC at Node 0x06 (repeat)
dd    2063F080h        ; Mute DAC at Node 0x06 (repeat)
```

These states could be reset to default values whenever codec reset or function group reset occurs.

Figure A.45 List of Eight Verbs Which Will Mute All DACs in the Codec

```
 [HdAudInit.AddReg]
; Number of verbs to be sent to codec
HKR,InitVerbs,NumVerbs,0x00010001,0x00000005

;--Codec ID#2, Mute DACs 0x02 thru 0x06
HKR,InitVerbs,0000,0x00010001,0x2023F080 ; Mute DAC 0x02
HKR,InitVerbs,0001,0x00010001,0x2033F080 ; Mute DAC 0x03
HKR,InitVerbs,0002,0x00010001,0x2043F080 ; Mute DAC 0x04
HKR,InitVerbs,0003,0x00010001,0x2053F080 ; Mute DAC 0x05
HKR,InitVerbs,0004,0x00010001,0x2063F080 ; Mute DAC 0x06
```

Specify the verb table in a copy of the UAA class driver INF file as a temporary workaround if the BIOS is not programming the pin configuration default registers properly. You cannot use this to pass Windows Vista Logo.

Figure A.46 Partial Verb Table specified in the INF file of the Microsoft UAA class driver for Intel HD Audio

Set All Pin Widgets to Disabled State

```
; Set all Pin Widgets on Codec ID #2
; to disable input, output, and VRefOut
;
; the verbs are formed in groups of four in case the BIOS
; uses the count of pin widgets to determine how big the
; verb table is. The pin widget count in the BIOS should
; increase by two to accommodate these additional verbs
;
dd    20A70700h         ; Disable Pin Widget 0x0A
dd    20B70700h         ; Disable Pin Widget 0x0B
dd    20C70700h         ; Disable Pin Widget 0x0C
dd    20D70700h         ; Disable Pin Widget 0x0D

dd    20E70700h         ; Disable Pin Widget 0x0E
dd    20F70700h         ; Disable Pin Widget 0x0F
dd    21070700h         ; Disable Pin Widget 0x10
dd    21170700h         ; Disable Pin Widget 0x11
```

These states could be reset to default values whenever codec reset or function group reset occurs.

Figure A.47 Verb List to Disable Input, Output and VRefOut for All Pin Widgets

```
[HdAudInit.AddReg]
; Number of verbs to be sent to codec
HKR,InitVerbs,NumVerbs,0x00010001,0x00000008

;--Codec ID#2, Disable Pins A thru H
HKR,InitVerbs,0000,0x00010001,0x20A70700 ; Disable Pin 0x0A
HKR,InitVerbs,0001,0x00010001,0x20B70700 ; Disable Pin 0x0B
HKR,InitVerbs,0002,0x00010001,0x20C70700 ; Disable Pin 0x0C
HKR,InitVerbs,0003,0x00010001,0x20D70700 ; Disable Pin 0x0D
HKR,InitVerbs,0004,0x00010001,0x20E70700 ; Disable Pin 0x0A
HKR,InitVerbs,0005,0x00010001,0x20F70700 ; Disable Pin 0x0B
HKR,InitVerbs,0006,0x00010001,0x21070700 ; Disable Pin 0x0C
HKR,InitVerbs,0007,0x00010001,0x21170700 ; Disable Pin 0x0D
```

Specify the verb table in a copy of the UAA class driver INF file as a temporary work-around if the BIOS is not programming the pin configuration default registers properly. You cannot use this verb table and pass Windows Vista Logo testing.

Figure A.48 Partial Verb Table specified in the INF file of the Microsoft UAA class driver for Intel HD Audio

Appendix B

PC Audio Hardware History: Then and Now

When the first personal computers (PC) were introduced in the late 1970's, they had very limited sound capabilities—if they had any at all. As an example, the Apple II released in 1977 came standard with a simple speaker that could be toggled between two positions via software. To produce any sort of tone, a subroutine had to be written that would toggle the speaker at the de-sired frequency. The resulting motion generated monophonic square wave sound.

At the time, cassette tapes and long-playing (LP) records were the popular consumer audio formats. These formats provided audio fidelity that far exceeded that of the contemporary computers.

The sound capabilities of the computers improved over time. In 1981, Commodore introduced the VIC-20 computer, the first PC model to exceed a million units shipped. It offered three square wave generators that could be run simultaneously. Each generator spanned three octaves, but was limited to producing 128 different tones. The VIC-20 also included a white noise generator that could be combined with the square wave generators.

Launched in 1981, the IBM PC (Model 5150) was the first in a long-lived species of computers based on Intel® processors that survives to this day. The IBM PC sported a single-channel square wave generator using the 8253 timer chip that was present on every system. The resulting sound has come to be known as PC Speaker or PC Beep.

By 1987, IBM had introduced multiple successors to the original IBM PC. Furthermore, compatible IBM clones were being sold by an increasing number of companies around the world. All these computers continued to use monophonic PC Speaker sound. Meanwhile, competing computer systems offered superior sound capabilities. For instance, the Apple Macintosh II supported four channels of 8-bit, 44.1-kilohertz digital stereo sound.

The ISA Era

The year 1987 was a milestone in IBM PC sound: it marked the introduction of a new sound card from AdLib, which used a technique known as frequency modulation (FM) to reproduce the sound of musical instruments far more accurately than was possible with a single square wave. The AdLib card could play nine sound channels simultaneously, or six sound channels and five hit instruments, such as drums and cymbals. While the AdLib card dramatically improved the musical soundtracks of games, the remaining sound effects, such as a spaceship firing its weapons, still had to be rendered via the monophonic PC Speaker.

The AdLib card attached to the PC via the Industry Standard Architecture (ISA) bus. Originally an 8-bit bus running at 4.77 megahertz, the ISA bus was later enhanced to support a 16-bit width running at 8 megahertz, but no soundcards made use of this enhancement. ISA's bandwidth is very limited by today's standards, but at the time, it allowed for a huge leap forward in PC sound. The applications that made the most use of the new audio capabilities were computer games.

In 1989, Creative Labs introduced a new sound card, called the Sound Blaster, which contained the same FM synthesis chip used by AdLib and included the ability to play 8-bit, 22-kilohertz digital samples. While still a far cry from the built-in capabilities of the Apple computers, the $300 Sound Blaster marked the start of a whole new era of sound on PCs. The Sound Blaster quickly became the best-selling computer peripheral. A 1991 version of Sound Blaster added stereo sound support. A 1992 version supported stereo and 16-bit digital sound.

Even after the Sound Blaster was introduced, most games continued to use FM synthesis to generate sounds. However, ultimately FM synthesis was discarded and the vast majority of computer sound was generated using digital samples.

The PCI Era

With each passing year, computers increased in performance, and the ISA bus became a bottleneck for high-bandwidth applications. Higher performance buses, such as the Extended Industry Standard Architecture (EISA), were introduced, but the bus that became the real industry standard was the Peripheral Component Interconnect (PCI) bus, developed by Intel in the early 1990s.

PCI was intended to be a general-purpose bus, and indeed, it was used for a variety of applications including modems, video cards, SCSI cards, and sound cards. PCI is a 32-bit bus originally clocked at 33 megahertz, offering a bandwidth of 132 megabytes per second, four times more than EISA and over 15 times more than ISA. PCI was also upgraded to support a 64-bit width and 66-megahertz speed, but such extensions were not widely used outside of servers.

Another innovative feature of PCI was its Plug and Play capability, which allowed users to add cards to the computer without having to set jumpers on the cards or adjust low-level software configurations manually—as was the case with ISA.

Despite PCI's advanced capabilities, it was not until 1998 that the first PCI sound cards appeared. These first PCI sound cards offered support for up to 32 voices in hardware as well as 3-dimensional sound processing. But as PCs supporting ISA dwindled, PCI became the most popular interconnect for external sound cards. By 2001, PCI sound cards using 24-bit/96-kilohertz DACs were available, offering a potential SNR of better than 100 decibels. The fidelity of these cards was on par with consumer electronics (CE) audio equipment. The high-end sound cards surpassed low-end CE devices; high-end CE devices surpassed the low-end sound cards.

The Chipset Era

A typical computer built in the late 1990s has the components shown in Figure B.1. The central processing unit (CPU) is the brains of the computer; it performs most of the calculations on the system. The CPU attaches to a memory controller hub (MCH), sometimes known as a *Northbridge*. The MCH provides a high-speed interconnect between the CPU and main system memory. The memory stores the code and data that the CPU processes. A graphics controller that attaches to the MCH via an Accelerated Graphics Port (AGP) has the responsibility of for generating the image that is displayed on the attached monitor. The graphics card is connected to the MCH since it needs high-speed, high-bandwidth access to the system memory.

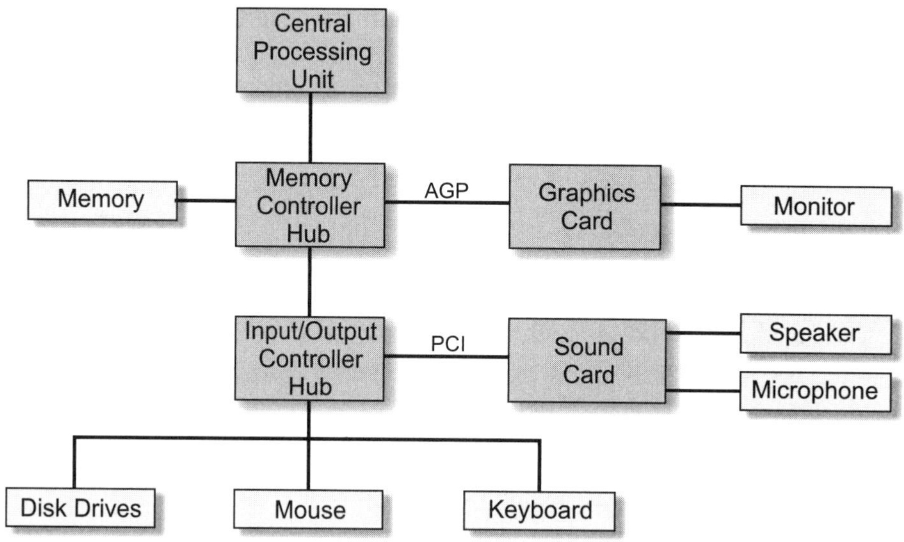

Figure B.1 PC Functional Blocks Prior to Introduction of Integrated Audio

Attached to the MCH is the Input/Output Controller Hub (ICH), also known as the *Southbridge*. With the exception of the graphics display, the ICH had responsibility for directing all data that exited and entered the computer. This input/output traffic included input from the mouse and keyboard, read and writes to disk drivers, sound coming in from microphones, and sound going out to speakers. The ICH did not communicate directly with all these peripherals. In the case of audio, the ICH included an embedded PCI bus controller and attached to this was a PCI sound card.

Conceptually, the fundamental components of a sound card can be broken down into three elements, as shown in Figure B.2. Computers work primarily in digital signals, so audio data that moves between the ICH and the sound card needs to be in digital format. Conversely, speakers and microphones can only handle analog signals. The ADC and the DAC that are shown in the figure convert data between the two domains.

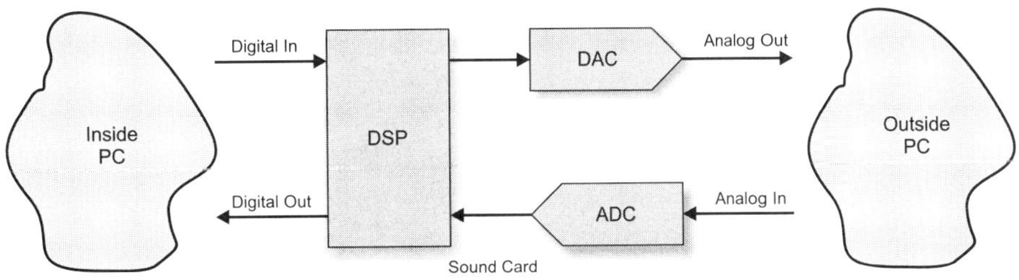

Figure B.2 Simplified Sound Card Block Diagram

The remaining element in our simplified sound card is the Digital Signal Processor (DSP). As implied by its name, the DSP operates on digital audio data. These operations included combining multiple voice channels into a single audio signal and converting the sampling rate or sampling depth of signals. The DSP was one of the most expensive pieces of hardware on the sound card. As such, it accounted for a non-trivial portion of the Bill of Materials (BOM) cost for a computer. Computer manufacturers are always looking for ways to lower the BOM cost.

As noted, the computer already has another processor on it. The CPU is capable of performing all the operations done in the DSP. In the era of the ISA sound cards, however, the CPU did not have enough computational bandwidth to spare for doing sound processing; it had its hands full performing other operations.

But time marches on. And CPU manufacturers were improving the computational power of their products in accordance with Moore's Law, which translated into CPU performance doubling every 12–18 months.

So in the mid-1990s, sound cards were expensive and CPUs had some computational bandwidth to spare. Hence, the stage was set for Intel to release the Audio Controller 97 (AC97) standard in 1997.

AC97

AC97 allows sound processing tasks such as sample rate conversion and mixing to be handled by the CPU. AC97 is implemented by adding logic known as the *AC97 digital controller* to the ICH, as shown in Figure B.3. The digital controller logic sends and receives processed digital audio to an external piece of silicon known as an *AC97 analog codec*. The purpose of the codec is to convert the digital audio data into analog signals, which were used to drive speakers. The codec also converts external analog sources into digital data that is fed back to the main memory space via the AC97 link.

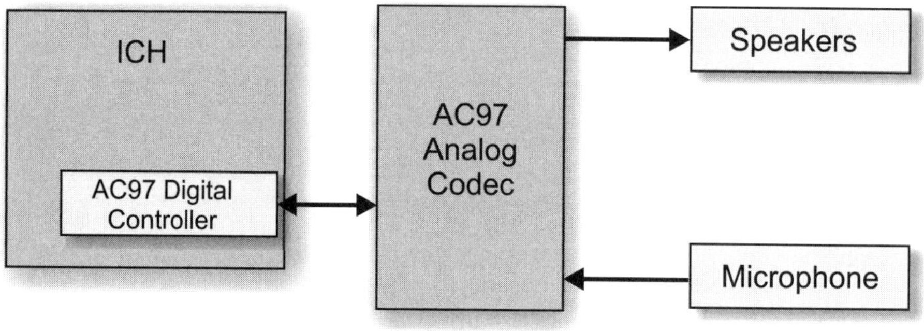

Figure B.3 Addition of AC97

Because AC97 offloads many of the sound-processing tasks from dedicated hardware to software that is run on the general purpose CPU, it was originally known as *soft audio* or *host audio*. An AC97 analog codec is significantly cheaper than a full-blown sound chip, so it is an inexpensive way to add sound to a PC. The decreased price comes at the cost of some of the CPU's computational bandwidth being used to process sound. Typically, the CPU usage is negligible.

The original AC97 specification supported 18-bit stereo sound output at 48 kilohertz. The specification was expanded in subsequent years to include support for 20-bit, 96-kilohertz stereo sound output, 4- and 6-channel sound configurations, and a separate S/PDIF channel.

CNR

PC manufacturers often prefer flexibility in their designs, such as the ability to use a single motherboard design as the basis of multiple products. Having an AC97 codec soldered directly on the motherboard means that it is not efficient to use that same motherboard for a system with a PCI sound card. The system has the expense of the AC97 hardware, even when the external card is used to generate sounds. In the context of AC97, this flexibility issue is addressed via a Communication Network Riser (CNR) interface.

The CNR interface defines a motherboard connector and card form factor (see Figure B.4) that can be used to carry AC97, network, USB, or

System Management Bus (SMB) signals. CNR allows PC manufacturers to have a stuffing option for a single motherboard.

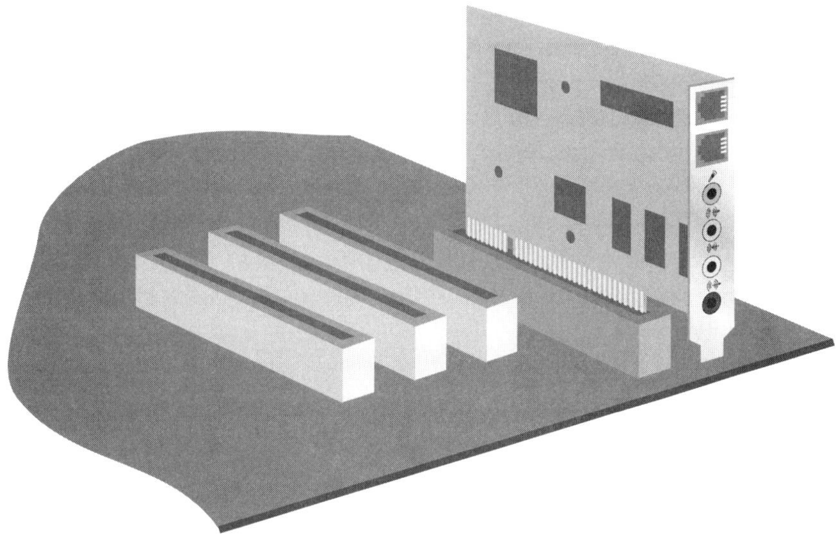

Figure B.4 CNR Card with AC97 Codec

In terms of sound, manufacturers could use the same motherboard for a low-cost sound solution such as a single AC97 codec on the CNR card or a higher-performance sound solution like 6-channel sound provided by two AC97 codecs on the CNR card. Alternatively, sound could be provided by a PCI sound card. Another benefit of CNR is that it allowed for higher fidelity via AC97 by moving the codecs further away noisy motherboard components. Conversely, a poor CNR design could introduce more noise into the audio subsystem.

In practice, it turned out that the CNR slot was used much less for AC97 than many had hoped, and now it is used only in audio laboratories for switching between different devices. While CNR is technically capable of supporting AC97's successor, Intel® HD Audio, CNR is not formally supported for Intel HD Audio.

The earlier Audio Modem Riser (AMR), a predecessor to CNR and the competing Audio Communications Riser (ACR) were functionally very similar and differed from CNR only in the pinout, the Plug and Play support that required an external EEPROM, and the support for various non-audio devices. These connectors are no longer used in modern designs.

AC97 in Practice

Initially, most people considered AC97 solutions to be capable of providing only entry level sound with poor fidelity. This perception was certainly justified; the early years of AC97 were plagued by software and operating system issues, as was the case for the early years of discrete cards as well. But the fundamental problem with early AC97 products was rooted in hardware. Motherboard designers and manufacturers did not understand how to design a quality audio solution—or they did not care about doing so. They mostly focused on the low cost offered by AC97 solutions. Many of the products, including CNR-based products, suffered from crosstalk, electromagnetic interface, hums, and other types of noise.

Ultimately, the quality of many AC97 solutions improved, and the benefits of dedicated sound cards diminished, especially for those cards that still used on-board DSPs for mixing. The parity between AC97 and discrete sound solutions came about in part because the PCI bus speed matched the 33-megahertz system memory at the time PCI was introduced, but it stayed fixed at 33 megahertz for desktop PCs while memory bus speeds soared. As a result, transferring multiple streams of audio across the PCI bus and mixing them in hardware became very inefficient. Instead, the CPU load could be reduced as much as an order of magnitude by mixing in software and only sending the final two channels of mixed audio over the PCI bus.

OEMs began caring more about sound quality, and AC97 expanded from entry-level to mainstream PCs. AC97 sound quality became on par with the average external sound card. However, high-end sound cards offered larger sampling rates, greater sample depths, and more channels than AC97 supported.

High Definition Audio

The Intel® High Definition Audio Specification replaced AC97 in early 2004. You can read more about it elsewhere in this book.

Appendix C

Audio Drivers from DOS to Windows[†] XP

The existing Windows[†] XP audio subsystem contains a rich legacy driven by backwards compatibility. Many of today's Windows XP audio "features" exist only because they were useful long ago and could not be removed. Windows Vista will completely restructure the audio subsystem and its release will be a much larger break from legacy applications than any that has ever taken place in Windows audio. However, to understand why the audio in Windows XP works that way it does, you need to first understand how it evolved.

Early PC soundcards intended for DOS games were implemented in many different ways, and game software typically included direct support for one or more popular soundcards. Some soundcards would load Terminate and Stay Resident (TSR) programs to support the cards, and others would simply talk directly to the application. Early versions of Windows were built on top of DOS, and they made little effort to provide a unified approach to audio. The drivers that did exist at this time were implemented using 16-bit code with segmented addressing.

Windows 3.0 and Multi-Media Extensions

Windows 3.0 made the shift to multiple protection modes and 32-bit linear addressing. While applications continued to be written in 16-bit code with segmented addressing, new Virtual Device Drivers known as VxDs were capable of running at Ring 0 and addressing up to 2 gigabytes of memory linearly. The VxDs were used to virtualize the hardware, to make each application function as if it owned all of the hardware. The VxD would provide a layer between the hardware and the application to allow the application to operate this way.

This new architecture made possible the introduction of MME, or Windows Multimedia Extensions. This audio driver framework for Windows was the first to abstract the interface to the sound card in a generalized way. A generalized media player interface called Multimedia Control Interface was introduced at part of this package, along with a Media Player application.

Windows† 3.1

MME was initially made available to developers as an add-on to Windows 3.0, but was included with the Windows 3.1 release in March of 1992. The three main functional groups were Wave, MIDI, and Aux. Wave had to do with the data coming through the DMA channel, and it also controlled the volume of the DAC. MIDI controlled the serial MIDI port on the soundcard at first, and as higher quality General MIDI synthesizers were added to soundcards, it was used to control the synthesizer itself. Aux was used to control analog signal paths on the soundcard. A complete driver package included 16-bit DLLs with an extension of .DRV for Wave, MIDI, and Aux, as well as a 32-bit VxD driver that usually was shared by all three.

The Windows Sound System, a soundcard sold with bundled software from Microsoft, also included the first implementation of the Microsoft MIXERLINE interface, which replaced the Aux interface for controlling analog volume controls on the soundcard. This MIXERLINE interface for the first time enabled the SNDVOL32.EXE application to provide a standardized volume control GUI to the user. It has changed very little since then. WHQL testing for audio drivers was started in this timeframe.

Windows NT

In parallel, Microsoft was also developing Windows NT—the NT designation originally stood for New Technology. This development effort spun off from the co-development of OS/2† with IBM, and the new OS was released in May of 1993, with version number "3.1" because it used the same user interface as Windows 3.1. It was designed from the bottom up as 32-bit protected mode operating system. Audio drivers in Windows NT were similar in concept to the 16-bit .DRV files in Windows 3.11, but were implemented in 32-bit code. Windows NT contained no VxDs. Therefore a driver codebase could not be shared easily between the two, and separate drivers and applications needed to be maintained for each. Because NT was primarily focused on business applications, the audio on the platform had little reason to evolve beyond the basics. Windows NT4 followed in 1996, but this was basically the same kernel with the Windows 95 look and feel. Audio functionality was basically identical to earlier versions.

DirectSound

In parallel with Windows NT, Microsoft began their DirectX initiative to wean game developers from DOS and direct communication with sound cards. DirectX provides a comprehensive set of interfaces for optimizing game performance. DirectSound and DirectSound3D are the portions of DirectX that focus on audio and provide consistent APIs for controlling all aspects of how a sound is played. DirectMusic includes a software-based MIDI synthesizer and does much the same sound-control for MIDI and musical events. Drivers need to add special support for DirectSound, and a number of soundcards developed for DirectSound3D can play sounds from either main memory or from an independent RAM buffer without loading down the CPU. Many of these chips can also perform 3D-positional effects, such as creating the sound of a bee buzzing around your head.

Applications can choose to play audio through the DirectSound interface or through the Windows Multimedia interface. Behavior differs depending on which interface is used. For instance, you may get different results when playing a multi-channel file using Windows Sound Recorder rather than Windows Media Player, because each one uses a different audio API. Table C.1 shows the a few types of Windows audio applications and the system component that each type of application uses. Some applications offer the option to use either interface, but others do not.

Table C.1 APIs Used by Some Windows Applications

Audio Application	System Component
Windows Sound Recorder	Windows Multimedia (winmm.sys)
Windows Media Player v7 & higher	DirectSound (dsound.dll)

DirectX titles, including most games	DirectSound
Most high-end wave editors	Windows Multimedia

Windows 95

In August of 1995, the introduction of Windows 95 included Plug and Play, which provided a big boost to the end-user's ability to successfully install a soundcard in a PC. In the OS installer, Microsoft† also included drivers for a number of popular soundcards. Windows 95 also introduced pre-emptive multi-tasking and the Win32 programming model, allowing 32-bit applications to be written so that they could run on either Windows 95 or Windows NT 3.5. Changes between Windows 3.11 and Windows 95 were small as far as the audio driver stack was concerned.

Around this time, Steinberg† introduced their Audio Stream I/O (ASIO†) driver model to get around some of the limitations of Wave drivers. Intended to work on both Mac and PC, this API is designed primarily for multi-track recording and playback. Most of the functionality is implemented in user-mode, rather than in kernel mode. This standard has become popular enough that ASIO drivers are included with virtually every sound card capable of recording more than two channels simultaneously.

Windows 98 and WDM Drivers

Windows 98 introduced the concept of the Win32 Driver Model, or WDM driver. Just as applications could be written to run on both Windows 98 and Windows NT, the same could now be done for drivers. The older NT 32-bit driver model would be retired in favor of WDM, and the DRV/VxD based driver model would also be retired in favor of WDM.

WDM also introduced the concept of a kernel mixer, also known as "KMixer," and the concept of digital input ripped directly from a CD. It standardized most of the driver stack, including all of the older 16-bit and 32-bit DRV files, so that third party drivers needed to include only a miniport driver that was specific to the hardware. A full emulation of a Sound Blaster Pro 8-bit stereo sound card was included so that most DOS games could be run from a DOS box inside Windows, and no longer needed to be run from real-mode DOS. DirectX was also included as part of Windows 98. Windows 98 SE (Second Edition) resolved some design issues with WDM audio drivers and became the first viable platform to use WDM drivers, though VxD-based drivers could continue to be logoed until the end of 1999.

Windows 2000

In February of 2000, Microsoft released Windows 2000, often called Win2k for short, renamed from its earlier Windows NT 5 designation. A WDM audio driver was a hard requirement for those wanting to receive the Designed for Windows Logo for Windows 2000, though older NT4 drivers would usually work. VxD drivers do not work with Windows 2000. While initially slated to have both a home and professional version, only the professional version was released. Though Windows 2000 is very similar to Windows XP in many regards, it does not contain full support for multi-channel audio. Because of this characteristic, you should limit audio support for Windows 2000 to a single stream of stereo audio whenever possible.

Windows Millennium Edition (ME)

The Windows Millennium Edition (Windows ME) that followed was derived from Windows 98 rather than Windows 2000. It added support for multi-channel analog output, non-PCM support for outputting multi-channel compressed audio over S/PDIF, and the first version of the Secure Audio Path (SAP). Also implemented was a software input splitter module that would allow multiple applications to record from the same input source simultaneously. The Windows ME OS was still based on VxDs, just like Windows 98, so only corporate users were getting the benefits of the stability of the NT-based OS.

Windows XP

Nineteen months after the release of Windows 2000, Microsoft released Windows XP in both Professional and Home versions, which made the NT kernel available to the home user for the first time. This release also brought the audio improvements from Windows ME to the NT kernel, including full multi-channel support and a fully implemented Secure Audio Path (SAP). As a result, it became possible to qualify for a second digital signature as part of the Windows Logo process, with a DRM level of 1200. See Chapter 10 for details on SAP and DRM.

Windows XP also supports DirectKS, which is a special interface made available for recording studio applications that are capable of taking over all of the audio functions in the system. DirectKS is usually not appropriate for audio applications that must coexist with other audio applications, but can be useful for professional recording studio applications.

Universal Audio Architecture

In support of Intel HD Audio, Microsoft has developed a Universal Audio Architecture (UAA) Intel HD Audio class function driver and bus driver. This class driver has the ability to create logical devices based on the hardware discoverability of Intel HD Audio and the Intel HD Audio codec's pin configuration defaults registers. These defaults must be programmed to meet Microsoft Logo program specifications.

Just as the standard VGA driver on the PC ensures a basic level of compatibility with any video card or chipset, the Microsoft UAA class driver for Intel HD Audio ensures a base level of audio functionality after a fresh install of the operating system, even if the codec vendor's audio drivers aren't available. Microsoft has selected this approach to ensure consistent support for all audio devices in future PCs. Codec vendors are allowed to substitute their own audio function drivers, which communicate with the Intel HD Audio hardware through the Intel HD Audio bus driver included with the OS.

Following the Intel HD Audio specification, both the controller and the codec are capable of fully identifying their capabilities to the OS and of supporting standard methods for adjusting codec settings. Thus no code paths in the OS are specific to a controller or codec. Instead, everything is controlled by the capabilities exposed by the hardware. Windows Vista will extend this concept, requiring full WHQL testing with both the UAA Class Driver and with the driver supplied by the codec vendor, if one is present.

Appendix D

Jack Retasking

Retaskable jacks, sometimes known as Universal Jacks, were introduced in the final 2.3 revision of the AC97 specification, and they are more fully supported under the Intel HD Audio specification.

The concept of retaskable jacks is actually a combination of four different but complementary technologies:

- *Jack Detection or Jack Sense*—The capability to detect jack insertions, which is a requirement of both the Intel HD Audio specification and Windows Vista logo program
- *Switchable Microphone Bias*—The capability to independently turn microphone bias off and on for each port
- *Redirection*—The ability for a port to function as either an analog input or analog output
- *Impedance Sensing*—The optional ability to sense the impedance of an analog device and to determine the class of device being used: e.g., microphone, headphone, or line-level input or output
- *Analog Device Classification*—A somewhat imprecise method of determining what type of a device is at the other end of a cable plugged into the jack, according to the following classifications: microphone, headphone, and high-impedance line-level device, such as a powered speaker or a stereo receiver

Automatic jack retasking builds on these technologies to allow a system to detect automatically what is plugged into a jack and then automatically reconfigure the jack. While automatic jack retasking seems promising, you face considerable technical and usability challenges in getting it to work properly, especially in a manner that minimizes expensive customer support incidents.

Early expectations for jack retasking included the possibility of reducing cost and saving space by reducing the number of jacks on the system, as well as making it easier for users to simply plug cables into any available jack and let the computer sort out what was plugged into each jack. In practice, retaskable jacks have proved unlikely to save costs over dedicated jacks, and fully automatic retasking has proven to be quite difficult.

Think carefully before including retaskable jacks in your design. The best reason for using retaskable jacks is its potential for minimizing the number of jacks on the system. This minimization is especially useful for subcompact laptop and tablet PCs, where space is a significant consideration. Unless you need to save space, you usually find that implementing retaskable jacks results in more problems than they solve, either in additional component costs, additional development and validation efforts, or additional customer support calls. Retaskability should only be used with 3.5-millimeter jacks; avoid retasking RCA jacks.

Jack Detection

"Jack Detection" in Chapter 4 explains in detail how Intel HD Audio codecs provide the software with the capability to detect which ports have a plug inserted into their associated jack. The Windows[†] Vista logo program requires this capability for each analog port in the system, even on fixed-function jacks which are not retaskable. Jack detection is also required for systems which support impedance detection, allowing an impedance sense cycle to be triggered whenever a jack is inserted.

Switchable Microphone Bias

If a jack is to be retasked between a microphone input and any other function, then the jack needs the ability to supply a bias voltage for the microphone whenever a microphone is in use and to remove this bias voltage whenever a line input, line output, or headphone output is used. This bias voltage is the most problematic aspect of retaskable jacks.

Avoid adding this microphone bias circuitry whenever possible because of the poor interactions with other circuitry. In some cases, special types of capacitors are needed, along with additional current-limiting resistors.

The microphone bias circuitry degrades the crosstalk performance when operating in line-in or line-out modes because the two 4-kiloohm resistors provide an inadvertent crosstalk path between the left and right channels. To get better crosstalk measurements, some designs include diodes in the microphone bias power supply as shown in Figure D.1. Adding these diodes could result in some types of distortion on higher-level signals, which would be a much worse source of audible problems than the crosstalk, which is relatively benign.

Avoid using diodes in the microphone bias circuit. If you do decide to use diodes in the circuit, make sure to perform analog full-scale fidelity testing with and without the diodes installed. In almost all cases, the fidelity is better without the diodes. Even if the design includes microphone bias components, you should only populate microphone bias circuits on jacks which the software exposes to the user as retaskable. If the jack cannot be retasked when the system is running normally, then be sure to depopulate the microphone bias circuit.

Avoid sharing a microphone jack with an output to a high-powered speaker system, especially the LFE channel of a 5.1 system. If the microphone bias is mistakenly turned on, the result is a VERY loud pop, and that noise could damage the speakers.

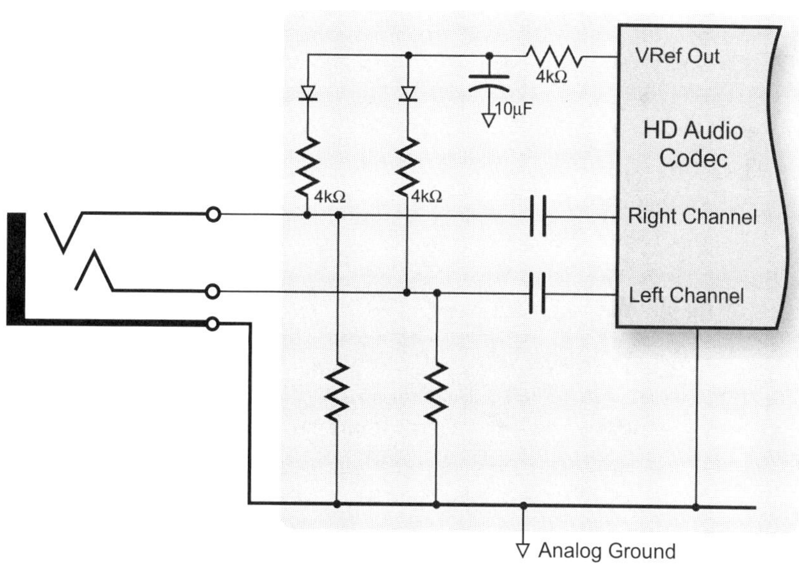

Avoid using diodes like these in the microphone bias circuitry.

Figure D.1 Microphone Bias Circuitry Incorporating Diodes

The VRefControl bit field in the Pin Capabilities register and the VRefEn bit field in the Pin Widget Control register control different modes for the VRefOut pin which provides microphone bias for each pin widget. Depending on the codec design and the motherboard wiring, the bias may be set to 100 percent of the analog power supply, 80 percent, 50 percent, ground, and Hi-Z (floating). These various settings are in support of different retasking and microphone bias configurations.

- *100 percent* is not practical in most codec designs, and the voltage could be higher than expected by some microphones. The codec has no opportunity to filter the microphone bias supply at this setting. *Not recommended*.
- *80 percent* is a good value for most microphones, but you must use a non-polarized coupling capacitor in the design, since the bias voltage is higher than the normal DC voltage at the codec output. Avoid tantalum capacitors and use only non-polarized aluminum electrolytic capacitors in any circuit that has switchable microphone bias.
- *50 percent* is also a good choice. While most microphones exhibit lower output due to the lower voltage, this setting should prevent the output coupling capacitor from being reverse biased.
- *Ground* is used to minimize crosstalk through the microphone bias resistors, by pulling the center point of this crosstalk path to ground. This configuration could be useful when operating in line-in or line-out mode.
- *Hi-Z* is used during impedance sensing to minimize loading of the microphone bias circuit. This configuration increases the range of impedances that can be detected, though it could take many seconds for the microphone bias to drop to zero, allowing a clean impedance measurement.

Because the driver can set the microphone bias to any or all of these different levels, you should design your systems to ensure that nothing can be damaged by these different settings. To do so, *never* use tantalum coupling capacitors, and always make sure that the coupling capacitor is non-polarized. Design your circuit so that the DC voltage at the jack can be anywhere from zero to 5 volts without damaging any components.

Redirection

Intel HD Audio codecs typically have one or more ports that can switch between input and output modes. The Intel HD Audio specification allows for the input and output sections to be enabled and operated independently and even simultaneously, although this usage is rare. In most Intel HD Audio codecs, each ADC has the ability to select its stereo input signal from any of the analog stereo I/O ports.

Each port usually has one or more DACs associated with it for output, though only one can be selected at a time. Sometimes a port is designed for input-only, but it's rare to find a codec port which is output only.

Because microphone bias is never used on output circuits, changing between an output and a microphone input causes the microphone bias to turn on. It could take several seconds for the bias levels to settle at the new settings before the microphone begins to work properly, which might confuse the end user.

Impedance Sensing

The most controversial and confusing aspect of retaskable jacks is impedance sensing, and its use for device classification. The Intel HD Audio specification uses the unsolicited response to enable each port on a codec to announce a change in the impedance of the device connected to the port. The specification does not describe any specific impedance sensing technique. Instead, the specification includes an "Execute" verb which is sent to the pin widget to start a sense cycle. Usually, the unsolicited response containing an impedance measurement is the result of a sense cycle triggered by this verb.

The driver triggers a sense cycle by sending an *Execute* verb to a pin widget whenever it detects a jack insertion. Usually a brief sine wave tone is played using a combination of level and frequency that is difficult for humans to hear. The impedance measurement is taken, and the unsolicited response is sent to the Intel HD Audio bus driver, which sends it on up the audio stack.

The surrounding circuitry can have a significant effect on impedance sensing, especially when trying to sense devices which have higher impedances. For instance, if you are trying to determine the impedance of a device with a 10-kiloohm input impedance, you need to be sure that the shunt resistance in your circuit is no lower than 20 kiloohms. Be sure to keep the shunt resistance of your circuit at least twice as high as the highest impedance for which you plan to test, though reliably sensing impedances higher than 20 kiloohms is often impractical.

Analog Device Classification

Analog audio devices used with a computer typically fall into several categories of impedance.

- *Line Input*—typical impedance for devices in this category is between 3 and 11 kiloohms. However, some devices might be much higher or much lower.
- *Microphone*—typical impedance for devices in this category is between 400 and 1200 ohms. However, some microphones could have very high impedance, which might be mistaken for a line input.
- *Headphone*—typical impedance for devices in this category is between 16 and 32 ohms. However, some studio-quality headphones have impedances up to 300 ohms, which might be mistaken for microphone impedance.

While most devices fall into one of these categories, you cannot assume these ranges apply for the devices that you are trying to detect unless they are shipped as part of the system. In that case, you can choose devices with clearly defined impedances that do not overlap with one another.

Usability

You should perform usability testing on any retaskable jack implementation. Systems with automatic retasking using impedance sensing and device classification should be designed by a human factors or usability expert, and a full suite of usability testing should be employed. It is certainly possible to build a software framework that provides an appropriate level of usability for automatic retasking jacks, but no truly usable system has been built to date. Chapter 11 contains more information on usability testing.

UAA Class Driver Support

Current versions of the UAA class driver do not support retasking or impedance sensing. While the pin configuration registers are capable of describing the primary usage for the retaskable jack, the pin configuration registers contain too little information to adequately define the alternate configurations for each jack. Therefore you should always set the pin configuration register to the default usage model that is supported by the class driver. Any retasking capabilities only become available when used with a third party driver.

Types of Retasking Circuits

Six basic retasking configurations cover all useful retasking configurations. Generally speaking, retasking between two different inputs or two different outputs is simpler, while retasking between headphones and microphones is more difficult.

The following six circuits are generally codec-agnostic, and they should work with any Intel HD Audio codec currently in production. Variations between these circuits include the presence or absence of the microphone bias circuitry, the size of the output coupling capacitors, and the configuration of the EMI filter.

Line Out and Headphone Out (LO/HP)

Figure D.2 shows the standard headphone (HP) output circuit, capable of driving HP or line out signals. This retaskable circuit is the baseline on which all other retaskable circuits are built, though some may omit headphone capability.

Some codecs have a special Line Out (LO) mode which has better THD+N or dynamic range when compared to the headphone output mode; when possible, the UAA class driver disengages the headphone amp if the pin configuration is set to Line Out rather than Headphone.

Note that all shunt resistances and impedances are 20 kiloohms or higher throughout the frequency range of 20 hertz to 24 kilohertz. Keeping the shunt resistance above 20 kiloohms allows automatic impedance sensing to detect line level devices in addition to microphones and headphones.

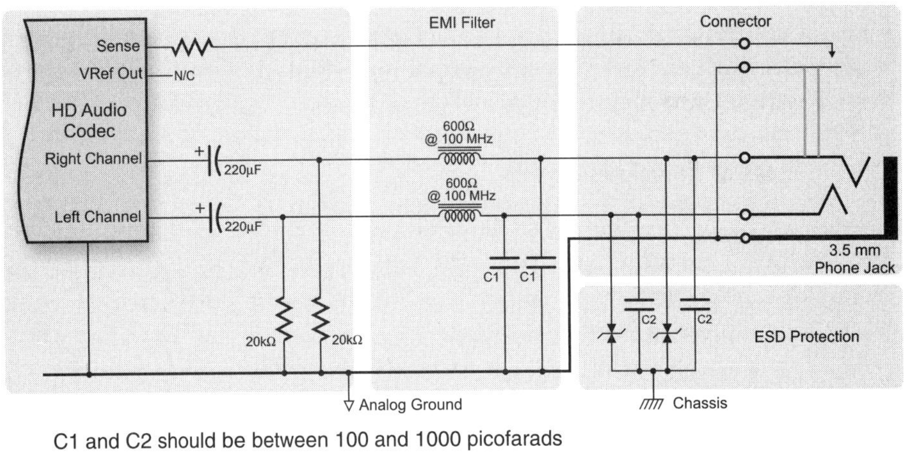

Figure D.2 Schematic for retasking Headphone Out and Line Out

The coupling capacitors are 220 microfarads, which are large enough to drive 32 ohm headphones at lower frequencies. Table D.1 shows two usage scenarios for this jack: the primary in white and alternate in gray. Since a headphone configuration is always capable of driving line out while the line out configuration does not drive headphones well, the headphone output always should be the default.

Table D.1 Usage scenarios for LO/HP

Primary Device	Color	Alternates	Not Supported
HP – Headphone	Green	LO	MI, LI
LO – Line Out	Green†	HP	MI, LI

†Line Out may also be orange, black, or grey when used in 5.1 or 7.1 systems

Since Microphone In and Line In are not supported by this configuration; the unneeded microphone bias circuitry should be omitted. Only two EMI shunt capacitors are needed, and they are placed on the high-impedance side of the ferrite bead, which in this case is the side nearest the jack.

If you are implementing impedance sensing, make sure that the shunt resistors are at least 20 kiloohms in value. If you are not implementing impedance sensing, you could decrease this value, which might help eliminate a pop when power is applied to the codec. However, don't use a value lower than 5 kiloohms or so—the exact value depends on the codec—because this low impedance loads down the line output and causes excessive distortion when in line output mode. If you are concerned about the pop, the best solution is to dedicate this jack to headphone-out capability only. It can still drive line out, but does so at a slightly lower fidelity in most cases.

This configuration is a subset of the LI/LO/HP configuration which adds two shunt capacitors to the EMI filter to support redirection. You should lay out your board for the LI/LO/HP configuration and then depopulate the two shunt capacitors if you decide to not support line in.

Line In, Line Out, and HP Out (LI/LO/HP)

While basically the same as the previous configuration, LI/LO/HP has added EMI suppression treatment for when the jack is used as an input. Otherwise, the schematics for these two configurations do not differ (see Figure D.3).

The EMI shunt capacitors only have an effect on the high-impedance side of the ferrite bead. When the port is in Line Out mode, the capacitors on the jack side of the ferrite bead filter any EMI signals. When the port is in Line In (LI) mode the capacitors on the codec side of the ferrite bead act as an EMI filter.

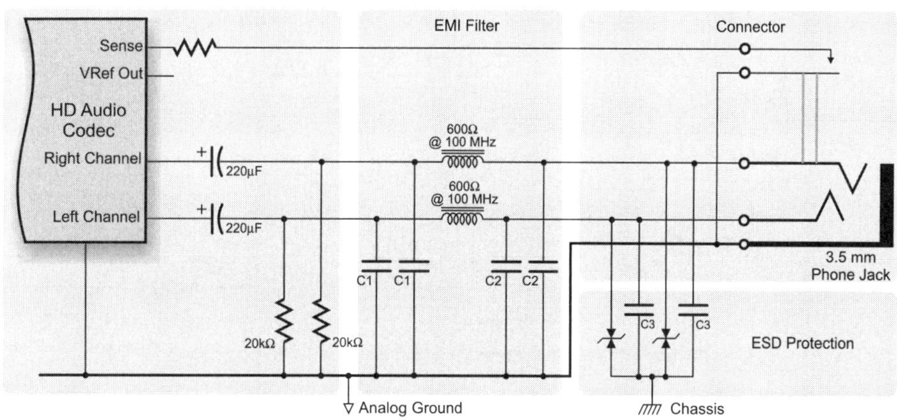

C1, C2, and C3 should be between 100 and 10,000 picofarads

Figure D.3 Schematic for retasking Line In, Line Out, and HP Out

Table D.2 shows the three usage scenarios for this jack: primary in white and the alternates in gray. The headphone output should always be the default.

Table D.2 Usage scenarios for LI/LO/HP

Primary Device	Color	Alternates	Not Supported
LI – Line In	Blue	LO, HP	MI
LO – Line Out	Green†	LI, HP	MI
HP – Headphone	Green	LI, LO	MI

†Line Out may also be orange, black, or grey when used in 5.1 or 7.1 systems

Line In and Line Out (LI/LO)

If headphone output is not required, you can replace the 220 microfarad output coupling capacitor with a 3.3- or 4.7-microfarad capacitor, which is sufficiently large to provide a good low-frequency output response into a 10-kiloohm input device. Figure D.4 provides the schematic for the LI/LO configuration.

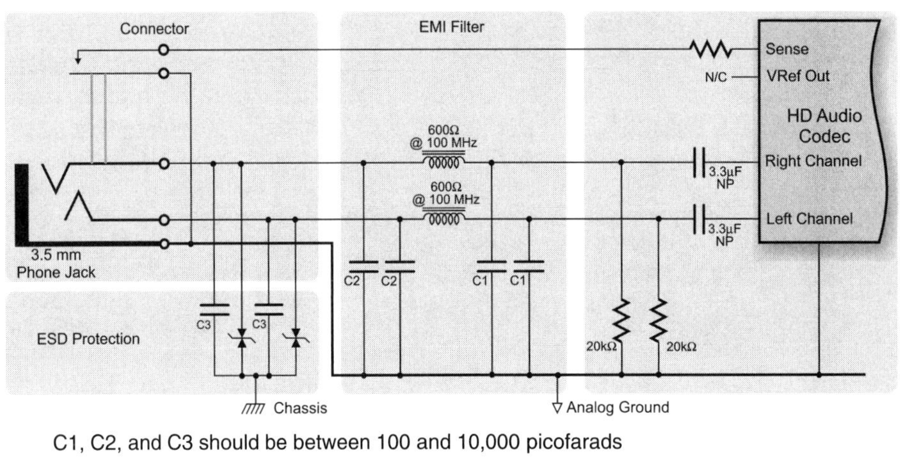

Figure D.4 Schematic for retasking Line In and Line Out

Table D.3 shows the primary usage in white and the alternate usage in gray. The line output should be the default because line-out jacks are more commonly used than line-in jacks.

Table D.3 Usage scenarios for LI/LO

Primary Device	Color	Alternates	Not Supported
LI – Line In	Blue	LO	MI, HP
LO – Line Out	Green†	LI	MI, HP

†Line Out may also be orange, black, or grey when used in 5.1 or 7.1 systems

Impedance sensing is not particularly useful for this circuit, since both line input and line output signals may be high impedance, and you have no easy way to distinguish between the two unless an incoming signal is present, which is an indicator of line-in functionality.

Microphone In and Line In (MI/LI)

The configuration shown in Figure D.5 supports only inputs. Because the codec has a very high input impedance, a 1-microfarad coupling capacitor can be used for both microphone and line inputs. The EMI filter capacitors are placed on the high-impedance side of the ferrite beads, which in this case is the codec input side of the ferrite beads.

The switchable VRefOut pin provides microphone bias only when the microphone is used. Otherwise the circuitry is the same for both microphone and line. A preamp in the codec becomes engaged when microphone is used. The 1-microfarad coupling capacitors must be nonpolarized, since the DC voltage at the jack may be higher than the DC voltage at the codec when the microphone bias voltage is switched on. When switched off, the voltage at the jack goes to zero, which is lower than the DC voltage at the codec.

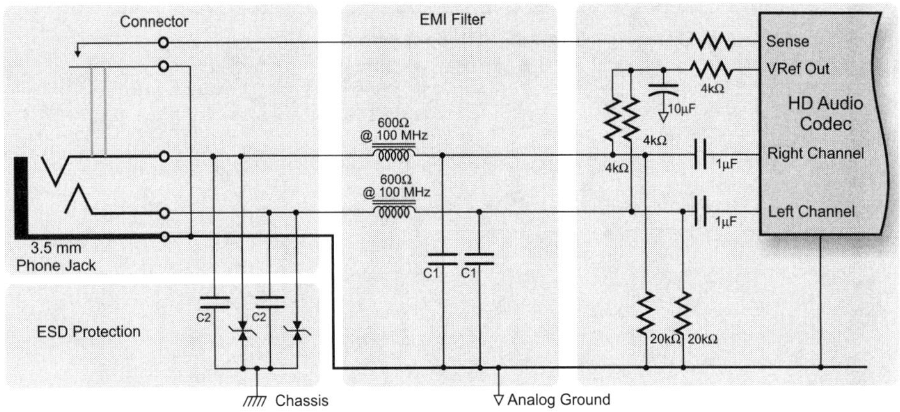

C1 and C2 should be between 100 and 10,000 picofarads

Figure D.5 Schematic for retasking Microphone In and Line In

The two 4-kiloohm resistors have the potential to create a crosstalk path. Be sure to measure the crosstalk during development with the 4-kiloohm resistors installed and removed. Measure the crosstalk with the VRefOut voltage turned both off and on. With VRefOut turned off, make sure that the crosstalk measurements for Line-In comply with applicable logo and certification requirements. While adding diodes in series with the 4-kiloresistors might help with the crosstalk issue, these diodes can often cause distortion artifacts and you should avoid using them.

Table D.4 shows the possible options for using this configuration. Because of the presence of the microphone bias circuit, this configuration should default to microphone input. Line out and headphone out are not supported because of the small 1-microfarad coupling capacitor, which attenuates the low frequencies of these output signals.

Table D.4 Usage scenarios for MI/LI

Primary Device	Color	Alternates	Not Supported
MI – Microphone In	Pink	LI	LO, HP
LI – Line In	Blue	MI	LO, HP

Impedances above the 4-kiloohms value of the microphone bias resistors cannot be easily detected. You could work around this limitation by adding discrete transistors to isolate the right channel from the left channel when VRefOut is set to zero, but this extra effort is usually not warranted.

Impedance sensing results often are difficult or impossible if the microphone bias is switched on. Also, if the bias voltage is higher than the normal DC output voltage of the codec's virtual analog ground (VAG), you should be aware that the output coupling capacitor could end up being reverse-biased, which could cause a polarized capacitor to degrade or fail

This configuration is a subset of the MI/LI/LO configuration which uses a larger coupling capacitor and two additional EMI shunt capacitors. If you lay out your motherboard for the MI/LI/LO configuration you can adjust stuffing options to create this MI/LI configuration.

Microphone In, Line In, and Line Out (MI/LI/LO)

Figure D.6 shows the primary change from the previous configuration, which is the substitution of a 3.3- or 4.7-microfarad coupling capacitor in place of the 1-microfarad capacitor. This configuration also adds two shunt capacitors in the EMI filter to block interference when operating in output mode instead of input mode.

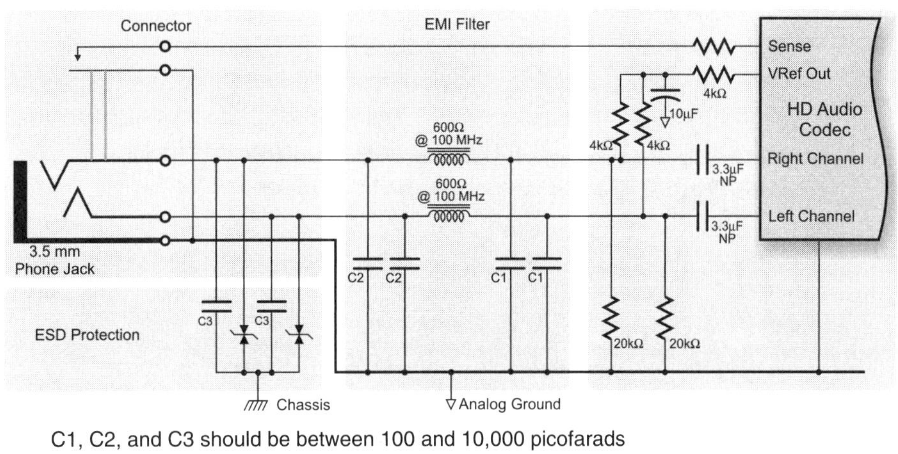

Figure D.6 Schematic for retasking Microphone In, Line In, and Line Out

Table D.5 shows the possible options for using this configuration. Because of the presence of the microphone bias circuit, this configuration should default to microphone input. Headphone out is not supported because of the relatively small 3.3- or 4.7-microfarad coupling capacitor. Impedance sensing is usually difficult when a microphone bias network is present, especially if the microphone bias is turned on.

Table **D.5** **Usage scenarios for MI/LI/LO**

Primary Device	Color	Alternates	Not Supported
MI – Microphone In	Pink	LI, LO	HP
LI – Line In	Blue	MI, LO	HP
LO – Line Out	Green†	MI, LI	HP

† Line Out may also be orange, black, or grey when used in 5.1 or 7.1 systems

This configuration is a superset of both the LI/LO configuration and the MI/LI configuration. It adds the microphone bias circuit to the LI/LO configuration and increases the coupling capacitor in the MI/LI configuration from 1-microfarad to 3.3- or 4.7-microfarads. If your circuit board and schematic is laid out to use the MI/LI/LO configuration, you can easily depopulate the circuit to generate these two related configurations.

Mic In, Line In, Line Out, & HP Out (MI/LI/LO/HP)

The most difficult retasking configuration by far is one which supports both headphone and microphone. The difficulty comes from the current surges that are a result of the interaction between the microphone bias circuit and the large coupling capacitor required for headphones. Such surges might damage the codec or the output coupling capacitor, which would require the motherboard to be replaced.

After reading through the previous configurations, you might have expected this circuit simply to substitute a 220-microfarad coupling capacitor. However, that substitution doesn't work very well because large capacitors, such as a 220-microfarad capacitor, are usually aluminum electrolytic or tantalum, which are regularly available only in polarized versions. While non-polarized capacitors of this size are available, they are expensive and are typically through-hole mounted, which requires a manual assembly step that cannot be automated.

The best compromise between non-polarized, surface-mount, and sufficient capacitance to drive a headphone is a 47-microfarad non-polarized capacitor. Several sources for such a capacitor are available.

It's very important that the capacitor is non-polarized, as the microphone bias voltage is typically higher than the codec DC operating level, which will cause the capacitor to become reverse biased. In turn, this reverse bias can cause the capacitor to fail unless it is a non-polarized capacitor.

Figure D.7 shows the MI/LI/LOP/HP configuration's schematics.

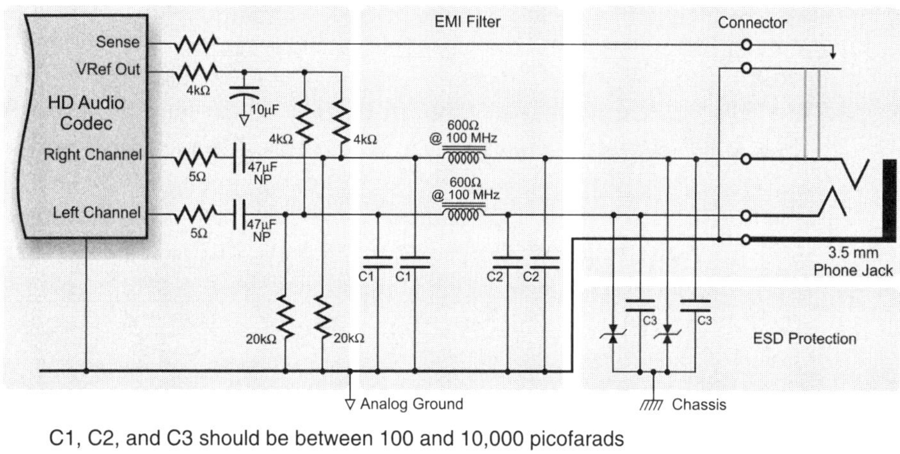

Figure D.7 Schematic for retasking Microphone In, Line In, Line Out, and HP Out

Table D.6 shows the various usages for this configuration. While all modes are supported in hardware, the software may choose to limit which alternate modes can be set by the user to simplify operation and enhance usability. The default usage should be either microphone input or headphone output. Choose microphone in as the default if you plan to have the microphone bias on at startup; choose headphone out if you plan to leave the microphone bias off.

Table D.6 Usage scenarios for MI/LI/LO/HP

Primary Device	Color	Alternates	Not Supported
MI – Microphone In	Pink	LI, LO, HP	
LI – Line In	Blue	MI, LO, HP	
LO – Line Out	Green†	MI, LI, HP	
HP – Headphone	Green	MI, LI, LO	

† Line Out may also be orange, black, or grey when used in 5.1 or 7.1 system

You might feel some concern that 47 microfarads is not large enough to drive most headphones, but it is important to consider the characteristics of the headphones being driven. Most earbud-style headphones have an impedance between 24 and 32 ohms. Earbuds are not usually capable of producing low frequencies below 100 hertz without specially fitted ear molds, which are rare.

On the other hand, the better hi-fi headphone brands such as Sennheiser and AKG have impedances between 90 and 600 ohms. These headphones are physically large enough to reproduce the lower frequencies, but because of their higher impedance, they extend down to a 20 hertz frequency response when used with a 47-microfarad coupling capacitor in a retasking application. The 47-microfarad capacitor does not limit the low frequency response in the case of these higher headphone impedances.

Two 5-ohm resistors are placed between the codec and the non-polarized coupling capacitors, to limit current surges when switching between headphone and microphone modes. Unlike the previously described circuits with switchable VRefOut, the 47-microfarad capacitor can source enough current in some modes to damage the codec unless the current-limiting resistors are present.

The worst case event occurs when the jack is in microphone mode and the capacitor is reverse biased. That is, the microphone bias voltage at the jack, which typically is 3 to 4 volts, is higher than the DC output voltage at the codec pin. Sometimes when a jack is plugged in, it may momentarily short the left channel to ground. This short might send a significant surge of current into the codec. The 5-ohm resistors limit this surge to safe levels, and they don't have a large effect on the current that is delivered to the headphone while music is playing.

Impedance sensing is very difficult in this configuration, especially when the microphone bias is turned on. The only reliable way to measure impedances above 4 kiloohms is to add additional silicon switches to the microphone bias circuit, thereby completely isolating the 4-kiloohm resistors in the microphone bias network from the remainder of the audio path whenever the microphone bias is disabled. Otherwise the 4-kiloohm resistance of these resistors dominates and you won't be able to detect line-level impedances.

Recommendations for Retasking

Use fixed-function jacks and avoid retaskable jacks for most systems. If you decide that you need retaskable jacks on your system, consider each jack in the system one by one and for each, you should determine what functions the software will expose. Try to keep as many fixed-function jacks in the system as possible.

Usually, the only good reason to implement retaskable jacks is that you don't have enough space to mount fixed-function jacks for surround-sound output, such as on a high-end laptop computer designed for gaming or media. Very few other good reasons can be cited for using retasking jacks.

Think carefully about whether to include the microphone bias circuitry on each port. Populate microphone bias components only on ports which software can set to microphone. Avoid using diodes in the microphone bias supply lines.

Don't use retaskable jacks to save cost. This attempt will almost always backfire on you. Any retasking implementation is more difficult than not: more factors are involved in testing, and the usability is often at risk, which can result in expensive technical support calls once the product is in the field.

If you do use retaskable jacks, it's much better if you limit the functions to input-only or output-only. Switching between Microphone In and Line In or Line Out and Headphone Out is much less risky than switching between input and output modes, and much easier for the user to understand.

Glossary

5.1. A surround sound format with five full range channels (front left, front center, front right, rear left, rear right) and one low frequency effects channel.

7.1. A surround sound format with seven full range channels (front left, front center, front right, rear left, rear right, side or surround left, side or surround right) and one low frequency effects channel

AAC. Advanced Audio Coding is an audio coding algorithm used for compressed audio in both MPEG-2 and MPEG-4 standards.

A-weighting filter. A specific noise-weighting filter (ANSI S1.4, IEC Recommendation 179) used to produce noise measurements which correlate well with human observations. See **weighting filter**.

absolute noise level. The noise level at the output of the converter. For DACs, this is specified in dBV, while for ADCs it is specified in dBFS.

AC-3. A multi-channel audio compression algorithm used in DTV and DVD. This term is no longer used, having been replaced by "Dolby Digital."

AC97. An audio bus and controller infrastructure developed by Intel® Corporation in 1997. This term has been superseded by the Intel High Definition Audio Specification.

acoustic echo cancellation (AEC). A technique used to remove room echoes of incoming speech during a VoIP call or other types of real-time communications.

acoustic energy. The amount of energy that an object emits in the form of sound.

ADAT. Alesis Digital Audio Tape is commonly used to refer to a digital optical interface capable of transporting eight channels of 24-bit audio over a standard TOSLINK† optical cable.

ADC. An acronym for an analog-to-digital converter, a device that converts an analog signal into a digital signal.

A-to-D converter. Another name for **ADC**.

AEC. See **acoustic echo cancellation**.

AES3. A digital interface standard for professional audio equipment interconnection. It is somewhat compatible with S/PDIF digital interfaces.

AES/EBU interface. Now called AES 3 after the AES standard that describes its characteristics.

AES-6id. A document from the Audio Engineering Society which focuses on the measurement of audio quality specifications in a PC environment. Each specification listed has a definition and an example measurement technique.

AES-17.. The Audio Engineering Society standard method for digital audio engineering measurement of digital audio equipment.

AES-17 brickwall filter. A specially designed 7-pole low-pass filter used to filter out-of-band noise when measuring sigma-delta DACs.

AES. Audio Engineering Society, with headquarters in New York City, a world-wide group of professional audio engineers with interests in audio technology, recording, and transmission. Also, this group is responsible for many industry-wide audio and audio measurement standards.

AES. The Advanced Encryption Standard was standardized by the National Institute of Standards and Technology in 2002, replacing the older Data Encryption Standard (DES). AES supports key sizes of 128, 192, and 256-bits.

AGC. See **automatic gain control**.

Aliasing. The introduction of spectral components into a reconstructed signal that did not exist in the original signal. Aliasing is caused by sampling a signal with spectral components above the **nyquist frequency**.

analog-to-digital converter. See **ADC**.

anechoic chamber. A specially-designed room with acoustically absorbent walls that is used for sound measurements. This room has no reflections, and hence no diffuse sounds.

APO. An Audio Processing Object in Windows† Vista can be either a Local Effect (LFX) which only affects a single application, or a Global Effect (GFX) which affects all audio going to a particular endpoint.

anti-aliasing filter. A low-pass filter designed to band-limit a signal prior to sampling. A properly designed anti-aliasing filter prevents aliasing during sampling.

audio controller. PC hardware responsible for transporting sound signals from within the computer out to speakers and for bringing external sound signals into the computer.

ANSI. American National Standards Institute, a U.S.-based standards organization.

ASCII. American Standard Code for Information Interchange, a standard for representing 127 alphabetic, numeric, and other characters and symbols as 7-bit binary numbers.

association. A method of grouping used when programming a pin widget's configuration defaults registers. See **sequence**.

attack time. The time interval required following a sudden increase in input level to a device for the output of the device to reach some stated percentage of the eventual signal level.

Attenuator. A passive network of resistors (plus possibly compensating capacitors), which reduces the amplitude of a signal by a precise amount. Often referred to as a pad.

automatic gain control. A technique for automatically varying the gain of a device, usually to maintain a relatively constant output level.

automatic volume control. A technique for maintaining output audio level (volume) relatively constant in spite of varying input levels.

average responding. A form of AC signal detection indicative of the average absolute value of a waveform, typical of analog meter movements.

backward masking. A type of masking that occurs when the signal precedes the masker in time.

Balanced. Refers to a transferring a signal using three wires where the signal is applied differentially between two conductors, each of which has equal impedances to ground or common. One wire carries a variable voltage that corresponds to the signal itself, a second wire carries then inverse of the signal on the first wire. The third wire serves as a zero reference, or ground.

band reject filter. A filter which attenuates the frequencies within a specified frequency range while passing essentially without attenuation the frequencies below and above that range. If the rejection range is narrow, a band reject filter is also often called a notch filter.

bandpass filter. A filter that passes a specific frequency band, essentially without attenuation, while attenuating frequencies both below and above the specified band.

band-limiting. In general, low and/or high-pass filters in a system cause band-limiting. For example, a 20-kilohertz low-pass filter creates a system that is limited by the audio band. In an analog to digital conversion application, you run a signal through a low-pass filter so that it contains no frequencies above the Nyquist frequency. Failure to band-limit a signal results in aliasing of the signal when it is sampled.

bass management. The process of routing the low frequencies from each satellite speaker in a surround system so that the LFE speaker can produce the low frequencies. Doing so allows the satellite speakers to be smaller.

Beamforming. The process of combining the signals from two or more matched microphones to focus the audio pickup in one specific direction, to avoid picking up audio from other directions.

Binaural. Two-channel sound that creates spatial cues by directly feeding pressure waves into the audio canals.

BIOS. Basic Input Output System, the firmware code that runs at system startup and "underneath" Windows or Linux. The BIOS is responsible for programming the Intel HD Audio codecs at startup by transmitting predefined verb tables to the Intel HD Audio codec.

bit depth. Same as **bits of resolution**.

BITCLK. The 24.000 Megahertz clock line of the Intel HD Audio bus.

bits of resolution. The number of bits in a binary word that represent signals in a digital recording or transmission system. Each bit adds approximately 6 decibels to the theoretical dynamic range available. Thus, a 16-bit digital system is capable of approximately 96 decibels dynamic range, etc.

bridging. A relatively high impedance input (usually balanced) which may be connected across a lower impedance circuit without significantly affecting the levels in the lower impedance circuit.

burning. Writing files to an optical disc. Often used to refer to placing audio files onto a CD-R disk in such a way that they can be played by a standard CD-Audio player.

bus driver. A special type of device driver used to enumerate a hardware bus and aggregate all the devices connected to that bus. The Intel HD Audio bus driver identifies all of the codecs on the Intel HD Audio bus, and also provides a software interface for function drivers to control these codecs.

C-message weighting filter. A weighting filter commonly used for noise measurements in the telephone industry. The shape of the C-message weighting filter is based on both the typical human ear frequency response and also on the response of a typical telephone receiver. The C-message weighting filter is described in the IEEE-743 and Bell 41009 specifications. See **weighting filter**.

CCIR 468. A CCIR specification which includes, among other things, standards for weighted and un-weighted noise measurements. The weighted standard specifies the CCIR weighting filter and a quasi-peak detector (see **weighting filter**). The un-weighted standard specifies a 22-hertz to 22-kilohertz bandwidth limiting filter and an RMS detector.

CCIR-ARM. A noise measurement technique developed by Dolby Laboratories, which uses the weighting filter shape specified in CCIR Recommendation 468 but with the unity-gain frequency at 2 kilohertz rather than at 1 kilohertz, and an average-responding detector.

CCIR. Comite Consultatif International des Radiocommunications (International Radio Consultative Committee), an international standards-setting organization with headquarters in Geneva, Switzerland.

CCITT Comite Consultatif International Telephonique et Telegraphique (International Telegraph and Telephone Consultative Committee), an international standards organization for telephone communications related industries.

cannon plug. See **XLR**.

capacitor. An electronic component which exhibits capacitive reactance.

Capsule. The actual transducer element in a microphone.

Capture. The act of recording an analog audio input signal.

Cardioid. A microphone pickup pattern that is most sensitive to sounds directly in front. The cardioid family includes the pure cardioid, the super-cardioid, and the hyper-cardioid.

channel status bits. The bits in the S/PDIF stream which contain information about the stream rather than actual audio data.

chipset. The combination of Northbridge and Southbridge chips used a glue logic to connect the CPU to various devices, such as memory, video, audio, networking, etc.

class driver. A driver included with the operating system which is capable of working with an entire class of devices rather than one specific device or configuration

clipping. The action of a system in flattening and squaring off signal peaks when driven with a signal whose peak amplitude is beyond its linear signal-handling capability.

CMRR. See **common mode rejection ratio**.

codec. 1. An integrated circuit connected to the Intel HD Audio bus containing both ADCs and DACs. 2. Short for compressor/decompressor: an algorithm that converts an audio stream into a smaller file size or bandwidth, and then restores the signal at the other end.

COM interface. The Common Object Model structure used for modern programming interfaces in Windows..

common mode rejection ratio. The ability of a balanced (differential) input circuit to reject signals on the two conductors which are in phase with respect to common or ground.

common mode voltage range. The maximum voltage between either side of a balanced pair and ground or common, which can be tolerated while still permitting full common mode rejection.

common mode. Signals on a balanced pair that are in phase with respect to ground, as opposed to differential signals that are developed across the balanced pair (normal mode). Common mode signals are sometimes also referred to as longitudinal signals.

companding. Independently scaling each sub-band in order to achieve optimal signal-to-noise ratios during compression.

compressor. A signal processing amplifier whose gain automatically reduces with higher amplitude input signals, making the dynamic signal range at its output less than the signal dynamic range at its input.

compression. Constraining the dynamic range of a signal into a smaller dynamic range. A compression ratio of 10:1 means that for every 10 decibels that the input signal increases, the output signal increases by one decibel.

compression. Using an algorithm to render audio data into a smaller format. MP3 files can easily achieve a compression ratio of 10:1, which means that the resulting file is one tenth the size of the original.

lossy compression. A method of compressing the size or bandwidth of an audio signal, in which the decompressed output sounds similar to the original content, but is not identical.

lossless compression. A method of compressing the size or bandwidth of an audio signal, in which the decompressed output is identical to the original content.

configuration default. A register in an Intel HD Audio codec pin widget that can be programmed with information pertaining to the associated analog port. This information includes color, location, type of jack, and intended functionality.

copy always. A protection state indicating the associated content can be freely copied an unlimited number of times.

copy never. A protection state indicating the associated content can never be copied.

copy once. A protection state indicating the associated content can be copied only once. Copies of the copy are not permitted.

crest factor. The ratio of a signal's peak amplitude to its RMS amplitude.

critical band. In psychoacoustics, the maximum bandwidth of noise, which is perceived by humans to be the same loudness as a sine wave of the same power at band center. A range of frequencies that stimulates the same portion of the basilar membrane.

critical bandwidth. The width of the auditory filter associated with a single critical band.

critical sampling. Refers to sampling a signal at exactly twice the frequency of the highest frequency in the signal.

crossover. A circuit that splits an incoming audio signal into two or more bands. For instance, a two-way crossover splits a signal into low-frequency and high-frequency components. The low-frequency output is sent to a woofer, and the high-frequency output to a tweeter.

crosstalk. Unwanted signal coupling from one channel of a multi-channel transmission or recording system to another.

CSS. Content Scramble System, a content protection scheme used by makers of DVD players.

DAC. An acronym for a digital-to-analog converter. A device that converts a digital signal into an analog signal.

D-to-A converter. Another name for DAC.

dB/octave. A standard means of referring to the ultimate rejection slope (attenuation versus frequency) of a band-limiting filter. Each pole of a band-limiting filter produces an ultimate rejection slope of 6 dB/octave (20 dB/decade). Thus, a 3-pole filter will have a rejection slope of 18 dB/octave (60 dB/decade).

dB. Abbreviation of decibel, a ratio unit for expressing signal amplitudes. If the amplitudes are expressed in voltage, dB = 20 log10 (V1/V2). If the amplitudes are expressed in power, dB = 10 log10 (P1/P2).

dBFS. Decibels with respect to digital full scale. The full scale amplitude (zero dBFS value) is the RMS value of a sine wave whose positive peak just reaches positive full scale.

dBm. Decibels relative to a reference value of 1.000 milliwatts at 600 ohms. dBm is thus a power unit and requires knowledge of power levels (voltage and current, or voltage and impedance, or current and impedance) rather than merely voltage.

dBr. Relative dB—decibels relative to an arbitrary reference value. The reference value must be stated for this to be a meaningful unit.

dBspl. Decibel sound pressure level, a standard unit in acoustical measurements. Zero dBspl corresponds to a sound pressure of 20 micropascal, that is 20 micronewtons per meter squared, 0.0002 dynes per square centimeter. Thus, +94 dBspl corresponds to one Pascal.

dBu. Decibels relative to a reference of 0.7746 Volts.

dBV. Decibels relative to a reference value of 1.000 Volts. This value is the most commonly used analog measurement unit for Intel HD Audio.

DCOM. The Distributed Common Object Model interface in Windows that allows a process on one computer to call into a process on another computer.

decade. The interval between two frequencies with a ratio of exactly 10:1, such as the range from 20 hertz to 200 hertz, or from 1 kilohertz to 10 kilohertz.

decimation. A mathematical process of reducing the clock rate and bandwidth content of a digital audio signal; the opposite of interpolation.

delta-sigma converter. See **sigma-delta converter**.

detector. The precision AC to DC conversion section of a measurement instrument, located following all AC signal processing and prior to the indicating portion. Detectors are classified according to which parameter of the input AC signal the output DC value linearly follows true RMS, average, peak, etc.

device classification. The use of impedance measurements to determine whether an analog device connected to a PC is a microphone, headphone, or line-level device.

diaphragm. A large thin surface designed to interact with the air. In a speaker, the diaphragm is the component that actually creates sound pressure waves. In a microphone, the diaphragm is the component that actually receives sound pressure waves.

diffraction. The tendency of sound waves to bend around obstructions in their path.

digital-to-analog converter. See **DAC**.

digital clipping. The mapping of an input signal to the highest or lowest quantization level when the signal is outside the quantization range.

digitizing. The process of discretely sampling a continuous signal.

DirectKS. An interface to the Windows XP audio subsystem that allows applications to bypass KMixer, for reduced latency and more control over the audio. Applications designed for Windows Vista should use the WASAPI interface instead of the DirectKS interface.

distortion. The addition of new unwanted signals related to the primary signal.

dither. Low amplitude noise, at approximately the one-half to one LSB range in amplitude, added prior to a signal quantization in order to reduce distortion, improve linearity, and extend the available dynamic range downwards below that of an undithered system of the same number of bits.

DMA. 1. Direct Memory Access, used as a way for a device to transfer data directly to and from system memory, without making use of the CPU for the transfer.

2. Digital media adapter, a remote device capable of playing an audio stream being delivered from another computer or device.

DPC. Deferred Procedure Call, scheduled by the interrupt service routine to carry out further processing triggered by the interrupt. In Windows XP, this location is where signal processing often occurs in the kernel. The DPC is limited to 25 microseconds in Windows Vista, which effectively prohibits signal processing in the kernel.

DSD. Direct Stream Digital, a digital audio transmission and storage format which uses one bit of data at a 64x oversampling rate.

driver. 1. A piece of software that converts high-level commands from an operating system or application into instructions that are specific to the hardware associated with the driver.

2. The actual transducer element in a speaker.

3. The portion of a circuit responsible for providing sufficient current or voltage output to the next circuit in the audio path.

DRM. Digital rights management, a term which encompasses all manner of copy protection and secure content.

DTCP. Digital Transmission Content Protection, a copy protection system developed by the 5C entity.

DTM. Driver Test Manager, a part of the Windows Driver Kit (WDK) for Windows Vista. The DTM automates testing of systems.

DTV. An acronym for digital television. Refers to the broadcast of video and sound in a digital format. Ancillary data may be included in the broadcast. The ancillary data may contain episode guides, detailed biographies of the actors, or even executable software that can be run on a computer.

DVD. A high quality audio and video optical disc format. Also used as a generic high-capacity storage medium. Variants are:

DVD+R. A write-once, read-many DVD format defined by the DVD+RW Alliance.

DVD+RW. A rewritable DVD format defined by the DVD+RW Alliance.

DVD-Audio A DVD designed primarily to store high quality audio.

DVD-R. A write-once, read-many DVD format.

DVD-RAM. A rewritable DVD format designed for random access.

DVD-RW. A rewritable DVD format designed for sequential access.

DVD-Video. A DVD designed primarily to store high quality video and associated audio.

DVI. Digital video interface, a digital interconnect between the PC and the video monitor, used only for video signals.

dynamic range. Generally, it's the difference, usually expressed in dB, between the highest and lowest amplitude portions of a signal, or between the highest amplitude signal which a device can linearly handle and the noise level of the device. Specifically, the term refers to a measurement technique that characterizes the signal to noise ratio of a digital audio system.

EAPD. External amplifier power down, an electrical signal used to turn a power amp on and off.

electret. a substance that has a permanent electrical charge. It is the electrical equivalent of a permanent magnet.

electrical overstress. See **EOS**.

electromagnetic interference. See **EMI**.

electrostatic discharge. See **ESD**.

EMI. Electro-magnetic interference, frequencies outside of the audio band which interact with the audio signals and cause distortion or noise.

EMI filter. Components added to an audio circuit to suppress EMI.

EOL. End of life, the state of a product or component which has been discontinued from manufacturing.

EOS. Electrical overstress, a failure condition in an integrated circuit caused from operating the circuit outside of its normal parameters.

EPC. Entertainment PC.

EQ. Equalization, or an equalizer.

Equalizer. Circuitry or equipment which produces a varying (usually adjustable) amplitude as a function of frequency.

equivalent noise level. The intensity an external sound source would need to have in order to generate a voltage level in the microphone equal to the voltage the microphone generates as self-noise. Also known as **equivalent noise rating** and **equivalent input noise (EIN)**.

ESD. Electrostatic discharge, an electrical event associated with static electricity. Typically, this discharge has very high voltage but low current, with the potential to damage the device or system subject to this event. A lightning strike is a severe example of electrostatic discharge.

even order distortion. A type of distortion produced by nonlinearities mathematically described by even value exponents. These nonlinearities produce an asymmetrical shape in the output versus input transfer characteristic of the device. Examples include second harmonic distortion and difference frequency intermodulation distortion.

excursion. The maximum range of diaphragm movement in a speaker driver.

expander. A signal-processing amplifier which has greater gain at high input amplitudes than at low inputs, producing an output dynamic range greater than the input dynamic range. Normally, an expander is used as part of an overall system with earlier compressors, to restore the original dynamic range of a signal which was reduced in a compressor.

fast Fourier transform. A mathematical optimization of the discrete Fourier transform, which converts a signal between the time domain and the frequency domain.

FET. Field Effect Transistor.

FFT. See **fast Fourier transform**.

foldback. The reflection of upper sideband signals above the Nyquist limit into the lower sideband.

formants. Resonant frequencies in the vocal tract that form a pivotal role in forming vowel sounds.

forward masking. A type of masking that occurs when the masker precedes the signal in time.

frequency domain. A means of representing a signal as a plot of amplitude (normally on the vertical axis) versus frequency (normally on the horizontal axis). Spectrum analyzers represent signals in the frequency domain.

frequency response. The measurement of a frequency-varying gain or response parameter across the spectrum. Commonly used to measure the sensitivity of a microphone or the intensity a speaker can create.

frequency selectivity. The ability to differentiate two pure tones. Also known as **frequency resolution**.

frequency. The rate at which a wave repeats. The inverse of period.

full duplex. The capability of a system to provide audio input and output simultaneously, with no interaction between the two.

full range. Refers to equipment that can handle sounds across the entire spectrum of human hearing.

full scale. The maximum signal level in a system. In an analog system, this level is usually the clipping level. In a digital system, it is usually the maximum level that can be represented by the audio coding scheme in use.

function driver. In Intel HD Audio, the function driver is the miniport driver that provides the basic audio control. It works in conjunction with the bus driver to control the hardware.

fundamental. The lowest or base frequency in a set of harmonics.

fundamental rejection. The amount, usually expressed in decibels, by which a THD+N analyzer rejects the fundamental component of the input signal. The lowest measurable distortion of a THD+N analyzer is limited by fundamental rejection, along with several other attributes.

fusion. The phenomenon of two sounds with similar frequencies being perceived as a single sound.

GFX. Global Effects, a user-mode signal processing block in Windows Vista used to process the final mix before sending it to the endpoint. The GFX is installed based on a plug and play ID.

GPIO. General purpose input/output. This digital signal on a codec can be used to control external binary logic or for the codec to monitor external binary inputs to the codec. In Windows Vista, the UAA class driver does not make use of any GPIOs, though a third-party function driver may choose to do so.

graphic equalizer. An equalizer in which the gain at each portion of the spectrum is controlled by a separate fader. The faders are typically vertically-mounted slide controls, so that the positions of the control knobs form an approximation to the frequency response of the equalizer.

Gerber plot. The graphical representation of the copper traces on each layer of a motherboard. It is derived from the schematic.

glitch. A momentary disruption in an audio or video signal.

ground loop. An inadvertent signal path formed when interconnecting the chassis of two or more pieces of equipment, each possessing a safety ground. Ground loops can cause hum-related interference.

ground plane. A trace on a printed circuit board that is widened to provide a shield for other layers in the motherboard. A ground plane may take up a significant portion of the layout on multi-layer printed circuit boards.

group delay. The relative time delay between different spectral portions of a signal.

hardware interrupt. See **interrupt**.

harmonic. A frequency that is an integer multiple of a fundamental. The second harmonic has twice the frequency of the fundamental. The third harmonic has three times the frequency of the fundamental. And so on. Sometimes, the fundamental is referred to as the first harmonic.

harmonic distortion. A type of non-linear distortion characterized by the presence of harmonics of the original signal. See **THD** and **THD+N**.

HBM. See **Human Body Model**.

HD. An acronym for high definition. Used to describe video or audio signals that have superior quality to standard definition signals.

HD Audio. Intel® High Definition Audio.

HDCP. High-Bandwidth Digital Content Protection.

HDMI. The High-Definition Multimedia Interface is an uncompressed, all-digital audio/video interface. HDMI provides an interface between any audio/video source, such as a set-top box, DVD player, or computer and an audio and/or video monitor, such as a digital television.

HDTV. An acronym for High Definition Television.

headroom. The difference between average program level and the highest level possible.

headphone. A set of small speakers worn directly on the ears.

heterodyning. Shifting the frequency of a signal. For instance, a sub-band with the range 1,000 to 2,000 hertz and a sub-band with the range 3,000 to 4,000 hertz can both be heterodyned to the range 0 to 1,000 hertz so that they can both be processed by a single device that only operates on frequencies in the range 0 to 1,000 hertz.

hertz. Denotes units of "per second," typically used when measuring frequency.

HID. Human interface device, a type of control used by USB audio devices. HID controls are not applicable for Intel HD Audio.

high-order filter. A filter that has two or more poles and zeroes. This type of filter has a steep cutoff, but it requires more processing blocks, whether they be analog resistors and capacitors or DSP cycles.

HP. See **headphone**.

Human Body Model. An electrical circuit which approximates the way a human body can create electrostatic discharges.

Hz. An abbreviation of hertz.

I^2S. The Inter-IC Sound is a serial bus for digital audio devices and technologies such as compact disc CD players, digital sound processors, and digital TV sound. 24-bit audio devices are usually connected with either the I2S or the Intel HD Audio bus.

I^2C. The Inter-IC bus is a control bus often used in conjunction with the I2S bus. There is no easy way to interface I^2C devices to Intel HD Audio devices.

IEC. International Electrotechnical Commission. A global organization that prepares and promotes electrical and electronic standards.

impedance. The opposition to the flow of alternating current.

impedance sensing. A method of determining the impedance of a device attached to a port of an Intel HD Audio codec. This technique can be used to provide **device classification**.

INF file. A text file used by a device driver to describe how the driver should be installed, and what plug and play devices it will match.

ISO. International Organization for Standardization. A network of national standards committees. You might think the proper acronym would be "IOS." Or perhaps the organization's name in another language forms "ISO." In fact, "ISO" is apparently not an acronym at all, but rather a reference to the root "iso-" which means "equal."

ITU-R. International Telecommunications Union, Radio Sector, which coordinates efforts within different countries in the field of radio communications.

jack. A connector attached to or embedded in a piece of equipment. See **plug**.

jack sense. The capability to know whether a plug is inserted in a particular jack. Sometimes incorrectly refers to impedance sense. Also known as **jack detect**.

JEDEC. The Joint Electron Device Engineering Council and is the semiconductor engineering standardization body of the Electronic Industries Alliance (EIA), a trade association that represents all areas of the electronics industry.

jitter. The undesirable cycle-to-cycle variation in the period of a reference clock, such as are used in digital audio converters. Jitter can cause modulation sidebands and noise if converters operate from a jittered clock. Excessive jitter in an interface can cause digitally interfaced equipment to malfunction.

JND. An acronym for just noticeable difference. Refers to the smallest consistently perceivable change for a given stimulus.

kernel mode. Refers to software running in a protected mode of the x86 architecture in Windows XP or Windows Vista. Device drivers normally run in kernel mode

kilohertz. One thousand hertz.

KMixer. The kernel mode mixer is a part of the WDM driver stack in Windows XP and Windows Vista, and provides a software-based method for mixing the audio outputs of multiple applications together

land. The flat region between bumps on an optical disk, such as a compact disk or DVD.

limiter. A signal-processing amplifier whose gain is sharply reduced above some critical threshold, so that the output signal does not exceed a specified value regardless of input amplitude.

LFE. An acronym for Low Frequency Effects. Refers to a sound channel that is designed to carry only low frequencies. LFE channels are typically played using a subwoofer.

LFX. Local Effects, a user-mode signal processing block in Windows Vista used to process the input or output of each individual The LFX is installed based on a plug and play ID.

longitudinal balance. An alternative method to common mode rejection ratio for measuring the degree of balance of a transmission line.

lossless. A system in which information is not lost. Typically, this term is used to describe compression algorithms in which the original signal can be exactly reconstructed from the compressed version.

lossy. A system in which information is lost. Typically, this term is used to describe compression algorithms in which the original signal cannot be exactly reconstructed from the compressed version.

loudness adaptation. The psycho-acoustical phenomenon of sounds of constant intensity decreasing in loudness over time.

loudness. The subjective equivalent of intensity.

low-pass filter. A filter that passes all frequencies below a specified frequency essentially without attenuation, while attenuating frequencies above that value.

Machine Model. An electrical circuit that approximates the way automated electronic assembly equipment can create electrostatic discharges.

maskee. The sound that is hidden by a masker.

masker. The sound that is responsible for rendering a signal undetectable.

masking. The phenomenon of a sound being rendered undetectable due to the presence of another sound.

masking, frequency. The psycho-acoustic effect wherein a strong signal causes weaker signals nearby in frequency to be inaudible.

masking, temporal. The psycho-acoustic effect wherein a strong signal causes weaker signals occurring just before or just after the strong signal to be inaudible.

matrixing. The process of encoding multiple audio channels into sound channels. For instance, surround channel information can be matrixed into two channels that also carry front stereo information.

maximum length sequence (MLS). A pseudo-random noise sequence designed such that every possible bit combination occurs once during each repetition cycle. An MLS sequence has the property that if it is passed through a linear device under test and a cross correlation computed between the output and input of the device, the result is the impulse response of the device. The MLS is used in quasi-anechoic acoustical testing.

maximum output level (MOL). The maximum output level that a device can deliver without exceeding a specified distortion value. Most commonly used with analog tape recorders, where maximum output level is typically defined as maximum level achievable without exceeding third harmonic distortion of 3 percent for a mid-band signal, which is usually 1 kilohertz.

MCI. Multimedia Control Interface, a simple-to-use interface to control media playback, present in every version of windows since 3.1.

mel. A unit of pitch. One thousand mels are defined to equal the pitch of a 1,000-hertz pure tone. A 2,000-mel tone is one that sounds to a listener twice as high as a 1,000-hertz tone. A 500-mel tone is one that sounds twice as low as a 1,000-mel tone.

MME multimedia extensions. The classic Windows audio subsystem introduced as part of Windows 3.1, and replaced in Windows Vista.

MME multimedia extender. A device capable of receiving a multimedia stream from a Media Center PC and rendering it in a location separate and distinct from the location where the Media Center PC is located.

MEMS. Micro-Electro-Mechanical Systems, the integration of mechanical elements, sensors, actuators, and electronics on a common silicon substrate through microfabrication technology. While the electronics are fabricated using integrated circuit (IC) process sequences (e.g., CMOS, Bipolar, or BICMOS processes), the micromechanical components are fabricated using compatible "micromachining" processes that selectively etch away parts of the silicon wafer or add new structural layers to form the mechanical and electromechanical devices.

MFT. Media Foundation Transform, an audio or video processing block in Windows Vista.

meridian lossless packing. The multi-channel lossless compression technology incorporated into DVD-Audio discs.

microphone. A collection of one or more capsules encased within an enclosure. A microphone converts sound pressure waves into electrical signals. Also known as a mike or mic.

microphone array. Two or more microphones used with a beamforming software algorithm to focus more tightly on an audio point source than is possible with a single microphone.

microphonic. Describes a circuit component which is sensitive to vibration and generates electrical signals in response to the vibration.

MIDI. Musical Instrument Digital Interface, a serial interface common on computerized musical equipment.

mid-range. A speaker driver optimized to create medium frequency sounds.

MIXERLINE. The legacy application programming interface used for volume controls in Windows.

MLS. See **maximum length sequence**.

MLP. see **meridian lossless packing**.

monophonic. Single-channel sound. Also known as mono.

Moore's Law. The observation made in 1965 by Gordon Moore, co-founder of Intel, that the number of transistors per square inch on integrated circuits had doubled every year since the integrated circuit was invented. Moore predicted that this trend would continue for the foreseeable future.

MP3. An acronym for MPEG-1 Layer III audio. A popular music compression format.

MPEG. Moving Pictures Experts Group. An ISO/IEC subcommittee that develops international standards for storing, transmitting, and organizing digital audio and video.

MPEG-1. A video and audio compression standard. It supports a maximum bit rate of 1.5 megabits per second.

MPEG-2. An extension of MPEG-1 that adds support for higher quality audio and video. The base format of DVD-Video.

MPEG-4. A versatile format that allows for multiple concurrent audio and video channels.

MPEG-7. An infrastructure for searching and managing multimedia. Unlike its predecessors, it is not an audio/video compression format.

multigenerational copying. Making a copy of a copy.

multiplexing. Chronologically interleaving packets of data together. For instance, MPEG-2 streams consist of discrete audio and video packets that contain information that are intended to be played back at the same time. For transmission or storage purposes, the packets are multiplexed: placed one after another in a single stream.

mute. When muted, an audio channel produces no output. When unmuted, the audio channel produces a normal volume level.

MUX. Multiplexer; an analog or digital switch selecting among several signal paths.

NMR. An acronym for noise-to-mask ratio. A measurement of the perceivable distortion of a compressed signal.

node ID. The numerical address of a codec widget

noise gate. A signal processing device whose output is disabled (infinite attenuation) when the input signal level falls below a critical threshold, so that noise in the absence of significant program material is not passed to the output.

noise reduction. A system, normally used with recording or transmission, which reduces overall noise by processing the signal prior to recording or transmission and again following transmission or a playback. Processing before recording or transmission is normally some combination of compression and high frequency boost. Processing after transmission or at playback is the opposite of the first processing in order to restore the initial dynamic range and frequency response, while reducing the effects of noise introduced in the recording or transmission medium.

noise shaping. Using a feedback loop and oversampling to change the spectrum of noise. Specifically, noise energy is redistributed so that most of it exists at higher frequencies than can be heard by the human ear. These can be easily removed by a low-pass filter.

noise suppression. Audio processing intended to remove background noise from a speech signal.

noise weighting. A filtering technique used in audio fidelity testing to match how the ear's sensitivity to high and low frequency noise at low levels is diminished.

non-PCM. A digital audio signal consisting of compressed or encoded audio to be passed over S/PDIF or HDMI outputs.

nonlinear PCM. A form of PCM wherein the quantization levels are unevenly spaced.

Northbridge. The chip in the chipset that attaches to the CPU, typically controls video and memory, and provides a connection to the Southbridge chip.

notch filter. A band reject filter with a narrow rejection band, often used to eliminate the fundamental frequency for THD+N measurements or to reject a specific spectral component such as power mains hum.

nyquist frequency. The maximum frequency that can be represented by a specific sample rate; normally half the sampling rate.

Octave. The interval between a 2:1 range of frequencies, such as 400 hertz to 800 hertz or 5 kilohertz to 10 kilohertz.

OATS. Open air test site used for EMI and RF testing.

odd order distortion. A type of distortion produced by nonlinearities mathematically described with odd order exponents. These nonlinearities cause a symmetrical shape of the output versus input transfer characteristic of a device. An example would be third harmonic distortion, or the 13 kilohertz product produced by 14 kilohertz and 15 kilohertz signals (2*F1 - F2).

off-axis. Any and all directions that are not directly in front of a microphone or speaker.

off-axis colorization. The tendency of microphones to have an increasingly distorted frequency response as sounds originate further away from on-axis.

ohm. The unit of resistance and impedance.

omnidirectional. A microphone pickup pattern that is equally sensitive to sounds in all directions.

on-axis. The direction directly in front of a microphone or speaker.

oversampling. Sampling a signal at a much higher rate than required by the Nyquist frequency, often with less bits of resolution.

out-of-band noise. The sigma-delta conversion process used in digital to analog converters can generate significant noise which can't be heard by the human ear. For audio fidelity testing, this noise can create errors, and must be filtered out.

parametric equalizer. An equalizer in which the center frequency, bandwidth (Q factor), and amount of gain or attenuation of a number of filters are all adjustable.

passband. The frequency band of a filter in which signals are essentially unattenuated.

passband ripple. The amount of amplitude variation within the passband, measured in plus or minus decibels.

PC Beep. See **PC Speaker.**

PC Speaker. The single-channel square wave sound generator using the 8253 chip, that originated on the IBM PC. Still present in most 32-bit PCs.

PCI. Peripheral Component Interconnect is a local bus standard developed by Intel. While PCI slots are popular for mounting sound cards, there are currently no Intel HD Audio solutions which incorporate a PCI slot.

PCI Express. A backward compatible high performance extension of the PCI local bus that addresses the increased I/O requirements for high-bandwidth applications such as Intel HD Audio, Gigabit Ethernet, Fibre Channel, Ultra3 SCSI and graphics.

PCI-SIG. The PCI Special Interest Group, which issues the plug and play vendor ID numbers used in Intel HD Audio products.

PCM. An acronym for pulse code modulation. A digital coding scheme wherein samples are stored as multi-bit data words at the sampling rate. This is the format used for most Wave files and audio streams.

peak-to-peak. The maximum amplitude difference between positive-going and negative-going peaks of a signal.

peak. The maximum instantaneous excursion of a signal.

peer-to-peer file sharing. A scheme for directly sending and receiving files among networked PCs.

perfect pitch. The ability to identify the pitch of a tone without a reference tone.

period. The time required for a wave to complete a cycle. The inverse of frequency.

phantom power. A technique for supplying power to microphones that need it over the very same lines used to transmit the sound signals. Phantom power is designed in such a way that it does not interfere with microphones that do not require power.

phase opposition. When two waves are 180 degrees out of phase.

phase quadrature. When two waves are ±90 degrees out of phase.

phone jack, ¼-inch. A female connector used for electric guitars and headphones.

phone jack, 3.5mm. A smaller version of a phone jack used for audio connections to a computer.

phoneme. A distinctive sound that is a fundamental unit of speech.

pickup pattern. A polar graph that indicates the sensitivity of a microphone to sounds originating from different directions.

piezoelectric. A material that physically changes shape when electricity is applied. Changing the shape of the material causes it to generate electricity.

pin. For software, it's a node in an audio device driver which exposes certain characteristics. For hardware, it's a physical connector on the outside of an integrated circuit which is usually soldered down to the printed circuit board.

pin complex. The set of hardware pins associated with a pin widget in an Intel HD Audio codec. A pin complex usually consists of a stereo left/right signal pair, a jack sense line (shared with other pins), and a VRefOut signal to provide switchable microphone bias.

pin configuration default. See **configuration default.**

pin widget. A control node in an Intel HD Audio codec associated with an analog input or output port.

pink noise. A type of noise whose spectral power distribution is such that the power per octave, per decade, or in any other equal-percentage section is the same anywhere across the spectrum. For example, pink noise has the same power in the octave between 50 hertz and 100 hertz as in the octave between 10 kilohertz and 20 kilohertz.

pitch. The subjective equivalent of frequency.

plug. A connector attached to a cable. See **jack**.

polar patterns. See **pickup pattern**.

POST. Power On Self Test routine executed by the BIOS when power is applied to a motherboard.

POST Tones. Audio tones generated by the BIOS on the 8253 timer chip. These tones are either directed to a piezoelectric buzzer mounted on the motherboard, or they are directed to the analog PC beep input of the codec, to be heard through speakers connected to the motherboard.

power supply rejection ratio. The ability of an integrated circuit to reject noise which is present on the power supply.

precedence effect. The psycho-acoustical phenomenon wherein two similar sounds arrive within milliseconds of each other at each ear and are fused together into a single perceived sound. The fused sound is localized in the direction of the sound the reaches the ears first. This effect is also known the **Haas effect**, and the **law of the first wave front**.

prediction. A compression technique in which the current value is determined from previous values.

preferred device. In Windows XP, the user can designate a device as the preferred device. Applications may choose to use the preferred device, or may provide the user with a choice of devices specific to that application.

protected user mode audio. In Windows Vista, all audio processing will be performed in a global user-mode audio engine (see **UMA**). The protected user mode audio path provides additional security layers to support digital rights management.

proximity effect. The phenomenon of certain microphones becoming increasingly sensitive to low frequencies as the sound source nears the diaphragm.

pseudorandom noise. A type of noise whose amplitude-vs.-time distribution appears to be random when examined over a short period of time, but which in fact exactly repeats a pattern of a certain duration. The spectrum of a pseudorandom noise signal has power only at the frequencies corresponding to integer multiples (harmonics) of a fundamental frequency whose period is equal to the repetition cycle duration. For example, a pseudorandom noise sequence with a two second repetition cycle will have a spectrum consisting of power at every harmonic of 0.5 hertz.

psophometric filter. A filter whose response is based on the frequency response of the human hearing system. Most noise weighting filters are psophometric filters.

PSRR. See **power supply rejection ratio.**

Psychoacoustics. The area of science combining acoustical stimulus and human response to that stimulus.

pulse code modulation. A form of data transmission in which amplitude samples of an analog signal are represented by digital numbers.

pulse width modulation. A form of data transmission in which amplitude samples of an analog signal are represented by the duty factor of a pulse train. Sometimes, it is used in high-power switching amplifiers.

PUMA. See **protected user mode audio.**

PWM. See **pulse width modulation**.

Q or **distance factor.** A measurement of a microphone's reach.

Q factor. A measurement of the selectivity or sharpness of a bandpass or band-reject filter. For a bandpass filter, the Q is equal to the ratio of the center frequency to the bandwidth at the •3 decibel points. For example, a bandpass filter with a Q of 5, tuned to a center frequency of 1,000 Hertz, would have a •3-decibel bandwidth of 200 Hertz.

quantization error. The difference in magnitude between the original signal and the quantized version of the signal.

Quantizing. The process of discretely sampling a signal's intensity.

quasi-anechoic. An electronic technique for eliminating the effect of acoustical reflections while testing in a normal space with reflections. Quasi-anechoic techniques all involve measuring signals whose arrival time corresponds to the acoustical propagation delay of the desired direct path, while attenuating or eliminating signals which arrive later due to the longer path length of the reflection. Quasi-anechoic techniques include impulse stimulus with gating, Maximum Length Sequence, and Time Delay Spectrometry.

quasi-peak. A fast-attack, slow-decay detector circuit which approximately responds to signal peaks. Specifically, the detector response called out in CCIR Recommendation 468.

random noise. A type of noise whose amplitude-vs.-time distribution is mathematically random and unpredictable, never repeating. The spectrum of a random noise signal is continuous with power at all frequencies, rather than power only at certain points as with pseudorandom noise.

RCA jack. An analog audio connector popular in A/V receivers.

real time analyzer. A piece of audio test equipment that displays the audio content in the frequency domain in real time, usually using 1/3 octave bands.

real time communications. Refers to two-way voice communications such as VoIP or Instant Messenger with speech.

rear wave. The sound wave created by the rear of a speaker diaphragm.

reconstruction filter. A low-pass filter following a D/A converter, used to remove the high frequency clock signal and smoothly integrate between the discrete voltage values from the D/A.

redirection. The ability of an codec analog port to operate either as an input or an output.

redirected headphone. An optional pin configuration defaults sequence which disables the line outputs or speakers whenever a headphone is plugged in and redirects the audio to the headphone as long as it remains plugged in.

reference level. An empirically determined operating level used as the baseline for a series of audio fidelity testing. For Intel HD Audio systems, an analog reference level of 0 dBV (1 volt RMS) is usually sufficient, while 0 dBFS (full scale) is used for the digital reference level.

render. In audio, the opposite of capture, the act of playing back or outputting audio.

RESET#. The wire on the Intel HD Audio link which determines whether the codec is in reset mode (and therefore disabled) or not.

residual. A term used in compression to denote the difference between a predicted value and the actual value, also known as an error.

residual distortion. The irreducible minimum distortion of an audio generator and analyzer. Residual distortion is thus the floor below which the instrument is not useful; measurements above but approaching within 6 to 10 decibels of the residual distortion value are less accurate.

residual noise. The irreducible noise in a measurement instrument, which sets a floor for amplitude measurements.

resistance. The opposition to the flow of direct current.

resolution. The smallest change in a measured parameter to which a measurement instrument can respond.

resume. The transition of the PC from a sleeping state to a waking state.

retasking. The ability of a 3.5 mm analog phone jack to support more than one type of device. For instance, the jack might be retasked from headphone to microphone.

ripping. Copying media files from an optical disc to a PC's hard drive. Often used to describe copying audio files from an audio CD to a PC, this practice is also used to describe copying video and audio from a DVD to a PC.

ripple. 1. Undesired AC variations on a DC power supply output. 2. Variations in frequency response in the passband of a filter.

RMS. Root mean square, the preferred form of AC signal detection, which measures amplitude in terms of its equivalent power content, regardless of signal's wave shape.

RTC. See **real time communications.**

rolloff frequency. The frequency considered the transition between the attenuated and non-attenuated portions of the frequency response of a high-pass or low-pass filter. The filter has a specified attenuation, usually either 3.01 dB or the magnitude of the ripple, at the rolloff frequency.

root node. The codec node or widget which describes the rest of the codec

sample clock. The time reference signal in a digital system which determines the intervals at which the signal will be sampled.

sample frequency, sample rate. The frequency at which the signal is sampled in a digital system. The sample rate must exceed twice the highest analog frequency to be converted. Commonly-used sample rates are 48 kilohertz, 44.1 kilohertz, and 32 kilohertz.

SACD. Super Audio CD, a newer CD format which stores audio in single-bit DSD format (see **DSD**).

SAP. Secure Audio Path, a secure media interconnect contained in Windows XP. Windows Vista replaces SAP with **Protected User Mode Audio.**

schematic. A set of symbols and connections used to describe an electrical circuit. In Intel HD Audio, the schematic determines how the pin configuration defaults registers are programmed.

SCMS. An acronym for Serial Copy Management System, which is a copy protection system in which compliant equipment prevents unlicensed multigenerational copies from being made.

SD. An acronym for standard definition that may be used to describe either video or audio signals.

SDI. Serial Data In line of the Intel HD Audio bus.

SDO. Serial Data Out line of the Intel HD Audio bus.

self-noise. The amount of sound a microphone generates when it is placed in an absolutely quiet environment. Self-noise originates from phenomenon such as thermal noise in electrical components.

separation. The isolation, usually stated in decibels, between the two channels of a stereo device.

sequence. A method of grouping used in setting pin configuration default registers in each pin widget of an Intel HD Audio codec. See **association.**

shielded cable. A construction technique for cables in which a metallic outer conductor completely surrounds one or more signal-carrying conductors. This outer shield is normally connected to ground (earth) at one or both ends.

sigma-delta converter. The most common type of digital to analog converter or analog to digital converter design currently in use.

signal-to-noise ratio (SNR). The difference in level between a reference output signal (typically at the normal or maximum operating level of the device) and the device output with no signal applied. Signal-to-noise ratio is normally stated in dB. The device input conditions for the noise measurement must be specified, such as "input short circuited" or with a specific value of resistance connected at the device input instead of a signal. In PC Audio, the dynamic range measurement is typically used instead of SNR.

SMI. System Management Interrupt, a type of interrupt serviced by the BIOS, and unknown to the OS. Overly long SMIs can cause audio glitches.

SMR. An acronym for signal-to-mask ratio. Refers to the distance between the intensity of the masker and the masking threshold.

SNR. See **signal-to-noise ratio.**

sonogram. A plot of how a sound's spectrum changes over time.

Southbridge. The chip in a chipset that services the audio device. See **Northbridge.**

S/PDIF. An acronym for the Sony/Philips Digital Interface Format, which is the most popular consumer digital audio interconnect. It carries a wide variety of formats including compressed multi-channel audio across a single cable. S/PDIF. Sometimes referred to as the EIAJ interface. The S/PDIF interface is similar to the professional AES 3 interface, but is normally an unbalanced coaxial signal of lower amplitude. Most of the status byte definitions are different between S/PDIF and AES 3.

speaker. A collection of one or more speaker drivers and potentially a crossover encased within an enclosure. Speakers convert electrical signals into sound pressure waves.

spectrum. a plot of a sound's intensity at different frequencies.

spider. The flexible structure in a speaker driver that attaches the voice coil to the frame. The spider keeps the voice coil centered within the permanent magnet.

star grounding. The technique of running separate ground returns for each signal and power supply path. This technique reduces induced noises in an audio circuit.

stream. A group of one or more related audio inputs or outputs currently being recorded or played in real-time.

stopband. The frequency band across which a filter has at least some minimum specified value of attenuation.

sub-band. A subset of the audible audio spectrum, which is used in compression schemes such as MPEG audio, to allow a different portion of the spectrum to be concurrently compressed with different quality.

subwoofer. A speaker driver optimized to create very low frequency sounds.

suspend. The transition of a PC to a sleeping or hibernating state.

suspension. The flexible component of a speaker driver that attaches the diaphragm to the frame.

sweet spot. Some 3D audio algorithms require the user to sit in a particular spot relative to the speakers in order to hear the 3D effects. This is the sweet spot.

termination impedance. A network consisting of one or more resistive or reactive components used to properly match the input or output of the system under test, to ensure consistent test measurements

THD. Total Harmonic Distortion, which is normally computed from a series of selective measurements of the amplitudes of all significant individual harmonic distortion products. The bandwidth of each measurement must be sufficiently narrow that noise has no significant effect on the measurement.

THD+N. Total Harmonic Distortion plus Noise, Which is measured by attenuating the fundamental signal with a narrow-band notch filter, then measuring the remaining signal which consists of harmonics of various order, wide-band noise, and possibly interfering signals. This measurement is the common harmonic distortion method implemented in most analyzers.

third octave. A bandwidth of 1/3 octave, or a frequency ratio of 1.2599:1. Three successive frequency changes by this ratio result in a total frequency change of 2:1 (one octave).

third order. Distortion products produced by a cube (exponent of 3) term in a device's nonlinear transfer function.

time domain. A means of representing a signal as a graph of amplitude (usually on the vertical axis) versus time (on the horizontal axis). An oscilloscope produces a time domain representation of a signal.

threshold of feeling. The highest intensity a sound can have before it causes sensations of prickling and pain. Nominally on the order of 120 to 130 dB-SPL. Also known as the **threshold of pain**.

threshold of hearing. The lowest intensity a sound can have and still be audible. Nominally, it's 0 dB-SPL, although the exact level varies from person to person.

timbre. The psycho-acoustical assessment that allows us to differentiate between two sounds that have the same pitch and loudness.

tip-ring-sleeve. A three-conductor phone plug typically used to carry unbalanced stereo audio.

tip-sleeve. A two-conductor phone plug typically used to carry unbalanced mono audio.

topology. The set of parameters used by the audio function driver to describes the audio flow and control nodes.

topology parser. A module contained in the UAA class driver which "walks" though an Intel HD Audio codec and uses the pin configuration defaults registers to determine how to configure the codec for a particular system.

TOSLINK.† Toshiba's trade name for a popular optical interconnect used for optical S/PDIF connections.

transducer. A device that converts energy from one medium to another. For instance, speakers convert energy from electricity to air.

tweeter. A speaker driver optimized to create high frequency sounds.

UAA. Universal Audio Architecture, which is the Microsoft† strategy to ensure consistent audio performance by providing class drivers for specific types of audio devices, include Intel HD Audio, USB, and IEEE-1394 interfaces.

UAA class driver. Commonly refers to the Intel HD Audio class driver.

UMA. User Mode Audio, the global audio engine in Windows Vista.

Unbalanced. Refers to a transferring a signal using two wires. One wire carries a variable voltage that corresponds to the signal itself, while the other wire serves as a zero reference, or ground.

Universal Audio Architecture. See **UAA.**

Universal Serial Bus. An interconnect standard for connecting external devices to a PC, including audio devices. Used instead of Intel HD Audio.

user mode. Refers to software that is not running in a protected mode of the X86 architecture in Windows XP or Windows Vista. Device drivers normally run in **kernel mode**, while applications run in user mode.

USB. See **Universal Serial Bus.**

VAG. Virtual Audio Ground, the DC level at the analog input or output pins of an Intel HD Audio codec.

verb table. A list of Intel HD Audio verbs that the BIOS sends to an Intel HD Audio codec's pin configuration default registers during startup and resume.

virtual analog ground. See **VAG.**

voice coil. The electromagnet in a speaker driver that is used to modulate the diaphragm.

VoIP. Voice over IP, a type of real-time speech communication where the speech signals travel over the Internet in the form of TCP/IP packets.

VRefOut. A pin on an Intel HD Audio codec which provides switchable microphone bias voltage.

WaveCylic. A type of audio miniport driver used in Windows XP which loops through a single DMA buffer.

WavePCI. A type of audio miniport driver used in Windows XP which uses a list of multiple scatter-gather DMA buffers.

WaveRT. The preferred type of audio miniport driver for use with Windows Vista.

Waveform. A plot of a sound's intensity over time.

WDK. The Windows Driver Kit, the driver test and development framework used for Windows Vista and for testing Windows XP once Windows Vista has launched.

WDM. Win32 Driver Model, the framework for Windows audio drivers for both Windows XP and Windows Vista.

weighting filter. A filter with varying attenuation as a function of frequency so as to produce a measurement where the various spectral components affect the measurement in a specified fashion. Most commonly used weighting filters are attempts to correspond to the varying response of the human hearing system in order to produce measurements (usually of noise) that correlate well with human observations.

white noise. A type of noise whose spectral power distribution is such that no equivalent power per hertz occurs anywhere in the spectrum. For example, white noise has the same power in the 30 hertz bandwidth between 70 hertz and 100 hertz as in the 30 hertz bandwidth between 10,000 hertz and 10,030 hertz.

WHQL. Windows Hardware Quality Labs, the Microsoft team which administers the various Windows logo testing programs.

widget. a control object in an Intel HD Audio codec which can be address through a Node ID.

Win32 Driver Model. See **WDM.**

WMA. Short for Windows Media Audio, a Microsoft file format for encoding digital audio files similar in concept to MP3.

WMA. Short for Windows Media Audio Professional, a set of extensions to the WMA format which includes all high definition audio formats and lossless compression.

woofer. A speaker driver optimized to create low frequency sounds.

XLR connector. A high-quality connector designed for audio applications. Most commonly used in a 3-pin variation to interconnect professional audio devices with balanced interfaces.

zipper noise. The noise made when moving a volume control, either analog or digital, which has a coarse set of volume settings. The presence of DC often makes the zipper noise more noticeable.

References

The following sources are cited in this book. On this book's page on the Intel Press Web site, you can find an extensive list of useful background and supplementary information for topics in each chapter. Intel® Corporation product manuals are generally available from the Intel developer Web site at developer.intel.com.

1394 Trade Association. DATE. *Audio and Music Data Transmission Protocol 2.1 (AMDTP2.1) Specification*. Document number 2001024. Available at: www.1394ta.org/Technology/Specifications/.

Audio Engineering Society. 2003. AES standard for digital audio—Digital input-output interfacing—Serial transmission format for two channel linearly represented digital audio data. AES3-200:3 Available from http://www.aes.org/publications/standards/.

———. 2004. AES standard method for digital audio engineering—Measurement of digital audio equipment. AES17-1998 (r2004). Available from http://www.aes.org/publications/standards/.

———. 2000. AES information document for digital audio—Personal computer audio quality measurements. AES-6id-2000. Available from http://www.aes.org/publications/standards/.

Dolby, Ray. David Robinson and Kenneth Gundry. 1979. "CCIR/ARM: A Practical Noise Measurement Method," *Journal of the Audio Engineering Society*, 27:149-157.

Harris, Steven, and Clif Sanchez. 1999. "Personal Computer Audio Quality Measurement," a white paper from Cirrus Logic. Available at: http://www.cirrus.com/en/pubs/whitePaper/meas100.pdf

IEEE Standards Association. 2005. IEEE Standard for High Performance Serial Bus Bridges, 1394.1-2004. Available at: http://standards.ieee.org/catalog/olis/busarch.html.

Intel Corporation. 2004. Intel® High-Definition Audio Specification, Santa Clara: Intel Corporation. Available at: http://www.intel.com/standards/hdaudio/.

———. 2005. *Intel® I/O Controller Hub 7 (ICH7) / Intel® High Definition Audio / AC'97 Programmer's Reference Manual (PRM)*. Santa Clara: Intel Corporation. Available at: http://www.intel.com/design/chipsets/manuals/307017.htm.

Intel Corporation and Microsoft Corporation. 2001. *PC 2001 System Design Guide: A Technical Reference for Designing PCs and Peripherals for the Microsoft® Windows® Family of Operating Systems*. Redmond: Microsoft Press. Available at: http://download.microsoft.com/download/win2000pro/PCG/1.0/NT5/EN-US/pc2001v10.exe.

International Electrotechnical Commission. 2005. Audio and audiovisual equipment—Digital audio parts—Basic measurements methods of audio characteristics—Part 4: Personal computer (TC 100), IEC 61606-4. Available at: http://www.iec.ch/.

———. 2002. Electroacoustics- Sound level meters—Part 1: specifications, IEC 61672-1, first edition. Available at: http://www.iec.ch/.

———. 2005. Consumer audio/video equipment—Digital interface—Part 6: Audio and music data transmission protocol, IEC 61883-6, Second edition. Available at: http://www.iec.ch/.

———. 2004. Digital audio interface—Part 1: General, IEC 60958-1, second edition. Available at: http://www.iec.ch/.

———. 2003. Digital audio interface—Part 3: Consumer applications, IEC 60958-3, second edition. Available at: http://www.iec.ch/.

———. 2003. Digital audio interface—Part 4: Professional applications (TA4), IEC 60958-4, second edition. Available at: http://www.iec.ch/.

International Organization for Standardization. 1987. Acoustics—Normal Equal-Loudness Level Contours, ISO 226:2003. Available at: http://www.iso.org/iso/.

International Telecommunication Union (ITU). 2001. Recommendation BS.1387-1 Method for objective measurements of perceived audio quality (PEAQ), November, Radiocommunication Sector. Available at: http://www.itu.int/publications/default.aspx.

———. 1986. ITU-R Recommendation BS.468-4, Measurement of Audio Frequency Noise in Broadcasting, Sound Recording Systems and on Sound Programme Circuits. Geneva, Switzerland. Available at: http://www.itu.int/publications/default.aspx.

———. 2005, Front Panel I/O Connectivity Design Guide. Available at: http://www.formfactors.org/devlist.asp?FFID=-1&CatID=10.

Janus, Scott. 2004. *Audio in the 21st Century*, Hillsboro: Intel Press.

Jones, Wayne. 2003. Testing Challenges in Personal Computer Audio Devices, Audio Engineering Society Convention Paper 5814, presented at the 114th Convention, March 22-25, Amsterdam, The Netherlands.

Metzler, Bob. 1993. *Audio Measurement Handbook*, Portland: Audio Precision, Inc.

Microsoft Corporation. 2005. *Windows Driver Kit Introduction*. Available from: http://msdn.microsoft.com/library/.

Schmidt, Kymberly, and Tony Doy. 2005. Quantitative analysis yields objective audio-amplifier click and pop measurement. *Electronic Data News*, March 17, 73-80.

Tremaine, Howard. 1969. *Audio Cyclopedia*, Indianapolis: Howard W. Sams & Co.

Index

B

C

D

L

M

Q

R

U

V

"As the pace of technology introduction increases, it's difficult to keep up. Intel Press has established an impressive portfolio. The breadth of topics is a reflection of both Intel's diversity as well as our commitment to serve a broad technical community.

I hope you will take advantage of these products to further your technical education."

Patrick Gelsinger
Senior Vice President
Intel Corporation

Turn the page to learn about titles from Intel Press for system developers

intel

PCI Express† Electrical Interconnect Design

Practical Solutions for Board-level Integration and Validation

By Dave Coleman, Scott Gardiner, Mohammad Kolbehdari, and Stephen Peters

ISBN 0-9743649-9-1

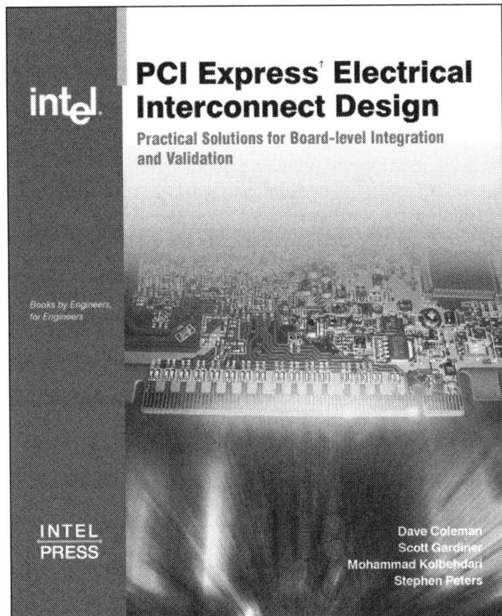

Intel and other companies throughout the computer and communications industries are adopting PCI Express† technology as the successor to today's Conventional PCI† and PCI-X† architectures. The PCI Express serial architecture offers scalable bandwidth and advanced features to meet the I/O needs of next-generation systems.

PCI Express† Electrical Interconnect Design is a how-to guide for system design engineers, board and layout designers, signal integrity engineers, designers of high-speed communication devices, test engineers and technicians, and validation engineers.

With design flowcharts, example implementations, and testing guidelines at your fingertips, you will learn how to translate PCI Express electrical specifications into a reliable and robust interface implementation.

Intel experts relate their insights and experience, thoroughly explaining each step from design through validation. Developers can directly apply this knowledge to improve both quality and time-to-market for desktop, server, workstation, mobile, and communication platform designs.

The range of topics includes:

- Overview and insight into the PCI Express Electrical Specification
- Modeling and simulation in both frequency and time domains
- Design guidelines and expert advice for PCB layout
- Validation of the final design using measurement and correlation procedures

> *"One can either spend a lot of time experimenting, or read this book. It offers the right level of details on the electrical guidelines. I especially find that chapters 5, 6 and 7 are a MUST READ for any hardware designers and CAD guys who want their board TO WORK!"*
>
> *Eric Duchesne, P.Eng, Professional Engineer, Avnet Design Services*

- ***Introduction to PCI Express†***
  A Hardware and Software Developer's Guide
  By Adam Wilen, Justin Schade, Ron Thornburg
  ISBN 0-9702846-9-1

  In this ground-breaking book on the new PCI Express technology, Intel insiders tell hardware and software developers how to overcome the performance limits of existing multi-drop, parallel bus technology in applications for desktop, mobile, server, and communications platforms.

“The book is good for every engineer who will be working on PCI Express-based systems.”

Ajay Kwatra,
Engineer Strategist,
Dell Computer Corporation

- ***UPnP† Design by Example***
  A Software Developer's Guide to Universal Plug and Play
  By Michael Jeronimo, Jack Weast
  ISBN 0-9717861-1-9

  Computer network devices should plug in, turn on, and just work! Two Intel experts show software developers how to make it happen with UPnP technology. With this book, software developers familiar with basic network programming concepts and protocols can design UPnP technology into their next product.

A must-have resource for building devices with UPnP technology

- ***USB Design by Example***

  A Practical Guide to Building I/O Devices

  By John Hyde

  ISBN 0-9702846-5-9

  Organized around a series of fully documented, real-world examples, this step-by-step guide provides designers with the expert knowledge and skills they need to design and implement USB I/O devices. It also serves as a complete reference to Universal Serial Bus classes and devices.

“We have used this book extensively to help us produce several USB devices. John Hyde’s insights are invaluable and he expresses them clearly. A must-have book.”

George T. Frueh, Software Engineer, Educational Computer Company, Inc.

- ***Serial ATA Storage Architecture and Applications***

  Designing High-Performance, Low-Cost I/O Solutions

  By Knut Grimsrud, Hubbert Smith

  ISBN 0-9717861-8-6

  In this definitive guide to Serial ATA, the new storage interconnect standard, two Intel experts show engineering professionals how to cope with changes and problems as the PC industry transitions from parallel interconnects to Serial ATA.

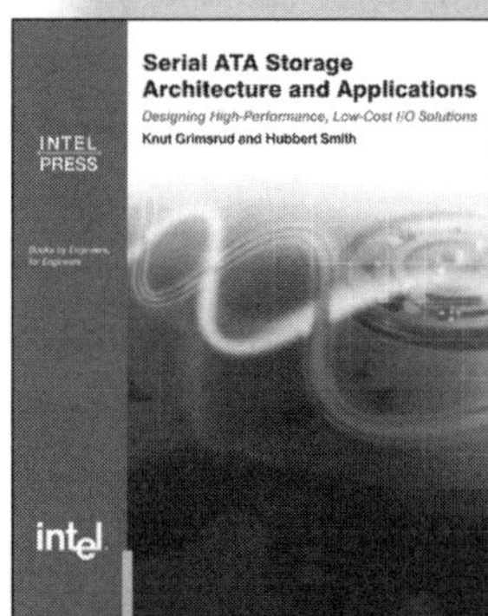

“If you’re designing products based upon Serial ATA, you’ve got to read this book. I recommend it to all my peers at Hitachi.”

Frank Chu, Senior Engineer, Hitachi Global Storage

About Intel Press

Intel Press is the authoritative source of timely, technical books to help software and hardware developers speed up their development process. We collaborate only with leading industry experts to deliver reliable, first-to-market information about the latest technologies, processes, and strategies.

Our products are planned with the help of many people in the developer community and we encourage you to consider becoming a customer advisor. If you would like to help us and gain additional advance insight to the latest technologies, we encourage you to consider the Intel Press Customer Advisor Program. You can register here:

www.intel.com/intelpress/register.htm

For information about bulk orders or corporate sales, please send email to **bulkbooksales@intel.com**

Other Developer Resources from Intel

At these Web sites you can also find valuable technical information and resources for developers:

developer.intel.com	general information for developers
www.intel.com/software	content, tools, training, and the Intel® Early Access Program for software developers
www.intel.com/software/products	programming tools to help you develop high-performance applications
www.intel.com/netcomms	solutions and resources for networking and communications
www.intel.com/technology/itj	Intel Technology Journal
www.intel.com/idf	worldwide technical conference, the Intel Developer Forum

Intel
PRESS

6164-0179-8931-8347

If serial number is missing, please send an e-mail to Intel Press at **intelpress@intel.com**

IMPORTANT

You can access the companion Web site for this book on the Internet at:

www.intel.com/intelpress/haud

Use the serial number located in the upper-right hand corner of this page to register your book and access additional material, including all code examples and pointers to development resources.